McGraw-Hill Connect®
Learn Without Limits

Connect is a teaching and learning platform that is proven to deliver better results for students and instructors.

Connect empowers students by continually adapting to deliver precisely what they need, when they need it, and how they need it, so your class time is more engaging and effective.

73% of instructors who use **Connect** require it; instructor satisfaction **increases** by 28% when **Connect** is required.

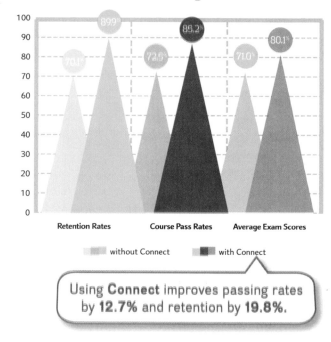

Connect's Impact on Retention Rates, Pass Rates, and Average Exam Scores

Retention Rates   Course Pass Rates   Average Exam Scores

without Connect   with Connect

Using **Connect** improves passing rates by **12.7%** and retention by **19.8%**.

Analytics

Connect Insight®

Connect Insight is Connect's new one-of-a-kind visual analytics dashboard—now available for both instructors and students—that provides at-a-glance information regarding student performance, which is immediately actionable. By presenting assignment, assessment, and topical performance results together with a time metric that is easily visible for aggregate or individual results, Connect Insight gives the user the ability to take a just-in-time approach to teaching and learning, which was never before available. Connect Insight presents data that empowers students and helps instructors improve class performance in a way that is efficient and effective.

Impact on Final Course Grade Distribution

without Connect		with Connect
22.9%	A	31.0%
27.4%	B	34.3%
22.9%	C	18.7%
11.5%	D	6.1%
15.4%	F	9.9%

Students can view their results for any **Connect** course.

Mobile

Connect's new, intuitive mobile interface gives students and instructors flexible and convenient, anytime–anywhere access to all components of the Connect platform.

Adaptive

THE **ADAPTIVE** **READING EXPERIENCE**
DESIGNED TO TRANSFORM THE WAY STUDENTS READ

More students earn **A's** and **B's** when they use McGraw-Hill Education **Adaptive** products.

SmartBook®

Proven to help students improve grades and study more efficiently, SmartBook contains the same content within the print book, but actively tailors that content to the needs of the individual. SmartBook's adaptive technology provides precise, personalized instruction on what the student should do next, guiding the student to master and remember key concepts, targeting gaps in knowledge and offering customized feedback, and driving the student toward comprehension and retention of the subject matter. Available on tablets, SmartBook puts learning at the student's fingertips—anywhere, anytime.

Over **8 billion questions** have been answered, making McGraw-Hill Education products more intelligent, reliable, and precise.

www.mheducation.com

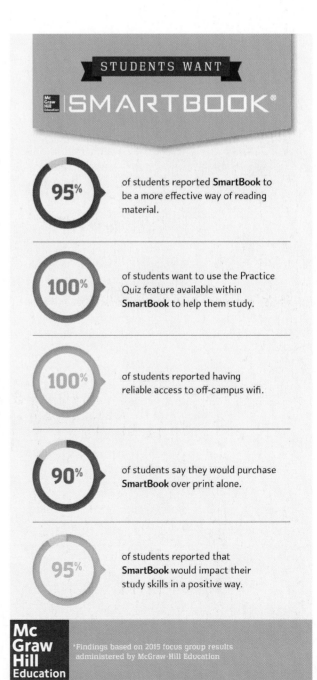

Business Driven Technology

SEVENTH EDITION

Paige Baltzan

Daniels College of Business

University of Denver

BUSINESS DRIVEN TECHNOLOGY, SEVENTH EDITION

Published by McGraw-Hill Education, 2 Penn Plaza, New York, NY 10121. Copyright © 2017 by McGraw-Hill Education. All rights reserved. Printed in the United States of America. Previous editions © 2015, 2013, 2010, and 2009. No part of this publication may be reproduced or distributed in any form or by any means, or stored in a database or retrieval system, without the prior written consent of McGraw-Hill Education, including, but not limited to, in any network or other electronic storage or transmission, or broadcast for distance learning.

Some ancillaries, including electronic and print components, may not be available to customers outside the United States.

This book is printed on acid-free paper.

2 3 4 5 6 7 8 9 0 LWI 21 20 19 18 17

ISBN 978-1-259-56732-2
MHID 1-259-56732-X

Chief Product Office, SVP Products & Markets: *G. Scott Virkler*
Director: *Scott Davidson*
Senior Brand Manager: *Wyatt Morris*
Development Editor: *Kevin White*
Digital Development Editor II: *Kevin White*
Senior Marketing Manager: *Tiffany Russell*
Director, Content Production: *Terri Schiesl*
Content Project Manager: *Rick Hecker*
Media Project Manager: *Evan Roberts*
Buyer: *Jennifer Pickel*
Design: *Matt Diamond*
Content Licensing Specialist: *Ann Marie Jannette (image); Shannon Manderscheid (text)*
Compositor: *SPi Global*
Printer: *LSC Communications*

All credits appearing on page or at the end of the book are considered to be an extension of the copyright page.

Library of Congress Cataloging-in-Publication Data
Names: Baltzan, Paige, author.
Title: Business driven technology / Paige Baltzan, Daniels College of
  Business, University of Denver.
Description: Seventh edition. | New York, NY : McGraw-Hill Education, [2018]
Identifiers: LCCN 2016038028 | ISBN 9781259567322 (alk. paper)
Subjects: LCSH: Information technology—Management. | Management information
  systems. | Information resources management. | Industrial
  management—Technological innovations.
Classification: LCC HD30.2 .H32 2018 | DDC 658.4/038—dc23 LC record available
at https://lccn.loc.gov/2016038028

The Internet addresses listed in the text were accurate at the time of publication. The inclusion of a website does not indicate an endorsement by the authors or McGraw-Hill Education, and McGraw-Hill Education does not guarantee the accuracy of the information presented at these sites.

www.mhhe.com

 **DEDICATION**

In memory of Allan R. Biggs, my father, my mentor, and my inspiration.
Paige

To my mother Sophie, my father Thomas, my brother Tom, and my wonderful husband Mel—without whom I would not be who I am today. Thank you all for your love, support, and undying confidence in me.
Patricia

UNITS

BUSINESS PLUG-INS

TECHNOLOGY PLUG-INS (CONNECT ONLY)

TABLE OF CONTENTS

Paige Baltzan

Paige Baltzan is an Assistant Teaching Professor in the department of Business Information and Analytics at the Daniels College of Business at the University of Denver. She holds a BSBA specializing in Accounting/MIS from Bowling Green State University and an MBA specializing in MIS from the University of Denver. She is a coauthor of several books, including *Business Driven Information Systems, Essentials of Business Driven Information Systems,* and *I-Series,* and is a contributor to *Management Information Systems for the Information Age.*

Before joining the Daniels College faculty in 1999, Paige spent several years working for a large telecommunications company and an international consulting firm where she participated in client engagements in the United States as well as South America and Europe. Paige lives in Lakewood, Colorado, with her husband, Tony, and daughters, Hannah and Sophie.

The overall goal of the Technology Plug-Ins is to provide additional information not covered in the text such as personal productivity using information technology, problem solving using Excel, and decision making using Access. These plug-ins also offer an all-in-one text to faculty, avoiding their having to purchase an extra book to support Microsoft Office. These plug-ins offer integration with the core chapters and provide critical knowledge using essential business applications, such as Microsoft Excel, Microsoft Access, and Microsoft Project with hands-on tutorials for comprehension and mastery. Plug-Ins T1 to T12 are located in McGraw-Hill Connect at **http://connect.mheducation.com.**

Plug-In	Description
T1. Personal Productivity Using IT	This plug-in covers a number of things to do to keep a personal computer running effectively and efficiently. The topics covered in this plug-in are: ■ Creating strong passwords. ■ Performing good file management. ■ Implementing effective backup and recovery strategies. ■ Using Zip files. ■ Writing professional emails. ■ Stopping spam. ■ Preventing phishing. ■ Detecting spyware. ■ Threads to instant messaging. ■ Increasing PC performance. ■ Using antivirus software. ■ Installing a personal firewall.
T2. Basic Skills Using Excel	This plug-in introduces the basics of using Microsoft Excel, a spreadsheet program for data analysis, along with a few fancy features. The topics covered in this plug-in are: ■ Workbooks and worksheets. ■ Working with cells and cell data. ■ Printing worksheets. ■ Formatting worksheets. ■ Formulas. ■ Working with charts and graphics.
T3. Problem Solving Using Excel	This plug-in provides a comprehensive tutorial on how to use a variety of Microsoft Excel functions and features for problem solving. The areas covered in this plug-in are: ■ Lists ■ Conditional Formatting ■ AutoFilter ■ Subtotals ■ PivotTables
T4. Decision Making Using Excel	This plug-in examines a few of the advanced business analysis tools used in Microsoft Excel that have the capability to identify patterns, trends, and rules, and create "what-if" models. The four topics covered in this plug-in are: ■ IF ■ Lookup ■ Goal Seek ■ Solver ■ Scenario Manager
T5. Designing Database Applications	This plug-in provides specific details on how to design relational database applications. One of the most efficient and powerful information management computer-based applications is the relational database. The topics covered in this plug-in are: ■ Entities and data relationships. ■ Documenting logical data relationships. ■ The relational data model. ■ Normalization.

Plug-in	Description
T6. Basic Skills Using Access	This plug-in focuses on creating a Microsoft Access database file. One of the most efficient information management computer-based applications is Microsoft Access. Access provides a powerful set of tools for creating and maintaining a relational database. The topics covered in this plug-in are: ■ Create a new database file. ■ Create and modify tables.
T7. Problem Solving Using Access	This plug-in provides a comprehensive tutorial on how to query a database in Microsoft Access. Queries are essential for problem solving, allowing a user to sort information, summarize data (display totals, averages, counts, and so on), display the results of calculations on data, and choose exactly which fields are shown. The topics in this plug-in are: ■ Create simple queries using the simple query wizard. ■ Create advanced queries using calculated fields. ■ Format results displayed in calculated fields.
T8. Decision Making Using Access	This plug-in provides a comprehensive tutorial on entering data in a well-designed form and creating functional reports using Microsoft Access. A form is essential to use for data entry and a report is an effective way to present data in a printed format. The topics in this plug-in are: ■ Creating, modifying, and running forms. ■ Creating, modifying, and running reports.
T9. Designing Web Pages	This plug-in provides a comprehensive assessment into the functional aspects of web design. Websites are beginning to look more alike and to employ the same metaphors and conventions. The web has now become an everyday thing whose design should not make users think. The topics in this plug-in are: ■ The World Wide Web. ■ Designing for the unknown(s). ■ The process of web design. ■ HTML basics. ■ Web fonts. ■ Web graphics.
T10. Creating Web Pages Using HTML	This plug-in provides an overview of creating web pages using the HTML language. HTML is a system of codes that you use to create interactive web pages. It provides a means to describe the structure of text-based information in a document—by denoting certain text as headings, paragraphs, lists, and so on. The topics in this plug-in are: ■ An introduction to HTML. ■ HTML tools. ■ Creating, saving, and viewing HTML documents. ■ Apply style tags and attributes. ■ Using fancy formatting. ■ Creating hyperlinks. ■ Displaying graphics.
T11. Creating Gantt Charts with Excel and Microsoft Project	This plug-in offers a quick and efficient way to manage projects. Excel and Microsoft Project are great for managing all phases of a project, creating templates, collaborating on planning processes, tracking project progress, and sharing information with all interested parties. The two topics in this plug-in are: ■ Creating Gantt Charts with Excel. ■ Creating Gantt Charts with Microsoft Project.

Unlike any other MIS text, *Business Driven Technology,* 7e, discusses various business initiatives first and how technology supports those initiatives second. The premise for this unique approach is that business initiatives should drive technology choices. Every discussion in the text first addresses the business needs and then addresses the technology that supports those needs.

Business Driven Technology offers you the flexibility to customize courses according to your needs and the needs of your students by covering only essential concepts and topics in the five core units, while providing additional in-depth coverage in the business and technology plug-ins.

Business Driven Technology contains 19 chapters (organized into five units), 12 business plug-ins, and 11 technology plug-ins offering you the ultimate flexibility in tailoring content to the exact needs of your MIS course. The unique construction of this text allows you to cover essential concepts and topics in the five core units while providing you with the ability to customize a course and explore certain topics in greater detail with the business and technology plug-ins.

Plug-ins are fully developed modules of text that include student learning outcomes, case studies, business vignettes, and end-of-chapter material such as key terms, individual and group questions and projects, and case study exercises.

We realize that instructors today require the ability to cover a blended mix of topics in their courses. While some instructors like to focus on networks and infrastructure throughout their course, others choose to focus on ethics and security. *Business Driven Technology* was developed to easily adapt to your needs. Each chapter and plug-in is independent so you can:

- Cover any or all of the *chapters* as they suit your purpose.
- Cover any or all of the *business plug-ins* as they suit your purpose.
- Cover any or all of the *technology plug-ins* as they suit your purpose.
- Cover the plug-ins in any order you wish.

LESS MANAGING. MORE TEACHING. GREATER LEARNING.

McGraw-Hill *Connect MIS* is an online assignment and assessment solution that connects students with the tools and resources they'll need to achieve success.

McGraw-Hill *Connect MIS* helps prepare students for their future by enabling faster learning, more efficient studying, and higher retention of knowledge.

MCGRAW-HILL *CONNECT MIS* FEATURES

Connect MIS offers a number of powerful tools and features to make managing assignments easier, so faculty can spend more time teaching. With *Connect MIS,* students can engage with their coursework anytime and anywhere, making the learning process more accessible and efficient. *Connect MIS* offers you the features described next.

Simple Assignment Management

With *Connect MIS,* creating assignments is easier than ever, so you can spend more time teaching and less time managing. The assignment management function enables you to:

- Create and deliver assignments easily with selectable interactive exercises, scenario-based questions, and test bank items.
- Streamline lesson planning, student progress reporting, and assignment grading to make classroom management more efficient than ever.
- Go paperless with the eBook and online submission and grading of student assignments.

Smart Grading

When it comes to studying, time is precious. *Connect MIS* helps students learn more efficiently by providing feedback and practice material when they need it, where they need it. When it comes to teaching, your time also is precious. The grading function enables you to:

- Have assignments scored automatically, giving students immediate feedback on their work and side-by-side comparisons with correct answers.
- Access and review each response; manually change grades or leave comments for students to review.
- Reinforce classroom concepts with practice tests and instant quizzes.

Instructor Library

The *Connect MIS* Instructor Library is your repository for additional resources to improve student engagement in and out of class. You can select and use any asset that enhances your lecture. The *Connect MIS* Instructor Library includes:

- Instructor's Manual with
  - Classroom openers and exercises for each chapter.
  - Case discussion points and solutions.
  - Answers to all chapter questions and cases.
  - Video guides–discussion points, questions and answers.
- PowerPoint Presentations with detail lecture notes.
- Solution files to all Apply Your Knowledge problems.

Student Study Center

- The *Connect MIS* Student Study Center is the place for students to access additional data files, student versions of the PowerPoint slides and more.

Student Progress Tracking

Connect MIS keeps instructors informed about how each student, section, and class is performing, allowing for more productive use of lecture and office hours. The progress-tracking function enables you to:

- View scored work immediately and track individual or group performance with assignment and grade reports.
- Access an instant view of student or class performance relative to learning objectives.
- Collect data and generate reports required by many accreditation organizations, such as AACSB.

Lecture Capture

Increase the attention paid to lecture discussion by decreasing the attention paid to note taking. For an additional charge Lecture Capture offers new ways for students to focus on the in-class discussion, knowing they can revisit important topics later. Lecture Capture enables you to:

- Record and distribute your lecture with a click of a button.
- Record and index PowerPoint presentations and anything shown on your computer so it is easily searchable, frame by frame.

- Offer access to lectures anytime and anywhere by computer, iPod, or mobile device.
- Increase intent listening and class participation by easing students' concerns about note taking. Lecture Capture will make it more likely you will see students' faces, not the tops of their heads.

McGraw-Hill *Connect Plus MIS*

McGraw-Hill reinvents the textbook learning experience for the modern student with *Connect Plus MIS*. A seamless integration of an eBook and *Connect MIS*, *Connect Plus MIS* provides all of the *Connect MIS* features plus the following:

- SmartBook, our adaptive eBook, allowing for anytime, anywhere access to the textbook.
- A powerful search function to pinpoint and connect key concepts in a snap.

In short, *Connect MIS* offers you and your students powerful tools and features that optimize your time and energies, enabling you to focus on course content, teaching, and student learning. *Connect MIS* also offers a wealth of content resources for both instructors and students. This state-of-the-art, thoroughly tested system supports you in preparing students for the world that awaits.

For more information about Connect, go to **connect.mheducation.com**, or contact your local McGraw-Hill sales representative.

Tegrity Campus: Lectures 24/7

 Tegrity Campus is a service that makes class time available 24/7 by automatically capturing every lecture in a searchable format for students to review when they study and complete assignments. With a simple one-click start-and-stop process, you capture all computer screens and corresponding audio. Students can replay any part of any class with easy-to-use browser-based viewing on a PC or Mac.

Educators know that the more students can see, hear, and experience class resources, the better they learn. In fact, studies prove it. With Tegrity Campus, students quickly recall key moments by using Tegrity Campus's unique search feature. This search helps students efficiently find what they need, when they need it, across an entire semester of class recordings. Help turn all your students' study time into learning moments immediately supported by your lecture.

Assurance of Learning Ready

Many educational institutions today are focused on the notion of *assurance of learning,* an important element of some accreditation standards. *Business Driven Technology,* 7e, is designed specifically to support your assurance of learning initiatives with a simple yet powerful solution.

Each test bank question for *Business Driven Technology* maps to a specific chapter learning outcome/objective listed in the text. You can use our test bank software, EZ Test, or in *Connect MIS* to easily query for learning outcomes/objectives that directly relate to the learning objectives for your course. You can then use the reporting features of EZ Test to aggregate student results in similar fashion, making the collection and presentation of assurance of learning data simple and easy.

McGraw-Hill Customer Contact Information

At McGraw-Hill, we understand that getting the most from new technology can be challenging. That's why our services don't stop after you purchase our products. You can email our Product Specialists 24 hours a day to get product-training online. Or you can search our knowledge bank of Frequently Asked Questions on our support website. For Customer Support, you can call **800-331-5094** or visit **www.mhhe.com/support.** One of our Technical Support Analysts will be able to assist you in a timely fashion.

Walkthrough

This text is organized around the traditional sequence of topics and concepts in information technology; however, the presentation of this material is nontraditional. That is to say, the text is divided into four major sections: (1) units, (2) chapters, (3) business plug-ins, and (4) technology plug-ins. This represents a substantial departure from existing traditional texts. The goal is to provide both students and faculty with only the most essential concepts and topical coverage in the text, while allowing faculty to customize a course by choosing from among a set of plug-ins that explore topics in more detail. All of the topics that form the core of the discipline are covered, including CRM, SCM, Porter's Five Forces Model, value chain analysis, competitive advantage, information security, and ethics.

Business Driven Technology
includes four major components:

- 5 Core Units
- 19 Chapters
- 12 Business Plug-Ins
- 11 Technology Plug-Ins

UNITS

1. **Achieving Business Success**
   Chapter 1: Business Driven Technology
   Chapter 2: Identifying Competitive Advantages
   Chapter 3: Strategic Initiatives for Implementing Competitive Advantages
   Chapter 4: Measuring the Success of Strategic Initiatives
   Chapter 5: Organizational Structures That Support Strategic Initiatives

2. **Exploring Business Intelligence**
   Chapter 6: Valuing and Storing Organizational Information—Databases
   Chapter 7: Accessing Organizational Information—Data Warehouses
   Chapter 8: Understanding Big Data and Its Impact on Business

3. **Streamlining Business Operations**
   Chapter 9: Enabling the Organization—Decision Making
   Chapter 10: Extending the Organization—Supply Chain Management
   Chapter 11: Building a Customer-Centric Organization—Customer Relationship Management
   Chapter 12: Integrating the Organization from End to End—Enterprise Resource Planning

4. **Building Innovation**
   Chapter 13: Creating Innovative Organizations
   Chapter 14: Ebusiness
   Chapter 15: Creating Collaborative Partnerships
   Chapter 16: Integrating Wireless Technology in Business

5. **Transforming Organizations**
   Chapter 17: Developing Software to Streamline Operations
   Chapter 18: Methodologies for Supporting Agile Organizations
   Chapter 19: Managing Organizational Projects

BUSINESS PLUG-INS

B1	Business Basics	B7	Ethics
B2	Business Process	B8	Operations Management
B3	Hardware and Software Basics	B9	Sustainable MIS Infrastructures
B4	MIS Infrastructures	B10	Business Intelligence
B5	Networks and Telecommunications	B11	Global Information Systems
B6	Information Security	B12	Global Trends

TECHNOLOGY PLUG-INS (CONNECT ONLY)

T1	Personal Productivity Using IT	T7	Problem Solving Using Access
T2	Basic Skills Using Excel	T8	Decision Making Using Access
T3	Problem Solving Using Excel	T9	Designing Web Pages
T4	Decision Making Using Excel	T10	Creating Web Pages Using HTML
T5	Designing Database Applications	T11	Creating Gantt Charts with Excel and Microsoft Project
T6	Basic Skills Using Access		

Apply Your Knowledge Projects   Notes
Glossary   Index

Format, Features, and Highlights

Business Driven Technology, 7e, is state of the art in its discussions, presents concepts in an easy-to-understand format, and allows students to be active participants in learning. The dynamic nature of information technology requires all students, more specifically business students, to be aware of both current and emerging technologies. Students are facing complex subjects and need a clear, concise explanation to be able to understand and use the concepts throughout their careers. By engaging students with numerous case studies, exercises, projects, and questions that enforce concepts, *Business Driven Technology* creates a unique learning experience for both faculty and students.

- **Logical Layout.** Students and faculty will find the text well organized with the topics flowing logically from one unit to the next and from one chapter to the next. The definition of each term is provided before it is covered in the chapter and an extensive glossary is included at the back of the text. Each core unit offers a comprehensive opening case study, introduction, learning outcomes, unit summary, closing case studies, key terms, and making business decision questions. The plug-ins follow the same pedagogical elements with the exception of the exclusion of opening case and closing case studies in the technology plug-ins.

- **Thorough Explanations.** Complete coverage is provided for each topic that is introduced. Explanations are written so that students can understand the ideas presented and relate them to other concepts presented in the core units and plug-ins.

- **Solid Theoretical Base.** The text relies on current theory and practice of information systems as they relate to the business environment. Current academic and professional journals and websites upon which the text is based are found in the References at the end of the book—a road map for additional, pertinent readings that can be the basis for learning beyond the scope of the unit, chapter, or plug-in.

- **Material to Encourage Discussion.** All units contain a diverse selection of case studies and individual and group problem-solving activities as they relate to the use of information technology in business. Two comprehensive cases at the end of each unit reflect the concepts from the chapters. These cases encourage students to consider what concepts have been presented and then apply those concepts to a situation they might find in an organization. Different people in an organization can view the same facts from different points of view and the cases will force students to consider some of those views.

- **Flexibility in Teaching and Learning.** While most textbooks that are "text only" leave faculty on their own when it comes to choosing cases, *Business Driven Technology* goes much further. Several options are provided to faculty with case selections from a variety of sources including *CIO, Harvard Business Journal, Wired, Forbes,* and *Time,* to name just a few. Therefore, faculty can use the text alone, the text and a complete selection of cases, or anything in between.

- **Integrative Themes.** Several themes recur throughout the text, which adds integration to the material. Among these themes are value-added techniques and methodologies, ethics and social responsibility, globalization, and gaining a competitive advantage. Such topics are essential to gaining a full understanding of the strategies that a business must recognize, formulate, and in turn implement. In addition to addressing these in the chapter material, many illustrations are provided for their relevance to business practice. These include brief examples in the text as well as more detail presented in the corresponding plug-in(s) (business or technical).

Visual Content Map

Introduction

Information is everywhere. Most organizations value information as a strategic asset. Organizational success depends heavily on the ability to gather and analyze information about operations, suppliers, customers, and markets. Information can answers such questions as who are your best and worst customers? How much inventory do you need to meet demand? Where can you source the cheapest raw materials? How can you increase sales or reduce costs? Answering these questions incorrectly can lead directly to business failure. Estimating too many buyers will lead to an excess of inventory; estimating too few buyers will potentially lead to lost sales due to lack of product (resulting in even more lost revenues).

Understanding the direct impact information has on an organization's bottom line is crucial to running a successful business. This text focuses on information, business, technology, and the integrated set of activities used to run most organizations. Many of these activities are the hallmarks of business today—supply chain management, customer relationship management, enterprise resource planning, outsourcing, integration, ebusiness, and others. The five core units of this text cover these important activities in detail. Each unit is divided into chapters that provide individual learning outcomes and case studies. In addition to the five core units, there are technology and business "plug-ins" (see Figure Unit 1.1) that further explore topics presented in the five core units.

The chapters in Unit 1 are:

- **Chapter One**—Business Driven Technology.
- **Chapter Two**—Identifying Competitive Advantages.
- **Chapter Three**—Strategic Initiatives for Implementing Competitive Advantages.
- **Chapter Four**—Measuring the Success of Strategic Initiatives.
- **Chapter Five**—Organizational Structures That Support Strategic Initiatives.

Introduction and Learning Outcomes

Introduction. Located after the Unit Opening Case, the introduction familiarizes students with the overall tone of the chapters. Thematic concepts are also broadly defined.

Learning Outcomes. These outcomes focus on what students should learn and be able to answer upon completion of the chapter or plug-in.

Introduction

Decision making and problem solving in today's electronic world encompass large-scale, opportunity-oriented, strategically focused solutions. The traditional "cookbook" approach to decisions simply will not work in the ebusiness world. Decision-making and problem-solving abilities are now the most sought-after traits in up-and-coming executives. To put it mildly, decision makers and problem solvers have limitless career potential.

Ebusiness is the conducting of business on the Internet, not only buying and selling, but also serving customers and collaborating with business partners. (Unit Four discusses ebusiness in detail.) With the fast growth of information technology and the accelerated use of the Internet, ebusiness is quickly becoming standard. This unit focuses on technology to help make decisions, solve problems, and find new innovative opportunities. The unit highlights how to bring people together with the best IT processes and tools in complete, flexible solutions that can seize business opportunities (see Figure Unit 3.1). The chapters in Unit 3 are:

- **Chapter Nine**—Enabling the Organization—Decision Making.
- **Chapter Ten**—Extending the Organization—Supply Chain Management.
- **Chapter Eleven**—Building a Customer-centric Organization—Customer Relationship Management.
- **Chapter Twelve**—Integrating the Organization from End to End—Enterprise Resource Planning.

LEARNING OUTCOMES

9.1. Explain the importance of decision making for managers at each of the three primary organization levels along with the associated decision characteristics.

9.2. Classify the different operational support systems, managerial support systems, and strategic support systems, and explain how managers can use these systems to make decisions and gain competitive advantages.

9.3. Describe artificial intelligence, and identify its five main types.

Unit Opening Case and Opening Case Study Questions

Unit Opening Case. To enhance student interest, each unit begins with an opening case study that highlights an organization that has been time-tested and value-proven in the business world. This feature serves to fortify concepts with relevant examples of outstanding companies. Discussion of the case is threaded throughout the chapters in each unit.

Opening Case Study Questions. Located at the end of each chapter, pertinent questions connect the Unit Opening Case with important chapter concepts.

UNIT ONE OPENING CASE

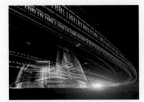  

© nadla/Getty Images   © Ariel Skelley/Blend Images LLC   © Hero Images/Getty Images

Buy Experiences, Not Things

Retail is one of the most competitive and stingiest industries in America boasting some of the most dissatisfied workers across the board. Walmart Stores employees began a week-long strike in Miami, Boston, and the San Francisco Bay Area to publicly display their immense dissatisfaction with the multinational corporation. Employees at Amazon.com fulfillment center in Leipzig, Germany went on strike demanding higher wages and better benefits. Just search retail strikes and you will find numerous examples of dissatisfied employees doing what they can to improve their situations. However, there is one company that will not appear on the list – Costco Wholesale!

Costco Wholesale, the second-largest retailer in the U.S. behind Walmart, is an anomaly in a world where retailers are closing their doors due to the inability to compete with online prices. Retail stores such as Aeropostale, Sears, and Macy's are all feeling the pressure of the online marketplaces of today's digital world. Costco requires a $55-a-year membership fee for access to its massive warehouses supplied floor to ceiling with generous portions of everything from olive oil to paper towels. While many businesses are losing customers to the Internet Costco's sales have grown 40 percent and its stock price has doubled.

Treating employees exceptionally well is the secret to Costco's success. Costco employees make an average of $20 an hour, not including overtime and eighty-eight percent of Costco

OPENING CASE STUDY QUESTIONS

1. What is the ebusiness model implemented by Slack?
2. What is the revenue model implemented by Slack?

Projects and Case Studies

Case Studies. This text is packed with case studies illustrating how a variety of prominent organizations and businesses have successfully implemented many of this text's concepts. All cases promote critical thinking. Company profiles are especially appealing and relevant to your students, helping to stir classroom discussion and interest.

Apply Your Knowledge Project Overview

Project Number	Project Name	Project Type	Plug-In	Focus Area	Project Level	Skill Set	Page Number
1	Financial Destiny	Excel	T2	Personal Budget	Introductory	Formulas	AYK.4
2	Cash Flow	Excel	T2	Cash Flow	Introductory	Formulas	AYK.4
3	Technology Budget	Excel	T1, T2	Hardware and Software	Introductory	Formulas	AYK.4
4	Tracking Donations	Excel	T2	Employee Relationships	Introductory	Formulas	AYK.4
5	Convert Currency	Excel	T2	Global Commerce	Introductory	Formulas	AYK.5
6	Cost Comparison	Excel	T2	Total Cost of Ownership	Introductory	Formulas	AYK.5
7	Time Management	Excel or Project	T12	Project Management	Introductory	Gantt Charts	AYK.6
8	Maximize Profit	Excel	T2, T4	Strategic Analysis	Intermediate	Formulas or Solver	AYK.6
9	Security Analysis	Excel	T3	Filtering Data	Intermediate	Conditional Formatting, Autofilter, Subtotal	AYK.7
10	Gathering Data	Excel	T3	Data Analysis	Intermediate	Conditional Formatting	AYK.8
11	Scanner System	Excel	T2	Strategic Analysis	Intermediate	Formulas	AYK.8

Chapter Three Case: Amazon Drone Knocking

Using drones to drop off packages could be great for buyers, who might want to get cer[tain items] fast as humanly possible. Back in 2013, when Amazon revealed plans to begin deliveri[ng] via flying drones through Prime Air, some seemed skeptical about the reality of deplo[ying such a] system. Recently, Amazon doubled down on those claims by releasing information on o[ne of their] drones in action, and it is seriously impressive.

A new video presented by former Top Gear host Jeremy Clarkson (who is working [with] Amazon), takes us through the entire process, from ordering, to warehouse launch, to deliv[ery. The] drone looks a lot different from the one Amazon showed us a couple of years ago. This on[e has a] commercial and streamlined look, and instead of showing the package hanging in open [air, the] drone hides the item in a square compartment. Just Google Amazon Prime Air Drone video [with] Clarkson to see for yourself this amazing new drone that will dramatically impact the supply [chain.]

According to Amazon, the drone reaches a height of about 400 feet in vertical mo[de before it] switches to horizontal mode to travel up to 15 miles away from the warehouse. During th[e flight the] drone uses what Amazon calls "sense and avoid technology" to avoid collisions with oth[er objects in] its flight path.

Toward the end of the video, the drone alights atop an Amazon logo in the yard of [a customer] and spits out the package (in this case, shoes) and then takes off in a matter of seconds. [The entire] process, which Amazon is careful to note is real and not a simulation, comes off seamle[ssly, making] the prospect of drone deliveries seem like something that will be viable just a few month[s away.]

However, despite the encouraging footage, Amazon is still holding off on announ[cing exactly] when its drones will take to the skies. On the updated Prime Air page featuring the new fli[ght video,] a message reads, "Putting Prime Air into service will take some time, but we will depl[oy when we] have the regulatory support needed to realize our vision."

The FAA's Unmanned Aircraft Systems (UAS) Registration Task Force Aviation Rulemak[ing Commit]tee is still hammering out rules for private and commercial drone use in U.S. air space, s[o the current] lack of a specific launch timeline for Prime Air is understandable. But based on the video [it is becom]ing increasingly clear that Prime Air might not be a mere marketing stunt but a real look [at the future] of Amazon deliveries.

Retailers Racing to the Drone Games

Wal-Mart recently applied to U.S. regulators for permission to test drones for home delive[ry, curbside] pickup and checking warehouse inventories, a sign it plans to go head-to-head with Ama[zon in using] drones to fill and deliver online orders.

Wal-Mart wants to start using drones in an effort to create a more efficient supply cha[in that con]nect their network of stores, distribution centers, fulfillment centers and transportatio[n fleet. The] world's largest retailer by revenue has for several months been conducting indoor te[sting of] unmanned aircraft systems (drones) and is now seeking for the first time to test the m[achines out]doors. In addition to having drones take inventory of trailers outside its warehouses [and perform] other tasks aimed at making its distribution system more efficient, Wal-Mart is asking the F[ederal Avia]tion Administration for permission to research drone use in "deliveries to customers at W[al-Mart facili]ties, as well as to consumer homes." The move comes as Amazon, Google and other co[mpanies...]

Apply Your Knowledge. At the end of this text is a set of 33 projects aimed at reinforcing the business initiatives explored in the text. These projects help to develop the application and problem-solving skills of your students through challenging and creative business-driven scenarios.

Making Business Decisions

 MAKING BUSINESS DECISIONS

1. Two Trillion Rows of Data Analyzed Daily—No Problem

eBay is the world's largest online marketplace, with 97 million global users selling anything to anyone at a yearly total of $62 billion—more than $2,000 every second. Of course with this many sales, eBay is collecting the equivalent of the Library of Congress worth of data every three days that must be analyzed to run the business successfully. Luckily, eBay discovered Tableau!

Tableau started at Stanford when Chris Stolte, a computer scientist; Pat Hanrahan, an Academy Award–winning professor; and Christian Chabot, a savvy business leader, decided to solve the problem of helping ordinary people understand big data. The three created Tableau, which bridged two computer science disciplines: computer graphics and databases. No more need to write code or understand the relational database keys and categories; users simply drag and drop pictures of what they want to analyze. Tableau has become one of the most successful data visualization tools on the market, winning multiple awards, international expansion, and millions in revenue and spawning multiple new inventions.

Tableau is revolutionizing business analytics, and this is only the beginning. Visit the Tableau website and become familiar with the tool by watching a few of the demos. Once you have a good understanding of the tool, create three questions eBay might be using Tableau to answer, including the analysis of its sales data to find patterns, business insights, and trends.

2. Track Your Life

With wearable technology, you can track your entire life. Nike's Fuelband and Jawbone's Up tracks all of your physical activity, caloric burn, and sleep patterns. You can track your driving patterns, tooth-brushing habits, and even laundry status. The question now becomes how to track all of your trackers.

A new company called Exist incorporates tracking devices with weather data, music choices, Netflix favorites, and Twitter activity all in one digital dashboard. Exist wants to understand every area of your life and provide correlation information between such things as your personal productivity and mood. As the different types of data expand, so will the breadth of correlations Exist can point out. For instance, do you tweet more when you are working at home? If so, does this increase productivity? Exist wants to track all of your trackers and analyze the information to help you become more efficient and more effective.

Create a digital dashboard for tracking your life. Choose four areas you want to track and determine three ways you would measure each area. For example, if you track eating habits, you might want to measure calories and place unacceptable levels in red and acceptable levels in green. Once completed, determine whether you can find any correlations among the areas in your life.

3. Butterfly Effects

End-of-Unit Elements

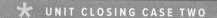

UNIT CLOSING CASE TWO

© C. Borland/PhotoLink/Getty Images   © F

Informing Information

Since the beginning of time, r

MAKING BUSINESS DECISIONS

1. Two Trillion Rows of Data Analyzed Daily—No Problem

eBay is the world's largest online marketplace, with 97 million global users selling anything
anyone at a yearly total of $62 billion—more than $2,000 every second. Of course with this
sales, eBay is collecting the equivalent of the Library of Congress worth of data every three
that must be analyzed to run

Tableau started at Stanfor
Award–winning professor; an
of helping ordinary people un
science disciplines: computer
relational database keys and
analyze. Tableau has become
multiple awards, internationa

KEY TERMS

Affinity grouping analysis, 137
Algorithms, 141
Analysis paralysis, 143
Analytical information, 100
Analytics, 141
Anomaly detection, 141
Attribute, 105
Backward integration, 112
Big data, 131
Business-critical integrity
  constraints, 109
Business intelligence dashboard,
  144
Business rule, 109

Content editor, 110
Cube, 140
Data-driven decision
  management, 126
Data aggregation, 121
Data artist, 143
Database, 104
Database management system
  (DBMS), 104
Data broker, 124
Data dictionary, 105
Data-driven website, 110
Data element (or data field, 104
Data gap analysis, 103

Each unit contains complete pedagogical support in the form of:

- **Unit Summary.** Revisiting the unit highlights in summary format.
- **Key Terms.** With page numbers referencing where they are discussed in the text.
- **Two Closing Case Studies.** Reinforcing important concepts with prominent examples from businesses and organizations. Discussion questions follow each case study.
- **Apply Your Knowledge.** In-depth projects that help students focus on applying the skills and concepts they have learned throughout the unit.
- **Apply Your Knowledge Application Projects.** Highlights the different AYK projects available at the end of the text that takes the MIS concepts and challenges the students to apply them using Excel, Access, and other tools.

About the Plug-Ins

The plug-ins are designed to allow faculty to customize their course and cover selected topics in more detail. Students will read core material related to all of the plug-ins in the five units.

As an example, students will learn about various facets of customer relationship management (CRM) most notably in Chapter 11. However, customer relationship management has its own business plug-in. The CRM business plug-in gives both faculty and students the ability to cover CRM in more detail if desired. Likewise, students will receive an introduction to decision making in Unit 3. The Excel technology plug-ins allow coverage of decision-making tools such as PivotTables, Goal Seek, and Scenario Manager.

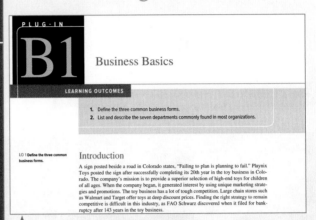

Management Focus. By focusing on the business plug-ins, your course will take on a managerial approach to MIS.

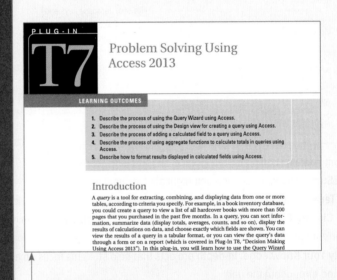

Technical Focus. If hands-on, technical skills are more important, include technical plug-ins in your MIS course.

End-of-Plug-In Elements

Each business plug-in contains complete pedagogical support in the form of:

- **Plug-in Summary.** Revisiting the plug-in highlights in summary format.
- **Key Terms.** With page numbers referencing where they are discussed in the text.
- **Making Business Decisions.** Small scenario-driven projects that help students focus individually on decision making as they relate to the topical elements in the chapters.

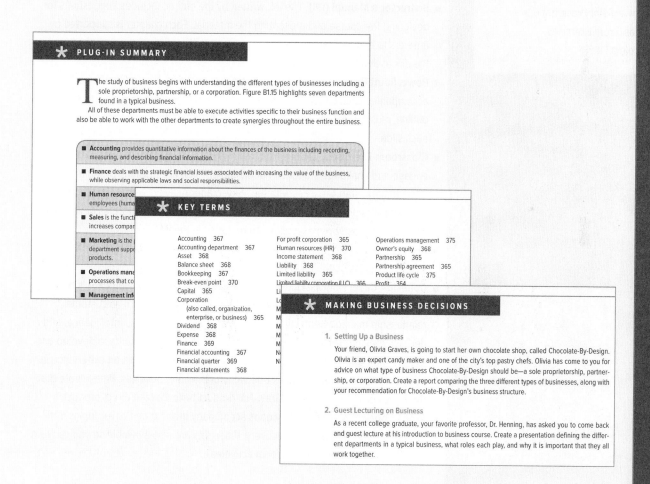

✱ PLUG-IN SUMMARY

The study of business begins with understanding the different types of businesses including a sole proprietorship, partnership, or a corporation. Figure B1.15 highlights seven departments found in a typical business.

All of these departments must be able to execute activities specific to their business function and also be able to work with the other departments to create synergies throughout the entire business.

- **Accounting** provides quantitative information about the finances of the business including recording, measuring, and describing financial information.
- **Finance** deals with the strategic financial issues associated with increasing the value of the business, while observing applicable laws and social responsibilities.
- **Human resource** employees (huma
- **Sales** is the functi increases compar
- **Marketing** is the department suppo products.
- **Operations mana** processes that co
- **Management info**

✱ KEY TERMS

Accounting 367	For profit corporation 365	Operations management 375
Accounting department 367	Human resources (HR) 370	Owner's equity 368
Asset 368	Income statement 368	Partnership 365
Balance sheet 368	Liability 368	Partnership agreement 365
Bookkeeping 367	Limited liability 365	Product life cycle 375
Break-even point 370	Limited liability corporation (LLC) 366	Profit 364
Capital 365	Li	
Corporation	Lo	
(also called, organization,	M	
enterprise, or business) 365	M	
Dividend 368	M	
Expense 368	M	
Finance 369	M	
Financial accounting 367	N	
Financial quarter 369	N	
Financial statements 368		

✱ MAKING BUSINESS DECISIONS

1. **Setting Up a Business**

   Your friend, Olivia Graves, is going to start her own chocolate shop, called Chocolate-By-Design. Olivia is an expert candy maker and one of the city's top pastry chefs. Olivia has come to you for advice on what type of business Chocolate-By-Design should be—a sole proprietorship, partnership, or corporation. Create a report comparing the three different types of businesses, along with your recommendation for Chocolate-By-Design's business structure.

2. **Guest Lecturing on Business**

   As a recent college graduate, your favorite professor, Dr. Henning, has asked you to come back and guest lecture at his introduction to business course. Create a presentation defining the different departments in a typical business, what roles each play, and why it is important that they all work together.

Support and Supplemental Material

All of the supplemental material supporting *Business Driven Technology* was developed by the author to ensure you receive accurate, high-quality, and in-depth content. Included are a complete set of materials that will assist students and faculty in accomplishing course objectives.

Video Exercises. Many of the videos that accompany the text are supported by detailed teaching notes on how to turn the videos into classroom exercises where your students can apply the knowledge they are learning after watching the videos.

Test Bank. This computerized package allows instructors to custom design, save, and generate tests. The test program permits instructors to edit, add, or delete questions from the test banks; analyze test results; and organize a database of tests and student results.

- **Instructor's Manual (IM).** The IM, written by the author, includes suggestions for designing the course and presenting the material. Each chapter is supported by answers to end-of-chapter questions and problems and suggestions concerning the discussion topics and cases.

- **PowerPoint Presentations.** A set of PowerPoint slides, created by the author, accompanies each chapter that features bulleted items that provide a lecture outline, plus key figures and tables from the text, and detailed teaching notes on each slide.

- **Classroom Exercises.** Choose from over 30 detailed classroom exercises that engage and challenge students. For example, if you are teaching systems development, start the class with the "Skyscraper Activity" where the students build a prototype that takes them through each phase of the systems development life cycle. All classroom exercises can be found in the IM.

- **Project Files.** The author has provided files for all projects that need further support, such as data files.

- **Cohesion Case.** Now assignable through Connect, The Broadway Cafe is a running case instructors can use to reinforce core material such as customer relationship management, supply chain management, business intelligence, and decision making. The case has 15 sections that challenge students to develop and expand their grandfather's coffee shop. Students receive hands-on experience in business and learn technology's true value of enabling business. Please note that the Cohesion Case is not a McGraw-Hill product but a Baltzan direct product.

- **Video Content.** More than 20 videos accompany this text and cover topics from entrepreneurship to disaster recovery. Video IMs are also available so you can turn the videos into engaging classroom activities.

Supplements:

- Business Driven Teaching Notes
- Instructor Resource Library in McGraw-Hill Connect
- Instructor's Manual and Video Case Guide
- PowerPoint Presentations
- Classroom Exercises
- Project Files

McGraw-Hill Higher Education and Blackboard have teamed up. What does this mean for you?

1. **Your life, simplified.** Now you and your students can access McGraw-Hill's Connect™ and Create™ right from within your Blackboard course—all with one single sign-on. Say good-bye to the days of logging in to multiple applications.

2. **Deep integration of content and tools.** Not only do you get single sign-on with Connect™ and Create™, you also get deep integration of McGraw-Hill content and content engines right in Blackboard. Whether you're choosing a book for your course or building Connect™ assignments, all the tools you need are right where you want them—inside of Blackboard.

3. **Seamless gradebooks.** Are you tired of keeping multiple gradebooks and manually synchronizing grades into Blackboard? We thought so. When a student completes an integrated Connect™ assignment, the grade for that assignment automatically (and instantly) feeds your Blackboard grade center.

4. **A solution for everyone.** Whether your institution is already using Blackboard or you just want to try Blackboard on your own, we have a solution for you. McGraw-Hill and Blackboard can now offer you easy access to industry leading technology and content, whether your campus hosts it or we do. Be sure to ask your local McGraw-Hill representative for details.

Craft your teaching resources to match the way you teach! With McGraw-Hill Create, www.mcgrawhillcreate.com, you can easily rearrange chapters, combine material from other content sources, and quickly upload content you have written, like your course syllabus or teaching notes. Find the content you need in Create by searching through thousands of leading McGraw-Hill textbooks. Arrange your book to fit your teaching style. Create even allows you to personalize your book's appearance by selecting the cover and adding your name, school, and course information. Order a Create book and you'll receive a complimentary print review copy in 3–5 business days or a complimentary electronic review copy (eComp) via email in about one hour. Go to www.mcgrawhillcreate.com today and register. Experience how McGraw-Hill Create empowers you to teach *your* students *your* way.

There are numerous people whom we want to heartily thank for their hard work, enthusiasm, and dedication on this edition of *Business Driven Technology*.

To the faculty at the Daniels College of Business at the University of Denver—Richard Scudder, Don McCubbrey, Paul Bauer, Hans Hultgren, Daivd Paul, Dan Connolly, and Amy Phillips—thank you. Your feedback, advice, and support are truly valued and greatly appreciated.

We offer our sincerest gratitude and deepest appreciation to our valuable reviewers, whose feedback was instrumental.

Etido Akpan
Freed Hardemann University

Dennis Anderson
Bentley University

Kaan Ataman
Chapman University–Orange

Vikram Bhadauria
Southern Arkansas University

Utpal Bose
University of Houston–Downtown

Traci Carte
University of Oklahoma

Carey Cole
James Madison University

Charles DeSassure
Tarrant County College–SE Campus

Mike Eom
University of Portland

Ahmed Eshra
St. John's University–Jamaica

Deborah Geil
Bowling Green State University

Naveen Gudigantala
University of Portland

Saurabh Gupta
University of North Florida

Vernard Harrington
Radford University

Shoreh Hashimi
University of Houston–Downtown

Tracey Hughes
Southern Arkansas University

Keri Larson
The University of Alabama–Birmingham

Linda Lynam
University of Central Missouri

Michael Magro
Shenandoah University

Richard McMahon
University of Houston–Downtown

Don Miller
Avila University

Allison Morgan
Howard University

Vincent Nestler
University of California–San Bernardino

Sandra Newton
Sonoma State University

Ahmet Ozkul
University of New Haven

Susan Peterson
University of California–San Diego

Julie Pettus
Missouri State University

Gerald Plumlee
Southern Arkansas University

Pauline Ratnasingham
University of Central Missouri

Julio Rivera
University of Alabama–Birmingham

Thomas Sandman
California State University–Sacramento

Dmitriy Shalteyev
Christopher Newport University

Lakisha Simmons
Belmont University

Ron Sones
Liberty University

Nathan Stout
University of Oklahoma

Stephen Taraszewski
Youngstown State University

Sharon Testa
Merrimack College

John Wee
University of Mississippi

Chuck West
Bradley University

Melody White
University of North Texas

Benjamin Yeo
Chapman University

Zehai Zhou
University of Houston–Downtown

Patricia A. McQuaid, Ph.D., CISA, is a Professor of Information Systems in the Orfalea College of Business at California Polytechnic State University (Cal Poly). She has a doctorate in Computer Science and Engineering, an MBA, and an undergraduate degree in Accounting. Patricia is a Certified Information Systems Auditor (CISA), and a Certified Tester - Foundation Level (CTFL), through the ISTQB, the International Software Testing Qualifications Board. She has over 25 years of experience in software engineering, having taught in both the Colleges of Business and Engineering throughout her career. She has worked in industry in the banking and manufacturing industries as an information systems auditor, is a consultant, and a trainer.

Her research interests include software quality, software testing, project management, and process improvement. She is a member of IEEE, and a Senior Member of the American Society for Quality (ASQ). She is an Associate Editor for the *Software Quality Professional* journal, and also participates on ASQ's Software Division Council. Patricia is a frequent speaker and author, both internationally and nationally. She is a frequent speaker, both nationally and internationally.

Business
Driven
Technology

Achieving Business Success

This unit sets the stage for diving into *Business Driven Technology*. It starts from the ground floor by providing a clear description of what information technology is and how IT fits into business strategies and organizational activities. It then provides an overview of how organizations operate in competitive environments and must continually define and redefine their business strategies to create competitive advantages. Doing so allows organizations to not only survive, but also thrive. Individuals who understand and can access and analyze the many different enterprisewide information systems dramatically improve their decision-making and problem-solving abilities. Most importantly, information technology is shown as a key enabler to help organizations operate successfully in highly competitive environments.

You, as a business student, must recognize the tight correlation between business and technology. You must first understand information technology's role in daily business activities, and then understand information technology's role in supporting and implementing enterprisewide initiatives and global business strategies. After reading this unit, you should have acquired a solid grasp of business driven information systems, technology fundamentals, and business strategies. You should also have gained an appreciation of the various kinds of information systems employed by organizations and how you can use them to help make strategically informed decisions. All leaders must appreciate the numerous ethical and security concerns voiced by customers today. These concerns directly influence a customer's likelihood to embrace electronic technologies and conduct business over the web. In this sense, these concerns affect a company's bottom line. You can find evidence in recent news reports about how the stock price of organizations dramatically falls when information privacy and security breaches are publicized. Further, organizations face potential litigation if they fail to meet their ethical, privacy, and security obligations concerning the handling of information in their companies.

© nadla/Getty Images

© Ariel Skelley/Blend Images LLC

© Hero Images/Getty Images

Buy Experiences, Not Things

Retail is one of the most competitive and stingiest industries in America boasting some of the most dissatisfied workers across the board. Walmart Stores employees began a week-long strike in Miami, Boston, and the San Francisco Bay Area to publicly display their immense dissatisfaction with the multinational corporation. Employees at Amazon.com fulfillment center in Leipzig, Germany went on strike demanding higher wages and better benefits. Just search retail strikes and you will find numerous examples of dissatisfied employees doing what they can to improve their situations. However, there is one company that will not appear on the list – Costco Wholesale!

Costco Wholesale, the second-largest retailer in the U.S. behind Walmart, is an anomaly in a world where retailers are closing their doors due to the inability to compete with online prices. Retail stores such as Aeropostale, Sears, and Macy's are all feeling the pressure of the online marketplaces of today's digital world. Costco requires a $55-a-year membership fee for access to its massive warehouses supplied floor to ceiling with generous portions of everything from olive oil to paper towels. While many businesses are losing customers to the Internet Costco's sales have grown 40 percent and its stock price has doubled.

Treating employees exceptionally well is the secret to Costco's success. Costco employees make an average of $20 an hour, not including overtime and eighty-eight percent of Costco employees have company-sponsored health insurance. Costco treats its employees well in the belief that a happier work environment will result in a more profitable company. It is obvious Costco is thriving in one of the toughest retail markets in history.

The style of Costco is minimalist with no-frills industrial shelving stocking the 4,000 different products. Products are marked up 14 percent or less over cost. Items like diapers, suitcases, and tissues, which it sells under its in-house Kirkland Signature brand, get a maximum 15 percent bump. After accounting for expenses such as real estate costs and wages, Costco barely ekes out a profit on many of its products. Eighty percent of its gross profit comes from membership fees; customers renew their memberships at a rate of close to 90 percent.

"They are buying and selling more olive oil, more cranberry juice, more throw rugs than just about anybody," says David Schick, an analyst at Stifel Nicolaus. And that allows Costco to get bulk discounts from its suppliers, often setting the industry's lowest price. Even Amazon can't beat Costco's prices, which means that "showrooming," or browsing in stores but buying online for the better price, isn't much of a concern for Costco.

The company's obsession with selling brand-name merchandise at cut-rate prices occasionally gets it into trouble. Tiffany filed a multi-million-dollar trademark infringement suit against Costco alleging it improperly labeled merchandise as "Tiffany engagement rings." Costco calls it "an honest mistake" and re-branded the label "Tiffany-style." The suit is pending.

Buying Happiness

When you work hard every single day you want to spend your hard-earned funds on what science says will make you happy. The Commerce Department released data showing that American consumers are spending their disposable income on eating out, upgrading cars, renovating houses, sports, health, and beauty. Data shows restaurant spending has increased 10 percent over the last year, and automotive sales have increased seven percent. Analysts say a wider shift is occurring in the mind of the American consumer, spurred by the popularity of a growing body of scientific studies that appear to show that experiences, not objects, bring the most happiness. The Internet is bursting with the "Buy Experiences, Not Things" type of stories that give retailing executives nightmares. Millennials - the 20- and 30-something consumers whom marketers covet are actively pursuing this new happiness mentality.

A 20-year study conducted by Dr. Thomas Gilovich, a psychology professor at Cornell University, reached a powerful and straightforward conclusion: don't spend your money on things. The trouble with things is that the happiness they provide fades quickly. New possessions quickly become old and what once seemed novel and exciting quickly becomes the norm. The bar is constantly rising and new purchases lead to new expectations. As soon as we get used to a new possession, we look for an even better one. And of course we are always comparing ourselves to the neighbors. By nature, we are always comparing our possessions and as soon as we buy a new car a friend buys a better one—and there's always someone with a better one.

Gilovich is not the only person believing experiences make us happier than possessions. Dr. Elizabeth Dunn at the University of British Columbia attributes the temporary happiness achieved by buying things to what she calls "puddles of pleasure." In other words, that kind of happiness evaporates quickly and leaves us wanting more. Things may last longer than experiences, but the memories that linger are what matter most![1]

Introduction

Information is everywhere. Most organizations value information as a strategic asset. Organizational success depends heavily on the ability to gather and analyze information about operations, suppliers, customers, and markets. Information can answers such questions as who are your best and worst customers? How much inventory do you need to meet demand? Where can you source the cheapest raw materials? How can you increase sales or reduce costs? Answering these questions incorrectly can lead directly to business failure. Estimating too many buyers will lead to an excess of inventory; estimating too few buyers will potentially lead to lost sales due to lack of product (resulting in even more lost revenues).

Understanding the direct impact information has on an organization's bottom line is crucial to running a successful business. This text focuses on information, business, technology, and the integrated set of activities used to run most organizations. Many of these activities are the hallmarks of business today—supply chain management, customer relationship management, enterprise resource planning, outsourcing, integration, ebusiness, and others. The five core units of this text cover these important activities in detail. Each unit is divided into chapters that provide individual learning outcomes and case studies. In addition to the five core units, there are technology and business "plug-ins" (see Figure Unit 1.1) that further explore topics presented in the five core units.

The chapters in Unit 1 are:

- **Chapter One**—Business Driven Technology.
- **Chapter Two**—Identifying Competitive Advantages.
- **Chapter Three**—Strategic Initiatives for Implementing Competitive Advantages.
- **Chapter Four**—Measuring the Success of Strategic Initiatives.
- **Chapter Five**—Organizational Structures That Support Strategic Initiatives.

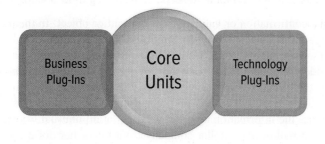

FIGURE UNIT 1.1

The Format and Approach of This Text.

Business Driven Technology

1.1. Describe the information age and the differences among data, information, business intelligence, and knowledge.

1.2. Identify the different departments in a company and why they must work together to achieve success.

1.3. Explain systems thinking and how management information systems enable business communications.

LO 1.1 Describe the information age and the differences among data, information, business intelligence, and knowledge.

Competing in the Information Age

Did you know that . . .

- The movie *Avatar* took more than four years to create and cost $450 million.
- Lady Gaga's real name is Stefani Joanne Angelina Germanotta.
- Customers pay $2.6 million for a 30-second advertising time slot during the Super Bowl.[2]

A *fact* is the confirmation or validation of an event or object. In the past, people primarily learned facts from books. Today, by simply pushing a button people can find out anything, from anywhere, at any time. We live in the *information age*, when infinite quantities of facts are widely available to anyone who can use a computer. The impact of information technology on the global business environment is equivalent to the printing press's impact on publishing and electricity's impact on productivity. College student startups were mostly unheard of before the information age. Now, it's not at all unusual to read about a business student starting a multimillion-dollar company from his or her dorm room. Think of Mark Zuckerberg, who started Facebook from his dorm, or Michael Dell (Dell Computers) and Bill Gates (Microsoft), who both founded their legendary companies as college students.

You may think only students well versed in advanced technology can compete in the information age. This is simply not true. Many business leaders have created exceptional opportunities by coupling the power of the information age with traditional business methods. Here are just a few examples:

- Amazon is not a technology company; its original business focus was to sell books, and it now sells nearly everything including technology services.
- Netflix is not a technology company; its primary business focus is to rent videos.
- Zappos is not a technology company; its primary business focus is to sell shoes, bags, clothing, and accessories.

Amazon's founder, Jeff Bezos, at first saw an opportunity to change the way people purchase books. Using the power of the information age to tailor offerings to each customer and speed the payment process, he in effect opened millions of tiny virtual bookstores, each with a vastly larger selection and far cheaper product than traditional bookstores. The success of his original business model led him to expand Amazon to carry many other types of products.

The founders of Netflix and Zappos have done the same thing for videos and shoes. All these entrepreneurs were business professionals, not technology experts. However, they understood enough about the information age to apply it to a particular business, creating innovative companies that now lead entire industries.

Over 20 years ago a few professors at MIT began describing the *Internet of Things (IoT)* a world where interconnected Internet-enabled devices or "things" have the ability to collect and share data without human intervention. Another term commonly associated with The Internet of Things is *machine-to-machine (M2M),* which refers to devices that connect directly to other devices. With advanced technologies devices are connecting in ways not previously thought possible and researchers predict that over 50 billion IoT devices will be communicating by 2020. Kevin Ashton, cofounder and executive director of the Auto-ID Center at MIT, first mentioned the Internet of Things in a presentation he made to Procter & Gamble. Here's Ashton explanation of the Internet of Things:

"Today computers—and, therefore, the Internet—are almost wholly dependent on human beings for information. Nearly all of the roughly 50 petabytes (a petabyte is 1,024 terabytes) of data available on the Internet were first captured and created by human beings by typing, pressing a record button, taking a digital picture or scanning a bar code. The problem is, people have limited time, attention and accuracy—all of which means they are not very good at capturing data about things in the real world. If we had computers that knew everything there was to know about things—using data they gathered without any help from us—we would be able to track and count everything and greatly reduce waste, loss and cost. We would know when things needed replacing, repairing or recalling and whether they were fresh or past their best."[3]

IoT is transforming our world into a living information system as we control our intelligent lighting from our smart phone to a daily health check from our smart toothbrush. Of course with all great technological advances come unexpected risks and you have to be prepared to encounter various security issues with IoT. Just imagine if your devices are hacked by someone who now has the ability to shut off your water, take control of your car, or unlock the doors of your home from thousands of miles away. We are just beginning to understand the security issues associated with IoT and M2M and you can be sure that sensitive data leakage from your IoT device is something you will most likely encounter in your life.

Students who understand business along with the power associated with the information age will create their own opportunities and perhaps even new industries. Realizing the value of obtaining real-time data from connected "things" will allow you to make more informed decisions, identify new opportunities, and analyze customer patterns to predict new behaviors. Our primary goal in this course is to arm you with the knowledge you need to compete in the information age. The core drivers of the information age include:

- Data
- Information
- Business intelligence
- Knowledge (see Figure 1.1)

DATA

Data are raw facts that describe the characteristics of an event or object. Before the information age, managers manually collected and analyzed data, a time-consuming and complicated task without which they would have little insight into how to run their business. *Structured data* has a defined length, type, and format and includes numbers, dates, or strings such as Customer Address. Structured data is typically stored in a traditional system such as a relational database or spreadsheet and accounts for about 20 percent of the data that surrounds us. The sources of structured data include:

- *Machine-generated data* is created by a machine without human intervention. Machine-generated structured data includes sensor data, point-of-sale data, and web log data.
- *Human-generated data* is data that humans, in interaction with computers, generate. Human-generated structured data includes input data, click-stream data, or gaming data.

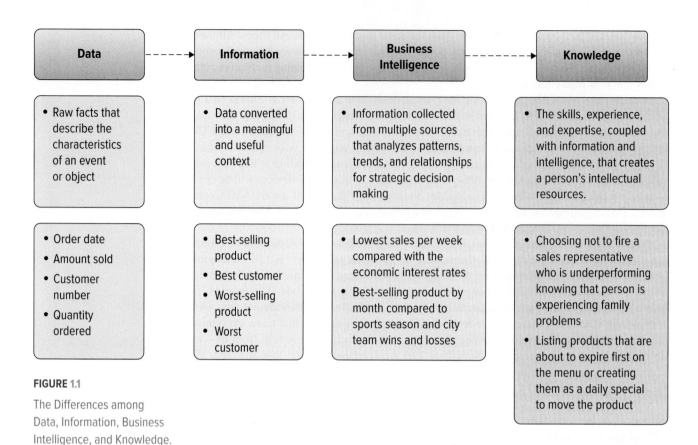

Data	Information	Business Intelligence	Knowledge
• Raw facts that describe the characteristics of an event or object	• Data converted into a meaningful and useful context	• Information collected from multiple sources that analyzes patterns, trends, and relationships for strategic decision making	• The skills, experience, and expertise, coupled with information and intelligence, that creates a person's intellectual resources.
• Order date • Amount sold • Customer number • Quantity ordered	• Best-selling product • Best customer • Worst-selling product • Worst customer	• Lowest sales per week compared with the economic interest rates • Best-selling product by month compared to sports season and city team wins and losses	• Choosing not to fire a sales representative who is underperforming knowing that person is experiencing family problems • Listing products that are about to expire first on the menu or creating them as a daily special to move the product

FIGURE 1.1

The Differences among Data, Information, Business Intelligence, and Knowledge.

Unstructured data is not defined and does not follow a specified format and is typically free-form text such as emails, Twitter tweets, and text messages. Unstructured data accounts for about 80 percent of the data that surrounds us. The sources of unstructured data include:

■ Machine-generated unstructured data includes satellite images, scientific atmosphere data, and radar data.

■ Human-generated unstructured data includes text messages, social media data, and emails.

Big data is a collection of large complex data sets, including structured and unstructured data, which cannot be analyzed using traditional database methods and tools. Lacking data, managers often found themselves making business decisions about how many products to make, how much material to order, or how many employees to hire based on intuition or gut feelings. In the information age, successful managers compile, analyze, and comprehend massive amounts of data daily, which helps them make more successful business decisions.

A *snapshot* is a view of data at a particular moment in time. Figure 1.2 provides a snapshot of sales data for Tony's Wholesale Company, a fictitious business that supplies snacks to stores. The data highlight characteristics such as order date, customer, sales representative, product, quantity, and profit. The second line in Figure 1.2, for instance, shows that Roberta Cross sold 90 boxes of Ruffles to Walmart for $1,350, resulting in a profit of $450 (note that Profit = Sales − Costs). These data are useful for understanding individual sales; however, they do not provide us much insight into how Tony's business is performing as a whole. Tony needs to answer questions that will help him manage his day-to-day operations such as:

■ Who are my best customers?

■ Who are my least-profitable customers?

■ What is my best-selling product?

■ What is my slowest-selling product?

FIGURE 1.2

Tony's Snack Company Data.

Order Date	Customer	Sales Representative	Product	Qty	Unit Price	Total Sales	Unit Cost	Total Cost	Profit
4-Jan	Walmart	PJHelgoth	Doritos	41	$24	$ 984	$18	$738	$246
4-Jan	Walmart	Roberta Cross	Ruffles	90	$15	$1,350	$10	$900	$450
5-Jan	Safeway	Craig Schultz	Ruffles	27	$15	$ 405	$10	$270	$135
6-Jan	Walmart	Roberta Cross	Ruffles	67	$15	$1,005	$10	$670	$335
7-Jan	7-Eleven	Craig Schultz	Pringles	79	$12	$ 948	$ 6	$474	$474
7-Jan	Walmart	Roberta Cross	Ruffles	52	$15	$ 780	$10	$520	$260
8-Jan	Kroger	Craig Schultz	Ruffles	39	$15	$ 585	$10	$390	$195
9-Jan	Walmart	Craig Schultz	Ruffles	66	$15	$ 990	$10	$660	$330
10-Jan	Target	Craig Schultz	Ruffles	40	$15	$ 600	$10	$400	$200
11-Jan	Walmart	Craig Schultz	Ruffles	71	$15	$1,065	$10	$710	$355

- Who is my strongest sales representative?
- Who is my weakest sales representative?

What Tony needs, in other words, is not data but *information*.

INFORMATION

Information is data converted into a meaningful and useful context. The simple difference between data and information is that computers or machines need data and humans need information. Data is a raw building block that has not been shaped, processed, or analyzed and frequently appears disorganized and unfriendly. Information gives meaning and context to analyzed data making it insightful for humans providing context and structure that is extremely valuable when making informed business decisions.

A *report* is a document containing data organized in a table, matrix, or graphical format allowing users to easily comprehend and understand information. Reports can cover a wide range of subjects or specific subject for a certain time period or event. A *static report* is created once based on data that does not change. Static reports can include a sales report from last year or salary report from five years ago. A *dynamic report* changes automatically during creation. Dynamic reports can include updating daily stock market prices or the calculation of available inventory.

Having the right information at the right moment in time can be worth a fortune. Having the wrong information at the right moment; or the right information at the wrong moment can be disastrous. The truth about information is that its value is only as good as the people who use it. People using the same information can make different decisions depending on how they interpret or analyze the information. Thus information has value only insofar as the people using it do as well.

Tony can analyze his sales data and turn them into information to answer all the above questions and understand how his business is operating. Figures 1.3 and 1.4, for instance, show us that Walmart is Roberta Cross's best customer, and that Ruffles is Tony's best product measured in terms of total sales. Armed with this information, Tony can identify and then address such issues as weak products and under-performing sales representatives.

A *variable* is a data characteristic that stands for a value that changes or varies over time. For example, in Tony's data, price and quantity ordered can vary. Changing variables allows managers to create hypothetical scenarios to study future possibilities. Tony may find it valuable to anticipate how sales or cost increases affect profitability. To estimate how a 20 percent increase in prices might improve profits, Tony simply changes the price variable for all orders, which automatically calculates the amount of new profits. To estimate how a 10 percent increase in costs hurts profits, Tony changes the cost variable for all

Order Date	Customer	Sales Representative	Product	Quantity	Unit Price	Total Sales	Unit Cost	Total Cost	Profit
26-Apr	Walmart	Roberta Cross	Fritos	86	$ 19	$ 1,634	$ 17	$ 1,462	$ 172
29-Aug	Walmart	Roberta Cross	Fritos	76	$ 19	$ 1,444	$ 17	$ 1,292	$ 152
7-Sep	Walmart	Roberta Cross	Fritos	20	$ 19	$ 380	$ 17	$ 340	$ 40
22-Nov	Walmart	Roberta Cross	Fritos	39	$ 19	$ 741	$ 17	$ 663	$ 78
30-Dec	Walmart	Roberta Cross	Fritos	68	$ 19	$ 1,292	$ 17	$ 1,156	$ 136
7-Jul	Walmart	Roberta Cross	Pringles	79	$ 18	$ 1,422	$ 8	$ 632	$ 790
6-Aug	Walmart	Roberta Cross	Pringles	21	$ 12	$ 252	$ 6	$ 126	$ 126
2-Oct	Walmart	Roberta Cross	Pringles	60	$ 18	$ 1,080	$ 8	$ 480	$ 600
15-Nov	Walmart	Roberta Cross	Pringles	32	$ 12	$ 384	$ 6	$ 192	$ 192
21-Dec	Walmart	Roberta Cross	Pringles	92	$ 12	$ 1,104	$ 6	$ 552	$ 552
28-Feb	Walmart	Roberta Cross	Ruffles	67	$ 15	$ 1,005	$ 10	$ 670	$ 335
6-Mar	Walmart	Roberta Cross	Ruffles	8	$ 15	$ 120	$ 10	$ 80	$ 40
16-Mar	Walmart	Roberta Cross	Ruffles	68	$ 15	$ 1,020	$ 10	$ 680	$ 340
23-Apr	Walmart	Roberta Cross	Ruffles	34	$ 15	$ 510	$ 10	$ 340	$ 170
4-Aug	Walmart	Roberta Cross	Ruffles	40	$ 15	$ 600	$ 10	$ 400	$ 200
18-Aug	Walmart	Roberta Cross	Ruffles	93	$ 15	$ 1,395	$ 10	$ 930	$ 465
5-Sep	Walmart	Roberta Cross	Ruffles	41	$ 15	$ 615	$ 10	$ 410	$ 205
12-Sep	Walmart	Roberta Cross	Ruffles	8	$ 15	$ 120	$ 10	$ 80	$ 40
28-Oct	Walmart	Roberta Cross	Ruffles	50	$ 15	$ 750	$ 10	$ 500	$ 250
21-Nov	Walmart	Roberta Cross	Ruffles	79	$ 15	$ 1,185	$ 10	$ 790	$ 395
29-Jan	Walmart	Roberta Cross	Sun Chips	5	$ 22	$ 110	$ 18	$ 90	$ 20
12-Apr	Walmart	Roberta Cross	Sun Chips	85	$ 22	$ 1,870	$ 18	$ 1,530	$ 340
16-Jun	Walmart	Roberta Cross	Sun Chips	55	$ 22	$ 1,210	$ 18	$ 990	$ 220
				1,206	$383	$20,243	$273	$14,385	$5,858

Sorting the data reveals the information that Roberta Cross's total sales to Walmart were $20,243 resulting in a profit of $5,858.
(Profit $5,858 = Sales $20,243 – Costs $14,385)

FIGURE 1.3

Tony's Data Sorted by Customer "Walmart" and Sales Representative "Roberta Cross".

orders, which automatically calculates the amount of lost profits. Manipulating variables is an important tool for any business.

BUSINESS INTELLIGENCE

Business intelligence (BI) is information collected from multiple sources such as suppliers, customers, competitors, partners, and industries that analyzes patterns, trends, and relationships for strategic decision making. BI manipulates multiple variables and in some cases even hundreds of variables including such items as interest rates, weather conditions, and even gas prices. Tony could use BI to analyze internal data such as company sales, along with external data about the environment such as competitors, finances, weather, holidays, and even sporting events. Both internal and external variables affect snack sales, and analyzing these variables will help Tony determine ordering levels and sales forecasts. For instance, BI can predict inventory requirements for Tony's business for the week before the Super Bowl if, say,

Tony's Business Information	Name	Total Profit
Who is Tony's best customer by total sales?	Walmart	$ 560,789
Who is Tony's least-valuable customer by total sales?	Walgreens	$ 45,673
Who is Tony's best customer by profit?	7-Eleven	$ 324,550
Who is Tony's least-valuable customer by profit?	King Soopers	$ 23,908
What is Tony's best-selling product by total sales?	Ruffles	$ 232,500
What is Tony's weakest-selling product by total sales?	Pringles	$ 54,890
What is Tony's best-selling product by profit?	Tostitos	$ 13,050
What is Tony's weakest-selling product by profit?	Pringles	$ 23,000
Who is Tony's best sales representative by profit?	R. Cross	$1,230,980
Who is Tony's weakest sales representative by profit?	Craig Schultz	$ 98,980
What is the best sales representative's best-selling product by total profit?	Ruffles	$ 98,780
Who is the best sales representative's best customer by total profit?	Walmart	$ 345,900
What is the best sales representative's weakest-selling product by total profit?	Sun Chips	$ 45,600
Who is the best sales representative's weakest customer by total profit?	Krogers	$ 56,050

FIGURE 1.4

Information Gained after Analyzing Tony's Data.

the home team is playing, average temperature is above 80 degrees, and the stock market is performing well. This is BI at its finest, incorporating all types of internal and external variables to anticipate business performance.

Analytics is the science of fact-based decision making. A big part of business intelligence is called *predictive analytics*, which extracts information from data and uses it to predict future trends and identify behavioral patterns. Top managers use predictive analytics to define the future of the business, analyzing markets, industries, and economies to determine the strategic direction the company must follow to remain profitable. *Behavioral analytics* uses data about people's behaviors to understand intent and predict future actions. Tony will set the strategic direction for his firm, which might include introducing new flavors of potato chips or sports drinks as new product lines or schools and hospitals as new market segments based on both predictive and behavioral analytics.

KNOWLEDGE

Knowledge includes the skills, experience, and expertise, coupled with information and intelligence, that creates a person's intellectual resources. *Knowledge workers* are individuals valued for their ability to interpret and analyze information. Today's workers are commonly referred to as knowledge workers and they use BI along with personal experience to make decisions based on both information and intuition, a valuable resource for any company.

Imagine that Tony analyzes his data and finds his weakest sales representative for this period is Craig Schultz. If Tony considered only this information, he might conclude that firing Craig was a good business decision. However, because Tony has knowledge about how the company operates, he knows Craig has been out on medical leave for several weeks; hence, his sales numbers are low. Without this additional knowledge, Tony might have executed a bad business decision, delivered a negative message to the other employees, and sent his best sales representatives out to look for other jobs.

The key point in this scenario is that it is simply impossible to collect all the information about every situation, and yet without that, it can be easy to misunderstand the problem. Using data, information, business intelligence, and knowledge to make decisions and solve

FIGURE 1.5

Transformation of Data to Knowledge.

DATA: I have one item.

INFORMATION: The item I have is a product that has the most sales during the month of December.

BUSINESS INTELLIGENCE: The month of December this year is going to see interest rates rise by 10 percent and snow stores are expected to cause numerous problems throughout the East coast.

KNOWLEDGE: Given the unexpected financial issues caused by the storms and the interest rate hike we will offer a discount on purchase in November and December to ensure sales levels increase by 10 percent.

problems is the key to finding success in business. These core drivers of the information age are the building blocks of business systems. Figure 1.5 offers a few different examples of data through knowledge.

LO 1.2 Identify the different departments in a company and why they must work together to achieve success.

The Challenge: Departmental Companies

A *business unit* is a segment of a company (such as accounting, production, marketing) representing a specific business function. The terms department, functional area, and business unit are used interchangeably and corporations are typically organized by business unit such as:

- **Accounting:** Records, measures, and reports monetary transactions.
- **Finance:** Deals with strategic financial issues including money, banking, credit, investments, and assets.
- **Human resources:** Maintains policies, plans, and procedures for the effective management of employees.
- **Marketing:** Supports sales by planning, pricing, and promoting goods or services.
- **Operations management:** Manages the process of converting or transforming resources into goods or services.
- **Sales:** Performs the function of selling goods or services.

An *information silo* occurs when one business unit is unable to freely communicate with other business units making it difficult or impossible for organizations to work cross-functionally. Information silos exist because management does not believe there to be enough benefit from sharing information across business units and because information might not be useful to personnel in other business units. Figure 1.6 provides an example of how an organization operates functionally causing information silos as each department performs its own activities. Sales and marketing focus on moving goods or services into the hands of consumers; they maintain transactional data. Finance and accounting focus on managing the company's resources and maintain monetary data. Operations management focuses on manufacturing and maintains production data, while human resources focuses on hiring and training people and maintains employee data. Although each department has its own focus and data, none can work independently if the company is to operate as a whole.

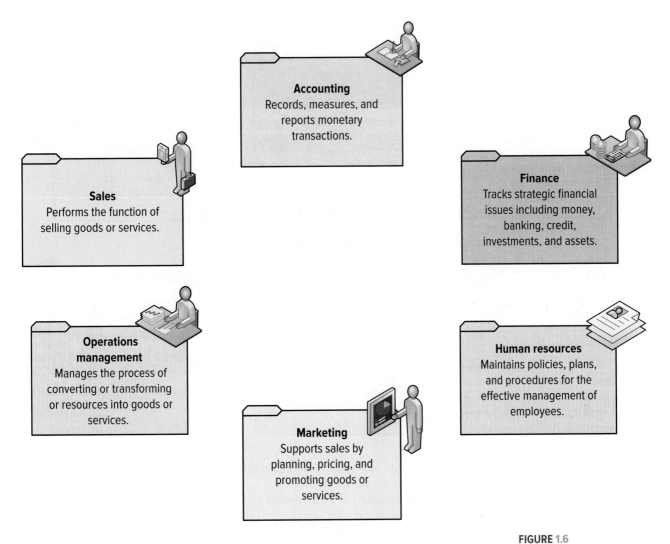

Accounting
Records, measures, and reports monetary transactions.

Sales
Performs the function of selling goods or services.

Finance
Tracks strategic financial issues including money, banking, credit, investments, and assets.

Operations management
Manages the process of converting or transforming or resources into goods or services.

Marketing
Supports sales by planning, pricing, and promoting goods or services.

Human resources
Maintains policies, plans, and procedures for the effective management of employees.

FIGURE 1.6

Departments Working Independently.

It is easy to see how a business decision made by one department can affect other departments. Marketing needs to analyze production and sales data to come up with product promotions and advertising strategies. Production needs to understand sales forecasts to determine the company's manufacturing needs. Sales needs to rely on information from operations to understand inventory, place orders, and forecast consumer demand. All departments need to understand the accounting and finance departments' information for budgeting. For the firm to be successful, all departments must work together as a single unit sharing common information and not operate independently or in a silo (see Figure 1.7).

The Solution: Management Information Systems

LO 1.3 **Explain systems thinking and how management information systems enable business communications.**

You probably recall the old story of three blind men attempting to describe an elephant. The first man, feeling the elephant's girth, said the elephant seemed very much like a wall. The second, feeling the elephant's trunk, declared the elephant was like a snake. The third man felt the elephant's tusks and said the elephant was like a tree or a cane. Companies that operate departmentally are seeing only one part of the elephant, a critical mistake that hinders successful operation.

Successful companies operate cross-functionally, integrating the operations of all departments. Systems are the primary enabler of cross-functional operations. A *system* is a collection of parts that link to achieve a common purpose. A car is a good example of a system, since removing a part, such as the steering wheel or accelerator, causes the entire system to stop working.

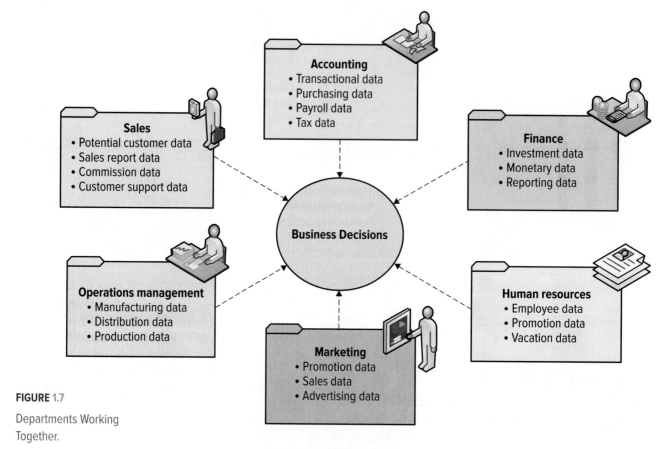

FIGURE 1.7

Departments Working
Together.

Before jumping into how systems work, it is important to have a solid understanding of the basic production process for goods and services. *Goods* are material items or products that customers will buy to satisfy a want or need. Clothing, groceries, cell phones, and cars are all examples of goods that people buy to fulfill their needs. *Services* are tasks performed by people that customers will buy to satisfy a want or need. Waiting tables, teaching, and cutting hair are all examples of services that people pay for to fulfill their needs (see Figure 1.8).

FIGURE 1.8

Different Types of Goods and
Services.

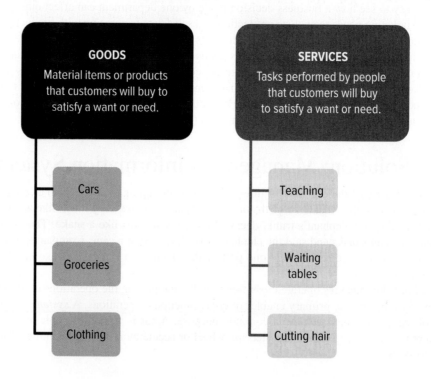

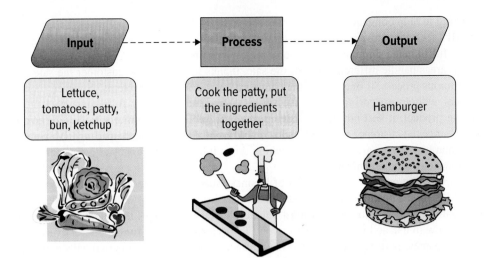

FIGURE 1.9

Input, Process, Output
Example.

Production is the process where a business takes raw materials and processes them or converts them into a finished product for its goods or services. Just think about making a hamburger (see Figure 1.9). First, you must gather all of the *inputs* or raw materials such as the bun, patty, lettuce, tomato, and ketchup. Second, you *process* the raw materials, so in this example you would need to cook the patty, wash and chop the lettuce and tomato, and place all of the items in the bun. Finally, you would have your *output* or finished product—your hamburger! *Productivity* is the rate at which goods and services are produced based upon total output given total inputs. Given our previous example, if a business could produce the same hamburger with less expensive inputs or more hamburgers with the same inputs it would see a rise in productivity and possibly an increase in profits. Ensuring the input, process, and output of goods and services work across all of the departments of a company is where systems add tremendous value to overall business productivity.

Systems thinking is a way of monitoring the entire system by viewing multiple inputs being processed or transformed to produce outputs while continuously gathering feedback on each part (see Figure 1.10). *Feedback* is information that returns to its original transmitter (input, transform, or output) and modifies the transmitter's actions. Feedback helps the system maintain stability. For example, a car's system continuously monitors the fuel level and turns on a warning light if the gas level is too low. Systems thinking provides an end-to-end view of how operations work together to create a product or service. Business students who understand systems thinking are valuable resources because they can implement solutions that consider the entire process, not just a single component.

Management information systems (MIS) is a business function, like accounting and human resources, which moves information about people, products, and processes across the company to facilitate decision making and problem solving. MIS incorporates systems

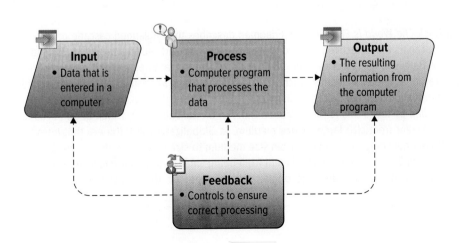

FIGURE 1.10

Overview of Systems
Thinking.

thinking to help companies operate cross-functionally. For example, to fulfill product orders, an MIS for sales moves a single customer order across all functional areas including sales, order fulfillment, shipping, billing, and finally customer service. Although different functional areas handle different parts of the sale, thanks to MIS, to the customer the sale is one continuous process. If one part of the company is experiencing problems, however, then, like the car without a steering wheel, the entire system fails. If order fulfillment packages the wrong product, it will not matter that shipping, billing, and customer service did their jobs right, since the customer will not be satisfied when he or she opens the package. Management information systems are the key to breaking down information silos by allowing information to flow across the organization.

MIS can be an important enabler of business success and innovation. This is not to say that MIS *equals* business success and innovation, or that MIS *represents* business success and innovation. MIS is a tool that is most valuable when it leverages the talents of people who know how to use and manage it effectively. To perform the MIS function effectively, almost all companies, particularly large and medium-sized ones, have an internal MIS department, often called information technology (IT), information systems (IS), or management information systems (MIS). For the purpose of this text, we will refer to it as MIS.

OPENING CASE STUDY QUESTIONS

1. Imagine you are working for Costco as a manager in its Chicago store. Your boss does not understand the difference between data, information, business intelligence, and knowledge. Using examples of products and services available at Costco provide examples of each to help your boss understand these important concepts.

2. Explain why it is important for Costco's corporate accounting, marketing, and operations management business units to access and analyze information about your store's sales. What could happen if your store sales were not shared with the different business units at Costco's headquarters?

3. Explain systems thinking and how MIS solves the issue with information silos throughout Costco's entire worldwide organization.

Chapter One Case: The World Is Flat—Thomas Friedman

In his book *The World Is Flat,* Thomas Friedman describes the unplanned cascade of technological and social shifts that effectively leveled the economic world and "accidentally made Beijing, Bangalore, and Bethesda next-door neighbors." Chances are good that Bhavya in Bangalore will read your next X-ray, or as Friedman learned firsthand, "Grandma Betty in her bathrobe" will make your JetBlue plane reservation from her Salt Lake City home.

Friedman believes this is Globalization 3.0. "In Globalization 1.0, which began around 1492, the world went from size large to size medium. In Globalization 2.0, the era that introduced us to multinational companies, it went from size medium to size small. And then around 2000 came Globalization 3.0, in which the world went from being small to tiny. There is a difference between being able to make long-distance phone calls cheaper on the Internet and walking around

Riyadh with a PDA where you can have all of Google in your pocket. It is a difference in degree that's so enormous it becomes a difference in kind," Friedman states. Below are Friedman's list of "flatteners."

1. Fall of the Berlin Wall	Opened the world to free markets.
2. Netscape IPO	Began the gigantic investments in connecting the world with fiber-optic cables.
3. Work flow software	Allowed employees to communicate and collaborate from all over the world.
4. Open-sourcing	Open source communities began creating free software.
5. Outsourcing	Using labor from third world countries allowed companies to grow while helping grow economies.
6. Offshoring	Using China to manufacture goods helped the world-wide global economy.
7. Supply-chaining	Businesses gained monumental efficiencies by connecting networks of suppliers, retailers, distributors, and customers.
8. Insourcing	Small business gained global momentum.
9. Informing	Search gave the intelligence to the masses.
10. Wireless	Business mobility gave the power of collaboration to the people.

Friedman says these flatteners converged around the year 2000 and "created a flat world: a global, Web-enabled platform for multiple forms of sharing knowledge and work, irrespective of time, distance, geography, and increasingly, language." At the very moment this platform emerged, three huge economies materialized—those of India, China, and the former Soviet Union—"and 3 billion people who were out of the game, walked onto the playing field." A final convergence may determine the fate of the United States in this chapter of globalization. A "political perfect storm," as Friedman describes it—the dot-com bust, the attacks of 9/11, and the Enron scandal—"distract us completely as a country." Just when we need to face the fact of globalization and the need to compete in a new world, "we're looking totally elsewhere."

Friedman believes that the next great breakthrough in bioscience could come from a 5-year-old who downloads the human genome in Egypt. Bill Gates's view is similar: "Twenty years ago, would you rather have been a B-student in Poughkeepsie or a genius in Shanghai? Twenty years ago you'd rather be a B-student in Poughkeepsie. Today, it is not even close. You'd much prefer to be the genius in Shanghai because you can now export your talents anywhere in the world."[4]

Questions

1. Do you agree or disagree with Friedman's assessment that the world is flat? Be sure to justify your answer.

2. What are the potential impacts of a flat world for a student performing a job search?

3. What can students do to prepare themselves for competing in a flat world?

4. Identify a current flattener not mentioned on Friedman's list.

1.1. Describe the information age and the differences among data, information, business intelligence, and knowledge.

We live in the information age, when infinite quantities of facts are widely available to anyone who can use a computer. The core drivers of the information age include data, information, business intelligence, and knowledge. Data are raw facts that describe the characteristics of an event or object. Information is data converted into a meaningful and useful context. Business intelligence (BI) is information collected from multiple sources such as suppliers, customers, competitors, partners, and industries that analyzes patterns, trends, and relationships for strategic decision making. Knowledge includes the skills, experience, and expertise, coupled with information and intelligence, that create a person's intellectual resources. As you move from data to knowledge, you include more and more variables for analysis, resulting in better, more precise support for decision making and problem solving.

1.2. Identify the different departments in a company and why they must work together to achieve success.

- **Accounting:** Records, measures, and reports monetary transactions.
- **Finance:** Deals with strategic financial issues including money, banking, credit, investments, and assets.
- **Human resources:** Maintains policies, plans, and procedures for the effective management of employees.
- **Marketing:** Supports sales by planning, pricing, and promoting goods or services.
- **Operations management:** Manages the process of converting or transforming resources into goods or services.
- **Sales:** Performs the function of selling goods or services.

It is easy to see how a business decision made by one department can affect other departments. Marketing needs to analyze production and sales data to come up with product promotions and advertising strategies. Production needs to understand sales forecasts to determine the company's manufacturing needs. Sales needs to rely on information from operations to understand inventory, place orders, and forecast consumer demand. All departments need to understand the accounting and finance departments' information for budgeting. For the firm to be successful, all departments must work together as a single unit sharing common information and not operate independently or in a silo.

1.3. Explain systems thinking and how management information systems enable business communications.

A system is a collection of parts that link to achieve a common purpose. Systems thinking is a way of monitoring the entire system by viewing multiple inputs being processed or transformed to produce outputs while continuously gathering feedback on each part. Feedback is information that returns to its original transmitter (input, transform, or output) and modifies the transmitter's actions. Feedback helps the system maintain stability. Management information systems (MIS) is a business function, like accounting and human resources, which moves information about people, products, and processes across the company to facilitate decision making and problem solving. MIS incorporates systems thinking to help companies operate cross-functionally. For example, to fulfill product orders, an MIS for sales moves a single customer order across all functional areas, including sales, order fulfillment, shipping, billing, and finally customer service. Although different functional areas handle different parts of the sale, thanks to MIS, to the customer the sale is one continuous process.

1. What is data? Why is data important to a business?
2. How can a manager turn data into information?
3. What is the relationship between data, information, business intelligence, and knowledge?
4. Why is it important for a company to operate cross-functionally?
5. What is MIS and what role does it plays in an organization?
6. Do you agree that MIS is essential for businesses operating in the information age? Why or why not?
7. What type of career are you planning to pursue? How will your specific career use data, information, business intelligence, and knowledge?
8. How does system thinking support business operations?

★ MAKING BUSINESS DECISIONS

1. View from a Flat World

Bill Gates, founder of Microsoft, stated that 20 years ago most people would rather have been a B student in New York City than a genius in China because the opportunities available to students in developed countries were limitless. Today, many argue that the opposite is now true due to technological advances making it easier to succeed as a genius in China than a B student in New York. As a group, discuss whether you agree or disagree with Bill Gates's statement.

2. Is Technology Making Us Dumber or Smarter?

There are numerous articles on how Facebook can make you dumber and Twitter can impede your ability to make sound decisions. Do you believe technology is making mankind dumber? Choose a side and debate the following:

Side A Living in the information age has made us smarter because we have a huge wealth of knowledge at our fingertips whenever or wherever we need it.

Side B Living in the information age has caused people to become lazy and dumber because they are no longer building up their memory banks to solve problems; machines give them the answers they need to solve problems.

3. IOT in the Room

Each day you are surrounded by millions of bits of data flying around you and you probably have not even noticed! As a collective group analyze all of the IOT devices currently in your classroom. What types of data are they sending and receiving? How frequently are they sending and receiving the data? What types of IOT device information are you using to manage your life? What types of IOT devices will be in the room in 5 years and how will they help future students analyze and manage their lives?

4. Working for the Best

Each year, *Fortune* magazine creates a list of the top 100 companies to work for. Find the most recent list. What types of data do you think *Fortune* analyzed to determine the company ranking? What issues could occur if the analysis of the data was inaccurate? What types of information can you gain by analyzing the list? Create five questions a student performing a job search could answer by analyzing this list.

5. People in China and India Are Starving for Your Jobs

"When I was growing up in Minneapolis, my parents always said, 'Tom, finish your dinner. There are people starving in China and India.' Today I tell my girls, 'Finish your homework, because people in China and India are starving for your jobs.' And in a flat world, they can have them, because there's no such thing as an American job anymore." Thomas Friedman.

In his book, *The World Is Flat,* Thomas Friedman describes the unplanned cascade of technological and social shifts that effectively leveled the economic world, and "accidentally made Beijing, Bangalore, and Bethesda next-door neighbors." The video of Thomas Friedman's lecture at MIT discussing the flat world is available at http://mitworld.mit.edu/video/266. If you want to be prepared to compete in a flat world you must watch this video and answer the following questions:

- Do you agree or disagree with Friedman's assessment that the world is flat?
- What are the potential impacts of a flat world for a student performing a job search?
- What can students do to prepare themselves for competing in a flat world?

6. Teddy The Guardian

Two London-based entrepreneurs are building an Internet of huggable things for sick children to make any hospital visit more like a trip to Disneyland. Teddy The Guardian captures heart rate, temperatures, and blood-oxygen levels when a child grabs it by the paw to give it a cuddle. All measurements are sent wirelessly to nurses and parents, mobile devices. The new cute, cuddly teddy bear is packed full of sensors designed to track children's vital signs and help quickly find out potential issues. Teddy The Guardian takes from 5 to 7 seconds to record measurements and is programmed to run five times per hour. Future versions of Teddy The Guardian will be interactive, using machine learning to find out the child's favorite song or bedtime story and then play the related content for a more soothing hospital visit. Big pharmaceutical companies in the United States have already placed over $500,000 in orders and plan to donate the bears to hospitals and clinics.

This is clearly a brilliant idea, and soon we will see Teddy The Guardian in many local hospitals and clinics. Can you identify any additional markets where Teddy The Guardian should focus? Can you think of any ethical issues related to huggable things? Can you think of any security issues related to huggable things?

Identifying Competitive Advantages

2.1. Explain why competitive advantages are temporary along with the four key areas of a SWOT analysis.

2.2. Describe Porter's Five Forces Model and explain each of the five forces.

2.3. Compare Porter's three generic strategies.

2.4. Demonstrate how a company can add value by using Porter's value chain analysis.

Identifying Competitive Advantages

LO 2.1 Explain why competitive advantages are temporary along with the four key areas of a SWOT analysis.

Running a company today is similar to leading an army; the top manager or leader ensures all participants are heading in the right direction and completing their goals and objectives. Companies lacking leadership quickly implode as employees head in different directions attempting to achieve conflicting goals. To combat these challenges, leaders communicate and execute business strategies (from the Greek word *stratus* for army and *ago* for leading).

A *business strategy* is a leadership plan that achieves a specific set of goals or objectives such as increasing sales, decreasing costs, entering new markets, or developing new products or services. A *stakeholder* is a person or group that has an interest or concern in an organization. Stakeholders drive business strategies, and depending on the stakeholder's perspective, the business strategy can change. It is not uncommon to find stakeholders' business strategies have conflicting interests such as investors looking to increase profits by eliminating employee jobs. Figure 2.1 displays the different stakeholders found in an organization and their common business interests.

Good leaders also anticipate unexpected misfortunes, from strikes and economic recessions to natural disasters. Their business strategies build in buffers or slack, allowing the company the ability to ride out any storm and defend against competitive or environmental threats. Of course, updating business strategies is a continuous undertaking as internal and external environments rapidly change. Business strategies that match core company competencies to opportunities result in competitive advantages, a key to success!

A *competitive advantage* is a feature of a product or service on which customers place a greater value than they do on similar offerings from competitors. Competitive advantages provide the same product or service either at a lower price or with additional value that can fetch premium prices. Unfortunately, competitive advantages are typically temporary, because competitors often quickly seek ways to duplicate them. In turn, organizations must develop a strategy based on a new competitive advantage. Ways that companies duplicate competitive advantages include acquiring the new technology, copying the business operations, and hiring away key employees. The introduction of Apple's iPod and iTunes, a brilliant merger of technology, business, and entertainment, offers an excellent example.

In early 2000, Steve Jobs was fixated on developing video editing software when he suddenly realized that millions of people were using computers to listen to music, a new trend

FIGURE 2.1

Stakeholders' Interests.

in the industry catapulted by illegal online services such as Napster. Jobs was worried that he was looking in the wrong direction and had missed the opportunity to jump on the online music bandwagon. He moved fast, however, and within four months he had developed the first version of iTunes for the Mac. Jobs's next challenge was to make a portable iTunes player that could hold thousands of songs and be completely transportable. Within nine months the iPod was born. With the combination of iTunes and iPod, Apple created a significant competitive advantage in the marketplace. Many firms began following Apple's lead by creating portable music players to compete with the iPod. In addition, Apple continues to create new and exciting products to gain competitive advantages, such as its iPad, a larger version of the iPod that functions more as a computer than a music player.[1]

When a company is the first to market with a competitive advantage, it gains a particular benefit, such as Apple did with its iPod. This *first-mover advantage* occurs when a company can significantly increase its market share by being first with a new competitive advantage. FedEx created a first-mover advantage by developing its customer self-service software, which allows people to request parcel pickups, print mailing slips, and track parcels online. Other parcel delivery companies quickly began creating their own online services. Today, customer self-service on the Internet is a standard feature of the parcel delivery business.

Competitive intelligence is the process of gathering information about the competitive environment, including competitors' plans, activities, and products, to improve a company's ability to succeed. It means understanding and learning as much as possible as soon as possible about what is occurring outside the company to remain competitive. Frito-Lay, a premier provider of snack foods such as Cracker Jacks and Cheetos, does not send its sales representatives into grocery stores just to stock shelves; they carry handheld computers and record the

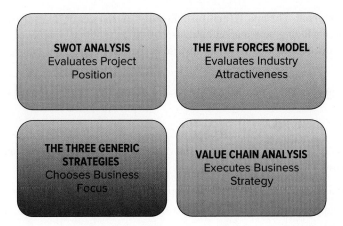

FIGURE 2.2

Business Tools for Analyzing
Business Strategies.

product offerings, inventory, and even product locations of competitors. Frito-Lay uses this information to gain competitive intelligence on everything from how well competing products are selling to the strategic placement of its own products.[2] Managers use four common tools to analyze competitive intelligence and develop competitive advantages as displayed in Figure 2.2.

SWOT ANALYSIS: UNDERSTANDING BUSINESS STRATEGIES

A *SWOT analysis* evaluates an organization's **s**trengths, **w**eaknesses, **o**pportunities, and **t**hreats to identify significant influences that work for or against business strategies (see Figure 2.3). Strengths and weaknesses originate inside an organization, or internally. Opportunities and threats originate outside an organization, or externally, and cannot always be anticipated or controlled.

- **Potential Internal Strengths (Helpful):** Identify all key strengths associated with the competitive advantage including cost advantages, new and/or innovative services, special expertise and/or experience, proven market leader, and improved marketing campaigns.

- **Potential Internal Weaknesses (Harmful):** Identify all key areas that require improvement. Weaknesses focus on the absence of certain strengths, including absence of an Internet marketing plan, damaged reputation, problem areas for service, and outdated technology employee issues.

- **Potential External Opportunities (Helpful):** Identify all significant trends along with how the organization can benefit from each, including new markets, additional customer groups, legal changes, innovative technologies, population changes, and competitor issues.

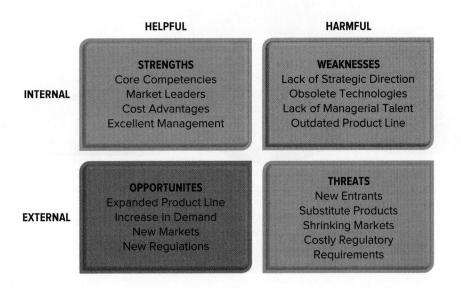

FIGURE 2.3

Sample SWOT Analysis

- **Potential External Threats (Harmful):** Identify all threats or risks detrimental to your organization, including new market entrants, substitute products, employee turnover, differentiating products, shrinking markets, adverse changes in regulations, and economic shifts.

LO 2.2 Describe Porter's Five Forces Model and explain each of the five forces.

The Five Forces Model—Evaluating Industry Attractiveness

Michael Porter, a university professor at Harvard Business School, identified the following pressures that can hurt potential sales:

- Knowledgeable customers can force down prices by pitting rivals against each other.
- Influential suppliers can drive down profits by charging higher prices for supplies.
- Competition can steal customers.
- New market entrants can steal potential investment capital.
- Substitute products can steal customers.

Formally defined, ***Porter's Five Forces Model*** analyzes the competitive forces within the environment in which a company operates to assess the potential for profitability in an industry. Its purpose is to combat these competitive forces by identifying opportunities, competitive advantages, and competitive intelligence. If the forces are strong, they increase competition; if the forces are weak, they decrease competition. This section details each of the forces and its associated MIS business strategy (see Figure 2.4).[3]

BUYER POWER

Buyer power is the ability of buyers to affect the price they must pay for an item. Factors used to assess buyer power include number of customers, their sensitivity to price, size of orders, differences between competitors, and availability of substitute products. If buyer power is high, customers can force a company and its competitors to compete on price, which typically drives prices down.

One way to reduce buyer power is by manipulating ***switching costs,*** costs that make customers reluctant to switch to another product or service. Switching costs include financial as well as intangible values. The cost of switching doctors, for instance, includes the powerful intangible components of having to build relationships with the new doctor and nurses, as well

FIGURE 2.4

Porter's Five Forces Model.

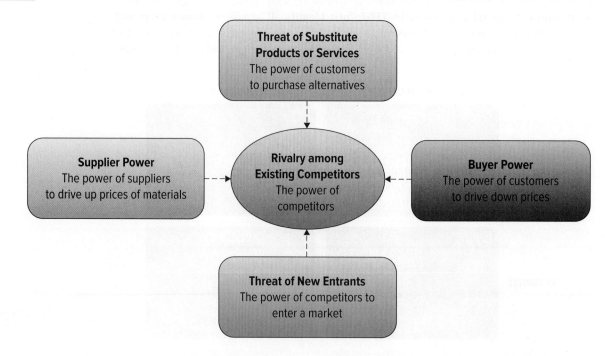

as transferring all your medical history. With MIS, however, patients can store their medical records on DVDs or thumb drives, allowing easy transferability. The Internet also lets patients review websites for physician referrals, which takes some of the fear out of trying someone new.[4]

Companies can also reduce buyer power with **loyalty programs**, which reward customers based on their spending. The airline industry is famous for its frequent-flyer programs, for instance. Because of the rewards travelers receive (free airline tickets, upgrades, or hotel stays), they are more likely to be loyal to or give most of their business to a single company. Keeping track of the activities and accounts of many thousands or millions of customers covered by loyalty programs is not practical without large-scale business systems, however. Loyalty programs are thus a good example of using MIS to reduce buyer power.[5]

SUPPLIER POWER

A **supply chain** consists of all parties involved, directly or indirectly, in obtaining raw materials or a product. In a typical supply chain, a company will be both a supplier (to customers) and a customer (of other suppliers), as illustrated in Figure 2.5. **Supplier power** is the suppliers' ability to influence the prices they charge for supplies (including materials, labor, and services). Factors used to appraise supplier power include number of suppliers, size of suppliers, uniqueness of services, and availability of substitute products. If supplier power is high, the supplier can influence the industry by:

- Charging higher prices.
- Limiting quality or services.
- Shifting costs to industry participants.[6]

Typically, when a supplier raises prices, the buyers will pass on the increase to their customers by raising prices on the end product. When supplier power is high, buyers lose revenue because they cannot pass on the raw material price increase to their customers. Some powerful suppliers, such as pharmaceutical companies, can exert a threat over an entire industry when substitutes are limited and the product is critical to the buyers. Patients who need to purchase cancer-fighting drugs have no power over price and must pay whatever the drug company asks because there are few available alternatives.

Using MIS to find alternative products is one way of decreasing supplier power. Cancer patients can now use the Internet to research alternative medications and practices, something that was next to impossible just a few decades ago. Buyers can also use MIS to form groups or collaborate with other buyers, increasing the size of the buyer group and reducing supplier power. For a hypothetical example, the collective group of 30,000 students from a university has far more power over price when purchasing laptops than a single student.[7]

THREAT OF SUBSTITUTE PRODUCTS OR SERVICES

The **threat of substitute products or services** is high when there are many alternatives to a product or service and low when there are few alternatives from which to choose. For example, travelers have numerous substitutes for airline transportation including automobiles, trains, and boats. Technology even makes videoconferencing and virtual meetings possible, eliminating the need for some business travel. Ideally, a company would like to be in a market in which there are few substitutes for the products or services it offers.

Polaroid had this unique competitive advantage for many years until it forgot to observe competitive intelligence. Then the firm went bankrupt when people began taking digital pictures with everything from video cameras to cell phones.

A company can reduce the threat of substitutes by offering additional value through wider product distribution. Soft-drink manufacturers distribute their products through vending

FIGURE 2.5

Traditional Supply Chain.

machines, gas stations, and convenience stores, increasing the availability of soft drinks relative to other beverages. Companies can also offer various add-on services, making the substitute product less of a threat. For example, iPhones include capabilities for games, videos, and music, making a traditional cell phone less of a substitute.[8]

THREAT OF NEW ENTRANTS

The *threat of new entrants* is high when it is easy for new competitors to enter a market and low when there are significant entry barriers to joining a market. An *entry barrier* is a feature of a product or service that customers have come to expect and entering competitors must offer the same for survival. For example, a new bank must offer its customers an array of MIS-enabled services, including ATMs, online bill paying, and online account monitoring. These are significant barriers to new firms entering the banking market. At one time, the first bank to offer such services gained a valuable first-mover advantage, but only temporarily, as other banking competitors developed their own MIS services.[9]

RIVALRY AMONG EXISTING COMPETITORS

Rivalry among existing competitors is high when competition is fierce in a market and low when competitors are more complacent. Although competition is always more intense in some industries than in others, the overall trend is toward increased competition in almost every industry. The retail grocery industry is intensively competitive. Kroger, Safeway, and Albertsons in the United States compete in many different ways, essentially trying to beat or match each other on price. Most supermarket chains have implemented loyalty programs to provide customers special discounts while gathering valuable information about their purchasing habits. In the future, expect to see grocery stores using wireless technologies that track customer movements throughout the store to determine purchasing sequences.

Product differentiation occurs when a company develops unique differences in its products or services with the intent to influence demand. Companies can use differentiation to reduce rivalry. For example, while many companies sell books and videos on the Internet, Amazon differentiates itself by using customer profiling. When a customer visits Amazon.com repeatedly, Amazon begins to offer products tailored to that particular customer based on his or her profile. In this way, Amazon has reduced its rivals' power by offering its customers a differentiated service.

To review, the Five Forces Model helps managers set business strategy by identifying the competitive structure and economic environment of an industry. If the forces are strong, they increase competition; if the forces are weak, they decrease it (see Figure 2.6).[10]

ANALYZING THE AIRLINE INDUSTRY

Let us bring Porter's five forces together to look at the competitive forces shaping an industry and highlight business strategies to help it remain competitive. Assume a shipping company is

FIGURE 2.6

Strong and Weak Examples of Porter's Five Forces.

	Weak Force: Decreases Competition or Few Competitors	Strong Force: Increases Competition or Lots of Competitors
Buyer Power	An international hotel chain purchasing milk	A single consumer purchasing milk
Supplier Power	A company that makes airline engines	A company that makes pencils
Threat of Substitute Products or Services	Cancer drugs from a pharmaceutical company	Coffee from McDonald's
Threat of New Entrants	A professional hockey team	A dog walking business
Rivalry among Existing Competitors	Department of Motor Vehicles	A coffee shop

	Strong (High) Force: Increases Competition or Lots of Competitors
Buyer Power	Many airlines for buyers to choose from forcing competition based on price.
Supplier Power	Limited number of plane and engine manufacturers to choose from along with unionized workers.
Threat of Substitute Products or Services	Many substitutes including cars, trains, and buses. Even substitutes to travel such as video conferencing and virtual meetings.
Threat of New Entrants	Many new airlines entering the market all the time including the latest sky taxis.
Rivalry among Existing Competitors	Intense competition—many rivals.

FIGURE 2.7

Five Forces Model in the Airline Industry.

deciding whether to enter the commercial airline industry. If performed correctly, an analysis of the five forces should determine that this is a highly risky business strategy because all five forces are strong. It will thus be difficult to generate a profit.

- **Buyer power:** Buyer power is high because customers have many airlines to choose from and typically make purchases based on price, not carrier.

- **Supplier power:** Supplier power is high since there are limited plane and engine manufacturers to choose from, and unionized workforces (suppliers of labor) restrict airline profits.

- **Threat of substitute products or services:** The threat of substitute products is high from many transportation alternatives including automobiles, trains, and boats, and from transportation substitutes such as videoconferencing and virtual meetings.

- **Threat of new entrants:** The threat of new entrants is high because new airlines are continuously entering the market, including sky taxies offering low-cost on-demand air taxi service.

- **Rivalry among existing competitors:** Rivalry in the airline industry is high, and websites such as Travelocity.com force them to compete on price (see Figure 2.7).[11]

The Three Generic Strategies—Choosing a Business Focus

LO 2.3 Compare Porter's three generic strategies.

Once top management has determined the relative attractiveness of an industry and decided to enter it, the firm must formulate a strategy for doing so. If our sample company decided to join the airline industry, it could compete as a low-cost, no-frills airline or as a luxury airline providing outstanding service and first-class comfort. Both options offer different ways of achieving competitive advantages in a crowded marketplace. The low-cost operator saves on expenses and passes the savings along to customers in the form of low prices. The luxury airline spends on high-end service and first-class comforts and passes the costs on to the customer in the form of high prices.

Porter's three generic strategies are generic business strategies that are neither organization nor industry specific and can be applied to any business, product, or service. These three generic business strategies for entering a new market are: (1) broad cost leadership, (2) broad differentiation, and (3) focused strategy. Broad strategies reach a large market segment, while focused strategies target a niche or unique market with either cost leadership or differentiation. Trying to be all things to all people is a recipe for disaster, since doing so makes it difficult to project a consistent image to the entire marketplace. For this reason, Porter suggests adopting only one of the three generic strategies illustrated in Figure 2.8.[12]

FIGURE 2.8

Porter's Three Generic
Strategies.

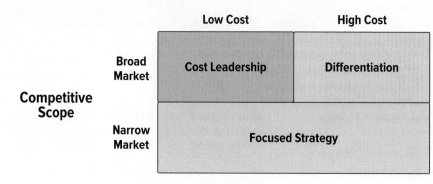

FIGURE 2.9

Examples of Porter's Three
Generic Strategies.

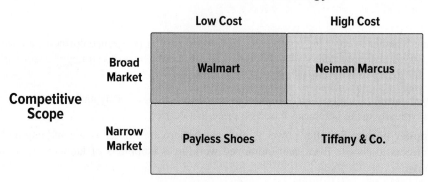

Figure 2.9 applies the three strategies to real companies, demonstrating the relationships among strategies (cost leadership versus differentiation) and market segmentation (broad versus focused).

- **Broad market and low cost:** Walmart competes by offering a broad range of products at low prices. Its business strategy is to be the low-cost provider of goods for the cost-conscious consumer.

- **Broad market and high cost:** Neiman Marcus competes by offering a broad range of differentiated products at high prices. Its business strategy offers a variety of specialty and upscale products to affluent consumers.

- **Narrow market and low cost:** Payless competes by offering a specific product, shoes, at low prices. Its business strategy is to be the low-cost provider of shoes. Payless competes with Walmart, which also sells low-cost shoes, by offering a far bigger selection of sizes and styles.

- **Narrow market and high cost:** Tiffany & Co. competes by offering a differentiated product, jewelry, at high prices. Its business strategy allows it to be a high-cost provider of premier designer jewelry to affluent consumers.

LO 2.4 Demonstrate how a company can add value by using Porter's value chain analysis.

Value Chain Analysis—Executing Business Strategies

Firms make profits by taking raw inputs and applying a business process to turn them into a product or service that customers find valuable. A ***business process*** is a standardized set of activities that accomplish a specific task, such as processing a customer's order. Once a firm identifies the industry it wants to enter and the generic strategy it will focus on, it must then choose the business processes required to create its products or services. Of course, the firm will want to ensure the processes add value and create competitive advantages. To identify these competitive advantages, Michael Porter created *value chain analysis*, which views a firm as a series of business processes that each add value to the product or service.

Value chain analysis is a useful tool for determining how to create the greatest possible value for customers (see Figure 2.10). The goal of value chain analysis is to identify processes in which the firm can add value for the customer and create a competitive advantage for itself, with a cost advantage or product differentiation.

The *value chain* groups a firm's activities into two categories, primary value activities, and support value activities. ***Primary value activities***, shown at the bottom of the value chain in Figure 2.10, acquire raw materials and manufacture, deliver, market, sell, and provide after-sales services.

1. **Inbound logistics:** acquires raw materials and resources and distributes to manufacturing as required.
2. **Operations:** transforms raw materials or inputs into goods and services.
3. **Outbound logistics:** distributes goods and services to customers.
4. **Marketing and sales:** promotes, prices, and sells products to customers.
5. **Service:** Provides customer support after the sale of goods and services.[13]

Support value activities, along the top of the value chain in Figure 2.10, include firm infrastructure, human resource management, technology development, and procurement. Not surprisingly, these support the primary value activities.

- **Firm infrastructure:** includes the company format or departmental structures, environment, and systems.
- **Human resource management:** provides employee training, hiring, and compensation.
- **Technology development:** applies MIS to processes to add value.
- **Procurement:** purchases inputs such as raw materials, resources, equipment, and supplies.

It is easy to understand how a typical manufacturing firm takes raw materials such as wood pulp and transforms it into paper. Adding value in this example might include using high-quality raw materials or offering next-day free shipping on any order. How, though, might a typical service firm take raw inputs such as time, knowledge, and MIS and transform them into valuable customer service knowledge? A hotel might use MIS to track customer reservations and then inform front-desk employees when a loyal customer is checking in so the employee can call the guest by name and offer additional services, gift baskets, or upgraded rooms. Examining the firm as a value chain allows managers to identify the important business processes that add value for customers and then find MIS solutions that support them.

FIGURE 2.10

The Value Chain.

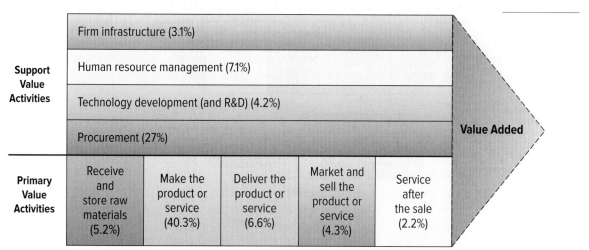

When performing a value chain analysis, a firm could survey customers about the extent to which they believe each activity adds value to the product or service. This step generates responses the firm can measure, shown as percentages in Figure 2.10, to describe how each activity adds (or reduces) value. Then the competitive advantage decision for the firm is whether to (1) target high value-adding activities to further enhance their value, (2) target low value-adding activities to increase their value, or (3) perform some combination of the two.

MIS adds value to both primary and support value activities. One example of a primary value activity facilitated by MIS is the development of a marketing campaign management system that could target marketing campaigns more efficiently, thereby reducing marketing costs. The system would also help the firm better pinpoint target market needs, thereby increasing sales. One example of a support value activity facilitated by MIS is the development of a human resources system that could more efficiently reward employees based on performance. The system could also identify employees who are at risk of quitting, allowing a manager time to find additional challenges or opportunities that would help retain these employees and thus reduce turnover costs.

Value chain analysis is a highly useful tool that provides hard and fast numbers for evaluating the activities that add value to products and services. Managers can find additional value by analyzing and constructing the value chain in terms of Porter's Five Forces Model (see Figure 2.11). For example, if the goal is to decrease buyer power, a company can construct its value chain activity of "service after the sale" by offering high levels of customer service. This will increase customers' switching costs and reduce their power. Analyzing and constructing support value activities can help decrease the threat of new entrants. Analyzing and constructing primary value activities can help decrease the threat of substitute products or services. Revising Porter's three business strategies is critical. Firms must continually adapt to their competitive environments, which can cause business strategy to shift.[14]

FIGURE 2.11

The Value Chain and Porter's Five Forces Model.

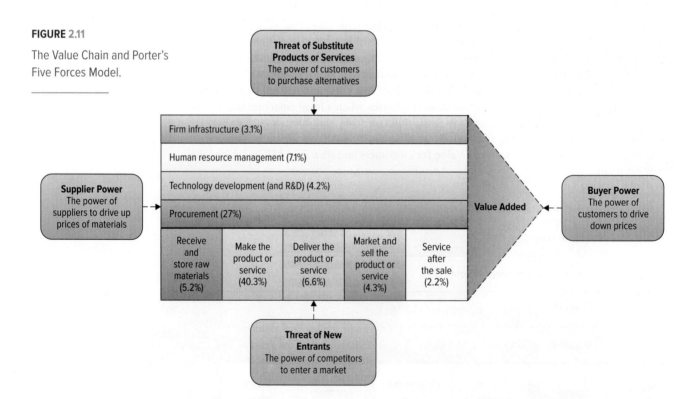

1. Imagine you are working for Costco as a manager in its Chicago store. Using Porter's Five Forces Model, analyze buyer power and supplier power for Costco.

2. Which of the three generic strategies is Costco following?

3. Only members of Costco can purchase products at Costco. Which of Porter's Five Forces did Costco address through the introduction of its members-only program?

Chapter Two Case: Michael Porter on TED—The Case for Letting Business Solve Social Problems

Micheal Porter is a university professor at Harvard Business School, where he leads the Institute on Strategy and Competitiveness, studying competitiveness for companies and nations—and as a solution to social problems. He is the founder of numerous nonprofits, including The Initiative for a Competitive Inner City, a nonprofit, private-sector organization to catalyze inner-city business development.

Fortune magazine calls Michael Porter simply "the most famous and influential business professor who has ever lived." His books are part of foundational coursework for business students around the world; he's applied sharp insight to health care systems, American competitiveness, development in rural areas. Now he's taking on a massive question: the perceived disconnect between corporations and society. He argues that companies must begin to take the lead in reconceiving the intersection between society and corporate interests—and he suggests a framework, that of "shared value," which involves creating economic value in a way that also creates value for society.[15]

Visit TED.com to watch Michael Porter's video on why business can be good at solving social problems.

https://www.ted.com/talks/michael_porter_why_business_can_be_good_at_solving_social_problems

Questions

1. In today's global business environment, does the physical location of a business matter?

2. Do you agree or disagree that business can solve social problems? Justify your answer.

2.1. Explain why competitive advantages are temporary along with the four key areas of a SWOT analysis.

A competitive advantage is a feature of a product or service on which customers place a greater value than they do on similar offerings from competitors. Competitive advantages provide the same product or service either at a lower price or with additional value that can fetch premium prices. Unfortunately, competitive advantages are typically temporary because competitors often quickly seek ways to duplicate them. In turn, organizations must develop a strategy based on a new competitive advantage. Ways that companies duplicate competitive advantages include acquiring the new technology, copying business processes, and hiring away employees.

A SWOT analysis evaluates an organization's strengths, weaknesses, opportunities, and threats to identify significant influences that work for or against business strategies. Strengths and weaknesses originate inside an organization, or internally. Opportunities and threats originate outside an organization, or externally, and cannot always be anticipated or controlled.

2.2. Describe Porter's Five Forces Model and explain each of the five forces.

Porter's Five Forces Model analyzes the competitive forces within the environment in which a company operates, to assess the potential for profitability in an industry.

- Buyer power is the ability of buyers to affect the price they must pay for an item.
- Supplier power is the suppliers' ability to influence the prices they charge for supplies (including materials, labor, and services).
- Threat of substitute products or services is high when there are many alternatives to a product or service and low when there are few alternatives from which to choose.
- Threat of new entrants is high when it is easy for new competitors to enter a market and low when there are significant entry barriers to entering a market.
- Rivalry among existing competitors is high when competition is fierce in a market and low when competition is more complacent.

2.3. Compare Porter's three generic strategies.

Organizations typically follow one of Porter's three generic strategies when entering a new market: (1) broad cost leadership, (2) broad differentiation, and (3) focused strategy. Broad strategies reach a large market segment. Focused strategies target a niche market. Focused strategies concentrate on either cost leadership or differentiation.

2.4. Demonstrate how a company can add value by using Porter's value chain analysis.

To identify competitive advantages, Michael Porter created value chain analysis, which views a firm as a series of business processes, each of which adds value to the product or service. The goal of value chain analysis is to identify processes in which the firm can add value for the customer and create a competitive advantage for itself, with a cost advantage or product differentiation. The value chain groups a firm's activities into two categories—primary value activities and support value activities. Primary value activities acquire raw materials and manufacture, deliver, market, sell, and provide after-sales services. Support value activities, along the top of the value chain in the figure, include firm infrastructure, human resource management, technology development, and procurement. Not surprisingly, these support the primary value activities.

1. What is the relationship between a business strategy and stakeholders?
2. Who are the top three most important stakeholders in a business?
3. When would you use a SWOT analysis to help you make business decisions?
4. What is the role Porter's Five Forces Model plays in decision making?
5. How could a company use loyalty programs to influence buyer power?
6. How could a company use switching costs to lock in customers and suppliers?
7. What are Porter's three generic strategies and why would a company want to follow only one?
8. How can a company use Porter's value chain analysis to measure customer satisfaction?

MAKING BUSINESS DECISIONS

1. SWOT Your Students

What is your dream job? Do you have the right skills and abilities to land the job of your dreams? If not, do you have a plan to acquire those sought-after skills and abilities? Do you have a personal career plan or strategy? Just like a business, you can perform a personal SWOT analysis to ensure your career plan will be successful. You want to know your strengths and recognize career opportunities while mitigating your weaknesses and any threats that can potentially derail your career plans. A key area where many people struggle is technology, and without the right technical skills, you might find you are not qualified for your dream job. One of the great benefits of this course is its ability to help you prepare for a career in business by understanding the key role technology plays in the different industries and functional areas. Regardless of your major, you will all use business driven information systems to complete the tasks and assignments associated with your career.

Perform a personal SWOT analysis for your career plan, based on your current skills, talents, and knowledge. Be sure to focus on your personal career goals, including the functional business area in which you want to work and the potential industry you are targeting, such as health care, telecommunications, retail, or travel.

PERSONAL CAREER SWOT ANALYSIS

STRENGTHS	WEAKNESSES
OPPORTUNITIES	THREATS

Personal Career SWOT Analysis

After completing your personal SWOT analysis, take a look at the table of contents in this text and determine whether this course will eliminate any of your weaknesses or create new strengths. Determine whether you can find new opportunities or mitigate threats based on the material we cover over the next several weeks. For example, project management is a key skill for any business professional who must run a team. Learning how to assign and track work status will be a key tool for any new business professional. Where would you place this great skill in your SWOT analysis? Did it help eliminate any of your weaknesses? When you have finished this exercise, compare your SWOT with your peers to see what kind of competition you will encounter when you enter the workforce.

2. Keeping Sensitive Data Safe When It's Not in a Safe

In the past few years, data collection rates have skyrocketed, and some estimate we have collected more data in the past four years than since the beginning of time. According to International Data Corporation (IDC), data collection amounts used to double every four years. With the massive growth of smart phones, tablets, and wearable technology devices, it seems as though data is being collected from everything, everywhere, all the time. It is estimated that data collection is doubling every two years, and soon it will double every six months. That is a lot of data! With the explosion of data collection, CTOs, CIOs, and CSOs are facing extremely difficult times as the threats to steal corporate sensitive data grows. Hackers and criminals have recently stolen sensitive data from retail giant Target, Home Depot, TJ Maxx, and even the Federal Reserve Bank.

To operate, sensitive data has to flow outside an organization to partners, suppliers, community, government, and shareholders. List 10 types of sensitive data found in a common organization. Review the list of stakeholders; determine which types of sensitive data each has access to and whether you have any concerns about sharing this data. Do you have to worry about employees and sensitive data? How can using one of the four business strategies discussed in this section help you address your data leakage concerns?

3. Pursuing Porter

There is no doubt that Michael Porter is one of the more influential business strategists of the 21st century. Research Michael Porter on the Internet for interviews, additional articles, and new or updated business strategies. Create a summary of your findings to share with your class. How can learning about people such as Thomas Friedman and Michael Porter help prepare you for a career in business? Name three additional business professionals you should follow to help prepare for your career in business.

4. Choosing a Career

Choosing a career can be an overwhelming task! Let's face facts, you are going to spend countless hours working day-and-night at your job. If you choose the right career you can lead a life filled with excitement, opportunities, and happiness. Choose the wrong career and you can lead a life filled with boredom, suffering, and pain. The good news is the choice is yours! Create a list of your top three career choices and then perform a SWOT analysis of each career. Be sure to include such things as expectations, longevity, perks, benefits, and personal career goals. Hopefully, this great little exercise can start you thinking about the numerous opportunties that will be available to you in the near future.

5. Death of a Product

Porter's Five Forces Model is an essential framework for understanding industries and market forces. Choose one of the categories listed here and analyze what happened to the market using Porter's Five Forces:

- PDA and laptop computer.
- On-Demand Movies and Blue-ray player.

- Digital camera and Polaroid camera.
- GPS device and a road atlas.
- Digital books and printed books.
- High-definition TV and radio.

6. Applying the Three Generic Strategies

The chapter discussed examples of companies that pursue differentiated strategies so that they are not forced into positions where they must compete solely on the basis of price. Pick an industry and have your team members find and compare two companies, one that is competing on the basis of price and another that has chosen to pursue a differentiated strategy enabled by the creative use of MIS. Some industries you may want to consider are clothing retailers, grocery stores, airlines, and personal computers. Prepare a presentation for the class on the ways that MIS is being used to help the differentiating company compete against the low-cost provider. Before you begin, spend some class time to make sure each team selects a different industry if at all possible.

7. IOT Time Management

There is no doubt about it, poor time management is one of the leading causes of failure among students. Without being able to manage due dates, deliverables, work, and of course life students find themselves sinking instead of swimming in the vast college pool. You have decided that enough is enough and you and a few friends are going to take advantage of technology to create an innovative new IOT device to solve this monumental problem. In a group, brainstorm your new time management IOT device and then apply a Porter's Five Forces model. Use the model to determine the chances of success for your new product.

<table>
<tr><td>**CHAPTER** 3</td><td># Strategic Initiatives for Implementing Competitive Advantages</td></tr>
</table>

LEARNING OUTCOMES

3.1. Identify how an organization can use business process reengineering to improve its business.

3.2. Explain supply chain management and its role in business.

3.3. Explain customer relationship management systems and how they can help organizations understand their customers.

3.4. Summarize the importance of enterprise resource planning systems.

LO 3.1 Identify how an organization can use business process reengineering to improve its business.

Business Process Reengineering

This chapter introduces high-profile strategic initiatives that an organization can undertake to help it gain competitive advantages and business efficiencies—business process reengineering, supply chain management, customer relationship management, and enterprise resource planning (see Figure 3.1). Each of these strategic initiatives is covered in detail throughout this text. This chapter provides a brief introduction only.

Most companies pride themselves on providing breakthrough products and services for customers. But if customers do not receive what they want quickly, accurately, and hassle-free, even fantastic offerings will not prevent a company from annoying customers and ultimately eroding its own financial performance. To avoid this pitfall and protect its competitive advantage, a company must continually evaluate all the business processes in its value chain.

FIGURE 3.1

Strategic Initiatives for Competitive Advantages.

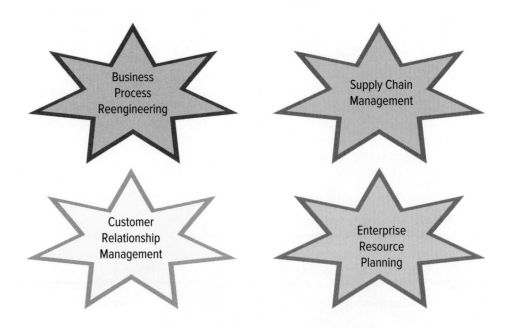

A business process is a standardized set of activities that accomplish a specific task, such as processing a customer's order. Business processes transform a set of inputs into a set of outputs—goods or services—for another person or process by using people and tools. *Workflow* includes the tasks, activities, and responsibilities required to execute each step in a business process. Understanding business processes, workflow, customers' expectations, and the competitive environment provides managers with the necessary ingredients to design and evaluate alternative business processes in order to maintain competitive advantages when internal or external circumstances change. *Workflow control systems* monitor processes to ensure tasks, activities, and responsibilities are executed as specified.

A *static process* uses a systematic approach in an attempt to improve business effectiveness and efficiency continuously. Managers constantly attempt to optimize static process. Examples of static processes include running payroll, calculating taxes, and creating financial statements. A *dynamic process* is continuously changing and provides business solutions to ever-changing business operations. As the business and its strategies change, so do the dynamic processes. Examples of dynamic processes include managing layoffs of employees, changing order levels based on currency rates, and canceling business travel due to extreme weather.

Systems thinking offers a great story to help differentiate between static and dynamic processes. If you throw a rock in the air, you can predict where it will land. If you throw a bird in the air you can't predict where it will land. The bird, a living dynamic, system, will sense its environment and fly in any direction. The bird gathers and processes input and interacts with its environment. The rock is an example of a static process and the bird is an example of a dynamic process. Organizations have people and are characteristically dynamic, making it difficult to predict how the business will operate. Managers must anticipate creating and deploying both static and dynamic processes to keep pace with the every changing business needs.

The business processes outlined in Figure 3.2 reflect functional thinking. Some processes, such as a programming process, may be contained wholly within a single department. However, most, such as ordering a product, are cross-functional or cross-departmental processes and span the entire organization. The process of "order to delivery" focuses on the entire customer order process across functional departments (see Figure 3.3). Another example is "product realization," which includes not only the way a product is developed, but also the way it is marketed and serviced. Some other cross-functional business processes are taking a product from concept to market, acquiring customers, loan processing, providing post-sales service, claim processing, and reservation handling.

Customer-facing processes, also called front-office processes, result in a product or service received by an organization's external customer. They include fulfilling orders, communicating with customers, and sending out bills and marketing information. *Business-facing processes*, also called back-office processes, are invisible to the external customer but essential to the effective management of the business; they include goal setting, day-to-day planning, giving performance feedback and rewards, and allocating resources. Figure 3.4 displays the different categories of customer-facing and business-facing processes along with an example of each. A company's strategic vision should provide guidance on which business processes are core, that is, which are directly linked to the firm's critical success factors. Mapping these core business processes to the value chain reveals where the processes touch the customers and affect their perceptions of value.

BUSINESS PROCESS REENGINEERING

Business process reengineering (BPR) is the analysis and redesign of workflow within and between enterprises. During a BPR effort a company begins with a blank sheet of paper evaluating existing processes to create new processes that deliver added-value to customers and eliminate redundancies in workflows. The primary goals of BPR efforts are to reduce organizational layers and eliminate unproductive activities by redesigning functional departments into cross-functional teams and promote the dissemination of information throughout the organizations.

FIGURE 3.2

Sample Business Processes.

Accounting and Finance

- Creating financial statements
- Paying of Accounts Payable
- Collecting of Accounts Receivable

Marketing and Sales

- Promoting of discounts
- Communicating marketing campaigns
- Attracting customers
- Processing sales

Operations Management

- Ordering inventory
- Creating production schedules
- Manufacturing goods

Human Resources

- Hiring employees
- Enrolling employees in health care
- Tracking vacation and sick time

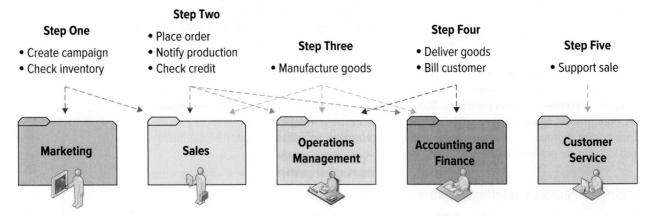

Step One
- Create campaign
- Check inventory

Step Two
- Place order
- Notify production
- Check credit

Step Three
- Manufacture goods

Step Four
- Deliver goods
- Bill customer

Step Five
- Support sale

| Marketing | Sales | Operations Management | Accounting and Finance | Customer Service |

FIGURE 3.3

Five Steps in the Order-to-Delivery Business Process.

Figure 3.5 highlights an analogy to business process reengineering by explaining the different means of traveling along the same route. A company could improve the way it travels by changing from foot to horse and then from horse to car. With a BPR mind-set, however, it would look beyond automating and streamlining to find a completely different approach. It would ignore the road and travel by air to get from point A to point B. Companies often

Customer-Facing Processes	Industry-Specific Customer Facing Processes	Business-Facing Processes
Order processing Customer service Sales process Customer billing Order shipping	Banking—Loan processing Insurance—Claims processing Government—Grant allocation Hotel—Reservation handling Airline—Baggage handling	Strategic planning Tactical planning Budget forecasting Training Purchasing raw materials

FIGURE 3.4

Customer-Facing, Industry-Specific, and Business-Facing Processes.

Better, Faster, Cheaper

FIGURE 3.5

Different Ways to Travel the Same Route.

follow the same indirect path for doing business, not realizing there might be a different, faster, and more direct way.

Creating value for the customer is the leading reason for instituting BPR, and MIS often plays an important enabling role. Fundamentally new business processes enabled Progressive Insurance to slash its claims settlement time from 31 days to four hours, for instance. Typically, car insurance companies follow this standard claims resolution process: The customer gets into an accident, has the car towed, and finds a ride home. The customer then calls the insurance company to begin the claims process, which includes an evaluation of the damage, assignment of fault, and an estimate of the cost of repairs, which usually takes about a month (see Figure 3.6). Progressive Insurance's innovation was to offer a mobile claims process. When a customer has a car accident, he or she calls in the claim on the spot. The Progressive claims adjuster comes to the accident site, surveys the scene, and takes digital photographs. The adjuster then offers the customer on-site payment, towing services, and a ride home. A true BPR effort does more for a company than simply improve

FIGURE 3.6

Auto Insurance Claims Processes Reengineering.

Company A: Claims Resolution Process

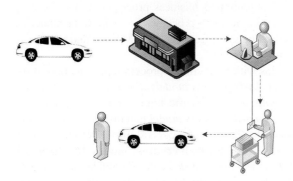

Resolution Cycle Time: 3–8 weeks

Progressive Insurance: Claims Resolution Process

Resolution Cycle Time: 30 minutes–3 hours

a process by performing it better, faster, and cheaper. Progressive Insurance's BPR effort redefined best practices for an entire industry.

When selecting a business process to reengineer, wise managers focus on those core processes that are critical to performance, rather than marginal processes that have little impact. The effort to reengineer a business process as a strategic activity requires a different mind-set than that required in continuous business process improvement programs. Because companies have tended to overlook the powerful contribution that processes can make to strategy, they often undertake process improvement efforts using their current processes as the starting point. Managers focusing on reengineering can instead use several criteria to identify opportunities:

- Is the process broken?
- Is it feasible that reengineering of this process will succeed?
- Does it have a high impact on the agency's strategic direction?
- Does it significantly impact customer satisfaction?
- Is it antiquated?
- Does it fall far below best-in-class?
- Is it crucial for productivity improvement?
- Will savings from automation be clearly visible?
- Is the return on investment from implementation high and preferably immediate?

A *business process patent* is a patent that protects a specific set of procedures for conducting a particular business activity. A firm can create a value chain map of the entire industry to extend critical success factors and business process views beyond its boundaries. *Core processes* are business processes, such as manufacturing goods, selling products, and providing service, that make up the primary activities in a value chain.

BUSINESS PROCESS MODELING

Business process modeling, or *mapping,* is the activity of creating a detailed flowchart or process map of a work process that shows its inputs, tasks, and activities in a structured sequence. A *business process model* is a graphic description of a process, showing the sequence of process tasks, which is developed for a specific purpose and from a selected viewpoint. A set of one or more process models details the many functions of a system or subject area with graphics and text, and its purpose is to:

- Expose process detail gradually and in a controlled manner.
- Encourage conciseness and accuracy in describing the process model.
- Focus attention on the process model interfaces.
- Provide a powerful process analysis and consistent design vocabulary. (See the end of the chapter for business process model examples.)

Business Process Model and Notation (BPMN) is a graphical notation that depicts the steps in a business process. BPMN provides businesses with a graphical view of the end-to-end flow of their business processes. Diagramming business processes allows for easy communication and understanding of how core business processes are helping or hindering the business. Figure 3.7 displays the standard notation from www.BPMN.org and Figure 3.8 displays a sample BPMN diagram for hiring a taxi cab.

Business process modeling usually begins with a functional process representation of the process problem, or an As-Is process model. *As-Is process models* represent the current state of the operation that has been mapped, without any specific improvements or changes to existing processes. The next step is to build a *To-Be process model* that displays how the process problem will be solved or implemented. To-Be process models show the results of applying change improvement opportunities to the current (As-Is) process model. This approach ensures that the process is fully and clearly understood before the details of a process solution are decided on. The To-Be process model shows how "the what" is to be realized. You need to be careful not to become inundated in excessive detail when creating an As-Is process model.

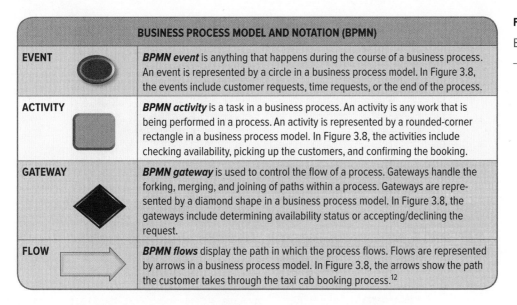

FIGURE 3.7

BPMN Notation.

BUSINESS PROCESS MODEL AND NOTATION (BPMN)	
EVENT	**BPMN event** is anything that happens during the course of a business process. An event is represented by a circle in a business process model. In Figure 3.8, the events include customer requests, time requests, or the end of the process.
ACTIVITY	**BPMN activity** is a task in a business process. An activity is any work that is being performed in a process. An activity is represented by a rounded-corner rectangle in a business process model. In Figure 3.8, the activities include checking availability, picking up the customers, and confirming the booking.
GATEWAY	**BPMN gateway** is used to control the flow of a process. Gateways handle the forking, merging, and joining of paths within a process. Gateways are represented by a diamond shape in a business process model. In Figure 3.8, the gateways include determining availability status or accepting/declining the request.
FLOW	**BPMN flows** display the path in which the process flows. Flows are represented by arrows in a business process model. In Figure 3.8, the arrows show the path the customer takes through the taxi cab booking process.[12]

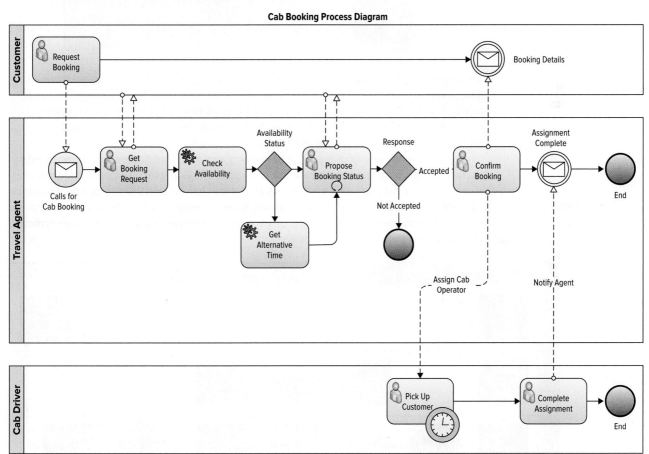

FIGURE 3.8

BPMN Sample Diagram for Hiring a Taxi Cab.

The primary goal is to simplify, eliminate, and improve the To-Be processes. Process improvement efforts focus on defining the most efficient and effective process identifying all of the illogical, missing, or irrelevant processes. Figure 3.9 displays the As-Is and To-Be process models for ordering a hamburger.

As-Is and To-Be process models are both integral in business process reengineering projects because these diagrams are very powerful in visualizing the activities, processes, and data flow of an organization. A *swimlane diagram* (or cross-functional diagram) documents the steps or activities of a workflow by grouping activities into swimlanes, which are

FIGURE 3.9

As-Is and To-Be Process
Models for Ordering a
Hamburger.

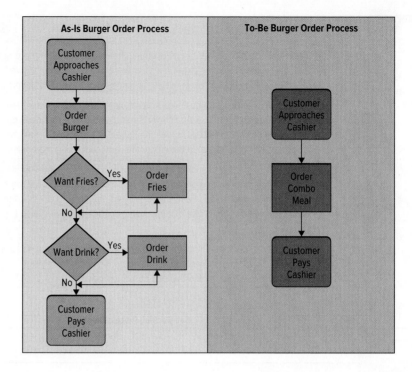

horizontal or vertical columns containing all associated activities for that category or department. A ***process owner*** is the person responsible for the end-to-end functioning of a business
process. Swimlane diagrams help identify process owners who can repair delays, bottlenecks,
or redundancies. Figure 3.10 illustrates an As-Is process model of the order-to-delivery process, using swimlanes to represent the relevant departments.

Investigating business processes can help an organization find bottlenecks, remove redundant tasks, and recognize smooth-running processes. For example, a florist might have a key
success factor of reducing delivery time. A florist that has an inefficient ordering process or
a difficult distribution process will be unable to achieve this goal. Taking down inaccurate
orders, recording incorrect addresses, or experiencing shipping delays can cause errors in
the delivery process.

FIGURE 3.10

As-Is Process Model for
Order Fulfillment.

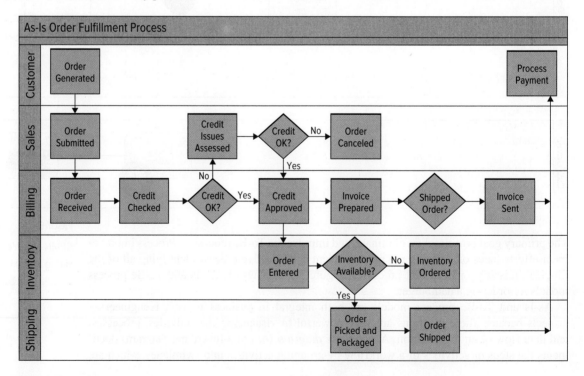

A)

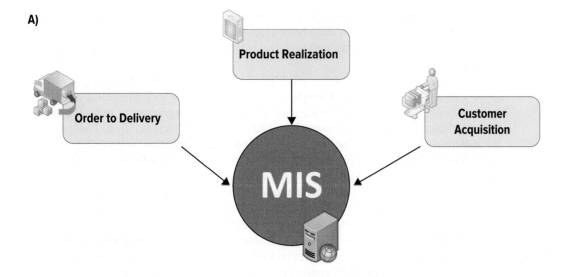

B)

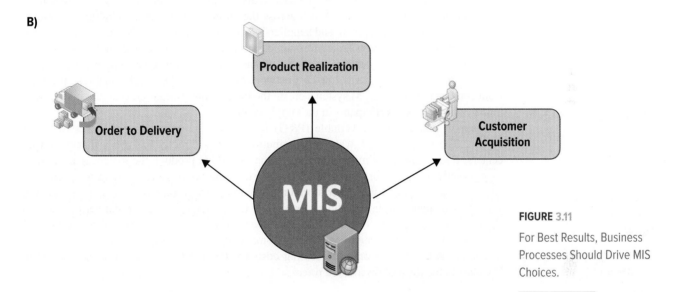

Improving order entry, production, or scheduling processes can improve the delivery process. Business processes should drive MIS choices and should be based on business strategies and goals (see Figure 3.11 A). Only after determining the most efficient and effective business process should an organization choose the MIS that supports that business process. Of course, this does not always happen, and managers may find themselves in the difficult position of changing a business process because the system cannot support the ideal solution (see Figure 3.11 B). Managers who make MIS choices and only then determine how their business processes should perform typically fail.

Supply Chain Management

LO 3.2 Explain supply chain management and its role in business.

Trek, a leader in bicycle products and accessories, gained more than 30 percent of the worldwide market by streamlining operations through the implementation of several MIS systems. According to Jeff Stang, director of MIS and operational accounting, the most significant improvement realized from the new systems was the ability to obtain key management information to drive business decisions in line with the company's strategic goals. Other system results included a highly successful website developed for the 1,400 Trek dealers where they could enter orders directly, check stock availability, and view accounts receivable and credit summaries. Tonja Green, Trek channel manager for North America, stated, "We wanted to give our dealers an easier and quicker way to enter their orders and get information. Every week the number of web orders increases by 25 to 30 percent due to the new system."

A supply chain includes all parties involved, directly or indirectly, in obtaining raw materials or a product. To understand a supply chain, consider a customer purchasing a Trek bike from a dealer. On one end, the supply chain has the customer placing an order for the bike with the dealer. The dealer purchases the bike from the manufacturer, Trek. Trek purchases raw materials such as packaging material, metal, and accessories from many different suppliers to make the bike. The supply chain for Trek encompasses every activity and party involved in the process of fulfilling the order from the customer for the new bike. Figure 3.12 displays a typical supply chain for a bike manufacturer including all processes and people required to fulfill the customer's order. Figure 3.13 highlights the five basic supply chain activities a company undertakes to manufacture and distribute products.

Supply chain management (SCM) is the management of information flows between and among activities in a supply chain to maximize total supply chain effectiveness and corporate profitability. Complex SCM systems provide demand forecasting, inventory control, and information flows between suppliers and customers.

In the past, manufacturing efforts focused primarily on quality improvement efforts within the company; today these efforts reach across the entire supply chain, including customers, customers' customers, suppliers, and suppliers' suppliers. Today's supply chain is an intricate network of business partners linked through communication channels and relationships. Supply chain management systems manage and enhance these relationships with the primary goal of creating a fast, efficient, and low-cost network of business relationships that take products from concept to market. SCM systems create the integrations or tight process and information linkages between all participants in the supply chain.

Walmart and Procter & Gamble (P&G) implemented a tremendously successful SCM system. The system linked Walmart distribution centers directly to P&G's manufacturing centers. Every time a Walmart customer purchases a P&G product, the system sends a message directly to the factory alerting P&G to restock the product. The system also sends an automatic alert to P&G whenever a product is running low at one of Walmart's distribution centers. This real-time information allows P&G to efficiently make and deliver products to Walmart without having to maintain large inventories in its warehouses. The system also generates invoices and receives payments automatically. The SCM system saves time, reduces inventory, and decreases order-processing costs for P&G. P&G passes on these savings to Walmart in the form of discounted prices.[1]

FIGURE 3.12

Supply Chain for a Bike Manufacturer.

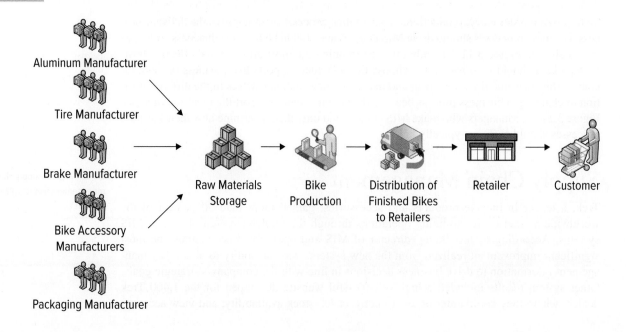

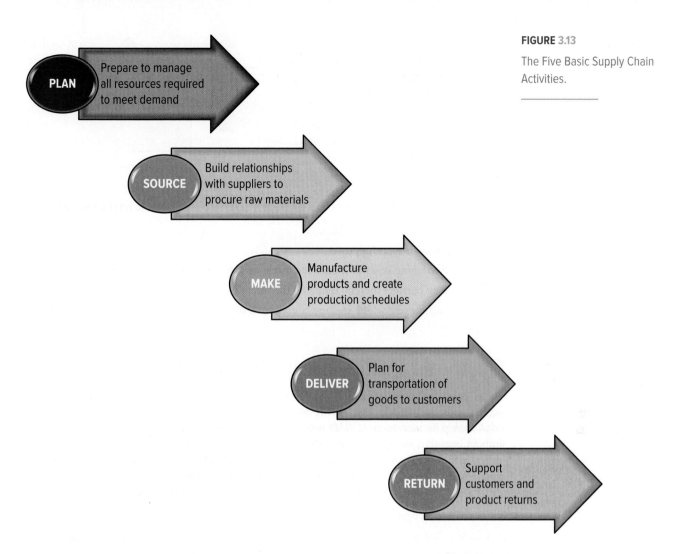

FIGURE 3.13

The Five Basic Supply Chain
Activities.

Figure 3.14 diagrams the stages of the SCM system for a customer purchasing a product from Walmart. The diagram demonstrates how the supply chain is dynamic and involves the constant flow of information between the different parties. For example, the customer generates order information by purchasing a product from Walmart. Walmart supplies the order information to its warehouse or distributor. The warehouse or distributor transfers the order information to the manufacturer, who provides pricing and availability information to the store and replenishes the product to the store. Payment funds among the various partners are transferred electronically.

FIGURE 3.14

Supply Chain for a Product
Purchased from Walmart.

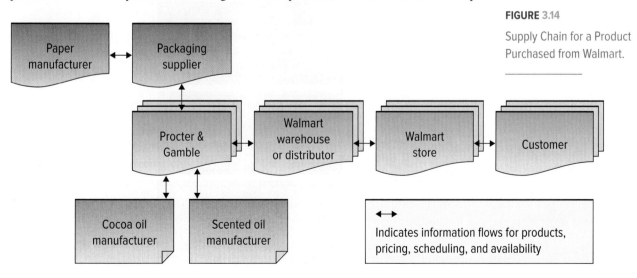

FIGURE 3.15

Effective and Efficient Supply
Chain Management's Effect
on Porter's Five Forces.

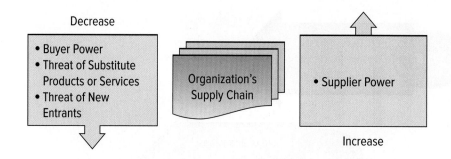

Effective and efficient supply chain management systems can enable an organization to:

- Decrease the power of its buyers.
- Increase its own supplier power.
- Increase switching costs to reduce the threat of substitute products or services.
- Create entry barriers thereby reducing the threat of new entrants.
- Increase efficiency while seeking a competitive advantage through cost leadership (see Figure 3.15).

LO 3.3 Explain customer relationship management systems and how they can help organizations understand their customers.

Customer Relationship Management

Today, most competitors are simply a mouse-click away. This intense marketplace has forced organizations to switch from being sales focused to being customer focused. ***Customer relationship management (CRM)*** involves managing all aspects of a customer's relationship with an organization to increase customer loyalty and retention and an organization's profitability. CRM allows an organization to gain insights into customers' shopping and buying behaviors in order to develop and implement enterprisewide strategies. The key players in CRM initiatives are outlined in Figure 3.16. CRM strategic goals include:

- Identify sales opportunities.
- Classify low-value customers and create marketing promotions to increase consumer spending.

FIGURE 3.16

Customer Relationship
Management Key Players.

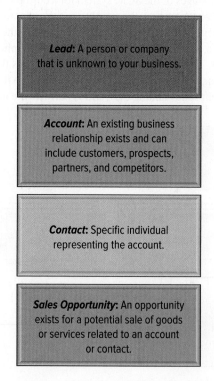

FIGURE 3.17

Customer Contact Points.

- Classify high-value customers and create marketing promotions to increase consumer loyalty.
- Analyze marketing promotions by product, market segment, and sales region.
- Identify customer relationship issues along with strategies for quick resolution.

The complicated piece of the CRM puzzle is identifying customers and the many communication channels they use to contact companies including call centers, web access, email, sales representatives, faxes, and cell phones. A single customer may access an organization multiple times through many different channels (see Figure 3.17). CRM systems can help to collect all of the points of customer contact along with sales and financial information to provide a complete view of each customer (see Figure 3.18). CRM systems track every communication between the customer and the organization and provide access to cohesive customer information for all business areas from accounting to order fulfillment. Understanding all customer communications allows the organization to communicate effectively with each customer. It gives the organization a detailed understanding of each customer's products and services record regardless of the customer's preferred communication channel. For example, a customer service representative can easily view detailed account information and history through a CRM system when providing information to a customer such as expected delivery dates, complementary product information, and customer payment and billing information.

Companies that understand individual customer needs are best positioned to achieve success. Of course, building successful customer relationships is not a new business practice; however, implementing CRM systems allows a company to operate more efficiently and effectively in the area of supporting customer needs. CRM moves far beyond technology by identifying customer needs and designing specific marketing campaigns tailored to each. This enables a firm to treat customers as individuals, gaining important insights into their buying preferences and shopping behaviors. Firms that treat their customers well reap the rewards and generally see higher profits and highly loyal customers. Identifying the most valuable customers allows a firm to ensure that these customers receive the highest levels of customer service and are offered the first opportunity to purchase new products. *Customer analytics* involves gathering, classifying, comparing, and studying customer data to identify buying trends, at-risk customers, and potential future opportunities. *Sales analytics* involves gathering, classifying, comparing, and studying company sales data to analyze product cycles, sales

FIGURE 3.18

CRM Overview.

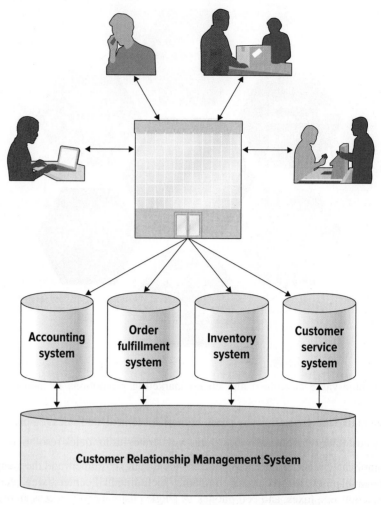

Customer Relationship Management System

◄──► Customer information flows
are represented by arrows.

pipelines, and competitive intelligence. Software with advanced analytics capabilities helps you attract and retain loyal and profitable customers and gives you the insight you need to increase revenues, customer satisfaction, and customer loyalty.

Firms can find their most valuable customers by using the RFM formula—recency, frequency, and monetary value. In other words, an organization must track:

- How *recently* a customer purchased items.
- How *frequently* a customer purchases items.
- The *monetary* value of each customer purchase.

After gathering this initial CRM information, the firm can analyze it to identify patterns and create marketing campaigns and sales promotions for different customer segments. For example, if a customer buys only at the height of the season, the firm should send a special offer during the off-season. If a certain customer segment purchases shoes but never accessories, the firm can offer discounted accessories with the purchase of a new pair of shoes. If the firm determines that its top 20 percent of customers are responsible for 80 percent of the revenue, it can focus on ensuring these customers are always satisfied and receive the highest levels of customer service.

There are three phases of CRM: (1) reporting, (2) analyzing, and (3) predicting. ***CRM reporting technologies*** help organizations identify their customers across other applications. ***CRM analysis technologies*** help organizations segment their customers into categories such as best and worst customers. ***CRM predicting technologies*** help organizations predict

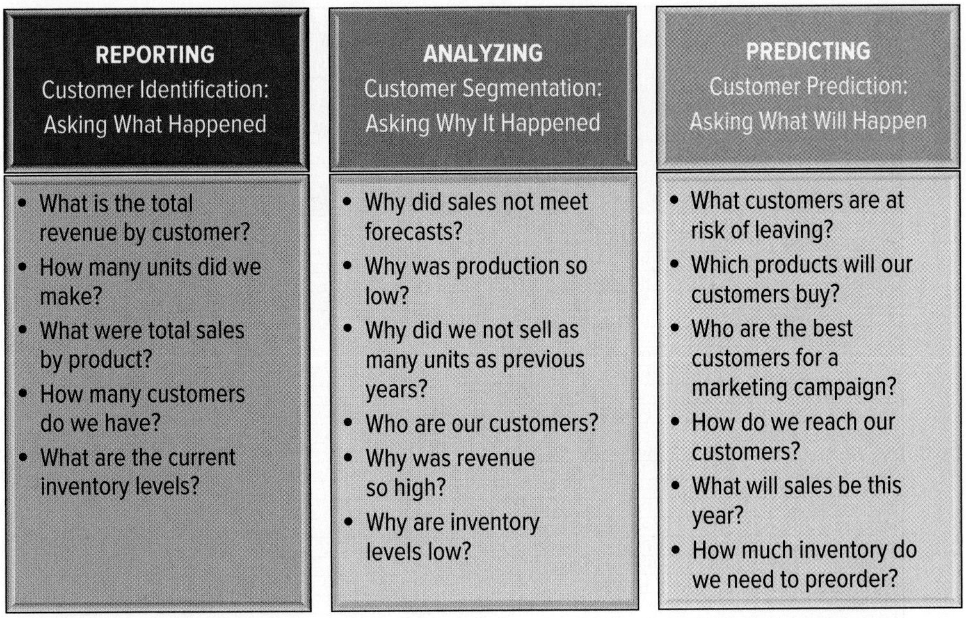

FIGURE 3.19

Three Phases of CRM.

REPORTING Customer Identification: Asking What Happened	ANALYZING Customer Segmentation: Asking Why It Happened	PREDICTING Customer Prediction: Asking What Will Happen
• What is the total revenue by customer? • How many units did we make? • What were total sales by product? • How many customers do we have? • What are the current inventory levels?	• Why did sales not meet forecasts? • Why was production so low? • Why did we not sell as many units as previous years? • Who are our customers? • Why was revenue so high? • Why are inventory levels low?	• What customers are at risk of leaving? • Which products will our customers buy? • Who are the best customers for a marketing campaign? • How do we reach our customers? • What will sales be this year? • How much inventory do we need to preorder?

customer behavior, such as which customers are at risk of leaving. Figure 3.19 highlights a few of the important questions an organization can answer in these areas by using CRM technologies.

Enterprise Resource Planning

Today's business leaders need significant amounts of information to be readily accessible with real-time views into their businesses so that decisions can be made when they need to be, without the added time of tracking data and generating reports. *Enterprise resource planning (ERP)* integrates all departments and functions throughout an organization into a single system (or integrated set of MIS systems) so that employees can make decisions by viewing enterprisewide information on all business operations. To truly understand the complexity of ERP systems you must think about the many different functional business areas and their associated business processes as well as cross-functional business processes such as supply chain management and customer relationship management and beyond. At its most basic level, ERP software integrates these various business functions into one complete system to streamline business processes and information across the entire organization. Essentially, ERP helps employees do their jobs more efficiently by breaking down barriers between business units.

Many organizations fail to maintain consistency across business operations. If a single department, such as sales, decides to implement a new system without considering the other departments, inconsistencies can occur throughout the company. Not all systems are built to talk to each other and share data, and if sales suddenly implements a new system that marketing and accounting cannot use or is inconsistent in the way it handles information, the company's operations become siloed. Figure 3.20 displays sample data from a sales database, and Figure 3.21 displays samples from an accounting database. Notice the differences in data formats, numbers, and identifiers. Correlating this data would be difficult, and the inconsistencies would cause numerous reporting errors from an enterprisewide perspective.

The two key components of an ERP system help to resolve these issues and include a common data repository and modular software design. A *common data repository* allows every department of a company to store and retrieve information in real-time allowing information to be more reliable and accessible. *Module software design* divides the system into a set of functional units (named modules) that can be used independently or combined with other modules for increased business flexibility. Module software design allows customers to mix-and-match modules so they purchase only the required modules. If a company wants to

FIGURE 3.20

Sales Information Sample.

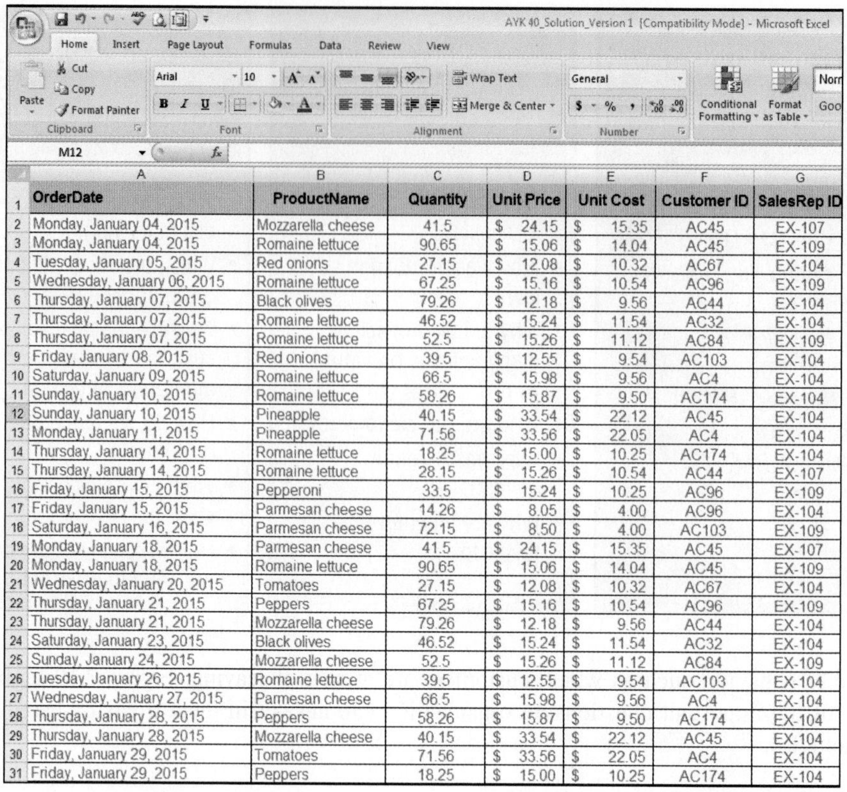

	A	B	C	D	E	F	G
1	OrderDate	ProductName	Quantity	Unit Price	Unit Cost	Customer ID	SalesRep ID
2	Monday, January 04, 2015	Mozzarella cheese	41.5	$ 24.15	$ 15.35	AC45	EX-107
3	Monday, January 04, 2015	Romaine lettuce	90.65	$ 15.06	$ 14.04	AC45	EX-109
4	Tuesday, January 05, 2015	Red onions	27.15	$ 12.08	$ 10.32	AC67	EX-104
5	Wednesday, January 06, 2015	Romaine lettuce	67.25	$ 15.16	$ 10.54	AC96	EX-109
6	Thursday, January 07, 2015	Black olives	79.26	$ 12.18	$ 9.56	AC44	EX-104
7	Thursday, January 07, 2015	Romaine lettuce	46.52	$ 15.24	$ 11.54	AC32	EX-104
8	Thursday, January 07, 2015	Romaine lettuce	52.5	$ 15.26	$ 11.12	AC84	EX-109
9	Friday, January 08, 2015	Red onions	39.5	$ 12.55	$ 9.54	AC103	EX-104
10	Saturday, January 09, 2015	Romaine lettuce	66.5	$ 15.98	$ 9.56	AC4	EX-104
11	Sunday, January 10, 2015	Romaine lettuce	58.26	$ 15.87	$ 9.50	AC174	EX-104
12	Sunday, January 10, 2015	Pineapple	40.15	$ 33.54	$ 22.12	AC45	EX-104
13	Monday, January 11, 2015	Pineapple	71.56	$ 33.56	$ 22.05	AC4	EX-104
14	Thursday, January 14, 2015	Romaine lettuce	18.25	$ 15.00	$ 10.25	AC174	EX-104
15	Thursday, January 14, 2015	Romaine lettuce	28.15	$ 15.26	$ 10.54	AC44	EX-107
16	Friday, January 15, 2015	Pepperoni	33.5	$ 15.24	$ 10.25	AC96	EX-109
17	Friday, January 15, 2015	Parmesan cheese	14.26	$ 8.05	$ 4.00	AC96	EX-104
18	Saturday, January 16, 2015	Parmesan cheese	72.15	$ 8.50	$ 4.00	AC103	EX-109
19	Monday, January 18, 2015	Parmesan cheese	41.5	$ 24.15	$ 15.35	AC45	EX-107
20	Monday, January 18, 2015	Romaine lettuce	90.65	$ 15.06	$ 14.04	AC45	EX-109
21	Wednesday, January 20, 2015	Tomatoes	27.15	$ 12.08	$ 10.32	AC67	EX-104
22	Thursday, January 21, 2015	Peppers	67.25	$ 15.16	$ 10.54	AC96	EX-109
23	Thursday, January 21, 2015	Mozzarella cheese	79.26	$ 12.18	$ 9.56	AC44	EX-104
24	Saturday, January 23, 2015	Black olives	46.52	$ 15.24	$ 11.54	AC32	EX-104
25	Sunday, January 24, 2015	Mozzarella cheese	52.5	$ 15.26	$ 11.12	AC84	EX-109
26	Tuesday, January 26, 2015	Romaine lettuce	39.5	$ 12.55	$ 9.54	AC103	EX-104
27	Wednesday, January 27, 2015	Parmesan cheese	66.5	$ 15.98	$ 9.56	AC4	EX-104
28	Thursday, January 28, 2015	Peppers	58.26	$ 15.87	$ 9.50	AC174	EX-104
29	Thursday, January 28, 2015	Mozzarella cheese	40.15	$ 33.54	$ 22.12	AC45	EX-104
30	Friday, January 29, 2015	Tomatoes	71.56	$ 33.56	$ 22.05	AC4	EX-104
31	Friday, January 29, 2015	Peppers	18.25	$ 15.00	$ 10.25	AC174	EX-104

Source: Microsoft Office 2016

FIGURE 3.21

Accounting Information Sample.

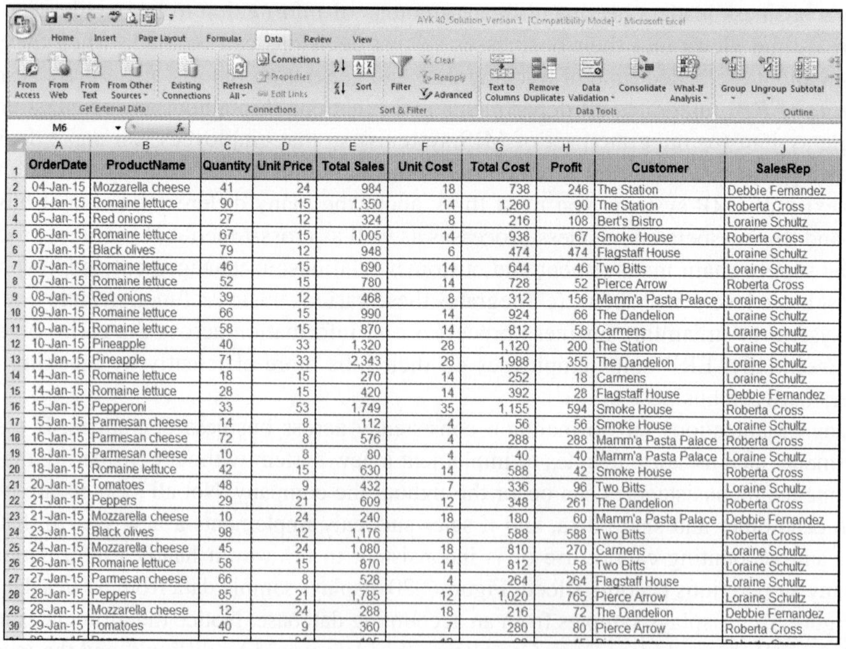

	A	B	C	D	E	F	G	H	I	J
1	OrderDate	ProductName	Quantity	Unit Price	Total Sales	Unit Cost	Total Cost	Profit	Customer	SalesRep
2	04-Jan-15	Mozzarella cheese	41	24	984	18	738	246	The Station	Debbie Fernandez
3	04-Jan-15	Romaine lettuce	90	15	1,350	14	1,260	90	The Station	Roberta Cross
4	05-Jan-15	Red onions	27	12	324	8	216	108	Bert's Bistro	Loraine Schultz
5	06-Jan-15	Romaine lettuce	67	15	1,005	14	938	67	Smoke House	Roberta Cross
6	07-Jan-15	Black olives	79	12	948	6	474	474	Flagstaff House	Loraine Schultz
7	07-Jan-15	Romaine lettuce	46	15	690	14	644	46	Two Bitts	Loraine Schultz
8	07-Jan-15	Romaine lettuce	52	15	780	14	728	52	Pierce Arrow	Roberta Cross
9	08-Jan-15	Red onions	39	12	468	8	312	156	Mamm'a Pasta Palace	Loraine Schultz
10	09-Jan-15	Romaine lettuce	66	15	990	14	924	66	The Dandelion	Loraine Schultz
11	10-Jan-15	Romaine lettuce	58	15	870	14	812	58	Carmens	Loraine Schultz
12	10-Jan-15	Pineapple	40	33	1,320	28	1,120	200	The Station	Loraine Schultz
13	11-Jan-15	Pineapple	71	33	2,343	28	1,988	355	The Dandelion	Loraine Schultz
14	14-Jan-15	Romaine lettuce	18	15	270	14	252	18	Carmens	Loraine Schultz
15	14-Jan-15	Romaine lettuce	28	15	420	14	392	28	Flagstaff House	Debbie Fernandez
16	15-Jan-15	Pepperoni	33	53	1,749	35	1,155	594	Smoke House	Roberta Cross
17	15-Jan-15	Parmesan cheese	14	8	112	4	56	56	Smoke House	Loraine Schultz
18	16-Jan-15	Parmesan cheese	72	8	576	4	288	288	Mamm'a Pasta Palace	Roberta Cross
19	18-Jan-15	Parmesan cheese	10	8	80	4	40	40	Mamm'a Pasta Palace	Loraine Schultz
20	18-Jan-15	Romaine lettuce	42	15	630	14	588	42	Smoke House	Roberta Cross
21	20-Jan-15	Tomatoes	48	9	432	7	336	96	Two Bitts	Loraine Schultz
22	21-Jan-15	Peppers	29	21	609	12	348	261	The Dandelion	Roberta Cross
23	21-Jan-15	Mozzarella cheese	10	24	240	18	180	60	Mamm'a Pasta Palace	Debbie Fernandez
24	23-Jan-15	Black olives	98	12	1,176	6	588	588	Two Bitts	Roberta Cross
25	24-Jan-15	Mozzarella cheese	45	24	1,080	18	810	270	Carmens	Loraine Schultz
26	26-Jan-15	Romaine lettuce	58	15	870	14	812	58	Two Bitts	Loraine Schultz
27	27-Jan-15	Parmesan cheese	66	8	528	4	264	264	Flagstaff House	Loraine Schultz
28	28-Jan-15	Peppers	85	21	1,785	12	1,020	765	Pierce Arrow	Loraine Schultz
29	28-Jan-15	Mozzarella cheese	12	24	288	18	216	72	The Dandelion	Debbie Fernandez
30	29-Jan-15	Tomatoes	40	9	360	7	280	80	Pierce Arrow	Roberta Cross

Source: Microsoft Office 2016

implement the system slowly it can begin with just one module, such as accounting, and then incorporate additional modules such as purchasing and scheduling.

ERP systems share data supporting business processes within and across departments. In practice, this means that employees in different divisions—for example, accounting and sales—can rely on the same information for their specific needs. ERP software also offers some degree of synchronized reporting and automation. Instead of forcing employees to maintain separate databases and spreadsheets that have to be manually merged to generate reports, some ERP solutions allow staff to pull reports from one system. For instance, with sales orders automatically flowing into the financial system without any manual re-keying, the order management department can process orders more quickly and accurately, and the finance department can close the books faster. Other common ERP features include a portal or dashboard to enable employees to quickly understand the business's performance on key metrics.

Figure 3.22 shows how an ERP system takes data from across the enterprise, consolidates and correlates it, and generates enterprisewide organizational reports. Original ERP implementations promised to capture all information onto one true "enterprise" system, with the ability to touch all the business processes within the organization. Unfortunately, ERP solutions have fallen short of these promises, and typical implementations have penetrated only 15 to 20 percent of the organization. The issue ERP intends to solve is that knowledge within a majority of organizations currently resides in silos that are maintained by a select few, without the ability to be shared across the organization, causing inconsistency across business operations.

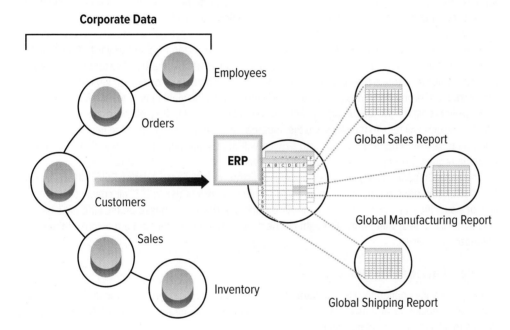

FIGURE 3.22

Enterprise Resource Planning System.

OPENING CASE STUDY QUESTIONS

1. Imagine you are working for Apple as a manager in its Chicago store. Explain how you could use a CRM system to help support customers.

2. Create an argument against the following statement: "Apple should not invest any resources to build a supply chain management system."

3. Explain how an ERP system can help Apple run its business.

Chapter Three Case: Amazon Drone Knocking

Using drones to drop off packages could be great for buyers, who might want to get certain items as fast as humanly possible. Back in 2013, when Amazon revealed plans to begin delivering packages via flying drones through Prime Air, some seemed skeptical about the reality of deploying such a system. Recently, Amazon doubled down on those claims by releasing information on one of its new drones in action, and it is seriously impressive.

A new video presented by former Top Gear host Jeremy Clarkson (who is working on a show for Amazon), takes us through the entire process, from ordering, to warehouse launch, to delivery. The new drone looks a lot different from the one Amazon showed us a couple of years ago. This one has a more commercial and streamlined look, and instead of showing the package hanging in open air, the new drone hides the item in a square compartment. Just Google Amazon Prime Air Drone video with Jeremy Clarkson to see for yourself this amazing new drone that will dramatically impact the supply chain.

According to Amazon, the drone reaches a height of about 400 feet in vertical mode and then switches to horizontal mode to travel up to 15 miles away from the warehouse. During the flight, the drone uses what Amazon calls "sense and avoid technology" to avoid collisions with other objects in its flight path.

Toward the end of the video, the drone alights atop an Amazon logo in the yard of a consumer and spits out the package (in this case, shoes) and then takes off in a matter of seconds. The delivery process, which Amazon is careful to note is real and not a simulation, comes off seamlessly, making the prospect of drone deliveries seem like something that will be viable just a few months from now.

However, despite the encouraging footage, Amazon is still holding off on announcing exactly when its drones will take to the skies. On the updated Prime Air page featuring the new flight footage, a message reads, "Putting Prime Air into service will take some time, but we will deploy when we have the regulatory support needed to realize our vision."

The FAA's Unmanned Aircraft Systems (UAS) Registration Task Force Aviation Rulemaking Committee is still hammering out rules for private and commercial drone use in U.S. air space, so Amazon's lack of a specific launch timeline for Prime Air is understandable. But based on the video, it's becoming increasingly clear that Prime Air might not be a mere marketing stunt but a real look at the future of Amazon deliveries.

Retailers Racing to the Drone Games

Wal-Mart recently applied to U.S. regulators for permission to test drones for home delivery, curbside pickup and checking warehouse inventories, a sign it plans to go head-to-head with Amazon in using drones to fill and deliver online orders.

Wal-Mart wants to start using drones in an effort to create a more efficient supply chain, and connect their network of stores, distribution centers, fulfillment centers and transportation fleet. The world's largest retailer by revenue has for several months been conducting indoor tests of small unmanned aircraft systems (drones) and is now seeking for the first time to test the machines outdoors. In addition to having drones take inventory of trailers outside its warehouses and perform other tasks aimed at making its distribution system more efficient, Wal-Mart is asking the Federal Aviation Administration for permission to research drone use in "deliveries to customers at Walmart facilities, as well as to consumer homes." The move comes as Amazon, Google and other companies test drones in the expectation that the FAA will soon establish rules for their widespread commercial use.[2]

Questions

1. How will drones impact the supply chain?

2. Why are big retailers racing to be the first to market with drone home delivery?

3. How can a CRM system help communicate issues in the supply chain between customers and drones?

4. How could BPR help uncover issues in a company's supply chain that uses drones?

5. What are the pros and cons of using a drone to deliver packages?

3.1. Identify how an organization can use business process reengineering to improve its business.

A business process is a standardized set of activities that accomplish a specific task, such as processing a customer's order. Business processes transform a set of inputs into a set of outputs (goods or services) for another person or process by using people and tools. Without processes, organizations would not be able to complete activities.

3.2. Explain supply chain management and its role in business.

A supply chain consists of all parties involved, directly or indirectly, in obtaining raw materials or a product. To automate and enable sophisticated decision making in these critical areas, companies are turning to systems that provide demand forecasting, inventory control, and information flows between suppliers and customers. Supply chain management (SCM) is the management of information flows between and among activities in a supply chain to maximize total supply chain effectiveness and corporate profitability. In the past, manufacturing efforts focused primarily on quality improvement efforts within the company; today these efforts reach across the entire supply chain, including customers, customers' customers, suppliers, and suppliers' suppliers. Today's supply chain is an intricate network of business partners linked through communication channels and relationships. Improved visibility across the supply chain and increased profitability for the firm are the primary business benefits received when implementing supply chain management systems. Supply chain visibility is the ability to view all areas up and down the supply chain in real time. The primary challenges associated with supply chain management include costs and complexity. The next wave in supply chain management will be home-based supply chain fulfillment. No more running to the store to replace your products because your store will come to you as soon as you need a new product.

3.3. Explain customer relationship management systems and how they can help organizations understand their customers.

Customer relationship management (CRM) is a means of managing all aspects of a customer's relationship with an organization to increase customer loyalty and retention and an organization's profitability. CRM allows an organization to gain insights into customers' shopping and buying behaviors. Every time a customer communicates with a company, the firm has the chance to build a trusting relationship with that particular customer. Companies that understand individual customer needs are best positioned to achieve success. Building successful customer relationships is not a new business practice; however, implementing CRM systems allows a company to operate more efficiently and effectively in the area of supporting customer needs. CRM moves far beyond technology by identifying customer needs and designing specific marketing campaigns tailored to each.

3.4. Summarize the importance of enterprise resource planning systems.

Enterprise resource planning (ERP) integrates all departments and functions throughout an organization into a single IT system (or integrated set of IT systems) so employees can make decisions by viewing enterprisewide information about all business operations.

1. What is a business process and what role does it play in an organization?
2. Why do managers need to understand business processes? Can you make a correlation between systems thinking and business processes?
3. Why would a manager need to review an As-Is and To-Be process model?
4. How can a manager use automation, streamlining, and business process reengineering to gain operational efficiency and effectiveness?
5. Explain the difference between customer-facing processes and business-facing processes. Which one is more important to an organization?
6. Explain how finding different ways to travel the same road relates to automation, streamlining, and business process reengineering.
7. What is supply chain management and why is it important to a company?
8. What are the five primary activities in a supply chain?
9. What is a supply chain inventory visibility system?
10. Why are customer relationships important to an organization? Do you agree that every business needs to focus on customers to survive in the information age?
11. What is an enterprise resource planning system?
12. What does a company need to integrate to become connected?

✳ MAKING BUSINESS DECISIONS

1. Cool College Start-Ups

Not long ago, people would call college kids who started businesses quaint. Now they call them the boss. For almost a decade, *Inc.* magazine has been watching college start-ups and posting a list of the nation's top start-ups taking campuses by storm. Helped in part by low-cost technologies and an increased prevalence of entrepreneurship training at the university level, college students—and indeed those even younger—are making solid strides at founding companies. And they're not just launching local pizza shops and fashion boutiques. They are starting up businesses that could scale into much bigger companies and may already cater to a national audience.

Research *Inc.* magazine at www.inc.com and find the year's current Coolest College Start-up listing. Choose one of the startups and explain how the business can use BPR, CRM, SCM, and ERP to help it gain traction in the market. Be sure to explain how the company can gain a competitive advantage by using each enterprise system efficiently and effectively.

2. Managing Bad Customer Relationships

There is a common saying that the customer is always right. Clearly this can create many issues with customer relationship management as many times the customer is actually incorrect, but you can't tell the customer they are wrong. Research the Internet and find an example of a customer relationship gone wrong and determine if the customer was at fault for the problem. What can you do as a manager when a customer is angry but clearly wrong about a situation? What strategies can a manager use when dealing with angry customers?

3. Fixing Broken School Processes

There are numerous simultaneous business processes occurring to keep your school running. Choose one area of your school and diagram all of the business processes occurring in one common day. For example, administration is registering students, creating class schedules, hiring faculty, recruiting students, and finding graduates jobs. Imagine the level of effort it takes to keep your school running day after day. List all of the processes associated with your chosen area.

4. School Supply Chains

The food industry has to operate tough schedules with supplies that have limited shelf-life and quickly approaching expiration dates. Imagine all of the food coming into your school to feed the students living in the dorms. List the different types of products being sourced by your school and what types of issues they might be encountering. What does your school do with out-dated products? How does your school estimate the food demand? What does your school do with leftover food? How can you improve your school's supply chain?

CHAPTER 4

Measuring the Success of Strategic Initiatives

4.1. Define the primary MIS roles along with their associated responsibilities.

4.2. Define critical success factors (CSFs) and key performance indicators (KPIs), and explain how managers use them to measure the success of MIS projects.

4.3. Explain why a business would use metrics to measure the success of strategic initiatives.

LO 4.1 Define the primary MIS roles along with their associated responsibilities.

MIS Roles and Responsibilities

Management information systems is a relatively new functional area, having been around formally in most organizations only for about 40 years. Job titles, roles, and responsibilities often differ dramatically from organization to organization. Nonetheless, clear trends are developing toward elevating some MIS positions within an organization to the strategic level.

Most organizations maintain positions such as chief executive officer (CEO), chief financial officer (CFO), and chief operations officer (COO) at the strategic level. Recently there are more MIS-related strategic positions such as chief information officer (CIO), chief data officer (CDO), chief technology officer (CTO), chief security officer (CSO), chief privacy officer (CPO), and chief knowledge officer (CKO). See Figure 4.1.

The ***chief information officer (CIO)*** is responsible for (1) overseeing all uses of information technology and (2) ensuring the strategic alignment of MIS with business goals and objectives. The CIO often reports directly to the CEO. CIOs must possess a solid and detailed understanding of every aspect of an organization coupled with tremendous insight into the capability of MIS. Broad functions of a CIO include:

1. *Manager*—ensure the delivery of all MIS projects, on time and within budget.
2. *Leader*—ensure the strategic vision of MIS is in line with the strategic vision of the organization.
3. *Communicator*—advocate and communicate the MIS strategy by building and maintaining strong executive relationships.

The ***chief data officer (CDO)*** is responsible for determining the types of information the enterprise will capture, retain, analyze, and share. The difference between the CIO and CDO is that the CIO is responsible for the *information systems* through which data is stored and processed, while the CDO is responsible for the *data,* regardless of the information system.

The ***chief technology officer (CTO)*** is responsible for ensuring the throughput, speed, accuracy, availability, and reliability of an organization's information technology. CTOs are similar to CIOs, except that CIOs take on the additional responsibility for effectiveness of ensuring that MIS is aligned with the organization's strategic initiatives. CTOs have direct responsibility for ensuring the *efficiency* of MIS systems throughout the organization.

Chief security officer (CSO)

Responsible for ensuring the security of business systems and developing strategies and safeguards against attacks by hackers and viruses.

Chief knowledge officer (CKO)

Responsible for collecting, maintaining, and distributing company knowledge.

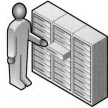

Chief technology officer (CTO)

Responsible for ensuring the speed, accuracy, availability, and reliability of the MIS.

MIS Department Roles and Responsibilities

Chief information officer (CIO)

Responsible for (1) overseeing all uses of MIS and (2) ensuring that MIS strategically aligns with business goals and objectives.

Chief privacy officer (CPO)

Responsible for ensuring the ethical and legal use of information within a company.

Chief data officer (CDO)

Responsible for determining the types of information the enterprise will capture, retain, analyze, and share.

FIGURE 4.1

The Roles and Responsibilities of MIS.

Most CTOs possess well-rounded knowledge of all aspects of MIS, including hardware, software, and telecommunications.

The *chief security officer (CSO)* is responsible for ensuring the security of MIS systems and developing strategies and MIS safeguards against attacks from hackers and viruses. The role of a CSO has been elevated in recent years because of the number of attacks from hackers and viruses. Most CSOs possess detailed knowledge of networks and telecommunications because hackers and viruses usually find their way into MIS systems through networked computers.

The *chief privacy officer (CPO)* is responsible for ensuring the ethical and legal use of information within an organization. CPOs are the newest senior executive position in MIS. Recently, 150 of the *Fortune* 500 companies added the CPO position to their list of senior executives. Many CPOs are lawyers by training, enabling them to understand the often complex legal issues surrounding the use of information.[1]

The *chief knowledge officer (CKO)* is responsible for collecting, maintaining, and distributing the organization's knowledge. The CKO designs programs and systems that make it easy for people to reuse knowledge. These systems create repositories of organizational documents, methodologies, tools, and practices, and they establish methods for filtering the information. The CKO must continuously encourage employee contributions to keep the systems up-to-date. The CKO can contribute directly to the organization's bottom line by reducing the learning curve for new employees or employees taking on new roles.

Danny Shaw was the first CKO at Children's Hospital in Boston. His initial task was to unite information from disparate systems to enable analysis of both the efficiency and effectiveness of the hospital's care. Shaw started by building a series of small, integrated information systems that quickly demonstrated value. He then gradually built on those successes, creating a knowledge-enabled organization one layer at a time. Shaw's information systems have enabled administrative and clinical operational analyses.[2]

With the election of President Barack Obama comes the appointment of the first-ever national chief technology officer (CTO). The job description, as listed on Change.gov, states that the first CTO must "ensure the safety of our networks and lead an interagency effort, working with chief technology and chief information officers of each of the federal agencies, to ensure that they use best-in-class technologies and share best practices." A federal-level CTO demonstrates the ongoing growth of technology positions outside corporate America. In the future expect to see many more technology positions in government and nonprofit organizations.

All the above MIS positions and responsibilities are critical to an organization's success. While many organizations may not have a different individual for each of these positions, they must have leaders taking responsibility for all these areas of concern. The individuals responsible for enterprisewide MIS and MIS-related issues must provide guidance and support to the organization's employees. According to *Fast Company* magazine a few executive levels you might see created over the next decade include:

- *Chief intellectual property officer* will manage and defend intellectual property, copyrights, and patents. The world of intellectual property law is vast and complicated as new innovations continually enter the market. Companies in the near future will need a core leadership team member who can not only wade through the dizzying sea of intellectual property laws and patents to ensure their own compliance, but also remain vigilant to protect their own company against infringement.

- *Chief automation officer* determines if a person or business process can be replaced by a robot or software. As we continue to automate jobs a member of the core leadership team of the future will be put in charge of identifying opportunities for companies to become more competitive through automation.

- *Chief user experience officer* will create the optimal relationship between user and technology. User experience used to be an afterthought for hardware and software designers. Now that bulky instruction manuals are largely (and thankfully) a thing of the past, technology companies need to ensure that their products are intuitive from the moment they are activated.[3]

MIS skills gap is the difference between existing MIS workplace knowledge and the knowledge required to fulfill the business goals and strategies. Closing the MIS skills gap by aligning the current workforce with potential future business needs is a complicated proposition. Today, employers often struggle to locate and retain qualified MIS talent, especially individuals with application development, information security, and data analysis skills.

Common approaches to closing an MIS skills gap include social recruiting, off-site training, mentoring services, and partnerships with universities. In many instances, an MIS job will remain unfilled for an extended period of time when an employer needs to hire someone who has a very specific set of skills. In recruiting lingo, such candidates are referred to as purple squirrels. Because squirrels in the real world are not often purple, the implication is that finding the perfect job candidate with exactly the right qualifications, education and salary expectations can be a daunting—if not impossible—task.

Metrics: Measuring Success

LO 4.2 Define critical success factors (CSFs) and key performance indicators (KPIs), and explain how managers use them to measure the success of MIS projects.

A *project* is a temporary activity a company undertakes to create a unique product, service, or result. For example, the construction of a new subway station is a project, as is a movie theater chain's adoption of a software program to allow online ticketing. Peter Drucker, a famous management writer, once said that if you cannot measure something, you cannot manage it. How do managers measure the progress of a complex business project?

Metrics are measurements that evaluate results to determine whether a project is meeting its goals. Two core metrics are critical success factors and key performance indicators. *Critical success factors (CSFs)* are the crucial steps companies perform to achieve their goals and objectives and implement their strategies (see Figure 4.2). *Key performance indicators (KPIs)* are the quantifiable metrics a company uses to evaluate progress toward critical success factors. KPIs are far more specific than CSFs.

It is important to understand the relationship between critical success factors and key performance indicators. CSFs are elements crucial for a business strategy's success. KPIs measure the progress of CSFs with quantifiable measurements, and one CSF can have several KPIs. Of course, both categories will vary by company and industry. Imagine *improve graduation rates* as a CSF for a college. The KPIs to measure this CSF can include:

- Average grades by course and gender.
- Student dropout rates by gender and major.
- Average graduation rate by gender and major.
- Time spent in tutoring by gender and major.

KPIs can focus on external and internal measurements. A common external KPI is *market share*, or the proportion of the market that a firm captures. We calculate it by dividing the firm's sales by the total market sales for the entire industry. Market share measures a firm's external performance relative to that of its competitors. For example, if a firm's total sales (revenues) are $2 million and sales for the entire industry are $10 million, the firm has captured 20 percent of the total market (2/10 = 20%) or a 20 percent market share.

FIGURE 4.2

CSF and KPI Metrics.

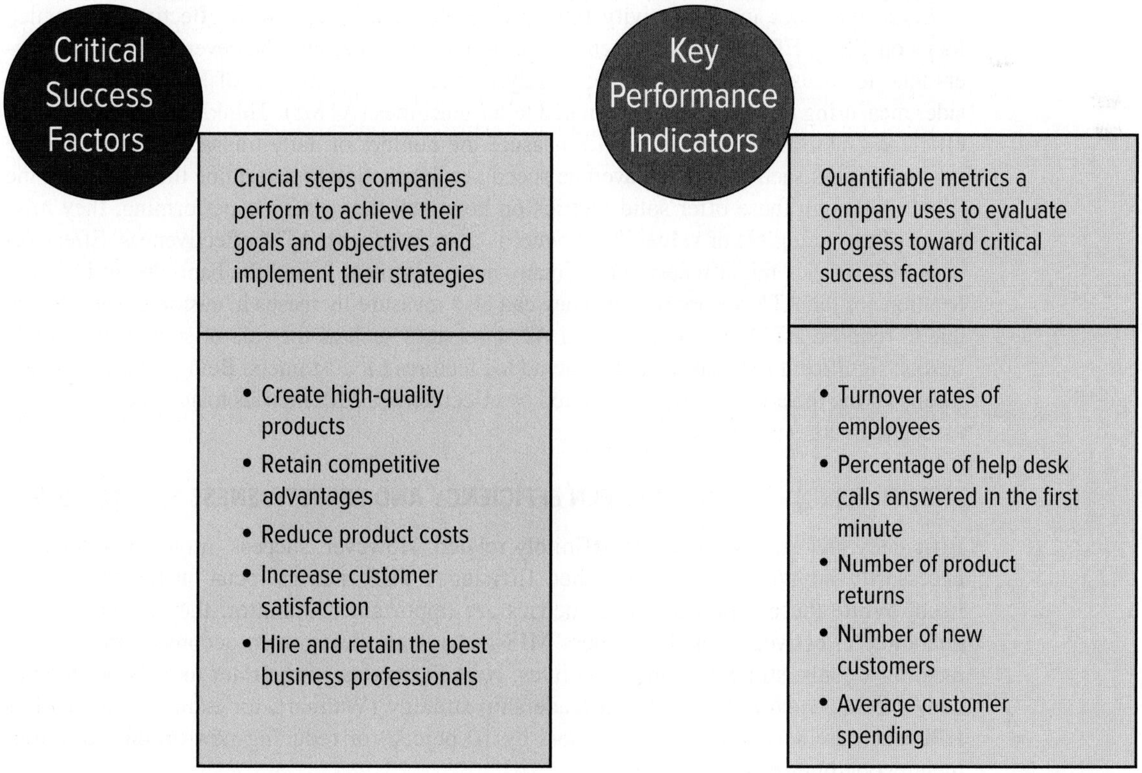

Critical Success Factors

Crucial steps companies perform to achieve their goals and objectives and implement their strategies

- Create high-quality products
- Retain competitive advantages
- Reduce product costs
- Increase customer satisfaction
- Hire and retain the best business professionals

Key Performance Indicators

Quantifiable metrics a company uses to evaluate progress toward critical success factors

- Turnover rates of employees
- Percentage of help desk calls answered in the first minute
- Number of product returns
- Number of new customers
- Average customer spending

A common internal KPI is ***return on investment (ROI)***, which indicates the earning power of a project. We measure it by dividing the profitability of a project by the costs. This sounds easy, and for many departments where the projects are tangible and self-contained it is; however, for projects that are intangible and cross departmental lines (such as MIS projects), ROI is challenging to measure. Imagine attempting to calculate the ROI of a fire extinguisher. If the fire extinguisher is never used, its ROI is low. If the fire extinguisher puts out a fire that could have destroyed the entire building, its ROI is astronomically high.

Creating KPIs to measure the success of an MIS project offers similar challenges. Think about a firm's email system. How could managers track departmental costs and profits associated with company email? Measuring by volume does not account for profitability, because one sales email could land a million-dollar deal while 300 others might not generate any revenue. Non-revenue-generating departments such as human resources and legal require email but will not be using it to generate profits. For this reason, many managers turn to higher-level metrics, such as efficiency and effectiveness, to measure MIS projects. ***Best practices*** are the most successful solutions or problem-solving methods that have been developed by a specific organization or industry. Measuring MIS projects helps determine the best practices for an industry.

EFFICIENCY AND EFFECTIVENESS METRICS

Efficiency MIS metrics measure the performance of MIS itself, such as throughput, transaction speed, and system availability. ***Effectiveness MIS metrics*** measure the impact MIS has on business processes and activities, including customer satisfaction and customer conversion rates. Efficiency focuses on the extent to which a firm is using its resources in an optimal way, while effectiveness focuses on how well a firm is achieving its goals and objectives. Peter Drucker offers a helpful distinction between efficiency and effectiveness: Doing things right addresses efficiency—getting the most from each resource. Doing the right things addresses effectiveness—setting the right goals and objectives and ensuring they are accomplished. Figure 4.3 describes a few of the common types of efficiency and effectiveness MIS metrics. KPIs that measure MIS projects include both efficiency and effectiveness metrics. Of course, these metrics are not as concrete as market share or ROI, but they do offer valuable insight into project performance.[4]

Large increases in productivity typically result from increases in effectiveness, which focus on CSFs. Efficiency MIS metrics are far easier to measure, however, so most managers tend to focus on them, often incorrectly, to measure the success of MIS projects. Consider measuring the success of automated teller machines (ATMs). Thinking in terms of MIS efficiency metrics, a manager would measure the number of daily transactions, the average amount per transaction, and the average speed per transaction to determine the success of the ATM. Although these offer solid metrics on how well the system is performing, they miss many of the intangible or value-added benefits associated with ATM effectiveness. Effectiveness MIS metrics might measure how many new customers joined the bank due to its ATM locations or the ATMs' ease of use. They can also measure increases in customer satisfaction due to reduced ATM fees or additional ATM services such as the sale of stamps and movie tickets, significant time savers and value-added features for customers. Being a great manager means taking the added viewpoint offered by effectiveness MIS metrics to analyze all benefits associated with an MIS project.

THE INTERRELATIONSHIP BETWEEN EFFICIENCY AND EFFECTIVENESS MIS METRICS

Efficiency and effectiveness are definitely related. However, success in one area does not necessarily imply success in the other. Efficiency MIS metrics focus on the technology itself. While these efficiency MIS metrics are important to monitor, they do not always guarantee effectiveness. Effectiveness MIS metrics are determined according to an organization's goals, strategies, and objectives. Here, it becomes important to consider a company's CSFs, such as a broad cost leadership strategy (Walmart, for example), as well as KPIs such as increasing new customers by 10 percent or reducing new-product development cycle times to six months.

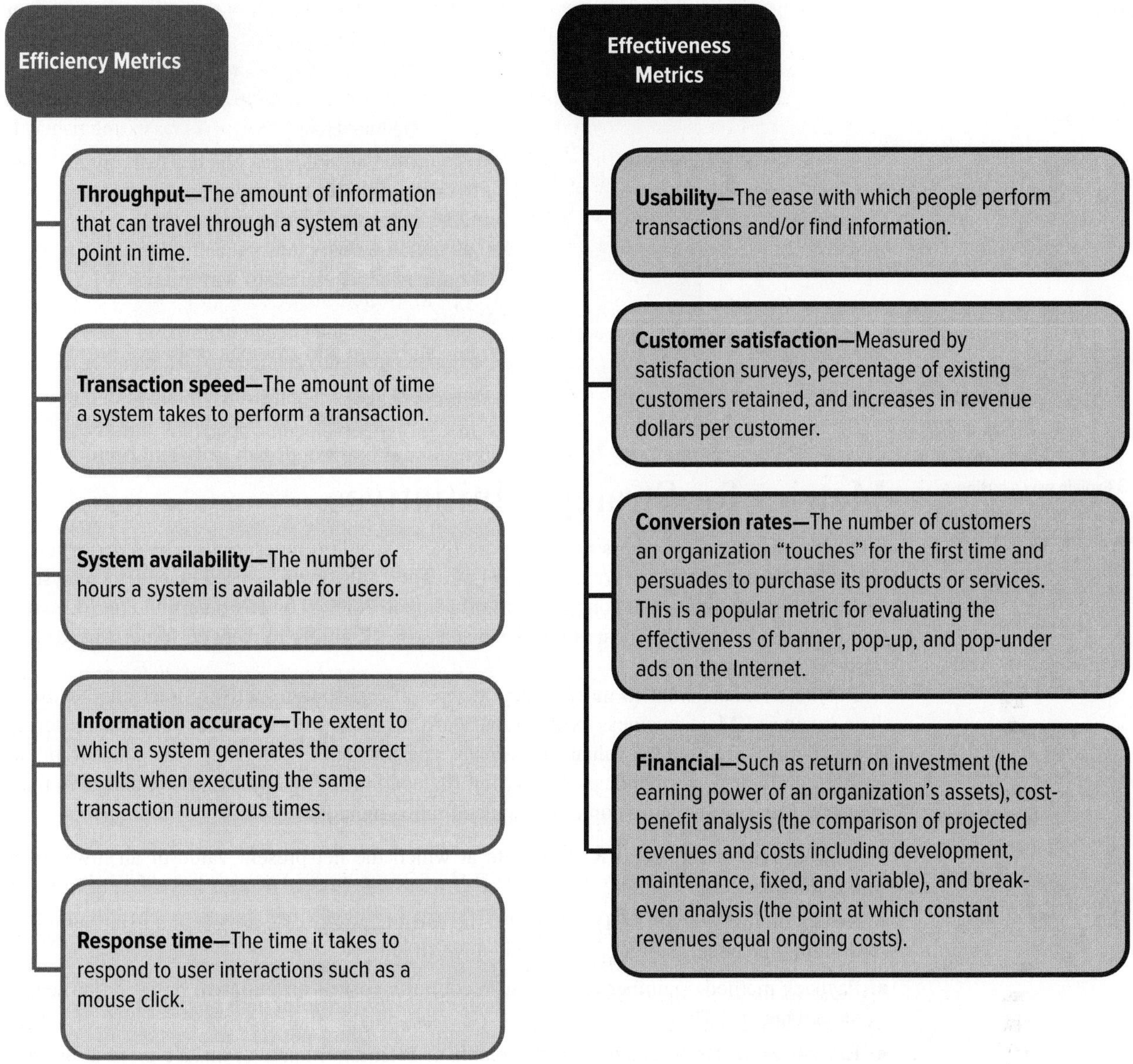

Efficiency Metrics

Throughput—The amount of information that can travel through a system at any point in time.

Transaction speed—The amount of time a system takes to perform a transaction.

System availability—The number of hours a system is available for users.

Information accuracy—The extent to which a system generates the correct results when executing the same transaction numerous times.

Response time—The time it takes to respond to user interactions such as a mouse click.

Effectiveness Metrics

Usability—The ease with which people perform transactions and/or find information.

Customer satisfaction—Measured by satisfaction surveys, percentage of existing customers retained, and increases in revenue dollars per customer.

Conversion rates—The number of customers an organization "touches" for the first time and persuades to purchase its products or services. This is a popular metric for evaluating the effectiveness of banner, pop-up, and pop-under ads on the Internet.

Financial—Such as return on investment (the earning power of an organization's assets), cost-benefit analysis (the comparison of projected revenues and costs including development, maintenance, fixed, and variable), and break-even analysis (the point at which constant revenues equal ongoing costs).

FIGURE 4.3

Common Types of Efficiency and Effectiveness Metrics.

Figure 4.4 depicts the interrelationships between efficiency and effectiveness. Ideally, a firm wants to operate in the upper right-hand corner of the graph, realizing both significant increases in efficiency and effectiveness. However, operating in the upper left-hand corner (minimal effectiveness with increased efficiency) or the lower right-hand corner (significant effectiveness with minimal efficiency) may be in line with an organization's particular strategies. In general, operating in the lower left-hand corner (minimal efficiency and minimal effectiveness) is not ideal for the operation of any organization.

Regardless of what process is measured, how it is measured, and whether it is performed for the sake of efficiency or effectiveness, managers must set **benchmarks**, or baseline values the system seeks to attain. **Benchmarking** is a process of continuously measuring system results, comparing those results to optimal system performance (benchmark values), and identifying steps and procedures to improve system performance. Benchmarks help assess how an MIS project performs over time. For instance, if a system held a benchmark for a response time of 15 seconds, the manager would want to ensure response time continued to decrease until it reached that point. If response time suddenly increased to 1 minute, the manager would know the system was not functioning correctly and could start looking into potential problems. Continuously measuring MIS projects against benchmarks provides feedback so managers can control the system.

FIGURE 4.4

The Interrelationships
between Efficiency and
Effectiveness.

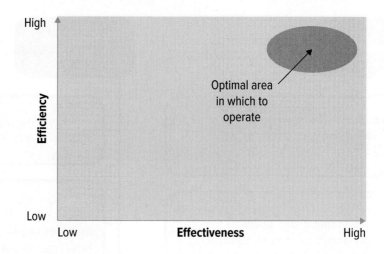

**LO 4.3 Explain why a business
would use metrics to measure the
success of strategic initiatives.**

Metrics for Strategic Initiatives

What is a metric? A metric is nothing more than a standard measure to assess performance in a particular area. Metrics are at the heart of a good, customer-focused management system and any program directed at continuous improvement. A focus on customers and performance standards shows up in the form of metrics that assess the ability to meet customers' needs and business objectives.

Business leaders want to monitor key metrics in real time to actively track the health of their business. Most business professionals are familiar with financial metrics. Different financial ratios are used to evaluate a company's performance. Companies can gain additional insight into their performance by comparing financial ratios against other companies in their industry. A few of the more common financial ratios include:

- Internal rate of return (IRR)—the rate at which the net present value of an investment equals zero.

- Return on investment (ROI)—indicates the earning power of a project and is measured by dividing the benefits of a project by the investment.

- Payback method—number of years to recoup the cost of an initiative based on projected annual net cash flow.

- Break-even analysis—determines the volume of business required to make a profit at the current prices charged for the products or services. For example, if a promotional mailing costs $1,000 and each item generates $50 in revenue, the company must generate 20 sales to break even and cover the cost of the mailing. The break-even point is the point at which revenues equal costs. The point is located by performing a break-even analysis. All sales over the break-even point produce profits; any drop in sales below that point will produce losses (see Figure 4.5).

FIGURE 4.5

Break-Even Analysis.

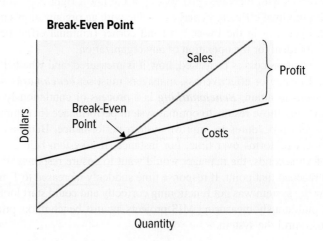

FIGURE 4.6

Website Metrics.

Website Metrics
■ **Abandoned registrations:** Number of visitors who start the process of completing a registration page and then abandon the activity.
■ **Abandoned shopping carts:** Number of visitors who create a shopping cart and start shopping and then abandon the activity before paying for the merchandise.
■ **Click-through:** Count of the number of people who visit a site, click on an ad, and are taken to the site of the advertiser.
■ **Conversion rate:** Percentage of potential customers who visit a site and actually buy something.
■ **Cost-per-thousand (CPM):** Sales dollars generated per dollar of advertising. This is commonly used to make the case for spending money to appear on a search engine.
■ **Page exposures:** Average number of page exposures to an individual visitor.
■ **Total hits:** Number of visits to a website, many of which may be by the same visitor.
■ **Unique visitors:** Number of unique visitors to a site in a given time. This is commonly used by Nielsen/Net ratings to rank the most popular websites.

Most managers are familiar with financial metrics but unfamiliar with information system metrics. Most companies measure the traffic on a website as the primary determinant of the website's success. However, heavy website traffic does not necessarily indicate large sales. Many organizations with lots of website traffic have minimal sales. A company can use web traffic analysis or web analytics to determine the revenue generated, the number of new customers acquired, any reductions in customer service calls, and so on. Figure 4.6 displays a few metrics managers should be familiar with to help measure website success along with an organization's strategic initiatives. A web-centric metric is a measure of the success of web and ebusiness initiatives. Of the hundreds of web-centric metrics available, some are general to almost any web or ebusiness initiative and others are dependent on the particular initiative.[5]

Supply chain management metrics can help an organization understand how it's operating over a given time period. Supply chain measurements can cover many areas including procurement, production, distribution, warehousing, inventory, transportation, and customer service. However, a good performance in one part of the supply chain is not sufficient. A supply chain is only as strong as its weakest link. The solution is to measure all key areas of the supply chain. Figure 4.7 displays common supply chain management metrics.[6]

Wondering what CRM metrics to track and monitor using reporting and real-time performance dashboards? Best practice is no more than seven (plus or minus two) metrics out

FIGURE 4.7

Supply Chain Management Metrics.

Supply Chain Management Metrics
■ **Back order:** An unfilled customer order. A back order is demand (immediate or past due) against an item whose current stock level is insufficient to satisfy demand.
■ **Customer order promised cycle time:** The anticipated or agreed upon cycle time of a purchase order. It is a gap between the purchase order creation date and the requested delivery date.
■ **Customer order actual cycle time:** The average time it takes to actually fill a customer's purchase order. This measure can be viewed on an order or an order line level.
■ **Inventory replenishment cycle time:** Measure of the manufacturing cycle time plus the time included to deploy the product to the appropriate distribution center.
■ **Inventory turns (inventory turnover):** The number of times that a company's inventory cycles or turns over per year. It is one of the most commonly used supply chain metrics.

FIGURE 4.8

CRM Metrics.

Sales Metrics	Service Metrics	Marketing Metrics
■ Number of prospective customers	■ Cases closed same day	■ Number of marketing campaigns
■ Number of new customers	■ Number of cases handled by agent	■ New customer retention rates
■ Number of retained customers	■ Number of service calls	■ Number of responses by marketing campaign
■ Number of open leads	■ Average number of service requests by type	■ Number of purchases by marketing campaign
■ Number of sales calls	■ Average time to resolution	■ Revenue generated by marketing campaign
■ Number of sales calls per lead	■ Average number of service calls per day	■ Cost per interaction by marketing campaign
■ Amount of new revenue	■ Percentage compliance with service-level agreement	■ Number of new customers acquired by marketing campaign
■ Amount of recurring revenue	■ Percentage of service renewals	■ Customer retention rate
■ Number of proposals given	■ Customer satisfaction level	■ Number of new leads by product

of the hundreds possible should be used at any given management level. Figure 4.8 displays common CRM metrics tracked by organizations.[7]

Business process reengineering and enterprise resource planning are large, organization-wide initiatives. Measuring these types of strategic initiatives is extremely difficult. One of the best methods is the balanced scorecard. This approach to strategic management was developed in the early 1990s by Dr. Robert Kaplan of the Harvard Business School and Dr. David Norton. Addressing some of the weaknesses and vagueness of previous measurement techniques, the balanced scorecard approach provides a clear prescription as to what companies should measure in order to balance the financial perspective.

The *balanced scorecard* is a management system, in addition to a measurement system, that enables organizations to clarify their vision and strategy and translate them into action. It provides feedback around both the internal business processes and external outcomes in order to continuously improve strategic performance and results. When fully deployed, the balanced scorecard transforms strategic planning from an academic exercise into the nerve center of an enterprise. Kaplan and Norton describe the innovation of the balanced scorecard as follows:

> The balanced scorecard retains traditional financial measures. But financial measures tell the story of past events, an adequate story for industrial age companies for which investments in long-term capabilities and customer relationships were not critical for success. These financial measures are inadequate, however, for guiding and evaluating the journey that information age companies must make to create future value through investment in customers, suppliers, employees, processes, technology, and innovation.[8]

The balanced scorecard views the organization from four perspectives, and users should develop metrics, collect data, and analyze their business relative to each of these perspectives:

- The learning and growth perspective.
- The internal business process perspective.
- The customer perspective.
- The financial perspective (see Figure 4.9).

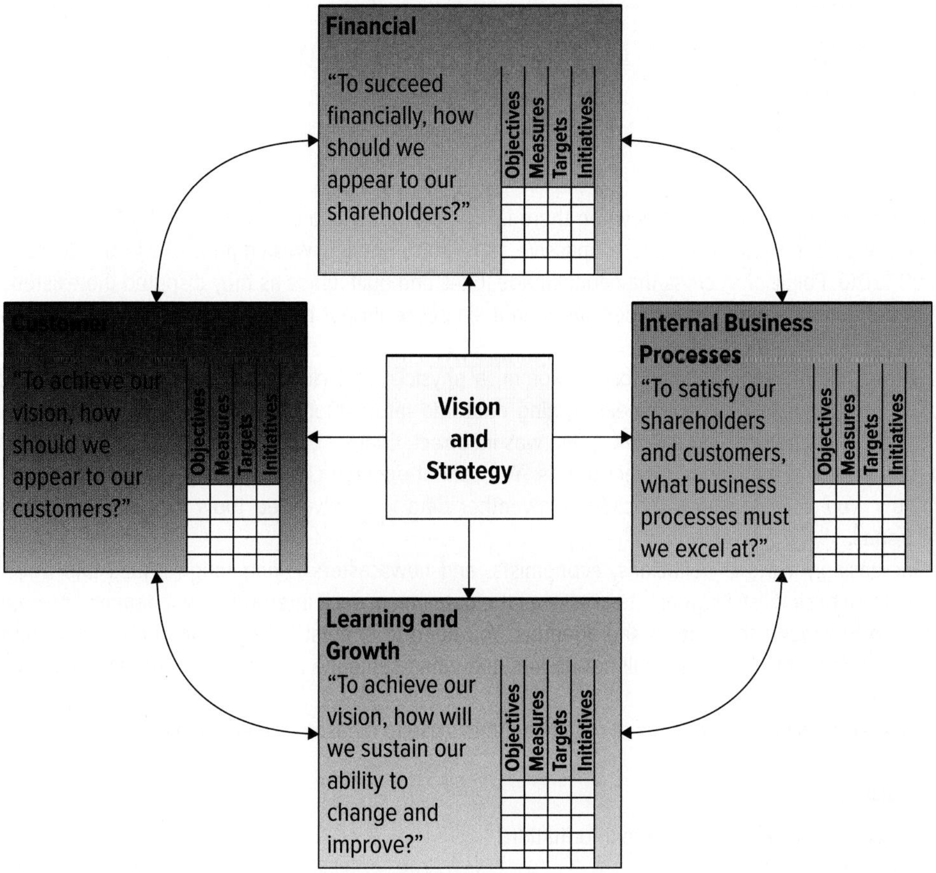

FIGURE 4.9

The Four Primary
Perspectives of the Balanced
Scorecard.

Financial

"To succeed financially, how should we appear to our shareholders?"

Objectives	Measures	Targets	Initiatives

Customer

"To achieve our vision, how should we appear to our customers?"

Objectives	Measures	Targets	Initiatives

Vision and Strategy

Internal Business Processes

"To satisfy our shareholders and customers, what business processes must we excel at?"

Objectives	Measures	Targets	Initiatives

Learning and Growth

"To achieve our vision, how will we sustain our ability to change and improve?"

Objectives	Measures	Targets	Initiatives

Recall that companies cannot manage what they cannot measure. Therefore, metrics must be developed based on the priorities of the strategic plan, which provides the key business drivers and criteria for metrics that managers most desire to watch.

One warning regarding metrics—do not go crazy. The trick is to find a few key metrics to track that provide significant insight. Remember to tie metrics to other financial and business objectives in the firm. The key is to get good insight without becoming a slave to metrics. The rule of thumb is to develop seven key metrics, plus or minus two.

OPENING CASE STUDY QUESTIONS

1. Explain the difference between efficiency MIS metrics and effectiveness MIS metrics.

2. Imagine you are working for Costco as a manager in its Chicago store. List three CRM metrics Costco should track, along with the reasons these metrics will add value to Costco's business strategy.

3. List three SCM metrics Costco should track, along with the reasons these metrics will add value to Costco's business strategy.

4. How can Costco use the balanced scorecard to make its business more efficient?

How can global warming be real when there is so much snow and cold weather? That's what some people wondered after a couple of massive snowstorms buried Washington, DC, in the winter of 2009–2010. Politicians across the capital made jokes and built igloos as they disputed the existence of climate change. Some concluded the planet simply could not be warming with all the snow on the ground.

These comments frustrated Joseph Romm, a physicist and climate expert with the Center for American Progress. He spent weeks turning data into information and graphs to educate anyone who would listen as to why this reasoning was incorrect. Climate change is all about analyzing data, turning it into information to detect trends. You cannot observe climate change by looking out the window; you have to review decades of weather data with advanced tools to really understand the trends.

Increasingly we see politicians, economists, and newscasters taking tough issues and boiling them down to simplistic arguments over what the data mean, each interpreting the data and spinning the data to support their views and agendas. You need to understand the data and turn them into useful information or else you will not understand when someone is telling the truth and when you are being lied to.

Brainstorm two or three types of data economists use to measure the economy.[9]

Questions

1. How do they turn the data into information?

2. What issues do they encounter when attempting to measure the economy?

3. As a manager, what do you need to understand when reading or listening to economic and business reports?

4.1. Define the primary MIS roles along with their associated responsibilities.

The chief information officer (CIO)is responsible for (1) overseeing all uses of information technology and (2) ensuring the strategic alignment of MIS with business goals and objectives. The chief data officer (CDO) is responsible for determining the types of information the enterprise will capture, retain, analyze, and share. The chief technology officer (CTO) is responsible for ensuring the throughput, speed, accuracy, availability, and reliability of an organization's information technology. The chief security officer (CSO) is responsible for ensuring the security of MIS systems and developing strategies and MIS safeguards against attacks from hackers and viruses. The chief privacy officer (CPO) is responsible for ensuring the ethical and legal use of information within an organization. The chief knowledge officer (CKO) is responsible for collecting, maintaining, and distributing the organization's knowledge.

4.2. Define critical success factors (CSFs) and key performance indicators (KPIs), and explain how managers use them to measure the success of MIS projects.

Metrics are measurements that evaluate results to determine whether a project is meeting its goals. Two core metrics are critical success factors and key performance indicators. Critical success factors (CSFs) are the crucial steps companies perform to achieve their goals and objectives and implement their strategies. Key performance indicators (KPIs) are the quantifiable metrics a company uses to evaluate progress toward critical success factors. KPIs are far more specific than CSFs.

4.3. Explain why a business would use metrics to measure the success of strategic initiatives.

Business leaders want to monitor key metrics in real time to actively track the health of their business. Most business professionals are familiar with financial metrics. Different financial ratios are used to evaluate a company's performance. Companies can gain additional insight into their performance by comparing financial ratios against other companies in their industry

1. What are the responsibilities of a chief information officer?
2. What are the responsibilities of a chief privacy officer?
3. What are the responsibilities of a chief data officer?
4. What are the responsibilities of a chief security officer?
5. Why would a company want to have a CIO, CPO, and CSO?
6. What is the difference between MIS efficiency metrics and MIS effectiveness metrics?
7. What is the difference between CSFs and KPIs?
8. How can metrics be used to measure the success of supply chain management systems and CRM systems?
9. What is the purpose of the balanced scorecard?

1. Who Really Won the Winter Olympics?

If you were watching the 2014 Winter Olympics, I bet you were excited to see your country and its amazing athletes compete. As you were following the Olympics day by day, you were probably checking different websites to see how your country ranked. And depending on the website you visited, you could get a very different answer to this seemingly easy question. On the NBC and ESPN networks, the United States ranked second, and on the official Sochie Olympic website, the United States ranked fourth. The simple question of who won the 2014 Winter Olympics changes significantly, depending on whom you asked.

In a group, take a look at the following two charts and brainstorm the reasons each internationally recognized source has a different listing for the top five winners. What measurement is each chart using to determine the winner? Who do you believe is the winner? As a manager, what do you need to understand when reading or listening to business forecasts and reports?

	Winter Olympics 2014 Medal Ranking According to NBC News				
Rank	**Country**	**Gold**	**Silver**	**Bronze**	**Total**
1	Russian Fed.	13	11	9	33
2	United States	9	7	12	28
3	Norway	11	5	10	26
4	Canada	10	10	5	25
5	Netherlands	8	7	9	24

	Winter Olympics 2014 Medal Ranking According to Official Sochie Olympic Website				
Rank	**Country**	**Gold**	**Silver**	**Bronze**	**Total**
1	Russian Fed.	13	11	9	33
2	Norway	11	5	10	26
3	Canada	10	10	5	25
4	United States	9	7	12	28
5	Netherlands	8	7	9	24

2. Starting Your Own Business

Josh James recently sold his web analytics company, Omniture, to Adobe for $1.8 billion. Yes, James started Omniture from his dorm room! Have you begun to recognize the unbelievable opportunities available to those students who understand the power of MIS, regardless of their major? What's stopping you from starting your own business today? You are living in the information age and, with the power of MIS, it is easier than ever to jump into the business game with very little capital investment. Why not start your own business today?

- Why is it so easy today for students to create start-ups while still in college and how can this course help prepare you to start your own business?

- Explain three CSFs and KPIs you would use to measure the success of your business.

- Choose two CRM and SCM metrics you could use to measure your business and explain how they can help you achieve success.

3. The Competitive Landscape for Students

According to the Economic Policy Institute, over the past decade the United States has lost an estimated 2.4 million factory jobs to China. Factories in South Korea, Taiwan, and China are producing toys, toothpaste, running shoes, computers, appliances, and cars. For a long time, U.S. firms did not recognize these products as competition; they regarded Asia's high-tech products as second-rate knockoffs and believed Asian countries maintained a factory culture—they could imitate but not innovate.

In hindsight, it is obvious that once these countries did begin designing and creating high-end products, they would have obvious competitive advantages, with high-value research and development coupled with low-cost manufacturing of unbeatable goods and services. Asia is now on the rise in all industries from wind turbines to high-speed bullet trains. According to *Bloomberg Businessweek* 's ranking of the most innovative companies, 15 of the top 50 are Asian, up from just 5 in the previous year. In fact, for the first time, the majority of the top 25 are based outside the United States.

How do you, as a business student, view these statistics? What type of global business climate will you be competing in when you graduate? If you wanted to gather competitive intelligence about the job market, where would you look and what types of data would you want to analyze? What can you do to create personal competitive advantages to differentiate yourself when searching for a job?

4. Roles and Responsibilities

You are the chief executive officer for a start-up telecommunications company. The company currently has 50 employees and plans to ramp up to 3,000 by the end of the year.

Your first task is to determine how you are going to model your organization. You decide to address the MIS department's organizational structure first. You need to consider if you want to have a CIO, CPO, CSO, CTO, CDO, and CKO, and if so, what their reporting structure will look like and why. You also need to determine the different roles and responsibilities for each executive position. Once you have compiled this information, put together a presentation describing your MIS department's organizational structure.

5. One Laptop per Child

Nicholas Negroponte is the founder of the MIT Media Lab and has spent his career pushing the edge of the information revolution as an inventor, thinker, and angel investor. His latest project, One Laptop per Child, plans to build $100 laptops that he hopes to put in the hands of the millions of children in developing countries around the globe. The XO (the "$100 laptop") is a wireless, Internet-enabled, pedal-powered computer costing roughly $100. What types of competitive advantages could children gain from Negroponte's $100 laptop? What types of issues could result from the $100 laptop? Explain each of the efficiency metrics and effectiveness metrics that are required for each laptop to be considered successful.

6. Is it Effective or Is It Efficient?

Making business decisions is a key skill for all managers. Review the following list and, in a group, determine whether the question is focusing on efficiency, effectiveness, or both.

Business Decision	Efficiency	Effectiveness
What is the best route for dropping off products?		
Should we change suppliers?		
Should we reduce costs by buying lower-quality materials?		
Should we sell products to a younger market?		
Did we make our sales targets?		
What was the turnover rate of employees?		
What is the average customer spending?		
How many new customers purchased products?		
Did the amount of daily transactions increase?		
Is there a better way to restructure a store to increase sales?		

Organizational Structures That Support Strategic Initiatives

5.1. Explain information ethics and its associated issues.

5.2. Describe information security and the difference between hackers and viruses.

Information Ethics

Ethics and security are two fundamental building blocks for all organizations. In recent years, enormous business scandals along with 9/11 have shed new light on the meaning of ethics and security. When the behavior of a few individuals can destroy billion-dollar organizations, the value of ethics and security should be evident.

Copyright is the legal protection afforded an expression of an idea, such as a song, book, or video game. *Intellectual property* is intangible creative work that is embodied in physical form and includes copyrights, trademarks, and patents. A *patent* is an exclusive right to make, use, and sell an invention and is granted by a government to the inventor. As it becomes easier for people to copy everything from words and data to music and video, the ethical issues surrounding copyright infringement and the violation of intellectual property rights are consuming the ebusiness world. Technology poses new challenges for our ethics—the principles and standards that guide our behavior toward other people.

The protection of customers' privacy is one of the largest, and murkiest, ethical issues facing organizations today. *Privacy* is the right to be left alone when you want to be, to have control over your personal possessions, and not to be observed without your consent. Privacy is related to *confidentiality*, which is the assurance that messages and information remain available only to those authorized to view them. Each time employees make a decision about a privacy issue, the outcome could sink the company.

Trust among companies, customers, partners, and suppliers is the support structure of ebusiness. Privacy is one of its main ingredients. Consumers' concerns that their privacy will be violated because of their interactions on the web continue to be one of the primary barriers to the growth of ebusiness.

Information ethics govern the ethical and moral issues arising from the development and use of information technologies as well as the creation, collection, duplication, distribution, and processing of information itself (with or without the aid of computer technologies). Ethical dilemmas in this area usually arise not as simple, clear-cut situations but as clashes among competing goals, responsibilities, and loyalties. Inevitably, there will be more than one socially acceptable or correct decision. The two primary areas concerning software include pirated software and counterfeit software. *Pirated software* is the unauthorized use, duplication, distribution, or sale of copyrighted software. *Counterfeit software* is software that is manufactured to look like the real thing and sold as such. *Digital rights management* is a technological solution that allows publishers to control their digital media to discourage, limit, or prevent illegal copying and distribution. Figure 5.1 contains examples of ethically questionable or unacceptable uses of information technology.

Individuals copy, use, and distribute software.
Employees search organizational databases for sensitive corporate and personal information.
Organizations collect, buy, and use information without checking the validity or accuracy of the information.
Individuals create and spread viruses that cause trouble for those using and maintaining IT systems.
Individuals hack into computer systems to steal proprietary information.
Employees destroy or steal proprietary organization information such as schematics, sketches, customer lists, and reports.

Unfortunately, few hard and fast rules exist for always determining what is ethical. Many people can either justify or condemn the actions in Figure 5.1, for example. Knowing the law is important, but that knowledge will not always help because what is legal might not always be ethical, and what might be ethical is not always legal. For example, Joe Reidenberg received an offer for AT&T cell phone service. AT&T used Equifax, a credit reporting agency, to identify potential customers such as Joe Reidenberg. Overall, this seemed like a good business opportunity between Equifax and AT&T wireless. Unfortunately, the Fair Credit Reporting Act (FCRA) forbids repurposing credit information except when the information is used for "a firm offer of credit or insurance." In other words, the only product that can be sold based on credit information is credit. A representative for Equifax stated, "As long as AT&T Wireless (or any company for that matter) is offering the cell phone service on a credit basis, such as allowing the use of the service before the consumer has to pay, it is in compliance with the FCRA." However, the question remains—is it ethical?[1]

Figure 5.2 shows the four quadrants where ethical and legal behaviors intersect. The goal for most businesses is to make decisions within quadrant I that are both legal and ethical. There are times when a business will find itself in the position of making a decision in quadrant III, such as hiring child labor in foreign countries, or in quadrant II when a business might pay a foreigner who is getting her immigration status approved because the company is in the process of hiring the person. A business should never find itself operating in quadrant IV. Ethics are critical to operating a successful business today.

INFORMATION DOES NOT HAVE ETHICS: PEOPLE DO

Information itself has no ethics. It does not care how it is used. It will not stop itself from spamming customers, sharing itself if it is sensitive or personal, or revealing details to third parties. Information cannot delete or preserve itself. Therefore, it falls to those who own the information to develop ethical guidelines about how to manage it.

FIGURE 5.2

Acting Ethically and Acting
Legally Are Not Always the
Same Thing.

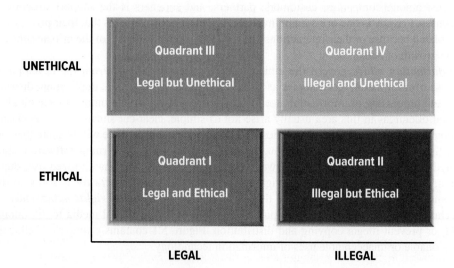

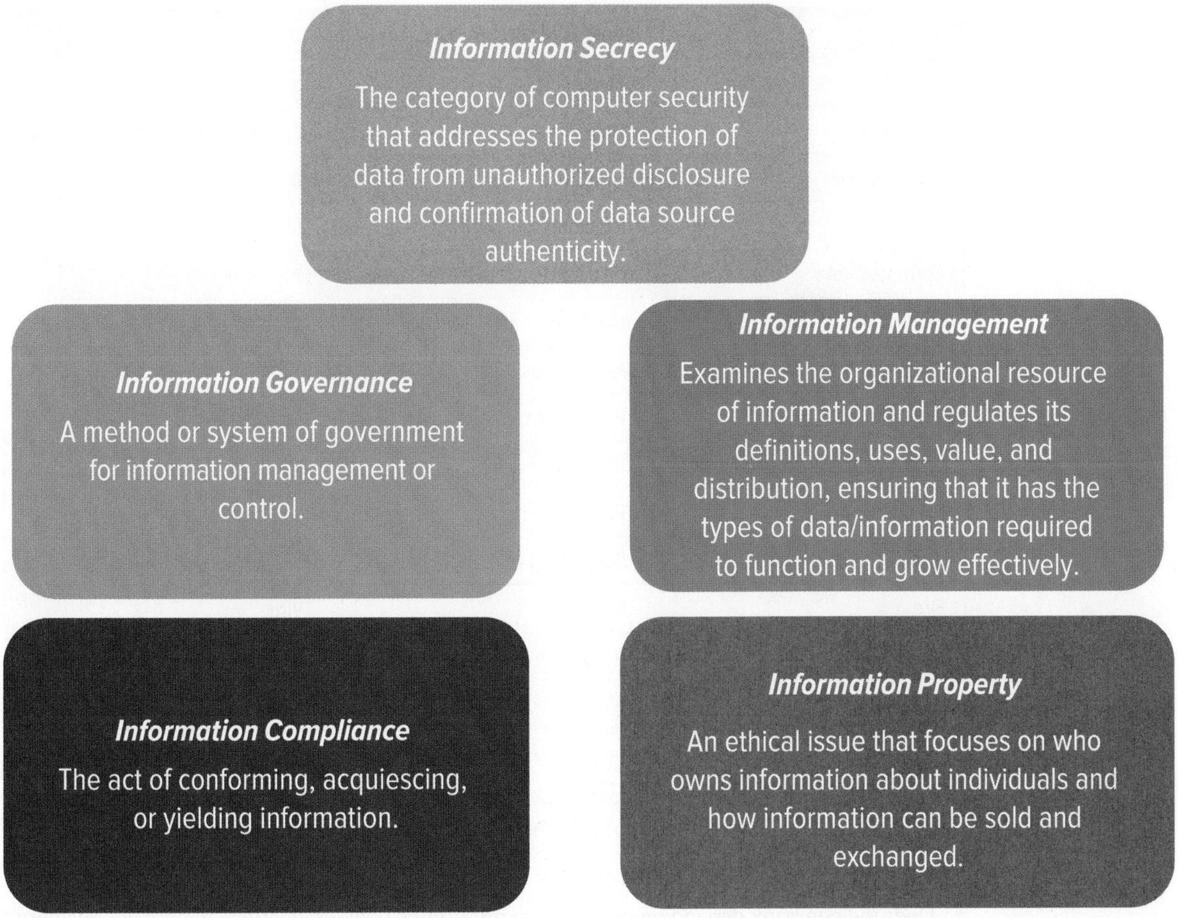

Information Secrecy

The category of computer security that addresses the protection of data from unauthorized disclosure and confirmation of data source authenticity.

Information Governance

A method or system of government for information management or control.

Information Management

Examines the organizational resource of information and regulates its definitions, uses, value, and distribution, ensuring that it has the types of data/information required to function and grow effectively.

Information Compliance

The act of conforming, acquiescing, or yielding information.

Information Property

An ethical issue that focuses on who owns information about individuals and how information can be sold and exchanged.

FIGURE 5.3

Ethical Guidelines for Information Management.

A few years ago, the ideas of information management, governance, and compliance were relatively obscure. Today, these concepts are a must for virtually every company, both domestic and global, primarily due to the role digital information plays in corporate legal proceedings or litigation. Frequently, digital information serves as key evidence in legal proceedings, and it is far easier to search, organize, and filter than paper documents. Digital information is also extremely difficult to destroy, especially if it is on a corporate network or sent by email. In fact, the only reliable way to obliterate digital information reliably is to destroy the hard drives on which the file was stored. *Ediscovery* (or electronic discovery) refers to the ability of a company to identify, search, gather, seize, or export digital information in responding to a litigation, audit, investigation, or information inquiry. As the importance of ediscovery grows, so does information governance and information compliance. The *Child Online Protection Act (COPA)* was passed to protect minors from accessing inappropriate material on the Internet. Figure 5.3 displays the ethical guidelines for information management.

Information Security

LO 5.2 Describe information security and the difference between hackers and viruses.

To reflect the crucial interdependence between MIS and business processes accurately, we should update the old business axiom "Time is money" to say "Uptime is money." *Downtime* refers to a period of time when a system is unavailable. Unplanned downtime can strike at any time for any number of reasons, from tornadoes to sink overflows to network failures to power outages (see Figure 5.4). Although natural disasters may appear to be the most devastating

FIGURE 5.4

Sources of Unplanned
Downtime.

Sources of Unplanned Downtime		
Bomb threat	Frozen Pipe	Snowstorm
Burst pipe	Hail	Sprinkler malfunction
Chemical spill	Hurricane	Static electricity
Construction	Ice storm	Strike
Corrupted data	Insects	Terrorism
Earthquake	Lightning	Theft
Electrical short	Network failure	Tornado
Epidemic	Plane crash	Train derailment
Equipment failure	Power interruption	Smoke damage
Evacuation	Power outage	Vandalism
Explosion	Power surge	Vehicle crash
Fire	Rodents	Virus
Flood	Sabotage	Water damage (various)
Fraud	Shredded data	Wind

causes of MIS outages, they are hardly the most frequent or most expensive. A few questions managers should ask when determining the cost of downtime are:

- How many transactions can the company afford to lose without significantly harming business?
- Does the company depend on one or more mission-critical applications to conduct business?
- How much revenue will the company lose for every hour a critical application is unavailable?
- What is the productivity cost associated with each hour of downtime?
- How will collaborative business processes with partners, suppliers, and customers be affected by an unexpected MIS outage?
- What is the total cost of lost productivity and lost revenue during unplanned downtime?

The reliability and resilience of MIS systems have never been more essential for success as businesses cope with the forces of globalization, 24/7 operations, government and trade regulations, global recession, and overextended MIS budgets and resources. Any unexpected downtime in today's business environment has the potential to cause both short- and long-term costs with far-reaching consequences. Figure 5.5 demonstrates that the costs of downtime are associated not only with lost revenues but also with financial performance, damage to reputations, and even travel or legal expenses.

Information security is a broad term encompassing the protection of information from accidental or intentional misuse by persons inside or outside an organization. Information security is perhaps the most fundamental and critical of all the technologies/disciplines an organization must have squarely in place to execute its business strategy. Without solid security processes and procedures, none of the other technologies can develop business advantages. Understanding how to secure information systems is critical to keeping downtime to a minimum and uptime to a maximum. Hackers and viruses are two of the hottest issues currently facing information security.

SECURITY THREATS CAUSED BY HACKERS AND VIRUSES

Hackers are experts in technology who use their knowledge to break into computers and computer networks, either for profit or simply for the challenge. Smoking is not just bad for a person's health; it seems it is also bad for company security because hackers regularly use

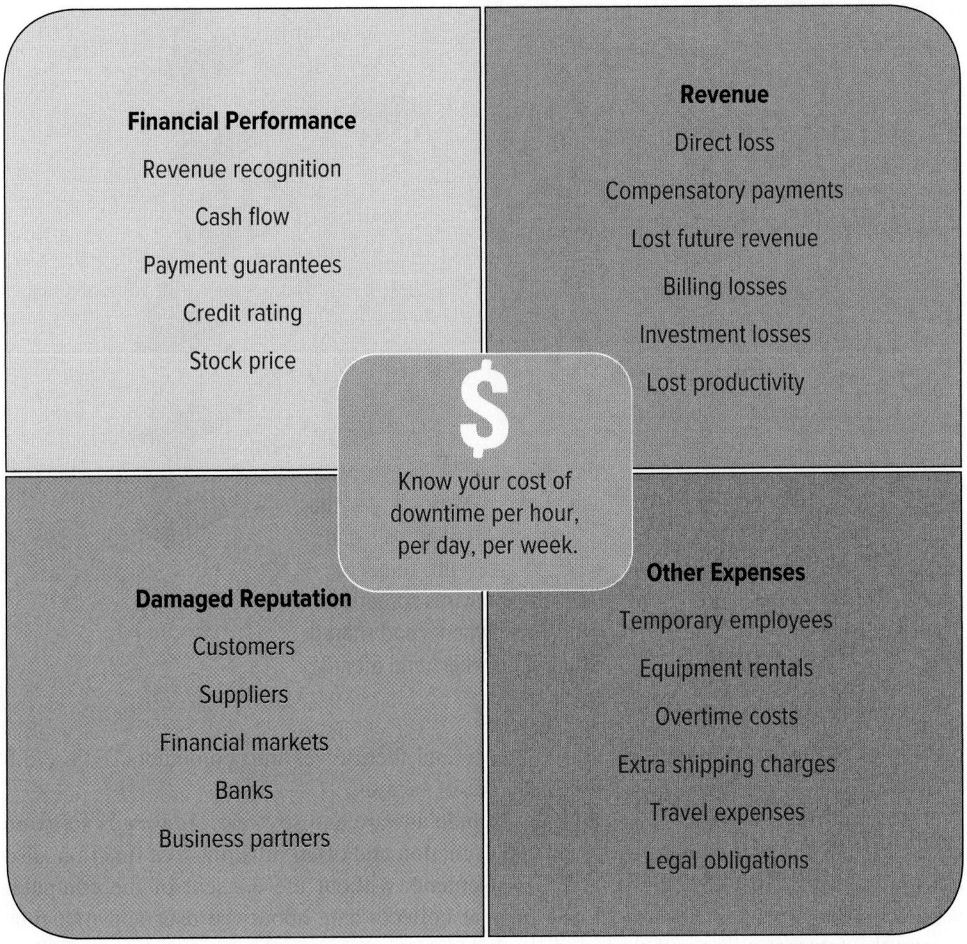

FIGURE 5.5

The Cost of Downtime.

Financial Performance

Revenue recognition

Cash flow

Payment guarantees

Credit rating

Stock price

Revenue

Direct loss

Compensatory payments

Lost future revenue

Billing losses

Investment losses

Lost productivity

$

Know your cost of
downtime per hour,
per day, per week.

Damaged Reputation

Customers

Suppliers

Financial markets

Banks

Business partners

Other Expenses

Temporary employees

Equipment rentals

Overtime costs

Extra shipping charges

Travel expenses

Legal obligations

smoking entrances to gain building access. Once inside, they pose as employees from the MIS department and either ask for permission to use an employee's computer to access the corporate network or find a conference room where they simply plugin their own laptop. ***Drive-by hacking*** is a computer attack by which an attacker accesses a wireless computer network, intercepts data, uses network services, and/or sends attack instructions without entering the office or organization that owns the network. Figure 5.6 lists the various types of hackers for organizations to be aware of, and Figure 5.7 shows how a virus is spread.

One of the most common forms of computer vulnerabilities is a virus. A ***virus*** is software written with malicious intent to cause annoyance or damage. Some hackers create and leave viruses, causing massive computer damage. A ***worm*** spreads itself not only from file to file but also from computer to computer. The primary difference between a virus and a worm is that a virus must attach to something, such as an executable file, to spread. Worms do not

FIGURE 5.6

Hacker Overview.

Common Types of Hackers
■ ***Black-hat hackers*** break into other people's computer systems and may just look around or may steal and destroy information.
■ ***Crackers*** have criminal intent when hacking.
■ ***Cyberterrorists*** seek to cause harm to people or to destroy critical systems or information and use the Internet as a weapon of mass destruction.
■ ***Hactivists*** have philosophical and political reasons for breaking into systems and will often deface the website as a protest.
■ ***Script kiddies*** or ***script bunnies*** find hacking code on the Internet and click-and-point their way into systems to cause damage or spread viruses.
■ ***White-hat hackers*** work at the request of the system owners to find system vulnerabilities and plug the holes.

FIGURE 5.7

How Computer Viruses
Spread.

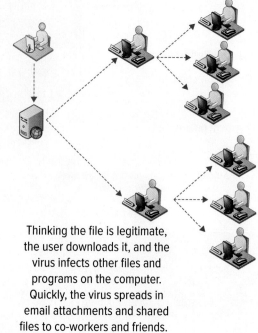

A hacker creates a virus and attaches it to a program, document, or website.

Thinking the file is legitimate, the user downloads it, and the virus infects other files and programs on the computer. Quickly, the virus spreads in email attachments and shared files to co-workers and friends.

need to attach to anything to spread and can tunnel themselves into computers. Figure 5.8 provides an overview of the most common types of viruses.

Two additional computer vulnerabilities include adware and spyware. *Adware* is software that, although purporting to serve some useful function and often fulfilling that function, also allows Internet advertisers to display advertisements without the consent of the computer user. *Spyware* is a special class of adware that collects data about the user and transmits it over the Internet without the user's knowledge or permission. Spyware programs collect specific data about the user, ranging from general demographics such as name, address, and browsing habits to credit card numbers, Social Security numbers, and user names and passwords. Not all adware programs are spyware and, used correctly, it can generate revenue for a company, allowing users to receive free products. Spyware is a clear threat to privacy. *Ransomware* is a form of malicious software that infects your computer and asks for money. Simplelocker is a new ransomware program that encrypts your personal files and demands payment for the files' decryption keys. Figure 5.9 displays a few additional weapons hackers use for launching attacks.

Organizational information is intellectual capital. Just as organizations protect their tangible assets—keeping their money in an insured bank or providing a safe working environment for employees—they must also protect their intellectual capital, everything from patents to transactional and analytical information. With security breaches and viruses on the rise and computer hackers everywhere, an organization must put in place strong security measures to survive.

FIGURE 5.8

Common Forms of Viruses.

Backdoor programs open a way into the network for future attacks.
Denial-of-service attack (DoS) floods a website with so many requests for service that it slows down or crashes.
Distributed denial-of-service attack (DDoS) attacks from multiple computers that flood a website with so many requests for service that it slows down or crashes. A common type is the Ping of Death, in which thousands of computers try to access a website at the same time, overloading it and shutting it down.
Polymorphic viruses and worms change their form as they propagate.
Trojan-horse virus hides inside other software, usually as an attachment or a downloadable file.

Elevation of privilege is a process by which a user misleads a system into granting unauthorized rights, usually for the purpose of compromising or destroying the system. For example, an attacker might log on to a network by using a guest account and then exploit a weakness in the software that lets the attacker change the guest privileges to administrative privileges.

Hoaxes attack computer systems by transmitting a virus hoax with a real virus attached. By masking the attack in a seemingly legitimate message, unsuspecting users more readily distribute the message and send the attack on to their co-workers and friends, infecting many users along the way.

Malicious code includes a variety of threats such as viruses, worms, and Trojan horses.

Packet tampering consists of altering the contents of packets as they travel over the Internet or altering data on computer disks after penetrating a network. For example, an attacker might place a tap on a network line to intercept packets as they leave the computer. The attacker could eavesdrop or alter the information as it leaves the network.

A **sniffer** is a program or device that can monitor data traveling over a network. Sniffers can show all the data being transmitted over a network, including passwords and sensitive information. Sniffers tend to be a favorite weapon in the hacker's arsenal.

Spoofing consists of forging the return address on an email so that the message appears to come from someone other than the actual sender. This is not a virus but rather a way by which virus authors conceal their identities as they send out viruses.

Splogs (spam blogs) are fake blogs created solely to raise the search engine rank of affiliated websites. Even blogs that are legitimate are plagued by spam, with spammers taking advantage of the Comment feature of most blogs to comment with links to spam sites.

Spyware is software that comes hidden in free downloadable software and tracks online movements, mines the information stored on a computer, or uses a computer's CPU and storage for some task the user knows nothing about.

FIGURE 5.9

Hacker Weapons.

OPENING CASE STUDY QUESTIONS

1. Imagine you are working for Apple as a manager in its Chicago store. Explain why it would be unethical for Apple to allow its customers to download free music from iTunes.

2. Evaluate the effects on Apple's business if it failed to secure its customer information and all of it was accidentally posted to an anonymous website.

Chapter Five Case: Targeting Target

The biggest retail hack in U.S. history wasn't particularly inventive, nor did it appear destined for success. In the days prior to Thanksgiving 2013, someone installed malware in Target's security and payments system designed to steal every credit card used at the company's 1,797 U.S. stores. At the critical moment—when the Christmas gifts had been scanned and bagged and the cashier asked for a swipe—the malware would step in, capture the shopper's credit card number, and store it on a Target server commandeered by the hackers.

It's a measure of how common these crimes have become, and how conventional the hackers' approach in this case, that Target was prepared for such an attack. Six months earlier, the company began installing a $1.6 million malware detection tool made by the computer security firm FireEye, whose customers also include the CIA and the Pentagon. Target had a team of security specialists in Bangalore to monitor its computers around the clock. If Bangalore noticed anything suspicious, Target's security operations center in Minneapolis would be notified.

On Saturday, Nov. 30, 2013, the hackers had set their traps and had just one thing to do before starting the attack: plan the data's escape route. As they uploaded exfiltration malware to move stolen credit card numbers—first to staging points spread around the U.S. to cover their tracks, then into their computers in Russia—FireEye spotted them. Bangalore got an alert and flagged the security team in Minneapolis. And then . . .

Nothing Happened!

For some reason, Minneapolis didn't react to the sirens. Bloomberg Businessweek spoke to more than 10 former Target employees familiar with the company's data security operation, as well as eight people with specific knowledge of the hack and its aftermath, including former employees, security researchers, and law enforcement officials. The story they tell is of an alert system, installed to protect the bond between retailer and customer, that worked beautifully. But then, Target stood by as 40 million credit card numbers—and 70 million addresses, phone numbers, and other pieces of personal information—gushed out of its mainframes.

When asked to respond to a list of specific questions about the incident and the company's lack of an immediate response to it, Target chairman, president, and chief executive officer Gregg Steinhafel issued an emailed statement: "Target was certified as meeting the standard for the payment card industry (PCI) in September 2013. Nonetheless, we suffered a data breach. As a result, we are conducting an end-to-end review of our people, processes and technology to understand our opportunities to improve data security and are committed to learning from this experience. While we are still in the midst of an ongoing investigation, we have already taken significant steps, including beginning the overhaul of our information security structure and the acceleration of our transition to chip-enabled cards. However, as the investigation is not complete, we don't believe it's constructive to engage in speculation without the benefit of the final analysis."

More than 90 lawsuits have been filed against Target by customers and banks for negligence and compensatory damages. That's on top of other costs, which analysts estimate could run into the billions. Target spent $61 million through February 1, 2014, responding to the breach, according to its fourth-quarter report to investors. It set up a customer response operation, and in an effort to regain lost trust, Steinhafel promised that consumers won't have to pay any fraudulent charges stemming from the breach. Target's profit for the holiday shopping period fell 46 percent from the same quarter the year before; the number of transactions suffered its biggest decline since the retailer began reporting the statistic in 2008.15 Questions How did the hackers steal Target's customer data? What types of technology could big retailers use to prevent identity thieves from stealing information? What can organizations do to protect themselves from hackers looking to steal account data? In a team, research the Internet and find the best ways to protect yourself from identity theft.

Questions

1. Identify the different types of hackers and viruses and explain how a company can protect itself from hackers looking to steal account data.

2. Authorities frequently tap online service providers to track down hackers. Do you think it is ethical for authorities to tap an online service provider and read people's email? Why or why not?

3. Do you think it was ethical for authorities to use one of the high-ranking members to trap other gang members? Why or why not?

4. In a team, research the Internet and find the best ways to protect yourself from identity theft.

5.1. Explain information ethics and its associated issues.

Information ethics govern the ethical and moral issues arising from the development and use of information technologies as well as the creation, collection, duplication, distribution, and processing of information itself (with or without the aid of computer technologies). Ethical dilemmas in this area usually arise not as simple, clear-cut situations but as clashes among competing goals, responsibilities, and loyalties. Inevitably, there will be more than one socially acceptable or correct decision.

5.2. Describe information security and the difference between hackers and viruses.

Information security is a broad term encompassing the protection of information from accidental or intentional misuse by persons inside or outside an organization. Information security is perhaps the most fundamental and critical of all the technologies/disciplines an organization must have squarely in place to execute its business strategy. Without solid security processes and procedures, none of the other technologies can develop business advantages. Understanding how to secure information systems is critical to keeping downtime to a minimum and uptime to a maximum. Hackers and viruses are two of the hottest issues currently facing information security. Hackers are experts in technology who use their knowledge to break into computers and computer networks, either for profit or simply for the challenge. A virus is software written with malicious intent to cause annoyance or damage.

 REVIEW QUESTIONS

1. What are ethics and why are they important to a company?
2. What is the correlation between privacy and confidentiality?
3. What is the difference between pirated software and counterfeit software?
4. What are the reasons a company experiences downtime?
5. What are the costs associated with downtime?
6. What is the relationship between adware and spyware?
7. What are the positive and negative effects associated with monitoring employees?
8. What is the relationship between hackers and viruses?

 MAKING BUSINESS DECISIONS

1. The Internet of Things Is Wide Open—for Everyone!

IoT is transforming our world into a living information system as we control our intelligent lighting from our smartphone to a daily health check from our smart toilet. Of course, with all great technological advances come unexpected risks, and you have to be prepared to encounter various security issues with IoT. Just imagine if your devices are hacked by someone who now can shut off your water, take control of your car, or unlock the doors of your home from thousands of miles away.

U nderstanding and working with technology have become an integral part of business. Most students take courses in various disciplines in their educational careers, such as in marketing, operations management, management, finance, accounting, and information systems, each of which is designed to provide insight into the tasks of each functional area. In the business world, these are all intertwined and inextricably linked.

Management information systems can be an important enabler of business success and innovation and is most useful when it leverages the talents of people. Technology in and of itself is not useful unless the right people know how to use and manage it effectively.

Organizations use management information systems to capture, process, organize, distribute, and massage information. MIS enables an organization to:

- Integrate all functional areas and the tasks they perform.
- Gain an enterprisewide view of its operations.
- Efficiently and effectively utilize resources.
- Realize tremendous market and industry growth by gaining insight into the market at large (through environmental scanning) and insight into internal operations.

✴ KEY TERMS

Adware   76
Analytics   11
As-Is Process Model   40
Balanced scorecard   64
Behavioral analytics   11
Benchmark   61
Benchmarking   61
Best practices   60
Business-facing processes   37
Business intelligence (BI)   10
Business process   28
Business process model   40
Business process modelling   40
Business Process Model and
    Notation (BPMN)   40
Business process patent   40
Business process reengineering
    (BPR)   37
Business strategy   21
Buyer power   24
Business unit   12
Chief automation officer   58
Chief data officer (CDO)   56
Chief information officer (CIO)   56
Chief intellectual property
    officer   58
Chief knowledge officer (CKO)   58
Chief privacy officer (CPO)   57
Chief security officer (CSO)   57
Chief technology officer (CTO)   56
Chief user experience officer   58
Child Online Protection Act
    (COPA)   73

Common data repository   49
Competitive advantage   21
Competitive intelligence   22
Confidentiality   71
Copyright   71
Counterfeit software   71
Critical success factors (CSFs)   59
CRM reporting technologies   48
CRM analysis technologies   48
CRM predicting technologies   48
Customer analytics   47
Customer-facing processes   37
Customer relationship
    management (CRM)   46
Data   7
Digital rights management   71
Downtime   73
Drive-by hacking   75
Dynamic process   37
Dynamic report   9
Ediscovery   73
Efficiency MIS metrics   60
Effectiveness MIS metrics   60
Enterprise resource planning
    (ERP)   49
Entry barrier   26
Fact   6
Feedback   15
First-mover advantage   22
Goods   14
Hacker   74
Human-generated data   7
Information   9

Information age   6
Information ethics   71
Information security   74
Information silo   12
Intellectual property   71
Internet of things (IOT)   7
Key performance indicator
    (KPI)   59
Knowledge   11
Knowledge workers   11
Loyalty program   25
Machine-to-machine (M2M)   7
Machine-generated data   7
Management information systems
    (MIS)   15
Market share   59
Metrics   59
MIS skills gap   58
Module software design   49
Patent   71
Pirated software   71
Porter's Five Forces Model   24
Predictive analytics   11
Primary value activities   29
Privacy   71
Process owner   42
Production   15
Productivity   15
Project   59
Product differentiation   26
Ransomware   76
Report   9
Return on investment (ROI)   60

✳ UNIT CLOSING CASE ONE

© C. Sherburne/Photo Link/Getty Images   © Ariel Skelley/Blend Images LLC   © Phil Boorman/Getty Images

The Internet of Things

Over 20 years ago a few professors at MIT began describing The Internet of Things (IoT), which is a world where interconnected Internet-enabled devices or "things" have the ability to collect and share data without human intervention. Another term for The Internet of Things is machine-to-machine (M2M), which allows devices to connect directly to other devices. With advanced technologies devices are connecting in ways not previously thought possible and researchers predict that over 50 billion IoT devices will be communicating by 2020. Kevin Ashton, cofounder and executive director of the Auto-ID Center at MIT, first mentioned the Internet of Things in a presentation he made to Procter & Gamble. Here's Ashton explanation of the Internet of Things:

"Today computers—and, therefore, the Internet—are almost wholly dependent on human beings for information. Nearly all of the roughly 50 petabytes (a petabyte is 1,024 terabytes) of data available on the Internet were first captured and created by human beings by typing, pressing a record button, taking a digital picture or scanning a bar code.

The problem is, people have limited time, attention and accuracy—all of which means they are not very good at capturing data about things in the real world. If we had computers that knew everything there was to know about things—using data they gathered without any help from us—we would be able to track and count everything and greatly reduce waste, loss and cost. We would know when things needed replacing, repairing or recalling and whether they were fresh or past their best."

Imagine your toothbrush telling you to visit your dentist because it senses a cavity. How would you react if your refrigerator placed an order at your local grocery store because your milk and eggs had expired? Predictions indicate that over the next decade almost every device you own—and almost every object imaginable—will be connected to the Internet as people share, store, and manage their lives online. Smoke detectors, alarms, refrigerators, stoves, and windows are just a few home devices already connected to the Internet sharing information on how to make everything in your life more efficient, effective, safe, and healthy. The Internet of Things is reaching further into our daily lives by combining data from sensors in wearable devices and equipment with analytic programs to help improve the performance of individuals by gaining insights that were traditionally impossible to detect. A few examples of the incredible power of the IoT era include:

- **Smart Yoga Mat:** Smart yoga mats include sensors that provide feedback on yoga postures, calories burned, and can even provide users with guided practice in the comfort of their own home.

- **Smart Thermostats:** IoTs share information in real-time to help homeowners manage energy more efficiently. The system will notify the homeowner if a door is left open, change the temperature in each room when it is occupied, and turn the furnace up or down depending on the weather and homeowner preferences.

- **Smart Diapers:** Pixie Scientific created disposable diapers with sensors that monitor babies' urine for signs of infection, dehydration, or kidney problems before symptoms appear.

- **Smart Trash Cans:** In Allentown, Pennsylvania, the city connected community trash and recycling cans allowing them to monitor fill rates, which are then used to recommend the most efficient routes for trash pickup services.

- **Smart Tennis Racket:** Babolat, a French tennis racket manufacturer, created the Play Pure Drive, a $400 smart tennis racket that has the capability to record data on every single shot a user takes and sends the data along with an analysis to the user's smartphone.

- **Smart Frying Pan:** Pantelligent is an innovative sensor-embedded frying pan that actually helps its users learn how to cook by measuring the temperature of the food and communicating with a smartphone when to add ingredients, change heat, flip, cover, and even when the food is done.

The future of business will focus on big data as IoT devices create, capture, and share massive amounts of data. The business environment is currently collecting more data from IoT devices in one second than all of the data collected from the beginning of time until the year 2000. In fact, over 90% of the data in the world was created over the last two years. Every minute over 204 million emails are sent and 200 thousand photos are uploaded to Facebook. The terms *analytics, data analysis,* and *business intelligence* are all referring to big data and the massive volumes of data being generated around the globe.

Understanding big data will be a critical skill for knowledge workers in every business regardless of size, focus, or industry. Future managers will be responsible for analyzing data in ways that were not even possible a decade ago allowing managers to predict customer behaviors, optimize and improve business processes, and analyze multiple variables for trends and patterns. The total amount of business data roughly doubles every 1.2 years. Estimates predict that a total of 6 million new jobs were created thanks to big data and will assist companies by the following:

- Understand consumer behaviors by combining purchasing data with social media data, weather data, competitor data, and economic data.

- Improve the delivery of products by combining delivery process information with current traffic data, vehicle maintenance data, and map data.

- Optimize health care treatments by capturing diagnosis, tracking pharmaceuticals, and eventually predicting diseases.

- Prevent cyber-attacks by analyzing credit card fraud, security system data, and police data.[2]

Questions

1. Explain the Internet of Things along with its potential impact on business. Also, list three IoT devices that you are currently using in your own personal life.

2. Explain why it is important for business managers to understand that data collection rates from IoT devices is increasing exponentially.

3. Demonstrate how data from an IoT device can be transformed into information and business intelligence.

4. Propose a plan for how a start-up company can use IoT device data to make better business decisions.

5. Argue for or against the following statement: "The Internet of Things is just a passing fad and will be gone within a decade."

Five Ways Hackers Can Get Into Your Business

Did you know:

- Once every 3 minutes, the average company comes into contact with viruses and malware.
- One in every 291 email messages contains a virus.
- Three things hackers want most are customer data, intellectual property, and bank account information.
- The top five file names used in phishing scams are Details.zip, UPS_document.zip, DCIM.zip, Report.zip, and Scan.zip.
- The average annual cost of a cyberattack on a small or medium-sized business is $188,242.

Cyberthieves are always looking for new ways to gain access to your business data, business networks, and business applications. The best way to protect your business from cybertheft is to build

FIGURE UNIT 1.2

Five ways hackers gain access to your business.

WEAK PASSWORDS

- With a $300 graphics card, a hacker can run 420 billion simple, lowercase, eight-character password combinations a minute.
- Cyberattacks involve weeak passwords 80% of the time, 55% of people use one password for all logins
- In 2012, hackers cracked 6.4 million LinkedIn passwords and 1.5 million eHarmony passwords in separate attacks.

Your Best Defense:

- Use a unique password for each account.
- Aim for at least 20 characters and preferably gibberish, not real words.
- Insert special characters: @#$*&.
- Try a password manager such as LastPass or Dashlane.

MALWARE ATTACKS

- An infected website, USB drive, or application delivers software that can capture keystrokes, passwords, and data.
- An 8% increase in malware attacks against small businesses has occurred since 2012; the average loss from a targeted attack was $92,000.
- In February, hackers attacked about 40 companies, including Apple, Facebook, and Twitter, by first infecting a mobile developer's site.

Your Best Defense:

- Run robust malware-detection software such as Norton Toolbar.
- Keep existing software updated.
- Use an iPhone— Android phones are targeted more than any other mobile operating system.

PHISHING EMAILS

- Bogus but official-looking emails prompt you to enter your password or click links to infected websites.
- A 125% rise in social-media phishing attacks has occurred since 2012. Phishers stole $1 billion from small businesses in 2012.
- Many small businesses were targeted in 2012 with phishing emails designed to look like Better Business Bureau warnings.

Your Best Defense:

- Keep existing software, operating systems, and browsers updated with the latest patches.
- Don't automatically click links in emails to external sites—retype the URL in your browser.

SOCIAL ENGINEERING

- Think 21st-century con artist tactics, e.g., hackers pretend to be you to reset your passwords.
- Twenty-nine percent of all security breaches involve some form of social engineering. Average loss is $25,000 to $100,000 per incident.
- In 2009, social engineers posed as Coca-Cola's CEO, persuading an exec to open an email with software that infiltrated the network.

Your Best Defense:

- Rethink what you reveal on social media—it's all fodder for social engineers.
- Develop policies for handling sensitive requests such as password resets over the phone.
- Have a security audit done.

RANSOMWARE

- Hackers hold your website hostage, often posting embarrassing content such as porn, until you pay a ransom.
- Five million dollars is extorted each year. The real cost is the data loss—paying the ransom doesn't mean you get your files back.
- Hackers locked the network at an Alabama ABC TV station, demanding a ransom to remove a red screen on every computer.

Your Best Defense:

- As with malware, do not click suspicious links or unknown websites.
- Regularly back up your data.
- Use software that specifically checks for new exploits.[1]

a strong defense and be able to identify vulnerabilities and weak spots. According to John Brandon of *Inc.* magazine, the top five ways hackers will try to gain access to your businesses are highlighted in Figure Unit 1.2. (Please note that there are far more than five ways; these are just the five most common.)

Questions

1. Explain why data, information, business intelligence, and knowledge are important to successfully running a business. Be sure to list examples of for each.

2. Why would hackers want to steal organizational information?

3. What problems can occur for a business that experiences a data theft from a CRM system? Would the problems be the same is the data theft occurred from an SCM system? Why or why not?

4. Define information ethics and information security and explain whether they are important to help prevent hackers from gaining access to an organization.

5. What type of metrics would an organization gather to help identify illegal system access?

1. Capitalizing on Your Career

Business leaders need to be involved in information technology—any computer-based tool that people use to work with information and support the information and information-processing needs of an organization—for the following (primary) reasons:

- The sheer magnitude of the dollars spent on MIS must be managed to ensure business value.
- Research has consistently shown that when business leaders are involved in information technology, it enables a number of business initiatives, such as gaining a competitive advantage, streamlining business processes, and even transforming entire organizations.
- Research has consistently shown that when business leaders are not involved in MIS, systems fail, revenue is lost, and even entire companies can fail as a result of poorly managed MIS.

One of the biggest challenges facing organizations is, "How do we get general business leaders involved in MIS?" Research has shown that involvement is highly correlated with personal experience with MIS and MIS education, including university classes and MIS executive seminars. Once general business leaders understand MIS through experience and education, they are more likely to be involved in MIS, and more likely to lead their organizations in achieving business success through MIS.

1. Search the Internet to find examples of the types of technologies that are currently used in the field or industry that you plan to pursue. For example, if you are planning on a career in accounting or finance, you should become familiar with financial systems such as Oracle Financials. If you are planning a career in logistics or distribution, you should research supply chain management systems. If you are planning a career in marketing, you should research customer relationship management systems, blogs, and emarketing.
2. MIS is described as an enabler/facilitator of competitive advantage, organizational effectiveness, and organizational efficiency. As a competitive tool, MIS can differentiate an organization's products, services, and prices from its competitors by improving product quality, shortening product development or delivery time, creating new MIS-based products and services, and improving customer service before, during, and after a transaction. Search the Internet and find several examples of companies in the industry where you plan to work that have achieved a competitive advantage through MIS.
3. Create a simple report of your findings; include a brief overview of the type of technologies you found and how organizations are using them to achieve a competitive advantage.

2. Achieving Alignment

Most companies would like to be in the market-leading position of JetBlue, Dell, or Walmart, all of which have used information technology to secure their respective spots in the marketplace. These companies have a relentless goal of keeping the cost of technology down by combining the best of MIS and business leadership.

It takes more than a simple handshake between groups to start on the journey toward financial gains; it requires operational discipline and a linkage between business and technology units. Only recently have companies not on the "path for profits" followed the lead of their successful counterparts, requiring more operational discipline from their MIS groups as well as more MIS participation from their business units. Bridging this gap is one of the greatest breakthroughs a company can make.

Companies that master the art of finely tuned, cost-effective MIS management will have a major advantage. Their success will force their competitors to also master the art or fail miserably. This phenomenon has already occurred in the retail and wholesale distribution markets, which have had to react to Walmart's MIS mastery, as one example. Other industries will follow. This trend will change not only the face of MIS, but also the future of corporate America.

As world markets continue to grow, the potential gains are greater than ever. However, so are the potential losses. The future belongs to those who are perceptive enough to grasp the significance of MIS and resourceful enough to synchronize business management and information technology.

1. Use any resource to answer the question, "Why is business-MIS alignment so difficult?" Use the following questions to begin your analysis:
   a. How do companies prioritize the demands of various business units as they relate to MIS?
   b. What are some of the greatest MIS challenges for the coming year?
   c. What drives MIS decisions?
   d. Who or what is the moving force behind MIS decisions?
   e. What types of efficiency metrics and effectiveness metrics might these companies use to measure the impact of MIS?
   f. How can a company use financial metrics to monitor and measure MIS investments?
   g. What are some of the issues with using financial metrics to evaluate MIS?

3. Market Dissection

To illustrate the use of the three generic strategies, consider Figure AYK.1. The matrix shown demonstrates the relationships among strategies (cost leadership versus differentiation) and market segmentation (broad versus focused).

- Hyundai is following a broad cost leadership strategy. Hyundai offers low-cost vehicles, in each particular model stratification, that appeal to a large audience.

- Audi is pursuing a broad differentiation strategy with its Quattro models available at several price points. Audi's differentiation is safety and it prices its various Quattro models (higher than Hyundai) to reach a large, stratified audience.

- Kia has a more focused cost leadership strategy. Kia mainly offers low-cost vehicles in the lower levels of model stratification.

- Hummer offers the most focused differentiation strategy of any in the industry (including Mercedes-Benz).

FIGURE AYK.1

Porter's Three Generic Strategies

(top left): © otomobil/Shutterstock   (top right): © Yauhen_D/Shutterstock
(bottom left): © Zavatskiy Aleksandr/Shutterstock   (bottom right): © Getty Images.

Create a similar graph displaying each strategy for a product of your choice. The strategy must include an example of the product in each of the following markets: (1) cost leadership, broad market, (2) differentiation, broad market, (3) cost leadership, focused market, and (4) differentiation, focused market. Potential products include:

- Cereal
- Dog food
- Soft drinks
- Computers
- Shampoo
- Snack foods
- Jeans
- Sneakers
- Sandals
- Mountain bikes
- TV shows
- Movies

4. Measuring Efficiency and Effectiveness

In a group, create a plan to measure the efficiency and effectiveness of this course and recommendations on how you could improve the course to make it more efficient and more effective. You must determine ways to benchmark current efficiency and effectiveness and ways to continuously monitor and measure against the benchmarks to determine if the course is becoming more or less efficient and effective (class quizzes and exams are the most obvious benchmarks). Be sure your plan addresses the following:

- Design of the classroom.
- Room temperature.
- Lighting and electronic capabilities of the classroom.
- Technology available in the classroom.
- Length of class.
- Email and instant messaging.
- Students' attendance.
- Students' preparation.
- Students' arrival time.
- Quizzes and exams (frequency, length, grades).

5. Adding Value

To identify these competitive advantages, Michael Porter created value chain analysis, which views a firm as a series of business processes that each add value to the product or service. Value chain analysis is a useful tool for determining how to create the greatest possible value for customers. The goal of value chain analysis is to identify processes in which the firm can add value for the customer and create a competitive advantage for itself, with a cost advantage or product differentiation.

Starbucks has hired you after your graduation for a temporary position that could turn into a full-time opportunity. With new cafés and juice shops popping up on every corner, coupled with the global recession, Starbucks is worried about losing market share to competitors. Your boss, Heather Sweitzer, is out of ideas for ways to improve the company's profitability. You decide that one of the most useful tools for identifying competitive advantages is Porter's value chain analysis. Of course, you do not yet have the detailed knowledge to complete all of the elements required, but you know enough to get started and plan to take your draft to Sweitzer next week. Using your knowledge of Starbucks, create a value chain analysis. Feel free to make assumptions about operations; just be sure to list any that you make. Also, be sure to write an overview of the tool and its potential value so Sweitzer can understand how it works.

6. I Love TED!

A small nonprofit started in 1984, TED (Technology, Entertainment, Design) hosts conferences for Ideas Worth Spreading. TED brings people from all over the globe to share award-winning talks covering the most innovative, informative, and exciting speeches ever given in 20 minutes. You can find TED talks by Al Gore, Bill Gates, Steve Jobs, Douglas Adams, Steven Levitt, Seth Godin, Malcolm Gladwell, and so on.

Visit www.ted.com and peruse the thousands of videos that are available; then answer the following:

- Review the TED website and find three talks you would want to watch. Why did you pick these three and will you make time outside of class to watch them?

- How can you gain a competitive advantage by watching TED?

- How can you find innovative ideas for a start-up by watching TED?

- How can you find competitive intelligence by watching TED?

7. Listen to Spider-Man; He Knows What He's Talking About!

Spider-Man's infamous advice—"With great power comes great responsibility"—should be applied to every type of technology you encounter in business. Technology provides countless opportunities for businesses, but it can also lead to countless pitfalls and traps. A great example is how many companies profited from online trading and how many people lost their life savings in online trading scams. For example, Bernard Madoff, the owner of a high-profile New York investment company, was able to forge investment statements and allegedly spent almost $50 billion of his client's money.

Texting and email are great assets for any company that require instant communication, but they also digitize conversations that can be tracked and retrieved. David Petraeus, director of the CIA, resigned after investigators found evidence from his emails indicating an extramarital affair with his biographer, Paula Broadwell. It should be crystal clear that email is a dangerous tool if it has the ability to take down the director of the CIA.

Craigslist allows anyone to become a provider of goods and services. Unfortunately, Craigslist does not describe exactly what types of goods and services are allowed. Adam Vitale was sentenced to two years in prison after he found a way to bypass Craigslist security and was caught running an online prostitution ring through Craigslist.

When competing in business, you must analyze the good and the bad associated with every technology you encounter. Choose a company that primarily operates online—such as eBay, Netflix, or Amazon—and analyze all of the business opportunities along with the potential pitfalls you might encounter if you were the owner of the company.

8. Fixing the Post Office

Is there anything more frustrating than waiting in line at the post office? Not only are those lines frustrating, but they are also unprofitable. The U.S. Postal Service has faced multibillion-dollar losses every year for the past few years, making for one of the greatest challenges in its history. What is killing the post office? Perhaps it is Stamps.com, a website that allows you to customize and print your own stamps 24 hours a day. Getting married? Place a photo of the happy couple right on the stamp for the invitations. Starting a business? Place your business logo on your stamps. Stamps.com even keeps track of a customer's postal spending and can recommend optimal delivery methods. Plus, Stamps.com gives you postage discounts you can't get at the post office or with a postage meter. Evaluate the U.S. Postal Service, using Porter's Five Forces Model. How could the Postal Service create new products and services to help grow its business? What types of competitive advantages can you identify for the Postal Service? Can you fix or create any new business processes that could fundamentally change the way the post office operates to reduce costs or increase revenues?

9. The iPad—the Greatest Product in History or Just Another Gadget?

Apple sold 300,000 units of its highly anticipated iPad in the first 15 hours it was available for sale. Hundreds of thousands of Apple devotees flocked to stores during Passover and Easter to be the first to obtain the new device, even though it is neither a phone nor a laptop computer and many people are still wondering what it's for. The controversy over the usefulness of Apple's portable tablet began as soon as Apple announced the device was heading to market. At first glance, the iPad is little more than a touch screen the size of a slim book, with a few control buttons along the edges and a home button at the bottom. Shrink it, and it would look like an iPod Touch. What is the value of this device? That's the question everyone wants to answer.

The iPad's modest features might represent an entirely new way of consuming media—video, web pages, music, pictures, and even books. Break into groups and review the current value of the iPad for business. Find three examples of the ways businesses are using, or could use, the iPad. Do you consider it the next revolutionary device or just an overpriced music player?

10. Finding Your College Start-up

Derek Johnson, a student at the University of Houston, was having lunch with his friend who happened to be the communications director for her sorority. During lunch, Derek's friend was telling him how hard it was to communicate with all of her sisters in the sorority. She had to send out important announcements about meetings, charitable events, and even dues. She had tried everything, including Facebook, email, and message boards, but so far nothing was working. As Derek pondered his friend's dilemma, he came up with a solution: mass text messaging. Johnson began researching mass text messaging products and was surprised to find that none existed for the average consumer. Spotting an entrepreneurial opportunity, Derek quickly began working on a product. Within a few months, he launched his website, Tatango, and began offering group text messaging at a reasonable price. Now, a few years later, Tatango offers customers subscription plans starting under $20 a month that allow groups to send text messages to all members at once—whether 10 or 10,000—from any device.

In a group, brainstorm a list of problems you are currently experiencing. Decide whether any present potential new business opportunities and, if so, analyze the potential, using the tools introduced in this unit. Be prepared to present your new business to the class.

11. Get the Cow Out of the Ditch

Fortune magazine asked Anne Mulcahy, former Chairman and CEO of Xerox, what the best advice she had ever received in business was. She said it occurred at a breakfast meeting in Dallas, to which she had invited a group of business leaders. One of them, a plainspoken, self-made, streetwise guy, came up to Mulcahy and said:

When everything gets really complicated and you feel overwhelmed, think about it this way. *You gotta do three things. First, get the cow out of the ditch. Second, find out how the cow got into the ditch. Third, make sure you do whatever it takes so the cow doesn't go into the ditch again.*

You are working for an international app developer that produces games. For months, you have been collecting metrics on usage by players from all over the world. You notice the metrics on the Asian and European players are falling sharply and sales are dropping. The United States and Canada metrics are still growing strongly, and sales are increasing. What can you do to get this cow out of the ditch?

If you are looking for Excel projects to incorporate into your class, try any of the following to test your knowledge.

Project Number	Project Name	Project Type	Plug-In Focus Area	Project Level	Skill Set	Page Number
1	Financial Destiny	Excel	T2	Personal Budget	Introductory Formulas	AYK.4
2	Cash Flow	Excel	T2	Cash Flow	Introductory Formulas	AYK.4
3	Technology Budget	Excel	T1, T2	Hardware and Software	Introductory Formulas	AYK.4
4	Tracking Donations	Excel	T2	Employee Relationships	Introductory Formulas	AYK.4
5	Convert Currency	Excel	T2	Global Commerce	Introductory Formulas	AYK.5
6	Cost Comparison	Excel	T2	Total Cost of Ownership	Introductory Formulas	AYK.5
7	Time Management	Excel or Project	T12	Project Management	Gantt Charts	AYK.6

2

Exploring Business Intelligence

What's in IT for Me?

This unit introduces the concept of information and its relative importance to organizations. It distinguishes between data stored in transactional databases and information housed in enterprise data warehouses. This unit also provides an overview of database fundamentals and the steps required to integrate various bits of data stored across multiple, operational data stores into a comprehensive and centralized repository of summarized information, which can be turned into powerful business intelligence.

You, as a business student, must understand the difference between transactional data and summarized information and the different types of questions you would use a transactional database or enterprise data warehouse to answer. You need to be aware of the complexity of storing data in databases and the level of effort required to transform operational data into meaningful, summarized information. You need to realize the power of information and the competitive advantage a data warehouse brings an organization in terms of facilitating business intelligence. Understanding the power of information will help you prepare to compete in a global marketplace. Armed with the power of information, you will make smart, informed, and data-supported managerial decisions.

© Image Source/Getty Images RF

© Maciej Frolow/Getty Images RF

© C. Zachariasen/PhotoAlto

Big Data, Big Business, Big Opportunities

Imagine working 10 years to become the lead marketing executive at a large retail organization to find that your competitor is invading your market share by 20 percent each year. You quickly decided to launch several online marketing promotions while improving your products only to find your efforts are fruitless as your competitor continues to steal your customers destroying your profits while raising its own.

As you begin to analyze your competitor's business strategy you find that while you were focused on sales reports, product inventory analysis, and other traditional marketing efforts your competitor was making a massive investment in upgrading all of its management information systems. This included systems capable of collecting, storing, and analyzing data from every store, product, and sales representative in the market. In fact, your competitor now knows more about your products and sales cycles than you do. The new systems not only collect data throughout its company, but also from a group of suppliers, retailers, and distributors around the globe. These new systems provide your competitor with the ability to adjust prices instantly based on daily customer traffic patterns, reorder automatically from every entity in the supply chains, and even move items within a store or between stores for maximum selling efficiencies.

Your competitor has won and not because it had a higher quality product or better sales and marketing strategies, but because it identified the value of management information systems coupled with the ability to instantly access big data within and beyond the organization. You quickly realize that your competitor's agility simply cannot be mimicked offering it a huge competitive advantage. You sigh as you realize your company is in big trouble because it did not understand the dynamics of the big data age.

We are all familiar with the information age and the improvements made to organizations around the world as they are able to better manage employees, track sales information, and analyze customer purchasing patterns. However, this scenario is an example of the game-changing impact of big data, the massive amounts of data being collected by humans and machines over the last few years. Companies are now capturing hundreds of terabytes of data on everything from operations and finances to weather patterns and stock market trends. Sensors are now embedded in everything from products and machines to store floors collecting real time data on operations and customers. Radical customization, continuous experimentation, and information-driven business models are the new trademarks of competition as organizations analyze massive volumes of data. Data volumes are exploding and more data has been created in the past two years than in the entire previous history of the human race. Here are the top twenty facts every manager should know about big data according to *Forbes* magazine.[1]

- Data volumes are exploding and more data has been created in the past 2 years than in the entire previous history of the human race.
- Data is growing faster than ever before and by the year 2020, about 1.7 megabytes of new information will be created every second for every human being on the planet.
- By 2020 our accumulated digital universe of data will grow from 4.4 zettabytes today to around 44 zettabytes, or 44 trillion gigabytes.
- Every second we create new data. For example, we perform 40,000 search queries every second (on Google alone), which makes it 3.5 searches per day and 1.2 trillion searches per year.
- In 2015 over 1 billion people used Facebook each day.
- Facebook users send on average 31.25 million messages and view 2.77 million videos every minute.
- Every minute up to 300 hours of video are uploaded to YouTube alone.
- In 2015, a staggering 1 trillion photos will be taken and billions of them will be shared online. By 2017, nearly 80% of photos will be taken on smart phones.
- This year, over 1.4 billion smart phones will be shipped—all packed with sensors capable of collecting all kinds of data, not to mention the data the users create themselves.
- By 2020, we will have over 6.1 billion smartphone users globally (overtaking basic fixed phone subscriptions).
- Within five years there will be over 50 billion smart connected devices in the world, all developed to collect, analyze, and share data.
- By 2020, at least a third of all data will pass through the cloud (a network of servers connected over the Internet).
- Distributed computing (performing computing tasks using a network of computers in the cloud) is very real. Google uses it every day to involve about 1,000 computers in answering a single search query, which takes no more than a second to complete.
- The Hadoop (open source software for distributed computing) market is forecast to grow at a compound annual growth rate 58% surpassing $1 billion by 2020.
- Estimates suggest that by better integrating big data, healthcare could save as much as $300 billion a year—that's equal to reducing costs by $1,000 a year for every man, woman, and child.
- The White House has already invested more than $200 million in big data projects.

- For a typical Fortune 1000 company, just a 10% increase in data accessibility will result in more than $65 million additional net income.
- Retailers who leverage the full power of big data could increase their operating margins by as much as 60%.
- Almost eighty percent of organizations have already invested or plan to invest in big data.
- At the moment less than 0.5% of all data is ever analyzed or used.

Introduction

Information is powerful. Information is useful in telling an organization how its current operations are performing and estimating and strategizing how future operations might perform. New perspectives open up when people have the right information and know how to use it. The ability to understand, digest, analyze, and filter information is a key to success for any professional in any industry. Unit Two demonstrates the value an organization can uncover and create by learning how to manage, access, analyze, and protect organizational information. The chapters in Unit Two are:

- **Chapter Six**—Valuing and Storing Organizational Information—Databases
- **Chapter Seven**—Accessing Organizational Information—Data Warehouses
- **Chapter Eight**—Understanding Big Data and Its Impact on Business

© Digital Vision/Getty Images

Valuing and Storing Organizational Information—Databases

LEARNING OUTCOMES

6.1. Explain the four primary traits that determine the value of information.

6.2. Describe a database, a database management system, and the relational database model.

6.3. Identify the business advantages of a relational database.

6.4. Explain the business benefits of a data-driven website.

6.5. Explain why an organization would want to integrate its databases.

The Business Benefits of High-Quality Information

LO 6.1 **Explain the four primary traits that determine the value of information.**

Information is powerful. Information can tell an organization how its current operations are performing and help it estimate and strategize about how future operations might perform. The ability to understand, digest, analyze, and filter information is key to growth and success for any professional in any industry. Remember that new perspectives and opportunities can open up when you have the right data that you can turn into information and ultimately business intelligence.

Information is everywhere in an organization. Managers in sales, marketing, human resources, and management need information to run their departments and make daily decisions. When addressing a significant business issue, employees must be able to obtain and analyze all the relevant information so they can make the best decision possible. Information comes at different levels, formats, and granularities. *Information granularity* refers to the extent of detail within the information (fine and detailed or coarse and abstract). Employees must be able to correlate the different levels, formats, and granularities of information when making decisions. For example, a company might be collecting information from various suppliers to make needed decisions, only to find that the information is in different levels, formats, and granularities. One supplier might send detailed information in a spreadsheet, while another supplier might send summary information in a Word document, and still another might send a collection of information from emails. Employees will need to compare these different types of information for what they commonly reveal to make strategic decisions. Figure 6.1 displays the various levels, formats, and granularities of organizational information.

Successfully collecting, compiling, sorting, and finally analyzing information from multiple levels, in varied formats, and exhibiting different granularities can provide tremendous insight into how an organization is performing. Exciting and unexpected results can include potential new markets, new ways of reaching customers, and even new methods of doing business. After understanding the different levels, formats, and granularities of information, managers next want to look at the four primary traits that help determine the value of information (see Figure 6.2).

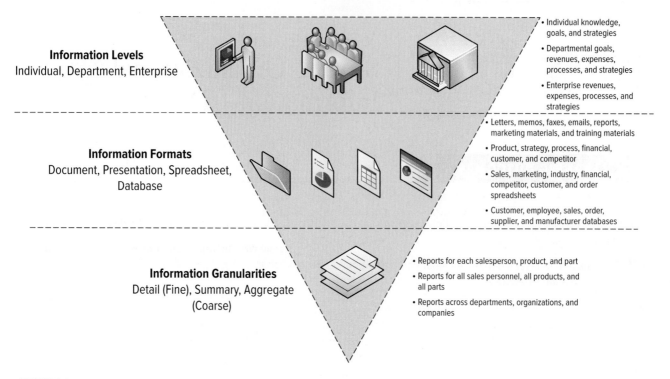

Information Levels
Individual, Department, Enterprise

- Individual knowledge, goals, and strategies
- Departmental goals, revenues, expenses, processes, and strategies
- Enterprise revenues, expenses, processes, and strategies

Information Formats
Document, Presentation, Spreadsheet, Database

- Letters, memos, faxes, emails, reports, marketing materials, and training materials
- Product, strategy, process, financial, customer, and competitor
- Sales, marketing, industry, financial, competitor, customer, and order spreadsheets
- Customer, employee, sales, order, supplier, and manufacturer databases

Information Granularities
Detail (Fine), Summary, Aggregate (Coarse)

- Reports for each salesperson, product, and part
- Reports for all sales personnel, all products, and all parts
- Reports across departments, organizations, and companies

FIGURE 6.1

Levels, Formats, and Granularities of Organizational Information.

INFORMATION TYPE: TRANSACTIONAL AND ANALYTICAL

Transactional information encompasses all of the information contained within a single business process or unit of work, and its primary purpose is to support daily operational tasks. Organizations need to capture and store transactional information to perform operational tasks and repetitive decisions such as analyzing daily sales reports and production schedules to determine how much inventory to carry. Consider Walmart, which handles more than 1 million customer transactions every hour, and Facebook, which keeps track of 400 million active users (along with their photos, friends, and web links). In addition, every time a cash register rings up a sale, a deposit or withdrawal is made from an ATM, or a receipt is given at the gas pump, capturing and storing of the transactional information are required.

    Analytical information encompasses all organizational information, and its primary purpose is to support the performing of managerial analysis tasks. Analytical information is useful when making important decisions such as whether the organization should build a new manufacturing plant or hire additional sales personnel. Analytical information makes it possible to do many things that previously were difficult to accomplish, such as spot business trends, prevent diseases, and fight crime. For example, credit card companies crunch through billions of transactional purchase records to identify fraudulent activity. Indicators such as charges in a foreign country or consecutive purchases of gasoline send a red flag highlighting potential fraudulent activity.

FIGURE 6.2

The Four Primary Traits of the Value of Information.

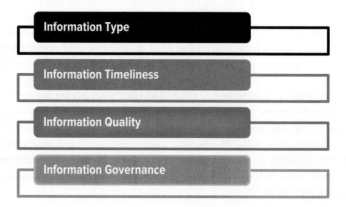

Information Type

Information Timeliness

Information Quality

Information Governance

Walmart was able to use its massive amount of analytical information to identify many unusual trends, such as a correlation between storms and Pop-Tarts. Yes, Walmart discovered an increase in the demand for Pop-Tarts during the storm season. Armed with the valuable information the retail chain was able to stock up on Pop-Tarts that were ready for purchase when customers arrived. Figure 6.3 displays different types of transactional and analytical information.

INFORMATION TIMELINESS

Timeliness is an aspect of information that depends on the situation. In some firms or industries, information that is a few days or weeks old can be relevant, while in others information that is a few minutes old can be almost worthless. Some organizations, such as 911 response centers, stock traders, and banks, require up-to-the-second information. Other organizations, such as insurance and construction companies, require only daily or even weekly information.

Real-time information means immediate, up-to-date information. *Real-time systems* provide real-time information in response to requests. Many organizations use real-time systems to uncover key corporate transactional information. The growing demand for real-time information stems from organizations' need to make faster and more effective decisions, keep smaller inventories, operate more efficiently, and track performance more carefully. Information also needs to be timely in the sense that it meets employees' needs, but no more. If employees can absorb information only on an hourly or daily basis, there is no need to gather real-time information in smaller increments.

Most people request real-time information without understanding one of the biggest pitfalls associated with real-time information—continual change. Imagine the following scenario: Three managers meet at the end of the day to discuss a business problem. Each manager has gathered information at different times during the day to create a picture of the situation. Each manager's picture may be different because of the time differences. Their views on the business problem may not match because the information they are basing their analysis on is continually changing. This approach may not speed up decision making, and it may actually slow it down. Business decision makers must evaluate the timeliness for the information for every decision. Organizations do not want to find themselves using real-time information to make a bad decision faster.

INFORMATION QUALITY

Business decisions are only as good as the quality of the information used to make them. *Information inconsistency* occurs when the same data element has different values. Take for example the amount of work that needs to occur to update a customer who had changed her last name due to marriage. Changing this information in only a few organizational systems will lead to data inconsistencies causing customer 123456 to be associated with two last names. *Information integrity* is a measure of the quality of information. Data integrity issues can cause managers to consider the system reports invalid and will make decisions based on other sources.

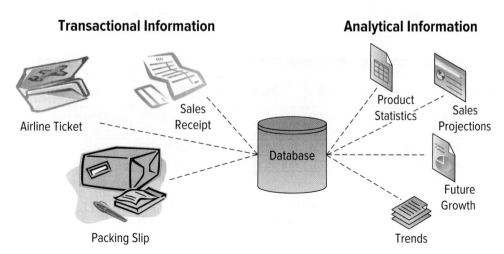

Transactional Information

Airline Ticket

Sales Receipt

Packing Slip

Database

Analytical Information

Product Statistics

Sales Projections

Future Growth

Trends

FIGURE 6.3

Transactional versus Analytical Information.

FIGURE 6.4

Five Common Characteristics
of High-Quality Information.

Accurate	• Is there an incorrect value in the information? • Example: Is the name spelled correctly? Is the dollar amount recorded properly?
Complete	• Is a value missing from the information? • Example: Is the address complete including street, city, state, and zip code?
Consistent	• Is aggregate or summary information in agreement with detailed information? • Example: Do all total columns equal the true total of the individual item?
Timely	• Is the information current with respect to business needs? • Example: Is information updated weekly, daily, or hourly?
Unique	• Is each transaction and event represented only once in the information? • Example: Are there any duplicate customers?

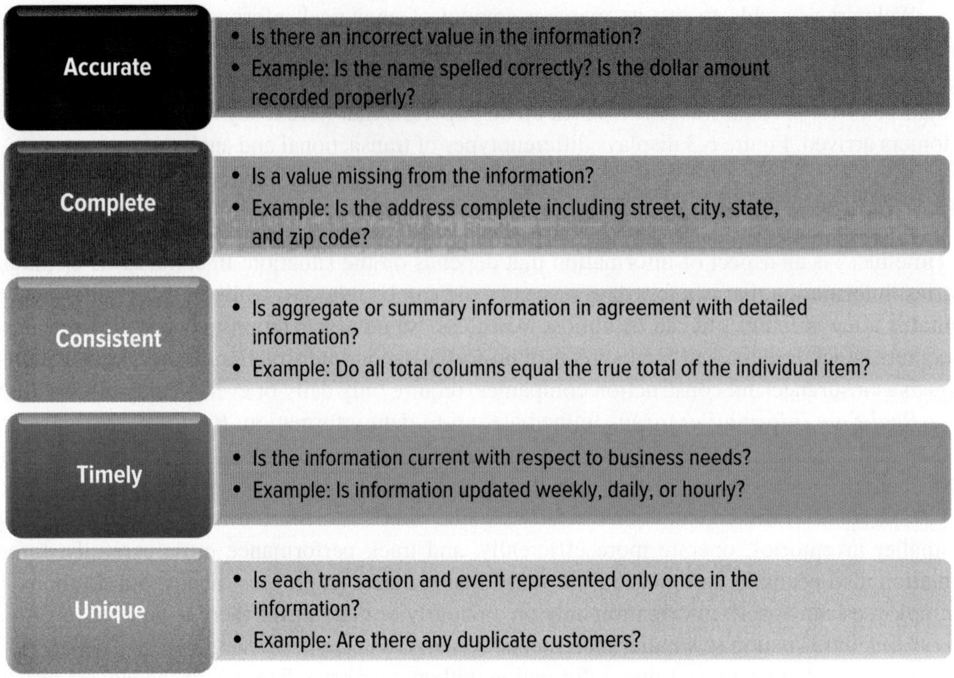

To ensure your systems do not suffer from data integrity issues, review Figure 6.4 for the five characteristics common to high-quality information: accuracy, completeness, consistency, timeliness, and uniqueness. Figure 6.5 provides an example of several problems associated with using low-quality information including:

1. *Completeness.* The customer's first name is missing.

2. Another issue with *completeness.* The street address contains only a number and not a street name.

3. *Consistency.* There may be a duplication of information since there is a slight difference between the two customers in the spelling of the last name. Similar street addresses and phone numbers make this likely.

4. *Accuracy.* This may be inaccurate information because the customer's phone and fax numbers are the same. Some customers might have the same number for phone and fax, but the fact that the customer also has this number in the email address field is suspicious.

FIGURE 6.5

Example of Low-Quality
Information.

1. Missing information (no first name) 2. Incomplete information (no street) 5. Inaccurate information (invalid email)

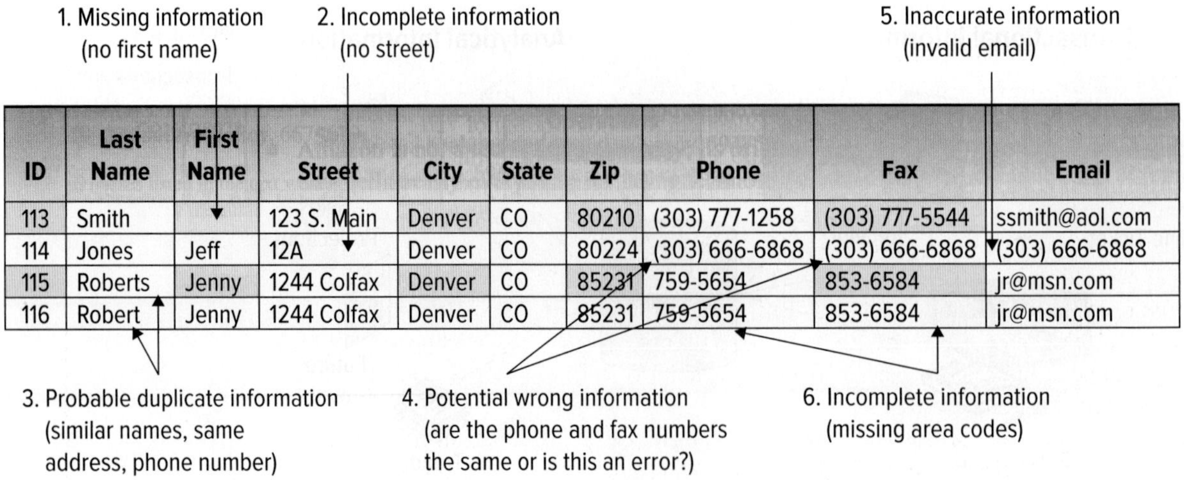

ID	Last Name	First Name	Street	City	State	Zip	Phone	Fax	Email
113	Smith		123 S. Main	Denver	CO	80210	(303) 777-1258	(303) 777-5544	ssmith@aol.com
114	Jones	Jeff	12A	Denver	CO	80224	(303) 666-6868	(303) 666-6868	(303) 666-6868
115	Roberts	Jenny	1244 Colfax	Denver	CO	85231	759-5654	853-6584	jr@msn.com
116	Robert	Jenny	1244 Colfax	Denver	CO	85231	759-5654	853-6584	jr@msn.com

3. Probable duplicate information (similar names, same address, phone number)

4. Potential wrong information (are the phone and fax numbers the same or is this an error?)

6. Incomplete information (missing area codes)

5. Another issue with *accuracy.* There is inaccurate information because a phone number is located in the email address field.

6. Another issue with *completeness.* The information is incomplete because there is not a valid area code for the phone and fax numbers.

Nestlé uses 550,000 suppliers to sell more than 100,000 products in 200 countries. However, due to poor information, the company was unable to evaluate its business effectively. After some analysis, it found that it had 9 million records of vendors, customers, and materials, half of which were duplicated, obsolete, inaccurate, or incomplete. The analysis discovered that some records abbreviated vendor names while other records spelled out the vendor names. This created multiple accounts for the same customer, making it impossible to determine the true value of Nestlé's customers. Without being able to identify customer profitability, a company runs the risk of alienating its best customers.[2]

Knowing how low-quality information issues typically occur can help a company correct them. Addressing these errors will significantly improve the quality of company information and the value to be extracted from it. The four primary reasons for low-quality information are:

1. Online customers intentionally enter inaccurate information to protect their privacy.

2. Different systems have different information entry standards and formats.

3. Data-entry personnel enter abbreviated information to save time or erroneous information by accident.

4. Third-party and external information contains inconsistencies, inaccuracies, and errors.

Understanding the Costs of Using Low-Quality Information

Using the wrong information can lead managers to make erroneous decisions. Erroneous decisions in turn can cost time, money, reputations, and even jobs. Some of the serious business consequences that occur due to using low-quality information to make decisions are:

- Inability to accurately track customers.
- Difficulty identifying the organization's most valuable customers.
- Inability to identify selling opportunities.
- Lost revenue opportunities from marketing to nonexistent customers.
- The cost of sending non-deliverable mail.
- Difficulty tracking revenue because of inaccurate invoices.
- Inability to build strong relationships with customers.

A *data gap analysis* occurs when a company examines its data to determine if it can meet business expectations, while identifying possible data gaps or where missing data might exist.

Understanding the Benefits of Using High-Quality Information

High-quality information can significantly improve the chances of making a good decision and directly increase an organization's bottom line. *Data stewardship* is the management and oversight of an organization's data assets to help provide business users with high-quality data that is easily accessible in a consistent manner. A *data steward* is responsible for ensuring the policies and procedures are implemented across the organization and acts as a liaison between the MIS department and the business. One company discovered that even with its large number of golf courses, Phoenix, Arizona, is not a good place to sell golf clubs. An analysis revealed that typical golfers in Phoenix are tourists and conventioneers who usually bring their clubs with them. The analysis further revealed that two of the best places to sell golf clubs in the United States are Rochester, New York, and Detroit, Michigan. Equipped with this valuable information, the company was able to strategically place its stores and launch its marketing campaigns.

High-quality information does not automatically guarantee that every decision made is going to be a good one, because people ultimately make decisions and no one is perfect.

However, such information ensures that the basis of the decisions is accurate. The success of the organization depends on appreciating and leveraging the true value of timely and high-quality information.

INFORMATION GOVERNANCE

Information is a vital resource and users need to be educated on what they can and cannot do with it. To ensure a firm manages its information correctly, it will need special policies and procedures establishing rules on how the information is organized, updated, maintained, and accessed. Every firm, large and small, should create an information policy concerning data governance. *Data governance* refers to the overall management of the availability, usability, integrity, and security of company data. *Master data management (MDM)* is the practice of gathering data and ensuring that it is uniform, accurate, consistent, and complete, including such entities as customers, suppliers, products, sales, employees, and other critical entities that are commonly integrated across organizational systems. MDM is commonly included in data governance. A company that supports a data governance program has a defined a policy that specifies who is accountable for various portions or aspects of the data, including its accuracy, accessibility, consistency, timeliness, and completeness. The policy should clearly define the processes concerning how to store, archive, back up, and secure the data. In addition, the company should create a set of procedures identifying accessibility levels for employees. Then, the firm should deploy controls and procedures that enforce government regulations and compliance with mandates such as Sarbanes-Oxley.

It is important to note the difference between data governance and data stewardship. Data governance focuses on enterprisewide policies and procedures, while data stewardship focuses on the strategic implementation of the policies and procedures. *Data validation* includes the tests and evaluations used to determine compliance with data governance polices to ensure correctness of data. Data validation helps to ensure that every data value is correct and accurate. In Excel you can use data validation to control the type of data or the values that users enter into a cell. For example, you may want to restrict data entry to a certain range of dates, limit choices by using a list, or make sure that only positive whole numbers are entered.

LO 6.2 Describe a database, a database management system, and the relational database model.

Storing Information Using a Relational Database Management System

The core component of any system, regardless of size, is a database and a database management system. Broadly defined, a *database* maintains information about various types of objects (inventory), events (transactions), people (employees), and places (warehouses). A *database management system (DBMS)* creates, reads, updates, and deletes data in a database while controlling access and security. Managers send requests to the DBMS, and the DBMS performs the actual manipulation of the data in the database. Companies store their information in databases, and managers access these systems to answer operational questions such as how many customers purchased Product A in December or what were the average sales by region. There are two primary tools available for retrieving information from a DBMS. First is a *query-by-example (QBE) tool* that helps users graphically design the answer to a question against a database. Second is a *structured query language (SQL)* that asks users to write lines of code to answer questions against a database. Managers typically interact with QBE tools, and MIS professionals have the skills required to code SQL. Figure 6.6 displays the relationship between a database, a DBMS, and a user. Some of the more popular examples of DBMS include MySQL, Microsoft Access, SQL Server, and Oracle.

A *data element (or data field)* is the smallest or basic unit of information. Data elements can include a customer's name, address, email, discount rate, preferred shipping method, product name, quantity ordered, and so on. *Data models* are logical data structures that detail the relationships among data elements using graphics or pictures.

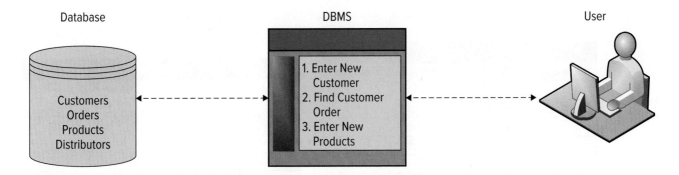

Database   DBMS   User

Customers
Orders
Products
Distributors

1. Enter New
   Customer
2. Find Customer
   Order
3. Enter New
   Products

FIGURE 6.6

Relationship of Database,
DBMS, and User.

Metadata provides details about data. For example, metadata for an image could include its size, resolution, and date created. Metadata about a text document could contain document length, data created, author's name, and summary. Each data element is given a description, such as Customer Name; metadata is provided for the type of data (text, numeric, alphanumeric, date, image, binary value) and descriptions of potential predefined values such as a certain area code; and finally the relationship is defined. A *data dictionary* compiles all of the metadata about the data elements in the data model. Looking at a data model along with reviewing the data dictionary provides tremendous insight into the database's functions, purpose, and business rules.

DBMS use three primary data models for organizing information—hierarchical, network, and the relational database, the most prevalent. A *relational database model* stores information in the form of logically related two-dimensional tables. A *relational database management system* allows users to create, read, update, and delete data in a relational database. Although the hierarchical and network models are important, this text focuses only on the relational database model.

STORING DATA ELEMENTS IN ENTITIES AND ATTRIBUTES

For flexibility in supporting business operations, managers need to query or search for the answers to business questions such as which artist sold the most albums during a certain month. The relationships in the relational database model help managers extract this information. Figure 6.7 illustrates the primary concepts of the relational database model—entities, attributes, keys, and relationships. An *entity* (also referred to as a table) stores information about a person, place, thing, transaction, or event. The entities, or tables, of interest in Figure 6.7 are *TRACKS, RECORDINGS, MUSICIANS,* and *CATEGORIES.* Notice that each entity is stored in a different two-dimensional table (with rows and columns).

Attributes (also called columns or fields) are the data elements associated with an entity. In Figure 6.7 the attributes for the entity *TRACKS* are *TrackNumber, TrackTitle, TrackLength,* and *RecordingID.* Attributes for the entity *MUSICIANS* are *MusicianID, MusicianName, MusicianPhoto,* and *MusicianNotes.* A *record* is a collection of related data elements (in the *MUSICIANS* table these include "3, Lady Gaga, gag.tiff, Do not bring young kids to live shows"). Each record in an entity occupies one row in its respective table.

CREATING RELATIONSHIPS THROUGH KEYS

To manage and organize various entities within the relational database model, you use primary keys and foreign keys to create logical relationships. A *primary key* is a field (or group of fields) that uniquely identifies a given record in a table. In the table *RECORDINGS,* the primary key is the field *RecordingID* that uniquely identifies each record in the table. Primary keys are a critical piece of a relational database because they provide a way of distinguishing each record in a table; for instance, imagine you need to find information on a customer named Steve Smith. Simply searching the customer name would not be an ideal way to find the information because there might be 20 customers with the name Steve Smith. This is

TRACKS

TrackNumber	TrackTitle	TrackLength	RecordingID
1	I Won't	3:45	1
2	Begin Again	4:14	1
3	You Got Me	4:00	1
4	Fallin For you	3:35	1
1	I Gotta Feelin	4:49	2
2	Imma Be	4:17	2
3	Boom Boom Pow	4:11	2
4	Meet Me Halfway	4:44	2

RECORDINGS

RecordingID	RecordingTitle	MuscianID	CategoryID
1	Breakthrough	1	1
2	The E.N.D.	2	1
3	Monkey Business	2	1
4	Elephunk	2	1
5	The Fame Monster	3	1
6	Raymond v. Raymond	4	2

Primary keys

Attributes

MUSICIANS

MusicianID	MusicianName	MusicianPhoto	MusicianNotes
1	Colby Caillat	Colby.jpg	Next concert in Boston 7/1/2011
2	Black Eyed Peas	BYP.bmp	New album due 12/25/2011
3	Lady Gaga	Gaga.tiff	Do not bring young kids to live shows
4	Usher	Usher.bmp	Current album #1 on Billboard

Records

CATEGORIES

CategoryID	CategoryName
1	Pop
2	R&B
3	Rock
4	Country
5	Blues
6	Classical

FIGURE 6.7

Primary Concepts of the Relational Database Model.

the reason the relational database model uses primary keys to uniquely identify each record. Using Steve Smith's unique ID allows a manager to search the database to identify all information associated with this customer.

A *foreign key* is a primary key of one table that appears as an attribute in another table and acts to provide a logical relationship between the two tables. For instance, Black Eyed Peas in Figure 6.7 is one of the musicians appearing in the *MUSICIANS* table. Its primary key, *MusicianID,* is "2." Notice that *MusicianID* also appears as an attribute in the *RECORD-INGS* table. By matching these attributes, you create a relationship between the *MUSICIANS* and *RECORDINGS* tables that states the Black Eyed Peas *(MusicianID 2)* have several recordings including The E.N.D., Monkey Business, and Elepunk. In essence, *MusicianID* in the *RECORDINGS* table creates a logical relationship (who was the musician that made the recording) to the *MUSICIANS* table. Creating the logical relationship between the tables allows managers to search the data and turn it into useful information.

COCA-COLA RELATIONAL DATABASE EXAMPLE

Figure 6.8 illustrates the primary concepts of the relational database model for a sample order of soda from Coca-Cola. Figure 6.8 offers an excellent example of how data is stored in a database. For example, the order number is stored in the *ORDER* table and each line item is stored in the *ORDER LINE* table. Entities include *CUSTOMER, ORDER, ORDER LINE, PRODUCT,* and *DISTRIBUTOR.* Attributes for *CUSTOMER* include *Customer ID, Customer Name, Contact Name,* and *Phone.* Attributes for *PRODUCT* include *Product ID, Description,* and *Price.* The columns in the table contain the attributes. Consider Hawkins Shipping, one of the distributors appearing in the *DISTRIBUTOR* table. Its primary key, *Distributor ID,* is DEN8001. Notice that *Distributor ID* also appears as an attribute in the *ORDER* table. This establishes the fact that Hawkins Shipping (*Distributor ID* DEN8001) was responsible for delivering orders 34561 and 34562 to the appropriate customer(s). Therefore, *Distributor ID* in the *ORDER* table creates a logical relationship (who shipped what order) between *ORDER* and *DISTRIBUTOR.*

FIGURE 6.8

Potential Relational Database for Coca-Cola Bottling Company of Egypt (TCCBCE).

Order Number: 34562

Coca-Cola Bottling Company of Egypt
Sample Sales Order

Customer: Dave's Sub Shop	Date: 8/6/2008		
Quantity	Product	Price	Amount
100	Vanilla Coke	$0.55	$55
		Distributor Fee	$12.95
		Order Total	$67.95

CUSTOMER

Customer ID	Customer Name	Contact Name	Phone
23	Dave's Sub Shop	David Logan	(555)333-4545
43	Pizza Palace	Debbie Fernandez	(555)345-5432
765	T's Fun Zone	Tom Repicci	(555)565-6655

ORDER

Order ID	Order Date	Customer ID	Distributor ID	Distributor Fee	Total Due
34561	7/4/2008	23	DEN8001	$22.00	$145.75
34562	8/6/2008	23	DEN8001	$12.95	$67.95
34563	6/5/2008	765	NY9001	$29.50	$249.50

ORDER LINE

Order ID	Line Item	Product ID	Quantity
34561	1	12345AA	75
34561	2	12346BB	50
34561	3	12347CC	100
34562	1	12349EE	100
34563	1	12345AA	100
34563	2	12346BB	100
34563	3	12347CC	50
34563	4	12348DD	50
34563	5	12349EE	100

DISTRIBUTOR

Distributor ID	Distributor Name
DEN8001	Hawkins Shipping
CHI3001	ABC Trucking
NY9001	Van Distributors

PRODUCT

Product ID	Product Description	Price
12345AA	Coca-Cola	$0.55
12346BB	Diet Coke	$0.55
12347CC	Sprite	$0.55
12348DD	Diet Sprite	$0.55
12349EE	Vanilla Coke	$0.55

Using a Relational Database for Business Advantages

Many business managers are familiar with Excel and other spreadsheet programs they can use to store business data. Although spreadsheets are excellent for supporting some data analysis, they offer limited functionality in terms of security, accessibility, and flexibility and can rarely scale to support business growth. From a business perspective, relational databases offer many advantages over using a text document or a spreadsheet, as displayed in Figure 6.9.

INCREASED FLEXIBILITY

Databases tend to mirror business structures, and a database needs to handle changes quickly and easily, just as any business needs to be able to do. Equally important, databases need to provide flexibility in allowing each user to access the information in whatever way best suits his or her needs. The distinction between logical and physical views is important in understanding flexible database user views. The ***physical view of information*** deals with the physical storage of information on a storage device. The ***logical view of information*** focuses on how individual users logically access information to meet their own particular business needs.

In the database illustration from Figure 6.7 , for example, one user could perform a query to determine which recordings had a track length of four minutes or more. At the same time, another user could perform an analysis to determine the distribution of recordings as they relate to the different categories. For example, are there more R&B recordings than rock, or are they evenly distributed? This example demonstrates that while a database has only one physical view, it can easily support multiple logical views that provides for flexibility.

Consider another example—a mail-order business. One user might want a report presented in alphabetical format, in which case last name should appear before first name. Another user, working with a catalog mailing system, would want customer names appearing as first name and then last name. Both are easily achievable, but different logical views of the same physical information.

INCREASED SCALABILITY AND PERFORMANCE

In its first year of operation, the official website of the American Family Immigration History Center, www.ellisisland.org, generated more than 2.5 billion hits. The site offers immigration information about people who entered America through the Port of New York and Ellis Island between 1892 and 1924. The database contains more than 25 million passenger names that are correlated to 3.5 million images of ships' manifests.[3]

FIGURE 6.9

Business Advantages of a Relational Database.

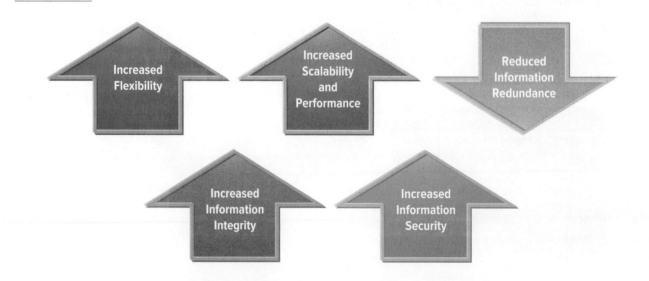

The database had to be scalable to handle the massive volumes of information and the large numbers of users expected for the launch of the website. In addition, the database needed to perform quickly under heavy use. *Data latency* is the time it takes for data to be stored or retrieved. Some organizations must be able to support hundreds or thousands of users including employees, partners, customers, and suppliers, who all want to access and share the same information with minimal data latency. Databases today scale to exceptional levels, allowing all types of users and programs to perform information-processing and information-searching tasks.

REDUCED INFORMATION REDUNDANCY

Information redundancy is the duplication of data, or the storage of the same data in multiple places. Redundant data can cause storage issues along with data integrity issues, making it difficult to determine which values are the most current or most accurate. Employees become confused and frustrated when faced with incorrect information causing disruptions to business processes and procedures. One primary goal of a database is to eliminate information redundancy by recording each piece of information in only one place in the database. This saves disk space, makes performing information updates easier, and improves information quality.

INCREASED INFORMATION INTEGRITY (QUALITY)

Information integrity is a measure of the quality of information. *Integrity constraints* are rules that help ensure the quality of information. The database design needs to consider integrity constraints. The database and the DBMS ensure that users can never violate these constraints. There are two types of integrity constraints: (1) relational and (2) business critical.

Relational integrity constraints are rules that enforce basic and fundamental information-based constraints. For example, a relational integrity constraint would not allow someone to create an order for a nonexistent customer, provide a markup percentage that was negative, or order zero pounds of raw materials from a supplier. A *business rule* defines how a company performs certain aspects of its business and typically results in either a yes/no or true/false answer. Stating that merchandise returns are allowed within 10 days of purchase is an example of a business rule. *Business-critical integrity constraints* enforce business rules vital to an organization's success and often require more insight and knowledge than relational integrity constraints. Consider a supplier of fresh produce to large grocery chains such as Kroger. The supplier might implement a business-critical integrity constraint stating that no product returns are accepted after 15 days past delivery. That would make sense because of the chance of spoilage of the produce. Business-critical integrity constraints tend to mirror the very rules by which an organization achieves success.

The specification and enforcement of integrity constraints produce higher-quality information that will provide better support for business decisions. Organizations that establish specific procedures for developing integrity constraints typically see an increase in accuracy, which then increases the use of organizational information by business professionals.

INCREASED INFORMATION SECURITY

Managers must protect information, like any asset, from unauthorized users or misuse. As systems become increasingly complex and highly available over the Internet on many different devices, security becomes an even bigger issue. Databases offer many security features including passwords to provide authentication, access levels to determine who can access the data, and access controls to determine what type of access they have to the information.

For example, customer service representatives might need read-only access to customer order information so they can answer customer order inquiries; they might not have or need the authority to change or delete order information. Managers might require access to employee files, but they should have access only to their own employees' files, not the employee files for the entire company. Various security features of databases can ensure that individuals have only certain types of access to certain types of information.

Identity management is a broad administrative area that deals with identifying individuals in a system (such as a country, a network, or an enterprise) and controlling their access to resources within that system by associating user rights and restrictions with the established identity. Security risks are increasing as more and more databases and DBMS systems are moving to data centers run in the cloud. The biggest risks when using cloud computing are ensuring the security and privacy of the information in the database. Implementing data governance policies and procedures that outline the data management requirements can ensure safe and secure cloud computing.

LO 6.4 Explain the business benefits of a data-driven website.

Driving Websites with Data

Websites change for site visitors depending on the type of information they request. Consider, for example, an automobile dealer. The dealer would create a database containing data elements for each car it has available for sale including make, model, color, year, miles per gallon, a photograph, and so on. Website visitors might click on Porsche and then enter their specific requests such as price range or year made. Once the user hits "go" the website automatically provides a custom view of the requested information. The dealer must create, update, and delete automobile information as the inventory changes.

A *data-driven website* is an interactive website kept constantly updated and relevant to the needs of its customers using a database. Data-driven capabilities are especially useful when a firm needs to offer large amounts of information, products, or services. Visitors can become quickly annoyed if they find themselves buried under an avalanche of information when searching a website. A data-driven website can help limit the amount of information displayed to customers based on unique search requirements. Companies even use data-driven websites to make information in their internal databases available to customers and business partners.

There are a number of advantages to using the web to access company databases. First, web browsers are much easier to use than directly accessing the database using a custom-query tool. Second, the web interface requires few or no changes to the database model. Finally, it costs less to add a web interface in front of a DBMS than to redesign and rebuild the system to support changes. Additional data-driven website advantages include:

- **Easy to manage content:** Website owners can make changes without relying on MIS professionals; users can update a data-driven website with little or no training.

- **Easy to store large amounts of data:** Data-driven websites can keep large volumes of information organized. Website owners can use templates to implement changes for layouts, navigation, or website structure. This improves website reliability, scalability, and performance.

- **Easy to eliminate human errors:** Data-driven websites trap data-entry errors, eliminating inconsistencies while ensuring all information is entered correctly.

WEBSITE DATA

A *content creator* is the person responsible for creating the original website content. A *content editor* is the person responsible for updating and maintaining website content. *Static information* includes fixed data incapable of change in the event of a user action. *Dynamic information* includes data that change based on user actions. For example, static websites supply only information that will not change until the content editor changes the information. Dynamic information changes when a user requests information. A dynamic website changes information based on user requests such as movie ticket availability, airline prices, or restaurant reservations. Dynamic website information is stored in a *dynamic catalog*, or an area of a website that stores information about products in a database.

Zappos credits its success as an online shoe retailer to its vast inventory of nearly 3 million products available through its dynamic data-driven website. The company built its data-driven website catering to a specific niche market: consumers who were tired of finding that their most-desired items were always out of stock at traditional retailers. Zappos's highly

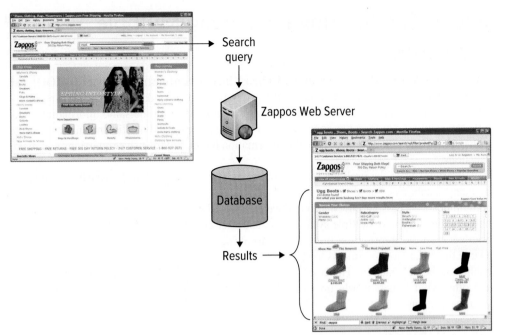

FIGURE 6.10

Zappos.com—a Data-Driven Website.

Source: Zappos.com

Search query

Zappos Web Server

Database

Results

flexible, scalable, and secure database helped it rank as the most-available Internet retailer. Figure 6.10 displays Zappos's data-driven website illustrating a user querying the database and receiving information that satisfies the user's request.[4]

Companies can gain valuable business knowledge by viewing the data accessed and analyzed from their website. Figure 6.11 displays how running queries or using analytical tools, such as a PivotTable, on the database that is attached to the website can offer insight into the business, such as items browsed, frequent requests, items bought together, and so on.

FIGURE 6.11

BI in a Data-Driven Website.

Source: Best Mobile

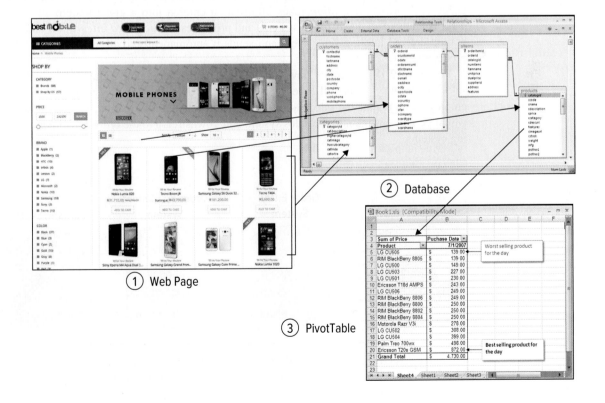

① Web Page

② Database

③ PivotTable

LO 6.5 Explain why an
organization would want to
integrate its databases.

Integrating Information among Multiple Databases

Until the 1990s, each department in the United Kingdom's Ministry of Defense (MOD) and army headquarters had its own systems, each system had its own database, and sharing information among the departments was difficult. Manually inputting the same information multiple times into the different systems was also time consuming and inefficient. In many cases, management could not even compile the information it required to answer questions and make decisions.

The army solved the problem by integrating its systems, or building connections between its many databases. These integrations allow the army's multiple systems to automatically communicate by passing information between the databases, eliminating the need for manual information entry into multiple systems because after entering the information once, the integrations send the information immediately to all other databases. The integrations not only enable the different departments to share information but have also dramatically increased the quality of the information. The army can now generate reports detailing its state of readiness and other vital issues, nearly impossible tasks before building the integrations among the separate systems.

DATA INTEGRATION

An *integration* allows separate systems to communicate directly with each other, eliminating the need for manual entry into multiple systems. Similar to the UK's army, an organization will probably maintain multiple systems, with each system having its own database. Without integrations, an organization will (1) spend considerable time entering the same information in multiple systems and (2) suffer from the low quality and inconsistency typically embedded in redundant information. While most integrations do not completely eliminate redundant information, they can ensure the consistency of it across multiple systems.

An organization can choose from two integration methods. The first is to create forward and backward integrations that link processes (and their underlying databases) in the value chain. A *forward integration* takes information entered into a given system and sends it automatically to all downstream systems and processes. A *backward integration* takes information entered into a given system and sends it automatically to all upstream systems and processes.

Figure 6.12 demonstrates how this method works across the systems or processes of sales, order entry, order fulfillment, and billing. In the order entry system, for example, an employee can update the information for a customer. That information, via the integrations, would be sent upstream to the sales system and downstream to the order fulfillment and billing systems.

FIGURE 6.12

A Forward and Backward Customer Information Integration Example.

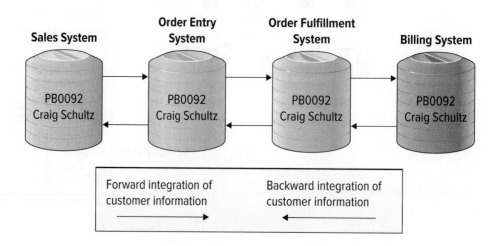

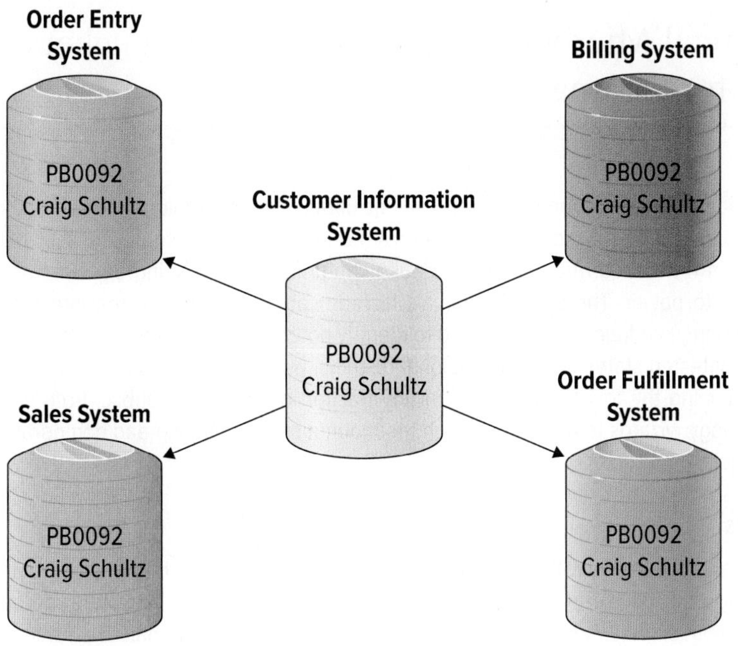

FIGURE 6.13

Integrating Customer
Information among
Databases.

Order Entry System

PB0092
Craig Schultz

Billing System

PB0092
Craig Schultz

Customer Information System

PB0092
Craig Schultz

Sales System

PB0092
Craig Schultz

Order Fulfillment System

PB0092
Craig Schultz

Ideally, an organization wants to build both forward and backward integrations, which provide the flexibility to create, update, and delete information in any of the systems. However, integrations are expensive and difficult to build and maintain and most organizations build only forward integrations (sales through billing in Figure 6.12). Building only forward integrations implies that a change in the initial system (sales) will result in changes occurring in all the other systems. Integration of information is not possible for any changes occurring outside the initial system, which again can result in inconsistent organizational information. To address this issue, organizations can enforce business rules that all systems, other than the initial system, have read-only access to the integrated information. This will require users to change information in the initial system only, which will always trigger the integration and ensure that organizational information does not get out of sync.

The second integration method builds a central repository for a particular type of information. Figure 6.13 provides an example of customer information integrated using this method across four different systems in an organization. Users can create, update, and delete customer information only in the central customer information database. As users perform these tasks on the central customer information database, integrations automatically send the new and/or updated customer information to the other systems. The other systems limit users to read-only access of the customer information stored in them. Again, this method does not eliminate redundancy—but it does ensure consistency of the information among multiple systems.

OPENING CASE STUDY QUESTIONS

1. Categorize the five common characteristics of high-quality information and rank them in order of importance for big data.

2. Explain how issues with low-quality information will impact big data.

3. Develop a list of some possible entities located in a database that tracks students and grades.

4. Develop a list of some possible attributes located in a database that tracks students and grades.

In his presidential inauguration speech, President Barack Obama spoke a word rarely expressed—*data*—referencing indicators of economic and other crises. It is not surprising that the word *data* was spoken in his inauguration speech because capturing and analyzing data has been crucial to Obama's rise to power. Throughout Obama's historic campaign he used the Internet not only for social networking and fund raising, but also to identify potential swing voters. Obama's team carefully monitored contested states and congressional districts, because 1,000 to 2,000 voters could prove decisive—meaning the focus was on only a tiny fraction of the voting public. Both political parties hired technology wizards to help sift through the mountains of consumer and demographic details to recognize these important voters.

Ten "Tribes"

Spotlight Analysis, a Democratic consultancy, used political microtargeting to analyze neighborhood details, family sizes, and spending patterns to categorize every American of voting age—175 million of us—into 10 "values tribes." Individual tribe members do not necessarily share the same race, religion, or income bracket, but they have common mind-sets about political issues: God, community, responsibility, opportunity. Spotlight identified a particular morally guided (but not necessarily religious) tribe of some 14 million voters that it dubbed "Barn Raisers." Barn Raisers comprise many races, religions, and ethnic groups and around 40 percent of Barn Raisers favor Democrats and 27 percent favor Republicans. Barn Raisers are slightly less likely to have a college education than Spotlight's other swing groups. They are active in community organizations, are ambivalent about government, and care deeply about "playing by the rules" and "keeping promises," to use Spotlight's definitions. Spotlight believed that the Barn Raisers held the key to the race between Obama and his Republican challenger, Arizona Senator John McCain.

Not typically seen outside of such corporate American icons as Google, Amazon, and eBay, political microtargeting, which depends on data, databases, and data analysis techniques, is turning political parties into sophisticated, intelligent, methodical machines. In nanoseconds, computers sort 175 million voters into segments and quickly calculate the potential that each individual voter has to swing from red or purple to blue or vice versa.

For some, political microtargeting signals the dehumanization of politics. For others, this type of sophisticated analysis is a highly efficient way of pinpointing potential voters. For example, analyzing a voter in Richmond, Virginia, traditionally simply identifies the number of school-age children, type of car, zip code, magazine subscriptions, and mortgage balance. But data crunching could even indicate if the voter has dogs or cats. (Cat owners lean slightly for Democrats, dog owners trend Republican.) After the analysis, the voter is placed into a political tribe, and analyzers can draw conclusions about the issues that matter to this particular voter. Is that so horrible?

Behavioral Grouping

For generations, governments lacked the means to study individual behaviors and simply placed all citizens into enormous groupings such as Hispanics, Jews, union members, hunters, soccer moms, etc. With the use of sophisticated databases and data analysis techniques, companies such as Spotlight can group individuals based more on specific behavior and choices and less on the names, colors, and clans that mark us from birth.

When Spotlight first embarked on its research, the company interviewed thousands of voters the old-fashioned way. At first, the Barn Raisers did not seem significant and the tribe represented about 9 percent of the electorate. However, when Spotlight's analysts dug deeper, they discovered that Barn Raisers stood at the epicenter of America's political swing. In 2004, 90 percent of them voted for President Bush, but then the group's political leanings shifted, with 64 percent of them saying they voted for Democrats in the 2006 election. Spotlight surveys showed that political scandals, tax-funded boondoggles like Alaska's Bridge to Nowhere, and the botched job on Hurricane Katrina sent them packing.

Suddenly, Spotlight identified millions of potential swing voters. The challenge then became locating the swing voters by states. For this, the company analyzed the demographics and buying patterns of the Barn Raisers they surveyed personally. Then it began correlating data from the numerous commercially available databases with matching profiles. By Spotlight's count, this approach nailed Barn Raisers three times out of four. So Democrats could bet that at least three-quarters of them would be likely to welcome an appeal stressing honesty and fair play.

Still Swing Voters

It is still undetermined to what extent Spotlight's strategy worked, and the company has not correlated the Barn Raisers to their actual votes. However, it is reasonable to presume that amid that sea of humanity stretched out before Obama on Washington's Mall on January 20, 2008, at least some were moved by microtargeted appeals. And if Obama and his team fail to honor their mathematically honed vows, the Barn Raisers may abandon them in droves. They are swing voters, after all.[5]

QUESTIONS

1. Describe the difference between transactional and analytical information, and determine which of these types Spotlight used to identify its 10 tribes.

2. Explain the importance of high-quality information for political microtargeting.

3. Review the five common characteristics of high-quality information, and rank them in order of importance for political microtargeting.

4. In terms of political microtargeting, explain the following sentence: It is never possible to have all of the information required to make a 100 percent accurate prediction.

5. Do you agree that political microtargeting signals the dehumanization of politics?

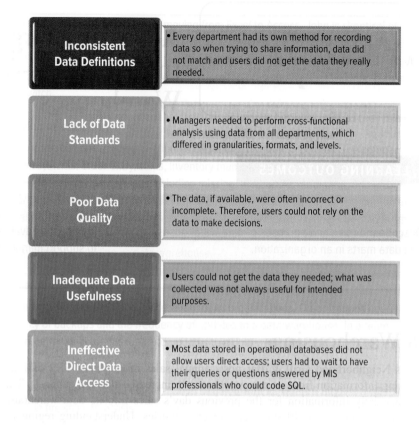

Inconsistent Data Definitions	• Every department had its own method for recording data so when trying to share information, data did not match and users did not get the data they really needed.
Lack of Data Standards	• Managers needed to perform cross-functional analysis using data from all departments, which differed in granularities, formats, and levels.
Poor Data Quality	• The data, if available, were often incorrect or incomplete. Therefore, users could not rely on the data to make decisions.
Inadequate Data Usefulness	• Users could not get the data they needed; what was collected was not always useful for intended purposes.
Ineffective Direct Data Access	• Most data stored in operational databases did not allow users direct access; users had to wait to have their queries or questions answered by MIS professionals who could code SQL.

organization into a single repository in such a way that the people who need that information can make decisions and undertake business analysis. A key idea within data warehousing is to collect information from multiple systems in a common location that uses a universal querying tool. This allows operational databases to run where they are most efficient for the business, while providing a common location using a familiar format for the strategic or enterprisewide reporting information.

Data warehouses go even a step further by standardizing information. Gender, for instance can be referred to in many ways (Male, Female, M/F, 1/0), but it should be standardized on a data warehouse with one common way of referring to each data element that stores gender (M/F). Standardization of data elements allows for greater accuracy, completeness, and consistency and increases the quality of the information in making strategic business decisions. The data warehouse then is simply a tool that enables business users, typically managers, to be more effective in many ways, including:

- Developing customer profiles.
- Identifying new-product opportunities.
- Improving business operations.
- Identifying financial issues.
- Analyzing trends.
- Understanding competitors.
- Understanding product performance. (See Figure 7.2.)

FIGURE 7.2

Data Warehousing
Components.

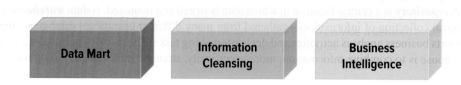

Data Mart	Information Cleansing	Business Intelligence

DATA MART

Data aggregation is the collection of data from various sources for the purpose of data processing. One example of a data aggregation is to gather information about particular groups based on specific variables such as age, profession, or income. Businesses collect a tremendous amount of transactional information as part of their routine operations. Marketing, sales, and other departments would like to analyze these data to understand their operations better. Although databases store the details of all transactions (for instance, the sale of a product) and events (hiring a new employee), data warehouses store that same information but in an aggregated form more suited to supporting decision-making tasks. Aggregation, in this instance, can include totals, counts, averages, and the like.

The data warehouse modeled in Figure 7.3 compiles information from internal databases or transactional/operational databases and external databases through *extraction, transformation, and loading (ETL),* which is a process that extracts information from internal and external databases, transforms the information using a common set of enterprise definitions, and loads the information into a data warehouse. The data warehouse then sends subsets of the information to data marts. A *data mart* contains a subset of data warehouse information. To distinguish between data warehouses and data marts, think of data warehouses as having a more organizational focus and data marts as having focused information subsets particular to the needs of a given business unit such as finance or production and operations. Figure 7.3 provides an illustration of a data warehouse and its relationship to internal and external databases, ETL, and data marts.

Lands' End created an organization-wide data warehouse so all its employees could access organizational information. Lands' End soon found out that there could be "too much of a good thing." Many of its employees would not use the data warehouse because it was simply too big, was too complicated, and had too much irrelevant information. Lands' End knew there was valuable information in its data warehouse, and it had to find a way for its employees to easily access the information. Data marts were the perfect solution to the company's information overload problem. Once the employees began using the data marts, they were ecstatic at the wealth of information. Data marts were a huge success for Lands' End.

FIGURE 7.3

Model of a Typical Data Warehouse.

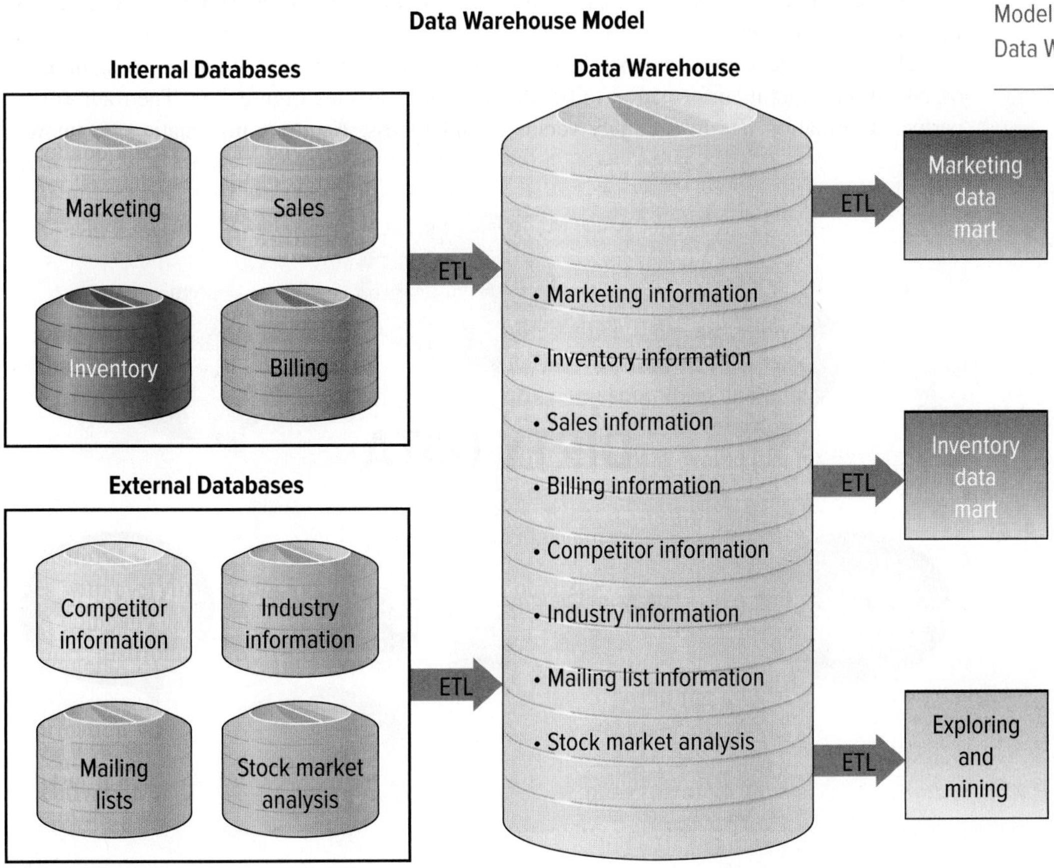

Data Warehouse Model

Internal Databases

- Marketing
- Sales
- Inventory
- Billing

External Databases

- Competitor information
- Industry information
- Mailing lists
- Stock market analysis

Data Warehouse

- Marketing information
- Inventory information
- Sales information
- Billing information
- Competitor information
- Industry information
- Mailing list information
- Stock market analysis

ETL → Marketing data mart

ETL → Inventory data mart

ETL → Exploring and mining

INFORMATION CLEANSING (OR SCRUBBING)

Maintaining quality information in a data warehouse or data mart is extremely important. The Data Warehousing Institute estimates that low-quality information costs U.S. businesses $600 billion annually. That number may seem high, but it is not. If an organization is using a data warehouse or data mart to allocate dollars across advertising strategies, low-quality information will definitely have a negative impact on its ability to make the right decision.

Dirty data is erroneous or flawed data (see Figure 7.4). The complete removal of dirty data from a source is impractical or virtually impossible. According to Gartner Inc., dirty data is a business problem, not an MIS problem. Over the next two years, more than 25 percent of critical data in Fortune 1000 companies will continue to be flawed; that is, the information will be inaccurate, incomplete, or duplicated.

Obviously, maintaining quality information in a data warehouse or data mart is extremely important. To increase the quality of organizational information and thus the effectiveness of decision making, businesses must formulate a strategy to keep information clean. *Information cleansing or scrubbing* is a process that weeds out and fixes or discards inconsistent, incorrect, or incomplete information.

Specialized software tools exist that use sophisticated procedures to analyze, standardize, correct, match, and consolidate data warehouse information. This step is vitally important because data warehouses often contain information from several databases, some of which can be external to the organization. In a data warehouse, information cleansing occurs first during the ETL process and again once the information is in the data warehouse. Companies can choose information cleansing software from several vendors, including Oracle, SAS, Ascential Software, and Group 1 Software. Ideally, scrubbed information is accurate and consistent.

Looking at customer information highlights why information cleansing is necessary. Customer information exists in several operational systems. In each system, all the details could change—from the customer ID to contact information—depending on the business process the user is performing (see Figure 7.5).

Figure 7.6 displays a customer name entered differently in multiple operational systems. Information cleansing allows an organization to fix these types of inconsistencies and cleans the information in the data warehouse. Figure 7.7 displays the typical events that occur during information cleansing.

Achieving perfect information is almost impossible. The more complete and accurate an organization wants its information to be, the more it costs (see Figure 7.8). The trade-off for perfect information lies in accuracy versus completeness. Accurate information means it is

FIGURE 7.4

Dirty Data Problems.

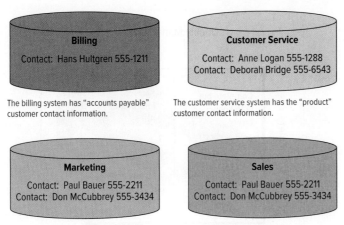

FIGURE 7.5

Contact Information in Operational Systems.

The billing system has "accounts payable" customer contact information.

The customer service system has the "product" customer contact information.

The marketing and sales system has "decision maker" customer contact information.

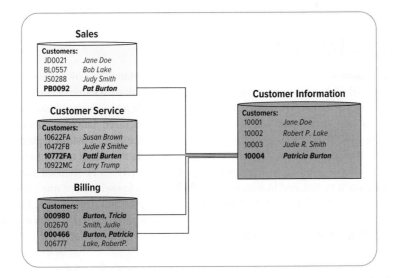

FIGURE 7.6

Standardizing Customer Name from Operational Systems.

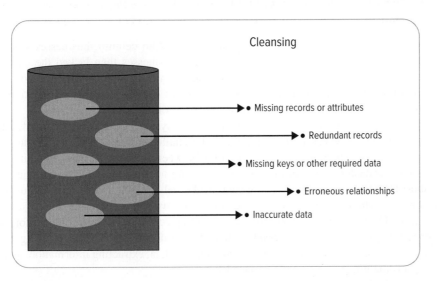

FIGURE 7.7

Information Cleansing Activities.

correct, while complete information means there are no blanks. A birth date of 2/31/10 is an example of complete but inaccurate information (February 31 does not exist). An address containing Denver, Colorado, without a zip code is an example of incomplete information that is accurate. For their information, most organizations determine a percentage high enough to make good decisions at a reasonable cost, such as 85 percent accurate and 65 percent complete.

FIGURE 7.8

Accurate and Complete
Information.

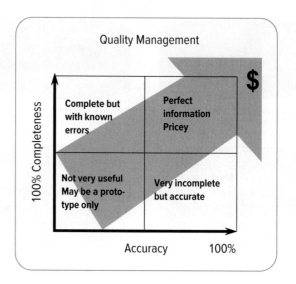

LO 7.2 **Identify the advantages
of using business intelligence
to support managerial
decision making.**

Business Intelligence

Many organizations today find it next to impossible to understand their own strengths and weaknesses, let alone their biggest competitors', because the enormous volume of organizational data is inaccessible to all but the MIS department. A ***data point*** is an individual item on a graph or a chart. Organizational data includes far more than simple structured data elements in a database; the set of data also includes unstructured data such as voice mail, customer phone calls, text messages, video clips, along with numerous new forms of data, such as tweets from Twitter.

An early reference to business intelligence occurs in Sun Tzu's book titled *The Art of War*. Sun Tzu claims that to succeed in war, one should have full knowledge of one's own strengths and weaknesses and full knowledge of the enemy's strengths and weaknesses. Lack of either one might result in defeat. A certain school of thought draws parallels between the challenges in business and those of war, specifically:

- Collecting information.
- Discerning patterns and meaning in the information.
- Responding to the resultant information.

Before the start of the information age in the late 20th century, businesses sometimes collected information from non-automated sources. Businesses then lacked the computing resources to properly analyze the information and often made commercial decisions based primarily on intuition. A ***data broker*** is a business that collects personal information about consumers and sells that information to other organizations.

As businesses started automating more and more systems, more and more information became available. However, collection remained a challenge due to a lack of infrastructure for information exchange or to incompatibilities between systems. Reports sometimes took months to generate. Such reports allowed informed long-term strategic decision making. However, short-term tactical decision making continued to rely on intuition. In modern businesses, increasing standards, automation, and technologies have led to vast amounts of available information. Data warehouse technologies have set up repositories to store this information. Improved ETL has increased the speedy collecting of information. Business intelligence has now become the art of sifting through large amounts of data, extracting information, and turning that information into actionable knowledge.

A ***data lake*** is a storage repository that holds a vast amount of raw data in its original format until the business needs it. While a traditional data warehouse stores data in files or folders, a data lake uses a flat architecture to store data. Each data element in a data lake is assigned a unique identifier and tagged with a set of extended metadata tags. When a business question arises, the data lake can be queried for all of the relevant data providing a smaller data set that can then be analyzed to help answer the question.

THE PROBLEM: DATA RICH, INFORMATION POOR

An ideal business scenario would be as follows: As a business manager on his way to meet with a client reviews historical customer data, he realizes that the client's ordering volume has substantially decreased. As he drills down into the data, he notices the client had a support issue with a particular product. He quickly calls the support team to find out all of the information and learns that a replacement for the defective part can be shipped in 24 hours. In addition, he learns that the client has visited the website and requested information on a new product line. Armed with all this information, the business manager is prepared for a productive meeting with his client. He now understands the client's needs and issues, and he can address new sales opportunities with confidence.

For many companies the above example is simply a pipe dream. Attempting to gather all of the client information would actually take hours or even days to compile. With so much data available, it is surprisingly hard for managers to get information, such as inventory levels, past order history, or shipping details. *Source data* identifies the primary location where data is collected. Source data can include invoices, spreadsheets, time-sheets, transactions, and electronic sources such as other databases. Managers send their information requests to the MIS department where a dedicated person compiles the various reports. In some situations, responses can take days, by which time the information may be outdated and opportunities lost. Many organizations find themselves in the position of being data rich and information poor. Even in today's electronic world, managers struggle with the challenge of turning their business data into business intelligence.

THE SOLUTION: BUSINESS INTELLIGENCE

Employee decisions are numerous and they include providing service information, offering new products, and supporting frustrated customers. A *data set* is an organized collection of data. A *comparative analysis* can compare two or more data sets to identify patterns and trends. Employees can base their decisions on data sets, experience, or knowledge and preferably a combination of all three. Business intelligence can provide managers with the ability to make better decisions. A few examples of how different industries use business intelligence include:

- **Airlines:** Analyze popular vacation locations with current flight listings.
- **Banking:** Understand customer credit card usage and nonpayment rates.
- **Health care:** Compare the demographics of patients with critical illnesses.
- **Insurance:** Predict claim amounts and medical coverage costs.
- **Law enforcement:** Track crime patterns, locations, and criminal behavior.
- **Marketing:** Analyze customer demographics.
- **Retail:** Predict sales, inventory levels, and distribution.
- **Technology:** Predict hardware failures.

Figure 7.9 displays how organizations using BI can find the cause to many issues and problems simply by asking "Why?" The process starts by analyzing a report such as sales amounts by quarter. Managers will drill down into the report looking for why sales are up or why sales are down. Once they understand why a certain location or product is experiencing an increase in sales, they can share the information in an effort to raise enterprisewide sales. Once they understand the cause for a decrease in sales, they can take effective action to resolve the issue. BI can help managers with *competitive monitoring* where a company keeps tabs of its competitor's activities on the web using software that automatically tracks all competitor website activities such as discounts and new products. Here are a few examples of how managers can use BI to answer tough business questions:

- **Where has the business been?** Historical perspective offers important variables for determining trends and patterns.
- **Where is the business now?** Looking at the current business situation allows managers to take effective action to solve issues before they grow out of control.
- **Where is the business going?** Setting strategic direction is critical for planning and creating solid business strategies.

FIGURE 7.9

How BI Can Answer Tough
Customer Questions.

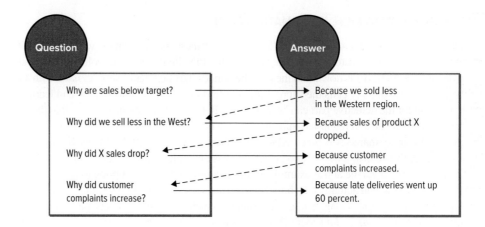

Ask a simple question—such as who is my best customer or what is my worst-selling product—and you might get as many answers as you have employees. Databases, data warehouses, and data marts can provide a single source of "trusted" data that can answer questions about customers, products, suppliers, production, finances, fraud, and even employees. A ***data map*** is a technique for establishing a match, or balance, between the source data and the target data warehouse. This technique identifies data shortfalls and recognizes data issues. They can also alert managers to inconsistencies or help determine the cause and effects of enterprisewide business decisions.

All business aspects can benefit from the added insights provided by business intelligence, and you, as a business student, will benefit from understanding how MIS can help you make data-driven decisions. ***Data-driven decision management*** is an approach to business governance that values decisions that can be backed up with verifiable data. The success of the data-driven approach is reliant upon the quality of the data gathered and the effectiveness of its analysis and interpretation.

In the early days of computing, it usually took a specialist with a strong background in technology to mine data for information because it was necessary for that person to understand how databases and data warehouses worked. Today, business intelligence tools often require very little, if any, support from the MIS department. Business managers can customize dashboards to display the data they want to see and run custom reports on the fly. The changes in how data can be mined and visualized allows business executives who have no technology backgrounds to be able to work with analytics tools and make data-driven decisions.

Data-driven decision management is usually undertaken as a way to gain a competitive advantage. A study from the MIT Center for Digital Business found that organizations driven most by data-based decision making had 4% higher productivity rates and 6% higher profits. However, integrating massive amounts of information from different areas of the business and combining it to derive actionable data in real time can be easier said than done. Errors can creep into data analytics processes at any stage of the endeavor, and serious issues can result when they do.

OPENING CASE STUDY QUESTIONS

1. Explain how a data warehouse stores enterprisewide data.

2. List the different types of dirty data and why it is important to cleanse data.

3. Describe how the marketing department could use a data mart that includes external and internal data to help analyze sales patterns.

Chapter Seven Case: Zillow

Zillow.com is an online, web-based real estate site helping homeowners, buyers, sellers, renters, real estate agents, mortgage professionals, property owners, and property managers find and share information about real estate and mortgages. Zillow allows users to access, anonymously and free of charge, the kinds of tools and information previously reserved for real estate professionals. Zillow's databases cover more than 90 million homes, which represents 95 percent of the homes in the United States. Adding to the sheer size of its databases, Zillow recalculates home valuations for each property every day, so it can provide historical graphs on home valuations over time. In some areas, Zillow is able to display 10 years of valuation history, a value-added benefit for many of its customers. This collection of data represents an operational data warehouse for anyone visiting the website.

As soon as Zillow launched its website, it immediately generated a massive amount of traffic. As the company expanded its services, the founders knew the key to its success would be the site's ability to process and manage massive amounts of data quickly, in real time. The company identified a need for accessible, scalable, reliable, secure databases that would enable it to continue to increase the capacity of its infrastructure indefinitely without sacrificing performance. Zillow's traffic continues to grow despite the weakened real estate market; the company is experiencing annual traffic growth of 30 percent, and about a third of all U.S. mortgage professionals visit the site in a given month.

Business Intelligence

Zestimate values on Zillow use data-mining features for spotting trends across property valuations. Data mining also allows the company to see how accurate Zestimate values are over time. Zillow has also built the industry's first search by monthly payment, allowing users to find homes that are for sale and rent based on a monthly payment they can afford. Along with the monthly payment search, users can also enter search criteria such as the number of bedrooms or bathrooms.

Zillow also launched a new service aimed at changing the way Americans shop for mortgages. Borrowers can use Zillow's new Mortgage Marketplace to get custom loan quotes from lenders without having to give their names, addresses, phone numbers, or Social Security numbers, or field unwanted telephone calls from brokers competing for their business. Borrowers reveal their identities only after contacting the lender of their choice. The company is entering a field of established mortgage sites such as LendingTree.com and Experian Group's Lowermybills.com, which charge mortgage companies for borrower information. Zillow, which has an advertising model, says it does not plan to charge for leads.

For mortgage companies, the anonymous leads come free; they can make a bid based on information provided by the borrower, such as salary, assets, credit score, and the type of loan. Lenders can browse borrower requests and see competing quotes from other brokers before making a bid.[1]

Questions

1. What is the source data for Zillow?

2. Describe how Zillow uses business intelligence to create a unique product for its customers.

3. Why would a person searching Zillow want to use a data mart?

4. Why would Zillow use a data lake?

5. Explain dirty data and its impact on a business.

6. What would happen to Zillow if it experienced dirty data?

7.1. Describe the roles and purposes of data warehouses and data marts in an organization.

A data warehouse is a logical collection of information, gathered from many different operational databases, that supports business analysis and decision making. The primary value of a data warehouse is to combine information, more specifically, strategic information, throughout an organization into a single repository in such a way that the people who need that information can make decisions and undertake business analysis.

7.2. Identify the advantages of using business intelligence to support managerial decision making.

Many organizations today find it next to impossible to understand their own strengths and weaknesses, let alone their biggest competitors', due to enormous volumes of organizational data being inaccessible to all but the MIS department. Organizational data includes far more than simple structured data elements in a database; the set of data also includes unstructured data such as voice mail, customer phone calls, text messages, video clips, along with numerous new forms of data, such as tweets from Twitter. Managers today find themselves in the position of being data rich and information poor, and they need to implement business intelligence systems to solve this challenge.

✴ REVIEW QUESTIONS

1. What is a data warehouse and why would a business want to implement one?
2. How does ETL help transfer data in and out of the data warehouse?
3. What is the purpose of information cleansing (or scrubbing)?
4. What are the causes of dirty data?
5. What is business intelligence and how can it help a company achieve success?
6. What is the difference between business intelligence and data?
7. Why would a marketing department want a data mart instead of just accessing the entire data warehouse?
8. Why would a business be data rich but information poor?

1. Gathering Business Intelligence

When considering new business opportunities, you need knowledge about the competition. One of the things many new business owners fail to do is to gather business intelligence on their competitors, such as how many there are and what differentiates each of them. You may find there are too many and that they would be tough competition for you. Or, you may find that there are few competitors and the ones who are out there offer very little value.

Generate a new business idea you could launch on the Internet. Research the Internet to find similar businesses in the area you have chosen. How many sites did you find that are offering the same products or services you are planning to offer? Did you come across any sites from another country that have a unique approach that you did not see on any of the sites in your own country? How would you use this information in pursuing your business idea?

2. Information—Business Intelligence or a Diversion from the Truth?

President Obama used part of his commencement address at Virginia's Hampton University to criticize the flood of incomplete information or downright incorrect information that flows in the 24-hour news cycle. The president said, "You're coming of age in a 24/7 media environment that bombards us with all kinds of content and exposes us to all kinds of arguments, some of which don't always rank all that high on the truth meter. With iPods and iPads and Xboxes and PlayStations—none of which I know how to work—information becomes a distraction, a diversion, a form of entertainment, rather than a tool of empowerment, rather than the means of emancipation."

Do you agree or disagree with President Obama's statement? Who is responsible for verifying the accuracy of online information? What should happen to companies that post inaccurate information? What should happen to individuals who post inaccurate information? What should you remember when reading or citing sources for online information?

3. Google Books

Google is scanning all or parts of the book collections of the University of Michigan, Harvard University, Stanford University, the New York Public Library, and Oxford University as part of its Google Print Library Project. It intends to make those texts searchable on Google. The Authors Guild filed a lawsuit against Google, alleging that its scanning and digitizing of library books constitutes a "massive" copyright infringement. Do you view Google's Print Library Project as a violation of copyright laws? If you were a publisher, how would you feel about Google's project? If you were an author, how would you feel about having your book posted for free on Google Books? What do you think the future of the book publishing industry will look like based on Google's radical new Google Book's website?

4. That Is Not My Mother in the Casket

Information—you simply can't put a value on having the right (or the cost of having the wrong) information. Just look at the mistake made at the Crib Point cemetery in Victoria, Australia, when they were burying Mrs. Ryan, an 85-year-old woman with almost 70 children, grandchildren, and great-grandchildren attending her funeral. The bereaved family of Mrs. Ryan was shocked to lift the lid of her coffin during the funeral to discover another woman lying in her clothes and jewelry. Where was the body of Mrs. Ryan? Mrs. Ryan had been buried earlier that day in the other woman's clothes, jewelry, and plot. What type of information blunder could possibly occur to allow someone to be buried in the wrong clothes, coffin, and plot? What could the cemetery do to ensure its customers are buried in the correct places? Why is the quality of information important to any business? What issues can occur when a business uses low-quality information to make decisions?

5. Data Storage

Information is one of the most important assets of any business. Businesses must ensure information accuracy, completeness, consistency, timeliness, and uniqueness. In addition, business must have a reliable backup service. In part thanks to cloud computing, there are many data storage services on the Internet. These sites offer storage of information that can be accessed from anywhere in the world. These data storage services include Google Docs, Box, and DropBox to name a few.

Visit a few of these sites along with several others you find through research. Which sites are free? Are there limits to how much you can store? If so, what is the limit? What type of information can you store (video, text, photos, etc.)? Can you allow multiple users with different passwords to access your storage area? Are you contractually bound for a certain duration (annual, etc.)? Does it make good business sense to store business data on the Internet? What about personal data?

6. Sorry, I Didn't Mean to Post Your Social Security Number on the Internet

Programming 101 teaches all students that security is the crucial part of any system. You must secure your data! It appears that some people working for the State of Oklahoma forgot this important lesson when tens of thousands of Oklahoma residents had their sensitive data—including numbers—posted on the Internet for the general public to access. You have probably heard this type of report before, but have you heard that the error went unnoticed for three years? A programmer reported the problem, explaining how he could easily change the page his browser was pointing to and grab the entire database for the State of Oklahoma. Also, because of the programming, malicious users could easily tamper with the database by changing data or adding fictitious data. If you are still thinking that isn't such a big deal, it gets worse. The website also posted the Sexual and Violent Offender Registry. Yes, the Department of Corrections employee data were also available for the general public to review.

In a group, discuss the following:

- Why is it important to secure data?
- What can happen if someone accesses your customer database?
- What could happen if someone changes the information in your customer database and adds fictitious data?
- Who should be held responsible for the State of Oklahoma data breech?
- What are the business risks associated with database security?

Understanding Big Data and Its Impact on Business

8.1. Identify the four common characteristics of big data.

8.2. Explain data mining and identify the three elements of data mining.

8.3. Explain the importance of data analytics and data visualization.

The Power of Big Data

LO 8.1 **Identify the four common characteristics of big data.**

Big data is a collection of large, complex data sets, including structured and unstructured data, which cannot be analyzed using traditional database methods and tools. Big data came into fruition primary due to the last 50 years of technology evolution. Revolutionary technological advances in software, hardware, storage, networking, and computing models have transformed the data landscape, making new opportunities for data collection possible. Big data is one of the latest trends emerging from the convergence of technological factors. For example, cell phones generate tremendous amounts of data and much of it is available for use with analytical applications. Big data includes data sources that include extremely large volumes of data, with high velocity, wide variety, and an understanding of the data veracity. The four common characteristics of big data are detailed in Figure 8.1 and Figure 8.2.

The move to big data combines business with science, research, and government activities. A company can now analyze petabytes of data for patterns, trends, and anomalies gaining insights into data in new and exciting ways. A petabyte of data is equivalent to 20 million four-drawer file cabinets filled with text files or 13 years of HDTV content. Big data requires sophisticated tools to analyze all of the structured and unstructured data from millions of customers, devices, and machine interactions (see Figure 8.3). The two primary computing models that have shaped the collection of big data include distributed computing and vitalization.

DISTRIBUTED COMPUTING

Distributed computing processes and manages algorithms across many machines in a computing environment (see Figure 8.4). A key component of big data is a distributed computing environment that shares resources ranging from memory to networks to storage. With distributed computing individual computers are networked together across geographical areas and work together to execute a workload or computing processes as if they were one single computing environment. For example, you can distribute a set of programs on the same physical server and use a message service to allow them to communicate and pass information. You can also have a distributed computing environment where many different systems or servers, each with its own computing memory, work together to solve a common problem.

FIGURE 8.10

Market Basket Analysis
Example.

© Purestock/Superstock

assign a level of importance to each segment. Zip codes offer valuable insight into such things as income levels, demographics, lifestyles, and spending habits. With target marketing, a business can decrease its costs while increasing the success rate of the marketing campaign.

Classification Analysis

Classification analysis is the process of organizing data into categories or groups for its most effective and efficient use. For example, groups of political affiliation and charity donors. The primary goal of a classification analysis is not to explore data to find interesting segments, but

FIGURE 8.11

Example of Cluster Analysis.

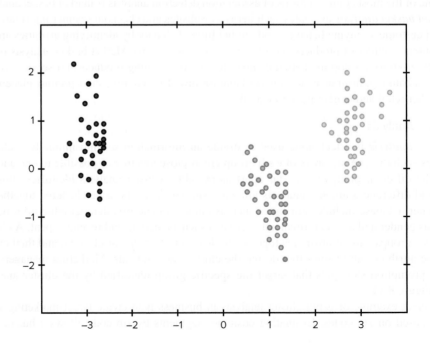

to decide the best way to classify records. It is important to note that classification analysis is similar to cluster analysis because it segments data into distinct segments called classes; however, unlike cluster analysis, a classification analysis requires that all classes are defined before the analysis begins. For example, in a classification analysis the analyst defines two classes: (1) a class for customers who default on a loan; (2) a class for customers who did not default on a loan. Cluster analysis is exploratory analysis and classification analysis is much less exploratory and more grouping. (See Figure 8.12.)

DATA MINING MODELING TECHNIQUES FOR PREDICTIONS

To perform data mining, users need data-mining tools. *Data mining tools* use a variety of techniques to find patterns and relationships in large volumes of information that predict future behavior and guide decision making. Data mining uncovers trends and patterns, which analysts use to build models that, when exposed to new information sets, perform a variety of information analysis functions. Data-mining tools for data warehouses help users uncover business intelligence in their data. Data mining uncovers patterns and trends for business analysis such as:

- Analyzing customer buying patterns to predict future marketing and promotion campaigns.
- Building budgets and other financial information.
- Detecting fraud by identifying deceptive spending patterns.
- Finding the best customers who spend the most money.
- Keeping customers from leaving or migrating to competitors.
- Promoting and hiring employees to ensure success for both the company and the individual.

A *prediction* is a statement about what will happen or might happen in the future, for example, predicting future sales or employee turnover. Figure 8.13 displays the three common data-mining techniques for predictions. Please note the primary difference between forecasts

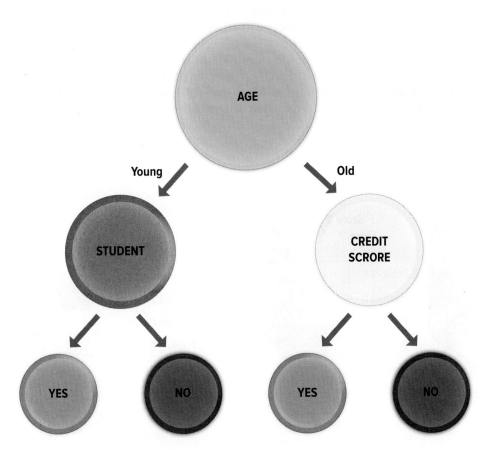

FIGURE 8.12

Classification Analysis Example.

Prediction Model	Definition	Example
Optimization Model	A statistical process that finds the way to make a design, system, or decision as effective as possible, for example, finding the values of controllable variables that determine maximal productivity or minimal waste.	■ Determine which products to produce given a limited amount of ingredients ■ Choose a combination of projects to maximize overall earnings
Forecasting Model	*Time-series information* is time-stamped information collected at a particular frequency. Forecasts are predictions based on time-series information allowing users to manipulate the time series for forecasting activities.	■ Web visits per hour ■ Sales per month ■ Customer service calls per day
Regression Model	A statistical process for estimating the relationships among variables. Regression models include many techniques for modeling and analyzing several variables when the focus is on the relationship between a dependent variable and one or more independent variables.	■ Predict the winners of a marathon based on gender, height, weight, hours of training ■ Explain how the quantity of weekly sales of a popular brand of beer depends on its price at a small chain of supermarkets

FIGURE 8.13

Data Mining Modeling
Techniques for Predictions.

and predictions. All forecasts are predictions, but not all predictions are forecasts. For example, when you would use regression to explain the relationship between two variables this is a prediction but not a forecast.

LO 8.3 **Explain the importance of data analytics and data visualization.**

Data Analysis

A relational database contains information in a series of two-dimensional tables. With big data information is multidimensional, meaning it contains layers of columns and rows. A dimension is a particular attribute of information. Each layer in big data represents information according to an additional dimension. A **cube** is the common term for the representation of multidimensional information. Figure 8.14 displays a cube (cube *a*) that represents store information (the layers), product information (the rows), and promotion information (the columns).

FIGURE 8.14

A Cube of Information
for Performing a
Multidimensional Analysis
on Three Different Stores,
for Five Different Products,
and Four Different
Promotions.

Once a cube of information is created, users can begin to slice and dice the cube to drill down into the information. The second cube (cube *b*) in Figure 8.14 displays a slice representing promotion II information for all products, at all stores. The third cube (cube *c*) in Figure 8.14 displays only information for promotion III, product B, at store 2. By using multidimensional analysis, users can analyze information in a number of different ways and with any number of different dimensions. For example, users might want to add dimensions of information to a current analysis including product category, region, and even forecasts for

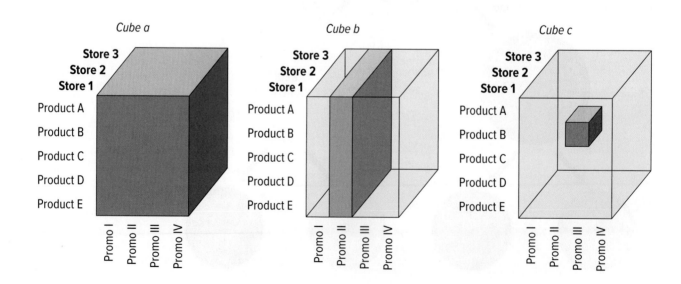

actual weather. The true value of big data is its ability to provide multidimensional analysis that allows users to gain insights into their information.

Big data is ideal for off-loading some of the querying against a database. For example, querying a database to obtain an average of sales for product B at store 2 while promotion III is under way might create a considerable processing burden for a database, essentially slowing down the time it takes another person to enter a new sale into the same database. If an organization performs numerous queries against a database (or multiple databases), aggregating that information into big data databases could be beneficial.

ADVANCED DATA ANALYTICS

Algorithms are mathematical formulas placed in software that performs an analysis on a data set. *Analytics* is the science of fact-based decision making. Analytics uses software-based algorithms and statistics to derive meaning from data. Advanced analytics uses data patterns to make forward-looking predictions to explain to the organization where it is headed. *Anomaly detection* is the process of identifying rare or unexpected items or events in a data set that do not conform to other items in the data set. One of the key advantages of performing advanced analytics is to detect anomalies in the data to ensure they are not used in models creating false results. An *outlier* is a data value that is numerically distant from most of the other data points in a set of data. Anomaly detection helps to identify outliers in the data that can cause problems with mathematical modeling.

Fast data is the application of big data analytics to smaller data sets in near-real or real-time in order to solve a problem or create business value. The term fast data is often associated with business intelligence and the goal is to quickly gather and mine structured and unstructured data so that action can be taken. As the flood of data from sensors, actuators and machine-to-machine (M2M) communication in the Internet of Things (IoT) continues to grow, it has become more important than ever for organizations to identify what data is time-sensitive and should be acted upon right away and what data can sit in a data warehouse or data lake until there is a reason to mine it.

A *data scientist* extracts knowledge from data by performing statistical analysis, data mining, and advanced analytics on big data to identify trends, market changes, and other relevant information. Figure 8.15 displays the techniques a data scientist will use to perform big data advanced analytics.

FIGURE 8.15

Advanced Data Analytics.

Analytics	Description
Behavioral Analysis	Using data about people's behaviors to understand intent and predict future actions.
Correlation Analysis	Determines a statistical relationship between variables, often for the purpose of identifying predictive factors among the variables.
Exploratory Data Analysis	Identifies patterns in data, including outliers, uncovering the underlying structure to understand relationships between the variables.
Pattern Recognition Analysis	The classification or labeling of an identified pattern in the machine learning process.
Social Media Analysis	Analyzes text flowing across the Internet, including unstructured text from blogs and messages.
Speech Analysis	The process of analyzing recorded calls to gather information; brings structure to customer interactions and exposes information buried in customer contact center interactions with an enterprise. Speech analysis is heavily used in the customer service department to help improve processes by identifying angry customers and routing them to the appropriate customer service representative.
Text Analysis	Analyzes unstructured data to find trends and patterns in words and sentences. Text mining a firm's customer support email might identify which customer service representative is best able to handle the question, allowing the system to forward it to the right person.
Web Analysis	Analyzes unstructured data associated with websites to identify consumer behavior and website navigation.

a business perspective. Data visualization is a powerful way to simplify complex data sets by placing data in a format that is easily grasped and understood far quicker than the raw data alone. **Data visualization tools** move beyond Excel graphs and charts into sophisticated analysis techniques such as controls, instruments, maps, time-series graphs, and more. Data visualization tools can help uncover correlations and trends in data that would otherwise go unrecognized.

Business intelligence dashboards track corporate metrics such as critical success factors and key performance indicators and include advanced capabilities such as interactive controls, allowing users to manipulate data for analysis. The majority of business intelligence software vendors offer a number of data visualization tools and business intelligence dashboards.

Big data is one of the most promising technology trends occurring today. Of course, notable companies such as Facebook, Google, and Netflix are gaining the most business insights from big data currently, but many smaller markets are entering the scene, including retail, insurance, and health care. Over the next decade, as big data starts to improve your everyday life by providing insights into your social relationships, habits, and careers, you can expect to see the need for data scientists and data artists dramatically increase.

OPENING CASE STUDY QUESTIONS

1. List the reasons a business would want to display big data in a graphic or visual format.

2. Describe how a business could use a few of the data analysis techniques to understand how the business is operating.

3. Explain how a marketing department could use data visualization tools to help with the release of a new product.

Chapter Eight Case: Mining the Data Warehouse

According to a Merrill Lynch survey in 2006, business intelligence software and data-mining tools were at the top of CIOs' technology spending list. Following are a few examples of how companies are using data warehousing and data-mining tools to gain valuable business intelligence.

Ben & Jerry's

These days, when we all scream for ice cream, Ben & Jerry's cuts through the din by using integrated query, reporting, and online analytical processing technology from BI software vendor Business Objects. Through an Oracle database and with BI from Business Objects, Ben & Jerry's tracks the ingredients and life of each pint. If a consumer calls in with a complaint, the consumer affairs staff matches the pint with which supplier's milk, eggs, cherries, or whatever did not meet the organization's near-obsession with quality.

The BI tools let Ben & Jerry's officials access, analyze, and act on customer information collected by the sales, finance, purchasing, and quality-assurance departments. The company can determine what milk customers prefer in the making of the ice cream. The technology helped Ben & Jerry's track more than 12,500 consumer contacts in 2005. The information ranged from comments about the ingredients used in ice cream to queries about social causes supported by the company.

California Pizza Kitchen

California Pizza Kitchen (CPK) is a leading casual dining chain in the premium pizza segment with a recognized consumer brand and an established, loyal customer base. Founded in 1985, there are currently more than 130 full-service restaurants in more than 26 states, the District of Columbia, and five foreign countries.

Before implementing its BI tool, Cognos, CPK used spreadsheets to plan and track its financial statements and line items. The finance team had difficulty managing the volumes of data, complex calculations, and constant changes to the spreadsheets. It took several weeks of two people working full-time to obtain one version of the financial statements and future forecast. In addition, the team was limited by the software's inability to link cells and calculations across multiple spreadsheets, so updating other areas of corporate records became a time-consuming task. With Cognos, quarterly forecasting cycles have been reduced from eight days to two days. The finance team can now spend more time reviewing the results rather than collecting and entering the data.

Noodles & Company

Noodles & Company has more than 70 restaurants throughout Colorado, Illinois, Maryland, Michigan, Minnesota, Texas, Utah, Virginia, and Wisconsin. The company recently purchased Cognos BI tools to help implement reporting standards and communicate real-time operational information to field management throughout the United States.

Before implementing the first phase of the Cognos solution, IT and finance professionals spent days compiling report requests from numerous departments including sales and marketing, human resources, and real estate. Since completing phase one, operational Cognos reports are being accessed on a daily basis through the Noodles & Company website. This provides users with a single, 360-degree view of the business and consistent reporting throughout the enterprise.

Noodles & Company users benefit from the flexible query and reporting capabilities, allowing them to see patterns in the data to leverage new business opportunities. Cognos tools can pull information directly from a broad array of relational, operational, and other systems.[1]

Questions

1. Explain how Ben & Jerry's is using business intelligence tools to remain successful and competitive in a saturated market.

2. Identify why information cleansing is critical to California Pizza Kitchen's business intelligence tool's success.

3. Illustrate why 100 percent accurate and complete information is impossible for Noodles & Company to obtain.

4. Describe how each of the companies above is using BI to gain a competitive advantage.

8.1. Identify the four common characteristics of big data.

The four V's of big data include variety, veracity, voluminous, and velocity. Variety includes different forms of structured and unstructured data. Veracity includes the uncertainty of data, including biases, noise, and abnormalities. Voluminous is the scale of data. Velocity is the analysis of streaming data as it travels around the Internet.

8.2. Explain data mining and identify the three elements of data mining.

Data mining is the process of analyzing data to extract information not offered by the raw data alone. The three elements of data mining include data, discovery, and deployment.

- ■ Data: Foundation for data-directed decision making.
- ■ Discovery: Process of identifying new patterns, trends, and insights.
- ■ Deployment: Process of implementing discoveries to drive success.

8.3. Explain the importance of data analytics and data visualization.

Algorithms are mathematical formulas placed in software that performs an analysis on a data set. Analytics is the science of fact-based decision making. Analytics uses software-based algorithms and statistics to derive meaning from data. Advanced analytics uses data patterns to make forward-looking predictions to explain to the organization where it is headed. Data visualization describes technologies that allow users to see or visualize data to transform information into a business perspective. Data visualization is a powerful way to simplify complex data sets by placing data in a format that is easily grasped and understood far quicker than the raw data alone.

 REVIEW QUESTIONS

1. What is big data?
2. What are the four common characteristics of big data?
3. What is distributed computing and how has it helped drive the big data era?
4. What is virtualization and how has it helped drive the big data era?
5. What are the six steps in the data-mining process and why is each important?
6. What are the four data-mining techniques? Provide examples of how you would use each one in business.
7. What is data-driven decision management?
8. What are the four data-mining techniques for predictions and why are they important to a business?

1. Two Trillion Rows of Data Analyzed Daily—No Problem

eBay is the world's largest online marketplace, with 97 million global users selling anything to anyone at a yearly total of $62 billion—more than $2,000 every second. Of course with this many sales, eBay is collecting the equivalent of the Library of Congress worth of data every three days that must be analyzed to run the business successfully. Luckily, eBay discovered Tableau!

Tableau started at Stanford when Chris Stolte, a computer scientist; Pat Hanrahan, an Academy Award–winning professor; and Christian Chabot, a savvy business leader, decided to solve the problem of helping ordinary people understand big data. The three created Tableau, which bridged two computer science disciplines: computer graphics and databases. No more need to write code or understand the relational database keys and categories; users simply drag and drop pictures of what they want to analyze. Tableau has become one of the most successful data visualization tools on the market, winning multiple awards, international expansion, and millions in revenue and spawning multiple new inventions.

Tableau is revolutionizing business analytics, and this is only the beginning. Visit the Tableau website and become familiar with the tool by watching a few of the demos. Once you have a good understanding of the tool, create three questions eBay might be using Tableau to answer, including the analysis of its sales data to find patterns, business insights, and trends.

2. Track Your Life

With wearable technology, you can track your entire life. Nike's Fuelband and Jawbone's Up tracks all of your physical activity, caloric burn, and sleep patterns. You can track your driving patterns, tooth-brushing habits, and even laundry status. The question now becomes how to track all of your trackers.

A new company called Exist incorporates tracking devices with weather data, music choices, Netflix favorites, and Twitter activity all in one digital dashboard. Exist wants to understand every area of your life and provide correlation information between such things as your personal productivity and mood. As the different types of data expand, so will the breadth of correlations Exist can point out. For instance, do you tweet more when you are working at home? If so, does this increase productivity? Exist wants to track all of your trackers and analyze the information to help you become more efficient and more effective.

Create a digital dashboard for tracking your life. Choose four areas you want to track and determine three ways you would measure each area. For example, if you track eating habits, you might want to measure calories and place unacceptable levels in red and acceptable levels in green. Once completed, determine whether you can find any correlations among the areas in your life.

3. Butterfly Effects

The butterfly effect, an idea from chaos theory in mathematics, refers to the way a minor event—like the movement of a butterfly's wing—can have a major impact on a complex system like the weather. Dirty data can have the same impact on a business as the butterfly effect. Organizations depend on the movement and sharing of data throughout the organization, so the impact of data quality errors are costly and far-reaching. Such data issues often begin with a tiny mistake in one part of the organization, but the butterfly effect can produce disastrous results, making its way through MIS systems to the data warehouse and other enterprise systems. When dirty data or low-quality data enters organizational systems, a tiny error such as a spelling mistake can lead to revenue loss, process inefficiency, and failure to comply with industry and government regulations. Explain how the following errors can affect an organization:

- A cascading spelling mistake.
- Inaccurate customer records.
- Incomplete purchasing history.

- Inaccurate mailing address.
- Duplicate customer numbers for different customers.

4. Unethical Data Mining

Mining large amounts of data can create a number of benefits for business, society, and governments, but it can also create a number of ethical questions surrounding an invasion of privacy or misuse of information. Facebook recently came under fire for its data-mining practices as it followed 700,000 accounts to determine whether posts with highly emotional content are more contagious. The study concluded that highly emotional texts are contagious, just as with real people. Highly emotional positive posts received multiple positive replies, whereas highly emotional negative posts received multiple negative replies. Although the study seems rather innocent, many Facebook users were outraged; they felt the study was an invasion of privacy because the 700,000 accounts had no idea Facebook was mining their posts.

As a Facebook user, you willingly consent that Facebook owns every bit and byte of data you post and, once you press submit, Facebook can do whatever it wants with your data. Do you agree or disagree that Facebook has the right to do whatever it wants with the data its 1.5 billion users post on its site?

5. News Dots

Gone are the days of staring at boring spreadsheets and trying to understand how the data correlate. With innovative data visualization tools, managers can arrange different ways to view the data, providing new forms of pattern recognition not offered by simply looking at numbers. *Slate,* a news publication, developed a new data visualization tool, called News Dots, that offers readers a different way of viewing the daily news through trends and patterns. The News Dots tool scans about 500 stories a day from major publications and then tags the content with important keywords such as people, places, companies, and topics. Surprisingly, the majority of daily news overlaps as the people, places, and stories are frequently connected. Using News Dots, you can visualize how the news fits together, almost similar to a giant social network. News Dots uses circles (or dots) to represent the tagged content and arranges them according to size. The more frequently a certain topic is tagged, the larger the dot and its relationship to other dots. The tool is interactive and users simply click a dot to view which stories mention that topic and which other topics it connects to in the network such as a correlation among the U.S. government, Federal Reserve, Senate, bank, and Barack Obama.

How can data visualization help identify trends? What types of business intelligence could you identify if your college used a data visualization tool to analyze student information? What types of business intelligence could you identify if you used a data visualization tool to analyze the industry in which you plan to compete?

6. Free Data!

The U.S. Bureau of Labor Statistics states that its role is as the "principal fact-finding agency for the federal government in the broad field of labor economics and statistics." And the data that the bureau provides via its website are available to anyone, free. This can represent a treasure trove of business intelligence and data mining for those who take advantage of this resource.

Visit the website www.bls.gov. What type of information does the site provide? What information do you find most useful? What sort of information concerning employment and wages is available? How is this information categorized? How would this type of information be helpful to a business manager? What type of demographic information is available? How could this benefit a new start-up business?

7. Follow the Data

There is a classic line in the movie *All the President's Men,* which covers the Watergate investigation, where Deep Throat meets with Bob Woodward and coolly advises him to "follow the money." Woodward follows the money, and the Watergate investigation ends with President Nixon's resignation. If you want to find out what is happening in today's data-filled world, you could probably change those words to "follow the data."

One of the newest forms of legal requirements emerging from the data explosion is ediscovery, the legal requirements mandating that an organization must archive all forms of software communications, including email, text messages, and multimedia. Yes, the text message you sent four years ago could come back to haunt you.

Organizations today have more data than they know what to do with and are frequently overwhelmed with data management. Getting at such data and presenting them in a useful manner for cogent analysis is a tremendous task that haunts managers. What do you think is involved in data management? What is contained in the zettabytes of data stored by organizations? Why would an organization store data? How long should an organization store its data? What are the risks associated with failing to store organizational data?

UNIT SUMMARY

The five common characteristics of quality information are accuracy, completeness, consistency, uniqueness, and timeliness. The costs to an organization of having low-quality information can be enormous and could result in revenue losses and ultimately business failure. Databases maintain information about various types of objects, events, people, and places and help to alleviate many of the problems associated with low-quality information such as redundancy, integrity, and security.

A data warehouse is a logical collection of information—gathered from many different operational databases—that supports business analysis activities and decision-making tasks. Data marts contain a subset of data warehouse information. Organizations gain tremendous insight into their business by mining the information contained in data warehouses and data marts. As we enter the era of big data the data-mining and data analysis techniques will become of critical importance to any company that wants to succeed in business.

Understanding the value of information is key to business success. Employees must be able to optimally access and analyze organizational information. The more knowledge employees have concerning how the organization stores, maintains, provides access to, and protects information the better prepared they will be when they need to use that information to make critical business decisions.

KEY TERMS

✳ UNIT CLOSING CASE ONE

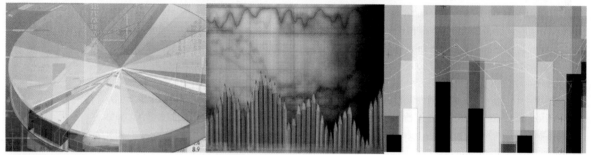

© Roz Woodward/Getty Images © Getty Images/Digital Vision © Epoxy/Getty Images

Data Visualization: Stories for the Information Age

At the intersection of art and algorithm, data visualization schematically abstracts information to bring about a deeper understanding of the data, wrapping it in an element of awe. While the practice of visually representing information is arguably the foundation of all design, a newfound fascination with data visualization has been emerging. After *The New York Times* and *The Guardian* recently opened their online archives to the public, artists rushed to dissect nearly two centuries worth of information, elevating this art form to new prominence.

For artists and designers, data visualization is a new frontier of self-expression, powered by the proliferation of information and the evolution of available tools. For enterprise, it is a platform for displaying products and services in the context of the cultural interaction that surrounds them, reflecting consumers' increasing demand for corporate transparency.

"Looking at something ordinary in a new way makes it extraordinary," says Aaron Koblin, one of the more recent pioneers of the discipline. As technology lead of Google's Creative Labs in San Francisco, he spearheaded the search giant's Chrome Experiments series designed to show off the speed and reliability of the Chrome browser.

Forget Pie Charts and Bar Graphs

Data visualization has nothing to do with pie charts and bar graphs. And it's only marginally related to "infographics," information design that tends to be about objectivity and clarification. Such representations simply offer another iteration of the data—restating it visually and making it easier to digest. Data visualization, on the other hand, is an interpretation, a different way to look at and think about data that often exposes complex patterns or correlations.

Data visualization is a way to make sense of the ever-increasing stream of information with which we're bombarded and provides a creative antidote to the analysis paralysis that can result from the burden of processing such a large volume of information. "It's not about clarifying data," says Koblin. "It's about contextualizing it."

Today algorithmically inspired artists are reimagining the art-science continuum through work that frames the left-brain analysis of data in a right-brain creative story. Some use data visualization as a bridge between alienating information and its emotional impact—see Chris Jordan's portraits of global mass culture. Others take a more technological angle and focus on cultural utility—the Zoetrope project offers a temporal and historical visualization of the ephemeral web. Still others are pure artistic indulgence—like Koblin's own Flight Patterns project, a visualization of air traffic over North America.

How Business Can Benefit

There are real implications for business here. Most cell phone providers, for instance, offer a statement of a user's monthly activity. Most often it's an overwhelming table of various numerical measures of how much you talked, when, with whom, and how much it cost. A visual representation of these data might help certain patterns emerge, revealing calling habits and perhaps helping users save money.

Companies can also use data visualization to gain new insight into consumer behavior. By observing and understanding what people do with the data—what they find useful and what they dismiss as worthless—executives can make the valuable distinction between what consumers say versus what they do. Even now, this can be a tricky call to make from behind the two-way mirror of a traditional qualitative research setting.

It's essential to understand the importance of creative vision along with the technical mastery of software. Data visualization isn't about using all the data available, but about deciding which patterns and elements to focus on, building a narrative, and telling the story of the raw data in a different, compelling way.

Ultimately, data visualization is more than complex software or the prettying up of spreadsheets. It's not innovation for the sake of innovation. It's about the most ancient of social rituals: storytelling. It's about telling the story locked in the data differently, more engagingly, in a way that draws us in, makes our eyes open a little wider and our jaw drop ever so slightly. And as we process it, it can sometimes change our perspective altogether.[2]

Questions

1. Identify the effects poor information might have on a data visualization project.

2. How does data visualization use database technologies?

3. How could a business use data visualization to identify new trends?

4. What is the correlation between data mining and data visualization?

5. Is data visualization a form of business intelligence? Why or why not?

6. What security issues are associated with data visualization?

7. What could happen to a data visualization project if it failed to cleanse or scrub its data?

© C. Borland/PhotoLink/Getty Images   © Fuse/Getty Images   Source: NPS photo by Jim Peaco

Informing Information

Since the beginning of time, man has been using pictures and images to communicate, moving from caveman drawings to hieroglyphics to the Internet. Today, it is easier than ever to paint a picture worth 100,000 words, thanks to technological advances. The primary advantages are databases and data warehouses that capture enormous amounts of data. Informing means accessing large amounts of data from different management information systems. According to a recent analysis of press releases by *PR Newswire,* an article or advertisement that uses visual images can significantly improve the number of views a message generates. This can be a true competitive advantage in the digital age.

An infographic (or information graphic) displays information graphically so it can be more easily understood. Infographics cut straight to the point by taking complex information and presenting it in a simple visual format. Infographics can present the results of large data analysis, looking for patterns and relationships that monitor changes in variables over time. Because infographics can easily become overwhelming, users need to be careful to not display too much data or the resulting infographics can result in information overload. Effective infographics can achieve outstanding results for marketing, advertising, and public relations. According to *PR Newswire,* infographics gain the greatest competitive advantage when they have the following:

- Survey results that are too hard to understand in text format.

- Statistical data that are not interesting for readers.

- Comparison research where the impact can be far more dramatic when presented visually.

- Messages for multilingual audiences.

- Any information that can use a visual element to make it more interesting (see Figure Unit 6.1 through Figure Unit 6.3 for examples).[3]

Bi-Annual Price Index

U.S. Travelers, Data from Early 2011

The hotels.com® Hotel Price Index™ (HPI™) is a regular survey of hotel prices in major city destinations across the world. The HPI is based on bookings made on hotels.com and prices shown are those actually paid by customers (rather than advertised rates) for the first half of 2011. The report largely compares prices paid in 2010 with prices paid in 2011. The following maps and charts illustrate some notable and interesting trends found in the survey.

Top International Destinations by U.S. Travelers

The hotel industry is seeing a global 3% price increase which is lending to the gradual recovery of the travel industry.

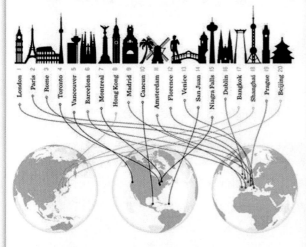

London 1 · Paris 2 · Rome 3 · Toronto 4 · Vancouver 5 · Barcelona 6 · Montreal 7 · Hong Kong 8 · Madrid 9 · Cancun 10 · Amsterdam 11 · Florence 12 · Venice 13 · San Juan 14 · Niagra Falls 15 · Dublin 16 · Bangkok 17 · Shanghai 18 · Prague 19 · Beijing 20

Hotel Prices Paid by **Home** and **Away** Travelers

Traveling outside the U.S. can be more expensive due to the weak U.S. dollar in comparison to other currencies – although Americans pay more to visit some countries abroad, they can find hidden deals in places like New Zealand, Ireland and Portugal.

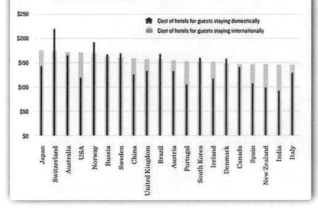

🏠 Cost of hotels for guests staying domestically
🏨 Cost of hotels for guests staying internationally

(Japan, Switzerland, Australia, USA, Norway, Russia, Sweden, China, United Kingdom, Brazil, Austria, Portugal, South Korea, Ireland, Denmark, Canada, Spain, New Zealand, India, Italy)

Travel Destinations in the United States

	MOST EXPENSIVE HOTEL RATES	MOST POPULAR *with* FOREIGN TRAVELERS	MOST POPULAR *with* DOMESTIC TRAVELERS	
1	New York	New York	Las Vegas	1
2	Honolulu	Las Vegas	New York	2
3	Boston	Orlando	Orlando	3
4	Miami	Miami	Chicago	4
5	New Orleans	San Francisco	San Diego	5
6	Washington D.C.	Los Angeles	San Francisco	6
7	Panama City	Honolulu	Los Angeles	7
8	Santa Barbara	Chicago	Washington D.C.	8
9	Anchorage	San Diego	Houston	9
10	Idaho Falls	Washington D.C.	San Antonio	10

not in U.S. Foreign Top 10

not in U.S. Domestic Top 10

Highest and **Lowest** Hotel Prices in the United States

U.S. travelers love visiting California – three cities within the top ten are located in The Golden State. Travel within the U.S. is affordable with about one third of U.S. cities reporting a decrease in hotel room rates. For a good bargain, head to the South. The South is still less expensive on average, than the rest of the U.S.

● Highest Priced   ○ Greatest Price Increases   ● Lowest Priced   ○ Greatest Price Decreases

Circles sized according to rank. Top Ten for each category shown.
10th 5th 1st

© 2011 Hotels.com L.P.   SOURCE: hotels.com® Hotel Price Index™ (HPI™) 2011   www.hotel-price-index.com

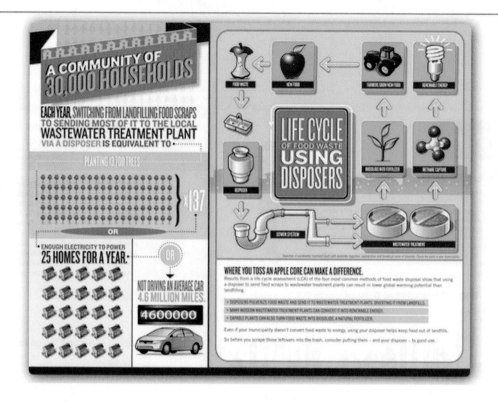

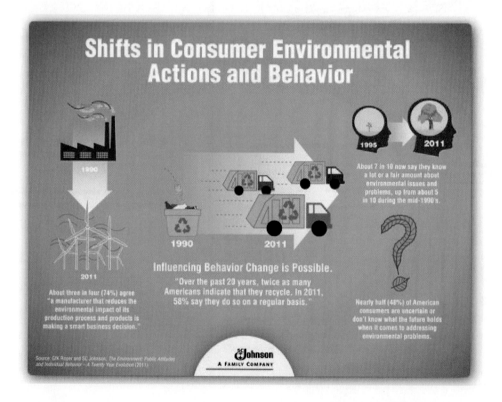

1. Mining the Data Warehouse

Alana Smith is a senior buyer for a large wholesaler that sells different types of arts and crafts to greeting card stores such as Hallmark. Alana's latest marketing strategy is to send all of her customers a new line of hand-made picture frames from Russia. Alana's data support her decision for the new line. Her analysis predicts that the frames should sell an average of 10 to 15 per store, per day. Alana is excited about the new line and is positive it will be a success.

One month later Alana learns that the frames are selling 50 percent below expectations and averaging between five and eight frames sold daily in each store. Alana decides to access the company's data warehouse to determine why sales are below expectations. Identify several different dimensions of data that Alana will want to analyze to help her decide what is causing the problems with the picture frame sales.

2. Cleansing Information

You are working for BI, a start-up business intelligence consulting company. You have a new client that is interested in hiring BI to clean up its information. To determine how good your work is, the client would like your analysis of the spreadsheet in Figure AYK.1.

3. Different Dimensions

The focus of data warehousing is to extend the transformation of data into information. Data warehouses offer strategic-level, external, integrated, and historical information so businesses can make projections, identify trends, and make key business decisions. The data warehouse collects and stores integrated sets of historical information from multiple operational systems and feeds them to one or more data marts. It may also provide end-user access to support enterprisewide views of information.

Project Focus

You are currently working on a marketing team for a large corporation that sells jewelry around the world. Your boss has asked you to look at the following dimensions of data to determine which ones you want in your data mart for performing sales and market analysis (see Figure AYK.2). As a team, categorize the different dimensions, ranking them from 1 to 5, with 1 indicating that the dimension offers the highest value and must be in your data mart and 5 indicating that the dimension offers the lowest value and does not need to be in your data mart.

4. Understanding Search

Pretend that you are a search engine. Choose a topic to query. It can be anything such as your favorite book, movie, band, or sports team. Search your topic on Google, pick three or four pages from the results, and print them out. On each printout, find the individual words from your query (such as "Boston Red Sox" or "The Godfather") and use a highlighter to mark each word with color. Do that for each of the documents that you print out. Now tape those documents on a wall, step back a few feet, and review your documents. If you did not know what the rest of a page said and could only judge by the colored words, which document do you think would be most relevant? Is there anything that would make a document look more relevant? Is it better to have the words be in a large heading or to occur several times in a smaller font? Do you prefer it if the words are at the top or the bottom of the page? How often do the words need to appear? Come up with two or three things you would look for to see if a document matched a query well. This exercise mimics search engine processes and should help you understand why a search engine returns certain results over others.

CUST ID	First Name	Last Name	Address	City	State	ZIP	Phone	Last Order Date
233620	Christopher	Lee	12421 W Olympic Blvd	Los Angeles	CA	75080-1100	(972)680-7848	4/18/2002
233621	Bruce	Brandwen	268 W 44th St	New York	PA	10036-3906	(212)471-6077	5/3/2002
233622	Glr	Johnson	4100 E Dry Creek Rd	Littleton	CO	80122-3729	(303)712-5461	5/6/2002
233623	Dave	Owens	466 Commerce Rd	Staunton	VA	24401-4432	(540)851-0362	3/19/2002
233624	John	Coulbourn	124 Action St	Maynard	MA	1754	(978)987-0100	4/24/2002
233629	Dan	Gagliardo	2875 Union Rd	Cheektowaga	NY	14227-1461	(716)558-8191	5/4/2002
23362	Damanceee	Allen	1633 Broadway	New York	NY	10019-6708	(212)708-1576	
233630	Michael	Peretz	235 E 45th St	New York	NY	10017-3305	(212)210-1340	4/30/2002
							(608)238-9690	
233631	Jody	Veeder	440 Science Dr	Madison	WI	53711-1064	X227	3/27/2002
233632	Michael	Kehrer	3015 SSE Loop 323	Tyler	TX	75701	(903)579-3229	4/28/
233633	Erin	Yoon	3500 Carillon Pt	Kirkland	WA	98033-7354	(425)897-7221	3/25/2002
233634	Madeline	Shefferly	4100 E Dry Creek Rd	Littleton	CO	80122-3729	(303)486-3949	3/33/2002
233635	Steven	Conduit	1332 Enterprise Dr	West Chester	PA	19380-5970	(610)692-5900	4/27/2002
233636	Joseph	Kovach	1332 Enterprise Dr	West Chester	PA	19380-5970	(610)692-5900	4/28/2002
233637	Richard	Jordan	1700 N	Philadelphia	PA	19131-4728	(215)581-6770	3/19/2002
233638	Scott	Mikolajczyk	1655 Crofton Blvd	Crofton	MD	21114-1387	(410)729-8155	4/28/2002
233639	Susan	Shragg	1875 Century Park E	Los Angeles	CA	90067-2501	(310)785-0511	4/29/2002
233640	Rob	Ponto	29777 Telegraph Rd	Southfield	MI	48034-1303	(810)204-4724	5/5/2002
			1211 Avenue Of The					
233642	Lauren	Butler	Americas	New York	NY	10036-8701	(212)852-7494	4/22/2002
233643	Christopher	Lee	12421 W Olympic Blvd	Los Angeles	CA	90064-1022	(310)689-2577	3/25/2002
233644	Michelle	Decker	6922 Hollywood Blvd	Hollywood	CA	90028-6117	(323)817-4655	5/8/2002
			1211 Avenue Of The					
233647	Natalia	Galeano	Americas	New York	NY	10036-8701	(646)728-6911	4/23/2002
233648	Bobbie	Orchard	4201 Congress St	Charlotte	NC	28209-4617	(704)557-2444	5/11/2002
233650	Ben	Konfino	1111 Stewart Ave	Bethpage	NY	11714-3533	(516)803-1406	3/19/2002
233651	Lenee	Santana	1050 Techwood Dr NW	Atlanta	GA	30318-KKRR	(404)885-2000	3/22/2002
233652	Lauren	Monks	7700 Wisconsin Ave	Bethesda	MD	20814-3578	(301)771-4772	3/19/2005
			10950 Washington					
233653	Mark	Woolley	Blvd	Culver City	CA	90232-4026	(310)202-2900	4/20/2002
233654	Stan	Matthews	1235 W St NE	Washington	DC	20018-1107	(202)608-2000	3/25/2002

FIGURE AYK.1

Data Cleansing.

Dimension	Value (1–5)	Dimension	Value (1–5)
Product number		Season	
Store location		Promotion	
Customer net worth		Payment method	
Number of sales personnel		Commission policy	
Customer eating habits		Manufacturer	
Store hours		Traffic report	
Salesperson ID		Customer language	
Product style		Weather	
Order date		Customer gender	
Product quantity		Local tax information	
Ship date		Local cultural demographics	
Current interest rate		Stock market closing	
Product cost		Customer religious affiliation	
Customer's political affiliation		Reason for purchase	
Local market analysis		Employee dress code policy	
Order time		Customer age	
Customer spending habits		Employee vacation policy	
Product price		Employee benefits	
Exchange rates		Current tariff information	
Product gross margin			

5. Predicting Movie

The Netflix Prize is a $1,000,000 prize for any person that can help Netflix improve the data in its recommendation engine. The Netflix Prize sought to substantially improve the accuracy of predictions about how much someone is going to enjoy a movie based on their movie preferences. On September 21, 2009 Netflix awarded the $1M Grand Prize to team BellKor's Pragmatic Chaos.

Project Focus

The ability to search, analyze, and comprehend information is vital for any organization's success. It certainly was for Netflix, as it was happy to pay anyone $1 million to improve the quality of its information. In a group explain how Netflix might use databases, data warehouses, and data marts to predict customer movie recommendations. Here are a few characteristics you might want to analyze to get you started:

- Customer demographics.
- Movie genre, rating, year, producer, type.
- Actor information.
- Internet access.
- Location for mail pickup.

6. The Crunch Factory

The Crunch Factory is one of the fourth-largest gyms operating in Australia, and each gym operates its own system with its own database. Unfortunately, the company failed to develop any data-capturing standards and now faces the challenges associated with low-quality enterprisewide information. For example, one system has a field to capture email addresses, while another system does not. Duplicate customer information among the different systems is another major issue, and the company continually finds itself sending conflicting or competing messages to customers from different gyms. A customer could also have multiple accounts within the company, one representing a membership, another representing additional classes, and yet another for a personal trainer. The Crunch Factory has no way to identify that the different customer accounts are actually for the same customer.

Project Focus

To remain competitive and be able to generate business intelligence The Crunch Factory has to resolve these challenges. The Crunch Factory has just hired you as its data quality expert. Your first task is to determine how the company can turn its low-quality information into high-quality business intelligence. Create a plan that The Crunch Factory can implement that details the following:

- Challenges associated with low-quality information.
- Benefits associated with high-quality information.
- Recommendations on how the company can clean up its data.

7. Too Much of a Good Thing

The Castle, a premium retailer of clothes and accessories, created an enterprisewide data warehouse so all its employees could access information for decision making. The Castle soon discovered that it is possible to have too much of a good thing. The Castle employees found themselves inundated with data and unable to make any decisions, a common occurrence called analysis paralysis. When sales representatives queried the data warehouse to determine if a certain product in the size, color, and category was available, they would get hundreds of results showing everything from production orders to supplier contracts. It became easier for the sales representatives to look in the warehouse themselves than to check the system. Employees found the data warehouse was simply too big and too complicated, and it contained too much irrelevant information.

Project Focus

The Castle is committed to making its data warehouse system a success and has come to you for help. Create a plan that details the value of the data warehouse to the business, how it can be easier for all employees to use, along with the potential business benefits the company can derive from its data warehouse.

8. Twitter Buzz

Technology tools that can predict sales for the coming week, decide when to increase inventory, and determine when additional staff is required are extremely valuable. Twitter is not just for tweeting your whereabouts anymore. Twitter and other social-media sites have become great tools for gathering business intelligence on customers, including what they like, dislike, need, and want. Twitter is easy to use, and businesses can track every single time a customer makes a statement about a particular product or service. Good businesses turn this valuable information into intelligence spotting trends and patterns in customer opinion.

Project Focus

Do you agree that a business can use Twitter to gain business intelligence? How many companies do you think are aware of Twitter and exactly how they can use it to gain BI? How do you think Twitter uses a data warehouse? How do you think companies store Twitter information? How would a company use Twitter in a data mart? How would a company use cubes to analyze Twitter data?

✱ AYK APPLICATION PROJECTS

If you are looking for Access projects to incorporate into your class, try any of the following to test your knowledge.

Project Number	Project Name	Project Type	Plug-In	Focus Area	Project Level	Skill Set	Page Number
28	Daily Invoice	Access	T5, T6, T7, T8	Business Analysis	Introductory	Entities, Relationships, and Databases	AYK.17
29	Billing Data	Access	T5, T6, T7, T8	Business Intelligence	Introductory	Entities, Relationships, and Databases	AYK.19
30	Inventory Data	Access	T5, T6, T7, T8	SCM	Intermediate	Entities, Relationships, and Databases	AYK.20
31	Call Center	Access	T5, T6, T7, T8	CRM	Intermediate	Entities, Relationships, and Databases	AYK.21
32	Sales Pipeline	Access	T5, T6, T7, T8	Business Intelligence	Advanced	Entities, Relationships, and Databases	AYK.23
33	Online Classified Ads	Access	T5, T6, T7, T8	Ecommerce	Advanced	Entities, Relationships, and Databases	AYK.23

3

Streamlining Business Operations

Information is a powerful asset. It is a key organizational asset that enables companies to carry out business initiatives and strategic plans. Companies that manage information are primed for competitive advantage and success. Information systems provide the key tools allowing access to and flow of information across enterprises. This unit emphasizes the important role strategic decision-making information systems play in increasing efficiency and effectiveness across global enterprises and providing the infrastructure required for supply chain management, customer relationship management, and enterprise resource planning. These systems facilitate interactions among customers, suppliers, partners, and employees providing new communication channels beyond those traditionally used by organizations such as face-to-face or paper-based methods.

A supply chain consists of all direct and indirect parties involved in the procurement of products and raw material. These parties can be internal groups or departments within an organization or external partner companies and end customers. You, as a business student, need to know the significance of a supply chain to organizational success and the critical role information technology plays in ensuring smooth operations of a supply chain.

You, as a business student, must understand the critical relationship your business will have with its customers. You must understand how to analyze your organizational data to ensure you are not just meeting, but exceeding, your customers' expectations. Business intelligence is the best way to understand your customers' current and—more importantly—future needs. Like never before, enterprises are technologically empowered to reach their goals of integrating, analyzing, and making intelligent business decisions based on their data.

You, as a business student, must understand how to give employees, customers, and business partners access to information by means of newer technologies such as enterprise resource planning systems and enterprise portals. Creating access to information with the help of information systems facilitates completion of current tasks while encouraging the sharing and generation of new ideas that lead to the development of innovations, improved work habits, and best practices.

© JGI/Blend Images/Getty Images RF

© Steve Cole/Getty Images RF

© Steve Cole/Getty Images RF

The Connected Car Revolution

We are currently in the middle of the connected car revolution, a vehicle equipped with smart sensors, Internet access, and a number of information systems that make driving easy, intelligent, and safe. Connected cars share information with individuals inside and outside the car via smart networks in a seamless and safe manner. Connected cars have the power of 20 modern PCs and contain more than 100 million lines of code that can process up to 25 gigabytes of data in an hour. From automobile manufacturers to software vendors to telecommunication companies, everyone is excited about the connected car phenomenon. Connected cars are not some futuristic auto technology; in fact, the connected car is already on the market and generating significant revenue for car makers and technology companies. A few benefits of the connected car include:

- Driver and passenger safety are the key benefits of a Connected Car, which warn the driver of external hazards and internal responses of the vehicle to hazards. The central monitoring system tracks multiple sensors for warning signs and indications related to the health of the car. It can even check external weather conditions and hazardous road conditions to alert the drivers in time.

- Car crashes are the leading cause of death for U.S. teens, and speeding is a contributing factor in about a third of those crashes. Mom and Dad cannot always be there to influence their teen driver's judgment, but a new application developed for Hyundai's in-car infotainment system allows parents to monitor and set restrictions on the car's speed, hours of operation and where it travels. If the driver exceeds a preset speed limit, for example, the parent will receive an alert via text, email and soon, a mobile app. The teenage driver also will see a notification on the vehicle's multimedia screen.

- Connected Cars take the infotainment to the next level by delivering popular content to the passengers. Today, car entertainment is mostly confined to FM radio and Bluetooth connectivity. With the availability of high-speed networks, popular streaming services such as Pandora, Spotify, and Hulu become available. Consumers will have a huge choice of digital content.

- Apple and Google are competing to becoming the brain behind in-car infotainment. Apple's Car Play embeds familiar iOS experience in the dashboard which gives access to a variety of third-party apps available in the App Store. Android Auto can stream music from Google Play Music straight into your car. It also makes it easy to access your favorite apps and content in the car. Passengers can purchase or rent media on the go. Consumers can use familiar voice-activated technologies such as Siri and Google Now to interact with the infotainment system. Amazon is partnering with Ford to bring its popular Alexa engine to the car.
- Connected Cars allow the driver to reach a destination quickly, safely, and in a cost-efficient manner. By communicating with the traffic signals and the road infrastructure, a smart car can slow down before reaching a signal. It can even automatically stop and start the car just before the lights turn green. This feature translates to a greater fuel efficiency.
- By tracking the driving patterns, Connected Cars can assess the wear and tear of a vehicle. This information can be leveraged by insurance agencies in calculating the premium that's based on usage and the maintenance of the car.
- Service stations can periodically gather the diagnostic information over the air to perform predictive analysis. They can proactively reach out to the vehicle owners to schedule a service appointment.

Over the next five to 10 years, the connected car market is expected to explode creating a new platform for consumers to access content and revolutionize the auto industry. Industry experts equate the connected car market is similar to where the smartphone was in 2010—it's just taken off and is ready to explode with an estimate of over 380 million connected cars will be on the road by 2021. Technology companies will play a major role in the future of the automotive market. The big question now is whether technology companies will eventually manufacture cars?

Next up, a world where cars drive themselves? Although fully autonomous vehicles are not yet mainstream, they are only a few years away. Technological, regulatory, and consumer adoption hurdles still remain, but there have been many strides towards a car that can drive itself from point A to point B with little to no human interaction. In the UK, KPMG estimates autonomous vehicles will lead to 2,500 fewer deaths between 2014 and 2030.[1]

Introduction

Decision making and problem solving in today's electronic world encompass large-scale, opportunity-oriented, strategically focused solutions. The traditional "cookbook" approach to decisions simply will not work in the ebusiness world. Decision-making and problem-solving abilities are now the most sought-after traits in up-and-coming executives. To put it mildly, decision makers and problem solvers have limitless career potential.

Ebusiness is the conducting of business on the Internet, not only buying and selling, but also serving customers and collaborating with business partners. (Unit Four discusses ebusiness in detail.) With the fast growth of information technology and the accelerated use of the Internet, ebusiness is quickly becoming standard. This unit focuses on technology to help make decisions, solve problems, and find new innovative opportunities. The unit highlights how to bring people together with the best IT processes and tools in complete, flexible solutions that can seize business opportunities (see Figure Unit 3.1). The chapters in Unit 3 are:

- **Chapter Nine**—Enabling the Organization—Decision Making.
- **Chapter Ten**—Extending the Organization—Supply Chain Management.
- **Chapter Eleven**—Building a Customer-centric Organization—Customer Relationship Management.
- **Chapter Twelve**—Integrating the Organization from End to End—Enterprise Resource Planning.

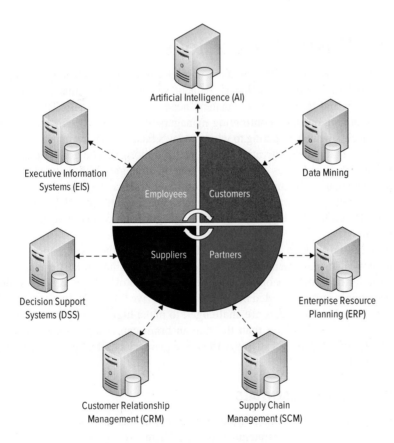

FIGURE UNIT 3.1

Decision-Enabling, Problem-Solving, and Opportunity-Seizing Systems.

CHAPTER 9

Enabling the Organization—Decision Making

9.1. Explain the importance of decision making for managers at each of the three primary organization levels along with the associated decision characteristics.

9.2. Classify the different operational support systems, managerial support systems, and strategic support

systems, and explain how managers can use these systems to make decisions and gain competitive advantages.

9.3. Describe artificial intelligence, and identify its five main types.

LO 9.1 Explain the importance of decision making for managers at each of the three primary organization levels along with the associated decision characteristics.

Making Business Decisions

Porter's strategies suggest entering markets with a competitive advantage in either overall cost leadership, differentiation, or focus. To achieve these results, managers must be able to make decisions and forecast future business needs and requirements. The most important and most challenging question confronting managers today is how to lay the foundation for tomorrow's success while competing to win in today's business environment. A company will not have a future if it is not cultivating strategies for tomorrow. The goal of this section is to expand on Porter's Five Forces Model, three generic strategies, and value chain analysis to demonstrate how managers can learn the concepts and practices of business decision making to add value. It will also highlight how companies heading into the 21st century are taking advantage of advanced MIS capable of generating significant competitive advantages across the value chain.

As we discussed in Unit 1, decision making is one of the most important and challenging aspects of management. Decisions range from routine choices, such as how many items to order or how many people to hire, to unexpected ones such as what to do if a key employee suddenly quits or needed materials do not arrive. Today, with massive volumes of information available, managers are challenged to make highly complex decisions—some involving far more information than the human brain can comprehend—in increasingly shorter time frames. Figure 9.1 displays the three primary challenges managers face when making decisions.

THE DECISION-MAKING ESSENTIALS

The process of making decisions plays a crucial role in communication and leadership for operational, managerial, and strategic projects. There are numerous academic decision-making models; Figure 9.2 presents just one example.[2]

A few key concepts about organizational structure will help our discussion of MIS decision-making tools. The structure of a typical organization is similar to a pyramid, and the different levels require different types of information to assist in decision making, problem solving, and opportunity capturing (see Figure 9.3).

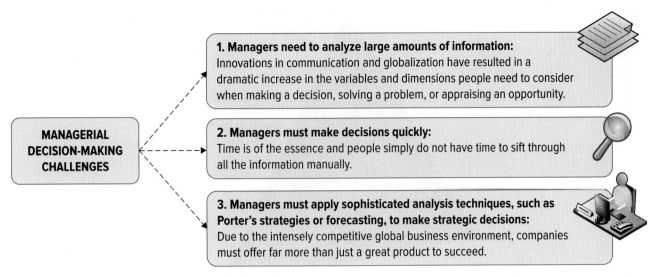

1. Managers need to analyze large amounts of information:
Innovations in communication and globalization have resulted in a dramatic increase in the variables and dimensions people need to consider when making a decision, solving a problem, or appraising an opportunity.

2. Managers must make decisions quickly:
Time is of the essence and people simply do not have time to sift through all the information manually.

3. Managers must apply sophisticated analysis techniques, such as Porter's strategies or forecasting, to make strategic decisions:
Due to the intensely competitive global business environment, companies must offer far more than just a great product to succeed.

FIGURE 9.1

Managerial Decision-Making Challenges.

Operational

At the *operational level*, employees develop, control, and maintain core business activities required to run the day-to-day operations. Operational decisions are considered *structured decisions*, which arise in situations where established processes offer potential solutions. Structured decisions are made frequently and are almost repetitive in nature; they affect short-term business strategies. Reordering inventory and creating the employee staffing and weekly production schedules are examples of routine structured decisions. Figure 9.4 highlights the essential elements required for operational decision making.

FIGURE 9.2

The Six-Step Decision-Making Process.

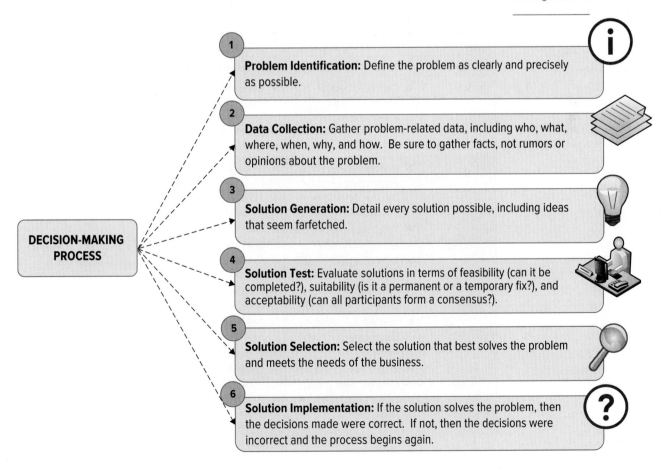

1 Problem Identification: Define the problem as clearly and precisely as possible.

2 Data Collection: Gather problem-related data, including who, what, where, when, why, and how. Be sure to gather facts, not rumors or opinions about the problem.

3 Solution Generation: Detail every solution possible, including ideas that seem farfetched.

4 Solution Test: Evaluate solutions in terms of feasibility (can it be completed?), suitability (is it a permanent or a temporary fix?), and acceptability (can all participants form a consensus?).

5 Solution Selection: Select the solution that best solves the problem and meets the needs of the business.

6 Solution Implementation: If the solution solves the problem, then the decisions made were correct. If not, then the decisions were incorrect and the process begins again.

FIGURE 9.3

Common Company
Structure.

FIGURE 9.4

Overview of Decision
Making.

	STRATEGIC LEVEL	MANAGERIAL LEVEL	OPERATIONAL LEVEL
Employee Types	■ Senior management, presidents, leaders, executives	■ Middle management, managers, directors	■ Lower management, department managers, analysts, staff
Focus	■ External, industry, cross company	■ Internal, crossfunctional (sometimes external)	■ Internal, functional
Time Frame	■ Long term—yearly, multiyear	■ Short term, daily, monthly, yearly	■ Short term, day-to-day operations
Decision Types	■ Unstructured, nonrecurring, one time	■ Semistructured, ad hoc (unplanned) reporting	■ Structured, recurring, repetitive
MIS Types	■ Knowledge	■ Business intelligence	■ Information
Metrics	■ Critical success factors focusing on effectiveness	■ Key performance indicators focusing on efficiency, and critical success factors focusing on effectiveness	■ Key performance indicators focusing on efficiency
Examples	■ How will changes in employment levels over the next 3 years affect the company? ■ What industry trends are worth analyzing? ■ What new products and new markets does the company need to create competitive advantages? ■ How will a recession over the next year affect business? ■ What measures will the company need to prepare for due to new tax laws?	■ Who are our best customers by region, by sales representative, by product? ■ What are the sales forecasts for next month? How do they compare to actual sales for last year? ■ What was the difference between expected sales and actual sales for each month? ■ What was the impact of last month's marketing campaign on sales? ■ What types of ad hoc or unplanned reports might the company require next month?	■ How many employees are out sick? ■ What are next week's production requirements? ■ How much inventory is in the warehouse? ■ How many problems occurred when running payroll? ■ Which employees are on vacation next week? ■ How many products need to be made today?

Managerial

At the *managerial level*, employees are continuously evaluating company operations to hone the firm's abilities to identify, adapt to, and leverage change. A company that has a competitive advantage needs to constantly adjust and revise its strategy to remain ahead of fast-following competitors. Managerial decisions cover short- and medium-range plans, schedules, and budgets along with policies, procedures, and business objectives for the firm. They also allocate resources and monitor the performance of organizational subunits, including departments, divisions, process teams, project teams, and other work groups. These types of decisions are considered *semistructured decisions* they occur in situations in which a few established processes help to evaluate potential solutions, but not enough to lead to a definite recommended decision. For example, decisions about producing new products or changing employee benefits range from unstructured to semistructured. Figure 9.4 highlights the essential elements required for managerial decision making.

Strategic

At the *strategic level*, managers develop overall business strategies, goals, and objectives as part of the company's strategic plan. They also monitor the strategic performance of the organization and its overall direction in the political, economic, and competitive business environment. Strategic decisions are highly *unstructured decisions*, occurring in situations in which no procedures or rules exist to guide decision makers toward the correct choice. They are infrequent, extremely important, and typically related to long-term business strategy. Examples include the decision to enter a new market or even a new industry over, say, the next three years. In these types of decisions, managers rely on many sources of information, along with personal knowledge, to find solutions. Figure 9.4 highlights the essential elements required for strategic decision making.

Support: Enhancing Decision Making with MIS

LO 9.2 Classify the different operational support systems, managerial support systems, and strategic support systems, and explain how managers can use these systems to make decisions and gain competitive advantages.

Now that we've reviewed the essentials of decision making, we are ready to understand the powerful benefits associated with using MIS to support managers making decisions.

A *model* is a simplified representation or abstraction of reality. Models help managers calculate risks, understand uncertainty, change variables, and manipulate time to make decisions. MIS support systems rely on models for computational and analytical routines that mathematically express relationships among variables. For example, a spreadsheet program, such as Microsoft Office Excel, might contain models that calculate market share or ROI. MIS have the capability and functionality to express far more complex modeling relationships that provide information, business intelligence, and knowledge. Figure 9.5 highlights the three primary types of management information systems available to support decision making across the company levels.

OPERATIONAL SUPPORT SYSTEMS

Transactional information encompasses all the information contained within a single business process or unit of work, and its primary purpose is to support the performance of daily operational or structured decisions. Transactional information is created, for example, when customers are purchasing stocks, making an airline reservation, or withdrawing cash from an ATM. Managers use transactional information when making structured decisions at the operational level, such as when analyzing daily sales reports to determine how much inventory to carry.

Online transaction processing (OLTP) is the capture of transaction and event information using technology to (1) process the information according to defined business rules, (2) store the information, and (3) update existing information to reflect the new information. During OLTP, the organization must capture every detail of transactions and events. A *transaction processing system (TPS)* is the basic business system that serves the operational level (analysts) and assists in making structured decisions. The most common

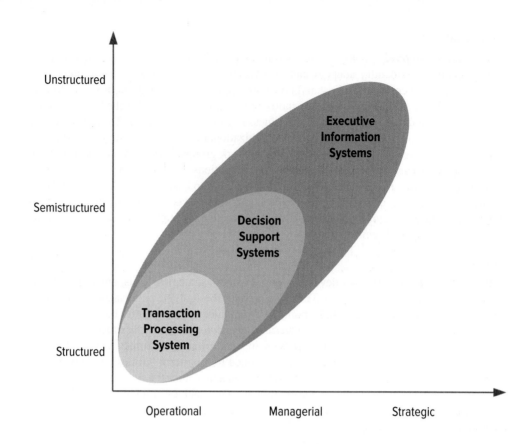

FIGURE 9.5

Primary Types of MIS
Systems for Decision
Making.

Unstructured

Semistructured

Structured

**Executive
Information
Systems**

**Decision
Support
Systems**

**Transaction
Processing
System**

Operational   Managerial   Strategic

example of a TPS is an operational accounting system such as a payroll system or an order-entry system.

Using systems thinking, we can see that the inputs for a TPS are *source documents*, which describes the original transaction record along with details such as its date, purpose, and amount spent and includes cash receipts, canceled checks, invoices, customer refunds, employee time sheet, etc.. Source documents for a payroll system can include time sheets, wage rates, and employee benefit reports. Transformation includes common procedures such as creating, reading, updating, and deleting (commonly referred to as CRUD) employee records, along with calculating the payroll and summarizing benefits. The output includes cutting the paychecks and generating payroll reports. Figure 9.6 demonstrates the systems thinking view of a TPS.[3]

FIGURE 9.6

Systems Thinking Example
of a TPS.

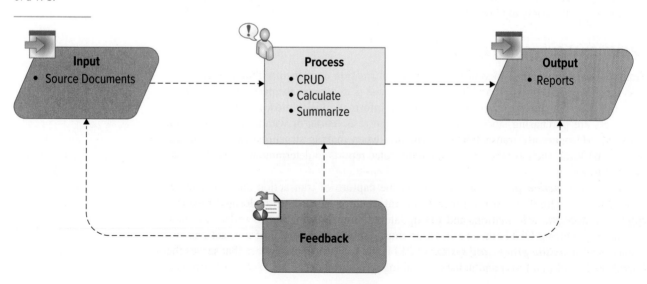

Input
• Source Documents

Process
• CRUD
• Calculate
• Summarize

Output
• Reports

Feedback

MANAGERIAL SUPPORT SYSTEMS

Analytical information encompasses all organizational information, and its primary purpose is to support the performance of managerial analysis or semistructured decisions. Analytical information includes transactional information along with other information such as market and industry information. Examples of analytical information are trends, sales, product statistics, and future growth projections. Managers use analytical information when making important semistructured decisions, such as whether the organization should build a new manufacturing plant or hire additional sales reps.

Online analytical processing (OLAP) is the manipulation of information to create business intelligence in support of strategic decision making. *Decision support systems (DSSs)* model information using OLAP, which provides assistance in evaluating and choosing among different courses of action. DSSs enable high-level managers to examine and manipulate large amounts of detailed data from different internal and external sources. Analyzing complex relationships among thousands or even millions of data items to discover patterns, trends, and exception conditions is one of the key uses associated with a DSS. For example, doctors may enter symptoms into a decision support system so it can help diagnose and treat patients. Insurance companies also use a DSS to gauge the risk of providing insurance to drivers who have imperfect driving records. One company found that married women who are homeowners with one speeding ticket are rarely cited for speeding again. Armed with this business intelligence, the company achieved a cost advantage by lowering insurance rates to this specific group of customers. The following are common DSS analysis techniques.

What-If Analysis

What-if analysis checks the impact of a change in a variable or assumption on the model. For example, "What will happen to the supply chain if a hurricane in South Carolina reduces holding inventory from 30 percent to 10 percent?" A user would be able to observe and evaluate any changes that occurred to the values in the model, especially to a variable such as profits. Users repeat this analysis with different variables until they understand all the effects of various situations.

Sensitivity Analysis

Sensitivity analysis, a special case of what-if analysis, is the study of the impact on other variables when one variable is changed repeatedly. Sensitivity analysis is useful when users are uncertain about the assumptions made in estimating the value of certain key variables. For example, repeatedly changing revenue in small increments to determine its effects on other variables would help a manager understand the impact of various revenue levels on other decision factors.

Goal-Seeking Analysis

Goal-seeking analysis finds the inputs necessary to achieve a goal such as a desired level of output. It is the reverse of what-if and sensitivity analysis. Instead of observing how changes in a variable affect other variables, goal-seeking analysis sets a target value (a goal) for a variable and then repeatedly changes other variables until the target value is achieved. For example, goal-seeking analysis could determine how many customers must purchase a new product to increase gross profits to $5 million.

Optimization Analysis

Optimization analysis, an extension of goal-seeking analysis, finds the optimum value for a target variable by repeatedly changing other variables, subject to specified constraints. By changing revenue and cost variables in an optimization analysis, managers can calculate the highest potential profits. Constraints on revenue and cost variables can be taken into consideration, such as limits on the amount of raw materials the company can afford to purchase and limits on employees available to meet production needs.

Figure 9.7 shows the common systems view of a DSS. Figure 9.8 shows how TPSs supply transactional data to a DSS. The DSS then summarizes and aggregates the information from the different TPSs, which assist managers in making semistructured decisions.

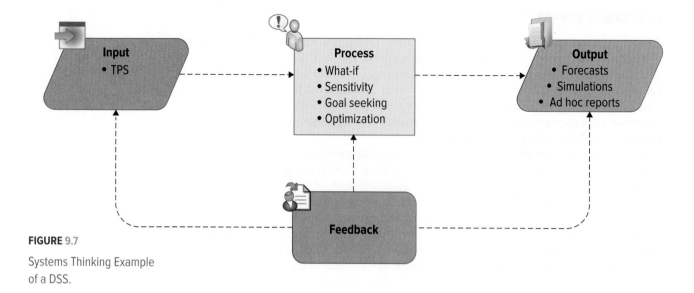

FIGURE 9.7

Systems Thinking Example
of a DSS.

STRATEGIC SUPPORT SYSTEMS

Decision making at the strategic level requires both business intelligence and knowledge to support the uncertainty and complexity associated with business strategies. An *executive information system (EIS)* is a specialized DSS that supports senior-level executives and unstructured, long-term, nonroutine decisions requiring judgment, evaluation, and insight. These decisions do not have a right or wrong answer, only efficient and effective answers. Moving up through the organizational pyramid, managers deal less with the details ("finer" information) and more with meaningful aggregations of information ("coarser" information). *Granularity* refers to the level of detail in the model or the decision-making process. The greater the granularity, the deeper the level of detail or fineness of data (see Figure 9.9).

A DSS differs from an EIS in that an EIS requires data from external sources to support unstructured decisions (see Figure 9.10). This is not to say that DSSs never use data from external sources, but typically DSS semistructured decisions rely on internal data only.

Visualization produces graphical displays of patterns and complex relationships in large amounts of data. Executive information systems use visualization to deliver specific key information to top managers at a glance, with little or no interaction with the system. A common tool that supports visualization is a *digital dashboard*, which tracks key performance

FIGURE 9.8

Interaction Between
TPS and DSS to Support
Semistructured Decisions.

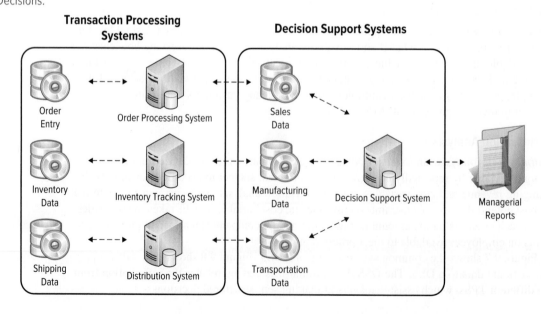

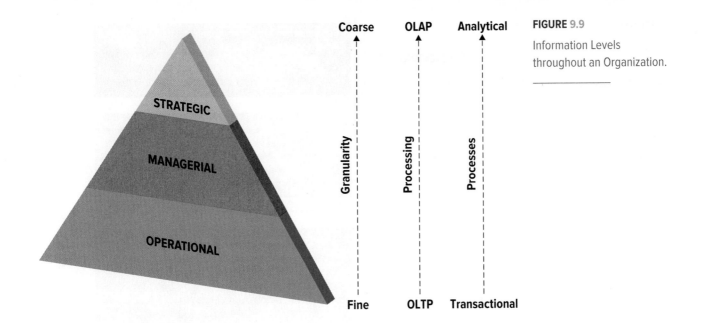

FIGURE 9.9

Information Levels throughout an Organization.

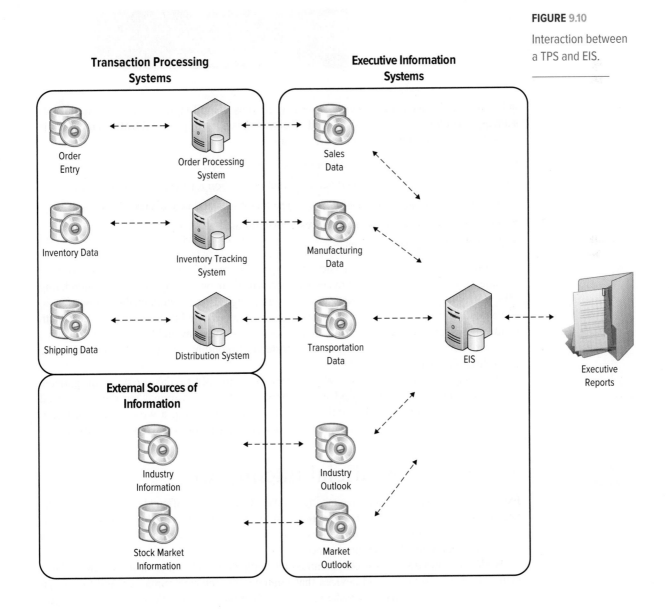

FIGURE 9.10

Interaction between a TPS and EIS.

FIGURE 9.11

Digital Dashboard Analytical
Capabilities.

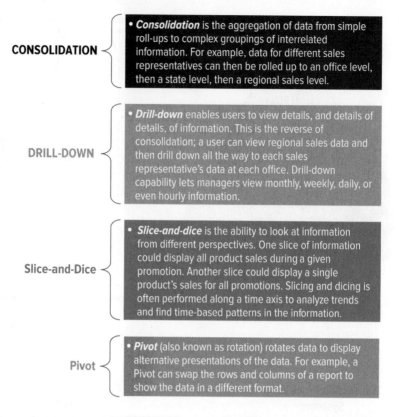

CONSOLIDATION {
- *Consolidation* is the aggregation of data from simple roll-ups to complex groupings of interrelated information. For example, data for different sales representatives can then be rolled up to an office level, then a state level, then a regional sales level.

DRILL-DOWN {
- *Drill-down* enables users to view details, and details of details, of information. This is the reverse of consolidation; a user can view regional sales data and then drill down all the way to each sales representative's data at each office. Drill-down capability lets managers view monthly, weekly, daily, or even hourly information.

Slice-and-Dice {
- *Slice-and-dice* is the ability to look at information from different perspectives. One slice of information could display all product sales during a given promotion. Another slice could display a single product's sales for all promotions. Slicing and dicing is often performed along a time axis to analyze trends and find time-based patterns in the information.

Pivot {
- *Pivot* (also known as rotation) rotates data to display alternative presentations of the data. For example, a Pivot can swap the rows and columns of a report to show the data in a different format.

indicators (KPIs) and critical success factors (CSFs) by compiling information from multiple sources and tailoring it to meet user needs. Following is a list of potential features included in a dashboard designed for a manufacturing team:

- A hot list of key performance indicators, refreshed every 15 minutes.
- A running line graph of planned versus actual production for the past 24 hours.
- A table showing actual versus forecasted product prices and inventories.
- A list of outstanding alerts and their resolution status.
- A graph of stock market prices.

Digital dashboards, whether basic or comprehensive, deliver results quickly. As they become easier to use, more employees can perform their own analyses without inundating MIS staff with questions and requests for reports. Digital dashboards enable employees to move beyond reporting to using information to directly increase business performance. With them, employees can react to information as soon as it becomes available and make decisions, solve problems, and change strategies daily instead of monthly. Digital dashboards offer the capabilities detailed in Figure 9.11.

One thing to remember when making decisions is the old saying "Garbage in, garbage out." If the transactional data used in the support system are wrong, then the managerial analysis will be wrong and the DSS will simply assist in making a wrong decision faster. Managers should also ask, "What is the DSS *not* telling me before I make my final decision?"

The Future: Artificial Intelligence

Executive information systems are starting to take advantage of artificial intelligence to facilitate unstructured strategic decision making. *Artificial intelligence (AI)* simulates human thinking and behavior, such as the ability to reason and learn. Its ultimate goal is to build a system that can mimic human intelligence.

Intelligent systems are various commercial applications of artificial intelligence. They include sensors, software, and devices that emulate and enhance human capabilities, learn or understand from experience, make sense of ambiguous or contradictory information, and even use reasoning to solve problems and make decisions effectively. Intelligent systems perform such tasks as boosting productivity in factories by monitoring equipment and signaling when preventive maintenance is required. They are beginning to show up everywhere:

- At Manchester Airport in England, the Hefner AI Robot Cleaner alerts passengers to security and nonsmoking rules while it scrubs up to 65,600 square feet of floor per day. Laser scanners and ultrasonic detectors keep it from colliding with passengers.

- Shell Oil's SmartPump keeps drivers in their cars on cold, wet winter days. It can service any automobile built after 1987 that has been fitted with a special gas cap and a windshield-mounted transponder that tells the robot where to insert the pump.

- Matsushita's courier robot navigates hospital hallways, delivering patient files, X-ray films, and medical supplies.

- The FireFighter AI Robot can extinguish flames at chemical plants and nuclear reactors with water, foam, powder, or inert gas. The robot puts distance between human operators and the fire.[4]

AI systems increase the speed and consistency of decision making, solve problems with incomplete information, and resolve complicated issues that cannot be solved by conventional computing. There are many categories of AI systems; five of the most familiar are (1) expert systems, (2) neural networks, (3) genetic algorithms, (4) intelligent agents, and (5) virtual reality (see Figure 9.12).

EXPERT SYSTEMS

Expert systems are computerized advisory programs that imitate the reasoning processes of experts in solving difficult problems. Typically, they include a knowledge base containing various accumulated experience and a set of rules for applying the knowledge base to each particular situation. Expert systems are the most common form of AI in the business arena because they fill the gap when human experts are difficult to find or retain or are too expensive. The best-known systems play chess and assist in medical diagnosis.

NEURAL NETWORKS

A *neural network*, also called an artificial neural network, is a category of AI that attempts to emulate the way the human brain works. Neural networks analyze large quantities of information to establish patterns and characteristics in situations where the logic or rules are unknown. Neural networks' many features include:

- Learning and adjusting to new circumstances on their own.
- Lending themselves to massive parallel processing.

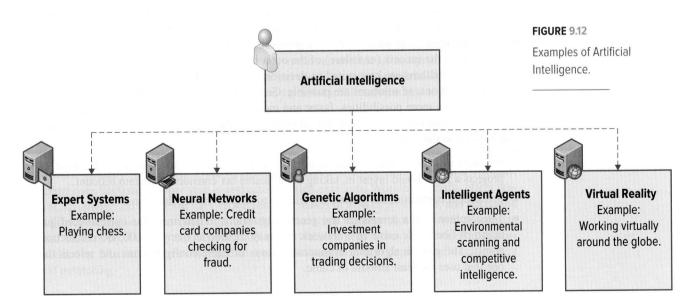

FIGURE 9.12

Examples of Artificial Intelligence.

Artificial Intelligence

Expert Systems
Example: Playing chess.

Neural Networks
Example: Credit card companies checking for fraud.

Genetic Algorithms
Example: Investment companies in trading decisions.

Intelligent Agents
Example: Environmental scanning and competitive intelligence.

Virtual Reality
Example: Working virtually around the globe.

1. What are the three levels of management found in a company? What types of decisions are made at each level?

2. Define transaction processing systems and describe the role they play in a business.

3. Define decision support systems and describe the role they play in a business.

4. Define expert systems and describe the role they play in a business.

5. What are the capabilities associated with digital dashboards?

6. What are the common DSS analysis techniques?

7. How does an electronic spreadsheet program, such as Excel, provide decision support capabilities?

8. What is artificial intelligence?

9. What are the five types of AI systems?

✱ MAKING BUSINESS DECISIONS

1. Long-Distance Hugs

Haptic technology digitizes touch. CuteCircuit created the Hug shirt that you can hug and send the exact hug, including strength, pressure, distribution, and even heartbeat, to a long-distance friend who is wearing the partner to your Hug shirt. Ben Hui at Cambridge University is creating hand-squeezes that can be sent by mobile phones. You simply squeeze the phone and your friend feels it, in some form, at the other end. The value of these haptic devices is based on the idea that physical touch is an important element to all human interactions, and if you can transfer the physical touch, you can replicate the emotion. In a group, create a new business product that uses a haptic inter-face. Share your product idea with your peers.

2. IBM Watson

In 2011, the IBM Watson computer defeated the two best contestants in the game show Jeopardy. What made the achievement so remarkable was that the computer had to read the question, understand what was being asked, search through 200 million pages of text, figure out what the best answer would be, and then hit a buzzer before the other contestants. It accomplished all these steps in about 3 seconds. IBM predicts that Watson could be the ultimate researcher, helping professionals in various industries find the information they are looking for in a matter of seconds. What do you think about Watson's powerful services? Do you think you could one day have access to htis powerful technology on your favorite serach engine. How would having an IBM Watson help you in your college career?

3. DSS and EIS

Dr. Rosen runs a large dental conglomerate—Teeth Doctors—that staffs more than 700 dentists in six states. Dr. Rosen is interested in purchasing a competitor called Dentix that has 150 dentists in three additional states. Before deciding whether to purchase Dentix, Dr. Rosen must consider several issues:

- The cost of purchasing Dentix.
- The locations of the Dentix offices.
- The current number of customers per dentist, per office, and per state.
- The merger between the two companies.

- The professional reputation of Dentix.
- Other competitors.

Explain how Dr. Rosen and Teeth Doctors can benefit from the use of information systems to make an accurate business decision in regard to the potential purchase of Dentix.

4. Finding Information on Decision Support Systems

You are working on the sales team for a small catering company that maintains 75 employees and generates $1 million in revenues per year. The owner, Pam Hetz, wants to understand how she can use decision support systems to help grow her business. Pam has an initial understanding of DSS systems and is interested in learning more about what types are available, how they can be used in a small business, and the cost associated with different DSS systems. In a group, create a presentation that discusses DSS systems in detail. Be sure to answer all Pam's questions on DSS systems in the presentation.

5. Searching Telephone Calls

Imagine being able to search a database of customer phone calls to find specific requests or to be able to sort through digital customer complaints to detect the exact moment when the interaction between the customer service representative and the customer went wrong. A new tool called Find It allows the sorting of digital voice records as easily as using Google to sift through documents. Find It is opening limitless business opportunities as organizations begin to understand how they can use this technology to help employees search voice mails or recorded calls for keywords and phrases.

You have recently started your own marketing firm and you want to use the power of Find It to help your customers query all of their unique data records, including digital voice recordings. Now all you need is to prepare your marketing materials to send to potential customers. Create a marketing pitch that you will deliver to customers detailing the business opportunities they could uncover if they purchased Find It. Your marketing pitch can be a one-page document, a catchy tune, a video, or a PowerPoint presentation.

Extending the Organization— Supply Chain Management

10.1. Describe supply chain management along with its impact on business.

10.2. Identify the three components of supply chain management along with the technologies reinventing the supply chain.

LO 10.1 Describe supply chain management along with its impact on business.

Information Technology's Role in the Supply Chain

Supply chain management systems can increase profitability across an organization. For example, a manufacturing plant manager might focus on keeping the inventory of Product A as low as possible, which will directly reduce the manufacturing costs and make the plant manager look great. However, the plant manager and the business might not realize that these savings are causing increased costs in other areas, such as having to pay more to procure raw materials for immediate production needs or increasing costs due to expedited shipping services. Only an end-to-end view or an integrated supply chain would uncover these issues, allowing a firm to adjust business strategies to increase profitability across the enterprise. Supply chain management performs three main business processes (see Figure 10.1):

1. Materials flow from suppliers and their upstream suppliers at all levels.
2. Materials are transformed into semifinished and finished products—the organization's own production processes.
3. Products are distributed to customers and their downstream customers at all levels.

FIGURE 10.1

Typical Supply Chain.

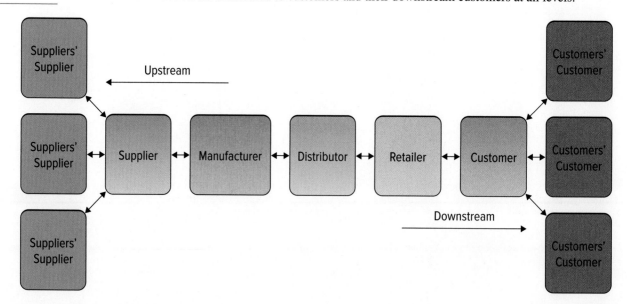

The supply chain is only as strong as its weakest link. Companies use supply chain management metrics to measure the performance of supply chains to identify weak links quickly. A few of the common supply chain management metrics include:

- **Back order:** An unfilled customer order for a product that is out of stock.
- **Inventory cycle time:** The time it takes to manufacture a product and deliver it to the retailer.
- **Customer order cycle time:** The agreed-upon time between the purchase of a product and the delivery of the product.
- **Inventory turnover:** The frequency of inventory replacement.

As companies evolve into extended organizations, the roles of supply chain participants are changing. It is now common for suppliers to be involved in product development and for distributors to act as consultants in brand marketing. The notion of virtually seamless information links within and between organizations is an essential element of integrated supply chains.

Information technology's primary role in SCM is creating the integrations or tight process and information linkages between functions within a firm—such as marketing, sales, finance, manufacturing, and distribution—and between firms, which allow the smooth, synchronized flow of both information and product between customers, suppliers, and transportation providers across the supply chain. Information technology integrates planning, decision-making processes, business operating processes, and information sharing for business performance management (see Figure 10.2).

Supply chain design determines how to structure a supply chain including the product, selection of partners, the location and capacity of warehouses, transportation methods, and supporting management information systems. Considerable evidence shows that this type of supply chain design results in superior supply chain capabilities and profits.

Supply chain visibility is the ability to view all areas up and down the supply chain in real time. To react to demand, an organization needs to know all customer events triggered upstream and downstream and so must their suppliers and their suppliers' suppliers. Without this information, supply chain participants are blind to the supply and demand needs occurring in the marketplace, a factor required to implement successful business strategies. To improve

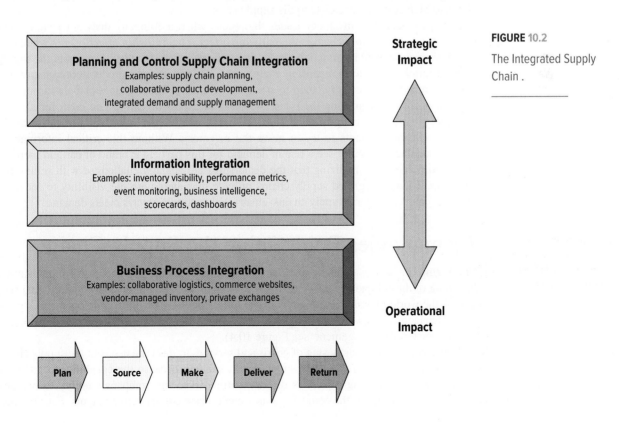

FIGURE 10.2

The Integrated Supply Chain.

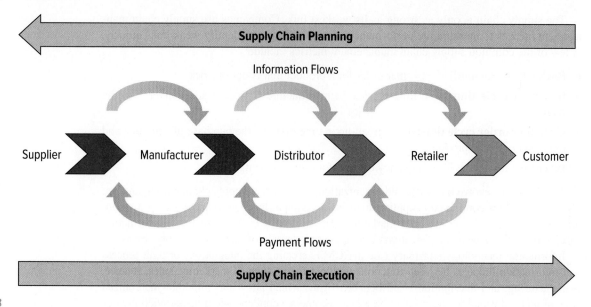

Supply Chain Planning

Information Flows

Supplier → Manufacturer → Distributor → Retailer → Customer

Payment Flows

Supply Chain Execution

FIGURE 10.3

Supply Chain Planning and Supply Chain Execution: Software's Correlation to the Supply Chain.

visibility across the supply chain, firms can use supply chain planning systems and supply chain execution systems.

Supply chain planning systems use advanced mathematical algorithms to improve the flow and efficiency of the supply chain while reducing inventory. To yield accurate results, however, supply chain planning systems require information inputs that are correct and up to date regarding customers, orders, sales, manufacturing, and distribution capabilities.

Ideally, the supply chain consists of multiple firms that function as efficiently and effectively as a single firm, with full information visibility. ***Supply chain execution systems*** ensure supply chain cohesion by automating the different activities of the supply chain. For example, a supply chain execution system might electronically route orders from a manufacturer to a supplier using ***electronic data interchange (EDI)***, a standard format for the electronic exchange of information between supply chain participants. Figure 10.3 details how SCP and SCE software correlate to the supply chain.

A good example of inventory issues that occur when a company does not have a clear vision of its entire supply chain is the bullwhip effect. The ***bullwhip effect*** occurs when distorted product-demand information ripples from one partner to the next throughout the supply chain. The misinformation regarding a slight rise in demand for a product could cause different members in the supply chain to stockpile inventory. These changes ripple throughout the supply chain, magnifying the issue and creating excess inventory and costs for all. For example, if a car dealership is having a hard time moving a particular brand of car, it might offer significant discounts to try to move the inventory. Without this critical information, the car manufacturer might see a rise in demand for this particular brand of car and increase production orders, not realizing that the dealerships are actually challenged with selling the inventory. Today, integrated supply chains provide managers with the visibility to see their suppliers' and customers' supply chains, ensuring that supply always meets demand.

LO 10.2 Identify the three components of supply chain management along with the technologies reinventing the supply chain.

Technologies Reinventing the Supply Chain

Optimizing the supply chain is a critical business process for any successful organization. Just think of the complexity of Walmart's supply chain and the billions of products being sent around the world guaranteeing every shelf is fully stocked. The three components of supply chain management on which companies focus to find efficiencies include procurement, logistics, and materials management (see Figure 10.4).

Procurement is the purchasing of goods and services to meet the needs of the supply chain. The procurement process is a key supply chain strategy because the capability to purchase input materials at the right price is directly correlated to the company's ability to operate. Without the right inputs, the company simply can't create cost-effective outputs. For example,

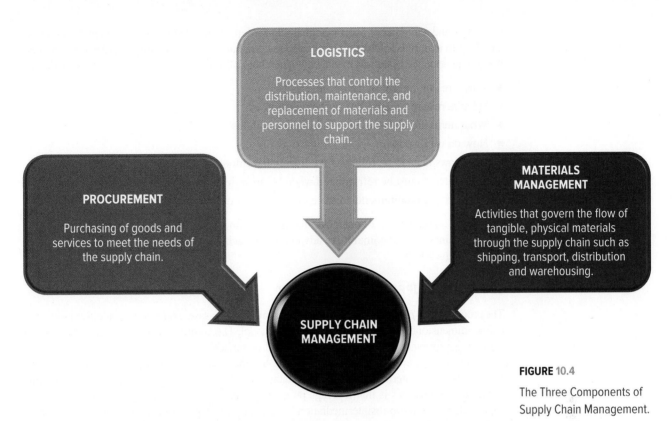

LOGISTICS

Processes that control the distribution, maintenance, and replacement of materials and personnel to support the supply chain.

PROCUREMENT

Purchasing of goods and services to meet the needs of the supply chain.

MATERIALS MANAGEMENT

Activities that govern the flow of tangible, physical materials through the supply chain such as shipping, transport, distribution and warehousing.

SUPPLY CHAIN MANAGEMENT

FIGURE 10.4

The Three Components of Supply Chain Management.

if McDonald's could not procure potatoes or had to purchase potatoes at an outrageous price, it would be unable to create and sell its famous french fries. In fact, procuring the right size potatoes that can produce the famous long french fries is challenging in some countries where locally grown potatoes are too small. Procurement can help a company answer the following questions:

- What quantity of raw materials should we purchase to minimize spoilage?
- How can we guarantee that our raw materials meet production needs?
- At what price can we purchase materials to guarantee profitability?
- Can purchasing all products from a single vendor provide additional discounts?

Logistics includes the processes that control the distribution, maintenance, and replacement of materials and personnel to support the supply chain. Recall from the value chain analysis in Chapter 1 that the primary value activities for an organization include inbound and outbound logistics. *Inbound logistics* acquires raw materials and resources and distributes them to manufacturing as required. *Outbound logistics* distributes goods and services to customers. Logistics controls processes inside a company (warehouse logistics) and outside a company (transport logistics) and focuses on the physical execution part of the supply chain. Logistics includes the increasingly complex management of processes, information, and communication to take a product from cradle to grave. *Cradle-to-grave* provides logistics support throughout the entire system or life of the product. Logistics can help a company answer the following questions:

- What is the quickest way to deliver products to our customers?
- What is the optimal way to place items in the warehouse for picking and packing?
- What is the optimal path to an item in the warehouse?
- What path should the vehicles follow when delivering the goods? What areas or regions are the trucks covering?

Materials management includes activities that govern the flow of tangible, physical materials through the supply chain such as shipping, transport, distribution, and warehousing. In materials management, you focus on quality and quantity of materials as well as on how you will plan, acquire, use, and dispose of such materials. It can include the handling of liquids, fuel, produce, and plants and a number of other potentially hazardous items. Materials management focuses on handling all materials safely, efficiently, and in compliance with regulatory requirements and disposal requirements. Materials management can help a company answer the following concerns:

- What are our current inventory levels?
- What items are running low in the warehouse?
- What items are at risk of spoiling in the warehouse?
- How do we dispose of spoiled items?
- What laws need to be followed for storing hazardous materials?
- Which items must be refrigerated when being stored and transported?
- What are the requirements to store or transport fragile items?

As with all other areas of business, disruptive technologies are continuously being deployed to help businesses find competitive advantages in each component of the supply chain, as outlined in Figure 10.5.

3D PRINTING SUPPORTS PROCUREMENT

The process of *3D printing* (additive manufacturing) builds—layer by layer in an additive process— a three-dimensional solid object from a digital model. The additive manufacturing process of 3D printing is profoundly different from traditional manufacturing processes. The *Financial Times* and other sources are stating that 3D printing has the potential to be vastly more disruptive to business than the Internet. That is a bold statement! The reason people are betting on 3D printing to disrupt business is that it brings production closer to users, thus eliminating steps in the supply chain similar to disintermediation by the Internet. Three-dimensional printing also promotes mass customization, small production batches, and reduction in inventory. Traditionally, the costs associated with 3D printing made it accessible only to large corporations. Now with

FIGURE 10.5

Disruptive Business Technologies.

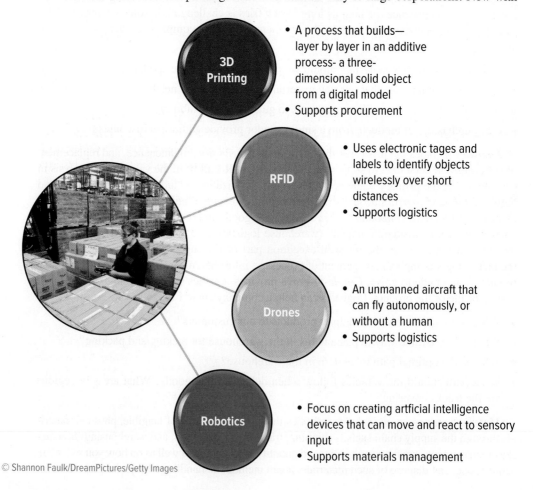

- **3D Printing**
  - A process that builds— layer by layer in an additive process- a three- dimensional solid object from a digital model
  - Supports procurement

- **RFID**
  - Uses electronic tages and labels to identify objects wirelessly over short distances
  - Supports logistics

- **Drones**
  - An unmanned aircraft that can fly autonomously, or without a human
  - Supports logistics

- **Robotics**
  - Focus on creating artficial intelligence devices that can move and react to sensory input
  - Supports materials management

© Shannon Faulk/DreamPictures/Getty Images

inexpensive printers, scanners, and applications, the technology is accessible to small and mid-sized businesses and home users. With the advances in 3D printing, the need to procure materials will become far easier because businesses can simply print the parts and components required for the production process. There is no doubt about it—3D printing will affect production process and supply chains and cause business disruption. These printers are creating auto parts, cell phone covers, jewelry, toys, bicycles, and manufacturing prototypes for testing purposes.

To print a 3D product, users create a digital model that is sliced into thin cross-sections called layers. During the printing process, the 3D printer starts at the bottom of the design and adds successive layers of material to complete the project. *Computer-aided design/computer-aided manufacturing (CAD/CAM)* systems are used to create the digital designs and then manufacture the products. For example, a user creates a design with a CAD application and then manufactures the product by using CAM systems. Before 3D printers existed, creating a prototype was time-consuming and expensive, requiring skilled craftsmen and specific machinery. Instead of sending modeling instructions to a production company, advances in 3D printing allow users to create prototypes and products on demand from their desks. Shipping required parts from around the world could become obsolete because the spare parts can now be 3D printed on demand. This could have a major impact on how businesses large and small operate and interact on a global scale in the future.

The ***maker movement*** is a cultural trend that places value on an individual's ability to be a creator of things as well as a consumer of things. In this culture, individuals who create things are called "makers." The movement is growing rapidly and is expected to be economically disruptive; as ordinary people become more self-sufficient, they will be able to make their own products instead of procuring brand-name products from retail stores. Makers come from all walks of life, with diverse skill sets and interests. The thing they have in common is creativity, an interest in design, and access to tools and raw materials that make production possible. The growth of the maker movement is often attributed to the rise of community ***makerspaces***, a community center that provides technology, manufacturing equipment, and educational opportunities to the public that would otherwise be inaccessible or unaffordable. Although the majority of makers are hobbyists, entrepreneurs and small manufacturers are also taking advantage of the classes and tools available in makerspaces.

RFID SUPPORTS LOGISTICS

A television commercial shows a man in a uniform quietly moving through a family home. The man replaces the empty cereal box with a full one just before a hungry child opens the cabinet; he then opens a new sack of dog food as the hungry bulldog eyes him warily; and, finally, he hands a full bottle of shampoo to the man in the shower whose bottle had just run out. The next wave in supply chain management will be home-based supply chain fulfillment. Walgreens is differentiating itself from other national chains by marketing itself as the family's just-in-time supplier. Consumers today are becoming incredibly comfortable with the idea of going online to purchase products when they want, how they want, and at the price they want. Walgreens is developing custom websites for each household, which allow families to order electronically and then at their convenience go to the store to pick up their goods at a special self-service counter or the drive-through window. Walgreens is making a promise that goes beyond low prices and customer service and extends right into the home.

Radio-frequency identification (RFID) uses electronic tags and labels to identify objects wirelessly over short distances. It holds the promise of replacing existing identification technologies such as the bar code. RFID tags are evolving, too, and the advances will provide more granular information to enterprise software. Today's tags can store an electronic product code. In time, tags could hold more information, making them portable mini-databases. *RFID's electronic product code (RFID EPC)* promotes serialization or the ability to track individual items by using the unique serial number associated with each RFID tag. Although a bar code might identify a product such as a bottle of salad dressing, an RFID EPC tag can identify each specific bottle and allow item-level tracking to determine whether the product has passed its expiration date. Businesses can tell automatically where all its items are in the supply chain just by gathering the data from the RFID chips. The possibilities of RFID are endless, and one area it is affecting is logistics. RFID tags for applications such as highway toll collection and container tracking remain in continuous use for several years. Like regular electronic components, the tags are adhered to rigid substrates and packaged in plastic enclosures. In contrast, tags on shipping cartons are used for a much shorter time and are then destroyed. Disposable tags are adhered to printed, flexible labels pasted onto the carton, and these smart labels contain an RFID chip and antenna on the back. A thermal printer/encoder prints alphanumeric and bar code data on the labels while encoding the chip at the same time. Figures 10.6. and 10.7 display how an RFID system works in the supply chain.

FIGURE 10.6

Three RFID Components.

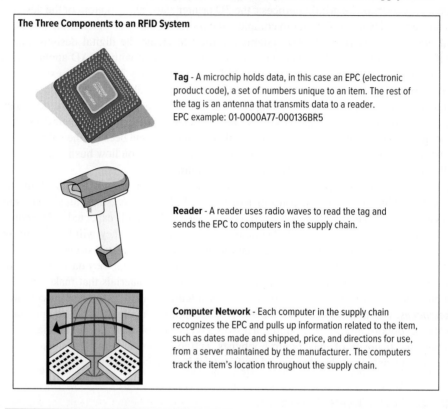

The Three Components to an RFID System

Tag - A microchip holds data, in this case an EPC (electronic product code), a set of numbers unique to an item. The rest of the tag is an antenna that transmits data to a reader. EPC example: 01-0000A77-000136BR5

Reader - A reader uses radio waves to read the tag and sends the EPC to computers in the supply chain.

Computer Network - Each computer in the supply chain recognizes the EPC and pulls up information related to the item, such as dates made and shipped, price, and directions for use, from a server maintained by the manufacturer. The computers track the item's location throughout the supply chain.

FIGURE 10.7

RFID in the Supply Chain.

RFID in the Retail Supply Chain
RFID tags are added to every product and shipping box. At every step of an item's journey, a reader scans one of the tags and updates the information on the server.

The Manufacturer
A reader scans the tags
as items leave the factory.

The Distribution Center
Readers in the unloading area scan the tags on arriving boxes and update inventory, avoiding the need to open packages.

The Store
Tags are scanned upon arrival to update inventory. At the racks, readers scan tags as shirts are stocked. At the checkout counter, a cashier can scan individual items with a handheld reader. As items leave the store, inventory is updated. Manufacturers and retailers can observe sales patterns in real time and make swift decisions about production, ordering, and pricing.

The Home
The consumer can have the tag disabled at the store for privacy or place readers in closets to keep track of clothes. With customers' approval, stores can follow purchasing patterns and notify them of sales.

FIGURE 10.8

Amazon Drones Delivering Packages.

© Mopic/Shutterstock

DRONES SUPPORT LOGISTICS

A *drone* is an unmanned aircraft that can fly autonomously, or without a human. Amazon.com is piloting drone aircraft that could someday deliver customers' packages in half an hour or less (see Figure 10.8). UPS and FedEx have also been experimenting with their own versions of flying parcel carriers. Drones are already here and use GPS to help coordinate the logistics of package delivery. The problems with drones include FAA approval and the advanced ability to detect and avoid objects. GPS coordinates can easily enable the drone to find the appropriate package delivery location, but objects not included in the GPS, such as cars, dogs, and children, will need to be detected and avoided.

FedEx founder Fred Smith stated that his drones are up and running in the lab; all he requires to move his fleet of drones from the lab to production is approval from regulators. "We have all this stuff working in the lab right now, we don't need to reinvent the wheel," remarks Smith. "We need a set of rules from the FAA. It's just a matter of getting the laws in place so companies can begin building to those specifications and doing some real field testing."

ROBOTICS SUPPORTS MATERIALS MANAGEMENT

Robotics focuses on creating artificial intelligence devices that can move and react to sensory input. The term *robot* was coined by Czech playwright Karl Capek in his play *R.U.R.* (*Rossum's Universal Robots*), which opened in Prague in 1921. *Robota* is the Czech word for "forced labor." The term *robotics* was introduced by writer Isaac Asimov; in his science fiction book *I, Robot,* published in 1950, he presented three laws of robotics:

1. A robot may not injure a human being, or, through inaction, allow a human being to come to harm.

2. A robot must obey the orders given it by human beings except where such orders would conflict with the First Law.

3. A robot must protect its own existence as long as such protection does not conflict with the First or Second Law.

You can find robots in factories performing high-precision tasks, in homes vacuuming the floor and the pool, and in dangerous situations such as cleaning toxic wastes or defusing bombs. Amazon alone has more than 10,000 robots in its warehouses, picking, packing, and managing materials to fulfill customer orders (see Figure 10.9). The robots are made by Kiva Systems, a company Amazon bought for $775 million in 2012. Kiva pitches its robots—which can cost between a few million dollars and as much as roughly $20 million—as simplifying and reducing costs via materials management. The robots are tied into a complex grid that optimizes item placement in the warehouse and allows the robots to pick the inventory items and bring them to the workers for packing. Watching an order fulfillment center equipped with Kiva robots is amazing; the operators stand still while the products come to them. Inventory pods store the products that are carried and transferred by a small army of little orange robots, eliminating the need for traditional systems such as conveyors and sorters. Though assessing the costs and benefits of robots versus human labor can be difficult, Kiva boasts that a packer working with its robots can fulfill three to four times as many orders per hour. Zappos, Staples, and Amazon are just a few of the companies taking advantage of the latest innovation in warehouse management by replacing traditional order fulfillment technologies such as conveyor belts with Kiva's little orange robots.

THE EXTENDED SUPPLY CHAIN

As the supply chain management market matures, it is becoming even more sophisticated and incorporating additional functionality such as marketing, customer service, and even product development to its extended supply chain. Advanced communications tools, easy-to-use decision support systems, and building trust among participants when sharing information are all making the home-based supply chain possible. A few of the fastest-growing extensions for supply chain management are included in Figure 10.11.

FIGURE 10.9

Kiva Robots.

© Beth Hall/Bloomberg via Getty Images

Supply chain event management (SCEM)

Enables an organization to react more quickly to resolve supply chain issues. SCEM software increases real-time information sharing among supply chain partners and decreases their response time to unplanned events. SCEM demand will skyrocket as more and more organizations begin to discover the benefits of real-time supply chain monitoring.

Selling chain management

Applies technology to the activities in the order life cycle from inquiry to sale.

Collaborative engineering

Allows an organization to reduce the cost and time required during the design process of a product.

Collaborative demand planning

Helps organizations reduce their investment in inventory, while improving customer satisfaction through product availability.

FIGURE 10.11

Extending the Supply Chain.

OPENING CASE STUDY QUESTIONS

1. Identify how connected cars can impact the supply chain.

2. Explain how connected cars can use RFID to improve the efficiency and effectiveness of drivers in the supply chain.

3. Explain how connected cars can use robotics to improve the supply chain?

Chapter Ten Case: ETSY

What does orthopedic surgery and governing a country have in common with knitting socks, scarves, and headbands? Nothing except the salary. Hobbyist Alicia Shaffer is earning $80,000 a month selling her handmade goods on Etsy, which adds up to an annual revenue of $960,000. That is the same amount as an orthopedic surgeon makes, and more than twice as much as the United States president makes.

Etsy is an online craft makerspace for handmade goods. ETSY is building a human, authentic, and community-centric makerspace that uses the power of business to create a better world. In an Etsy

Economy, creative entrepreneurs can find meaningful work selling their goods in both global and local markets, where thoughtful consumers can discover those goods and build relationships with the people who make and sell them. It's an ecosystem that connects buyers around the world to the communities where Etsy shop owners live, work, and create. As Etsy grows it is committed to its mission ensuring its core values are woven into all decisions it makes for the long-term health of its business, from the sourcing of office supplies to employee benefits to the items sold in its marketspace.

Shaffer's company ThreeBirdNest is named after her bird tattoo that honors her three children. Shaffer attributes her success to deep-seated motivation and access to a global supply chain through Etsy. ThreeBirdNest launched in 2011, when she made a few headbands for the small women's clothing boutique she ran in Livermore, California. Her headbands were so popular she decided to start selling them online. "I opened an Etsy shop, figuring I'd help pay for my kids' soccer and dance lessons to supplement the boutique's sales," states Shaffer. "I was recovering from the failure of a business I'd run selling baby products—handmade slings, carriers, and blankets. After that business tanked in the recession, I'd lost a little bit of confidence in my ability to be an entrepreneur."

In the first few weeks after its launch, ThreeBirdNest made 90 sales. Shaffer credits much of the traffic to Pinterest—she pinned her items. Still, "It was absolutely mindboggling. I thought it was a complete fluke." But a few months later Shaffer found herself hiring a friend to help with shipping as orders began flowing like water. Through its independent website and Etsy shop, ThreeBirdNest receives an average of 150 orders per day, with most orders consisting of three items. Around the holidays, that number goes up to 700 to 1,200 orders per day. Last January, the business raked in a total of $128,000 in sales. Since its launch, it has made 100,000 sales on Etsy alone. ThreeBirdNest is unusually successful on Etsy, as most Etsy shop owners feel lucky to sell 10 pieces a month, and 65% of Etsy sellers make less than $100 from their shops in a year. Etsy makerspace crafters usually need day jobs to support their hobbies. [1]

Questions

1. Without makerspace's like Etsy how would crafters market and sell their products?

2. Explain how the bullwhip effect could impact a crafter on Etsy.

3. Explain procurement, logistics, and materials management for ThreeBirdNest.

4. What are some advantages and disadvantages of using Etsy to sell good and access its global supply chain?

10.1. Describe supply chain management along with its impact on business.

A supply chain consists of all parties involved, directly or indirectly, in obtaining raw materials or a product. To automate and enable sophisticated decision making in these critical areas, companies are turning to systems that provide demand forecasting, inventory control, and information flows between suppliers and customers. Supply chain management (SCM) is the management of information flows between and among activities in a supply chain to maximize total supply chain effectiveness and corporate profitability. In the past, manufacturing efforts focused primarily on quality improvement efforts within the company; today these efforts reach across the entire supply chain, including customers, customers' customers, suppliers, and suppliers' suppliers. Today's supply chain is an intricate network of business partners linked through communication channels and relationships.

Improved visibility across the supply chain and increased profitability for the firm are the primary business benefits received when implementing supply chain management systems. Supply chain visibility is the ability to view all areas up and down the supply chain in real time. The primary challenges associated with supply chain management include costs and complexity. The next wave in supply chain management will be home-based supply chain fulfillment. No more running to the store to replace your products because your store will come to you as soon as you need a new product.

10.2. Identify the three components of supply chain management along with the technologies reinventing the supply chain.

The three components of supply chain management on which companies focus to find efficiencies include procurement, logistics, and materials management. Procurement is the purchasing of goods and services to meet the needs of the supply chain. Materials management includes activities that govern the flow of tangible, physical materials through the supply chain such as shipping, transport, distribution, and warehousing. The technologies reinventing the supply chain include 3D printing, RFID, drones, and robotics.

1. What are the five primary activities in a supply chain?
2. What is the bullwhip effect and how can it affect a supply chain and a firm's profitability?
3. Where are the customer's customers in a typical supply chain?
4. Where are the supplier's suppliers in a typical supply chain?
5. What is procurement and how does it impact the supply chain?
6. What is logistics and how does it impact the supply chain?
7. What is materials management and how does it impact the supply chain?
8. What is RFID's primary purpose in the supply chain?

1. 3D Printing for Poverty

Thirty-three-year-old Kodjo Afate Grikou wanted to help his community in West Africa to print necessities that they can't source locally, such as kitchen utensils for cooking. The structure of the 3D printer he had in mind uses very little in terms of new parts because it is mostly made up of ewaste and scrap metal. Before building this printer, he set up his project on the European social funding website, ulule. The project received more than $10,000, despite the printer costing only $1,000, mostly through purchasing new parts that he couldn't find locally. Grikou hopes that his innovation will inspire teenagers and young people in his community to attend school and gain an education so they can make further life-changing developments that will benefit not only their lives but also others around them. In a group, brainstorm ways 3D printing can help rural communities fight poverty.

- What is the quickest way to deliver products to our customers?
- What is the optimal way to place items in the warehouse for picking and packing?
- What is the optimal path to an item in the warehouse?
- What path should the vehicles follow when delivering the goods?
- What areas or regions are the trucks covering?

2. 3D Printing Weapons

In 1976, the big movie studios sued Sony for releasing the first VCR because it advertised it as "a way of recording feature-length movies from TV to VHS tape for watching and taking over to friends' houses." Over the next eight years Universal Studios, along with other powerful media groups, fought Sony over creating the device because it could allow users to violate copyright laws. The courts went back and forth for years attempting to determine whether Sony would be held liable for creating a device that enabled users to break copyright laws. In 1984, the U.S. Supreme Court ruled in favor of Sony: "If a device is capable of sustaining a substantial noninfringing use, then it is lawful to make and sell that device. That is, if the device is merely capable of doing something legit, it is legal to make no matter how it is used in practice."

Just think of cars, knives, guns, and computers as they are all used to break the law, and nobody would be allowed to produce them if they were held responsible for how people used them. Do you agree that if you make a tool and sell it to someone who goes on to break the law, you should be held responsible? Do you agree that 3D printers will be used to infringe copyright, trademark, and patent protections? If so, should 3D printers be illegal?

3. Analyzing Dell's Supply Chain Management System

Dell's supply chain strategy is legendary. Essentially, if you want to build a successful SCM system your best bet is to model your SCM system after Dell's. In a team, research Dell's supply chain management strategy on the web and create a report discussing any new SCM updates and strategies the company is using that were not discussed in this text. Be sure to include a graphical presentation of Dell's current supply chain model.

4. Robots Took My Job

Kiva's little orange robots are becoming the latest craze and a truly fascinating innovation in warehouse management. Kiva's robots are replacing conveyor belts and carousels at the order fulfillment warehouses of retailers such as Zappos, Staples, and Amazon. Kiva Mobile Fulfillment System uses a breakthrough parallel processing approach to order fulfillment with a unique material handling system that simultaneously improves productivity, speed, accuracy, and flexibility.

- How can Kiva robots help distribution centers attain flexible, efficient order fulfillment?
- What other types of businesses could use Kiva robots to improve distribution productivity?
- How would warehouse employees react if they were told the company was implementing Kiva robots?

5. Fixing the Post Office

Is there anything more frustrating than waiting in line at the Post Office? Well, not only are those lines frustrating, they are also becoming unprofitable. The United States Postal Service is looking at a $13 billion loss in 2011, one of the greatest catastrophes in its history. What is killing the Post Office? Perhaps it is Stamps.com, a website that allows you to customize and print your own stamps 24 hours a day. Getting married? You can place a photo of the happy couple right on the stamp for the invitations. Starting a business? You can place your business logo on your stamps. Stamps.com even keeps track of all of a customer's postal spending using client codes, and it can recommend optimal delivery methods. Plus, Stamps.com gives you postage discounts you can't even get at the Post Office or with a postage meter.

- What new products are stealing business from the Post Office?
- How could the Post Office create new products and services to help grow its business?
- How could the Post Office use cost, quality, delivery, flexibility, and service to revamp its operations management processes?

Building a Customer-centric Organization—Customer Relationship Management

11.1. Describe customer relationship management along with its importance to a business.

11.2. Differentiate between operational and analytical customer relationship management.

11.3. Identify the three current trends extending customer relationship management.

LO 11.1 Describe customer relationship management along with its importance to a business.

Customer Relationship Management

Today, most competitors are simply a mouse-click away, and this intense competition is forcing firms to switch from sales-focused business strategies to customer-focused business strategies. Customers are one of a firm's most valuable assets, and building strong, loyal customer relationships is a key competitive advantage. Harley-Davidson offers an excellent example of a company that knows the value of customer loyalty, and it finds itself in the coveted position of demand outweighing its supply. No other motorcycle in the world has the look, feel, and sound of a Harley-Davidson. Demand for Harley-Davidson motorcycles outweighs supply and some models have up to a two-year waiting list. Knowing the value of its customers, Harley-Davidson started the Harley's Owners Group (HOG), which is the largest motorcycle club in the world with more than 600,000 members. HOG offers a wide array of events, rides, and benefits to its members and is a key competitive advantage as it helps to build a strong sense of community among Harley-Davidson owners. Harley-Davidson has built a customer following that is extremely loyal, a difficult task to accomplish in any industry.

Customer relationship management (CRM) is a means of managing all aspects of a customer's relationship with an organization to increase customer loyalty and retention and an organization's profitability. CRM allows an organization to gain insights into customers' shopping and buying behaviors. Every time a customer communicates with a company, the firm has the chance to build a trusting relationship with that particular customer. Harley-Davidson realizes that it takes more than just building and selling motorcycles to fulfill the dreams of its loyal customers. For this reason, the company strives to deliver unforgettable experiences along with its top-quality products. When the company began selling products online it found itself facing a dilemma—its online strategy for selling accessories directly to consumers would bypass Harley-Davidson's dealers, who depend on the high-margin accessories for store revenues. The solution was to deploy Harley-Davidson.com, which prompts customers to select a participating Harley-Davidson dealership before placing any online orders. The selected dealership is then responsible for fulfilling the order. This strategy ensured that the dealers remained the focus point of each customer's buying experiences. To guarantee that every customer has a highly satisfying online buying experience, the company asks the dealers to agree to a number of standards including:

- Checking online orders twice daily.
- Shipping online orders within 24 hours.
- Responding to customer inquiries within 24 hours.

Harley-Davidson still monitors online customer metrics such as time taken to process orders, number of returned orders, and number of incorrect orders, guaranteeing that the company delivers on its critical success factor of providing prompt, excellent customer service consistently to all its loyal customers.

A primary component of managing a customer relationship is knowing when and why the customer is communicating with the company. Imagine an irate customer who has just spent an hour on the phone with your call center complaining about a defective product. While the customer is on the phone, your sales representative decides to drop by the customer's office in an attempt to sell additional products. Obviously, this is not the ideal time to try to up-sell or cross-sell products to this particular customer. A customer relationship management system would inform the sales representative that the customer was on the phone with customer service and even provide details of the call. Then your sales representative could stop by and offer assistance in resolving the product issue, which might help restore the relationship with the customer and provide opportunities for future sales.

THE POWER OF THE CUSTOMER

A standard rule of business states that the customer is always right. Although most businesses use this as their motto, they do not actually mean it. Ebusiness firms, however, must adhere to this rule as the power of the customer grows exponentially in the information age. Various websites and videos on YouTube reveal the power of the individual consumer (see Figure 11.1). A decade ago if you had a complaint against a company, you could make a phone call or write a letter. Now you can contact hundreds or thousands of people around the globe and voice your complaint or anger with a company or product. You—the customer— can now take your power directly to millions of people, and companies have to listen.

Using CRM metrics to track and monitor performance is a best practice for many companies. Figure 11.2 displays a few common CRM metrics a manager can use to track the success of the system. Just remember that you only want to track between five and seven of the hundreds of CRM metrics available.

Operational and Analytical CRM

LO 11.2 Differentiate between operational and analytical customer relationship management.

The two primary components of a CRM strategy are operational CRM and analytical CRM. *Operational CRM* supports traditional transactional processing for day-to-day front-office operations or systems that deal directly with the customers. *Analytical CRM* supports back-office operations and strategic analysis and includes all systems that do not deal directly with the customers. Figure 11.3 provides an overview of the two. Figure 11.4 shows the different technologies marketing, sales, and customer service departments can use to perform operational CRM.

MARKETING AND OPERATIONAL CRM

Companies are no longer trying to sell one product to as many customers as possible; instead, they are trying to sell one customer as many products as possible. Marketing departments switch to this new way of doing business by using CRM technologies that allow them to gather and analyze customer information to tailor successful marketing campaigns. In fact, a marketing campaign's success is directly proportional to the organization's ability to gather and analyze the right customer information. The three primary operational CRM technologies a marketing department can implement to increase customer satisfaction are:

1. List generator
2. Campaign management
3. Cross-selling and up-selling

List Generator

List generators compile customer information from a variety of sources and segment it for different marketing campaigns. These sources include website visits, questionnaires, surveys,

FIGURE 11.1

The Power of You—Websites
Demonstrating the Power of
the People.

———————————

www.
dontbuydodgechryslervehicles.
com
www.jetbluehostage.com

Sales Metrics	Customer Service Metrics	Marketing Metrics
Number of prospective customers	Cases closed same day	Number of marketing campaigns
Number of new customers	Number of cases handled by agent	New customer retention rates
Number of retained customers	Number of service calls	Number of responses by marketing campaign
Number of open leads	Average number of service requests by type	Number of purchases by marketing campaign
Number of sales calls	Average time to resolution	Revenue generated by marketing campaign
Number of sales calls per lead	Average number of service calls per day	Cost per interaction by marketing campaign
Amount of new revenue	Percentage compliance with service-level agreement	Number of new customers acquired by marketing campaign
Amount of recurring revenue	Percentage of service renewals	Customer retention rate
Number of proposals given	Customer satisfaction level	Number of new leads by product

FIGURE 11.2

Common CRM Metrics.

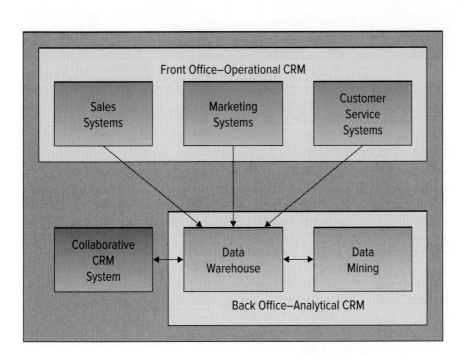

FIGURE 11.3

Operational CRM and Analytical CRM.

marketing mailers, and so on. After compiling the customer list, it can be filtered based on criteria such as household income, gender, education level, political facilitation, age, or other factors. List generators provide the marketing department with valuable information on the type of customer it must target to find success for a marketing campaign.

Campaign Management

Campaign management systems guide users through marketing campaigns by performing such tasks as campaign definition, planning, scheduling, segmentation, and success analysis. These advanced systems can even calculate the profitability and track the results for each marketing campaign.

FIGURE 11.4

Operational CRM
Technologies.

Cross-Selling and Up-Selling

Two key sales strategies a marketing campaign can deploy are cross-selling and up-selling. *Cross-selling* is selling additional products or services to an existing customer. For example, if you were to purchase Tim Burton's movie *Alice in Wonderland* on Amazon, you would also be asked whether you want to purchase the movie's soundtrack or the original book. Amazon is taking advantage of cross-selling by offering customers goods across its book, movie, and music product lines. *Up-selling* is increasing the value of the sale. McDonald's performs up-selling by asking customers whether they would like to super-size their meals for an extra cost. CRM systems offer marketing departments all kinds of information about customers and products, which can help identify up-selling and cross-selling opportunities to increase revenues.

SALES AND OPERATIONAL CRM

Sales departments were the first to begin developing CRM systems. They had two primary motivations to track customer sales information electronically. First, sales representatives were struggling with the overwhelming amount of customer account information they were required to maintain and track. Second, managers found themselves hindered because much of their vital customer and sales information remained in the heads of their sales representatives, even if the sales representative left the company. Finding a way to track customer information became a critical success factor for many sales departments. *Customer service and support (CSS)* is a part of operational CRM that automates service requests, complaints, product returns, and information requests.

Figure 11.5 depicts the typical sales process, which begins with an opportunity and ends with billing the customer for the sale. Leads and potential customers are the lifeblood of all sales organizations, whether they sell computers, clothing, consulting, or cars. How leads are handled can make the difference between revenue growth and decline.

Sales force automation (SFA) automatically tracks all the steps in the sales process. SFA products focus on increasing customer satisfaction, building customer relationships, and improving product sales. The three primary operational CRM technologies a sales department can adopt are:

1. Sales management CRM systems.
2. Contact management CRM systems.
3. Opportunity management CRM systems.

Sales Management CRM Systems

Sales management CRM systems automate each phase of the sales process, helping individual sales representatives coordinate and organize all their accounts. Features include calendars, reminders for important tasks, multimedia presentations, and document generation. These systems can even provide an analysis of the sales cycle and calculate how each sales representative is performing during the sales process.

Contact Management CRM Systems

A *contact management CRM system* maintains customer contact information and identifies prospective customers for future sales, using tools such as organizational charts, detailed customer notes, and supplemental sales information. For example, a contact management system can take an incoming telephone number and automatically display the person's name along with a comprehensive history, including all communications with the company. This allows the sales representative to personalize the phone conversation and ask such things as, "How is your new laptop working, Sue?" or "How was your family vacation to Colorado?" The customer feels valued, since the sales associate knows her name and even remembers details of their last conversation.

Opportunity Management CRM Systems

Opportunity management CRM systems target sales opportunities by finding new customers or companies for future sales. They determine potential customers and competitors and define selling efforts, including budgets and schedules. Advanced systems can even calculate the probability of a sale, which can save sales representatives significant time and money when

FIGURE 11.5

A Typical Sales Process.

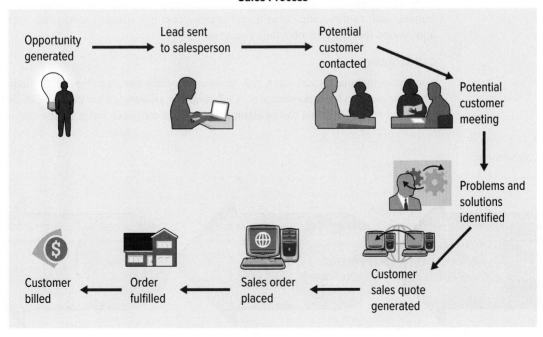

Sales Process

qualifying new customers. The primary difference between contact management and opportunity management is that contact management deals with existing customers and opportunity management with new or potential customers.

CUSTOMER SERVICE AND OPERATIONAL CRM

Most companies recognize the importance of building strong customer relationships during the marketing and sales efforts, but they must continue this effort by building strong post-sale relationships also. A primary reason firms lose customers is due to negative customer service experiences. Providing outstanding customer service is challenging, and many CRM technologies can assist organizations with this important activity. The three primary ones are:

1. Contact center.
2. Web-based self-service.
3. Call scripting.

Contact Center

A *contact center* (or call center) is where customer service representatives answer customer inquiries and solve problems, usually by email, chat, or phone. It is one of the best assets a customer-driven organization can have because maintaining a high level of customer support is critical to obtaining and retaining customers. Figure 11.6 highlights a few of the services contact center systems offer.

Contact centers also track customer communication histories along with problem resolutions—information critical for providing a comprehensive customer view to the service representative. Representatives who can quickly comprehend the customer's concerns provide tremendous value to the customer and to the company. Nothing makes frustrated customers happier than not having to explain their problems all over again to yet another customer service representative.

Web-Based Self-Service

Web-based self-service systems allow customers to use the web to find answers to their questions or solutions to their problems. FedEx uses web-based self-service systems to let customers electronically track packages without having to talk to a customer service representative. Another feature of web-based self-service is *click-to-talk* functions, which allow customers to click a button and talk with a representative via the Internet. Powerful customer-driven features such as these add value to any organization by providing customers with real-time information that helps resolve their concerns.

Call Scripting

Companies that market and sell highly technical products have a difficult time finding competent customer service representatives. *Call scripting systems* gather product details and issue resolution information that can be automatically generated into a script for the representative to

FIGURE 11.6

Contact Center Services.

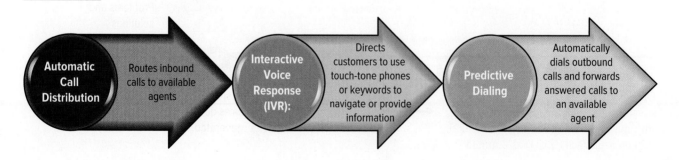

read to the customer. These systems even provide questions the representative can ask the customer to troubleshoot the problem and find a resolution. This feature not only helps reps answer difficult questions quickly but also presents a uniform response so customers don't receive different answers.

ANALYTICAL CRM

Analytical CRM provides information about customers and products that was once impossible to locate, such as which type of marketing and sales campaign to launch and which customers to target and when. Unlike operational CRM, which automates call centers and sales forces with the aim of enhancing customer service, analytical CRM works by using business intelligence to identify patterns in product sales and customer behaviors. *Uplift modeling* is a form of predictive analytics for marketing campaigns that attempts to identify target markets or people who could be convinced to buy products. The "uplift" refers to the increased sales that can follow after this form of analytical CRM analysis. Analytical CRM provides priceless customer information, supports important business decisions, and plays a vital role in your organization's success.

Analytical CRM tools can slice and dice vast amounts of information to create custom views of customers, products, and market segments, highlighting opportunities for cross-selling and up-selling. Analytical CRM provides *customer segmentation*, which divides a market into categories that share similar attributes such as age, location, gender, habits, and so on. By segmenting customers into groups, it becomes easier to create targeted marketing and sales campaigns, ensuring that you are not wasting resources marketing products to the wrong customers. *Website personalization* occurs when a website has stored enough data about a person's likes and dislikes to fashion offers more likely to appeal to that person. Many marketers use CRM to personalize customer communications and decide which customers are worth pursuing. Here are a few examples of the information insights analytical CRM can help an organization gain.

■ Find new profitable customers: Analytical CRM could highlight that the most profitable market segment consists of women between 35 and 45 years old who drive SUVs and live within 30 miles of the city limits. The firm could then find a way to locate these customers for mailings and other opportunities.

■ Exceed customer expectations: Analytical CRM helps a firm move past the typical "Dear Mr. Smith" greeting by personalizing communications. For example, if the firm knows the customer's favorite brand and size of shoe, it can notify the customer that a pair of size 12 Nike cross trainers is available for him to try on the next time he visits the store.

■ Discover the activities the firm performs the best: Analytical CRM can determine what an organization does better than its competitors. If a restaurant caters more lunches to mid-sized companies than its competition does, it can purchase a specialized mailing targeting these customers for future mailings.

■ Eliminate competition: Analytical CRM can determine sales trends, enabling the company to provide customers with special deals and outsmarting its competition. A sports store might identify its best customers for outdoor apparel and invite them to a private sale right before the competition runs its sale.

■ Care about customers: Analytical CRM can determine what customers want and need, so a firm can contact them with an invitation to a private sale, remind them that a product needs a tune-up, or send them a personalized letter along with a discount coupon to help spark a renewed relationship.

Extending Customer Relationship Management

LO 11.3 Identify the three current trends extending customer relationship management.

Organizations are discovering a wave of other key business areas where it is beneficial to take advantage of building strong relationships. These emerging areas include supplier relationship management (SRM), partner relationship management (PRM), and employee relationship management (ERM) as outlined in Figure 11.7.

FIGURE 11.7

Extending Customer
Relationship Management.

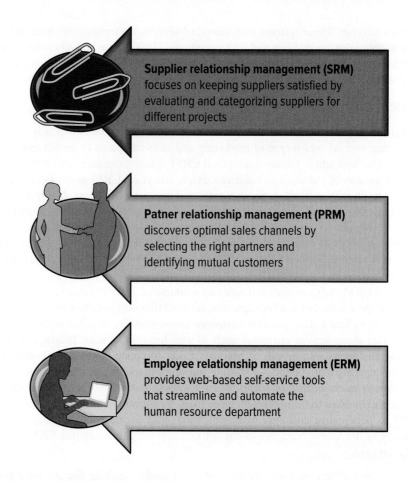

Supplier relationship management (SRM) focuses on keeping suppliers satisfied by evaluating and categorizing suppliers for different projects

Patner relationship management (PRM) discovers optimal sales channels by selecting the right partners and identifying mutual customers

Employee relationship management (ERM) provides web-based self-service tools that streamline and automate the human resource department

SUPPLIER RELATIONSHIP MANAGEMENT

Supplier relationship management (SRM) focuses on keeping suppliers satisfied by evaluating and categorizing suppliers for different projects, which optimizes supplier selection. SRM applications help companies analyze vendors based on a number of key variables including strategy, business goals, prices, and markets. The company can then determine the best supplier to collaborate with and can work on developing strong relationships with that supplier. The partners can then work together to streamline processes, outsource services, and provide products that they could not provide individually.

With the merger of the Bank of Halifax and Bank of Scotland, the new company, HBOS, implemented an SRM system to supply consistent information to its suppliers. The system integrates procurement information from the separate Bank of Halifax and Bank of Scotland operational systems, generating a single repository of management information for consistent reporting and analysis. Other benefits HBOS derived from the SRM solution include:

- A single consolidated view of all suppliers.
- Consistent, detailed management information allowing multiple views for every executive.
- Elimination of duplicate suppliers.

PARTNER RELATIONSHIP MANAGEMENT

Organizations have begun to realize the importance of building relationships with partners, dealers, and resellers. *Partner relationship management (PRM)* focuses on keeping vendors satisfied by managing alliance partner and reseller relationships that provide customers with the optimal sales channel. PRM's business strategy is to select and manage partners to optimize their long-term value to an organization. In effect, it means picking the right partners, working with them to help them be successful in dealing with mutual customers, and ensuring that partners and the ultimate end customers are satisfied and successful. Many of the features of a PRM application include real-time product information on availability, marketing materials, contracts, order details, and pricing, inventory, and shipping information.

PRM is one of the smaller segments of CRM that has superb potential. PRM has grown to more than a $1 billion industry. This is a direct reflection of the growing interdependency of organizations in the new economy. The primary benefits of PRM include:

- Expanded market coverage.

- Offerings of specialized products and services.

- Broadened range of offerings and a more complete solution.

CRM suites will also incorporate PRM and SRM modules as enterprises seek to take advantage of these initiatives. Automating interactions with distributors, resellers, and suppliers will enhance the corporation's ability to deliver a quality experience to its customers.

EMPLOYEE RELATIONSHIP MANAGEMENT

Employee relationship management (ERM) provides employees with a subset of CRM applications available through a web browser. Many of the ERM applications assist the employee in dealing with customers by providing detailed information on company products, services, and customer orders.

At Rackspace, a San Antonio–based web-hosting company, customer focus borders on the obsessive. Joey Parsons, 24, won the Straightjacket Award, the most coveted employee distinction at Rackspace. The award recognizes the employee who best lives up to the Rackspace motto of delivering "fanatical support," a dedication to customers that is so intense it borders on the loony. Rackspace motivates its staff by treating each team as a separate business, which is responsible for its own profits and losses and has its own ERM website. Each month, employees can earn bonuses of up to 20 percent of their monthly base salaries depending on the performance of their units by both financial and customer-centric measurements such as customer turnover, customer expansion, and customer referrals. Daily reports are available through the team's ERM website.

CRM revenue forecast for 2018 is $21.5 billion. In the future, CRM applications will continue to change from employee-only tools to tools used by suppliers, partners, and even customers. Providing a consistent view of customers and delivering timely and accurate customer information to all departments across an organization will continue to be the major goal of CRM initiatives.

As technology advances (intranet, Internet, extranet, wireless), CRM will remain a major strategic focus for companies, particularly in industries whose product is difficult to differentiate. Some companies approach this problem by moving to a low-cost producer strategy. CRM will be an alternative way to pursue a differentiation strategy with a nondifferentiable product.

CRM applications will continue to adapt wireless capabilities supporting mobile sales and mobile customers. Sales professionals will be able to access email, order details, corporate information, inventory status, and opportunity information all from a PDA in their car or on a plane. Real-time interaction with human CSRs over the Internet will continue to increase.

OPENING CASE STUDY QUESTIONS

1. Why is CRM important to the technology companies, automobile manufactures and telecommunication companies all competing for the connected car market? How can they use CRM to improve sales?

2. Identify a few different metrics a connected car will use to monitor driver activity.

3. How will automobile manufactures measure the success of customer satisfaction?

4. Argue for or against the following statement: Technology companies will invade driver privacy by collecting data from connected cars without the consent of the driver.

Tony Hsieh's first entrepreneurial effort began at the age of 12 when he started his own custom button business. Realizing the importance of advertising, Hsieh began marketing his business to other kids through directories, and soon his profits soared to a few hundred dollars a month. Throughout his adolescence, Hsieh started several businesses, and by the time he was in college he was making money selling pizzas out of his Harvard dorm room. Another entrepreneurial student, Alfred Lin, bought pizzas from Hsieh and resold them by the slice, making a nice profit. Hsieh and Lin quickly became friends.

After Harvard, Hsieh founded LinkExchange in 1996, a company that helped small businesses exchange banner ads. A mere two years later, Hsieh sold LinkExchange to Microsoft for $265 million. Using the profits from the sale, Hsieh and Lin formed a venture capital company that invested in start-up businesses. One investment that caught their attention was Zappos, an online etailer of shoes. Both entrepreneurs viewed the $40 billion shoe market as an opportunity they could not miss, and in 2000 Hsieh took over as Zappos's CEO with Lin as his chief financial officer.

Today, Zappos is leading its market and offering an enormous selection of more than 90,000 styles of handbags, clothing, and accessories for more than 500 brands. One reason for Zappos's incredible success was Hsieh's decision to use the advertising and marketing budget for customer service, a tactic that would not have worked before the Internet. Zappos's passionate customer service strategy encourages customers to order as many sizes and styles of products as they want, ships them for free, and offers free return shipping. Zappos encourages customer communication, and its call center receives more than 5,000 calls a day with the longest call to date lasting more than four hours.

Zappos's extensive inventory is stored in a warehouse in Kentucky right next to a UPS shipping center. Only available stock is listed on the website, and orders as late as 11 P.M. are still guaranteed next-day delivery. To facilitate supplier and partner relationships, Zappos built an extranet that provides its vendors with all kinds of product information, such as items sold, times sold, price, customer, and so on. Armed with these kinds of details, suppliers can quickly change manufacturing schedules to meet demand.

Zappos Culture

Along with valuing its partners and suppliers, Zappos also places a great deal of value on its employee relationships. Zappos employees have fun, and walking through the offices you will see all kinds of things not normally seen in business environments—bottle-cap pyramids, cotton-candy machines, and bouncing balls. Building loyal employee relationships is a critical success factor at Zappos, and to facilitate this relationship the corporate headquarters are located in the same building as the call center (where most employees work) in Las Vegas. All employees receive 100 percent company-paid health insurance along with a daily free lunch.

Of course, the Zappos culture does not work for everyone, and the company pays to find the right employees through "The Offer," which extends to new employees the option of quitting and receiving payment for time worked plus an additional $1,000 bonus. Why the $1,000 bonus for quitting? Zappos management believes that is a small price to pay to find those employees who do not have the sense of commitment Zappos requires. Less than 10 percent of new hires take The Offer. Zappos's unique culture stresses the following:

- Delivering WOW through service.
- Embracing and driving change.
- Creating fun and a little weirdness.
- Being adventurous, creative, and open-minded.
- Pursuing growth and learning.
- Building open and honest relationships with communication.

- Building a positive team and family spirit.
- Doing more with less.
- Being passionate and determined.
- Being humble.

Zappos's Sale to Amazon

Amazon.com purchased Zappos for $880 million. Zappos employees shared $40 million in cash and stock, and the Zappos management team remained in place. Having access to Amazon's world-class warehouses and supply chain is sure to catapult Zappos's revenues, though many wonder whether the Zappos culture will remain. It'll be interesting to watch![1]

Questions

1. Why would Zappos benefit from the implementation of a CRM system?

2. Why are customers at the heart of Zappos's business strategy?

3. Analyze the merger between Zappos and Amazon and assess potential issues for Zappos customers.

4. Propose a plan for how Zappos can use Amazon's supply chain to increase sales and customer satisfaction.

5. Argue for or against the following statement: "In the electronic age, customer relationships are more important than ever, and Zappos provides the new benchmark that all corporations should follow."

11.1. Describe customer relationship management along with its importance to a business.

Customer relationship management (CRM) is a means of managing all aspects of a customer's relationship with an organization to increase customer loyalty and retention and an organization's profitability. CRM allows an organization to gain insights into customers' shopping and buying behaviors. Every time a customer communicates with a company, the firm has the chance to build a trusting relationship with that particular customer.

11.2. Differentiate operational and analytical customer relationship management.

The two primary components of a CRM strategy are operational CRM and analytical CRM. Operational CRM supports traditional transactional processing for day-to-day front-office operations or systems that deal directly with the customers. Analytical CRM supports back-office operations and strategic analysis and includes all systems that do not deal directly with the customers.

11.3. Identify the three current trends extending customer relationship management.

Supplier relationship management (SRM) focuses on keeping suppliers satisfied by evaluating and categorizing suppliers for different projects, which optimizes supplier selection. Partner relationship management (PRM) focuses on keeping vendors satisfied by managing alliance partner and reseller relationships that provide customers with the optimal sales channel. Employee relationship management (ERM) provides employees with a subset of CRM applications available through a web browser. Many of the ERM applications assist the employee in dealing with customers by providing detailed information on company products, services, and customer orders.

 REVIEW QUESTIONS

1. Why are customer relationships important to an organization?
2. Do you agree that every business needs to focus on customers to survive?
3. What is the difference between operational and analytical CRM?
4. How can a sales department use CRM to improve operations?
5. How can a marketing department use CRM to improve operations?
6. How can a company use partner relationship management to create a successful business?
7. Why would a company want to implement an employee relationship management system?

 MAKING BUSINESS DECISIONS

1. Straightjacket Customer Service

You might not want to put the fact that you won the Straightjacket Award on your résumé unless you worked for Rackspace, a Texas company that specializes in hosting websites. At Rackspace, the coveted Straightjacket Award is won by the employee who best delivers "fanatical customer support," one of the firm's critical success factors. The company motivates its customer service representatives by dividing them into teams, each responsible for its own profitability. The company then measures such things as customer turnover, up-selling, cross-selling, and referrals. The team with the highest scores wins the Straightjacket Award and each member receives a 20 percent bonus.

Assume your professor has hired you as the employee relationship manager for your class. What type of award would you create to help increase class participation? What type of award would you create to help increase the overall average on exams? What type of award would you create to help increase student collaboration? Be sure to name your awards and describe their details. Also, what type of metrics would you create to measure your awards? How could a CRM system help you implement your awards?

2. Nice Emotions

New emotion-detection software called Perform, created by Nice Systems, helps firms improve customer service by identifying callers who are displeased or upset. Perform determines a baseline of emotion and can detect emotional issues during the first few seconds of a call; any variation from the baseline activates an alert. When an elderly person who was highly distressed over medical costs hung up during a phone call to the insurance company, Perform identified the customer's frustration and automatically emailed a supervisor. The supervisor was able to review a recording of the conversation and immediately called the customer back suggesting ways to lower the costs.

How do you think emotion-detection software will affect customer relationships? What other departments or business processes could benefit from its use? Create a new product that uses emotion-detection software. What business problem would your product solve and who would be your primary customers?

3. Ruby Receptionists

Great businesses are driven by exceptional customer experiences and interactions. Ruby is a company operating from Portland, Oregon, that has a team of smart and cheerful virtual receptionists that you can hire to carry out all your customer interactions—remotely. Ruby aims to deliver the perfect mix of friendliness, charm, can-do attitude, and professionalism to all its clients' customer calls. Best of all, customers believe the Ruby receptionists are working right in your office, not in Portland, Oregon. Ruby promises to bring back the lost art of human interaction by delighting each and every customer who calls.

Explain the importance of customer service for customer relationship management. Do you agree that a company can improve customer service by hiring Ruby receptionists? If you owned a small business, would you be comfortable hiring Ruby receptionists?

4. I'm Stuck in London and I've Been Robbed—Help Me!

There are so many people using Facebook that people can quickly become overwhelmed with friend requests. Without knowing who your friends are, it is easy to find yourself a victim of a scam. Internet impostors are perfecting the technique of impersonating friends on social networking sites like Facebook with lucrative results and suckering individuals out of thousands of dollars. Emotional email pleas sent by imposters, such as "I'm stuck in London and I've been robbed, help me," have become so effective that the FBI has issued warnings to consumers about social networking sites. "Fraudsters continue to hijack accounts on social networking sites and spread malicious software by using various techniques," the FBI stated after logging 3,200 complaints about such incidents within a week.

When Barry Schwartz logged on to Twitter, he had 20 messages waiting for him, all with the unwelcome news: someone was impersonating his company on Twitter. Schwartz runs RustyBrick, a 15-employee, $2 million website development company. The impostor had set up a profile using a slight variation of the company's name and started following Schwartz's 4,000 customer contacts with a message similar to spam: "Hey guys, you have to get this new Twitter Success Guide—it's priceless." A devastated Schwartz stated, "The last thing I want is to have people thinking that I'm following them and I'm selling a Twitter Success Guide."

Internet impostors impersonate organizations as well as individuals. What could happen to an organization whose customers are contacted by an impostor asking for money or selling a product? What happens when the relationship with a customer turns sour? What type of power does a disgruntled customer or employee have against a company? Why is it more important than ever to build strong relationships with your customers, employees, partners, and suppliers?

5. Customer Relationship Management Strategies

On average, it costs an organization six times more to sell to a new customer than to sell to an existing customer. As the co-owner of a medium-sized luggage distributor, you have recently been notified by your EIS systems that sales for the past three months have decreased by an average of 17 percent. The reasons for the decline in sales are numerous, including a poor economy, people's aversion to travel because of the terrorist attacks, and some negative publicity your company received regarding a defective product line. In a group, explain how implementing a CRM system can help you understand and combat the decline in sales. Be sure to justify why a CRM system is important to your business and its future growth.

6. My Customers Hate Me

The web contains numerous examples of customer power. Customers are using YouTube, Myspace, blogs, and a number of other web tools to slam or praise companies. Do you believe that the most influential person in your business is the customer? How could customers hurt or help your business? Will your employees agree that customers are the most important part of the business?

7. Times They Are A Changing!

Change.org, a social activist website, is a resource for researching and organizing groups around social and political causes, called "Changes." Changes allow members with similar beliefs to post images, videos, blogs, and even donations to their nonprofit cause. Politicians need to find donors to help them raise campaign funds so they can compete in elections. In fact, politicians in the last election raised upwards of $3 billion, with about $50 million spent on finding the donors. Change.org wants to lower those fund-raising costs, neutralize large donors' "special interest" money, and provide a place where the "average Joe" who can't afford a $2,500 fund-raising dinner can be heard. Change.org's strategy is to create a database of politician profiles that align with each Change group. The Change groups are now empowered to pool together a pot of money to donate to relevant charities or political candidates, as well as the power to lobby representatives.

Describe the differences between operational CRM and analytical CRM. What types of operational CRM would Change.org need to function? What types of analytical CRM would Change.org need to function? How could Change.org use marketing, sales, and customer service CRM technologies to help raise awareness and donations for nonprofit causes? Why is creating a social activist website a risky decision? Would you want to have your personal information stored on this website?

12 Integrating the Organization from End to End—Enterprise Resource Planning

12.1. Describe the role information plays in enterprise resource planning systems.

12.2. Identify the core and extended areas of enterprise resource planning.

12.3. Discuss the current technologies organizations are integrating in enterprise resource planning systems.

Enterprise Resource Planning (ERP)

LO 12.1 Describe the role information plays in enterprise resource planning systems.

Enterprise resource planning systems serve as the organization's backbone in providing fundamental decision-making support. In the past, departments made decisions independent of each other. ERP systems provide a foundation for collaboration between departments, enabling people in different business areas to communicate. ERP systems have been widely adopted in large organizations to store critical knowledge used to make the decisions that drive performance.

To be competitive, organizations must always strive for excellence in every business process enterprisewide, a daunting challenge if the organization has multisite operations worldwide. To obtain operational efficiencies, lower costs, improve supplier and customer relations, and increase revenues and market share, all units of the organization must work together harmoniously toward congruent goals. An ERP system will help an organization achieve this.

The heart of an ERP system is a central database that collects information from and feeds information into all the ERP system's individual application components (called modules), supporting diverse business functions such as accounting, manufacturing, marketing, and human resources. When a user enters or updates information in one module, it is immediately and automatically updated throughout the entire system, as illustrated in Figure 12.1.

ERP automates business processes such as order fulfillment—taking an order from a customer, shipping the purchase, and then billing for it. With an ERP system, when a customer service representative takes an order from a customer, he or she has all the information necessary to complete the order (the customer's credit rating and order history, the company's inventory levels, and the delivery schedule). Everyone else in the company sees the same information and has access to the database that holds the customer's new order. When one department finishes with the order, it is automatically routed via the ERP system to the next department. To find out where the order is at any point, a user need only log in to the ERP system and track it down, as illustrated in Figure 12.2. The order process moves like a bolt of lightning through the organization, and customers get their orders faster and with fewer errors than ever before. ERP can apply that same magic to the other major business processes, such as employee benefits or financial reporting.

FIGURE 12.1

ERP Integration Data Flow.

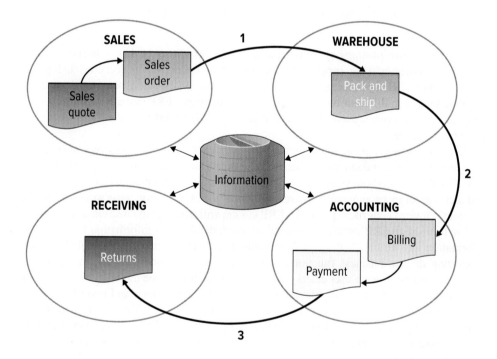

FIGURE 12.2

ERP Process Flow.

BRINGING THE ORGANIZATION TOGETHER

In most organizations, information has traditionally been isolated within specific departments, whether on an individual database, in a file cabinet, or on an employee's PC. ERP enables employees across the organization to share information across a single, centralized database. With extended portal capabilities, an organization can also involve its suppliers and customers to participate in the workflow process, allowing ERP to penetrate the entire value chain, and help the organization achieve greater operational efficiency (see Figures 12.3 and 12.4).

FIGURE 12.3

The Organization before ERP.

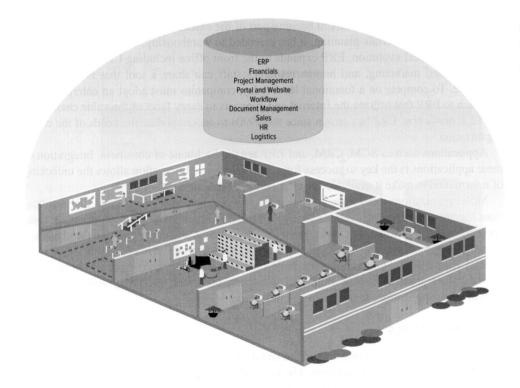

ERP

Logistics

Project Management

Workflow

Financials

Document Management

Sales

Portal and
Website

HR

FIGURE 12.4

ERP—Bringing the
Organization Together.

ERP
Financials
Project Management
Portal and Website
Workflow
Document Management
Sales
HR
Logistics

THE EVOLUTION OF ERP

Originally, ERP solutions were developed to deliver automation across multiple units of an organization, to help facilitate the manufacturing process and address issues such as raw materials, inventory, order entry, and distribution. However, ERP was unable to extend to other functional areas of the company such as sales, marketing, and shipping. It could not tie in any CRM capabilities that would allow organizations to capture customer-specific information, nor did it work with websites or portals used for customer service or order fulfillment. Call center or quality assurance staff could not tap into the ERP solution, nor could ERP handle document management, such as cataloging contracts and purchase orders.

LO 12.2 **Identify the core and extended areas of enterprise resource planning.**

Core and Extended ERP Components

Turner Industries grew from $300 million in sales to $800 million in sales in less than 10 years thanks to the implementation of an ERP system. Ranked number 369 on the *Forbes* 500 list of privately held companies, Turner Industries is a leading industrial services firm. Turner Industries develops and deploys advanced software applications designed to maximize the productivity of its 25,000 employees and construction equipment valued at more than $100 million.

The company considers the biggest challenges in the industrial services industry to be completing projects on time, within budget, while fulfilling customers' expectations. To meet these challenges the company invested in an ERP system and named the project Interplan. Interplan won Constructech's Vision award for software innovation in the heavy construction industry. Interplan runs all of Turner's construction, turnaround, shutdown, and maintenance projects and is so adept at estimating and planning jobs that Turner Industries typically achieves higher profit margins on projects that use Interplan. As the ERP solution makes the company more profitable, the company can pass on the cost savings to its customers, giving the company an incredible competitive advantage.

Figure 12.8 provides an example of an ERP system with its core and extended components. ***Core ERP components*** are the traditional components included in most ERP systems and they primarily focus on internal operations. ***Extended ERP components*** are the extra components that meet the organizational needs not covered by the core components and primarily focus on external operations.

CORE ERP COMPONENTS

The three most common *core* ERP components focusing on internal operations are:

1. Accounting and finance.
2. Production and materials management.
3. Human resources.

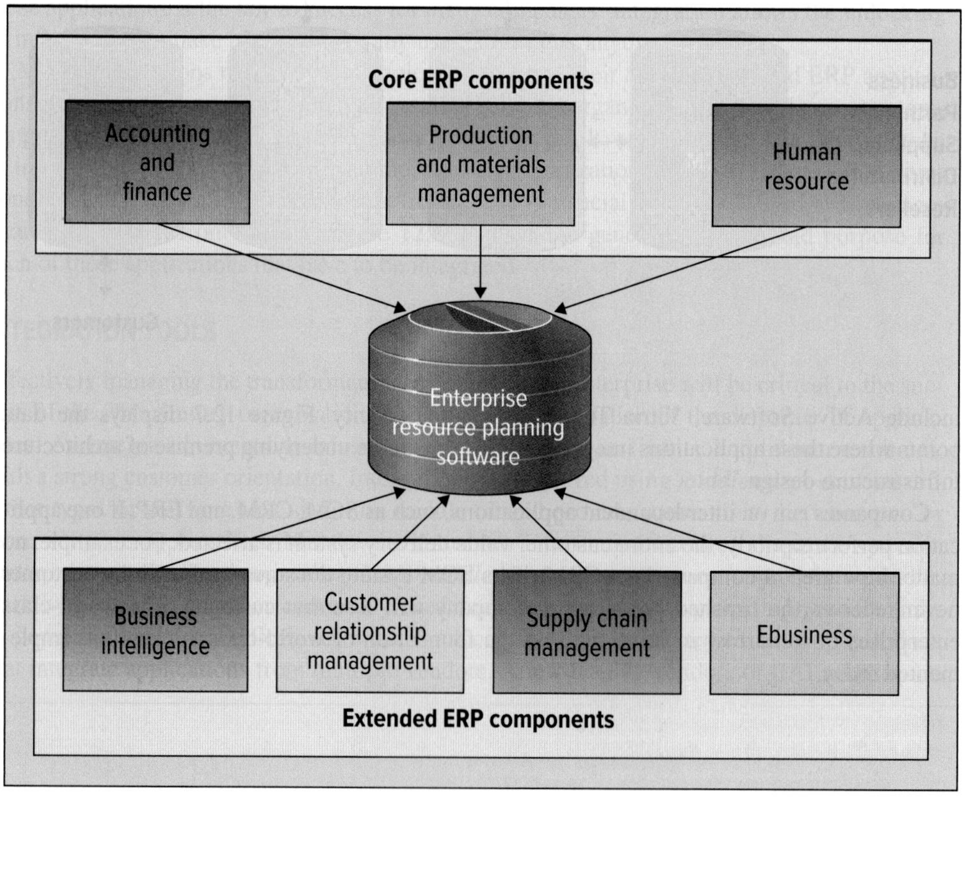

FIGURE 12.8

Core ERP Components and Extended ERP Components.

Accounting and Finance ERP Components

Deeley Harley-Davidson Canada (DHDC), the exclusive Canadian distributor of Harley-Davidson motorcycles, has improved inventory, turnaround time, margins, and customer satisfaction—all with the implementation of a financial ERP system. The system has opened up the power of information to the company and is helping it make strategic decisions when it still has the time to change things. The ERP system provides the company with ways to manage inventory, turnaround time, and warehouse space more effectively.

Accounting and finance ERP components manage accounting data and financial processes within the enterprise with functions such as general ledger, accounts payable, accounts receivable, budgeting, and asset management. One of the most useful features included in an ERP accounting/finance component is its credit-management feature. Most organizations manage their relationships with customers by setting credit limits, or a limit on how much a customer can owe at any one time. The company then monitors the credit limit whenever the customer places a new order or sends in a payment. ERP financial systems help to correlate customer orders with customer account balances determining credit availability. Another great feature is the ability to perform product profitability analysis. ERP financial components are the backbone behind product profitability analysis and allow companies to perform all types of advanced profitability modeling techniques.

Production and Materials Management ERP Components

One of the main functions of an ERP system is streamlining the production planning process. *Production and materials management ERP components* handle the various aspects of production planning and execution such as demand forecasting, production scheduling, job cost accounting, and quality control. Companies typically produce multiple products, each of which has many different parts. Production lines, consisting of machines and employees, build the different types of products. The company must then define sales forecasting for each product to determine production schedules and materials purchasing. Figure 12.9 displays the typical ERP production planning process. The process begins with forecasting sales in order to plan operations. A detailed production schedule is developed if the product is produced and a materials requirement plan is completed if the product is purchased.

Grupo Farmanova Intermed, located in Costa Rica, is a pharmaceutical marketing and distribution company that markets nearly 2,500 products to approximately 500 customers in Central and South America. The company identified a need for software that could unify product logistics management in a single country. It decided to deploy PeopleSoft financial and distribution ERP components allowing the company to improve customer data management, increase confidence among internal and external users, and coordinate the logistics of inventory. With the software the company enhanced its capabilities for handling, distributing, and marketing its pharmaceuticals.

Human Resources ERP Components

Human resources ERP components track employee information including payroll, benefits, compensation, and performance assessment, and assure compliance with the legal requirements of multiple jurisdictions and tax authorities. Human resources components even offer features that allow the organization to perform detailed analysis on its employees to determine such things as the identification of individuals who are likely to leave the company unless additional compensation or benefits are provided. These components can also identify which employees are using which resources, such as online training and long-distance telephone services. They can also help determine whether the most talented people are working for those business units with the highest priority—or where they would have the greatest impact on profit.

FIGURE 12.9

The Production Planning Process.

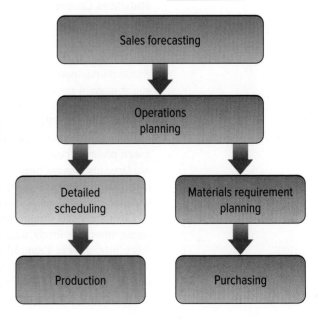

EXTENDED ERP COMPONENTS

Extended ERP components are the extra components that meet the organizational needs not covered by the core components and primarily focus on external operations. Many of the numerous extended ERP components are Internet enabled and require interaction with customers, suppliers, and business partners outside the organization. The four most common extended ERP components are:

1. Business intelligence
2. Customer relationship management
3. Supply chain management
4. Ebusiness

Business Intelligence Components

ERP systems offer powerful tools that measure and control organizational operations. Many organizations have found that these valuable tools can be enhanced to provide even greater value through the addition of powerful business intelligence systems. The business intelligence components of ERP systems typically collect information used throughout the organization (including data used in many other ERP components), organize it, and apply analytical tools to assist managers with decisions. Data warehouses are one of the most popular extensions to ERP systems, with over two-thirds of U.S. manufacturers adopting or planning such systems.

Customer Relationship Management Components

ERP vendors are expanding their functionality to provide services formerly supplied by customer relationship management (CRM) vendors such as Siebel. CRM components provide an integrated view of customer data and interactions allowing organizations to work more effectively with customers and be more responsive to their needs. CRM components typically include contact centers, sales force automation, and marketing functions. These improve the customer experience while identifying a company's most (and least) valuable customers for better allocation of resources.

Supply Chain Management Components

ERP vendors are expanding their systems to include SCM functions that manage the information flows between and among supply chain stages, maximizing total supply chain effectiveness and profitability. SCM components allow a firm to monitor and control all stages in the supply chain from the acquisition of raw materials to the receipt of finished goods by customers.

Ebusiness Components

The original focus of ERP systems was the internal organization. In other words, ERP systems are not fundamentally ready for the external world of ebusiness. The newest and most exciting extended ERP components are the ebusiness components. Two of the primary features of ebusiness components are elogistics and eprocurement. *Elogistics* manages the transportation and storage of goods. *Eprocurement* is the business-to-business (B2B) purchase and sale of supplies and services over the Internet.

Ebusiness and ERP complement each other by allowing companies to establish a web presence and fulfill orders expeditiously. A common mistake made by many businesses is deploying a web presence before the integration of back-office systems or an ERP system. For example, one large toy manufacturer announced less than a week before Christmas that it would be unable to fulfill any of its web orders. The company had all the toys in the warehouse, but it could not organize the basic order processing function to get the toys delivered to the consumers on time.

Customers and suppliers are now demanding access to ERP information including order status, inventory levels, and invoice reconciliation. Plus, the customers and partners want all this information in a simplified format available through a website. This is a difficult task to accomplish because most ERP systems are full of technical jargon, which is why employee training is one of the hidden costs associated with ERP implementations. Removing the jargon to accommodate untrained customers and partners is one of the more difficult tasks when web-enabling an ERP system. To accommodate the growing needs of the ebusiness world, ERP vendors need to build two new channels of access into the ERP system information—one channel for customers (B2C) and one channel for businesses, suppliers, and partners (B2B).

MEASURING ERP SUCCESS

There is no guarantee of success for an ERP system. It is difficult to measure the success of an ERP system because one system can span an entire organization, including thousands of employees across the globe. ERPs focus on how a corporation operates internally, and optimizing these operations takes significant time and energy.

Two of the primary forces driving ERP failure include software customization and ERP costs. *Software customization* modifies existing software according to the business's or user's requirements. Since ERP systems must fit business processes, many enterprises choose to customize their ERP systems to ensure that they meet business and user needs. Figure 12.10 displays the different forms of software customization a business will undertake to ensure the success of an ERP implementation. Heavy customization leads to complex code that must be continuously maintained and upgraded. It should be noted that customizing an ERP system is costly and complex and should only be done when there is a specific business advantage. According to Meta Group, it takes the average company 8 to 18 months to see any benefits from an ERP system. The primary risk for an ERP implementation includes the associated costs displayed in Figure 12.11.

SOFTWARE CUSTOMIZATION	
Business Processes or Workflows	Software can be customized to support the needs of business process workflows unique to each business or department.
Code Modifications	The most expensive customization occurs when application code is changed and should only be done if the code changes provide specific competitive advantages.
Integrations	Data integration is key for business process support that spans functional areas and legacy systems.
Reports, Documents, Forms	Customization to reports, documents, and forms can consist of simple layout or design changes or complex logic programming rules for specific business requirements.
User-Interface Changes	An ERP system can be customized to ensure that each user has the most efficient and effective view of the application.

FIGURE 12.10

Software Customization Examples.

ERP COSTS	
Software Costs	Purchasing the software can cost millions of dollars for a large enterprise.
Consulting Fees	Hiring external experts to help implement the system correctly can cost millions of dollars.
Process rework	Redefine processes to ensure that the company is using the most efficient and effective processes.
Customization	If the software package does not meet all of the company's needs, customizing the software may be required.
Integration	Ensuring that all software products, including disparate systems not part of the ERP system, are working together or are integrated.
Testing	Testing that all functionality works correctly along with testing all integrations.
Training	Training all new users and creating the training user manuals.
Data warehouse integration and data conversions	Moving data from an old system into the new ERP system.

FIGURE 12.11

ERP Costs.

sources, magazine sources, billboard sources, and now online sources. You notice that each system works independently to perform its job of creating, updating, and maintaining sales information, but you are wondering how he operates his business as a whole. Create a list of issues Kern will encounter if he continues to run his business with four systems performing the same operations. What could happen to the business if he cannot correlate the details of each? Be sure to highlight at least 10 issues by which separate systems could cause problems.

✳ UNIT SUMMARY

Today, organizations of various sizes are proving that systems that support decision making and opportunity seizing are essential to thriving in the highly competitive electronic world. We are living in an era when information technology is a primary tool, knowledge is a strategic asset, and decision making and problem solving are paramount skills. The tougher, larger, and more demanding a problem or opportunity is, and the faster and more competitive the environment is, the more important decision-making and problem-solving skills become. This unit discussed numerous tools and strategic initiatives that an organization can take advantage of to assist in decision making:

- Supply chain management (SCM)—managing information flows within the supply chain to maximize total supply chain effectiveness and profitability.

- Customer relationship management (CRM)—managing all aspects of customers' relationships with an organization to increase customer loyalty and retention and an organization's profitability.

- Enterprise resource planning (ERP)—integrating all departments and functions throughout an organization into a single IT system (or integrated set of IT systems) so that managers and leaders can make enterprisewide decisions by viewing enterprisewide information on all business operations.

✳ KEY TERMS

3D printing, 184	Cross-selling, 198	Executive information system
Accounting and finance ERP	Customer relationship	(EIS), 170
component, 215	management (CRM), 194	Expert system, 173
Analytical CRM, 195	Customer segmentation, 201	Extended ERP component, 214
Artificial intelligence (AI), 172	Customer service and support	Fuzzy logic, 174
Augmented reality, 175	(CSS), 198	Genetic algorithm, 174
Bullwhip effect, 182	Decision support system (DSS),	Goal-seeking analysis, 169
Call scripting system, 200	177	Granularity, 170
Campaign management system,	Digital dashboard, 170	Human resources ERP
197	Drill-down, 172	component, 215
Click-to-talk, 200	Drone, 187	Hybrid ERP, 220
Cloud computing, 218	Ebusiness, 163	Intelligent agent, 175
Computer-aided design/	Electronic data interchange	Intelligent system, 172
computer-aided	(EDI), 182	Legacy system, 218
manufacturing (CAD/CAM,	Elogistics, 216	List generator, 195
185	Employee relationship	Logistics, 183
Consolidation, 172	management (ERM), 203	Maker movement, 185
Contact center, 200	Enterprise application	Makerspace, 185
Contact management CRM	integration (EAI)	Managerial level, 167
system, 199	middleware, 212	Materials management, 183
Core ERP component, 214	Eprocurement, 216	Middleware, 212
Cradle to grave, 183	Extended ERP component, 214	Model, 167

✴ UNIT CLOSING CASE ONE

© Ryan McVay/Getty Images

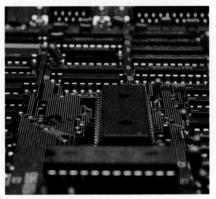
© C. Sherburne/PhotoLink/Getty Images

© Digital Vision/Getty Images

Action Finally

Data are all over the Internet! Tons and tons and tons of data! For example, over 152 million blogs are created each year, along with 100 million Twitter accounts resulting in 25 billion Tweets, 107 trillion emails are sent, and 730 billion hours of YouTube videos are watched. Known as the social media sector, this arena is by far one of the fastest growing and most influential sectors in business. Companies are struggling to understand how the social media sector impacts it both financially and strategically.

Data are valuable to any company and the data on the Internet are unique because the information comes directly from customers, suppliers, competitors, and even employees. As the social media sector takes off, companies are finding themselves at a disadvantage when attempting to keep up with all of the "online chatter" about their goods and services on the many different social media websites, including Facebook, Twitter, LinkedIn, Yelp, Google, blogs, etc.

Anytime there is a problem there is a potential business solution, and Actionly.com chooses to capitalize on the data glut problem. Actionly monitors multiple social media channels through one tracking service looking for specific keywords for industries, brands, companies, and trends. Actionly customers choose a keyword to monitor—such as a brand, product names, industry terms, or competitors—and then Actionly constantly collects the data from these social channels and pulls that data into a cohesive digital dashboard. The digital dashboard tracks the desired information, such as marketplace trends, specific companies, competitive brands, entire industries (for example, clean technology), by simultaneously searching Twitter, Facebook, Google, YouTube, Flickr, and blogs. After completing a search, Actionly.com uses Google Analytics to create graphs and charts indicating how frequently each keyword was found throughout the various channels. Additionally, it links each respective channel to the dashboard and filters them with "positive" and "negative" connections, allowing users to respond to any comments.

Actionly.com's business model sets it up for success in this emerging industry. Actionly has a first-mover advantage because it was the first online brand management company offering this service to customers. And the company benefits by using its own services to ensure its brand stays number one on all social media websites. Actionly uses Google Analytics to help transform the data it collects from the various social media websites into valuable business intelligence. Its digital dashboard monitors several key metrics, including:

- **Reputation Management:** Actionly's easy to use digital dashboard allows customers to observe and analyze trends and track mentions about brands based on historical data as well as continuously updated data. For example, a customer can view graphs that highlight key trends across 30 days for specific brands, products, or companies.

- **Social ROI:** By connecting to Google Analytics from Actionly, a customer can analyze its campaign performance for individual tweets or Facebook posts to determine which are successful and which are failing. Actionly analyzes every post and click to track page views, visitor information, goal completions, and so on, through its digital dashboard, allowing users to customize reports tracking the performance of daily posts.

- **Twitter Analytics:** After adding Twitter accounts to the dashboard, a user can drill down into the data to view graphs of followers, mentions, and retweets. This eliminates the need to manually track a number of Twitter accounts, and a user can view the data in graphs or export the data in Excel for further analysis.

- **Marketing Campaign Tracking:** If a company is launching a big promotion or contest, it can post messages across multiple Facebook or Twitter accounts; all the user has to do is select which Twitter or Facebook accounts it wants to use and when. Actionly's Campaign Tracking helps a user view which posts are resonating well with customers and measure metrics such as page views, signups, conversions, and revenue by post. Actionly even segments the data by post, account, campaign, or channel, allowing users to measure performance over time.

- **Click Performance:** Actionly tracks performance by hour and day of week, allowing customers to view which clicks are getting the most attention. Actionly's algorithm automatically assigns a sentiment to tweets, allowing the customer to immediately filter positive or negative or neutral posts to react to information quickly.

- **Sentiment Analysis:** Reviewing positive and negative feedback helps gauge how a brand is doing over time, allowing the client to try to increase the positive sentiment. However, no sentiment scoring is 100 percent accurate due to the complexities of interpretation, culture, sarcasm, and other language nuances. For example, if Actionly is incorrectly tracking a metric, it can change it, allowing users to assign their unique sentiments directly to their tweets. A user can also select to have positive or negative alerts for keywords emailed as soon as the keyword is posted to help manage online brand and company reputations.

- **Competitive Analysis:** Actionly tracks competitor intelligence by watching new-product releases, acquisitions, or customer feedback, allowing a company to stay on top of market entrants, market-related blogs, news, or industry-related seminars/webinars.

- **Find Influencers:** Actionly's digital dashboard allows a user to engage directly with key influencers or people who are driving the online chatter about goods and services. Actionly identifies influencers and determines their relevance to the company, brand, or product. It then compiles a list of influencers based on users with the most followers and who have been most active for the specific searches in the past 30 days.[2]

Questions

1. Describe the difference between transnational and analytical information, and determine which types Actionly uses to create a customer's digital dashboard.

2. Explain why virtual companies such as Actionaly would need to worry about supply chain management.

3. If you ran an apparel company, such as Nike or REI, how could you use RFID to improve the supply chain?

4. Identify the different metrics Actionly uses to measure the success of a customer marketing campaign.

5. Argue for or against the following statement: Actionly invades consumer privacy by taking data from different websites such as Twitter and Flickr without the consent of the customer who posted the information.

 UNIT CLOSING CASE TWO

© Cultura Creative (RF) / Alamy Stock Photo   © scanrail/Getty Images   © Izabela Habur/E+/Getty Images

Dream It, Design It, 3D Print It

Have you ever lost a beloved pet? No worries, just draw a picture of your pet and print a plastic replica from your 3D desktop printer so your cat or dog can sit on your desk forever. Can you imagine printing your drawing in 3D? Well, there is no need to imagine this because you can do it today for as little as $300. Just think of all the problems you can solve by having your own 3D printer. Did you recently lose the key to your car's roof rack? No worries, just download the specifications and print one. Did you forget your girlfriend's birthday? No worries, just download and customize a silver bracelet with her initials and in less than 30 minutes, you'll have the beautiful custom piece of jewelry on her wrist— without ever leaving your apartment.

Welcome to the wonderful world of 3D printing. For almost 30 years, 3D printing has been used by large manufacturing companies to create everything from custom parts to working prototypes. The medical industry uses 3D printing to create custom hearing aids, artificial limbs, and braces, and art designers and architects use 3D printers to create models and prototypes of statues and buildings. Traditionally, 3D printing was only available to large corporations and engineers who could code the intricate devices. Today, the first generation of consumer 3D printers is hitting the market at affordable prices with software easy enough for children to use.

The disruption occurring in the 3D printing world can, of course, be attributed to Moore's law as the technology has increased in capacity and processing power while decreasing in size and costs. Now you can purchase your own 3D printer for as little as $300 to $5,000; simply connect it to your Wi-Fi network and begin downloading files to create your own 3D objects. Current 3D printers offer a wide range of colors and materials, including plastics, metal, glass, and even chocolate. That's right—you can custom print your own valentine chocolates! The only barrier to 3D printing is that the software used to control the printer is still rather difficult for the average person to use, but you can expect that to change because software makers, such as Autodesk, are quickly releasing new, user-friendly applications. Autodesk just released 123D, a suite of free applications that enables ordinary people to design and customize objects on their PCs or even their iPads and then send them to a 3D printer.

3D printers work by first creating a digital computer-aided design (CAD) file, produced with a 3D modeling program or scanned into a 3D modeling program with a 3D scanner. To get from this digital file to instructions that the 3D printer understands, software then slices the design into hundreds or thousands of horizontal layers. Typically, the 3D printer uses either a fused deposition modeling printer, which applies the tiny layers of material, or a laser sintering process by which a laser fuses the material together. Names like 3DSystems, Afinia, and MakerBot produce 3D printers for just a few thousand dollars for consumers and small businesses alike. Figure Unit 3.2 represents a few of the best 3D printed objects according to PC Magazine and Wired. [3]

Questions

1. Define 3D printing and its impact on business.
2. Explain CRM and how 3D printing could affect customer relations.
3. Provide an example of how 3D printing might affect the global economy.
4. Analyze how 3D printing is affecting supply chains.
5. Propose a plan for how a company can use 3D printing to increase sales and customer satisfaction.
6. Argue for or against the following statement: "3D printing will be more disruptive to business than the Internet."

APPLY YOUR KNOWLEDGE

1. Great Stories

With the advent of the Internet, when customers have an unpleasant customer experience, the company no longer has to worry about them telling a few friends and family; the company has to worry about them telling everyone. Internet service providers are giving consumers frustrated with how they were treated by a company another means of fighting back. Free or low-cost computer space for Internet websites is empowering consumers to tell not only their friends, but also the world about the way they have been treated. A few examples of disgruntled customer stories from the Internet include:

- **Bad Experience with Blue Marble Biking**—Tourist on biking tour is bitten by dog, requires stitches. Company is barred from hotel because of incident, and in turn it bars the tourist from any further tours.
- **Best Buy Receipt Check**—Shopper declines to show register receipt for purchase to door guard at Lakewood Best Buy, which is voluntary. Employees attempt to seize cart, stand in shopper's path, and park a truck behind shopper's car to prevent departure.
- **Enterprise Rent-A-Car Is a Failing Enterprise**—Enterprise Rent-A-Car did not honor reservations, did not have cars ready as stated, rented cars with nearly empty tanks, and charged higher prices to corporate account holders.

The Internet is raising the stakes for customer service. With the ability to create a website dedicated to a particular issue, a disgruntled customer can have nearly the same reach as a manufacturer. The pervasive nature of the Internet is increasing customer power and changing business from product-focused to customer-focused. Explain the difference between product-focused business and

Acoustic guitar

Why print a guitar? Well, a little-known fact is that the supplies of exotic woods are running considerably low, so manufacturers of instruments need to start researching for alternative materials. Scott Summit, cofounder of Bespoke Innovations, says that the good news is that there is no gold standard for guitars compared to other stringed instruments such as the violin, so they can be made of anything. In addition, guitarists prefer to have their own unique sound in addition to a customized guitar face, something that will be available with a truly original, 3D-printed guitar.

Bikinis

The N12 is named after Nylon 12, the material in which the bikini was 3D printed by Continuum Fashion. Nylon 12 makes an ideal swimsuit material because it is innately waterproof. As well as being the first 3D printed bikini, it is also the first bikini that actually becomes more comfortable when it gets wet.

Bionic ear

To construct the ear, Princeton University researchers print the polymer gel onto an approximate ear shape and implant calf cells onto the matrix. The silver nanoparticles fuse to create an antenna, which picks up radio signals before being transferred to the cochlea, which translates the sound into brain signals. Despite all of this, researchers have yet to draw up plans to attach the ear to the human head.

Cars

In 2010, Stratasys and Kor Ecologic teamed up to develop Urbee, the first car ever to have its entire body 3D printed by printing layers of material on top of each other until a finished product appeared.

Car parts for Jay Leno

Comedian and car nut Jay Leno had a 1907 White Steamer with a badly damaged feedwater heater, a part that bolts onto the cylinders. Using a NextEngine 3D scanner and Dimension 3D printer, he was able to whip up a new one in 33 hours. "It's an amazingly versatile technology," Leno said on his website. "My EcoJet supercar needed air-conditioning ducts. We used plastic parts we designed, right out of the 3D copier. We didn't have to make these scoops out of aluminum—plastic is what they use in a real car. And the finished ones look like factory production pieces."

Chocolate heads

Some people give roses, some people give 3D-printed jewelry, some people give their undying love. But in Japan, you can give your lover your chocolate head so they can bite into your brain as the ultimate expression of love.

Clothes

Dutch designer Iris van Herpen was at Fashion Week in Paris, accompanied by MIT Media Lab's Neri Oxman, to showcase a dress that was fabricated using 3D printing technology. It was printed on an Objet Connex500 multimaterial 3D printer. Most 3D printers require creations to be printed using only one type of fabric or material, but the Connex500 allows mixing of different types of material.

Google Glasses

Chinese entrepreneur Sunny Gao printed a fully functioning pair of Google Glasses at a hackathon event in Shanghai. Unfortunately, the 3D printed version of the glasses doesn't boast Wi-Fi or Bluetooth support, unlike the real thing—but they are identical in every other way.

Meat (yes, meat)

U.S. start-up Modern Meadow believes it can make artificial raw meat using a 3D bioprinter, the BBC reported. Peter Thiel, one of Silicon Valley's most prominent venture capitalists, PayPal cofounder, and early Facebook investor, has just backed the company with $350,000. The team reportedly has a prototype, but it's "not ready for consumption."

Robotic prosthetic

Easton LaChappelle, a 17-year-old high school student from Colorado, used free online resources for 3D printers to construct a fully functional prosthetic arm and hand. The high school student found inspiration from one of his past projects, which involved building a robotic hand made entirely of LEGOs when he was 14. His creation was able to open and close its fingers using two things: fishing line and servomotors.[2]

customer-focused business and why CRM is more important than ever before. In a group, search the web for the most outrageous story of a disgruntled customer. A few places to start include:

- **Complain Complain**—provides professionally written, custom complaint letters to businesses.
- **The Complaint Department**—a for-fee consumer complaint resolution and letter writing service.
- **The Complaint Station**—provides a central location to complain about issues related to companies' products, services, employment, and get rich quick scams.
- **Complaints.com Consumer Complaints**—database of consumer complaints and consumer advocacy.
- **Baddealings.com**—forum and database on consumer complaints and scams on products and services.

2. Classic Car Problems

Classic Cars Inc. operates high-end automotive dealerships that offer luxury cars along with luxury service. The company is proud of its extensive inventory, top-of-the-line mechanics, and especially its exceptional service, which even includes a cappuccino bar at each dealership.

The company currently has 40 sales representatives at four locations. Each location maintains its own computer systems, and all sales representatives have their own contact management systems. This splintered approach to operations causes numerous problems including customer communication issues, pricing strategy issues, and inventory control issues. A few examples include:

- A customer shopping at one dealership can go to another dealership and receive a quote for a different price for the same car.
- Sales representatives are frequently stealing each other's customers and commissions.
- Sales representatives frequently send their customers to other dealerships to see specific cars and when the customer arrives, the car is not on the lot.
- Marketing campaigns are not designed to target specific customers; they are typically generic, such as 10 percent off a new car.
- If a sales representative quits, all of his or her customer information is lost.

You are working for Customer One, a small consulting company that specializes in CRM strategies. The owner of Classic Cars Inc., Tom Jones, has hired you to help him formulate a strategy to put his company back on track. Develop a proposal for Tom detailing how a CRM system can alleviate the company's issues and create new opportunities.

3. Building Visibility

Visionary companies are building extended enterprises to best compete in the new Internet economy. An extended enterprise combines the Internet's power with new business structures and processes to eliminate old corporate boundaries and geographic restrictions. Networked supply chains create seamless paths of communication among partners, suppliers, manufacturers, retailers, and customers. Because of advances in manufacturing and distribution, the cost of developing new products and services is dropping, and time to market is speeding up. This has resulted in increasing customer demands, local and global competition, and increased pressure on the supply chain.

To stay competitive, companies must reinvent themselves so that the supply chain—sourcing and procurement, production scheduling, order fulfillment, inventory management, and customer care—is no longer a cost-based back-office exercise, but rather a flexible operation designed to effectively address today's challenges.

The Internet is proving an effective tool in transforming supply chains across all industries. Suppliers, distributors, manufacturers, and resellers now work together more closely and effectively than ever. Today's technology-driven supply chain enables customers to manage their own buying experiences, increases coordination and connectivity among supply partners, and helps reduce operating costs for every company in the chain.

In the past, assets were a crucial component of success in supply chain management. In today's market, however, a customer-centric orientation is key to retaining competitive advantage. Using the Internet and any other resources available, develop a strategic plan for implementing a networked, flexible supply chain management system for a start-up company of your choice. Research Netflix if you are unfamiliar with how start-up companies are changing the supply chain. Be sure that your supply chain integrates all partners—manufacturers, retailers, suppliers, carriers, and vendors—into a seamless unit and views customer relationship management as a key competitive advantage. There are several points to consider when creating your customer-centric supply chain strategy:

- Taking orders is only one part of serving customer needs.
- Businesses must fulfill the promise they make to customers by delivering products and information upon request—not when it is convenient for the company.
- Time to market is a key competitive advantage. Companies must ensure uninterrupted supply, and information about customer demands and activities is essential to this requirement.
- Cost is an important factor. Companies need to squeeze the costs from internal processes to make the final products less expensive.
- Reducing design-cycle times is critical, as this allows companies to get their products out more quickly to meet customer demand.

4. Finding Shelf Space at Walmart

Walmart's business strategy of being a low-cost provider by managing its supply chain down to the minutiae has paid off greatly. Each week, approximately 100 million customers, or one-third of the U.S. population, visit Walmart's U.S. stores. Walmart is currently the world's largest retailer and the second largest corporation behind ExxonMobil. It was founded by Sam Walton in 1962 and is the largest private employer in the United States and Mexico. Walmart is also the largest grocery retailer in the United States, with an estimated 20 percent of the retail grocery and consumables business, and the largest toy seller in the United States, with an estimated 45 percent of the retail toy business, having surpassed Toys "R" Us in the late 1990s.

Walmart's business model is based on selling a wide variety of general merchandise at "always low prices." The reason Walmart can offer such low prices is due to its innovative use of information technology tools to create its highly sophisticated supply chain. Over the past decade, Walmart has famously invited its major suppliers to jointly develop powerful supply chain partnerships. These are designed to increase product flow efficiency and, consequently, Walmart's profitability.

Many companies have stepped up to the challenge, starting with the well-known Walmart/ Procter & Gamble alliance, which incorporated vendor-managed inventory, category management, and other intercompany innovations. Walmart's CFO became a key customer as P&G's objective became maximizing Walmart's internal profitability. Unlike many other retailers, Walmart does not charge a slotting fee to suppliers for their products to appear in the store. Alternatively, Walmart focuses on selling more popular products and often pressures store managers to drop unpopular products in favor of more popular ones, as well as pressuring manufacturers to supply more popular products.

You are the owner of a high-end collectible toy company. You create everything from authentic sports figure replicas to famous musicians and movie characters including Babe Ruth, Hulk Hogan, Mick Jagger, Ozzy Osbourne, Alien, and the Terminator. It would be a huge win for your company if you could get your collectibles into Walmart. Compile a strategic plan highlighting the steps required to approach Walmart as your supply chain partner. Be sure to address the pros and cons of partnering with Walmart, including the cost to revamp your current supply chain to meet Walmart's tough supply chain requirements.

5. Shipping Problems

Entrepreneurship is in Alyssa Stuart's blood. Alyssa has been starting businesses since she was 10 years old, and she finally has the perfect business of custom-made furniture. Customers who visit Alyssa's shop can choose from a number of different fabrics and 50 different styles of couch and chair designs to create their custom-made furniture. Once the customer decides on a fabric pattern and furniture design, the information is sent to China where the furniture is built and shipped to the customer via the West Coast. Alyssa is excited about her business; all of her hard work has finally paid off as she has more than 17,000 customers and 875 orders currently in the pipe.

Alyssa's business is booming. Her high-quality products and outstanding customer service have created an excellent reputation for her business. But Alyssa's business is at risk of losing everything and she has come to you for help solving her supply chain issues.

Yesterday, a dockworkers' union strike began and shut down all of the West Coast shipping docks from San Francisco to Canada. Work will resume only when the union agrees to new labor contracts, which could take months. Alyssa has asked you to summarize the impact of the dock shutdown on her business and create a strategy to keep her business running, which is especially difficult because Alyssa guarantees 30-day delivery on all products or the product is free. What strategies do you recommend for Alyssa's business to continue working while her supply chain is disrupted by the dockworkers' strike?

6. Political Supply Chains

The U.S. government has crafted a deal with the United Arab Emirates (UAE) that would let a UAE-based firm, Dubai Ports World (DPW), run six major U.S. ports. If the approval is unchallenged, Dubai Ports World would run the ports of New York, New Jersey, Baltimore, New Orleans, Miami, and Philadelphia. Currently, London-based Peninsular and Oriental Steam Navigation Co. (P&O), the fourth largest port operator in the world, runs the six ports. But the $6.8 billion sale of P&O to DPW would effectively turn over North American operations to the government-owned company in Dubai.

Some citizens are worried that the federal government may be outsourcing U.S. port operations to a company prone to terrorist infiltration by allowing a firm from the United Arab Emirates to run port operations within the United States. You have been called in on an investigation to determine the potential effects on U.S. businesses' supply chains if these ports were shut down due to terrorist activities. The United Arab Emirates has had people involved in terrorism. In fact, some of its financial institutions laundered the money for the 9/11 terrorists. Create an argument for or against outsourcing these ports to the UAE. Be sure to detail the effect on U.S. businesses' supply chains if these ports are subjected to terrorist acts.

7. JetBlue on YouTube

JetBlue took an unusual and interesting CRM approach by using YouTube to apologize to its customers. JetBlue's founder and CEO, David Neeleman, apologized to customers via YouTube after a very, very bad week for the airline: 1,100 flights canceled due to snow storms and thousands of irate passengers. Neeleman's unpolished, earnest delivery makes this apology worth accepting. But then again, we were not stuck on a tarmac for eight hours. With all of the new advances in technology and the many ways to reach customers, do you think using YouTube is a smart approach? What else could JetBlue do to help gain back its customers' trust?

You are the founder and CEO of GoodDog, a large pet food manufacturing company. Recently, at least 16 pet deaths have been tied to tainted pet food, fortunately not manufactured by your company. A recall of potentially deadly pet food has dog and cat owners studying their animals for even the slightest hint of illness and swamping veterinarians nationwide with calls about symptoms both real and imagined. Create a strategy for using YouTube as a vehicle to communicate with your customers as they fear for their pets' lives. Be sure to highlight the pros and cons of using YouTube as a customer communication vehicle. Are there any other new technologies you could use as a customer communication vehicle that would be more effective than YouTube?

8. Lively's Home Cooking Catering

Having been employed by the same company for more than 20 years, Mary Lou Lively was shocked when she was suddenly terminated along with about 900 of her co-workers. It took Lively a few weeks to recover from the shock, and then she finally began focusing her efforts on searching for a new job. Lively was sure her loyal employment history and strong skill set would land her a new job in no time; however, after several months of searching, she wasn't having any luck. With her emergency funds quickly being depleted, Lively knew she had to find a new job soon or she'd need to start selling her assets or cashing in her retirement.

The one positive aspect of having so much free time was that she could focus on her true passion, cooking. Mary Lou began making a little money by catering lunches and dinners for local businesses and neighbors. One day she overheard a neighbor remark that she was hosting a large party and didn't have enough time to prepare the meal. Almost jokingly, Lively asked her how much she'd be willing to pay for a catered event. Soon Lively was catering for numerous neighbors and small businesses and she knew she had to make a decision about whether she would go into business for herself or continue searching for other employment.

After a year in the catering business, Lively was earning a good living and building a stellar reputation. She began catering for all types of events, including weddings, and business was so good that she hired several employees to help grow her business. As Lively begins to plan her expansion, she has asked for your help in answering the following questions:

1. How important is customer loyalty for Lively's business? What can she do to ensure that her customers remain loyal? How could one disgruntled customer hurt business? What can she do to combat this challenge?

2. Research the business Yelp.com. What service does Yelp.com perform? Would a small business see Yelp.com as an opportunity or a threat? What are the pros and cons a customer should be aware of when using Yelp.com?

3. Lively's responsibilities include forecasting, inventory control, scheduling, and ensuring high-quality products. What types of forecasts would she require to run her business? What types of inventory would she want to track? What might happen if her inventory tracking tool was off by 50 percent? What types of schedules does Lively need to generate? What things might occur to disrupt schedules and cause her to reschedule? How can a supply chain management system help run the business?

4. Lively wants to create a business based on loyal customers and loyal employees. She offers her employees bonuses for new ideas, recipes, or business referrals. What risks is Lively encountering by offering these bonuses? One employee idea that she has implemented is turning out to be a competitive advantage for her business; however, the employee has quit and is now working for a competitor. Should Lively still pay the employee the bonus? What should she do to ensure that she is building strong employee relationships?

5. Lively overheard one of her customers talking about enterprise systems such as CRM, SCM, and ERP. However, she is sure they are available only to big companies that have lots of capital. Research the Internet and find examples of enterprise systems for small business. Do you think she should invest in these types of systems to run her business? Why or why not?

If you are looking for Excel projects to incorporate into your class, try any of the following to test your knowledge.

Project Number	Project Name	Project Type	Plug-In	Focus Area	Project Level	Skill Set	Page Number
9	Security Analysis	Excel	T3	Filtering Data	Intermediate	Conditional Formatting, Autofilter, Subtotal	AYK.7
10	Gathering Data	Excel	T3	Data Analysis	Intermediate	Conditional Formatting	AYK.8
11	Scanner System	Excel	T2	Strategic Analysis	Intermediate	Formulas	AYK.8
12	Competitive Pricing	Excel	T2	Profit Maximization	Intermediate	Formulas	AYK.9
13	Adequate Acquisitions	Excel	T2	Break Even Analysis	Intermediate	Formulas	AYK.9
15	Assessing the Value of Information	Excel	T3	Data Analysis	Intermediate	PivotTable	AYK.10
16	Growth, Trends, and Forecasts	Excel	T2, T3	Data Forecasting	Advanced	Average, Trend, Growth	AYK.11
18	Formatting Grades	Excel	T3	Data Analysis	Advanced	If, LookUp	AYK.12
22	Turnover Rates	Excel	T3	Data Mining	Advanced	PivotTable	AYK.15
23	Vital Information	Excel	T3	Data Mining	Advanced	PivotTable	AYK.15
24	Breaking Even	Excel	T4	Business Analysis	Advanced	Goal Seek	AYK.16
25	Profit Scenario	Excel	T4	Sales Analysis	Advanced	Scenario Manager	AYK.16

13

Creating Innovative Organizations

13.1. Compare disruptive and sustaining technologies, and explain how the Internet and WWW caused business disruption.

13.2. Describe ebusiness and its associated advantages.

LO 13.1 **Compare disruptive and sustaining technologies, and explain how the Internet and WWW caused business disruption.**

Disruptive Technologies and Web 1.0

Polaroid, founded in 1937, produced the first instant camera in the late 1940s. The Polaroid camera, whose pictures developed themselves, was one of the most exciting technological advances the photography industry had ever seen. The company eventually went public, becoming one of Wall Street's most prominent enterprises, with its stock trading above $60 per share in 1997. In 2002, the stock dropped to 8 cents and the company declared bankruptcy.[2]

How could a company such as Polaroid, which had innovative technology and a captive customer base, go bankrupt? Perhaps company executives failed to use Porter's Five Forces Model to analyze the threat of substitute products or services. If they had, would they have noticed the two threats—one-hour film processing and digital cameras—which eventually stole Polaroid's market share? Would they have understood that their customers, people who want instant access to their pictures, would be the first to try these alternatives? Could the company have found a way to compete with one-hour film processing and the digital camera to save Polaroid?

Many organizations face the same dilemma as Polaroid—what's best for the current business might not be what's best for it in the long term. Some observers of our business environment have an ominous vision of the future—digital Darwinism. **Digital Darwinism** implies that organizations that cannot adapt to the new demands placed on them for surviving in the information age are doomed to extinction.

DISRUPTIVE VERSUS SUSTAINING TECHNOLOGY

A **disruptive technology** is a new way of doing things that initially does not meet the needs of existing customers. Disruptive technologies tend to open new markets and destroy old ones. A **sustaining technology**, on the other hand, produces an improved product customers are eager to buy, such as a faster car or larger hard drive. Sustaining technologies tend to provide us with better, faster, and cheaper products in established markets. Incumbent companies most often lead sustaining technology to market, but they virtually never lead in markets opened by disruptive technologies. Figure 13.1 positions companies expecting future growth from new investments (disruptive technology) and companies expecting future growth from existing investments (sustaining technology).

Disruptive technologies typically enter the low end of the marketplace and eventually evolve to displace high-end competitors and their reigning technologies. Sony is a perfect example. Sony started as a tiny company that built portable, battery-powered transistor radios. The sound

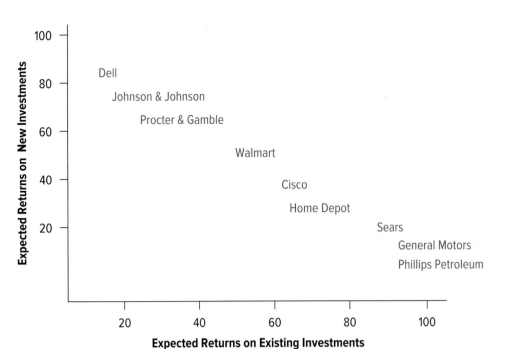

FIGURE 13.1

Disruptive and Sustaining
Technologies.

quality was poor, but customers were willing to overlook that for the convenience of portability. With the experience and revenue stream from the portables, Sony improved its technology to produce cheap, low-end transistor amplifiers that were suitable for home use and invested those revenues in improving the technology further, which produced still-better radios.

The Innovator's Dilemma, a book by Clayton M. Christensen, discusses how established companies can take advantage of disruptive technologies without hindering existing relationships with customers, partners, and stakeholders. Xerox, IBM, Sears, and DEC all listened to existing customers, invested aggressively in technology, had their competitive antennae up, and still lost their market-dominant positions. They may have placed too much emphasis on satisfying customers' current needs, while neglecting new disruptive technology to meet customers' future needs and thus losing market share. Figure 13.2 highlights several companies that launched new businesses by capitalizing on disruptive technologies.[3]

Company	Disruptive Technology
Apple	iPod, iPhone, iPad
Charles Schwab	Online brokerage
Hewlett-Packard	Microprocessor-based computers; ink-jet printers
IBM	Minicomputers; personal computers
Intel	Low-end microprocessors
Intuit	QuickBooks software; TurboTax software; Quicken software
Microsoft	Internet-based computing; operating system software; SQL and Access database software
Oracle	Database software
Quantum	3.5-inch disks
Sony	Transistor-based consumer electronics

FIGURE 13.2

Companies That Capitalized
on Disruptive Technologies.

THE INTERNET AND WORLD WIDE WEB—THE ULTIMATE BUSINESS DISRUPTORS

The *Internet* is a massive network that connects computers all over the world and allows them to communicate with one another. Computers connected via the Internet can send and receive information including text, graphics, voice, video, and software. Originally the Internet was essentially an emergency military communications system operated by the U.S. Department of Defense Advanced Research Project Agency (DARPA), which called the network ARPANET. No one foresaw the dramatic impact it would have on both business and personal communications. In time, all U.S. universities that had defense-related funding installed ARPANET computers, forming the first official Internet network. As users began to notice the value of electronic communications, the purpose of the network started shifting from a military pipeline to a communications tool for scientists.

The Internet and the World Wide Web are not synonymous. The WWW is just one part of the Internet, and its primary use is to correlate and disseminate information. The Internet includes the WWW and also other forms of communication systems such as email. Figure 13.3 lists the key terms associated with the WWW and Figure 13.4 lists the reasons for the massive growth of the WWW.

WEB 1.0: THE CATALYST FOR EBUSINESS

FIGURE 13.3

Overview of the WWW.

As people began learning about the WWW and the Internet, they understood that it enabled a company to communicate with anyone, anywhere, at anytime, creating a new way to participate

Term	Definition	Example
World Wide Web	Provides access to Internet information through documents, including text, graphics, and audio and video files that use a special formatting language called Hypertext Markup Language.	Tim Berners-Lee, a British computer scientist, is considered the inventor of the WWW on March 12, 1989.
Hypertext Markup Language (HTML)	Publishes hypertext on the WWW, which allows users to move from one document to another simply by clicking a hot spot or link.	HTML uses tags such as <h1> and </h1> to structure text into headings, paragraphs, lists, hypertext links, and so on.
HTML 5	The current version of HTML delivers everything from animation to graphics and music to movies; it can also be used to build complicated web applications and works across platforms, including a PC, tablet, smartphone, or smart TV.	Includes new tags such as doctype, a simple way to tell the browser what type of document is being looked at. <!DOCTYPE html PUBLIC>
Hypertext Transport Protocol (HTTP)	The Internet protocol web browsers use to request and display web pages using universal resource locators (URLs).	To retrieve the file at the URL http://www.somehost.com/path/file.html
World Wide Web Consortium (W3C)	An international community that develops open standards to ensure the long-term growth of the Web (www.w3.org).	Tim Berners-Lee founded the W3C to act as a steward of web standards, which the organization has done for more than 15 years.
Web browser	Allows users to access the WWW.	Internet Explorer, Mozilla's Firefox, Google Chrome
Universal resource locator (URL)	The address of a file or resource on the web.	www.apple.com www.microsoft.com www.amazon.com
Domain name hosting (web hosting)	A service that allows the owner of a domain name to maintain a simple website and provide email capacity.	GoDaddy.com, 1&1.com, Web.com
Applet	A program that runs within another application such as a website.	The common "Hello World" applet types Hello World across the screen
Internet Corporation for Assigned Names and Numbers (ICANN)	A nonprofit organization that has assumed the responsibility for Internet Protocol (IP) address space allocation, protocol parameter assignment, domain name system management, and root server system management functions previously performed under U.S. government contract.	https://www.icann.org/ Individuals, industry, noncommercial, and government representatives discuss, debate, and develop policies about the technical coordination of the Internet's Domain Name System.

The microcomputer revolution made it possible for an average person to own a computer.	
Advancements in networking hardware, software, and media made it possible for business computers to be connected to larger networks at a minimal cost.	
Browser software such as Microsoft's Internet Explorer and Netscape Navigator gave computer users an easy-to-use graphical interface to find, download, and display web pages.	
The speed, convenience, and low cost of email have made it an incredibly popular tool for business and personal communications.	
Basic web pages are easy to create and extremely flexible.	

FIGURE 13.4

Reasons for Growth of the World Wide Web.

in business. The competitive advantages for first movers would be enormous, thus spurring the beginning of the Web 1.0 Internet boom. **Web 1.0** is a term to refer to the World Wide Web during its first few years of operation between 1991 and 2003. **Ecommerce** is the buying and selling of goods and services over the Internet. Ecommerce refers only to online transactions. **Ebusiness** includes ecommerce along with all activities related to internal and external business operations such as servicing customer accounts, collaborating with partners, and exchanging real-time information. During Web 1.0, entrepreneurs began creating the first forms of ebusiness.

Ebusiness opened up a new marketplace for any company willing to move its business operations online. A **paradigm shift** occurs when a new radical form of business enters the market that reshapes the way companies and organizations behave. Ebusiness created a paradigm shift, transforming entire industries and changing enterprisewide business processes that fundamentally rewrote traditional business rules. Deciding not to make the shift to ebusiness proved fatal for many companies (see Figure 13.5 for an overview of industries revamped by the disruption of ebusiness).

FIGURE 13.5

Ebusiness Disruption of Traditional Industries.

Industry	Business Changes Due to Technology
Auto	AutoTrader.com is the world's largest used-car marketplace, listing millions of cars from both private owners and dealers. AutoTrader.com actually helps to increase used-car dealers' business as it drives millions of qualified leads (potential used-car buyers) to participating automotive dealers and private sellers.
Publishing	With the Internet, anyone can publish online content. Traditionally, publishers screened many authors and manuscripts and selected those that had the best chances of succeeding. Lulu.com turned this model around by providing self-publishing along with print-on-demand capabilities.
Education and Training	Continuing medical education is costly, and just keeping up-to-date with advances often requires taking training courses and traveling to conferences. Now continuing education in many fields is moving online, and by 2016 more than 50 percent of doctors will be building their skills through online learning. Companies such as Cisco save millions by moving training to the Internet.
Entertainment	The music industry was hit hard by ebusiness, and online music traders such as iTunes average billions of annual downloads. Unable to compete with online music, the majority of record stores closed. The next big entertainment industry to feel the effects of ebusiness will be the multibillion-dollar movie business. Video rental stores are closing their doors as they fail to compete with online streaming and home rental delivery companies such as Netflix.
Financial Services	Nearly every public efinance company makes money, with online mortgage service Lending Tree leading the pack. Processing online mortgage applications is more than 50 percent cheaper for customers.
Retail	Forrester Research predicts ebusiness retail sales will grow at a 10 percent annual growth rate through 2020. It forecasts U.S. online retail sales will be nearly $250 billion, up from $155 billion in 2009. Online retail sales were recently up 11 percent, compared to 2.5 percent for all retail sales.
Travel	Travel site Expedia.com is now the biggest leisure-travel agency, with higher profit margins than even American Express. The majority of travel agencies closed as a direct result of ebusiness.

Advantages of Ebusiness

Both individuals and organizations have embraced ebusiness to enhance productivity, maximize convenience, and improve communications. Companies today need to deploy a comprehensive ebusiness strategy, and business students need to understand its advantages, outlined in Figure 13.6. Let's look at each.

EXPANDING GLOBAL REACH

Easy access to real-time information is a primary benefit of ebusiness. *Information richness* refers to the depth and breadth of details contained in a piece of textual, graphic, audio, or video information. *Information reach* measures the number of people a firm can communicate with all over the world. Buyers need information richness to make informed purchases, and sellers need information reach to properly market and differentiate themselves from the competition.

Ebusinesses operate 24 hours a day, 7 days a week. This availability directly reduces transaction costs, since consumers no longer have to spend a lot of time researching purchases or traveling great distances to make them. The faster delivery cycle for online sales helps strengthen customer relationships, improving customer satisfaction and ultimately sales.

A firm's website can be the focal point of a cost-effective communications and marketing strategy. Promoting products online allows the company to precisely target its customers whether they are local or around the globe. A physical location is restricted by size and limited to those customers who can get there, while an online store has a global marketplace with customers and information seekers already waiting in line.

OPENING NEW MARKETS

Ebusiness is perfect for increasing niche-product sales. *Mass customization* is the ability of an organization to tailor its products or services to the customers' specifications. For example, customers can order M&M's in special colors or with customized sayings such as "Marry Me." *Personalization* occurs when a company knows enough about a customer's likes and dislikes that it can fashion offers more likely to appeal to that person, say by tailoring its website to individuals or groups based on profile information, demographics, or prior transactions. Amazon uses personalization to create a unique portal for each of its customers.

REDUCING COSTS

Chris Anderson, editor-in-chief of *Wired* magazine, describes niche-market ebusiness strategies as capturing the *long tail*, referring to the tail of a typical sales curve. This strategy demonstrates how niche products can have viable and profitable business models when selling via ebusiness. In traditional sales models, a store is limited by shelf space when selecting products to sell. For this reason, store owners typically purchase products that will be wanted or needed by masses, and the store is stocked with broad products as there is not room on the shelf for niche products that only a few customers might purchase. Ebusinesses such as Amazon and eBay eliminated the shelf-space dilemma and were able to offer infinite products.

FIGURE 13.6

Ebusiness Advantages.

Netflix offers an excellent example of the long tail. Let's assume that an average Block-buster store maintains 3,000 movies in its inventory, whereas Netflix, without physical shelf limitations, can maintain 100,000 movies in its inventory. Looking at sales data, the majority of Blockbuster's revenue comes from new releases that are rented daily, whereas older selections are rented only a few times a month and don't repay the cost of keeping them in stock. Thus Blockbuster's sales tail ends at title 3,000 (see Figure 13.7) However, Netflix, with no physical limitations, can extend its tail beyond 100,000 (and with streaming video perhaps 200,000). By extending its tail, Netflix increases sales, even if a title is rented only a few times.[4]

Intermediaries are agents, software, or businesses that provide a trading infrastructure to bring buyers and sellers together. The introduction of ebusiness brought about *disintermediation*, which occurs when a business sells directly to the customer online and cuts out the intermediary (see Figure 13.8). This business strategy lets the company shorten the order process and add value with reduced costs or a more responsive and efficient service. The disintermediation of the travel agent occurred as people began to book their own vacations online, often at a cheaper rate. At Amazon anyone can publish and sell print-on-demand books, online music, and custom calendars, making the publisher obsolete.[5]

In *reintermediation*, steps are *added* to the value chain as new players find ways to add value to the business process. Levi Strauss originally thought it was a good business strategy to limit all online sales to its own website. A few years later, the company realized it could

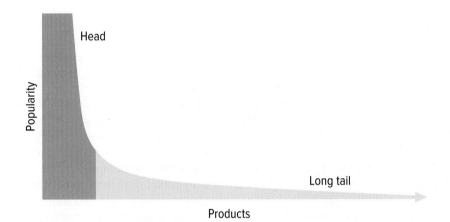

FIGURE 13.7

The Long Tail.

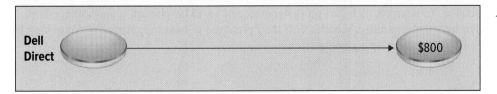
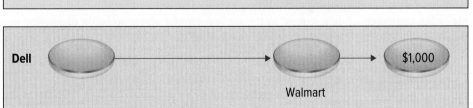
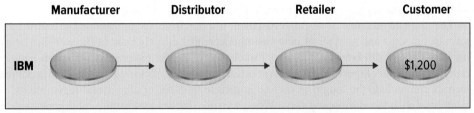

FIGURE 13.8

Business Value of Disintermediation.

The more intermediaries that are cut from the distribution chain, the lower the product price. When Dell decided to sell its PCs through Walmart many were surprised, because Dell's direct-to-customer sales model was the competitive advantage that had kept Dell the market leader for years.

gain a far larger market share by allowing all retailers to sell its products directly to customers. As ebusiness matures it has become evident that to serve certain markets in volume, some reintermediation may be desirable. **Cybermediation** refers to the creation of new kinds of intermediaries that simply could not have existed before the advent of ebusiness, including comparison-shopping sites such as Kelkoo and bank account aggregation services such as Citibank.

Operational benefits of ebusiness include business processes that require less time and human effort or can be eliminated. Compare the cost of sending out 100 direct mailings (paper, postage, labor) to the cost of a bulk email campaign. Think about the cost of renting a physical location and operating phone lines versus the cost of maintaining an online site. Switching to an ebusiness model can eliminate many traditional costs associated with communicating by substituting systems, such as Live Help, that let customers chat live with support or sales staff.

Online air travel reservations cost less than those booked over the telephone. Online ordering also offers the possibility of merging a sales order system with order fulfillment and delivery so customers can check the progress of their orders at all times. Ebusinesses can also inexpensively attract new customers with innovative marketing and retain present customers with improved service and support.

One of the most exciting benefits of ebusiness is its low start-up costs. Today, anyone can start an ebusiness with just a website and a great product or service. Even a dog-walking operation can benefit from being an ebusiness.

IMPROVING EFFECTIVENESS

Just putting up a simple website does not create an ebusiness. Ebusiness websites must create buzz, be innovative, add value, and provide useful information. In short, they must build a sense of community and collaboration.

MIS measures of efficiency, such as the amount of traffic on a site, don't tell the whole story. They do not necessarily indicate large sales volumes, for instance. Many websites with lots of traffic have minimal sales. The best way to measure ebusiness success is to use *effectiveness* MIS metrics, such as the revenue generated by web traffic, number of new customers acquired by web traffic, and reductions in customer service calls resulting from web traffic.

Interactivity measures advertising effectiveness by counting visitor interactions with the target ad, including time spent viewing the ad, number of pages viewed, and number of repeat visits to the advertisement. Interactivity measures are a giant step forward for advertisers, since traditional advertising methods—newspapers, magazines, radio, and television—provide few ways to track effectiveness. Figure 13.9 displays the ebusiness marketing initiatives allowing companies to expand their reach while measuring effectiveness.

The ultimate outcome of any advertisement is a purchase. Organizations use metrics to tie revenue amounts and number of new customers created directly back to the websites or banner ads. Through **clickstream data** they can observe the exact pattern of a consumer's navigation through a site. Figure 13.10 displays different types of clickstream metrics. Clickstream metrics can include the length of stay on a website, number of abandoned registrations, and number of abandoned shopping carts. When a visitor reaches a website, a hit is generated, and his or her computer sends a request to the site's computer server to begin displaying pages. Each element of a request page is recorded by the website's server log file as a hit. Stickiness is the length of time a visitor spends on a website.

Figure 3.11 provides definitions of common metrics based on clickstream data. Businesses want their websites to be sticky and keep their customer's attention. To interpret such data properly, managers try to benchmark against other companies. For instance, consumers seem to visit their preferred websites regularly, even checking back multiple times during a given session. To interpret such data properly, managers try to benchmark against other companies. For instance, consumers seem to visit their preferred websites regularly, even checking back multiple times during a given session.

TERM	DEFINITION	EXAMPLE
Associate (affiliate) program	Allows a business to generate commissions or referral fees when a customer visiting its website clicks a link to another merchant's website	If a customer to a company website clicks a banner ad to another vendor's website, the company will receive a referral fee or commission when the customer performs the desired action, typically making a purchase or completing a form.
Banner ad	A box running across a website that advertises the products and services of another business, usually another ebusiness.	The banner generally contains a link to the advertiser's website. Advertisers can track how often customers click a banner ad resulting in a click-through to their website. Often the cost of the banner ad depends on the number of customers who click the banner ad. Web-based advertising services can track the number of times users click the banner, generating statistics that enable advertisers to judge whether the advertising fees are worth paying.
Click-through	A count of the number of people who visit one site and click an advertisement that takes them to the site of the advertiser.	Tracking effectiveness based on click-throughs guarantees exposure to target ads; however, it does not guarantee that the visitor liked the ad, spent any substantial time viewing the ad, or was satisfied with the information contained in the ad.
Cookie	A small file deposited on a hard drive by a website, containing information about customers and their browsing activities.	Cookies allow websites to record the comings and goings of customers, usually without their knowledge or consent.
Pop-up ad	A small web page containing an advertisement that appears outside of the current website loaded in the browser.	A form of a pop-up ad that users do not see until they close the current web browser screen.
Viral marketing	A technique that induces websites or users to pass on a marketing message to other websites or users, creating exponential growth in the message's visibility and effect.	One example of successful viral marketing is Hotmail, which promotes its service and its own advertisers' messages in every user's email notes. Viral marketing encourages users of a product or service supplied by an ebusiness to encourage friends to join. Viral marketing is a word-of-mouth type of advertising program.

FIGURE 13.9

Marketing Benefits from Ebusiness.

FIGURE 13.10

Clickstream Data Metrics.

Types of Clickstream Data Metrics
The number of page views (i.e., the number of times a particular page has been presented to a visitor).
The pattern of websites visited, including most frequent exit page and most frequent prior website.
Length of stay on the website.
Dates and times of visits.
Number of registrations filled out per 100 visitors.
Number of abandoned registrations.
Demographics of registered visitors.
Number of customers with shopping carts.
Number of abandoned shopping carts.

FIGURE 14.5

Ebusiness Revenue Models.

Ebusiness Revenue Model	Benefits	Challenges
Advertising fees	■ Well-targeted advertisements can be perceived as value-added content by trading participants. ■ Easy to implement	■ Limited revenue potential ■ Overdone or poorly targeted advertisements can be disturbing elements on the website.
License fees	■ Creates incentives to do many transactions ■ Customization and back-end integration lead to lock-in of participants.	■ Up-front fee is a barrier to entry for participants. ■ Price differentiation is complicated.
Subscription fees	■ Creates incentives to do transactions ■ Price can be differentiated. ■ Possibility to build additional revenue from new user groups	■ Fixed fee is a barrier to entry for participants.
Transaction fees	■ Can be directly tied to savings (both process and price savings) ■ Important revenue source when high level of liquidity (transaction volume) is reached	■ If process savings are not completely visible, use of the system is discouraged (incentive to move transactions offline). ■ Transaction fees likely to decrease with time
Value-added services fees	■ Service offering can be differentiated. ■ Price can be differentiated. ■ Possibility to build additional revenue from established and new user groups (third parties)	■ Cumbersome process for customers to continually evaluate new services

Ebusinesses must have a revenue model, or a model for making money. Some companies charge a flat fee for access to the material or services and some business charge fees for use. For instance, will the ebusiness accept advertising or sell subscriptions or licensing rights? Figure 14.5 lists the different benefits and challenges of various ebusiness revenue models.[1]

LO 14.2 Describe the six ebusiness tools for connecting and communicating.

Ebusiness Tools for Connecting and Communicating

As firms began to move online, more MIS tools were created to support ebusiness processes and requirements. The tools supporting and driving ebusiness are highlighted in Figure 14.6 and covered below in detail.

EMAIL

Email, short for electronic mail, is the exchange of digital messages over the Internet. No longer do business professionals have to wait for the mail to receive important documents as email single-handedly increased the speed of business by allowing the transfer of documents with the same speed as the telephone. Its chief business advantage is the ability to inform and communicate with many people simultaneously, immediately, and with ease. There are no time or place constraints, and users can check, send, and view emails whenever they require.

FIGURE 14.6

Ebusiness Tools.

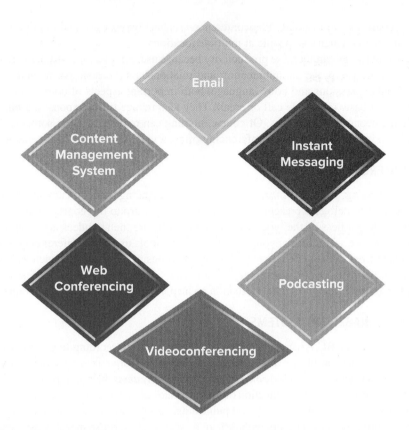

An *Internet service provider (ISP)* is a company that provides access to the Internet for a monthly fee. Major ISPs in the United States include AOL, AT&T, Comcast, Earthlink, and Netzero, as well as thousands of local ISPs including regional telephone companies.

INSTANT MESSAGING

Real-time communication occurs when a system updates information at the same rate it receives it. Email was a great advancement over traditional communication methods such as the U.S. mail, but it did not operate in real time. *Instant messaging (IMing)* is a service that enables instant or real-time communication between people. Businesses immediately saw what they could do:

- Answer simple questions quickly and easily.
- Resolve questions or problems immediately.
- Transmit messages as fast as naturally flowing conversation.
- Easily hold simultaneous IM sessions with multiple people.
- Eliminate long-distance phone charges.
- Quickly identify which employees are at their computers.

PODCASTING

Podcasting converts an audio broadcast to a digital music player. Podcasts can increase marketing reach and build customer loyalty. Companies use podcasts as marketing communication channels discussing everything from corporate strategies to detailed product overviews. The senior executive team can share weekly or monthly podcasts featuring important issues or expert briefings on new technical or marketing developments.

VIDEOCONFERENCING

A *videoconference* allows people at two or more locations to interact via two-way video and audio transmissions simultaneously as well as share documents, data, computer displays, and whiteboards. Point-to-point videoconferences connect two people, and multipoint conferences connect more than two people at multiple locations.

Videoconferences can increase productivity because users participate without leaving their offices. They can improve communication and relationships, because participants see each other's facial expressions and body language, both important aspects of communication that are lost with a basic telephone call or email. They also reduce travel expenses, a big win for firms facing economic challenges. Of course, nothing can replace meeting someone face-to-face and shaking hands, but videoconferencing offers a viable and cost-effective alternative.

WEB CONFERENCING

Web conferencing, or a *webinar*, blends videoconferencing with document sharing and allows the user to deliver a presentation over the web to a group of geographically dispersed participants. Regardless of the type of hardware or software the attendees are running, every participant can see what is on anyone else's screen. Schools use web conferencing tools such as Illuminate Live to deliver lectures to students, and businesses use tools such as WebEx to demonstrate products. Web conferencing is not quite like being there, but professionals can accomplish more sitting at their desks than in an airport waiting to make travel connections.

CONTENT MANAGEMENT SYSTEMS

In the fourth century BC Aristotle cataloged the natural world according to a systematic organization, and the ancient library at Alexandria was reportedly organized by subject, connecting like information with like. Today *content management systems* help companies manage the creation, storage, editing, and publication of their website content. Content management systems are user-friendly; most include web-based publishing, search, navigation, and indexing to organize information; and they let users with little or no technical expertise make website changes.

A search is typically carried out by entering a keyword or phrase (query) into a text field and clicking a button or a hyperlink. Navigation facilitates movement from one web page to another. Content management systems play a crucial role in getting site visitors to view more than just the home page. If navigation choices are unclear, visitors may hit the "Back" button on their first (and final) visit to a website. One rule of thumb to remember is that each time a user has to click to find search information, there is a 50 percent chance the user will leave the website instead. A key principle of good website design, therefore, is to keep the number of clicks to a minimum.

Taxonomy is the scientific classification of organisms into groups based on similarities of structure or origin. Taxonomies are also used for indexing the content on the website into categories and subcategories of topics. For example, car is a subtype of vehicle. Every car is a vehicle, but not every vehicle is a car; some vehicles are vans, buses, and trucks. Taxonomy terms are arranged so that narrower/more specific/"child" terms fall under broader/more generic/"parent" terms. *Information architecture* is the set of ideas about how all information in a given context should be organized. Many companies hire information architects to create their website taxonomies. A well-planned taxonomy ensures search and navigation are easy and user-friendly. If the taxonomy is confusing, the site will soon fail.

LO 14.3 Identify the four challenges associated with ebusiness.

The Challenges of Ebusiness

Although the benefits of ebusiness are enticing, developing, deploying, and managing ebusiness systems is not always easy. Figure 14.7 lists the challenges facing ebusiness.

IDENTIFYING LIMITED MARKET SEGMENTS

The main challenge of ebusiness is the lack of growth in some sectors due to product or service limitations. The online food sector has not grown in sales, in part because food products are perishable and consumers prefer to buy them at the supermarket as needed. Other sectors with limited ebusiness appeal include fragile or consumable goods and highly sensitive or confidential businesses such as government agencies.

MANAGING CONSUMER TRUST

Trust in the ebusiness exchange deserves special attention. The physical separation of buyer and seller, the physical separation of buyer and merchandise, and customer perceptions about the risk of doing business online provide unique challenges. Internet marketers must develop a trustworthy relationship to make that initial sale and generate customer loyalty. A few ways to build trust when working online include being accessible and available to communicate in person with your customers; using customers' testimonials that link to your client website or to provide their contact information; and accepting legitimate forms of payment such as credit cards.

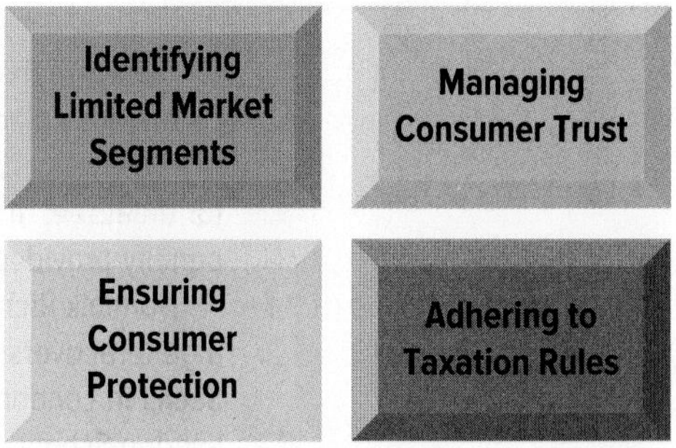

ENSURING CONSUMER PROTECTION

An organization that wants to dominate with superior customer service as a competitive advantage must not only serve but also protect its customers, guarding them against unsolicited goods and communication, illegal or harmful goods, insufficient information about goods and suppliers, invasion of privacy and misuse of personal information, and online fraud. System security, however, must not make ebusiness websites inflexible or difficult to use.

ADHERING TO TAXATION RULES

Many believe that U.S. tax policy should provide a level playing field for traditional retail businesses, mail-order companies, and online merchants. Yet the Internet marketplace remains mostly free of traditional forms of sales tax, partly because ecommerce law is vaguely defined and differs from state to state. For now, companies that operate online must obey a patchwork of rules about which customers are subject to sales tax on their purchases and which are not.

FIGURE 14.7

Challenges Facing Ebusiness.

OPENING CASE STUDY QUESTIONS

1. What is the ebusiness model implemented by Slack?
2. What is the revenue model implemented by Slack?

Chapter Fourteen Case: HelloFresh Hello Delicious

HelloFresh is at the forefront of disrupting a multi trillion-dollar industry at the very beginning of its online transition. HelloFresh is a truly local food product, uniquely suited to individual tastes and meal-time preferences offering delivery of a giant box of delicious food with recipes to enable easy and enjoyable meal preparation for a weekly fee.

HelloFresh aims to provide each and every household in its 7 markets with the opportunity to enjoy wholesome home-cooked meals with no planning, no shopping, and no hassle required. Everything required for weeknight meals, carefully planned, locally sourced and delivered to your door at the most convenient time for each subscriber. Behind the scenes, a huge data driven technology platform puts us in the prime position for disrupting the food supply chain and for fundamentally changing the way consumers shop for food. HelloFresh has local founders across the globe who are able to leverage the global platform, and at the same time ensure that the HelloFresh product in each market truly reflects the local community.

The soft subscription model business enables us to leverage our weekly subscriber touch points to consistently manage supply chains and demand, and to optimize the customer experience as well as our business economics. Customers sign-up for a box containing between 2 and 5 meals per week for a flat fee. If the customer is out of town or unavailable he can easily cancel any week without a penalty provided they notify HelloFresh in advance.

Dominik Richter has been CEO since starting HelloFresh in 2011. He has responsibility for keeping a general oversight of the business and strategy. Prior to HelloFresh, Dominik worked with Goldman Sachs in London. Dominik graduated with a degree in International Business in 2009, and from the London School of Economics in 2010 with a Masters in Finance.

Thomas Griesel has been responsible for the logistics and operations behind HelloFresh since founding with Dominik in 2011. Previously, Thomas had spent time at OC&C Strategy Consultants and worked on a range of his own businesses and ideas. He graduated from with a degree in International Business Administration in 2009, and from the London Business School in 2010 with a Masters in Management.

2011

All the way back in 2011, Dominik and Thomas arrived in Berlin, intent on starting a new and disruptive business. With a love of healthy food, nutrition, cooking, and a desire to make access to healthy food as easy as possible for as many people as possible - starting a Food at Home business seemed the natural choice.

2012

After examining business models from Sweden to Japan to very local ideas, they and a group of like-minded individuals formulated the recipe for HelloFresh. The team started early in 2012 packing shopping bags in Berlin, Amsterdam and London with a view to target the highest density population areas in Europe. Quite quickly, they started getting requests from people outside those areas who all wanted to become a part of the HelloFresh family. Wanting to serve as many people as possible, the team developed a logistics model that enabled them to deliver to every single household across a given country.

2013

The HelloFresh product started to rapidly gain in popularity, as subscribers shared the excitement about their weekly boxes, with friends and colleagues. Subscriber referrals accelerated, as it became clear that HelloFresh had finally solved the "What's for dinner tonight" problem for its subscribers.

2014

Having launched on the East Coast of the U.S in December 2012, HelloFresh moved to cover the entire country in September 2014. Over the short time since then, HelloFresh has grown rapidly to become one of the largest players in this market.

Questions

1. Do you consider HelloFresh a form of disruptive or sustaining technology?

2. Is HelloFresh an example of Web 1.0 (ebusiness) or Web 2.0 (Business 2.0)?

3. Describe the ebusiness model associated with HelloFresh.

4. Describe the revenue model associated with HelloFresh.

14.1. Compare the four categories of ebusiness models.

- Business-to-business (B2B) applies to businesses buying from and selling to each other over the Internet.

- Business-to-consumer (B2C) applies to any business that sells its products or services to consumers over the Internet.

- Consumer-to-business (C2B) applies to any consumer who sells a product or service to a business over the Internet.

- Consumer-to-consumer (C2C) applies to sites primarily offering goods and services to assist consumers interacting with each other over the Internet.

The primary difference between B2B and B2C are the customers; B2B customers are other businesses, whereas B2C markets to consumers. Overall, B2B relations are more complex and have higher security needs and is the dominant ebusiness force, representing 80 percent of all online business.

14.2. Describe the six ebusiness tools for connecting and communicating.

As firms began to move online, more MIS tools were created to support ebusiness processes and requirements. The ebusiness tools used to connect and communicate include email, instant messaging, podcasting, content management systems, videoconferencing, and web conferencing.

14.3. Identify the four challenges associated with ebusiness.

Although the benefits of ebusiness are enticing, developing, deploying, and managing ebusiness systems is not always easy. The challenges associated with ebusiness include identifying limited market segments, managing consumer trust, ensuring consumer protection, and adhering to taxation rules.

1. What is a business model?
2. How did ebusiness change traditional business models?
3. What are the benefits and challenges associated with ebusiness?
4. What is the difference between a B2B and C2C?
5. What is the difference between a C2B and B2C?
6. What is a pure-play? Provide an example.
7. What is a brick-and-mortar? Provide an example.
8. What is click-and-mortar? Provide an example.
9. Why is search engine ranking important to a company?
10. What is the difference between search engine ranking and search engine optimization?

1. Nasty Gal–Eight Years Old and Worth $100 Million

Sophia Amoruso is the founder and CEO of Nasty Gal, an eight-year-old online fashion retail company worth over $100 million. Nasty Gal sells new and vintage clothing, accessories, and shoes online. Founder Sophia Amoruso started the company on eBay, selling one-of-a-kind vintage pieces that she sourced, styled, photographed, and shipped herself. The following is excerpted from her new book, *#GIRLBOSS*.

"I never started a business. I started an eBay store, and ended up with a business. I never would have done it had I known it was going to become this big. I was 22 and, like most 22-year-olds, I was looking for a way to pay my rent and buy my Starbucks chai. Had someone shown me the future of where Nasty Gal would be in 2014, I would have gasped in revulsion, thinking, 'Oh, no, that is way too much work.'

There are different kinds of entrepreneurs. There are the ones who start a business because they're educated and choose to, and the ones who do it because it is really the only option. I definitely fall into the latter category."

The Internet is a great place to start a business! If Sophia Amoruso had started her business in a traditional store, would she have found success? List the advantages Sophia Amoruso gained by selling her items on eBay. If you could start a business on eBay, what would it be and how would you use ebusiness to your advantage?

2. Using Hashtags

If you have ever seen a word with a # before it in Facebook or Twitter, you have seen a hashtag. A hashtag is a keyword or phrase used to identify a topic and is preceded by a hash or pound sign (#). Hashtags provide an online audience to expand business exposure and directly engage with customers. Customers can type any search keyword in a social media site with a hashtag before the word and the search results will show all related posts. Hashtags can be used to reference promotions, observe market trends, and even provide links to helpful tips.

When you understand hashtags, you can use them to find business ideas and research potential employers. Pick a company you would like to work for and see whether you can find any related hashtags including what they are tweeting and posting. See whether you can find any information on partners and competitors. Which hashtags generate discussion or offer business insights? Check Twitter's and Facebook's trending topics and see whether there are any issues or insights on your career area.

3. Virtual Abandonment

Approximately 35 percent of online shopping carts are abandoned prior to checkout. Abandoned shopping carts relate directly to lost revenues for a business. It is like a customer walking out of the store, leaving his or her cart full of chosen items. Businesses need to focus on why the customers are virtually walking out of their stores. The problem typically lies in the checkout process and can be fixed by the following:

- Make sure the checkout button is easy to find.
- Make sure personal information is safe and the website's security is visible.
- Streamline the checkout process so the customer has as few clicks as possible.
- Do not ask shoppers to create an account prior to checkout, but you can ask them to create an account after checkout.
- Ensure your return policy is visible.

Have you ever abandoned a virtual shopping cart? In a group, visit a website that you or your peers have recently abandoned and review the checkout process. Was it difficult, cumbersome, or lacking security? Then visit Amazon.com and review its checkout process and determine whether Amazon is meeting the preceding recommendations.

4. Viral Foxes and Devil Babies

Viral marketing can be a company's greatest success or its worst nightmare. Here are a few popular examples:

- "What Does the Fox Say?" The video created by a pair of Norwegian variety show brothers displays people, dressed up as animals, dancing around in the woods and singing a catchy song. The video received over 400 million views on YouTube and skyrocketed the band Ylvis to virtual stardom.

- The video of a robotic devil baby left in an unattended stroller in the middle of the street in Manhattan attracted over 50 million views in a month. The creators of the devil baby video, Thinkmodo, was creating buzz for the 20th Century Fox movie it was promoting, *Devil's Due*.

- Domino's Pizza employees posted a video showing them making sandwiches with unsanitary ingredients. The video went viral and ended with the arrest of the employees and an apology from the CEO.

Research the web and find an example of a viral video that helped a business achieve success and one that caused a business to fail. Do you think it is important for a business to try to manage its online reputation actively? What can a company do if a negative video goes viral, such as the one concerning Domino's Pizza?

Creating Collaborative Partnerships

15.1. Explain Web 2.0, and identify its four characteristics.

15.2. Explain how Business 2.0 is helping communities network and collaborate.

15.3. Describe the three Business 2.0 tools for collaborating.

15.4. Explain the three challenges associated with Business 2.0.

15.5. Describe Web 3.0 and the next generation of online business.

LO 15.1 Explain Web 2.0, and identify its four characteristics.

Web 2.0: Advantages of Business 2.0

In the mid-1990s the stock market reached an all-time high as companies took advantage of ebusiness and Web 1.0, and many believed the Internet was the wave of the future. When new online businesses began failing to meet earning expectations, however, the bubble burst. Some then believed the ebusiness boom was over, but they could not have been more wrong.

Web 2.0 (or Business 2.0) is the next generation of Internet use—a more mature, distinctive communications platform characterized by new qualities such as collaboration, sharing, and free. Business 2.0 encourages user participation and the formation of communities that contribute to the content. In Business 2.0, technical skills are no longer required to use and publish information to the World Wide Web, eliminating entry barriers for online business.

Traditional companies tended to view technology as a tool required to perform a process or activity, and employees picked up information by walking through the office or hanging out around the water cooler. Business 2.0 technologies provide a virtual environment that, for many new employees, is just as vibrant and important as the physical environment. Figure 15.1 highlights the common characteristics of Business 2.0.[1]

CONTENT SHARING THROUGH OPEN SOURCING

An *open system* consists of nonproprietary hardware and software based on publicly known standards that allow third parties to create add-on products to plug into or interoperate with the system. Thousands of hardware devices and software applications created and sold by third-party vendors interoperate with computers, such as iPods, drawing software, and mice.

Source code contains instructions written by a programmer specifying the actions to be performed by computer software. *Closed source* is any proprietary software licensed under exclusive legal right of the copyright holder. *Open source* refers to any software whose source code is made available free (not on a fee or licensing basis as in ebusiness) for any third party to review and modify. Business 2.0 is capitalizing on open source software. Mozilla, for example, offers its Firefox web browser and Thunderbird email software free. Mozilla believes the Internet is a public resource that must remain open and accessible to all; it continuously develops free products by bringing together thousands of dedicated volunteers from

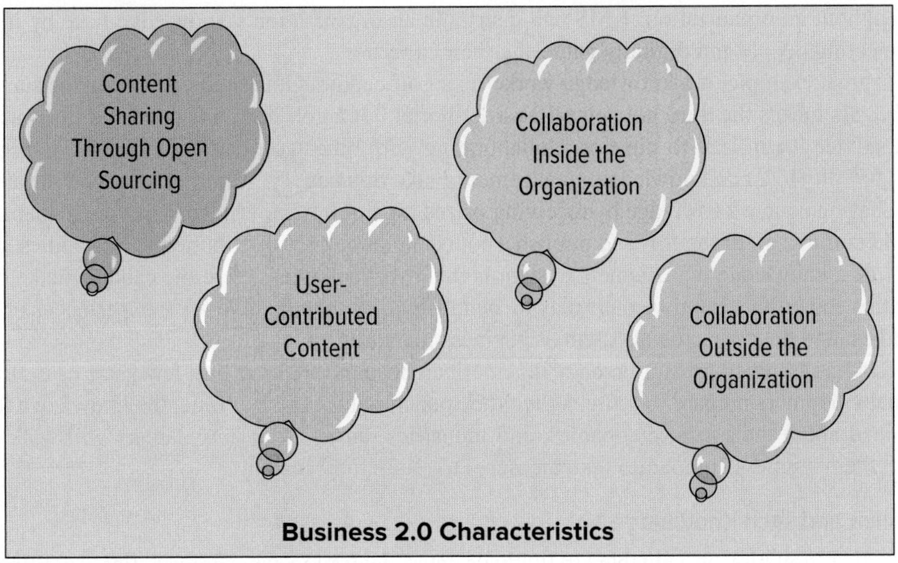

FIGURE 15.1

Characteristics of
Business 2.0.

Business 2.0 Characteristics

around the world. Mozilla's Firefox now holds more than 20 percent of the browser market and is quickly becoming a threat to Microsoft's Internet Explorer. How do open source software companies generate revenues? Many people are still awaiting an answer to this very important question.[2]

USER-CONTRIBUTED CONTENT

Ebusiness was characterized by a few companies or users posting content for the masses. Business 2.0 is characterized by the masses posting content for the masses. *User-contributed content* (or *user-generated content*) is created and updated by many users for many users. Websites such as Flickr, Wikipedia, and YouTube, for example, move control of online media from the hands of leaders to the hands of users. Netflix and Amazon both use user-generated content to drive their recommendation tools, and websites such as Yelp use customer reviews to express opinions on products and services. Companies are embracing user-generated content to help with everything from marketing to product development and quality assurance.

Native advertising is an online marketing concept in which the advertiser attempts to gain attention by providing content in the context of the user's experience in terms of its content, format, style, or placement. One of the most popular forms of user-generated content is a *reputation system*, where buyers post feedback on sellers. eBay buyers voluntarily comment on the quality of service, their satisfaction with the item traded, and promptness of shipping. Sellers comment about prompt payment from buyers or respond to comments left by the buyer. Companies ranging from Amazon to restaurants are using reputation systems to improve quality and enhance customer satisfaction.

COLLABORATION INSIDE THE ORGANIZATION

A *collaboration system* is a set of tools that supports the work of teams or groups by facilitating the sharing and flow of information. Business 2.0's collaborative mind-set generates more information faster from a wider audience. *Collective intelligence* is collaborating and tapping into the core knowledge of all employees, partners, and customers. Knowledge can be a real competitive advantage for an organization. The most common form of collective intelligence found inside the organization is *knowledge management (KM)*, which involves capturing, classifying, evaluating, retrieving, and sharing information assets in a way that provides context for effective decisions and actions. The primary objective of knowledge management is to be sure that a company's knowledge of facts, sources of information, and solutions are readily available to all employees whenever it is needed. A *knowledge management system (KMS)* supports the capturing, organization, and dissemination of knowledge (i.e., know-how) throughout an organization. KMS can distribute an organization's knowledge base by interconnecting people and digitally gathering their expertise.

A great example of a knowledge worker is a golf caddie. Golf caddies give advice such as "The rain makes the third hole play 10 yards shorter." If a golf caddie is good and gives accurate advice it can lead to big tips. Collaborating with other golf caddies can provide bigger tips for all. How can knowledge management make this happen? Caddies could be rewarded for sharing course knowledge by receiving prizes for sharing knowledge. The course manager could compile all of the tips and publish a course notebook for distribution to all caddies. The goal of a knowledge management system is that everyone wins. Here the caddies make bigger tips and golfers improve their play by benefiting from the collaborative experiences of the caddies, and the course owners win as business increases.

KM has assumed greater urgency in American business over the past few years as millions of baby boomers prepare to retire. When they punch out for the last time, the knowledge they gleaned about their jobs, companies, and industries during their long careers will walk out with them—unless companies take measures to retain their insights.

Explicit and Tacit Knowledge

Not all information is valuable. Individuals must determine what information qualifies as intellectual and knowledge-based assets. In general, intellectual and knowledge-based assets fall into one of two categories: explicit or tacit. As a rule, *explicit knowledge* consists of anything that can be documented, archived, and codified, often with the help of IT. Examples of explicit knowledge are assets such as patents, trademarks, business plans, marketing research, and customer lists. *Tacit knowledge* is the knowledge contained in people's heads. The challenge inherent in tacit knowledge is figuring out how to recognize, generate, share, and manage knowledge that resides in people's heads. While information technology in the form of email, instant messaging, and related technologies can help facilitate the dissemination of tacit knowledge, identifying it in the first place can be a major obstacle.

COLLABORATION OUTSIDE THE ORGANIZATION

The most common form of collective intelligence found outside the organization is *crowdsourcing*, which refers to the wisdom of the crowd. The idea that collective intelligence is greater than the sum of its individual parts has been around for a long time (see Figure 15.2). With Business 2.0 the ability to efficiently tap into its power is emerging. For many years organizations believed that good ideas came from the top. CEOs collaborated only with the heads of sales and marketing, the quality assurance expert, or the road warrior salesman. The organization chart governed who should work with whom and how far up the chain of command a suggestion or idea would travel. With Business 2.0 this belief is being challenged, as firms capitalize

FIGURE 15.2

Crowdsourcing: The Crowd Is Smarter Than the Individual.

© Punchstock/Digital Vision

on crowdsourcing by opening up a task or problem to a wider group to find better or cheaper results from outside the box. *Crowdfunding* sources capital for a project by raising many small amounts from a large number of individuals, typically via the Internet.

With Business 2.0, people can be continuously connected, a driving force behind collaboration. Traditional ebusiness communications were limited to face-to-face conversations and one-way technologies that used *asynchronous communications*, or communication such as email in which the message and the response do not occur at the same time. Business 2.0 brought *synchronous communication*, or communications that occur at the same time such as IM or chat. Ask a group of college students when they last spoke to their parents. For most the answer is less than hour ago, as opposed to the traditional response of a few days ago. In business, too, continuous connections are now expected in today's collaborative world.

Networking Communities with Business 2.0

LO 15.2 **Explain how Business 2.0 is helping communities network and collaborate.**

Social media refers to websites that rely on user participation and user-contributed content, such as Facebook, YouTube, and Digg. A *social network* is an application that connects people by matching profile information. Providing individuals with the ability to network is by far one of the greatest advantages of Business 2.0. *Social networking* is the practice of expanding your business and/or social contacts by constructing a personal network (see Figure 15.3). Social networking sites provide two basic functions. The first is the ability to create and maintain a profile that serves as an online identity within the environment. The second is the ability to create connections between other people within the network. *Social networking analysis (SNA)* maps group contacts (personal and professional), identifying who knows each other and who works together. In a company it can provide a vision of how employees work together. It can also identify key experts with specific knowledge such as how to solve a complicated programming problem or launch a new product.

Business 2.0 simplifies access to information and improves the ability to share it. Instead of spending $1,000 and two days at a conference to meet professional peers, business people can now use social networks such as LinkedIn to meet new contacts for recruiting, prospecting, and identifying experts on a topic. With executive members from all the *Fortune* 500 companies, LinkedIn has become one of the more useful recruiting tools on the web.

Social graph represents the interconnection of relationships in a social network. Social networking sites can be especially useful to employers trying to find job candidates with unique or highly specialized skill sets that may be harder to locate in larger communities. Many employers also search social networking sites to find "dirt" and character references for potential employees. Keep in mind that what you post on the Internet stays on the Internet.[4]

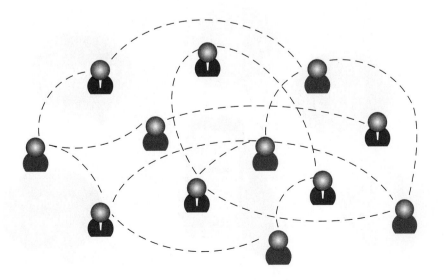

FIGURE 15.3

Social Network Example.[3]

SOCIAL TAGGING

Tags are specific keywords or phrases incorporated into website content for means of classification or taxonomy. An item can have one or more tags associated with it, to allow for multiple browseable paths through the items, and tags can be changed with minimal effort (see Figure 15.4). ***Social tagging*** describes the collaborative activity of marking shared online content with keywords or tags as a way to organize it for future navigation, filtering, or search. The entire user community is invited to tag, and thus essentially defines, the content. Flickr allows users to upload images and tag them with appropriate keywords. After enough people have done so, the resulting tag collection will identify images correctly and without bias. A *hashtag* is a keyword or phrase used to identify a topic and is preceded by a hash or pound sign (#). For example, the hashtag #sandiegofire helped coordinate emergency responses to a fire.

Folksonomy is similar to taxonomy except that crowdsourcing determines the tags or keyword-based classification system. Using the collective power of a community to identify and classify content significantly lowers content categorization costs, because there is no complicated nomenclature to learn. Users simply create and apply tags as they wish. For example, while cell phone manufacturers often refer to their products as mobile devices, the folksonomy could include mobile phone, wireless phone, smartphone, iPhone, Black-Berry, and so on. All these keywords, if searched, should take a user to the same site. Folksonomies reveal what people truly call things (see Figure 15.5). They have been a point of discussion on the web because the whole point of having a website is for your customers to find it. The majority of websites are found through search terms that match the content.[5]

A ***website bookmark*** is a locally stored URL or the address of a file or Internet page saved as a shortcut. ***Social bookmarking*** allows users to share, organize, search, and manage bookmarks. Del.icio.us, a website dedicated to social bookmarking, provides users with a place to store, categorize, annotate, and share favorites. StumbleUpon is another popular social bookmarking website that allows users to locate interesting websites based on their favorite subjects. The more you use the service, the more the system "learns" about your interests and the better it can show you websites that interest you. StumbleUpon represents a new social networking model in which content finds the users instead of the other way around. Stumble-Upon is all about the users and the content they enjoy.[6]

FIGURE 15.4

Social Tagging Occurs When Many Individuals Categorize Content.

———

© Radius Images/Corbis

FIGURE 15.5

Folksonomy Example: The User-Generated Names for Cellular Phones.

———

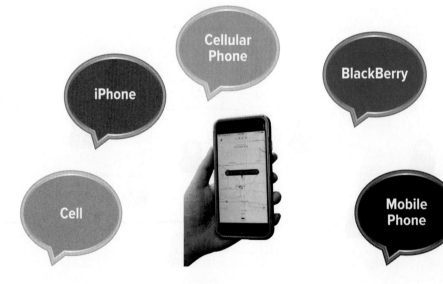

Business 2.0 Tools for Collaborating

LO 15.3 Describe the three Business 2.0 tools for collaborating.

Social networking and collaborating are leading businesses in new directions, and Figure 15.6 provides an overview of the tools that harness the "power of the people," allowing users to share ideas, discuss business problems, and collaborate on solutions.

BLOGS

A *blog*, or *web log,* is an online journal that allows users to post their own comments, graphics, and video. Unlike traditional HTML web pages, blog websites let writers communicate—and readers respond—on a regular basis through a simple yet customizable interface that does not require any programming. A *selfie* is a self-photograph placed on a social media website.

From a business perspective, blogs are no different from marketing channels such as video, print, audio, or presentations. They all deliver results of varying kinds. Consider Sun Microsystem's Jonathan Schwartz and GM's Bob Lutz, who use their blogs for marketing, sharing ideas, gathering feedback, press response, and image shaping. Starbucks has developed a blog called My Starbucks Idea, allowing customers to share ideas, tell Starbucks what they think of other people's ideas, and join discussions. Blogs are an ideal mechanism for many businesses because they can focus on topic areas more easily than traditional media, with no limits on page size, word count, or publication deadline.[7]

Microblogs

Microblogging is the practice of sending brief posts (140 to 200 characters) to a personal blog, either publicly or to a private group of subscribers who can read the posts as IMs or as text messages. The main advantage of microblogging is that posts can be submitted by a variety of means, such as instant messaging, email, or the web. By far the most popular microblogging tool is Twitter, which allows users to send microblog entries called tweets to anyone who has registered to "follow" them. Senders can restrict delivery to people they want to follow them or, by default, allow open access.

Real Simple Syndication (RSS)

Real Simple Syndication (RSS) is a web format used to publish frequently updated works, such as blogs, news headlines, audio, and video, in a standardized format. An RSS document or feed includes full or summarized text, plus other information such as publication date and authorship. News websites, blogs, and podcasts use RSS, constantly feeding news to consumers instead of having them search for it. In addition to facilitating syndication, RSS allows a website's frequent readers to track updates on the site.

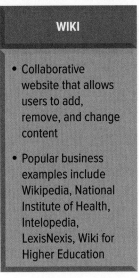

BLOG	WIKI	MASHUP
• An online journal that allows users to post their own comments, graphics, and videos	• Collaborative website that allows users to add, remove, and change content	• Content from more than one source to create a new product or service
• Popular business examples include Sweet Leaf Tea, Stoneyfield Farm, Nuts about Southwest, Disney Parks	• Popular business examples include Wikipedia, National Institute of Health, Intelopedia, LexisNexis, Wiki for Higher Education	• Examples include Zillow, Infopedia, Trendsmap, SongDNA, ThisWeKnow

FIGURE 15.6

Business 2.0 Communication and Collaboration Tools.

WIKIS

A *wiki* (the word is Hawaiian for quick) is a type of collaborative web page that allows users to add, remove, and change content, which can be easily organized and reorganized as required. While blogs have largely drawn on the creative and personal goals of individual authors, wikis are based on open collaboration with any- and everybody. Wikipedia, the open encyclopedia that launched in 2001, has become one of the 10 most popular web destinations, reaching an estimated 217 million unique visitors a month.[8]

A wiki user can generally alter the original content of any article, while the blog user can only add information in the form of comments. Large wikis, such as Wikipedia, protect the quality and accuracy of their information by assigning users roles such as reader, editor, administrator, patroller, policy maker, subject matter expert, content maintainer, software developer, and system operator. Access to some important or sensitive Wikipedia material is limited to users in these authorized roles.[9]

The *network effect* describes how products in a network increase in value to users as the number of users increases. The more users and content managers on a wiki, the greater the network effect because more users attract more contributors, whose work attracts more users, and so on. For example, Wikipedia becomes more valuable to users as the number of its contributors increases.

Wikis internal to firms can be vital tools for collecting and disseminating knowledge throughout an organization, across geographic distances, and between functional business areas. For example, what U.S. employees call a "sale" may be called "an order booked" in the United Kingdom, an "order scheduled" in Germany, and an "order produced" in France. The corporate wiki can answer any questions about a business process or definition. Companies are also using wikis for documentation, reporting, project management, online dictionaries, and discussion groups. Of course, the more employees who use the corporate wiki, the greater the network effect and valued added for the company.

MASHUPS

A *mashup* is a website or web application that uses content from more than one source to create a completely new product or service. The term is typically used in the context of music; putting Jay-Z lyrics over a Radiohead song makes something old new. The web version of a mashup allows users to mix map data, photos, video, news feeds, blog entries, and so on to create content with a new purpose. Content used in mashups is typically sourced from an *application programming interface (API)*, which is a set of routines, protocols, and tools for building software applications. A programmer then puts these building blocks together.

Most operating environments, such as Microsoft Windows, provide an API so that programmers can write applications consistent with them. Many people experimenting with mashups are using Microsoft, Google, eBay, Amazon, Flickr, and Yahoo! APIs, leading to the creation of mashup editors. *Mashup editors* are WYSIWYG, or What You See Is What You Get, tools. They provide a visual interface to build a mashup, often allowing the user to drag and drop data points into a web application. An *ezine* is a magazine published only in electronic form on a computer network. Flipboard is a social-network aggregation, magazine-format application software for multiple devices that collects content from social media and other websites, presents it in magazine format, and allows users to flip through the content.

Whoever thought technology could help sell bananas? Dole Organic now places three-digit farm codes on each banana and creates a mashup using Google Earth and its banana database. Socially and environmentally conscious buyers can plug the numbers into Dole's website and look at a bio of the farm where the bananas were raised. The site tells the story of the farm and its surrounding community, lists its organic certifications, posts some photos, and offers a link to satellite images of the farm in Google Earth. Customers can personally monitor the production and treatment of their fruit from the tree to the grocer. The process assures customers that their bananas have been raised to proper organic standards on an environmentally friendly, holistically minded plantation.[10]

The Challenges of Business 2.0

LO 15.4 Explain the three challenges associated with Business 2.0.

As much as Business 2.0 has positively changed the global landscape of business, a few challenges remain in open source software, user-contributed content systems, and collaboration systems, all highlighted in Figure 15.7. We'll briefly describe each one.

TECHNOLOGY DEPENDENCE

Many people today expect to be continuously connected, and their dependence on technology glues them to their web connections for everything from web conferencing for a university class or work project to making plans with friends for dinner. If a connection is down, how will they function? How long can people go without checking email, text messaging, or listening to free music on Pandora or watching on-demand television? As society becomes more technology-dependent, outages hold the potential to cause ever-greater havoc for people, businesses, and educational institutions.

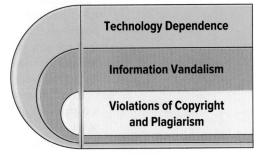

FIGURE 15.7

Challenges of Business 2.0.

INFORMATION VANDALISM

Open source and sharing are both major advantages of Business 2.0, and ironically they are major challenges as well. Allowing anyone to edit anything opens the door for individuals to purposely damage, destroy, or vandalize website content. One of the most famous examples of wiki vandalism occurred when a false biography entry read that John Seigenthaler Sr. was assistant to Attorney General Robert F. Kennedy in the early 1960s and was thought to have been directly involved in the assassinations of both Kennedy and his brother, President John F. Kennedy. Seigenthaler did work as an assistant to Robert Kennedy, but he was never involved in the assassinations. Wiki vandalism is a hot issue and for this reason wiki software can now store all versions of a web page, tracking updates and changes and ensuring the site can be restored to its original form if the site is vandalized. It can also color-code the background ensuring the user understands which areas have been validated and which areas have not. The real trick to wiki software is to determine which statements are true and which are false, a huge issue when considering how easily and frequently wiki software is updated and changed.[11]

VIOLATIONS OF COPYRIGHT AND PLAGIARISM

Online collaboration makes plagiarism as easy as clicking a mouse. Unfortunately a great deal of copyrighted material tends to find its ways to blogs and wikis where many times blame cannot be traced to a single person. Clearly stated copyright and plagiarism policies are a must for all corporate blogs and wikis.

Web 3.0: Defining the Next Generation of Online Business Opportunities

LO 15.5 Describe Web 3.0 and the next generation of online business.

While Web 1.0 refers to static text-based information websites and Web 2.0 is about user-contributed content, Web 3.0 is based on "intelligent" web applications using natural language processing, machine-based learning and reasoning, and intelligent applications. Web 3.0 is the next step in the evolution of the Internet and web applications. Business leaders who explore its opportunities will be the first to market with competitive advantages.

Web 3.0 offers a way for people to describe information such that computers can start to understand the relationships among concepts and topics. To demonstrate the power of Web 3.0, let's look at a few sample relationships, such as Adam Sandler is a comedian, Lady Gaga is a singer, and Hannah is friends with Sophie. These are all examples of descriptions that can be added to web pages allowing computers to learn about relationships while displaying the information to humans. With this kind of information in place, there will be a far richer interaction between people and machines with Web 3.0.

Applying this type of advanced relationship knowledge to a company can create new opportunities. After all, businesses run on information. Whereas Web 2.0 brings people closer together with information using machines, Web 3.0 brings *machines* closer together using *information*. These new relationships unite people, machines, and information so a business can be smarter, quicker, more agile, and more successful.

One goal of Web 3.0 is to tailor online searches and requests specifically to users' preferences and needs. For example, instead of making multiple searches, the user might type a complex sentence or two in a Web 3.0 browser, such as "I want to see a funny movie and then eat at a good Mexican restaurant. What are my options?" The Web 3.0 browser will analyze the request, search the web for all possible answers, organize the results, and present them to the user.

Tim Berners-Lee, one of the founders of the WWW, has described the **semantic web** as a component of Web 3.0 that describes things in a way that computers can understand. The semantic web is not about links between web pages; rather it describes the relationships between *things* (such as A is a part of B and Y is a member of Z) and the properties of things (size, weight, age, price). If information about music, cars, concert tickets, and so on is stored in a way that describes the information and associated resource files, semantic web applications can collect information from many different sources, combine it, and present it to users in a meaningful way. Although Web 3.0 is still a bit speculative, some topics and features are certain to be included in it, such as:[12]

- Integration of legacy devices: the ability to use current devices such as iPhones, laptops, and so on, as credit cards, tickets, and reservations tools.

- Intelligent applications: the use of agents, machine learning, and semantic web concepts to complete intelligent tasks for users.

- Open ID: the provision of an online identity that can be easily carried to a variety of devices (cell phones, PCs) allowing for easy authentication across different websites.

- Open technologies: the design of websites and other software so they can be easily integrated and work together.

- A worldwide database: the ability for databases to be distributed and accessed from anywhere.

EGOVERNMENT: THE GOVERNMENT MOVES ONLINE

Recent business models that have arisen to enable organizations to take advantage of the Internet and create value are within egovernment. *Egovernment* involves the use of strategies and technologies to transform government(s) by improving the delivery of services and enhancing the quality of interaction between the citizen-consumer and all branches of government.

One example of an egovernment portal, FirstGov.gov, the official U.S. gateway to all government information, is the catalyst for a growing electronic government. Its powerful search engine and ever-growing collection of topical and customer-focused links connect users to millions of web pages, from the federal government, to local and tribal governments, to foreign nations around the world. Figure 15.8 highlights and adds to our discussion specific egovernment models.

MBUSINESS: SUPPORTING ANYWHERE BUSINESS

Internet-enabled mobile devices are quickly outnumbering personal computers. *Mobile business* (or *mbusiness, mcommerce*) is the ability to purchase goods and services through a wireless Internet-enabled device. The emerging technology behind mbusiness is a mobile device equipped with a web-ready micro-browser that can perform the following services:

- Mobile entertainment—downloads for music, videos, games, voting, ring tones, as well as text-based messaging services.

- Mobile sales/marketing—advertising, campaigns, discounts, promotions, and coupons.

- Mobile banking—manage accounts, pay bills, receive alerts, and transfer funds.

	Business	**Consumer**	**Government**
Business	B2B conisint.com	B2C dell.com	B2G lockheedmartin.com
Consumer	C2B priceline.com	C2C ebay.com	C2G egov.com
Government	G2B export.gov	G2C medicare.gov	G2G disasterhelp.gov

FIGURE 15.8

Extended Ebusiness Models.

- Mobile ticketing—purchase tickets for entertainment, transportation, and parking including the ability to automatically feed parking meters.
- Mobile payments—pay for goods and services including in-store purchases, home delivery, vending machines, taxis, gas, and so on.

Organizations face changes more extensive and far reaching in their implications than anything since the modern industrial revolution occurred in the early 1900s. Technology is a primary force driving these changes. Organizations that want to survive must recognize the immense power of technology, carry out required organizational changes in the face of it, and learn to operate in an entirely different way.

OPENING CASE STUDY QUESTIONS

1. Categorize Slack as an example of Web 1.0 (ebusiness) or Web 2.0 (Business 2.0).
2. Explain the four characteristics of Business 2.0 and how each applies to Slack.
3. How could Slack use social networking analysis to help organizations function more efficiently?

Chapter Fifteen Case: Pinterest - Billboards for the Internet

Pinterest has been called the latest addiction for millions of people around the world. Pinterest, a visual social media network, allows users to create "interest boards" where they "pin" items of interests found on the web. Terms you need to understand to use Pinterest include:

- **Pin:** A link to an image from a computer or a website. Pins can include captions for other users. Users upload, or "pin," photos or videos to boards.
- **Board:** Pins live on boards and users can maintain separate boards, which can be categorized by activity or interests, such as cooking, do-it-yourself activities, fitness, music, movies, etc.
- **Repin:** After pinning an item, it can be repinned by other Pinterest users, spreading the content virally. Repinning allows users to share items they like with friends and family.

"Pinning" is simply done by clicking on a photo or video that captures the attention of a user, whether it be by uploading personal photos or repinning a photo or video from a fellow user. Started in 2010, Pinterest has already attracted over 10 million users with the majority being women between the ages of 25 and 54. Millions of people visit the website each day to find what new items will spark their interest as there are always more and more things to see.

Pinterest is considered a social network, but unlike other social networks, such as Twitter and Facebook, Pinterest is open to invited users only, meaning it is an invitation-only website and users must "ask" for an invitation before gaining access. Upon accepting the invitation, users can gain access to the website and begin inviting their own "friends" with whom they have connections on Facebook or Twitter. Pinterest's primary mission is to:

connect everyone in the world through the 'things' they find interesting. We think that a favorite book, toy, or recipe can reveal a common link between two people. With millions of new pins added every week, Pinterest is connecting people all over the world based on shared tastes and interests.

Just like on other social networks, Pinterest users can compile a list of people they want to follow. A user can link a Pinterest board to a Facebook account, allowing instant access to quickly see which of his or her Facebook friends are on the social network. Adding bookmarks allows the user to pin images to other websites such as a book at Barnes & Noble or a set of mugs at Pier 1 Imports. The image is automatically linked to the retailer's website, and if another user clicks on the image, that user receives additional information on the product or service. If users pin a specific image of a plate or sweater, they can add the item's price in the description, which will automatically place a banner ad on the image and show the listed price. If users are unsure of what they are looking for, they can search for a specific event or theme such as "twenty-first birthday party" for a whole array of ideas.

Essentially, Pinterest allows users to paint a visual picture. Just imagine a wedding planner talking to a bride about her upcoming event, and the bride mentions she would like a "classic modernism" wedding. If the wedding planner was confused on what exactly the bride meant by classic modernism, she could quickly visit Pinterest to find an entire suite of photos and videos to spark ideas of how to coordinate the event.

The Business Value of Pinterest

Visual Communication

Pinterest is by far one of the hottest social media spaces available today. Offering all kinds of valuable information from useful cleaning tips to fantastic recipes to beautiful photos and videos, the website is extremely valuable for sharing anything visual. Pinterest is in no way simply a passing fad as companies begin to use the website for social marketing.

One of the best business uses of Pinterest is allowing employees to visually communicate and brainstorm. Visual communication is a new experience for many employees and the phrase "A picture is worth a thousand words" can help a company perform many tasks from generating new products to transforming business processes. In fact, many companies are using Pinterest to solicit feedback directly from employees, customers, and suppliers to ensure the company is operating efficiently and effectively. Soliciting feedback directly from customers allows companies to have a customer service support team handle problems before they become mainstream issues. Providing customers with a new channel to post their thoughts and concerns about products or services can provide valuable feedback for any company. Companies typically state that they may not respond to every question or comment, but that they take each and every concern into account, demonstrating that they are devoted to creating a bond between themselves and their customers.

Driving Traffic

Pinterest drives traffic—it is that simple! Even though the website operates under an invitation-only model, it has attracted more than 10 million users in less than two years. That number might seem small compared to powerhouses such as Facebook, Twitter, or Google, but it demonstrates there is enough of an audience to send a decent amount of traffic to any business. The images a business pins up should be linked to the relevant page of its website. If users are attracted by it, they may click on it to find out more.

Pinterest also drives traffic by providing higher rankings on search engine optimization as companies appear higher and higher on search lists the more users are pinning to their boards. Linking is one of the key factors search engines consider, and with Pinterest gaining in popularity, it is also growing as a trustworthy domain. The number of Pinterest users combined with its ability to increase search rankings will play an important role when a company is looking to increase visibility and drive traffic to its website. Data from Shareholic found that Pinterest sent more referral traffic to bloggers than Google+, YouTube, and LinkedIn combined, falling just behind Twitter.

Product Branding

Pinterest is an extraordinary branding tool, offering a place where companies can create a presence and community around a product, idea, event, or company. Just like other social networking websites, Pinterest allows a company to reach out and engage its customers, vendors, suppliers, and even employees to communicate about its products and services. Recently the National Football League's Minnesota Vikings began using Pinterest to create a following of favorite photos, statistics, and even game-day recipes!

Pinterest recently deployed an iPhone application that allows users to pin photos and video from their cameras instantly on their boards. Pinterest's unique competitive advantage is its ability to host billions of images and redirect users to the appropriate sources in a user-friendly interface.

Pinterest's Dilemma

Since its inception, Pinterest has been under fire from sites such as Flikr, Photobucket, and Instagram over attributing credit to those who own the images that are pinned. Many users are concerned that they may one day be sued for the improper use of an image they pinned.

The Pinterest Terms of Use state, "If you are a copyright owner, or are authorized to act on behalf of one, or authorized to act under any exclusive right under copyright, please report alleged copyright infringements taking place on or through the Site by completing the following DMCA Notice of Alleged Infringement and delivering it to Pinterest's Designated Copyright Agent."

To protect Pinterest from third-party litigation claims (such as those from authors claiming copyright infringement), Pinterest has incorporated the following statement into its indemnity clause: "You agree to indemnify and hold harmless Pinterest and its officers, directors, employees and agents, from and against any claims, suits, proceedings, disputes, demands, liabilities, damages, losses, costs and expenses, including, without limitation, reasonable legal and accounting fees (including costs of defense of claims, suits or proceedings brought by third parties), arising out of or in any way related to (i) your access to or use of the Services or Pinterest Content, (ii) your User Content, or (iii) your breach of any of these Terms."

Pinterest is well aware of the probability that many of the pinned images might be violating copyright infringement and is attempting to protect itself against any litigation claims resulting from users intentionally or unintentionally breaking the law through its site. [13]

Questions

1. Do you consider Pinterest a form of disruptive or sustaining technology? Why or why not?
2. What types of security and ethical dilemmas are facing Pinterest?
3. Do you consider Pinterest an example of Web 1.0 or Web 2.0?
4. What are the mobility benefits and challenges facing Pinterest?

Philippines, Mexico, Argentina, and Malaysia—each of which showed about a 10 percent jump in Facebook membership in a single month. In a group answer the following:

- What potential business opportunities could be created by a worldwide social media network or phone book?

- Facebook, which contains personal data on each member, is becoming the world's phone book. What are the implications of a world phone book for social change?

- What do you think would be the benefits and challenges of global social networking?

4. Five Ways Google Docs Speeds Up Collaboration

Google Docs wants you to skip Microsoft Office and collaborate with your group in your browser for free, especially when you're not in the same physical space. Visit Google Docs and answer the following questions. What are five ways the new Google Docs can help your team accomplish work more efficiently, even when you're not in the same room together? Is Google Docs open source software? What revenue model is Google Docs following? Why would putting Google Docs and Microsoft Office on your résumé help differentiate your skills? What other applications does Google create that you are interested in learning to help collaborate and communicate with peers and co-workers?

5. Anti-Social Networking

Before the Internet, angry customers could write letters or make phone calls, but their individual power to find satisfaction or bring about change was relatively weak. Now, disgruntled consumers can create a website or upload a video bashing a product or service, and their efforts can be instantly seen by millions of people. Though many companies monitor the Internet and try to respond to such postings quickly, power has clearly shifted to the consumer. Create an argument for or against the following statement: "Social networking has given power to the consumer that benefits society and creates socially responsible corporations."

6. Collaborating for Nonprofits—Kiva

Kiva's mission is to connect people through lending for the sake of alleviating poverty. Kiva is a micro-lending online nonprofit organization that enables individuals to lend directly to entrepreneurs throughout the world. If you want to participate in Kiva you simply browse the website (www.kiva. org) and choose an entrepreneur that interests you, make a loan, then track your entrepreneur for the next 6 to 12 months while he or she builds the business and makes the funds to repay the loan. When the loan is up you can relend the money to someone else who is in need.[14]

Kiva is an excellent example of blending ethics and information technology. How is Kiva operating differently than traditional nonprofits? What are the risks associated with investing in Kiva? When you invest in Kiva you run three primary risks: entrepreneur risk, local field partner risk, and country risk. Analyze each of these risks for potential unethical issues that might arise when donating to Kiva.

7. Connectivity Breakdown

When you are considering connectivity services for your business, you need to take continuous access and connectivity seriously. What if one of your employees is about to close a multimillion-dollar deal and loses the Internet connection, jeopardizing the deal? What if a disgruntled employee decides to post your business's collective intelligence on an open source blog or wiki?

What if your patient-scheduling software crashes and you have no idea which patients are scheduled to which operating rooms with which doctors? These are far worse scenarios than a teenage boy not gaining access to his email or Facebook page. What management and technical challenges do you foresee as people and businesses become increasingly dependent on connectivity? What can managers do to meet these challenges and prevent problems?

8. Blogging for Dollars

You have purchased a financial investment company, The Financial Level, that caters to individuals and families. You would like to develop a few blogs for your customers, employees, and partners. The goals for your customer blog are to gather honest feedback, provide a place for customers to interact, and help find new opportunities for your businesses. The goals for the employee blog are to gather knowledge, collect employment feedback, and offer a place where employees can post anonymous feedback for issues and concerns so you can manage your staff better.

   a. Research the Internet and find several customer blogs and employee blogs.
   b. Determine the top three blogs for customers and for employees and critique the blogs for content, ease of use, and overall value.
   c. Design a prototype customer blog and a prototype employee blog for The Financial Level, using Word, PowerPoint, or a tool of your choice.

16 Integrating Wireless Technology in Business

16.1. Describe the different wireless network categories.

16.2. Explain the different wireless network business applications.

LO 16.1 **Describe the different wireless network categories.**

Wireless Network Categories

As far back as 1896, Italian inventor Guglielmo Marconi demonstrated a wireless telegraph, and in 1927, the first radiotelephone system began operating between the United States and Great Britain. Automobile-based mobile telephones were offered in 1947. In 1964, the first communications satellite, Telstar, was launched, and soon after, satellite-relayed telephone service and television broadcasts became available. Wireless networks have exploded since then, and newer technologies are now maturing that allow companies and home users alike to take advantage of both wired and wireless networks.[1]

Before delving into a discussion of wireless networks, we should distinguish between mobile and wireless, terms that are often used synonymously but actually have different meanings. *Mobile* means the technology can travel with the user, for instance, users can download software, email messages, and web pages onto a laptop or other mobile device for portable reading or reference. Information collected while on the road can be synchronized with a PC or company server. *Wireless,* on the other hand, refers to any type of operation accomplished without the use of a hard-wired connection. There are many environments in which the network devices are wireless but not mobile, such as wireless home or office networks with stationary PCs and printers. Some forms of mobility do not require a wireless connection; for instance, a worker can use a wired laptop at home, shut down the laptop, drive to work, and attach the laptop to the company's wired network.

In many networked environments today, users are both wireless and mobile; for example, a mobile user commuting to work on a train can maintain a VoIP call and multiple TCP/IP connections at the same time. Figure 16.1 categorizes wireless networks by type.

PERSONAL AREA NETWORKS

A *personal area network (PAN)* provides communication for devices owned by a single user that work over a short distance. PANs are used to transfer files, including email, calendar appointments, digital photos, and music. A PAN can provide communication between a wireless headset and a cell phone or between a computer and a wireless mouse or keyboard. Personal area networks generally cover a range of less than 10 meters (about 30 feet). *Bluetooth* is a wireless PAN technology that transmits signals over short distances among cell phones, computers, and other devices. The name is borrowed from Harald Bluetooth, a king in Denmark more than 1,000 years ago. Bluetooth eliminates the need for wires, docking stations, or cradles, as well as all the special attachments that typically accompany personal computing devices. Bluetooth operates at speeds up to 1 Mbps within a range of 33 feet or less. Devices that are Bluetooth-enabled communicate directly with each other in pairs, like a handshake.

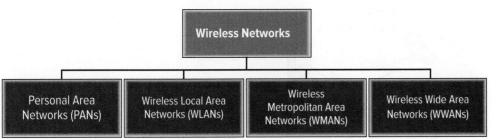

FIGURE 16.1

Wireless Communication
Network Categories.

Up to eight can be paired simultaneously. And Bluetooth is not just for technology devices. An array of Bluetooth-equipped appliances, such as a television set, a stove, and a thermostat, can be controlled from a cell phone—all from a remote location.[2]

WIRELESS LANS

A *wireless LAN (WLAN)* is a local area network that uses radio signals to transmit and receive data over distances of a few hundred feet. An *access point (AP)* is the computer or network device that serves as an interface between devices and the network. Each computer initially connects to the access point and then to other computers on the network. A *wireless access point (WAP)* enables devices to connect to a wireless network to communicate with each other. WAPs with *multiple-in/multiple-out (MIMO) technology* have multiple transmitters and receivers, allowing them to send and receive greater amounts of data than traditional networking devices. *Wireless fidelity (Wi-Fi)* is a means by which portable devices can connect wirelessly to a local area network, using access points that send and receive data via radio waves. Wi-Fi has a maximum range of about 1,000 feet in open areas such as a city park and 250 to 400 feet in closed areas such as an office building. *Wi-Fi infrastructure* includes the inner workings of a Wi-Fi service or utility, including the signal transmitters, towers, or poles, along with additional equipment required to send out a Wi-Fi signal. Most WLANs use a Wi-Fi infrastructure in which a wireless device, often a laptop, communicates through an access point or base station by means of, for instance, wireless fidelity.

Areas around access points where users can connect to the Internet are often called hotspots. *Hotspots* are designated locations where Wi-Fi access points are publically available. Hotspots are found in places such as restaurants, airports, and hotels—places where business professionals tend to gather. Hotspots are extremely valuable for those business professionals who travel extensively and need access to business applications. By positioning hotspots at strategic locations throughout a building, campus, or city, network administrators can keep Wi-Fi users continuously connected to a network or the Internet, no matter where they roam.[3]

In a Wi-Fi network, the user's laptop or other Wi-Fi-enabled device has a wireless adapter that translates data into a radio signal and transmits it to the wireless access point. The wireless access point, which consists of a transmitter with an antenna that is often built into the hardware, receives the signal and decodes it. The access point then sends the information to the Internet over a wired broadband connection, as illustrated in Figure 16.2. When receiving data, the wireless access point takes the information from the Internet, translates it into a radio signal, and sends it to the computer's wireless adapter. If too many people try to use the Wi-Fi network at one time, they can experience interference or dropped connections. Most laptop computers come with built-in wireless transmitters and software to enable computers to automatically discover the existence of a Wi-Fi network.

Wi-Fi operates at considerably higher frequencies than cell phones use, which allows greater bandwidth. The bandwidths associated with Wi-Fi are separated according to several wireless networking standards, known as 802.11, for carrying out wireless local area network communication. The *Institute of Electrical and Electronics Engineers (IEEE)* researches and institutes electrical standards for communication and other technologies. *IEEE 802.11n (orWireless-N)* is the standard for wireless networking. Compared with earlier standards such as 802.11b, Wireless-N offers faster speeds, more flexibility, and greater range.

FIGURE 16.2

Wi-Fi Networks.

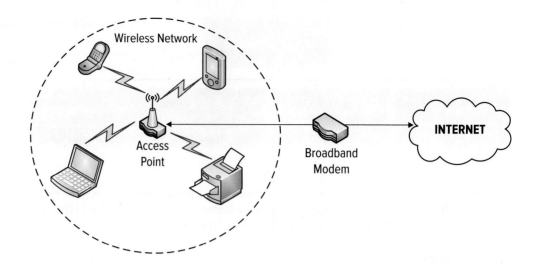

The organization denotes different versions of the standard—for example, Wireless-G and Wireless-N—by a lowercase letter at the end of this number. Figure 16.3 outlines the bandwidths associated with a few of these standards.[4]

An increasing number of digital devices, including most laptops, netbooks, tablets such as the iPad, and even printers are incorporating Wi-Fi technology into their design. Cell phones are incorporating Wi-Fi so they can automatically switch from the cell network to a faster Wi-Fi network where available for data communications. BlackBerrys and iPhones can connect to an access point for data communications such as email and web browsing, but not for voice unless they use the services of Skype or another VoIP.

WIRELESS MANs

A *wireless MAN (WMAN)* is a metropolitan area network that uses radio signals to transmit and receive data. WMAN technologies have not been highly successful to date, mainly because they are not widely available, at least in the United States. One with the potential for success is *Worldwide Interoperability for Microwave Access (WiMAX),* a communications technology aimed at providing high-speed wireless data over metropolitan area networks. In many respects, WiMAX operates like Wi-Fi, only over greater distances and with higher bandwidths. A WiMAX tower serves as an access point and can connect to the Internet or another tower. A single tower can provide up to 3,000 square miles of coverage, so only a few are needed to cover an entire city. WiMAX can support data communications at a rate of 70 Mbps. In New York City, for example, one or two WiMAX access points around the city might meet the heavy demand more cheaply than hundreds of Wi-Fi access points. WiMAX can also cover remote or rural areas where cabling is limited or nonexistent, and where it is too expensive or physically difficult to install wires for the relatively few users.[5]

WiMAX can provide both line-of-sight and non-line-of-sight service. A non-line-of-sight service uses a small antenna on a mobile device that connects to a WiMAX tower less than six miles away where transmissions are disrupted by physical obstructions. This form of service is similar to Wi-Fi but has much broader coverage area and higher bandwidths.

FIGURE 16.3

Wi-Fi Standards and Bandwidths.

Wi-Fi Standard	Bandwidth
802.11a	54 Mbps
802.11b	11 Mbps
802.11g	54 Mbps
802.11n	140 Mbps

A line-of-sight option offers a fixed antenna that points at the WiMAX tower from a rooftop or pole. This option is much faster than non-line-of-sight service, and the distance between the WiMAX tower and antenna can be as great as 30 miles. Figure 16.4 illustrates the WiMAX infrastructure.[6]

Some cellular companies are evaluating WiMAX as a means of increasing bandwidth for a variety of data-intensive applications such as those used by smartphones. Sprint Nextel and Clearwire are building a nationwide WiMAX network in the United States. WiMAX-capable gaming devices, laptops, cameras, and even cell phones are being manufactured by companies including Intel, Motorola, Nokia, and Samsung.[7]

WIRELESS WAN—CELLULAR COMMUNICATION SYSTEM

A *wireless WAN (WWAN)* is a wide area network that uses radio signals to transmit and receive data. WWAN technologies can be divided into two categories: cellular communication systems and satellite communication systems.

Although mobile communications have been around for generations, including the walkie-talkies of the 1940s and mobile radiophones of the 1950s, it was not until 1983 that cellular telephony became available commercially. A cell phone is a device for voice and data, communicating wirelessly through a collection of stationary ground-based sites called base stations, each of which is linked to its nearest neighbor stations. Base station coverage areas are about 10 square miles and are called cells, as Figure 16.5 illustrates.

The first cell phone was demonstrated in 1973 by Motorola (it weighed almost 2 pounds), but it took 10 years for the technology to become commercially available. The Motorola DynaTAC, marketed in 1983, weighed 1 pound and cost about $4,000. Cellular technology has come a long way since then.[8]

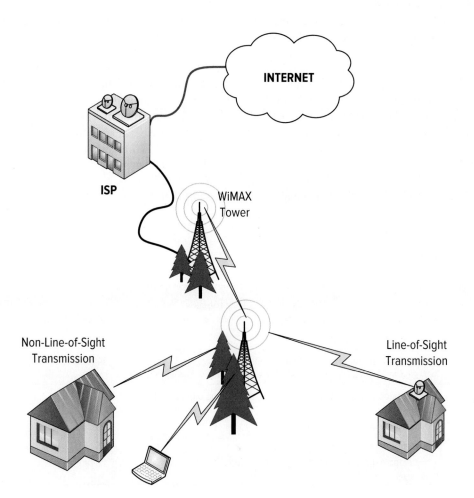

FIGURE 16.4

WiMAX Infrastructure.

FIGURE 16.5

Cell Phone Communication
System Overview.

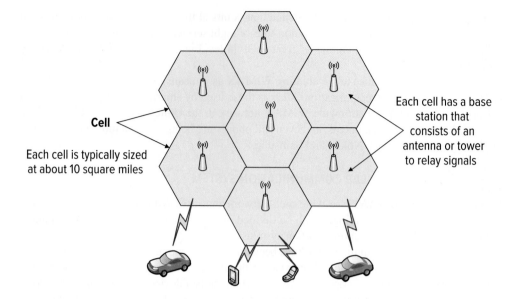

Cell

Each cell is typically sized
at about 10 square miles

Each cell has a base
station that
consists of an
antenna or tower
to relay signals

Cellular systems were originally designed to provide voice services to mobile customers and thus were designed to interconnect cells to the public telephone network. Increasingly, they provide data services and Internet connectivity. There are more cell phones than landline phones in many countries today, and it is no longer uncommon for cell phones to be the only phones people have.

Cell phones have morphed into *smartphones* that offer more advanced computing ability and connectivity than basic cell phones. They allow for web browsing, emailing, listening to music, watching video, computing, keeping track of contacts, sending text messages, and taking and sending photos. The Apple iPhone and RIM BlackBerry are examples of smartphones.

Streaming is a method of sending audio and video files over the Internet in such a way that the user can view the file while it is being transferred. Streaming is not limited to cellular usage; all wireless and even wired networks can take advantage of this method. The most obvious advantage is speed, a direct benefit for mobile and wireless devices since they are still not as fast as their wired counterparts. *Voice over LTE (VoLTE)* allows mobile voice calls to be made over broadband networks, creating—under the right network conditions—clearer audio and fewer dropped calls. One easy way to think of VoLTE is as, essentially, a VoIP call on your mobile phone. The functionality is still the same, but the data transfers in a faster and more efficient manner.

FIGURE 16.6

Cell Phone Generations.

	Wireless Communications	Speed
1G	– The original analog cell phone network	14.4 Kbps
2G	– Digital cell phone service	10 Kbps - 144 Kbps
3G	– Broadband Internet services over cellular networks – Added MMS (multimedia message services) or picture message services	144 Kbps - 4 Mbps
4G	– High-speed access, anywhere, anytime, to anything digital—audio, video, text – Improved video transmissions	100 Mbps
5G	– Superior data communication rate – Expected to provide artificial intelligence capabilities on wearable devices	1.5 Gbps over a distance of 90 meters

WIRELESS WAN—SATELLITE COMMUNICATION SYSTEM

The other wireless WAN technology is a satellite communication system. A *satellite* is a space station that orbits the Earth receiving and transmitting signals from Earth-based stations over a wide area. When satellite systems first came into consideration in the 1990s, the goal was to provide wireless voice and data coverage for the entire planet, without the need for mobile phones to roam between many different provider networks. But by the time satellite networks were ready for commercial use, they had already been overtaken by cellular systems.

The devices used for satellite communication range from handheld units to mobile base stations to fixed satellite dish receivers. The peak data transmission speeds range from 2.4 Kbps to 2 Mbps. For the everyday mobile professional, satellite communication may not provide a compelling benefit, but for people requiring voice and data access from remote locations or guaranteed coverage in nonremote locations, satellite technology is a viable solution.

Conventional communication satellites move in stationary orbits approximately 22,000 miles above Earth. A newer satellite medium, the low-orbit satellite, travels much closer to Earth and is able to pick up signals from weak transmitters. Low-orbit satellites also consume less power and cost less to launch than conventional satellites. With satellite networks, business people almost anywhere in the world have access to full communication capabilities, including voice, videoconferencing, and Internet access. Figure 16.7 briefly illustrates the satellite communication system.[9]

PROTECTING WIRELESS CONNECTIONS

Network intrusions can occur if access codes or passwords are stored on a device that is lost or stolen. However, anytime a wireless network connects to a wired one, the wireless network can serve as a conduit for a hacker to gain entry into an otherwise secure wired network. This risk is especially high if the wireless network is not sufficiently secured in its own right.

Before the emergence of the Internet, hackers generally had to be physically present within the corporate complex to gain access to a wired network. The thousands, if not millions, of access points enabled by the Internet now allow hackers to work from a distance. This threat has spawned a variety of security techniques, from firewalls to VPNs to SSL and HTTPS.

Several techniques can secure wireless networks from unauthorized access whether used separately or in combination. One method is authenticating Wi-Fi access points. Because Wi-Fi communications are broadcast, anyone within listening distance can intercept communications. Every time someone uses an unsecured website via a public Wi-Fi access point, his or her logon name and password are sent over the open airwaves with a high risk that someone might eavesdrop or capture logon names, passwords, credit card numbers, and other vital information. *Wired equivalent privacy (WEP)* is an encryption algorithm designed to protect wireless transmission data. If you are using a Wi-Fi connection, WEP encrypts the data by using a key that converts the data to a nonhuman readable form. The purpose of WEP was to provide wireless networks with the equivalent level of security as wired networks. Unfortunately, the

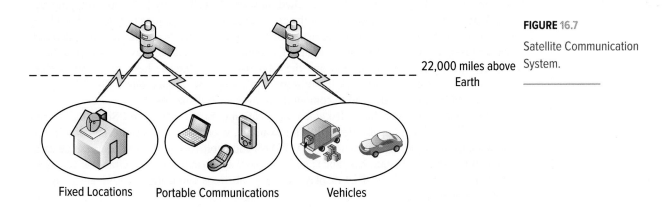

FIGURE 16.7

Satellite Communication System.

22,000 miles above Earth

Fixed Locations   Portable Communications   Vehicles

technology behind WEP has been demonstrated to be relatively insecure compared to newer protocols such as WPA. WLANs that use Wi-Fi have a built-in security mechanism called *Wi-Fi protected access (WPA)*, a wireless security protocol to protect Wi-Fi networks. It is an improvement on the original Wi-Fi security standard, wired equivalent privacy (WEP), and provides more sophisticated data encryption and user authentication. Anyone who wants to use an access point must know the WPA encryption key to access the Wi-Fi connection.

War chalking is the practice of tagging pavement with codes displaying where Wi-Fi access is available. The codes for war chalking tell other users the kind of access available, the speed of the network, and if the network is secured. *War driving* is deliberately searching for Wi-Fi signals while driving by in a vehicle. Many individuals who participate in war driving simply map where Wi-Fi networks are available. Other individuals have a more malicious intent and use war driving to hack or break into these networks. War driving has been a controversial practice since its inception and has raised the awareness of the importance of wireless network security.

MANAGING MOBILE DEVICES

IT consumerization is the blending of personal and business use of technology devices and applications. Today's workforce grew up with the Internet and its members do not differentiate between corporate and personal technology. Employees want to use the same technology they have at home in the office. This blending of personal and business technology is having a significant impact on corporate MIS departments, which traditionally choose all of the technology for the organization. Today, MIS departments must determine how to protect their networks and manage technology that they did not authorize or recommend. Two ways an MIS department can manage IT consumerization is through mobile device management and mobile application management.

Mobile device management(MDM) remotely controls smartphones and tablets, ensuring data security. MIS departments implement MDM by requiring passcodes on organizational smartphones to ensure data encryption and, in the event of a lost smartphone, that all data on the device can be deleted remotely. MDM tools can also enforce policies, track inventory, and perform real-time monitoring and reporting. One problem with MDM is that the full-device approach can be too heavy-handed in an era when employees, not their employers, own their smartphones and tablets. Users may wonder, "If I only use my phone to check email at night, why do I have to enter my work password every time I want to use the phone?" or "If I lose my phone, why does my IT department want to wipe pictures of my dog remotely?"

Mobile application management administers and delivers applications to corporate and personal smartphones and tablets. MAM software assists with software delivery, licensing, and maintenance and can limit how sensitive data can be shared among apps. An important feature of MAM is that it provides corporate network administrators with the ability to wipe corporate mobile apps from an end user's device remotely.

LO 16.2 Explain the different wireless network business applications.

Business Applications of Wireless Networks

Companies of all types and sizes have relied on wireless technology for years. Shipping and trucking companies developed some of the earliest wireless applications to help track vehicles and valuable cargo, optimize the logistics of their global operations, perfect their delivery capabilities, and reduce theft and damage. Government agencies such as the National Aeronautics and Space Administration and the Department of Defense have relied on satellite technologies for decades to track the movement of troops, weaponry, and military assets; to receive and broadcast data; and to communicate over great distances.

Wireless technologies have also aided the creation of new applications. Some build upon and improve existing capabilities. UPS, for example, is combining several types of wireless network technologies from Bluetooth to WWANs and deploying scanners and wearable data-collection terminals to automate and standardize package management and tracking across all its delivery centers. Figure 16.8 displays the three business applications taking advantage of wireless technologies.

FIGURE 16.8

Wireless Business
Applications.

Radio-Frequency
Identification
(RFID)

Global
Positioning
Systems (GPS)

Geographic
Information
Systems (GIS)

RADIO-FREQUENCY IDENTIFICATION (RFID)

Radio-frequency identification (RFID) uses electronic tags and labels to identify objects wirelessly over short distances. It holds the promise of replacing existing identification technologies such as the bar code. RFID wirelessly exchanges information between a tagged object and a reader/writer. An *RFID tag* is an electronic identification device that is made up of a chip and antenna. An *RFID reader (RFID interrogator)* is a transmitter/receiver that reads the contents of RFID tags in the area. A RFID system is comprised of one or more RFID tags, one or more RFID readers, two or more antennas (one on the tag and one on each reader), RFID application software, and a computer system or server, as Figure 16.9 illustrates. Tags, often smaller than a grain of rice, can be applied to books or clothing items as part of an adhesive bar-code label, or included in items such as ID cards or packing labels. Readers can be stand-alone devices, such as for self-checkout in a grocery store, integrated with a mobile device for portable use, or built in as in printers. The reader sends a wireless request that is received by all tags in the area that have been programmed to listen to wireless signals. Tags receive the signal via their antennas and respond by transmitting their stored data. The tag can hold many types of data, including a product number, installation instructions, and history of activity (such as the date the item was shipped). The reader receives a signal from the tag using its antenna, interprets the information sent, and transfers the data to the associated computer system or server.

Passive RFID tags do not have a power source, whereas *active RFID tags* have their own transmitter and a power source (typically a battery). The power source runs the microchip's circuitry and broadcasts a signal to the reader (similar to the way a cell phone transmits signals to a base station). Passive RFID tags draw power from the RFID reader, which sends out electromagnetic waves that induce a current in the tag's antenna. *Semi-passive RFID tags* use a battery to run the microchip's circuitry, but communicate by drawing power from the RFID reader. *Asset tracking* occurs when a company places active or semi-passive RFID tags on expensive products or assets to gather data on the items' location with little or no

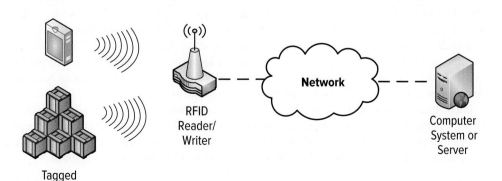

FIGURE 16.9

Elements of an RFID system.

Tagged
Products

RFID
Reader/
Writer

Network

Computer
System or
Server

manual intervention. Asset tracking allows a company to focus on its supply chain, reduce theft, identify the last known user of assets, and automate maintenance routines. Active and semi-passive tags are useful for tracking high-value goods that need to be scanned over long ranges, such as railway cars on a track. The cost of active and semi-passive RFID tags is significant; hence, low-cost items typically use passive RFID tags.

The *RFID accelerometer* is a device that measures the acceleration (the rate of change of velocity) of an item and is used to track truck speeds or taxi cab speeds. *Chipless RFID tags* use plastic or conductive polymers instead of silicon-based microchips, allowing them to be washed or exposed to water without damaging the chip. Examples of the innovative uses of RFID include:

- RFID chips injected under the skin of animals using a syringe can help ranchers meet regulations, track wild animals for ecological studies, and return lost pets to their owners.

- Retail stores use RFID to track and monitor inventory. Hospitals and pharmaceutical companies meet government regulations and standards with RFID. Even local libraries are using RFID to control theft and speed up the checkout process.

- Car manufacturers install RFID antitheft systems. Toll roads use RFID to collect payments from passing cars.

- Hospitals track patients', doctors', and nurses' locations to facilitate emergency situations and ensure safety. RFID also tracks equipment location to ensure quick response times during an emergency.

- American Express and MasterCard use RFID for automatic payments.

- Walmart and other large retailers use RFID to maintain inventory, stop shoplifting, and speed customer checkout processes.[10]

GLOBAL POSITIONING SYSTEM (GPS)

A *global positioning system (GPS)* is a satellite-based navigation system providing extremely accurate position, time, and speed information. The U.S. Department of Defense developed the technology in the early 1970s and later made it available to the public. GPS uses 24 global satellites that orbit Earth, sending signals to a receiver that can communicate with three or four satellites at a time. A GPS receiver can be a separate unit connected to a mobile device using cable or wireless technology such as Bluetooth, or it can be included in devices such as mobile phones or vehicle navigation systems. *Automatic vehicle location (AVL)* uses GPS tracking to track vehicles. AVL systems use a GPS receiver in the vehicle that links to a control center. Garmin is one of the more popular manufacturers of GPS tracking systems, offering vehicle tracking, phone and laptop integration, and hiker navigation for water and air.

The satellites broadcast signals constantly, while the receiver measures the time it takes for the signals to reach it. This measurement, which uses the speed of the signal to determine the distance, is taken from three distinct satellites to provide precise location information. The time measurements depend on high-powered clocks on each satellite and must be precise, because an error of one-thousandth of a second can result in a location variation of more than 200 miles. GPS can produce very accurate results, typically within 5 to 50 feet of the actual location (military versions have higher accuracy). GPS also provides latitude, longitude, and elevation information. *Latitude* represents a north/south measurement of position. *Longitude* represents an east/west measurement of position. *Geocache* is a GPS technology adventure game that posts the longitude and latitude location for an item on the Internet for users to find. GPS users find the geocache and typically sign a guest book or take an item and leave an item for the next adventure players to find. Caches are often placed in locations that are interesting or challenging for people to discover. A *geocoin*, a round, coin-sized object, is uniquely numbered and hidden in geocache. Geocoins can also be shaped to match a theme such as the state of Colorado or a birthday party hat. Geocoins are often decorative or commemorative, making them collectible and highly valuable for technology adventures.

GPS applications are in every kind of company vehicle these days—from police cars to bulldozers, from dump trucks to mayoral limousines. Emergency response systems use GPS to track each of their vehicles and so dispatch those closest to the scene of an accident. If a vehicle is missing, its GPS locator can help locate it. *Estimated time of arrival (ETA)* is the time of day of an expected arrival at a certain destination and is typically used for navigation applications. *Estimated time enroute (ETE)* is the time remaining before reaching a destination using the present speed and is typically used for navigation applications.

GEOGRAPHIC INFORMATION SYSTEMS (GIS)

GPS provides the foundation for geographic information systems. A *geographic information system (GIS)* stores, views, and analyzes geographic data creating multidimensional charts or maps. For example, GIS are monitoring global warming by measuring the speed of glaciers melting in Canada, Greenland, and Antarctica. *Cartography* is the science and art of making an illustrated map or chart. GIS allows users to interpret, analyze, and visualize data in different ways that reveal patterns and trends in the form of reports, charts, and maps. *Edge matching (warping, rubber sheeting)* occurs when paper maps are laid edge to edge and items that run across maps but do not match are reconfigured to match. Edge matching is a critical component of creating a GIS database because map misalignments occur frequently for many reasons, including survey error and cartographic errors. *GIS map automation* links business assets to a centralized system where they can be tracked and monitored over time.

Spatial data (geospatial data or geographic information) identifies the geographic location of features and boundaries on Earth, such as natural or constructed features, oceans, and more. Spatial data can be mapped and is stored as coordinates and topology. A GIS accesses, manipulates, and analyzes spatial data. *Geocoding* in spatial databases is a coding process that assigns a digital map feature to an attribute that serves as a unique ID (tract number, node number) or classification (soil type, zoning category). GIS professionals are certified in geocoding practices to ensure industry standards are met when classifying spatial data.

Companies that deal in transportation combine GISs with database and GPS technology. Airlines and shipping companies can plot routes with up-to-the-second information about the location of all their transport vehicles. Hospitals can locate their medical staff with GIS and sensors that pick up transmissions from ID badges. Automobiles have GPSs linked to GIS maps that display the car's location and driving directions on a dashboard screen. GM offers the OnStar system, which sends a continuous stream of information to the OnStar center about the car's exact location.

Some mobile phone providers combine GPS and GIS capabilities so they can locate users within a geographical area about the size of a tennis court to assist emergency services such as 911. Farmers can use GIS to map and analyze fields, telling them where to apply the proper amounts of seed, fertilizer, and herbicides.

A GIS can find the closest gas station or bank or determine the best way to get to a particular location. But it is also good at finding patterns, such as finding the most feasible location to hold a conference according to where the majority of a company's customers live and work. GIS can present this information in a visually effective way (see Figure 16.10).

A GIS can provide information and insight to both mobile users and people at fixed locations. Google Earth combines satellite imagery, geographic data, and Google's search capabilities to create a virtual globe that users can download to a computer or mobile device. Not only does this provide useful business benefits, but it also allows for many educational opportunities. Instead of just talking about the Grand Canyon, an instructor can use Google Earth to view that region.

GPS and GIS both utilize *location-based services (LBS)*, applications that use location information to provide a service. LBS is designed to give mobile users instant access to personalized local content and range from 911 applications to buddy finders ("Let me know when my friend is within 1,000 feet") to games (treasure hunts) to location-based advertising

FIGURE 16.10

GIS Uses.

GRAPHICAL INFORMATION SYSTEMS USES	
Finding what is nearby	Given a specific location, the GIS finds sources within a defined radius. These might be entertainment venues, medical facilities, restaurants, or gas stations. Users can also use GIS to locate vendors that sell a specific item they want and get the results as a map of the surrounding area or an address.
Routing information	Once users have an idea where they want to go, GIS can provide directions to get there using either a map or step-by-step instructions. Routing information can be especially helpful when combined with search services.
Sending information alerts	Users may want to be notified when information relevant to them becomes available near their location. A commuter might want to know that a section of the highway has traffic congestion, or a shopper might want to be notified when a favorite store is having a sale on a certain item.
Mapping densities	GIS can map population and event densities based on a standard area unit, such as square miles, making it easy to see distributions and concentrations. Police can map crime incidents to determine where additional patrolling is required, and stores can map customer orders to identify ideal delivery routes.
Mapping quantities	Users can map quantities to find out where the most or least of a feature may be. For example, someone interested in opening a specialty coffee shop can determine how many others are already in the area, and city planners can determine where to build more parks.

("Visit the Starbucks on the corner and get $1.00 off a latte"). Many LBS applications complement GPS and GIS, such as:

- Emergency services
- Field service management
- Find-it services
- Mapping
- Navigation
- Tracking assets
- Traffic information
- Vehicle location
- Weather information
- Wireless advertising[11]

Just as Facebook and Twitter helped fuel the Web 2.0 revolution, applications such as Foursquare, Gowalla, and Loopt are bringing attention to LBS. Each application is a mobile phone service that helps social media users find their friends' locations. Facebook and Twitter have added location-based services to complement their applications.

OPENING CASE STUDY QUESTIONS

1. What are the three different wireless business applications? How can Slack use each to provide value to its customers?

2. What are the mobility benefits and challenges facing Slack?

Chapter Sixteen Case: Square

Square is a little device that magically transforms a smartphone into a credit/debit card machine. It's changing the game for electronic payments and the way we traditionally send and receive money. Square allows you to buy, sell, and send money by using any Apple or Android mobile device. With three free mobile apps—Square Register, Square Wallet, and Square Cash—Square is designed to help small businesses and sole proprietorship's accept credit card payments and help consumers transition to a cashless lifestyle. Here is how Square works:

- **Request your free reader:** Sign up and Square will send you a free Square Reader to take payments on an iPhone, iPad, or Android. Activate your account and process payments in minutes.

- **Download Square Register:** Square Register is a free app that works with Square Reader to turn a smartphone or an iPad into a mobile point of sale. Payments, sales reports, and hardware—Register does all this and more.

- **Go places. Sell things:** Plug in Square Reader, sign in to Square Register, and start swiping. Send receipts via email or text message. Request more free Square Readers so staff can sell for your business, too.

Square is amazing technology, but the question you have to ask is whether Square is really changing how we process payments. If you own a small business and could traditionally only accept cash, then the answer is yes! Just think of the farmer's markets, street fair vendors, or flea market. Unfortunately, small business does not always equate to large profits. These types of customers are low volume and minimal transactions, which equate to low profits for a payment processor like Square, which makes its money by taking 2.75 percent of the total purchase. If you purchase $100 worth of t-shirts at the local street fair with your Visa card, Square collects $2.75 and has to pay Visa $2.20, making a mere $0.55. Square has to run its business on these profits, including expenses for marketing, sales, customer service, employees, accounting, and so on. For a viable business, Square needs to scale its way to massive payment volumes, and with PayPal and Intuit quickly building card readers of their own, the competition is growing.[12]

Questions

1. Would you categorize Square as a disruptive technology?

2. How is Square using wireless networks to gain a competitive advantage?

3. What type of network is Square using? What happens to Square's business if the network is hacked?

4. What can Square do to maintain its competitive advantage and become more profitable?

5. If you were given $1 million to invest in Square, would you do it? Why or why not?

16.1. Describe the different wireless network categories.

There are four types of wireless networks—PAN, WLAN, WMAN, and WWAN. A PAN provides communication over a short distance that is intended for use with devices that are owned and operated by a single user. A WLAN is a local area network that uses radio signals to transmit and receive data over distances of a few hundred feet. A WMAN is a metropolitan area network that uses radio signals to transmit and receive data, and a WWAN is a wide area network that uses radio signals to transmit and receive data.

16.2. Explain the different wireless network business applications.

Mobile and wireless business applications and services are using satellite technologies. These technologies are GPS, GIS, and LBS. GPS is a satellite-based navigation system providing extremely accurate position, time, and speed information. GIS is location information that can be shown on a map. LBSs are applications that use location information to provide a service that both GPS and GIS use.

1. What is a personal area network?
2. How does Wi-Fi work?
3. What are GIS, GPS, and LBS? How are businesses using these applications to compete?
4. What is RFID and how could it help a large retailer track inventory?
5. What are the advantages of mobile business?
6. Why would a company want to implement mobile device management?
7. What is IT consumerization and how does it impact an organization?
8. Why would a company want to use VoLTE?
9. What is the difference between WEP and WPA?
10. How could hackers use war chalking and war driving?

1. Sports Sensors

A sensor is a device that detects or measures a physical property such as heat, light, sound, or motion and records, indicates, or otherwise reacts to it in a particular way. With wireless apps and sensors, a number of new, high-tech tools for amateurs provide coach-quality feedback to athletes of all levels, including:

 Tennis (Sony): Sony recently created a tennis-tracking device and app that will let users collect the kind of game-play data that used to be available only to professionals.

 Golf (Swingbyte): The ultralight sensor clips to the club and monitors speed, acceleration, arc, and other statistics.

- **Hockey (Fwd Powershot):** The ultralight sensor fits into the handle end of the stick and measures swing speed, angle, and acceleration.
- **Basketball (94Fifty Smart Sensor):** Embedded in a standard ball, the sensor tracks shot speed, arc, and backspin plus dribble speed and force.
- **Baseball (Zepp):** Stuck to the knob of the bat, the sensor tracks the speed and plane of a swing and the angle of impact.

In a group, create a product that takes advantage of sensors, including what the sensor would measure and how it would deliver the feedback to the user.

2. Wi-Fi for Fishes

Not too long ago, the Seattle Aquarium decided it needed to take a deep dive into its network infrastructure and deploy wireless across its facilities. Now, a year and half in, the aquarium has found Wi-Fi to be a tool that not only lets it serve visitors in unique ways but enriches the exchanges possible between staff members and the community, says Pam Lamon, the aquarium's web and social media coordinator. For instance, there are long stretches when Umi, the aquarium's 40-pound giant Pacific octopus, doesn't move at all. Now, staff members armed with tablets can roam around the exhibit showing visitors videos of Umi feeding while they field questions.

Wireless even lets the aquarium interact with people who can't visit in person. For instance, during a recent Google + Hangout on Air, a young boy from an East Coast school asked an aquarium diver how many fish were swimming in the tank with her. The diver, wearing a wetsuit and a facemask with a microphone and speaker, began pointing out fish. "One, two, three, four, five, six, seven," she counted off, before giving up and telling him there were 500, give or take a few. "It's a little bit hard to know for sure because they just don't hold still while we count them," she joked.

The Seattle Aquarium is far from alone among businesses and organizations that are tapping into wireless to expand or improve services. As wireless has morphed from a pleasant perk to a necessity for employees and clients across industries, many businesses are finding they can no longer make do without wireless or with limited Wi-Fi services. Today, not only is there incentive to find better solutions, but companies have access to more sophisticated equipment to help them pinpoint network problems. From next-generation access points to cloud-based management systems, wireless tools can provide expanded capabilities, are easy to manage, and are available in a range of prices.

In a group, choose a business in your area that could benefit from wireless technology, such as the Seattle Aquarium, and create a plan detailing the additional services it could offer its customers.

3. Snapping a Theftie

Has your smartphone ever been stolen? If so, you are not alone; millions of cell phones are stolen every year and the numbers are increasing. Of course, every good entrepreneur can spot an opportunity, and a new antitheft app is one step ahead of criminals who are targeting smartphones.

Lookout is among the latest additions to the growing antitheft industry, and the app features some smart ways of helping you get one step ahead of thieves. A smartphone's front-facing camera is often regarded as merely a portal to endless selfie photographs. But Lookout puts the camera to good use by capturing a photo of you—or of any would-be thief—when someone inputs your phone's password incorrectly three times. That photo, or theftie, is instantly emailed to the phone's owner, along with the device's approximate location. The antitheft app is free to download, but this handy photo feature is not available on iPhones due to Apple restrictions and comes with an annual charge of $30.

Lookout's team has been adding new features to the app's alerts, based on the methods thieves use to steal phones undetected. The app also will send emails to its owner if anyone attempts to remove the phone's SIM card, enables Airplane mode, or turns off the device. From that point, the owner can choose to lock or wipe the phone remotely.

Do you agree that antitheft apps are smart business? Are any ethical issues involved in taking thefties? How would you feel if company security policy required you to install Lookout on your cell phone? If you could add a new feature to Lookout, how would it work and what would it do to deter smartphone theft?

4. Pandora Makes Users' Music Public

Pandora, the online music company, lets users create personalized music stations that they can stream online, but it also makes those stations viewable to anyone on the Internet who knows someone's email address. For example, someone with the email address sergey@google.com likes a band called Rise Against. Using the email address of Steve Jobs implies he likes country music legend Willie Nelson and jazz trumpeter Chris Botti.Do you view your music selection as private or public information? How could someone use this information unethically? Do you see this as a threat for Pandora? Do you think customers will stop using the service? What can Pandora do to ensure customer privacy?

Do you view your music selection as private or public information? How could someone use this information unethically? Do you see this as a threat for Pandora? Do you think customers will stop using the service? What can Pandora do to ensure customer privacy?

5. Cars Hacked

Who would have thought that a car could be hacked? But that is exactly what happened in Austin, Texas. About a hundred cars were broken into, not by the usual method of either picking the lock or smashing a window but instead through a Wi-Fi connection. A local dealership, where all the cars were purchased, had installed a Wi-Fi-enabled black box under the dashboard that could disable the car and set off the horn if the owner did not make payments. However, in this case, the owners were not in arrears but, rather, the victims of a recently laid-off employee at the dealership who was seeking revenge by using the web-based system to disable the cars one by one. After someone at the dealership figured out the cars had been hacked, the password that allowed authorization to the black boxes was quickly changed.

Is the black box a good idea? Do you consider this an ethical business practice? If you had bought a car with a black box, would you have had it removed? How many customers do you think will consider buying another car from that dealership?

6. Google TV

As more Internet-related services move beyond delivering content just to the computer, Google wants to bring that content into the living room. In a joint venture, Google is teaming with Sony and Intel to introduce IPTV services either through new Internet-accessible TVs or a new set-top box allowing consumers to search for content, browse the web, view photo albums, and more. Google would provide the needed software along with advertisement opportunities, Sony would manufacture the new TVs, and Intel would supply the processors that make it all happen. Although consumers can already watch TV shows on their computers as well as on a TV, porting Internet content to an HDTV screen seems like the next logical step, which is the magic of IPTV. However, this is a very crowded playing field with many firms competing for the living room space. Google is competing with the likes of VUDU, TiVo, Yahoo! Connected TV, Netflix, Roku, Rovi, DivX, Apple TV, Xbox 360, Boxee, CinemaNow, Popbox, and many others, with no clear winner, at least not at the moment. Brainstorm the advantages and disadvantages associated with IPTV. Do you think Google TV will be successful? Why or why not?

7. Shipment Routes

Mary Conzachi works in the logistics department for Loadstar, a large trucking company and barge operator in the Midwest. She has looked into a variety of systems to keep track of the location of trucks and barges so that the company can route shipments better and answer customer inquiries faster. Conzachi's major concern is with the trucks; the barges have commodities and take weeks to move something. She states that it is much harder to keep up with trucking. She needs to know the exact location of the truck at any given time. You have been hired to assist her in recommending a solution. What solution would you recommend? Why?

8. Google Collected Public Wi-Fi Data . . . By Mistake

Google has admitted to collecting data sent over unsecured Wi-Fi networks mistakenly, using its Street View cars. Google photographs homes from public streets, using a fleet of company cars. Google said it was trying to gather information about the location, strength, and configuration of Wi-Fi networks so it could improve the accuracy of location-based services such as Google Maps and driving directions. However, in the process, the cars were also collecting snippets of emails and other Internet activity from unprotected wireless networks in the homes. Google blamed this on a programming error, temporarily halted the Street View data collection, and announced it would stop collecting all Wi-Fi data. Do you believe this was a mistake by Google? If home users do not protect their wireless networks, what is to stop a neighbor from collecting the same information? Who is really at fault here?

 UNIT SUMMARY

In a remarkably short time, the Internet has grown from a virtual playground into a vital, sophisticated medium for business, more specifically, ebusiness. Online consumers are flooding to the Internet, and they come with very high expectations and a degree of control that they did not have with traditional bricks-and-mortar companies. The enticement of doing business online must be strengthened by the understanding that, to succeed online, businesses will have to be able to deliver a satisfying and consistent customer experience, building brand loyalty and guaranteeing high rates of customer retention.

Strategic alliances enable businesses to gain competitive advantage(s) through access to a partner's resources, including markets, technologies, and people. Teaming up with another business adds complementary resources and capabilities, enabling participants to grow and expand more quickly and efficiently.

 KEY TERMS

BitCoin

Bitcoin is a new currency that was created in 2009 by an unknown person using the alias Satoshi Nakamoto. Bitcoin isn't just a currency, like dollars or euros or yen. It's a way of making payments, like PayPal or the Visa credit card network. Bitcoins can be used to buy merchandise anonymously. Transactions are made with no middle men—meaning no banks, and bitcoins are not tied to any country or subject to regulation! There are no transaction fees and no need to give your real name. More merchants are beginning to accept them: You can buy webhosting services, pizza, or even manicures. There's now a Bitcoin ATM in Vancouver and one planned for Hong Kong.

It's not clear whether Bitcoin's inventor, who disappeared from the Internet in mid-2010, was prophetic enough to imagine what happened last year. The idea was to create a currency whose value couldn't be watered down by some central authority such as the Federal Reserve. The value of Bitcoin exploded, with the price of an individual coin jumping from $100 in July to $200 in October to more than $1,000 as of May 2014.

About five years ago, using the pseudonym Satoshi Nakamoto, an anonymous computer programmer or group of programmers built the Bitcoin software system and released it on the Internet. This was a system that was designed to run across a large network of machines—called Bitcoin miners—and anyone on Earth could operate one of these machines. This distributed software seeded the new currency, creating a small number of Bitcoins. Basically, Bitcoins are just long digital addresses and balances, stored in an online ledger called the blockchain. But the system was also designed so that the currency would slowly expand and encourage people to operate Bitcoin miners to keep the system itself growing.

When the system creates new Bitcoins, it gives them to the miners. Miners keep track of all the Bitcoin transactions and add them to the blockchain ledger; in exchange, they get the privilege of, every so often, awarding themselves a few extra Bitcoins. Right now, 25 Bitcoins are paid out to the world's miners about six times per hour, but that rate changes over time.

Why do these Bitcoins have value? It's pretty simple. They've evolved into something that a lot of people want—like a dollar or a yen or the cowry shells swapped for goods on the coast of Africa over 3,000 years ago—and they're in limited supply. Although the system continues to crank out Bitcoins, this will stop when it reaches 21 million, which was designed to happen in about the year 2140.

Bitcoins are stored in a digital wallet, a kind of virtual bank account that allows users to send or receive bitcoins, pay for goods, or save their money. Although each Bitcoin transaction is recorded in a public log, names of buyers and sellers are never revealed—only their wallet IDs. Although that keeps Bitcoin users' transactions private, it also lets them buy or sell anything without easily tracing it back to them. That's why it has become the currency of choice for people online buying drugs or other illicit activities. No one knows what will become of Bitcoin. It is mostly unregulated, but that could change. Governments are concerned about taxation and their lack of control over the currency.[13]

Questions

1. Do you consider Bitcoin a form of disruptive or sustaining technology?
2. How can web-based businesses benefit from Bitcoin?
3. Describe the revenue model for how miners receive Bitcoin currency.
4. Why are governments wary of Bitcoin?
5. What are the security issues surrounding Bitcoin?

✳ **UNIT CLOSING CASE TWO**

© fotog/Getty Images RF

© FocusTechnology/Alamy

© Ronnie Kaufman/Blend Images LLC RF

Disrupting the Taxi: Uber

Ray Markovich started driving a taxi in Chicago three years ago after shutting his struggling wireless phone store. Driving a cab wasn't particularly gratifying or lucrative—he had to pay $400 a week just to lease his white 2011 Ford Escape. It was predictable if monotonous work. Well, there's nothing monotonous about it now. In June, Markovich, a thin, well-dressed man with short brown hair and spots of gray in his mustache and goatee, walked into the local office of Uber, the San Francisco–based taxi technology start-up. Uber put him through an hour of orientation, gave him a free iPhone that carries its car dispatch app and some gear to mount it on the windshield, and sent him on his way.

Since then, Markovich has had to dodge flak from traditional cabbies who complain that they can no longer pick up riders in the city's tonier neighborhoods, and he's receiving a constant flood of emails from Uber itself, offering steep discounts on new cars and other perks to secure his loyalty. At the same time, he has increased his earnings by about 20 percent and says he's simply evolving along with his customers. "No one under the age of 40 with a smart phone is going out and getting a cab anymore," says Markovich. "I say if you can't beat 'em, join 'em."

A battle for the future of transportation is being waged outside our offices and homes. Uber and a growing collection of well-funded start-ups, such as the ride-sharing service Lyft, are trying to make getting a taxi as easy as booking a reservation on OpenTable or checking a price on Amazon—just another thing you do with your smartphone. Flush with Silicon Valley venture capital, these companies have an even grander ambition: They want to make owning a car completely unnecessary. They're battling each other, city regulators, entrenched taxi interests, and critics who claim they are succeeding only because they run roughshod over laws meant to protect public safety. "Being out in front of the taxi industry, putting a bull's-eye on our back, has not been easy," says Travis Kalanick, the 37-year-old chief executive of Uber. "The taxi industry has been ripe for disruption for decades. But only technology has allowed it to really kick in."

Nearly four years ago, Uber introduced the idea of allowing passengers to book the nearest town car by smartphone and then track the vehicle on a map as it approaches their location. After the ride, the service automatically compensates the driver from the customer's preloaded credit card—no awkward tipping required. It's a simple experience and a much more pleasant way to get a ride than stepping onto a busy street and waving at oncoming traffic.

Uber has raised $307 million from a group of backers that include Google Ventures, Google's investment arm, and Jeff Bezos, the founder of Amazon. It operates in 270 cities around the world and was on track to book more than $1 billion annually in rides in 2013, according to financial information that leaked to the gossip website Valleywag last November. In February alone, Uber expanded to Dubai; Honolulu; Lyon; Manila; Milwaukee; Pittsburgh; Tucson, Arizona; and Durban, South Africa.

In the process, Uber has managed to become one of the most loved and hated start-ups of the smartphone age. Its customers rave about the reliability and speed of the service even as they bitterly complain about so-called surge pricing, the elevated rates Uber charges during hours of high demand. Uber has also been blocked from operating in several markets by regulators out to protect the interests of consumers or entrenched incumbents, depending on whom you ask. After customers complained about the ban in Austin, Texas, the Austin City Council adopted a regulatory structure for ride sharing, enabling Uber to operate in the city. In Boston and Chicago, taxi operators have sued their cities for allowing unregulated companies to devalue million-dollar operating permits. Things grew especially heated recently in Paris when incensed taxi drivers shut down highway exits to the main airports and gridlocked city traffic.

Kalanick calls the cab industry a "protectionist scheme." He says these protests are not about the drivers but cab companies "that would prefer not to compete at all and like things the way they are."

His opponents are equally critical. They accuse Uber of risking passengers' lives by putting untested drivers on the road, offering questionable insurance, and lowering prices as part of a long-term conspiracy to kill the competition, among other alleged transgressions. Fueling the anti-Uber cause is the tragic case of a 6-year-old girl in San Francisco who was struck and killed by an Uber driver. "Would you feel comfortable if you had a 21-year-old daughter living alone in the city, using a smart phone app to get in a vehicle for hire, and that vehicle ends up being a 2001 Chevy Astro van with 300,000 miles on it?" says Trevor Johnson, one of the directors of the San Francisco Cab Drivers Association. "I've made it my personal mission to make it as difficult as possible for these guys to operate."

Kalanick calls himself the perfect man for the job of liberating drivers and riders. His previous company, video-streaming start-up Red Swoosh, was well ahead of its time, and Kalanick limped along for years, taking no salary before selling it to Akamai Technologies in 2007 for a modest sum. "Imagine hearing 'no' a hundred times a day for six years straight," he says. "When you go through an experience like that, you are sort of a hardened veteran. You only persevere if you are really hard-core and fight for what you believe in."[14]

Questions

1. Identify Uber's ebusiness model and explain how it is disruptive.
2. Explain why some market segments are not included in Uber's business model.
3. List the ways Uber is using collaboration and wireless technologies to improve its competitive advantage in the taxi market.
4. Describe the different types of networks Uber is using to run its business.
5. Develop a use for LBS that Uber customers can benefit from using when looking for a taxi.
6. Evaluate the security dilemmas that Uber faces in using the various forms of wireless technology.

1. Analyzing Website

Stars Inc. is a large clothing corporation that specializes in reselling clothes worn by celebrities. The company's four websites generate 75 percent of its sales. The remaining 25 percent of sales occur directly through the company's warehouse. You have recently been hired as the director of sales. The only information you can find about the success of the four websites is displayed in the table below.

You decide that maintaining four websites is expensive and adds little business value. You propose consolidating to one site. Create a report detailing the business value gained by consolidating to a single website, along with your recommendation for consolidation. Be sure to include your website profitability analysis. Assume that, at a minimum, 10 percent of hits result in a sale; at an average, 30 percent of hits result in a sale; and at a maximum, 60 percent of hits result in a sale.

Website	Classic	Contemporary	New Age	Traditional
Traffic analysis	5,000 hits/day	200 hits/day	10,000 hits/day	1,000 hits/day
Stickiness (average)	20 minutes	1 hour	20 minutes	50 minutes
Number of abandoned shopping carts	400/day	0/day	5,000/day	200/day
Number of unique visitors	2,000/day	100/day	8,000/day	200/day
Number of identified visitors	3,000/day	100/day	2,000/day	800/day
Average revenue per sale	$1,000	$1,000	$50	$1,300

2. Wiki Your Way

Wikis are web-based tools that make it easy for users to add, remove, and change online content. Employees at companies such as Intel, Motorola, IBM, and Sony use them for a host of tasks, from setting internal meeting agendas to posting documents related to new products.

Many companies rely on wikis to engage customers in ongoing discussions about products. Wikis for Motorola and T-Mobile handsets serve as continually updated user guides. TV networks, including ABC and CBS, created fan wikis that let viewers interact with each other as they unraveled mysteries from such shows as *Lost* and *CSI: Crime Scene Investigation*. You would like to implement wikis at your new company, The Consulting Edge, a small computer consulting company catering to mid- and large-sized businesses. Answer the following questions:

- How can a wiki help you attract customers and grow your business?
- How can a wiki help your partners and employees?
- What ethical and security concerns would you have with the wiki?
- What could you do to minimize these concerns?

3. Sticky Wiki

Wiki (Hawaiian for "quick") is software that allows users to create and edit web page content freely, using any web browser. The most common wiki is Wikipedia. Wikis offer a powerful yet flexible collaborative communication tool for developing websites. The best part of a wiki is that it grows and evolves by the collaborative community adding content—the owner of the wiki does not have to add all of the content as is typical in a standard web page.

Many sites offer free wiki software such as Socialtext, a group-editable website. As one of the first wiki companies, Socialtext wikis are designed for anyone who wants to accelerate team communications, enable knowledge sharing better, foster collaboration, and build online communities. Socialtext also offers WikiWidgets, which make it easy for nontechnical business users to create rich, dynamic wiki content. Today, more than 3,000 organizations use Socialtext, including Symantec, Nokia, IKEA, Conde Nast, Ziff-Davis, Kodak, University of Southern California, Boston College, and numerous others.

Create your own wiki. Wikis can address a variety of needs: student involvement, fraternities and sororities, group activities, sport team updates, local band highlights, and so on. Choose a free wiki software vendor from the Internet and create a wiki for something you are involved in or excited about and want to share with others. This could include a student organization; fraternity or sorority; academic organization; or favorite author, book, movie, band, musician, or sports team. If you have different wiki software you prefer, feel free to use it to create your wiki.

4. Securing Your Home Wireless Network

These days wireless networking products are so ubiquitous and inexpensive that anyone can easily build a wireless network with less than $100 worth of equipment. However, wireless networks are exactly that—wireless—they do not stop at walls. In fact, wireless networks often carry signals more than 300 feet from the wireless router. Living in an apartment, dorm, condominium, or house means that you might have dozens of neighbors who can access your wireless network.

It is one thing to let a neighbor borrow a lawn mower, but it is another thing to allow a neighbor to access a home wireless network. There are several good reasons for not sharing a home wireless network including:

- It may slow Internet performance.
- It allows others to view files on your computers and spread dangerous software such as viruses.
- It allows others to monitor the websites you visit, read your email and instant messages as they travel across the network, and copy your user names and passwords.
- It allows others to send spam or perform illegal activities with your Internet connection.

Securing a home wireless network is invaluable and allows you to enable security features that can make it difficult for uninvited guests to connect through your wireless network. Create a document detailing all of the features you can use to secure a home wireless network.

5. Weather Bots

Warren Jackson, an engineering graduate student at the University of Pennsylvania, was not interested in the weather until he started investigating how the National Weather Service collected weather data. The weather service has collected most of its information using weather balloons that carry a device to measure items such as pressure, wind speed, and humidity. When the balloon reaches about 100,000 feet and pressure causes it to pop, the device falls and lands a substantial distance from its launch point. The National Weather Service and researchers sometimes look for the $200 device, but of the 80,000 sent up annually, they write off many as lost.

Convinced there had to be a better way, Warren began designing a GPS-equipped robot that launches a parachute after the balloon pops and brings the device back down to Earth, landing it at a predetermined location set by the researchers. The idea is so inventive that the Penn's Weiss Tech House, a university organization that encourages students to innovate and bring their ideas to market, awarded Warren and some fellow graduate engineering students first prize in its third annual PennVention Contest. Warren won $5,000 and access to expert advice on prototyping, legal matters, and branding.

GPS and GIS can be used in all sorts of devices, in many different industries, for multiple purposes. You want to compete, and win first prize, in the PennVention next year. Create a product, using a GPS or GIS, that is not currently in the market today that you will present at the fourth annual PennVention.

6. Wireless Networks and Streetlamps

Researchers at Harvard University and BBN Technologies have designed CitySense, a wireless network capable of reporting real-time sensor data across the entire city of Cambridge, Massachusetts. CitySense is unique because it solves a constraint on previous wireless networks—battery life. The network mounts each node on a municipal streetlamp, where it draws power from city electricity. Researchers plan to install 100 sensors on streetlamps throughout Cambridge by 2011, using a grant from the National Science Foundation. Each node will include an embedded PC running the Linux operating system, an 802.11 Wi-Fi interface, and weather sensors.

One of the challenges in the design was how the network would allow remote nodes to communicate with the central server at Harvard and BBN. CitySense will do that by letting each node form a mesh with its neighbors, exchanging data through multiple-hop links. This strategy allows a node to download software or upload sensor data to a distant server hub using a small radio with only a 1-kilometer range.

You are responsible for deploying a CitySense network around your city. What goals would you have for the system besides monitoring urban weather and pollution? What other benefits could a CitySense network provide? How could local businesses and citizens benefit from the network? What legal and ethical concerns should you understand before deploying the network? What can you do to protect your network and your city from these issues?

7. Free Wi-Fi in Africa

Covering Africa with free and low-cost Wi-Fi may not seem like a smart thing, but that is exactly what Paul English, the cofounder of travel search engine Kayak.com, plans to do. English has created a hybrid nonprofit/for-profit company, JoinAfrica, to explore the creation of two tiers of Wi-Fi access in Africa. The first tier will be free and offer basic email service (from Gmail, Yahoo!, etc.) and web browsing (Wikipedia, BBC, etc.). The second tier will be fee-based and offer additional capabilities, including audio, video, and high-quality images.

Although many countries in Africa struggle to have proper drinking water or even efficient electrical power, English and the JoinAfrica initiative believe having access to the Internet is just as important. JoinAfrica will work with for-profit telecommunication companies in Africa to first branch out with existing connections in villages, providing residents with the first-tier services, and residents can pay money to upgrade to the second tier. More bandwidth-intensive services such as streaming video and pornography will be throttled to ensure a basic level of service for all as the networks grow.

- List 10 ways wireless access could hurt remote villages in Africa.
- What other infrastructure requirements will JoinAfrica need to implement to ensure the project's success?
- How will changes in technology over the next decade affect the JoinAfrica project?
- What types of security and ethical issues will JoinAfrica face?
- If you were given $1 million, would you invest it in JoinAfrica?

8. Never Run with Your iPod

Jennifer Goebel was disqualified from her first-place spot in the Lakefront Marathon in Milwaukee after race officials spotted her using an iPod. A controversial 2007 rule banned portable music devices by all U.S. Track and Field participants because music could give a runner a competitive advantage and cause safety issues if the runner can't hear announcements. The officials for the Lakefront Marathon took action after viewing online photos of Goebel using her iPod; ironically, the photos were posted by Goeble herself on her own website.

Do you agree with the USTAF's decision to disqualify Jennifer Goebel? How could an iPod give a runner a competitive advantage? With so many wireless devices entering the market, it is almost impossible to keep up with the surrounding laws. Do you think Goebel was aware of the headphone ban? In your state, what are the rules for using wireless devices while driving? Do you agree with these rules? How does a business keep up with the numerous, ever-changing rules surrounding wireless devices? What could happen to a company that fails to understand the laws surrounding wireless devices?

9. Ding-a-Ling Took My $400!

A satellite television customer requested her service to be disconnected due to poor reception. Soon after disconnecting the service, the customer noticed a direct bank withdrawal for a $430 early-termination fee from the satellite provider. To make matters worse, the unplanned charge caused hundreds of dollars in overdraft charges. To top it all off, a customer service representative apparently named Ding-a-Ling called the customer to see if she would consider reconnecting the service.

Never give any company your checking account number or direct access to your bank account. If you want to establish a good relationship with a company, give it your credit card number. When a relationship with a supplier turns sour, the last thing you want is for that company to have direct access to your checking account.

Do you think what the satellite provider did was ethical? What could the customer do when disconnecting her service to avoid this type of issue? Can credit card companies enter your bank account and take out as much money as you owe at any time they want? Why is it important to never give a supplier direct access to your business checking account?

10. 911 McNuggets

Cellular technologies have changed the way we do business, and it is hard to imagine life without them. There are many wonderful advantages of using wireless technologies in business, but there are also some serious disadvantages, like the ability to make a bad decision faster.

A woman in Florida called 911 three times after McDonald's employees told her they were out of Chicken McNuggets. The woman stated that this is an emergency and if she had known they didn't have any McNuggets, then she would not have given them any money. The woman said McDonald's offered her a McDouble, but that she didn't want one. The woman was cited on a misuse of 911 charge.

It is so easy to pick up the phone, from anywhere, at any time, and make a bad call. How many times do you see people making calls on their cell phones from inappropriate locations? If this woman had to wait in line to use a pay phone, do you think it would have given her time to calm down and rethink her decision? With technology and the ability to communicate at our fingertips, do you agree that it is easier than ever to make a bad decision? What can you do to ensure that you think before you communicate?

If you are looking for Excel projects to incorporate into your class, try any of the following to test your knowledge.

Project Number	Project Name	Project Type	Plug-In Focus Area	Project Focus	Project Skill Set	Page Number
1	Financial Destiny	Excel	T2	Personal Budget	Introductory Formulas	AYK.4
2	Cash Flow	Excel	T2	Cash Flow	Introductory Formulas	AYK.4
3	Technology Budget	Excel	T1, T2	Hardware and Software	Introductory Formulas	AYK.4
4	Tracking Donations	Excel	T2	Employee Relationships	Introductory Formulas	AYK.4
5	Convert Currency	Excel	T2	Global Commerce	Introductory Formulas	AYK.5
6	Cost Comparison	Excel	T2	Total Cost of Ownership	Introductory Formulas	AYK.5
7	Time Management	Excel or Project	T2 or T12	Project Management	Introductory Gantt Charts	AYK.6
8	Maximize Profit	Excel	T2, T4	Strategic Analysis	Intermediate Formulas or Solver	AYK.6
9	Security Analysis	Excel	T3	Filtering Data	Intermediate Conditional Formatting, Autofilter, Subtotal	AYK.7
10	Gathering Data	Excel	T3	Data Analysis	Intermediate Conditional Formatting, PivotTable	AYK.8
11	Scanner System	Excel	T2	Strategic Analysis	Intermediate	AYK.8
12	Competitive Pricing	Excel	T2	Profit Maximization	Intermediate	AYK.9
13	Adequate Acquisitions	Excel	T2	Break-Even Analysis	Intermediate	AYK.9
24	Electronic Resumes	HTML	T9, T10, T11	Electronic Personal Marketing	Introductory Structural Tags	AYK.16
25	Gathering Feedback	Dreamweaver	T9, T10, T11	Data Collection	Intermediate Organization of Information	AYK.16

5

Transforming Organizations

This unit provides an overview of how organizations build information systems to prepare for competing in the 21st century. You as a business student need to know about this because information systems are the underlying foundation of how companies operate. A basic understanding of the principles of building information systems will make you a more valuable employee. You will be able to identify trouble spots early during the design process and make suggestions that will result in a better delivered information systems project—one that satisfies both you and your business.

Building an information system is analogous to constructing a house. You could sit back and let the developers do all the design work, construction, and testing with hopes that the house will satisfy your needs. However, participating in the house building process helps to guarantee that your needs are not only being heard, but also being met. It is good business practice to have direct user input steering the development of the finished product. The same is true for building information systems. Your knowledge of the systems development process will allow you to participate and ensure you are building flexible enterprise architectures that support not only current business needs, but also your future business needs.

Have you ever dreamed of traveling to exotic cities like Paris, Tokyo, Rio de Janeiro, or Cairo? In the past, the closest many people ever got to working in such cities was in their dreams. Today, the situation has changed. Most major companies cite global expansion as a link to future growth and a recent study noted that 91 percent of the companies doing business globally believe it is important to send employees on assignments in other countries.

If a career in global business has crossed your mind, this unit will help you understand the nature of competition in the global business world. The United States is a market of about 300 million people, but there are more than 6 billion potential customers in the 193 countries that make up the global market. Perhaps more interesting is that approximately 75 percent of the world's population lives in developing areas where technology, education, and per capita income still lag considerably behind developed (or industrialized) nations such as the United States. Developing countries are still a largely untapped market.

You, the business student, should be familiar with the potential of global business, including its many benefits and challenges. The demand for students with training in global business is almost certain to grow as the number of businesses competing in global markets increases.

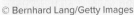

© Bernhard Lang/Getty Images   © Comstock/Jupiterimages RF   © altrendo images/Getty Images RF

Gamer Delight

It is a dream come true when you can make an incredible salary doing what you love and that is exactly what is happening in the gaming industry. To the gamer's delight profitable careers can be found for people with design, development, and programming skills. Video programmers are finding success in technology companies, marketing corporations, advertising agencies, and video game development companies. In fact, video games are a $30 billion industry in the U.S., especially as more people play games on their mobile phones, according to Reuters. Companies around the globe are paying application programmers, developers, and designers incredible salaries for their skills and capabilities.

Video Game Programmer

Video game programmers are software engineers who work on games for console or hand-held video gaming systems. In addition to understanding computer languages and structures, they must also be familiar with the specific target systems on which their games will be played, as well as the development platforms used to create games

Video game programming experts specializing in networking or graphic engines are seeing starting salaries as high as $100,000. One of the great benefits of the video game industry is that it is hardly affected by depression or bad economies. New college graduates are offered $60,000 annually without any industry experience.

Technical Directors

Technical directors for a game development company get high salaries even at the entry level. Those having the least experience are said to get an average of $60,000 every year and increase to more than $70, 000 for individuals who have more than three years of know-how. The highest compensation for this particular job description was $195,500 annually.

Video Games Designer

Video game designers work with a team developing and designing video games. Game designers are an important part of a comprehensive team of designers and developers that coordinate the complex task of creating a new video game. Game designers have duties like designing characters, levels, puzzles, art and animation. They may also write code, using various computer programming languages. Depending on their career duties, they may also be responsible for project management tasks and testing early versions of video games.

Video game designers also receives comparatively high compensation whether the knowledge comes from experience or formal education. The designer with fewer than three years of experience normally starts with $50,000 each year which increases to $75,000 after the third year. Once the video game design expert earns more than six years of on-the-job experience, this can go up to $100,000 annually. The creative director or lead designer earns up to $180,000 every year after getting substantial experience in the industry.

Video Game Producer

Video game producers supervise all aspects of creating a video game and are held liable for decisions from start to finish. These individuals coordinate the work of different departments involved, ensure that deadlines are met and the project remains within the budget. The minimum salary of producers is $62,000 while those with over six years of experience can earn up to $180,000 every year.

Video Game Artists and Animators

The artists and animators for video game development companies earn an average salary of $50,000 annually. Senior lead artists earn anywhere from $80,000 to $215,000 annually. Earning high income is quite easy in the video game industry if you have a good education, experience, determination, and creativity.[1]

Introduction

In a competitive business climate, an organization's ability to efficiently align resources and business activities with strategic objectives can mean the difference between succeeding and just surviving. To achieve strategic alignment, organizations increasingly manage their systems development efforts and project planning activities to monitor performance and make better business decisions. Fast-growing companies outsource many areas of their business to extend their technical and operational resources. By outsourcing, they save time and boost productivity by not having to develop their own systems from scratch. They are then free to concentrate on innovation and their core business. The chapters in Unit 5 are:

- **Chapter Seventeen**—Developing Software to Streamline Operations.
- **Chapter Eighteen**—Methodologies for Supporting Agile Organizations.
- **Chapter Nineteen**—Managing Organizational Projects.

© PhotoDisc Imaging/Getty Images

17

Developing Software to Streamline Operations

17.1. Describe the seven phases of the systems development life cycle.

LO 17.1 Describe the seven phases of the systems development life cycle.

The Systems Development Life Cycle (SDLC)

The multimillion-dollar Nike SCM system failure is legendary as Nike CEO Philip Knight famously stated, "This is what we get for our $400 million?" Nike partnered with i2 to implement an SCM system that never came to fruition. i2 blamed the failed implementation on the fact that Nike failed to use the vendor's implementation methodology and templates. Nike blamed the failure on faulty software.

It is difficult to get an organization to work if its systems do not work. In the information age, software success, or failure, can lead directly to business success, or failure. Companies rely on software to drive business operations and ensure work flows throughout the company. As more and more companies rely on software to operate, so do the business-related consequences of software successes and failures.

The potential advantages of successful software implementations provide firms with significant incentives to manage software development risks. However, an alarmingly high number of software development projects come in late or over budget, and successful projects tend to maintain fewer features and functions than originally specified. Understanding the basics of software development, or the systems development life cycle, will help organizations avoid potential software development pitfalls and ensure that software development efforts are successful.

Before jumping into software development, it is important to understand a few key terms. A legacy system is an old system that is fast approaching or beyond the end of its useful life within an organization. **Conversion** is the process of transferring information from a legacy system to a new system. Software customization modifies software to meet specific user or business requirements. **Off-the-shelf application software** supports general business processes and does not require any specific software customization to meet the organization's needs.

The **systems development life cycle (SDLC)** is the overall process for developing information systems, from planning and analysis through implementation and maintenance. The SDLC is the foundation for all systems development methods, and hundreds of different activities are associated with each phase. These activities typically include determining budgets, gathering system requirements, and writing detailed user documentation.

The SDLC begins with a business need, proceeds to an assessment of the functions a system must have to satisfy the need, and ends when the benefits of the system no longer outweigh its maintenance costs. This is why it is referred to as a life cycle. The SDLC is comprised of seven distinct phases: planning, analysis, design, development, testing, implementation, and maintenance (see Figure 17.1).

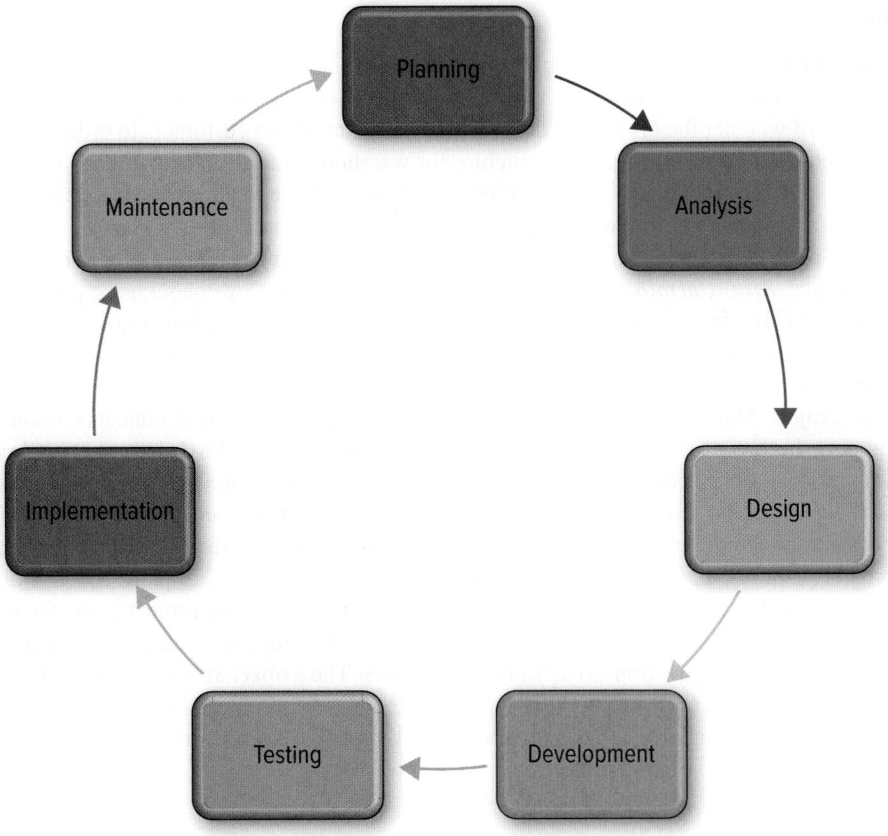

FIGURE 17.1

The SDLC and Its Associated Activities.

Phase	Associated Activity
Planning	■ Brainstorm issues and identify opportunities for the organization ■ Prioritize and choose projects for development ■ Set the project scope ■ Develop the project plan
Analysis	■ Gather the business requirement for the system ■ Define any constraints associated with the system
Design	■ Design the technical architecture required to support the system ■ Design the system models
Development	■ Build the technical architecture ■ Build the database ■ Build the applications
Testing	■ Write the test conditions ■ Perform system testing
Implementation	■ Write detailed user documentation ■ Provide training for the system users
Maintenance	■ Build a help desk to support the system users ■ Provide an environment to support system changes

PHASE 1: PLANNING

The *planning phase* establishes a high-level plan of the intended project and determines project goals. Planning is the first and most critical phase of any systems development effort, regardless of whether the effort is to develop a system that allows customers to order products online, determine the best logistical structure for warehouses around the world, or develop a strategic information alliance with another organization. Organizations must carefully plan the activities (and determine why they are necessary) to be successful. A *change agent* is a person or event that is the catalyst for implementing major changes for a system to meet business changes. *Brainstorming* is a technique for generating ideas by encouraging participants to offer as many ideas as possible in a short period without any analysis until all the ideas have been exhausted. Many times, new business opportunities are found as the result of a brainstorming session.

The Project Management Institute (PMI) develops procedures and concepts necessary to support the profession of project management (www.pmi.org). PMI defines a *project* as a temporary activity a company undertakes to create a unique product, service, or result. *Project management* is the application of knowledge, skills, tools, and techniques to project activities to meet project requirements. A *project manager* is an individual who is an expert in project planning and management, defines and develops the project plan, and tracks the plan to ensure the project is completed on time and on budget. The project manager is the person responsible for executing the entire project and defining the project scope that links the project to the organization's overall business goals. The *project scope* describes the business need (the problem the project will solve) and the justification, requirements, and current boundaries for the project. The *project plan* is a formal, approved document that manages and controls the entire project.

PHASE 2: ANALYSIS

In the *analysis phase* the firm analyzes its end-user business requirements and refines project goals into defined functions and operations of the intended system. *Business requirements* are the specific business requests the system must meet to be successful, so the analysis phase is critical because business requirements drive the entire systems development effort. A sample business requirement might state, "The CRM system must track all customer inquiries by product, region, and sales representative." The business requirement will state what the system must accomplish to be considered successful.

Gathering business requirements is basically conducting an investigation in which users identify all the organization's business needs and take measurements of these needs. Figure 17.2 displays a number of ways to gather business requirements. *Requirements management* is the process of managing changes to the business requirements throughout the project. Projects are typically dynamic in nature, and change should be expected and anticipated for successful project completion. A *requirements definition document* prioritizes all of the business requirements by order of importance to the company. *Sign-off* consists of the users' actual signatures indicating they approve all of the business requirements. If a system does not meet

FIGURE 17.2

Methods for Gathering Business Requirements.

Methods for Gathering Business Requirements
Perform a *joint application development (JAD)* session where employees meet, sometimes for several days, to define or review the business requirements for the system.
Interview individuals to determine current operations and current issues.
Compile questionnaires to survey employees to discover issues.
Make observations to determine how current operations are performed.
Review business documents to discover reports, policies, and how information is used throughout the organization.

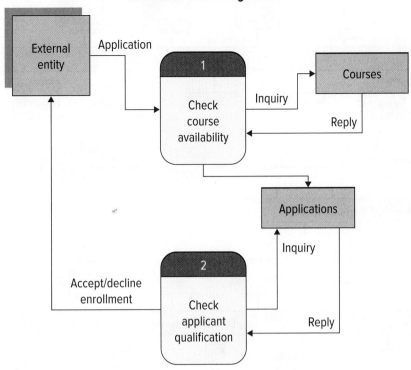

Automated Course Registration

FIGURE 17.3

Sample Data Flow Diagram.

the business requirements, it will be deemed a failed project. For this reason, the organization must spend as much time, energy, and resources as necessary to gather accurate and detailed business requirements.

Once a business analyst takes a detailed look at how an organization performs its work and its processes, the analyst can recommend ways to improve these processes to make them more efficient and effective. Process modeling involves graphically representing the processes that capture, manipulate, store, and distribute information between a system and its environment. One of the most common diagrams used in process modeling is the data flow diagram. A *data flow diagram (DFD)* illustrates the movement of information between external entities and the processes and data stores within the system (see Figure 17.3). Process models and data flow diagrams establish the specifications of the system. *Computer-aided software engineering (CASE)* tools are software suites that automate systems analysis, design, and development. Process models and data flow diagrams can provide the basis for the automatic generation of the system if they are developed using a CASE tool.

PHASE 3: DESIGN

The *design phase* establishes descriptions of the desired features and operations of the system, including screen layouts, business rules, process diagrams, pseudo code, and other documentation. During the analysis phase, end users and MIS specialists work together to gather the detailed business requirements for the proposed project from a logical point of view. That is, during analysis, business requirements are documented without respect to technology or the technical infrastructure that will support the system. Moving into the design phase turns the project focus to the physical or technical point of view, defining the technical architecture that will support the system, including data models, screen designs, report layouts, and database models (see Figure 17.4). The *graphical user interface (GUI)* is the interface to an information system. GUI screen design is the ability to model the information system screens for an entire system using icons, buttons, menus, and submenus. Data models represent a formal way to express data relationships to a database management system (DBMS). Entity relationship diagrams document the relationships between entities in a database environment (see Figure 17.5).

FIGURE 17.4

Sample Technical
Architecture.

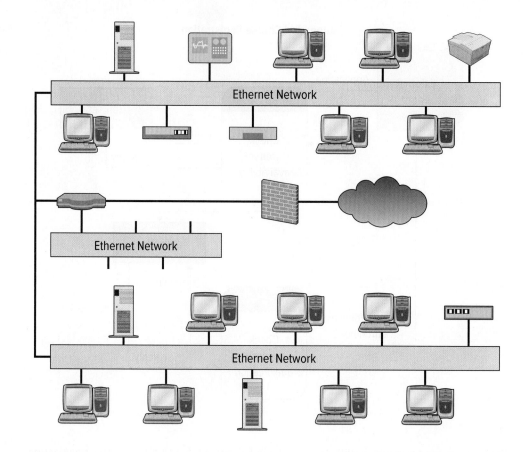

PHASE 4: DEVELOPMENT

The *development phase* takes all the detailed design documents from the design phase and transforms them into the actual system. In this phase, the project transitions from preliminary designs to actual physical implementation. During development, the company purchases and implements the equipment necessary to support the architecture. *Software engineering* is a disciplined approach for constructing information systems through the use of common methods, techniques, or tools. Software engineers use computer-aided software engineering (CASE) tools, which provide automated support for the development of the system. *Control objects for information and related technology (COBIT)* is a set of best practices that helps an organization to maximize the benefits of an information system, while at the same time establishing appropriate controls to ensure minimum errors.

During development, the team defines the programming language it will use to build the system. A *scripting language* is a programming method that provides for interactive modules to a website. *Object-oriented languages* group data and corresponding processes into objects. *Fourth-generation languages (4GL)* are programming languages that look similar to human languages. For example, a typical 4GL command might state, "FIND ALL RECORDS WHERE NAME IS "SMITH"." Programming languages are displayed in Figure 17.6.

PHASE 5: TESTING

The *testing phase* brings all the project pieces together into a special testing environment to eliminate errors and bugs and verify that the system meets all the business requirements defined in the analysis phase. *Bugs* are defects in the code of an information system. *Test conditions* detail the steps the system must perform along with the expected result of each step. Figure 17.7 displays several test conditions for testing user log-on functionality in a system. The tester will execute each test condition and compare the expected results with the actual results in order to verify that the system functions correctly. Notice in Figure 17.7

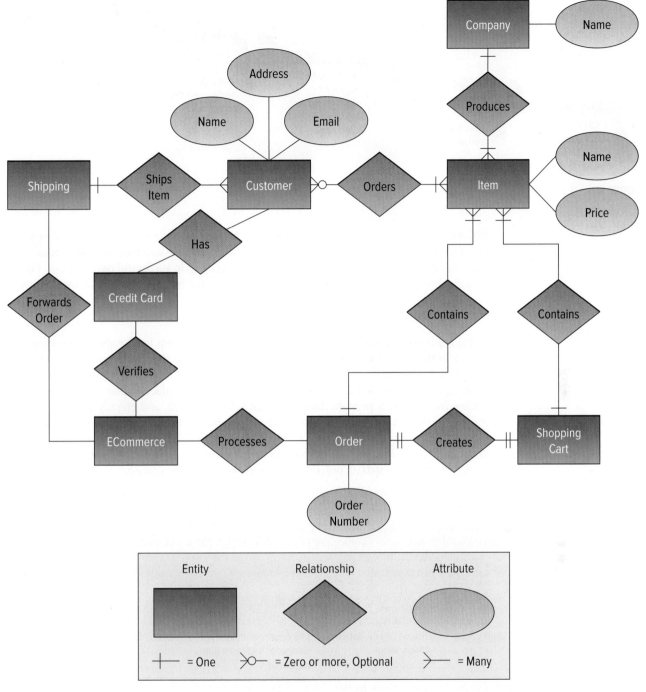

Entity   Relationship   Attribute

┼ = One   ⟩○─ = Zero or more, Optional   ⟩ = Many

FIGURE 17.5

Sample Entity Relationship Diagram.

how each test condition is extremely detailed and states the expected results that should occur when executing each test condition. Each time the actual result is different from the expected result, a "bug" is generated and the system goes back to development for a bug fix. Test condition 6 in Figure 17.7 displays a different actual result than the expected result because the system failed to allow the user to log on. After this test condition fails, it is obvious that the system is not functioning correctly, and it must be sent back to development for a bug fix.

A typical system development effort has hundreds or thousands of test conditions. Every single test condition must be executed to verify that the system performs as expected.

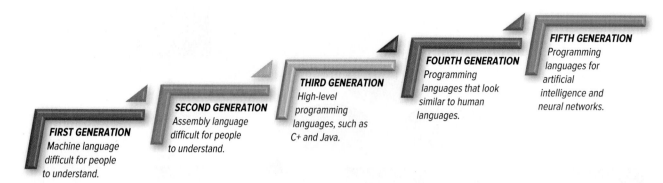

FIRST GENERATION
Machine language difficult for people to understand.

SECOND GENERATION
Assembly language difficult for people to understand.

THIRD GENERATION
High-level programming languages, such as C+ and Java.

FOURTH GENERATION
Programming languages that look similar to human languages.

FIFTH GENERATION
Programming languages for artificial intelligence and neural networks.

FIGURE 17.6

Overview of Programming Languages.

Writing all the test conditions and performing the actual testing of the software takes a tremendous amount of time and energy. After reviewing the massive level of effort required to test a system, it becomes obvious why this is a critical step in successful development. Figure 17.8 displays the different types of tests typically included in a systems development effort.

PHASE 6: IMPLEMENTATION

In the *implementation phase*, the organization places the system into production so users can begin to perform actual business operations with it. In this phase, the detailed *user documentation* is created that highlights how to use the system and how to troubleshoot issues or problems. Training is also provided for the system users and can take place online or in a classroom. *Online training* runs over the Internet or on a CD or DVD, and employees complete the training on their own time at their own pace. *Workshop training* is held in a classroom environment and led by an instructor. One of the best ways to support users is to create a *help desk*, or a group of people who respond to users' questions. Figure 17.9 displays the different implementation methods an organization can choose to ensure success.

FIGURE 17.7

Sample Test Conditions.

Test Condition Number	Date Tested	Tested	Test Condition	Expected Result	Actual Result	Pass/ Fail
1	1/1/20	Audry Sapp	Click on System Start Button	Main Menu appears	Same as expected result	Pass
2	1/1/20	Audry Sapp	Click on Log-on Button in Main Menu	Log-on screen appears asking for username and password	Same as expected result	Pass
3	1/1/20	Audry Sapp	Type Audry Sapp in the Username Field	Audry Sapp appears in the username field	Same as expected result	Pass
4	1/1/20	Audry Sapp	Type Password Miranda	XXXXXXXXX appears in the password field	Same as expected result	Pass
5	1/1/20	Audry Sapp	Click on OK	User log-on request is sent to database and username and password are verified	Same as expected result	Pass
6	1/1/20	Audry Sapp	Click on Start	Username and password are accepted and the system main menu appears	Screen appeared stating log-on failed and username and password were incorrect	Fail

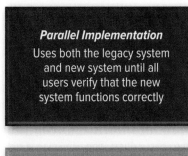

Alpha Testing
Assess if the entire system meets the design requirements of the users

Development Testing
Test the system to ensure it is bug-free

Integration Testing
Verify that separate systems can work together, passing data back and forth correctly

System Testing
Verify that the units or pieces of code function correctly when integrated

User Acceptance Testing (UAT)
Determine if the system satisfies the user and business requirements

Unit Testing
Test individual units or pieces of code for a system

FIGURE 17.8

Different Forms of System Testing.

Parallel Implementation
Uses both the legacy system and new system until all users verify that the new system functions correctly

Plunge Implementation
Discards the legacy system and immediately migrates all users to the new system

Pilot Implementation
Assigns a small group of people to use the new system until it is verified that it works correctly; then the remaining users migrate to the new system

Phased Implementation
Installs the new system in phases (for example, by department) until it is verified that it works correctly

FIGURE 17.9

System Implementation Methods.

PHASE 7: MAINTENANCE

Maintaining the system is the final sequential phase of any systems development effort. In the ***maintenance phase***, the organization performs changes, corrections, additions, and upgrades to ensure the system continues to meet business goals. This phase continues for the life of the system because the system must change as the business evolves and its needs change, which means conducting constant monitoring, supporting the new system with frequent minor changes (for example, new reports or information capturing), and reviewing the system to be sure it is moving the organization toward its strategic goals. ***Corrective maintenance*** makes system changes to repair design flaws, coding errors, or implementation issues. ***Preventive maintenance*** makes system changes to reduce the chance of future system failure. During the maintenance phase, the system will generate reports to help users and MIS specialists ensure it is functioning correctly (see Figure 17.10).

Report	Examples
Internal report	Presents data that are distributed inside the organization and intended for employees within an organization. Internal reports typically support day-to-day operations monitoring that supports managerial decision making.
Detailed internal report	Presents information with little or no filtering or restrictions of the data.
Summary internal report	Organizes and categorizes data for managerial perusal. A report that summarizes total sales by product for each month is an example of a summary internal report. The data for a summary report are typically categorized and summarized to indicate trends and potential problems.
Exception reporting	Highlights situations occurring outside of the normal operating range for a condition or standard. These internal reports include only exceptions and might highlight accounts that are unpaid or delinquent or identify items that are low in stock.
Information system control report	Ensures the reliability of information, consisting of policies and their physical implementation, access restrictions, or record keeping of actions and transactions.
Information systems audit report	Assesses a company's information system to determine necessary changes and to help ensure the information system's availability, confidentiality, and integrity.
Post-implementation report	Presents a formal report or audit of a project after it is up and running.

FIGURE 17.10

Examples of System Reports.

OPENING CASE STUDY QUESTIONS

1. Which phase in the systems development life cycle is the most critical when building a video game?

2. Which phase in the systems development life cycle is the least critical when building a video game?

Chapter Seventeen Case: Reducing Ambiguity in Business Requirements

The number one reason projects fail is bad business requirements. Business requirements are considered "bad" because of ambiguity or insufficient involvement of end users during analysis and design.

A requirement is unambiguous if it has the same interpretation for all parties. Different interpretations by different participants will usually result in unmet expectations. Here is an example of an ambiguous requirement and an example of an unambiguous requirement:

- **Ambiguous requirement:** The financial report must show profits in local and U.S. currencies.
- **Unambiguous requirement:** The financial report must show profits in local and U.S. currencies using the exchange rate printed in *The Wall Street Journal* for the last business day of the period being reported.

Ambiguity is impossible to prevent completely because it is introduced into requirements in natural ways. For example:

- Requirements can contain technical implications that are obvious to the IT developers but not to the customers.
- Requirements can contain business implications that are obvious to the customer but not to the IT developers.
- Requirements may contain everyday words whose meanings are "obvious" to everyone, yet different for everyone.
- Requirements are reflections of detailed explanations that may have included multiple events, multiple perspectives, verbal rephrasing, emotion, iterative refinement, selective emphasis, and body language—none of which are captured in the written statements.

Tips for Reviewing Business Requirements

When reviewing business requirements always look for the following words to help dramatically reduce ambiguity:

- **"And"** and **"or"** have well-defined meanings and ought to be completely unambiguous, yet they are often understood only informally and interpreted inconsistently. For example, consider the statement "The alarm must ring if button T is pressed and if button F is pressed." This statement may be intended to mean that to ring the alarm, both buttons must be pressed or it may be intended to mean that either one can be pressed. A statement like this should never appear in a requirement because the potential for misinterpretation is too great. A preferable approach is to be very explicit, for example, "The alarm must ring if both buttons T and F are pressed simultaneously. The alarm should not ring in any other circumstance."
- **"Always"** might really mean "most of the time," in which case it should be made more explicit. For example, the statement "We always run reports A and B together" could be challenged with "In other words, there is never any circumstance where you would run A without B and B without A?" If you build a system with an "always" requirement, then you are actually building the system to never run report A without report B. If a user suddenly wants report B without report A, you will need to make significant system changes.
- **"Never"** might mean "rarely," in which case it should be made more explicit. For example, the statement "We never run reports A and B in the same month" could be challenged with "So that means that if I see that A has been run, I can be absolutely certain that no one will want to run B." Again, if you build a system that supports a "never" requirement then the system users can never perform that requirement. For example, the system would never allow a user to run reports A and B in the same month, no matter what the circumstances.
- **Boundary conditions** are statements about the line between true and false and do and do not. These statements may or may not be meant to include end points, for example, "We want to use method X when there are up to 10 pages, but method Y otherwise." If you were building this system, would you include page 10 in method X or in method Y? The answer to this question will vary causing an ambiguous business requirement.

Questions

1. Why are ambiguous business requirements the leading cause of system development failures?
2. Why do the words "and" and "or" tend to lead to ambiguous requirements?
3. Research the web and determine other reasons for "bad" business requirements.
4. What is wrong with the following business requirement? "The system must support employee birthdays since every employee always has a birthday every year."

17.1. Describe the seven phases of the systems development life cycle.

The seven phases in the SDLC are:

- Planning—involves establishing a high-level plan of the intended project and determining project goals.

- Analysis—involves analyzing end-user business requirements and refining project goals into defined functions and operations of the intended system.

- Design—involves describing the desired features and operations of the system, including screen layouts, business rules, process diagrams, pseudocode, and other documentation.

- Development—involves transforming all the detailed design documents from the design phase into the actual system.

- Testing—involves bringing all the project pieces together into a special testing environment to test for errors, bugs, and interoperability and verifying that the system meets all the business requirements defined in the analysis phase.

- Implementation—involves placing the system into production so users can begin to perform actual business operations with the system.

- Maintenance—involves performing changes, corrections, additions, and upgrades to ensure that the system continues to meet the business goals.

1. What is the systems development life cycle?
2. What are the phases in the systems development life cycle?
3. Which phase in the systems development life cycle is the most important?
4. If you had to skip a phase during the development of a system, which phase would it be and why?
5. Which phase in the systems development life cycle contains the most risk? Be sure to explain your answer.
6. What are the different types of system testing?
7. What are the different types of system implementation methods?
8. Why should end users be involved in the systems development effort?

1. Missing Phases in the Systems Development Life Cycle

Hello Inc. is a large concierge service for executives operating in Chicago, San Francisco, and New York. The company performs all kinds of services from dog walking to airport transportation. Your manager, Dan Martello, wants to skip the testing phase during the company's financial ERP implementation. He feels that because the system came from a vendor, it should work correctly. Draft a memo explaining the importance of following the SDLC and the ramifications to the business if the financial system is not tested.

2. Refusing to Sign Off

You are the primary client on a large extranet development project. After carefully reviewing the requirements definition document, you are positive that there are missing, ambiguous, inaccurate, and unclear requirements. The project manager is pressuring you for your sign-off because he has already received sign-off from five of your co-workers. If you fail to sign off on the requirements, you are going to put the entire project at risk because the time frame is nonnegotiable. What would you do? Why?

3. Just Ask TED

You'll remember this day because it is the day you were introduced to TED (www.ted.com). TED is a nonprofit devoted to "ideas worth spreading." The company hosts a yearly conference focusing on technology, entertainment, and design (TED). It gathers the world's innovative minds and challenges them to give the talk of their lives in just 18 minutes. Each talk is posted to the TED website and includes such famous speakers as:

- Chris Anderson, editor of *Wired* and author of *The Long Tail: Why the Future of Business Is Selling Less of More.*
- Tim Berners-Lee, inventor of the World Wide Web.
- Jeff Bezos, founder of Amazon.com.
- Richard Branson, founder of Virgin.
- Bill Clinton, former president of the United States.
- Peter Diamandis, chairman of the X Prize Foundation.
- Sergey Brin and Larry Page, cofounders of Google.
- Malcolm Gladwell, author of *Blink* and *The Tipping Point.*
- Bill Gates, founder of Microsoft.
- Seth Godin, a marketing guru.
- Steven Levitt, author of *Freakonomics.*

As you brainstorm your future start-up, hoping to become the next Bill Gates or Steve Jobs, how can you use TED to generate ideas? Review the TED website and choose three talks that could help lead to the next great business idea.

4. Flawed Development

Data must be secure! A computer programming course would teach you that security is a critical component that must be included in every system. Apparently, the employees that developed the new system for the state of Oklahoma were out sick during this important class. The new system mistakenly posted confidential data, including Social Security numbers, for thousands of Oklahoma residents on the state's website. The really unfortunate part of this systems blunder is that the error went unnoticed for more than three years. A programmer found the error when he realized that by changing his web browser he could redirect his page to the entire database for the state of Oklahoma. To make matters even worse, due to development issues, a hacker could have easily changed all the data in the database or added false data to elements such as the state's Sexual and Violent Offender Registry.

Why is it important to secure data? What can happen if someone accesses your customer database? What could happen if someone changes the information in your customer database and adds fictitious data? What phases in the systems development life cycle should have found these errors? How could these errors go unnoticed for over three years? Who should be held responsible for the system issues?

18 Methodologies for Supporting Agile Organizations

18.1. Summarize the different software development methodologies.

18.2. Explain why a company would implement a service-oriented architecture.

Software Development Methodologies

Today, systems are so large and complex that teams of architects, analysts, developers, testers, and users must work together to create the millions of lines of custom-written code that drive enterprises. For this reason, developers have created a number of different systems development life cycle methodologies. A *methodology* is a set of policies, procedures, standards, processes, practices, tools, techniques, and tasks that people apply to technical and management challenges. Firms use a methodology to manage the deployment of technology with work plans, requirements documents, and test plans, for instance. A formal methodology can include coding standards, code libraries, development practices, and much more.

The oldest and the best known is the *waterfall methodology*, a sequence of phases in which the output of each phase becomes the input for the next (see Figure 18.1). In the SDLC, this means the steps are performed one at a time, in order, from planning through implementation and maintenance. The traditional waterfall method no longer serves most of today's development

LO 18.1 Summarize the different software development methodologies.

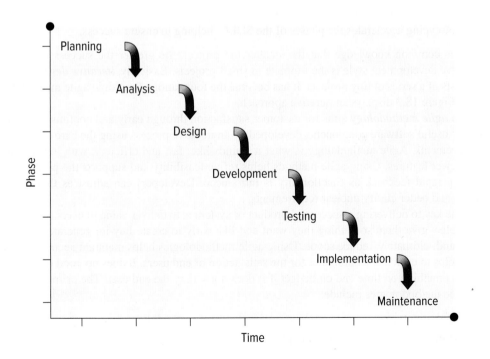

FIGURE 18.1

The Traditional Waterfall Methodology.

FIGURE 18.2

Disadvantages of the
Waterfall Methodology.

Issues Related to the Waterfall Methodology	
The business problem	Any flaws in accurately defining and articulating the business problem in terms of what the business users actually require flow onward to the next phase.
The plan	Managing costs, resources, and time constraints is difficult in the waterfall sequence. What happens to the schedule if a programmer quits? How will a schedule delay in a specific phase impact the total cost of the project? Unexpected contingencies may sabotage the plan.
The solution	The waterfall methodology is problematic in that it assumes users can specify all business requirements in advance. Defining the appropriate IT infrastructure that is flexible, scalable, and reliable is a challenge. The final IT infrastructure solution must meet not only current but also future needs in terms of time, cost, feasibility, and flexibility. Vision is inevitably limited at the head of the waterfall.

efforts, however; it is inflexible and expensive, and it requires rigid adherence to the sequence of steps. Its success rate is only about 1 in 10. Figure 18.2 explains some issues related to the waterfall methodology.

Today's business environment is fierce. The desire and need to outsmart and outplay competitors remain intense. Given this drive for success, leaders push internal development teams and external vendors to deliver agreed-upon systems faster and cheaper so they can realize benefits as early as possible. Even so, systems remain large and complex. The traditional waterfall methodology no longer serves as an adequate systems development methodology in most cases. Because this development environment is the norm and not the exception anymore, development teams use a new breed of alternative development methods to achieve their business objectives.

Prototyping is a modern design approach where the designers and system users use an iterative approach to building the system. *Discovery prototyping* builds a small-scale representation or working model of the system to ensure it meets the user and business requirements. The advantages of prototyping include:

- Prototyping encourages user participation.
- Prototypes evolve through iteration, which better supports change.
- Prototypes have a physical quality allowing users to see, touch, and experience the system as it is developed.
- Prototypes tend to detect errors earlier.
- Prototyping accelerates the phases of the SDLC, helping to ensure success.

It is common knowledge that the smaller the project, the greater the success rate. The iterative development style is the ultimate in small projects. Basically, *iterative development* consists of a series of tiny projects. It has become the foundation of multiple agile methodologies. Figure 18.3 displays an iterative approach.

An *agile methodology* aims for customer satisfaction through early and continuous delivery of useful software components developed by an iterative process using the bare minimum requirements. Agile methodology is what it sounds like: fast and efficient, with lower costs and fewer features. Using agile methods helps refine feasibility and supports the process for getting rapid feedback as functionality is introduced. Developers can adjust as they move along and better clarify unclear requirements.

One key to delivering a successful product or system is to deliver value to users as soon as possible—give them something they want and like early to create buy-in, generate enthusiasm, and, ultimately, reduce scope. Using agile methodologies helps maintain accountability and helps to establish a barometer for the satisfaction of end users. It does no good to accomplish something on time and on budget if it does not satisfy the end user. The primary forms of agile methodologies include:

- Rapid prototyping or rapid application development methodology.
- Extreme programming methodology.

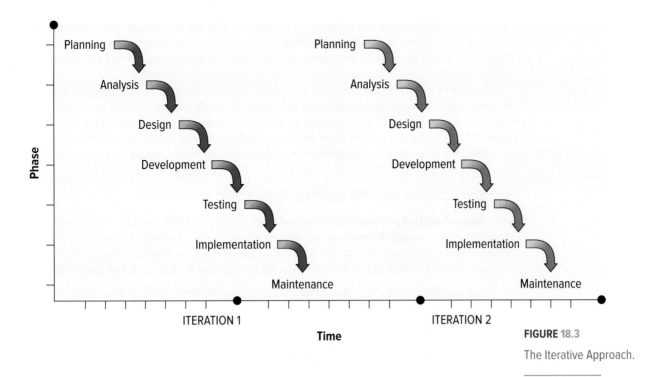

FIGURE 18.3

The Iterative Approach.

- Rational unified process (RUP) methodology.
- Scrum methodology.

It is important not to get hung up on the names of the methodologies—some are proprietary brand names; others are generally accepted names. It is more important to know how these alternative methodologies are used in today's business environment and the benefits they can deliver.

RAPID APPLICATION DEVELOPMENT (RAD) METHODOLOGY

In response to the faster pace of business, rapid application development has become a popular route for accelerating systems development. *Rapid application development (RAD) methodology* (also called rapid prototyping) emphasizes extensive user involvement in the rapid and evolutionary construction of working prototypes of a system, to accelerate the systems development process. Figure 18.4 displays the fundamentals of RAD.

EXTREME PROGRAMMING METHODOLOGY

Extreme programming (XP) methodology, like other agile methods, breaks a project into four phases, and developers cannot continue to the next phase until the previous phase is complete. The delivery strategy supporting XP is that the quicker the feedback the more improved the results. XP has four basic phases: planning, designing, coding, and testing. Planning can include user interviews, meetings, and small releases. During design, functionality is not added until it is required or needed. During coding, the developers work together soliciting continuous feedback from users, eliminating the communication gap that

Fundamentals of RAD
Focus initially on creating a prototype that looks and acts like the desired system.
Actively involve system users in the analysis, design, and development phases.
Accelerate collecting the business requirements through an interactive and iterative construction approach.

FIGURE 18.4

Fundamentals of RAD.

generally exists between developers and customers. During testing, the test requirements are generated before any code is developed. Extreme programming saves time and produces successful projects by continuously reviewing and revamping needed and unneeded requirements.

Customer satisfaction is the primary reason XP finds success as developers quickly respond to changing business requirements, even late in the life cycle. XP encourages managers, customers, and developers to work together as a team to ensure the delivery of high-quality systems. XP is similar to a puzzle; there are many small pieces and individually the pieces make no sense, but when they are pieced together they can create a new system.

RATIONAL UNIFIED PROCESS (RUP) METHODOLOGY

The *rational unified process (RUP) methodology*, owned by IBM, provides a framework for breaking down the development of software into four "gates." Each gate consists of executable iterations of the software in development. A project stays in a gate waiting for the stakeholder's analysis, and then it either moves to the next gate or is cancelled. The gates include:

- **Gate one: inception.** This phase ensures all stakeholders have a shared understanding of the proposed system and what it will do.
- **Gate two: elaboration.** This phase expands on the agreed-upon details of the system, including the ability to provide an architecture to support and build it.
- **Gate three: construction.** This phase includes building and developing the product.
- **Gate four: transition.** Primary questions answered in this phase address ownership of the system and training of key personnel.

Because RUP is an iterative methodology, the user can reject the product and force the developers to go back to gate one. RUP helps developers avoid reinventing the wheel and focuses on rapidly adding or removing reusable chunks of processes addressing common problems.

SCRUM METHODOLOGY

Another agile methodology, *scrum methodology*, uses small teams to produce small pieces of software using a series of "sprints," or 30-day intervals, to achieve an appointed goal. In rugby, a scrum is a team pack and everyone in the pack works together to move the ball down the field. In scrum methodology, each day ends or begins with a stand-up meeting to monitor and control the development effort.

LO 18.2 Explain why a company would implement a service-oriented architecture.

Developing a Service-Oriented Architecture

One of the latest trends in systems development is creating a service-oriented architecture. *Service-oriented architecture (SOA)* is a business-driven enterprise architecture that supports integrating a business as linked, repeatable activities, tasks, or services. SOA ensures that MIS systems can adapt quickly, easily, and economically to support rapidly changing business needs. SOA promotes a scalable and flexible enterprise architecture that can implement new or reuse existing MIS components, creating connections among disparate applications and systems. It is important to understand that SOA is not a concrete architecture; it is thought that leads to a concrete architecture. It might be described as a style, paradigm, concept, perspective, philosophy, or representation. That is, SOA is an approach, a way of thinking, a value system that leads to decisions that design a concrete architecture allowing enterprises to plug in new services or upgrade existing services in a granular approach. Figure 18.5 discusses the problems that can be addressed by implementing SOA. Figure 18.6 displays the three key technical concepts of SOA.

Service-Oriented Architecture Solutions	
■ Agents unable to see policy coverage information remotely ■ Calls/faxes used to get information from other divisions ■ Clinical patient information stored on paper ■ Complex access to supplier design drawings	Integrate information to make it more accessible to employees.
■ High cost of handling customer calls ■ Reconciliation of invoice deductions and rebates ■ Hours on hold to determine patient insurance eligibility ■ High turnover leading to excessive hiring and training costs	Understand how business processes interact to manage administrative costs better.
■ Decreasing customer loyalty due to incorrect invoices ■ Customers placed on hold to check order status ■ Inability to update policy endorsements quickly ■ Poor service levels	Improve customer retention and deliver new products and services through reuse of current investments.
■ Time wasted reconciling separate databases ■ Manual processes such as handling trade allocations ■ Inability to detect quality flaws early in cycle ■ High percentage of scrap and rework	Improve people productivity with better business integration and connectivity.

FIGURE 18.5

Business Issues and SOA Solutions.

_____

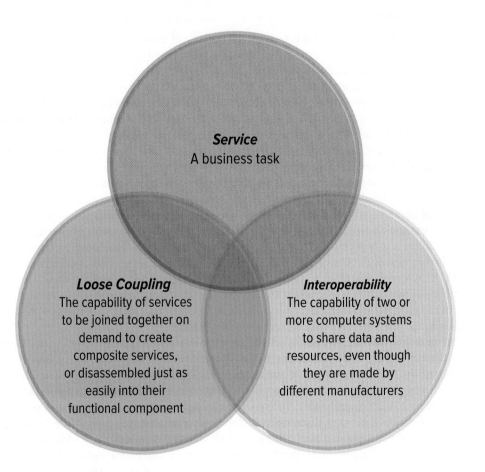

FIGURE 18.6

SOA Concepts.

_____

Service
A business task

Loose Coupling
The capability of services to be joined together on demand to create composite services, or disassembled just as easily into their functional component

Interoperability
The capability of two or more computer systems to share data and resources, even though they are made by different manufacturers

INTEROPERABILITY

As defined earlier, *interoperability* is the capability of two or more computer systems to share data and resources, even though they are made by different manufacturers. Businesses today use a variety of systems that have resulted in diverse operating environments. This diversity has inundated businesses with the lack of interoperability. With SOA, a business can create solutions that draw on functionality from these existing, previously isolated systems that are portable, interoperable, or both, regardless of the environment in which they exist.

A *web service* is an open-standards way of supporting interoperability. Web services are application programming interfaces (API) that can be accessed over a network, such as the Internet, and executed on a remote system hosting the requested services. SOA is a style of architecture that enables the creation of applications that are built by combining loosely coupled and interoperable services. In SOA, since the basic unit of communication is a message rather than an operation, web services are usually loosely coupled. Although SOA can exist without web services, the best-practice implementation of SOA for flexibility always involves web services.

Technically, web services are based on *Extensible Markup Language (XML)*, a markup language for documents, containing structured information. The technical specifics of XML's capabilities go beyond the scope of this book, but for our purposes, they support things such as ebusiness transactions, mathematical equations, and a thousand other kinds of structured data. XML is a common data representation that can be used as the medium of exchange between programs that are written in different programming languages and execute different kinds of machine instructions. In simple terms, think about XML as the official translator for structured information. Structured information is both the content (word, picture, and so on) and the role it plays. XML is the basis for all web service technologies and the key to interoperability; every web service specification is based on XML.

LOOSE COUPLING

Part of the value of SOA is that it is built on the premise of loose coupling of services. *Loose coupling* is the capability of services to be joined on demand to create composite services or disassembled just as easily into their functional components. Loose coupling is a way of ensuring that the technical details such as language, platform, and so on are decoupled from the service. For example, look at currency conversion. Today all banks have multiple currency converters, all with different rate refreshes at different times. By creating a common service, conversion of currency, that is loosely coupled to all banking functions that require conversion, the rates, times, and samplings can be averaged to ensure floating the treasury in the most effective manner possible. Another example is common customer identification. Most businesses lack a common customer ID and, therefore, have no way to determine who the customers are and what they buy for what reason. Creating a common customer ID that is independent of applications and databases allows loosely coupling the service, customer ID, to data and applications without the application or database ever knowing who it is or where it is.

The difference between traditional, tightly bound interactions and loosely coupled services is that, before the transaction occurs, the functional pieces (services) operating within the SOA are dormant and disconnected. When the business process initiates, these services momentarily interact with each other. They do so for just long enough to execute their piece of the overall process, and then they go back to their dormant state, with no long-standing connection to the other services with which they just interacted.

The next time the same service is called, it could be as part of a different business process with different calling and destination services. A great way to understand this is through the analogy of the telephone system. At the dawn of widespread phone usage, operators had to plug in a wire physically to create a semi-permanent connection between two parties. Callers were "tightly bound" to each other. Today you pick up your cell phone and put it to your ear, and there's no dial tone—it's disconnected. You enter a number, you push "Talk," and only then does the process initiate, establishing a loosely coupled connection just long enough for your conversation. Then when the conversation is over, your cell phone goes back to dormant mode until a new connection is made with another party. As a result, supporting a million cell phone subscribers does not require the cell phone service provider to support a million live connections; it requires supporting only the number of simultaneous conversations at any given time. It allows for a much more flexible and dynamic exchange.

SOA SERVICE

Service-oriented architecture begins with a service—an *SOA service* being simply a business task, such as checking a potential customer's credit rating when opening a new account. It is important to stress that this is part of a business process. Services are "like" software products; however, when describing SOA, do not think about software or MIS. Think about what a company does on a day-to-day basis, and break up those business processes into repeatable business tasks or components. SOA works with services that are not just software or hardware but, rather, business tasks. It is a pattern for developing a more flexible kind of software applications (see Figure 18.7).

SOA is a pattern for developing a more flexible kind of software application that can promote loose coupling among software components while reusing existing investments in technology in new, more valuable ways across the organization. SOA is based on standards that enable interoperability, business agility, and innovation to generate more business value for those who use these principles.

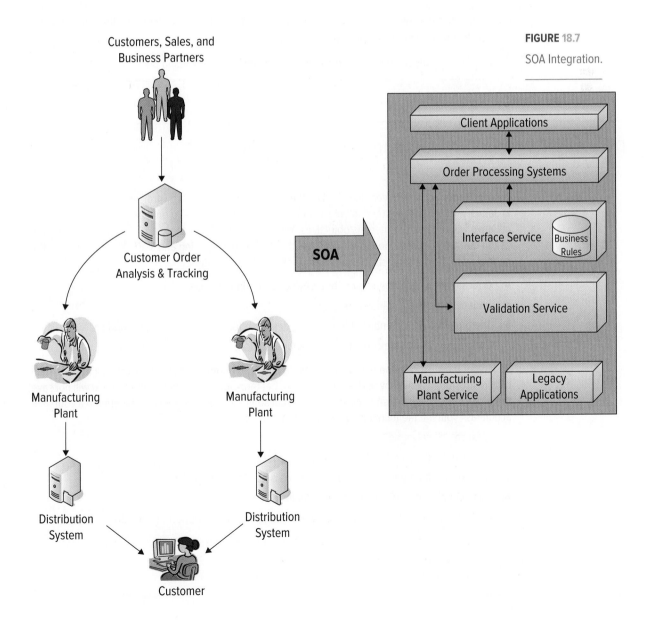

FIGURE 18.7

SOA Integration.

SOA helps companies become more agile by aligning business needs and the MIS capabilities that support these needs. Business drives requirements for MIS; SOA enables the MIS environment to respond to these requirements effectively and efficiently. SOA is about helping companies apply reusability and flexibility that can lower cost (of development, integration, and maintenance), increase revenue, and obtain sustainable competitive advantage through technology.

It is very important to note that SOA is an evolution. Although its results are revolutionary, it builds on many technologies used in the marketplace, such as web services, transactional technologies, information-driven principles, loose coupling, components, and object-oriented design. The beauty of SOA is that these technologies exist together in SOA through standards, well-defined interfaces, and organizational commitments to reuse key services instead of reinventing the wheel. SOA is not just about technology, but about how technology and business link themselves for a common goal of business flexibility.

OPENING CASE STUDY QUESTIONS

1. If you were consulting to a business that wanted to build a video game for the iPhone, which development methodology would you recommend and why?

2. What is a prototype and why would a new game benefit from building one?

Chapter Eighteen Case: Getting Your Project on Track

June is the perfect time of year to reflect on the current state of all the key projects that were approved in January. At this stage, you and your management team should have enough data to know if each initiative will successfully meet its objectives. You may already know there are projects in your organization that are not positioned to succeed, yet they still receive funding and staff. When you assess the current state of your projects, do you see any of the following signs?

- Critical issues keep opening up, but they're not getting resolved.
- Project scope is constantly changing.
- The project is consistently behind its plan, despite efforts to get it back on schedule.
- Competing deliverables are distracting your attention.

If all of these signs appear, it may be time to cut your losses and cut the project—or at least radically restructure it. You know better than anyone that throwing good money after the bad will not save the project because it doesn't address the root cause of the project's woes. To determine a course of action, ask yourself the following questions about the project:

- What can be salvaged?
- What can be delivered with the time and budget that are left?
- Do you have the right leadership in place to complete the project successfully?
- Is the plan for the initiative sound and realistic?
- Am I and my management team doing everything we can to support the initiative?

If part of or the entire project can be salvaged and delivered on time and with the remaining budget, if the right leaders are present to steer the project, if the new plan is solid, and if management will continue to support the project, the following four steps will help you regain control and deliver the revised project successfully. These steps are basic blocking and tackling, but the detail behind the plan—and more importantly, the execution and focus the project team brings to the effort—will determine whether the project recovery effort will succeed.

Step One: Assess the Situation

Get as much information about the current state of the project as possible. Use that data to make informed decisions about what needs to happen next. Don't be afraid if, at this stage, there are more questions than answers; that is normal. The key is to ask the right question to obtain as accurate a picture of the project's status as possible. The following questions address key data points you need to collect:

- How critical is the delivery date?
- What functionality is exactly required by the delivery date?
- What has been completed and what is still outstanding?
- How willing will people be to change scope, dates, and budget?

The last question about change is critical because it touches on the people and political issues that are present in any project and any organization. Even when faced with sure failure, people find it hard to change unless there is a direct benefit to them and their team. For recovery to have a chance, expectations need to change, especially those of the key stakeholders.

When gathering data about the current state of the project, remember to ask the current team for their opinions on what went wrong. It can be easy to ignore their input since they're associated with the current failure. In fact, each individual can provide great insight into why the project arrived in its current state. Reach out to key team members and get their suggestions for correcting the situation.

Step Two: Prepare the Team for Recovery

Everyone involved in the project—from executive management to stakeholders to project team members—needs to accept that the current project is broken and needs to be fixed. They also need to accept that the existing project plan and approach to delivering the project is flawed and needs to be restructured. If they don't accept these facts, they will likely resist the steps needed for recovery.

Once everyone has accepted the need to change course, define realistic expectations for what can be delivered given the current state and time frame. Also establish metrics for success and control of the recovery. If you had metrics at the outset of the project, you may need to establish new ones, or you may simply need to hold yourself and others accountable to them.

Both management and the project manager in charge of the recovery need to develop a supportive environment for team members. Giving them realistic goals and providing them with the needed space, equipment, and training will position them for success.

Finally, take advantage of the new momentum associated with the recovery and involve all the key parties in the status of the project. This involvement will keep everyone focused and engaged. It will assure project team members and stakeholders that they're needed for more than just executing tasks.

Step Three: Develop a Game Plan for Recovery

Think of the recovery as a new project, separate from the old one. This new project requires its own scope of work to make the expectations around what is being delivered and the new criteria for judging success crystal clear. The new scope may require you to determine if you have the right resources on the project team or if you need to re-staff some team members.

Based on the new project scope, the project manager and project team should lay out a clear and realistic road map to achieve the objectives. The main difference in the plan this time is that it must not fail. It will also be under much greater scrutiny by management. Consequently, it will be critical to make sure the milestones are shorter in duration to demonstrate success and to allow for course correction if needed. The shorter milestones will provide valuable data points to determine the health of the project early.

Step Four: Execute the Game Plan

With the new plan in hand, it's time to get down to business. Remember that during execution, it is not just the project team members who are accountable. Everyone from management on down is on the hook. All facets of the project, from environment to support, need to be in sync at all times, and everyone needs to know he or she is accountable for the project recovery to succeed.

To make sure everyone is on the same page during the recovery, the project communication needs to be clear, informative, and frequent. Clearly define in your communication plan how information will be disseminated, how urgent items will be addressed, and how key decisions will be made.

Given the added level of scrutiny on the plan and the project, being able to provide the latest on the metrics to show the improved control over the project will be key. The data will also allow you to quickly make corrections when any sign of trouble surfaces.

Getting a flailing project back on track is not easy. It requires sustained effort, focus, commitment, and objectivity. During the project recovery there is no time for personal agendas. The ability to see and do what is best for the project is required from every team member.

It is also important to not lose sight of the pressure that everyone is under. Make sure there is a positive focus on people. The team needs to have the ability to bond, release a little steam, and be focused on the task at hand.

When the project has been successfully delivered, celebrate and recognize the effort of each and every team member. Finally, learn from this successful project recovery so that you and your organization can avoid having to recover a project again. Pay attention to the warning signs and act swiftly and decisively to make corrections early in the project's life cycle so that successful delivery is ensured the first time.[1]

Questions

1. What signs identify if a current project is experiencing issues?

2. Which software development methodology would you choose to build a new accounting system? Explain why.

3. Which software development methodology would you choose to build a personal website? Explain why.

18.1. Summarize the different software development methodologies.

The oldest and the best known project management methodology is the waterfall methodology, a sequence of phases in which the output of each phase becomes the input for the next. In the SDLC, this means the steps are performed one at a time, in order, from planning through implementation and maintenance. The traditional waterfall method no longer serves most of today's development efforts, however; it is inflexible and expensive, and it requires rigid adherence to the sequence of steps. Its success rate is only about 1 in 10.

There are a number of software development methodologies:

- Agile methodology aims for customer satisfaction through early and continuous delivery of useful software components developed by an iterative process with a design point that uses the bare minimum requirements.

- Waterfall methodology follows an activity-based process in which each phase in the SDLC is performed sequentially from planning through implementation and maintenance.

- Rapid application development (RAD) methodology emphasizes extensive user involvement in the rapid and evolutionary construction of working prototypes of a system to accelerate the systems development process.

- Extreme programming (XP) methodology breaks a project into tiny phases, and developers cannot continue on to the next phase until the first phase is complete.

- Rational unified process (RUP) provides a framework for breaking down the development of software into four gates.

- Scrum uses small teams to produce small pieces of deliverable software by using sprints, or 30-day intervals, to achieve an appointed goal.

18.2. Explain why a company would implement a service-oriented architecture.

Service oriented architecture (SOA) is a business-driven enterprise architecture that supports integrating a business as linked, repeatable activities, tasks, or services. SOA ensures that MIS systems can adapt quickly, easily, and economically to support rapidly changing business needs. SOA promotes a scalable and flexible enterprise architecture that can implement new or reuse existing MIS components, creating connections among disparate applications and systems. It is important to understand that SOA is not a concrete architecture; it is a way of thinking that leads to a concrete architecture.

1. Which project management methodology would you choose to run your systems development project?

2. If you started on a new software development project and the project plan was using the waterfall methodology, would you remain on the project? Why or why not? What could you do to prepare your project better for success?

3. What do rapid application development, extreme programming, and the rational unified process all have in common?

4. How many gates are included in the RUP methodology?

5. What is the scrum methodology?

6. What is a service-oriented architecture?

7. What is a service?

8. Why is loose coupling and interoperability important to SOA?

1. Selecting a Systems Development Methodology

Exus Incorporated is an international billing outsourcing company. Exus currently has revenues of $5 billion, more than 3,500 employees, and operations on every continent. You have recently been hired as the CIO. Your first task is to increase the software development project success rate, which is currently at 20 percent. To ensure that future software development projects are successful, you want to standardize the systems development methodology across the entire enterprise. Currently, each project determines which methodology it uses to develop software.

Create a report detailing three systems development methodologies that were covered in this text. Compare each of these methodologies to the traditional waterfall approach. Finally, recommend which methodology you want to implement as your organizational standard. Be sure to highlight any potential roadblocks you might encounter when implementing the new standard methodology.

2. Planning for the Unexpected

Unexpected situations happen all the time, and the more you plan for them the better prepared you'll be when developing software. Your employees will get into accidents, contract viruses and diseases, and experience other life issues. All of these scenarios lead to unplanned absenteeism, which can throw your project plan into a tailspin. What can happen to a project when a key employee suddenly quits or is forced to go on short-term disability? When reviewing all the different SDLC methodologies, which one offers the greatest flexibility for unplanned employee downtime? If you could choose when your employee was absent, which phase in the SDLC would be the safest for your project to still continue and achieve success? What can you do to ensure that you are preparing for unplanned absenteeism on your project plan?

3. Scratch

Scratch is a visual programming language that is perfect for anyone learning to code. Scratch creates programs by connecting blocks of code by using a drag-and-drop GUI so users do not have to type programming languages. Users can simply select colored blocks of code that, when joined, create a script or a set of computer instructions that can make objects such as people and animals move and speak. Users can create interactive stories, games, and animations with the click of a button.

Scratch is a free project created by the Lifelong Kindergarten Group at the MIT Media Lab and currently has more than 8 million users. The goal of Scratch is to help young people learn to think creatively, reason systematically, and work collaboratively—essential skills for life in the 21st century.

In a group, visit the Scratch website at http://scratch.mit.edu/. What type of system development methodology is Scratch using? What skills can young people learn from creating Scratch programs?

4. DUI in a Golf Cart

Swedish police stopped Bill Murray and charged him with drunk driving when he attempted to drive his golf cart around the city. A golf cart hits top speed at three miles per hour and although it might seem odd that you can be issued a DUI for driving one, many countries have laws against such practices. A few other culture blunders you want to avoid include the following:

- One American company learned that the name of the cooking oil they were marketing translated as "jackass oil" in Spanish.

- A deodorant marketing campaign displayed images of a strong, courageous man washing his dog. The campaign failed in Islamic countries, where dogs are considered unclean.

- A sports equipment company packaged golf balls in groups of four for sales throughout Japan. Sales plummeted because the word *four* pronounced in Japanese sounds the same as the word *death* and items packaged in fours are considered unlucky.

Companies that are expanding globally are looking for opportunities, not problems. Yet local laws and procedures that come into play when setting up shop abroad—everything from hiring and firing to tax filings—can be a minefield. What types of culture, language, and legal issues should a company expect to encounter when dealing with outsourcing to another country? What can a company do to mitigate these risks?

5. Living the Dream

CharityFocus.org

Don't ask what the world needs. Ask what makes you come alive, and go do it. Because what the world needs is people who have come alive.—Howard Thurman

This is the quote found at the bottom of the website for CharityFocus.org. CharityFocus, created in 1999, partners volunteers with small nonprofit organizations to build custom web solutions. CharityFocus is completely run by volunteers, and the services of its volunteers are absolutely free. The nonprofit believes that it is impossible to create a better world without inner change resulting from selfless service. In the spirit of selfless service, volunteers created the following on the website to inspire and cultivate change:

- **DailyGood:** Email service that delivers a little bit of good news to thousands of people all over the world.

- **KarmaTube:** Site that uses the power of video to document multiple acts of compassion, generosity, and selflessness.

- **Conversations:** Site (Conversations.org) that hosts in-depth interviews of everyday heroes and a broad spectrum of artists.

- **HelpOthers:** A kindness portal based on the smile, a universally recognized symbol. People smile because they are happy and people smile because they want to become happy. The purpose of HelpOthers.org is to bring more of those smiles in the world through small acts of kindness.

Why is it important to give back to communities around the globe and share systems development methodologies? Would you volunteer for CharityFocus? What are the risks associated with volunteering for CharityFocus?

Managing Organizational Projects

19.1. Explain project management and identify the primary reasons projects fail.

19.2. Identify the primary project planning diagrams.

19.3. Identify the three different types of outsourcing along with their benefits and challenges.

LO 19.1 **Explain project management and identify the primary reasons projects fail.**

FIGURE 19.1

Types of Organizational Projects.

Using Project Management to Deliver Successful Projects

No one would think of building an office complex by turning loose 100 different construction teams to build 100 different rooms with no single blueprint or agreed-upon vision of the completed structure. Yet this is precisely the situation in which many large organizations find themselves when managing information technology projects. Organizations routinely overschedule their resources (human and otherwise), develop redundant projects, and damage profitability by investing in nonstrategic efforts that do not contribute to the organization's bottom line. Business leaders face a rapidly moving and unforgiving global marketplace that will force them to use every possible tool to sustain competitiveness; project management is one of those tools. For this reason, business personnel must anticipate being involved in some form of project management during their career. Figure 19.1 displays a few examples of the different types of projects organizations encounter.

Sales	Marketing	Finance	Accounting	MIS
Deploying a new service to help up-sell a current product	Creating a new TV or radio show	Requesting a new report summarizing revenue across departments	Adding system functionality to adhere to new rules or regulations	Upgrading a payroll system or adding a new sales force management system

a. © Ingram Publishing; b. © ColorBlind Images/Blend Images LLC; c-d. © Royalty-Free/Corbis; e.© webphotographeer/Getty Images

FIGURE 19.2

Examples of Tangible and Intangible Benefits.

Tangible benefits are easy to quantify and typically measured to determine the success or failure of a project. *Intangible benefits* are difficult to quantify or measure (see Figure 19.2 for examples). One of the most difficult decisions managers make is identifying the projects in which to invest time, energy, and resources. An organization must choose what it wants to do—justifying it, defining it, and listing expected results—and how to do it, including project budget, schedule, and analysis of project risks. *Feasibility* is the measure of the tangible and intangible benefits of an information system. Figure 19.3 displays several types of feasibility studies business analysts can use to determine the projects that best fit business goals.

With today's volatile economic environment, many businesses are being forced to do more with less. Businesses today must respond quickly to a rapidly changing business environment by continually innovating goods and services. Effective project management provides a controlled way to respond to changing market conditions, to foster global communications, and to provide key metrics to enable managerial decision making. Developing projects within budget and on time is challenging, and with the help of solid project management skills, managers can avoid the primary reasons projects fail, including:

- Unclear or missing business requirements.
- Skipped SDLC phases.
- Changing technology.
- The cost of finding errors.
- Balance of the triple constraints.

UNCLEAR OR MISSING BUSINESS REQUIREMENTS

The most common reason systems fail is because the business requirements are either missing or incorrectly gathered during the analysis phase. The business requirements drive the entire system. If they are not accurate or complete, the system will not be successful.

SKIPPED PHASES

The first thing individuals tend to do when a project falls behind schedule is to start skipping phases in the SDLC. For example, if a project is three weeks behind in the development phase, the project manager might decide to cut testing from six weeks to three weeks. Obviously, it is impossible to perform all the testing in half the time. Failing to test the system will lead to unfound errors, and chances are high that the system will fail. It is critical for an organization

FIGURE 19.3

Types of Feasibility Studies.

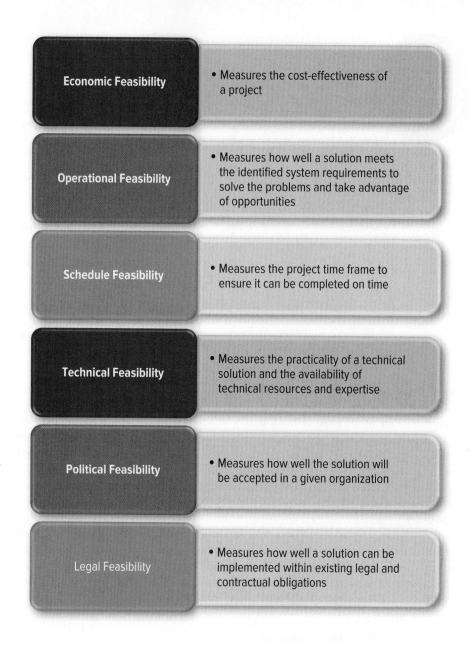

to perform all phases in the SDLC during every project. Skipping any of the phases is sure to lead to system failure.

CHANGING TECHNOLOGY

Many real-world projects have hundreds of business requirements, take years to complete, and cost millions of dollars. As Moore's Law states, technology changes at an incredibly fast pace; therefore, it is possible that an entire project plan will need to be revised in the middle of a project as a result of a change in technology. Technology changes so fast that it is almost impossible to deliver an information system without feeling the pain of updates.

THE COST OF FINDING ERRORS IN THE SDLC

It is important to discuss the relationship between the SDLC and the cost for the organization to fix errors. An error found during the analysis and design phase is relatively inexpensive to fix. All that is typically required is a change to a Word document. However, exactly the same error found during the testing or implementation phase will cost the organization an enormous amount to fix because it has to change the actual system. Figure 19.4 displays how the cost to fix an error grows exponentially the later the error is found in the SDLC.

BALANCE OF THE TRIPLE CONSTRAINTS

Figure 19.5 displays the relationships among the three primary and interdependent variables in any project—time, cost, and scope. All projects are limited in some way by these three constraints. The Project Management Institute calls the framework for evaluating these competing demands *the triple constraints.*

The relationship among these variables is such that if any one changes, at least one other is likely to be affected. For example, moving up a project's finish date could mean either increasing costs to hire more staff or decreasing the scope to eliminate features or functions. Increasing a project's scope to include additional customer requests could extend the project's time to completion or increase the project's cost—or both—to accommodate the

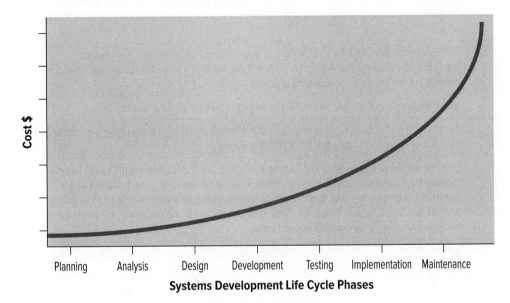

FIGURE 19.4

The Cost of Finding Errors.

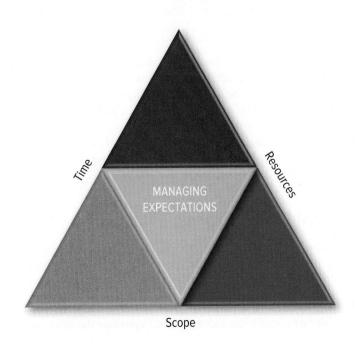

FIGURE 19.5

The Triple Constraints: Changing One Changes All.

Tool	Description
Communication plan	Defines the how, what, when, and who regarding the flow of project information to stakeholders and is key for managing expectations.
Executive sponsor	The person or group who provides the financial resources for the project.
Project assumption	Factors considered to be true, real, or certain without proof or demonstration. Examples include hours in a workweek or time of year the work will be performed.
Project constraint	Specific factors that can limit options, including budget, delivery dates, available skilled resources, and organizational policies.
Project deliverable	Any measurable, tangible, verifiable outcome, result, or item that is produced to complete a project or part of a project. Examples of project deliverables include design documents, testing scripts, and requirements documents.
Project management office (PMO)	An internal department that oversees all organizational projects. This group must formalize and professionalize project management expertise and leadership. One of the primary initiatives of the PMO is to educate the organization on techniques and procedures necessary to run successful projects.
Project milestone	Represents key dates when a certain group of activities must be performed. For example, completing the planning phase might be a project milestone. If a project milestone is missed, then chances are the project is experiencing problems.
Project objectives	Quantifiable criteria that must be met for the project to be considered a success.
Project requirements document	Defines the specifications for product/output of the project and is key for managing expectations, controlling scope, and completing other planning efforts.
Project scope statement	Links the project to the organization's overall business goals. It describes the business need (the problem the project will solve) and the justification, requirements, and current boundaries for the project. It defines the work that must be completed to deliver the product with the specified features and functions, and it includes constraints, assumptions, and requirements—all components necessary for developing accurate cost estimates.
Project stakeholder	Individuals and organizations actively involved in the project or whose interests might be affected as a result of project execution or project completion.
Responsibility matrix	Defines all project roles and indicates what responsibilities are associated with each role.
Status report	Periodic reviews of actual performance versus expected performance.

FIGURE 19.6

PMBOK Elements of Project Management.

changes. Project quality is affected by the project manager's ability to balance these competing demands. High-quality projects deliver the agreed-upon product or service on time and on budget. Project management is the science of making intelligent trade-offs between time, cost, and scope. Benjamin Franklin's timeless advice—*by failing to prepare, you prepare to fail*—applies to many of today's software development projects.

The Project Management Institute created the *Project Management Body of Knowledge (PMBOK)* for the education and certification of project managers. Figure 19.6 summarizes the key elements of project planning according to *PMBOK*.

LO 19.2 Identify the primary project planning diagrams.

Primary Project Planning Diagrams

Project planning is the process of detailed planning that generates answers to common operational questions such as why are we doing this project or what is the project going to accomplish for the business? Some of the key questions project planning can help answer include:

- How are deliverables being produced?
- What activities or tasks need to be accomplished to produce the deliverables?

- Who is responsible for performing the tasks?
- What resources are required to perform the tasks?
- When will the tasks be performed?
- How long will it take to perform each task?
- Are any tasks dependent upon other tasks being completed before they can begin?
- How much does each task cost?
- What skills and experience are required to perform each task?
- How is the performance of the task being measured including quality?
- How are issues being tracked?
- How is change being addressed?
- How is communication occurring and when?
- What risks are associated with each task?

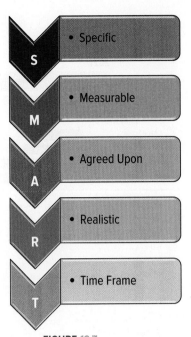

FIGURE 19.7

SMART Criteria for Successful Objective Creation.

The project objectives are among the most important areas to define because they are essentially the major elements of the project. When an organization achieves the project objectives, it has accomplished the major goals of the project and the project scope is satisfied. Project objectives must include metrics so that the project's success can be measured. The metrics can include cost, schedule, and quality metrics. Figure 19.7 lists the SMART criteria—useful reminders about how to ensure the project has created understandable and measurable objectives.

The project plan is a formal, approved document that manages and controls project execution. The project plan should include a description of the project scope, a list of activities, a schedule, time estimates, cost estimates, risk factors, resources, assignments, and responsibilities. In addition to these basic components, most project professionals also include contingency plans, review and communications strategies, and a *kill switch*—a trigger that enables a project manager to close the project before completion.

A good project plan should include estimates for revenue and strategic necessities. It also should include measurement and reporting methods and details as to how top leadership will engage in the project. It also informs stakeholders of the benefits of the project and justifies the investment, commitment, and risk of the project as it relates to the overall mission of the organization.

Managers need to continuously monitor projects to measure their success. If a project is failing, the manager must cancel the project and save the company any further project costs. Canceling a project is not necessarily a failure as much as it is successful resource management as it frees resources that can be used on other projects that are more valuable to the firm.

The most important part of the plan is communication. The project manager must communicate the plan to every member of the project team and to any key stakeholders and executives. The project plan must also include any project assumptions and be detailed enough to guide the execution of the project. A key to achieving project success is earning consensus and buy-in from all key stakeholders. By including key stakeholders in project plan development, the project manager allows them to have ownership of the plan. This often translates to greater commitment, which in turn results in enhanced motivation and productivity. The two primary diagrams most frequently used in project planning are PERT and Gantt charts.

A *PERT (Program Evaluation and Review Technique) chart* is a graphical network model that depicts a project's tasks and the relationships between them. A *dependency* is a logical relationship that exists between the project tasks, or between a project task and a milestone. PERT charts define dependency between project tasks before those tasks are scheduled (see Figure 19.8). The boxes in Figure 19.8 represent project tasks, and the project manager can adjust the contents of the boxes to display various project attributes such as schedule and actual start and finish times. The arrows indicate that a task depends on the start or the completion of a different task. The *critical path* estimates the shortest path through the project ensuring all critical tasks are completed from start to finish. The red line in Figure 19.8 displays the critical path for the project.

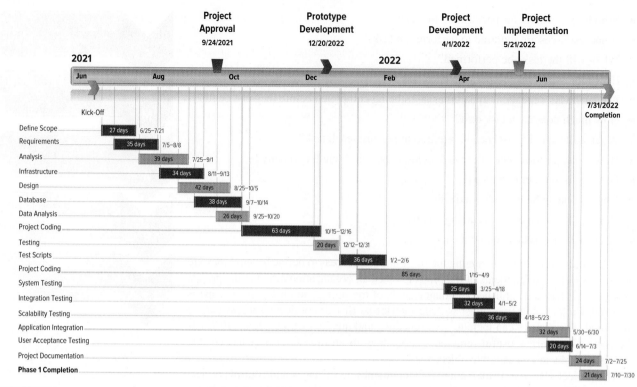

Project Approval
9/24/2021

Prototype Development
12/20/2022

Project Development
4/1/2022

Project Implementation
5/21/2022

2021   2022

Jun   Aug   Oct   Dec   Feb   Apr   Jun

7/31/2022
Completion

Kick-Off

Task	Duration	Dates
Define Scope	27 days	6/25–7/21
Requirements	35 days	7/5–8/8
Analysis	39 days	7/25–9/1
Infrastructure	34 days	8/11–9/13
Design	42 days	8/25–10/5
Database	38 days	9/7–10/14
Data Analysis	26 days	9/25–10/20
Project Coding	63 days	10/15–12/16
Testing	20 days	12/12–12/31
Test Scripts	36 days	1/2–2/6
Project Coding	85 days	1/15–4/9
System Testing	25 days	3/25–4/18
Integration Testing	32 days	4/1–5/2
Scalability Testing	36 days	4/18–5/23
Application Integration	32 days	5/30–6/30
User Acceptance Testing	20 days	6/14–7/3
Project Documentation	24 days	7/2–7/25
Phase 1 Completion	21 days	7/10–7/30

FIGURE 19.8

PERT Chart Expert, a PERT Chart Example.

Source: Microsoft Office 2016

A ***Gantt chart*** is a simple bar chart that lists project tasks vertically against the project's time frame, listed horizontally. A Gantt chart works well for representing the project schedule. It also shows actual progress of tasks against the planned duration. Figure 19.9 displays a software development project using a Gantt chart.

FIGURE 19.9

Microsoft Project, a Gantt Chart Example.

Source: Microsoft Office 2016

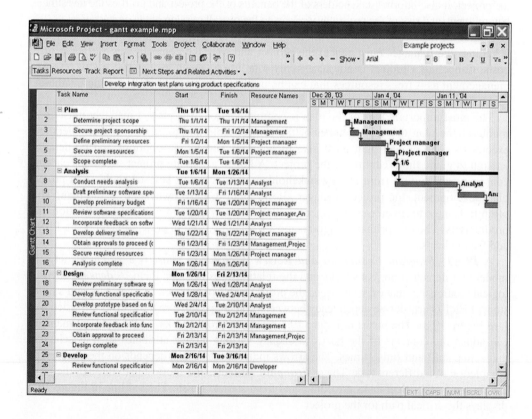

Outsourcing Projects

In the high-speed global business environment, an organization needs to increase profits, grow market share, and reduce costs. Two basic options are available to organizations wishing to develop and maintain their information systems—in-sourcing or outsourcing.

In-sourcing (in-house development) uses the professional expertise within an organization to develop and maintain its information technology systems. In-sourcing has been instrumental in creating a viable supply of IT professionals and in creating a better quality workforce combining both technical and business skills.

Outsourcing is an arrangement by which one organization provides a service or services for another organization that chooses not to perform them in-house. In some cases, the entire MIS department is outsourced, including planning and business analysis as well as the design, development, and maintenance of equipment and projects. Outsourcing can range from a large contract under which an organization such as IBM manages all MIS services for another company, to hiring contractors and temporary staff on an individual basis. Common reasons companies outsource include:

- **Core competencies.** Many companies have recently begun to consider outsourcing as a way to acquire best-practices and the business process expertise of highly skilled technology resources for a low cost. Technology is advancing at such an accelerated rate that companies often lack the technical resources required to keep current.

- **Financial savings.** It is far cheaper to hire people in China and India than pay the required salaries for similar labor in the United States.

- **Rapid growth.** Firms must get their products to market quickly and still be able to react to market changes. By taking advantage of outsourcing, an organization can acquire the resources required to speed up operations or scale to new demand levels.

- **The Internet and globalization.** The pervasive nature of the Internet has made more people comfortable with outsourcing abroad as India, China, and the United States become virtual neighbors.

Outsourcing MIS enables organizations to keep up with market and technology advances—with less strain on human and financial resources and more assurance that the IT infrastructure will keep pace with evolving business priorities (see Figure 19.10). The three forms of outsourcing options available for a project are:

1. *Onshore outsourcing*—engaging another company within the same country for services.

2. *Nearshore outsourcing*—contracting an outsourcing arrangement with a company in a nearby country. Often this country will share a border with the native country.

3. *Offshore outsourcing*—using organizations from developing countries to write code and develop systems. In offshore outsourcing the country is geographically far away.

Since the mid-1990s, major U.S. companies have been sending significant portions of their software development work offshore—primarily to vendors in India, but also to vendors in China, eastern Europe (including Russia), Ireland, Israel, and the Philippines. The big selling point for offshore outsourcing is inexpensive but good work. The overseas counterpart to an American programmer who earns as much as $63,000 per year is paid as little as $5,000 per year (see Figure 19.11). Developing countries in Asia and South Africa offer some outsourcing services but are challenged by language difference, inadequate telecommunication equipment, and regulatory obstacles. India is the largest offshore marketplace because it promotes English along with a technologically advanced population. Infosys, NIIT, Mahindra Satyam, Tata Consultancy Services, and Wipro are among the biggest Indian outsourcing service providers, each of which has a large presence in the United States.

FIGURE 19.10

Outsourcing Models.

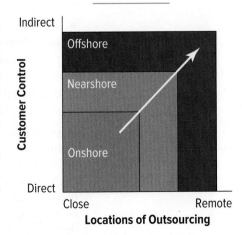

FIGURE 19.11

Typical Salary Ranges for
Computer Programmers.

Country	Salary Range per Year
China	$5,000–$9,000
India	6,000–10,000
Philippines	6,500–11,000
Russia	7,000–13,000
Ireland	21,000–28,000
Canada	25,000–50,000
United States	60,000–90,000

OUTSOURCING BENEFITS

The many benefits associated with outsourcing include:

- Increased quality and efficiency of business processes.
- Reduced operating expenses for head count and exposure to risk for large capital investments.
- Access to outsourcing service provider's expertise, economies of scale, best practices, and advanced technologies.
- Increased flexibility for faster response to market changes and less time to market for new products or services.

OUTSOURCING CHALLENGES

Outsourcing comes with several challenges. These arguments are valid and should be considered when a company is thinking about outsourcing. Many challenges can be avoided with proper research. The challenges include:

- **Length of contract.** Most companies look at outsourcing as a long-term solution with a time period of several years. Training and transferring resources around the globe is difficult and expensive; hence, most companies pursuing offshore outsourcing contract for multiple years of service. A few of the challenges facing the length of the contract include:

  1. It can be difficult to break the contract.
  2. Forecasting business needs for the next several years is challenging and the contract might not meet future business needs.
  3. Re-creating an internal MIS department if the outsource provider fails is costly and challenging.

- **Threat to competitive advantage.** Many businesses view MIS as a competitive advantage and view outsourcing as a threat because the outsourcer could share the company's trade secrets.

- **Loss of confidentiality.** Information on pricing, products, sales, and customers can be a competitive asset and often critical for business success. Outsourcing could place confidential information in the wrong hands. Although confidentiality clauses contained in the contracts are supposed to protect the company, the potential risk and costs of a breach must be analyzed.

Every type of organization in business today relies on software to operate and solve complex problems or create exciting opportunities. Software built correctly can support nimble organizations and transform with them as they and their businesses transform. Software that effectively meets employee needs will help an organization become more productive and enhance decision making. Software that does not meet employee needs might have a damaging effect on productivity and can even cause a business to fail. Employee involvement in software development, along with the right implementation, is critical to the success of an organization.

1. What are the three interdependent variables shaping project management? Why are these variables important to a video game software development project?

2. Why is the cost of finding errors important to a business when developing and designing video games?

3. What are the ethical and security issues associated with outsourcing the development of a video game to India or China?

Chapter Nineteen Case: Disaster at Denver International Airport

One good way to learn how to develop successful systems is to review past failures. One of the most infamous system failures is Denver International Airport's (DIA) baggage system. When the automated baggage system design for DIA was introduced, it was hailed as the savior of modern airport design. The design relied on a network of 300 computers to route bags and 4,000 cars to carry luggage across 21 miles of track. Laser scanners were to read bar-coded luggage tags, while advanced scanners tracked the movement of toboggan-like baggage carts.

When DIA finally opened its doors for reporters to witness its revolutionary baggage handling system, the scene was rather unpleasant. Bags were chewed up, lost, and misrouted in what has since become a legendary systems nightmare.

One of the biggest mistakes made in the baggage handling system fiasco was that not enough time was allowed to properly develop the system. In the beginning of the project, DIA assumed it was the responsibility of individual airlines to find their own way of moving the baggage from the plane to the baggage claim area. The automated baggage system was not involved in the initial planning of the DIA project. By the time the DIA developers decided to create an integrated baggage system, the time frame for designing and implementing such a complex and huge system was not possible.

Another common mistake that occurred during the project was that the airlines kept changing their business requirements. This caused numerous issues, including the implementation of power supplies that were not properly updated for the revised system design, which caused overloaded motors and mechanical failures. Besides the power supply design problem, the optical sensors did not read the bar codes correctly, causing issues with baggage routing.

Finally, BAE, the company that designed and implemented the automated baggage system for DIA, had never created a baggage system of this size before. BAE had created a similar system in an airport in Munich, Germany, where the scope was much smaller. Essentially, the baggage system had an inadequate IT infrastructure because it was designed for a much smaller system.

DIA simply could not open without a functional baggage system so the city had no choice but to delay the opening date for more than 16 months, costing taxpayers roughly $1 million per day, which totaled around $500 million.[1]

Questions

1. One problem with DIA's baggage system was inadequate testing. Why is testing important to a project's success? Why do so many projects decide to skip testing?

2. Evaluate the different systems development methodologies. Which one would have most significantly increased the chances of the project's success?

3. How could more time spent in the analysis and design phase have saved Colorado taxpayers hundreds of millions of dollars?

4. Why could BAE not take an existing IT infrastructure and simply increase its scale and expect it to work?

19.1. Explain project management and identify the primary reasons projects fail.

A project is a temporary or short-term endeavor undertaken to create a unique product, service, or result, such as developing a custom ecommerce site or merging databases. Project management is the application of knowledge, skills, tools, and techniques to project activities to meet project requirements. A project manager is an individual who is an expert in project planning and management, defines and develops the project plan, and tracks the plan to ensure that the project is completed on time and on budget. The primary reasons projects fail include unclear or missing business requirements, skipped phases, changing technology, the cost of finding errors in the SDLC, and imbalance of the triple constraints.

19.2. Identify the primary project planning diagrams.

A PERT (Program Evaluation and Review Technique) chart is a graphical network model that depicts a project's tasks and the relationships between those tasks. A dependency is a logical relationship that exists between the project tasks or between a project task and a milestone. A Gantt chart is a simple bar chart that depicts project tasks against a calendar. In a Gantt chart, tasks are listed vertically and the project's time frame is listed horizontally. A Gantt chart works well for representing the project schedule. It also shows actual progress of tasks against the planned duration.

19.3. Identify the three different types of outsourcing along with their benefits and challenges.

- Onshore outsourcing—engaging another company within the same country for services.
- Nearshore outsourcing—contracting an outsourcing arrangement with a company in a nearby country.
- Offshore outsourcing—using organizations from developing countries to write code and develop systems.

The many benefits associated with outsourcing include increased quality and efficiency of a process, service, or function; reduction of operating expenses and exposure to risks involved with large capital investments; and access to the outsourcing service provider's expertise, economies of scale, best practices, and advanced technologies. Outsourcing comes with several challenges, including length of contracts, losing competitive advantages, and risking a breach of confidential information.

* REVIEW QUESTIONS

1. What role does project management play in the systems development effort?
2. What role does the project manager play in determining a project's success?
3. Why would a project require an executive sponsor?
4. Why would a project manager use Gantt and PERT charts?
5. Why is gathering business requirements a challenge for most projects?
6. What are the different types of outsourcing available for a project?
7. What are the risks associated with outsourcing?
8. Explain the goals of the Project Management Institute and identify three key terms associated with PMBOK.
9. Explain the different types of feasibility studies a project manager can use to prioritize project importance.

1. Understanding Project Failure

You are the director of project management for Stello, a global manufacturer of high-end writing instruments. The company sells to primarily high-end customers, and the average price for one of its fine writing instruments is about $350. You are currently implementing a new customer relationship management system, and you want to do everything you can to ensure a successful systems development effort. Create a document summarizing the primary reasons this project could fail, along with your strategy to eliminate the possibility of system development failure on your project.

2. Saving Failing Systems

Crik Candle Company manufactures low-end candles for restaurants. The company generates more than $40 million in annual revenues and has more than 300 employees. You are in the middle of a large multimillion-dollar supply chain management implementation. Your project manager has just come to you with the information that the project might fail for the following reasons:

- Several business requirements were incorrect and the scope has to be doubled.
- Three developers recently quit.
- The deadline has been moved up a month.

Develop a list of options that your company can follow to ensure that the project remains on schedule and within budget.

3. Explaining Project Management

Prime Time Inc. is a large consulting company that specializes in outsourcing people with project management capabilities and skills. You are in the middle of an interview for a job with Prime Time. The manager performing the interview asks you to explain why managing a project plan is critical to a project's success. The manager also wants you to explain scope creep and feature creep and your tactics for managing them on a project. Finally, the manager wants you to elaborate on your strategies for delivering successful projects and reducing risks.

4. Applying Project Management Techniques

You have been hired by a medium-sized airline company, Sun Best. Sun Best currently flies more than 300 routes in the East. The company is experiencing tremendous issues coordinating its 3,500 pilots, 7,000 flight attendants, and 2,000 daily flights. Determine how Sun Best could use a Gantt chart to help it coordinate pilots, flight attendants, and daily flights. Using Excel, create a sample Gantt chart highlighting the different types of activities and resources Sun Best could track with the tool.

5. SharePoint

Life is good when you can complete all your projects by the due date and under budget. Life is not good when you miss your deadlines, exceed your budget, and fail to meet the business requirements. One tool that can help ensure that your life always stays good is Microsoft SharePoint. With SharePoint, you can connect with employees enterprisewide to collaborate, share ideas, and reinvent the way work flows. Whether working as a team or an individual, SharePoint helps you organize information, people, and projects. SharePoint can make any manager's life easier by organizing teamwork around common milestones. You can make sure that work is completed by assigning people tasks that can be tracked and prioritized. You can keep an eye on important details with real-time summaries of your projects that warn you about delays and keep next steps and milestones on your radar. Explain why using a project management/collaboration tool such as SharePoint can help ensure that you never fail as a manager. Be sure to explain any project management terms such as deliverables, dependencies, and milestones.

6. Edward Yourdon's book *Death March* describes the complete software developer's guide to surviving "mission impossible" projects. MIS projects are challenging, and project managers are expected to achieve the impossible by pulling off a successful project even when pitted against impossible challenges. In *Death March*, infamous software developer Edward Yourdon presents his project classification displayed here. Yourdon measures projects based on the level of pain and chances for success.[2]

- **Mission Impossible Project:** This project has a great chance of success and your hard work will pay off as you find happiness and joy in the work. For example, this is the type of project where you work all day and night for a year and become the project hero as you complete the mission impossible and reap a giant promotion as your reward.

- **Ugly Project:** This project has a high chance of success but is very painful and offers little happiness. For example, you work day and night to install a new accounting system and although successful, you hate accounting and dislike the company and its products.

- **Kamikaze Project:** This is a project that has little chance of success but you are so passionate about the content that you find great happiness working on the project. For example, you are asked to build a website to support a cancer foundation, a cause near to your heart, but the company is nonprofit and doesn't have any funds to help buy the software you need to get everything working. You patch the system together and implement many manual workarounds just to keep the system functioning.

- **Suicide Project:** This project has no chance of success and offers you nothing but pain. This is the equivalent of your worst nightmare project. Word of caution, avoid suicide projects![2]

    1. Analyze your school and work projects and find a project that would fit in each box in the accompanying figure.
    2. What could you have done differently on your suicide project to ensure its success?
    3. What can you do to avoid being placed on a suicide project? Given the choice, which type of project would you choose to work on and why?

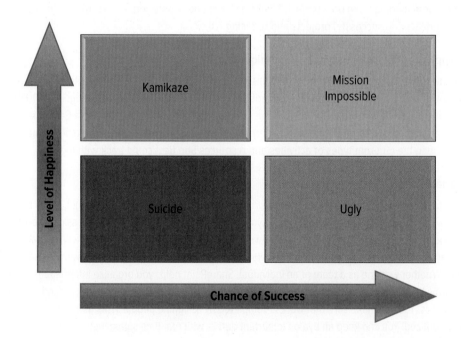

An organization must remain competitive in this quick-paced, constantly changing, global business environment. It must implement technology that is adaptive, disruptive, and transformable to meet new and unexpected customer needs. Focusing on the unexpected and understanding disruptive technologies can give an organization a competitive advantage.

Organizations need software that users can transform quickly to meet the requirements of the rapidly changing business environment. Software that effectively meets employee needs will help an organization become more productive and make better decisions. Software that does not meet employee needs may have a damaging effect on productivity. Employee involvement along with using the right implementation methodology in developing software is critical to the success of an organization.

Information technology has rapidly expanded from a backroom resource providing competitive advantage (e.g., cost, time, quality) to a front-office resource (e.g., marketing, sales) that is a competitive necessity. The dynamic business and technical environment of the 21st century is driving the need for technology infrastructures and applications architecture that are increasingly flexible, integrated, and maintainable (while always providing functionality, cost effectiveness, timeliness, and security).

* KEY TERMS

Agile methodology 326
Alpha testing 319
Analysis phase 314
Brainstorming 314
Bug 316
Business requirement 314
Change agent 314
Communication plan 342
Computer-aided software engineering (CASE) 315
Control objects for information and related technology (COBIT) 316
Conversion 312
Corrective maintenance 319
Critical path 343
Data flow diagram (DFD) 315
Dependency 343
Design phase 315
Development phase 316
Development testing 312
Discovery prototyping 326
Executive sponsor 342
Extensible Markup Language (XML) 330
Extreme programming (XP) methodology 327
Feasibility 339
Fourth-generation language (4GL) 316
Gantt chart 344
Graphical user interface (GUI) 315

Help desk 318
Implementation phase 318
In-sourcing (in-house development) 345
Intangible benefits 339
Integration testing 319
Interoperability 330
Iterative development 326
Joint application development (JAD) 314
Kill switch 343
Loose coupling 330
Maintenance phase 319
Methodology 325
Nearshore outsourcing 345
Object-oriented languages 316
Offshore outsourcing 345
Off-the-shelf application 312
Online training 318
Onshore outsourcing 345
Outsourcing 345
Parallel implementation 319
PERT (Program Evaluation and Review Technique) chart 343
Phased implementation 319
Pilot implementation 319
Planning phase 314
Plunge implementation 319
Preventive maintenance 319
Project 312
Project assumption 342

Project constraint 342
Project deliverable 342
Project management 000
Project management office (PMO) 342
Project manager 343
Project milestone 342
Project objective 342
Project plan 342
Project requirements document 342
Project scope 342
Project scope statement 342
Project stakeholder 342
Prototyping 326
Rapid application development (RAD) methodology (rapid prototyping) 327
Rational unified process (RUP) methodology 328
Requirements definition document 314
Requirements management 314
Responsibility matrix 342
Scripting language 316
Scrum methodology 328
Service-oriented architecture (SOA) 328
Sign-off 314
SOA service 331
Software customization 312
Software engineering 315

© Tetra Images/Getty Images

© The McGraw-Hill Companies, Inc./Lars A. Niki, photographer

© The McGraw-Hill Companies, Inc./ Christopher Kerrigan, photographer

To Share—Or Not To Share

People love social networks! Social networks are everywhere and a perfect way to share vacation photos, family events, and birthday parties with family, friends, and co-workers. About 40 percent of adults use at least one social media website, and 51 percent of those use more than one website. The majority of users are between the ages of 18 and 24. The Pew Research Center found that 89 percent of social network users primarily use the websites to update friends and family, while 57 percent use the websites to make plans with friends, and 49 percent use the websites to make new friends.

Facebook, Myspace, LinkedIn, Friendster, Urban Chat, and Black Planet are just a few of more than 100 websites connecting people around the world who are eager to share everything from photos to thoughts and feelings. But we need to remember that sometimes you can share too much; there can be too much information. Choosing whom you share with and what you share is something you want to think about for your personal social networks and corporate social networks. According to Pew Research, more than 40 percent of users allow open access to their social networking profiles, which allows anyone from anywhere to view all of their personal information. The remaining 60 percent restrict access to friends, family, and co-workers. The following are the top 10 things you should consider before posting information to your social networks.

1: If You Don't Want to Share It—Don't Post It

You can select all the privacy settings you want on social networking sites, but the fact is, if you post it, it has the potential to be seen by someone you don't want seeing it. You know all those fun Facebook applications, quizzes, and polls you can't help but fill out? A study performed by the University of Virginia found that of the top 150 applications on Facebook, 90 percent were given access to information they didn't need in order for the application to function. So when you sign up to find out what sitcom star you most identify with, the makers of that poll now have access to your personal information. It's anybody's guess where it goes from there. Social networking is all about sharing, so something you think is in confidence can easily be shared and then shared again, and before you know it, someone you don't even know has access to something private. "When in doubt, leave it out" is a good motto to follow. And always remember that anything you share has the potential to be leaked in some way.

2: Never Give Out Your Password Hints

Most websites that contain secure personal information require a password and have at least one password hint in case you forget. It typically goes like this: You sign up for something such as online banking and you get a log-in and password and then choose a security question for when you forget your password. What's the name of your first pet? What's your mother's maiden name? What was your high school mascot? What's the name of the first street you lived on? Including any of these details on a Facebook wall or status update may not seem like a big deal, but it could provide an identity thief with the last piece of the puzzle needed to hack into your bank account. Think before you post anything that could compromise this information.

3: Never Give Out Your Password

This one really seems like a no-brainer, but if it didn't happen, then Facebook probably wouldn't feel the need to list it in the No. 1 slot on its list of things you shouldn't share. Even sharing the password with a friend so he or she can log on and check something for you can be a risk. This is especially true with couples who feel like there's enough trust to share these kinds of things. Here's another scenario for you: You give your boyfriend your Facebook password because he wants to help you upload some vacation photos. A couple of months later, the relationship sours, he turns into a not-so-nice guy, and then there's a person out there who doesn't like you and has your log-in information. Time to cancel your account and get a new one. If you'd kept that information private, you could simply move on with your life. Now you have a compromised profile, and if you link to other sites or profiles, all that information is at risk as well. Keep your password to yourself, no matter what, and you never have to worry about it.

4: Never Provide Personal Financial Information

You would think that nobody would share things like where they do their banking or what their stock portfolio looks like, but it happens. It's easy for an innocent Facebook comment to reveal too much about your personal finances. Consider this scenario: You're posting to a long thread on a friend's wall about the bank crisis. You say something along the lines of, "We don't need to worry because we bank with a teacher's credit union," or even, "We put all our money into blue chip stocks and plan to ride it out." Again, if you're one of the 40 percent who allow open access to your profile, then suddenly identity thieves know where you bank and where you have the bulk of your investments. It's easy to forget that what may seem like a harmless comment on a Facebook wall could reveal a great deal about your personal finances. It's best to avoid that kind of talk.

5: Never Give Out Your Address or Phone Numbers

File this one under security risk. If you share your address and phone number on a social networking site, you open yourself up to threats of identity theft and other personal dangers such as burglaries. If you post that you're going on vacation and you have your address posted, then everyone knows you have an empty house. Identity thieves could pay a visit to your mailbox and open up a credit card in your name. Burglars could rid your home of anything of value. Even just posting your phone number gives people with Internet savvy easy access to your address. Reverse lookup services can supply anyone with your home address in possession of your phone number.

6: Never Share Photos of Your Children

Social networking sites are a common place for people to share pictures of their families, but if you're one of the 40 percent of users who don't restrict access to your profile, then those pictures are there for everyone to see. It's a sad fact, but a lot of predators use the Internet to stalk their prey. If you post pictures of your family and combine that with information like, "My husband is out of town this week-end" or "Little Johnny is old enough to stay at home by himself now," then your children's safety could be at risk. Nobody ever thinks it will happen to them until it does, so safety first is a good default mode when using social networking sites. Just like with other private matters, send family photos only to a select group of trusted friends and colleagues who you know won't share them.

7: Never Provide Company Information

You may be dying to tell the world about your new work promotion, but if it's news that could be advantageous to one of your company's competitors, then it's not something you should share. News of a planned expansion or a big project role and anything else about your workplace should be kept private. Sophos, a security software company, found that 63 percent of companies were afraid of what their employees were choosing to share on social networking sites. If you want to message it out, be selective and send private emails. Many companies are so serious about not being included in social networking sites that they forbid employees from using sites like Facebook at work. Some IT departments even filter the URLs and block access to these sites so employees aren't tempted to log on.

8: Never Give Links to Websites

With 51 percent of social network users taking advantage of more than one site, there's bound to be some crossover, especially if you have the sites linked. You may post something you find innocuous on Facebook, but then it's linked to your LinkedIn work profile and you've put your job at risk. If you link your various profiles, be aware that what you post in one world is available to the others. In 2009, a case of an employee caught lying on Facebook hit the news. The employee asked off for a weekend shift because he was ill and then posted pictures on his Facebook profile of himself at a party that same weekend. The news got back to his employer easily enough and he was fired. So if you choose to link your profiles, it's no longer a "personal life" and "work life" scenario.

9: Keep Your Social Plans to Yourself

Sharing your social plans for everybody to see isn't a good idea. Unless you're planning a big party and inviting all the users you're connected to, it will only make your other friends feel left out. There are also some security issues at stake here. Imagine a scenario where a jealous ex-boyfriend knows that you're meeting a new date out that night. What's to keep the ex from showing up and causing a scene or even potentially getting upset or violent? Nothing. If you're planning a party or an outing with a group of friends, send a personal "e-vite" for their eyes only and nobody is the wiser. If you're trying to cast a wide net by throwing out an idea for a social outing, just remember that anyone who has access to your profile sees it.

10: Do Not Share Personal Conversations

On Facebook, users can send personal messages or post notes, images, or videos to another user's wall. The wall is there for all to see, while messages are between the sender and the receiver, just like an email. Personal and private matters should never be shared on your wall. You wouldn't go around with a bullhorn announcing a private issue to the world, and the same thing goes on the Internet. This falls under the nebulous world of social networking etiquette. There is no official handbook for this sort of thing, but use your best judgment. If it's not something you'd feel comfortable sharing in person with extended family, acquaintances, work colleagues, or strangers, then you shouldn't share it on your Facebook wall.[3]

Questions

1. Which phase in the systems development life cycle is the most critical when building a social media website?

2. Which phase in the systems development life cycle is the least critical when building a social media website?

3. If you were consulting to a business that wanted to build a social networking website, which development methodology would you recommend and why?

4. What are the three interdependent variables shaping project management? Why are these variables important to a social media software development project?

5. What are the ethical and security issues associated with outsourcing the development of a social media website?

✳ UNIT CLOSING CASE TWO

© Shutterstock / Zurijeta

© Stockbyte/Getty Images

© Ingram Publishing/AGE Fotostock

Box Up Your Data

What happens when you need a file for a class that you have on your desktop back at home? What happens when you want to share your wedding video with your friends and family around the world? What happens when you want to safeguard the 4,000 selfies you have taken over the past year? Your best bet is to store your data in a Box! Box offers data storage services that: Help you securely store, share, and manage your files.

- Store unlimited data at the start.
- Securely send large files online.
- Take advantage of comprehensive security for mobile devices.
- Easily collaborate online with anyone, anywhere.
- Control who can access content.
- Edit documents and files online.

Box is a cloud data-sharing service that can increase your productivity by making it easy to create and collaborate with co-workers by using computers, iPhones, iPads, Androids, or other devices. With a Box site, you can access up to 50GB of files from anywhere. Through a web link, you can invite others to share your files or collaborate on your documents, and you can synchronize files from Box to your desktop and vice versa.

Another College Start-Up Box

Rachel King from InfoWorld interviewed Box founder Aaron Levie on how he and his childhood friends started the company. Box as a platform and company was born in 2005, but even that was well after the establishment of the friendship between Levie and his cofounder and Box's chief financial officer, Dylan Smith. Smith and Levie met as classmates at Islander Middle School on Mercer Island, Washington, a suburb southeast of Seattle, and then went to Mercer Island High School together. "Even back then he started getting me interested in entrepreneurship," Smith recalled. "He was much more interested in technology [than business] back then." Two other key members of the Box team were also childhood friends.

Jeff Queisser, currently vice president of Box's technical operations, met Levie when they were in the fourth and fifth grades, respectively, as neighbors. By high school, Queisser recalled that the two were starting "kinda crazy businesses." "[Levie] was a magician, and I was very much a hard core nerd and doing programming," Queisser laughed.

Sam Ghods, now vice president of technology at Box, joined the group in the tenth grade when his family relocated from Illinois to Mercer Island. The same year in school, Ghods recalled that he and Queisser became friends on the bus to school, eventually hanging out more frequently with Smith and Levie as well and getting involved in various business schemes.

In high school, Levie's parents' hot tub served as the discussion forum. "We would get a call at about 12:30, and it would be Aaron, 'What do you think about this? I think this could be absolutely insane. Like, come over right now. I got towels, just bring shorts, come over,'" Queisser remembers. "This would be at 12:30 and by like 12:40, we were in his hot tub just iterating ideas."

And although he built a lot of websites in high school, Levie doesn't brag about having a strong technical background, admitting, "They weren't very good websites." One example was a search engine dubbed Zizap, which Levie facetiously peddled as "the world's fastest search engine if you have never been to Google." Another project was Fastest.com, a website that let people buy and sell their homes online. Levie notes sarcastically that it "made sense as a high school senior to launch that company."

These early rumblings of entrepreneurship would soon pay dividends. Levie enrolled at the University of Southern California in 2003 to study business, which is where the idea that was to become Box began to develop. "It's not like a lightning bolt that hits you in the head, and all of a sudden you just get so obsessed with storing files online. It was a series of factors," he explained.

The first piece of the puzzle came from the basic difficulty of getting work done. He and his fellow students were working from lots of computers, collaborating on projects, and accessing files from different places, including libraries, classrooms, and dorm rooms.

"It felt unbelievably kind of painful and taxing to share data across those different systems and with other people. It seemed like there should be a simpler solution," Levie remarked.

A business school project in which students were asked to evaluate a particular industry added another piece to the puzzle. Levie chose the nascent online storage industry and wrote a paper on flaws with existing businesses in the market and what one could do to build a better business effectively. It didn't take long before he realized the massive potential. "It was very obvious that there should be a technology category that solved this problem," he said.

"When we were talking about just the things that we were doing and the stuff we were working on, Box came up," Levie described. "It's very, very early in the process, and Dylan Smith decided to join on board as the other half of the business and product side. He handled the finance and some of the early marketing stuff. That was how we started."[4]

Questions

1. List the different systems development methodologies and explain which one would be best supported by a service like Box.

2. Evaluate the following for Box.

   a. List and describe the seven phases in the systems development life cycle and determine which phase is most important for Box.

b. Review the primary principles of successful software development and prioritize them in order of importance to Box.

c. Explain how the company can use project management to ensure success.

d. Explain the pros and cons of outsourcing your data storage to a company like Box.

3. Why is building agile software important for all of the companies?

4. What types of information security issues should companies be aware as they use cloud services such as Box?

5. What types of ethical dilemmas should the companies be aware of as they use cloud services such as Box?

 APPLY YOUR KNOWLEDGE

1. Confusing Coffee

Business requirements are the detailed set of business requests that any new system must meet in order to be successful. A sample business requirement might state, "The system must track all customer sales by product, region, and sales representative." This requirement states what the system must do from the business perspective, giving no details or information on how the system is going to meet this requirement.

You have been hired to build an employee payroll system for a new coffee shop. Review the following business requirements and highlight any potential issues.

- All employees must have a unique employee ID.
- The system must track employee hours worked based on employee's last name.
- Employees must be scheduled to work a minimum of eight hours per day.
- Employee payroll is calculated by multiplying the employee's hours worked by $7.25.
- Managers must be scheduled to work morning shifts.
- Employees cannot be scheduled to work more than eight hours per day.
- Servers cannot be scheduled to work morning, afternoon, or evening shifts.
- The system must allow managers to change and delete employees from the system.

2. Picking Projects

You are a project management contractor attempting to contract work at a large telecommunications company, Hex Incorporated. Your interview with Debbie Fernandez, the senior vice president of IT, went smoothly. The last thing Debbie wants to see from you before she makes her final hiring decision is a prioritized list of the projects here. You are sure to land the job if Debbie is satisfied with your prioritization.

Create a report for Debbie prioritizing the following projects and be sure to include the business justifications for your prioritization.

- Upgrade accounting system.
- Develop employee vacation tracking system.
- Enhance employee intranet.
- Cleanse and scrub data warehouse information.
- Performance test all hardware to ensure 20 percent growth scalability.

- Implement changes to employee benefits system.
- Develop backup and recovery strategy.
- Implement supply chain management system.
- Upgrade customer relationship management system.
- Build executive information system for CEO.

3. Keeping Time

Time Keepers Inc. is a small firm that specializes in project management consulting. You are a senior project manager, and you have recently been assigned to the Tahiti Tanning Lotion account. The Tahiti Tanning Lotion company is currently experiencing a 10 percent success rate (90 percent failure rate) on all internal IT projects. Your first assignment is to analyze one of the current project plans being used to develop a new CRM system (see Figure AYK.1).

Review the project plan and create a document listing the numerous errors in the plan. Be sure to also provide suggestions on how to fix the errors.

4. Facing insurmountable troubles, some people turn to faking their own death to escape legal issues and even the Marines. Here are a few examples:

- Marcus Schrenker, a Wall Street investor whose company was under investigation for fraud, disappeared while flying his plane over Alabama. Schrenker's plane was found in a swamp, and the last anyone heard from Schrenker was a distressed radio call—until he was discovered in a campground a few weeks later.

- A Colorado man returning from a hike reported that his friend, Lance Hering, had been injured on the hike, and rescue teams were dispatched to find the hiker. All the rescuers found were blood, a water bottle, and Hering's shoes. Two years later, Hering was arrested with his father

FIGURE AYK.1

Sample Project Plan.

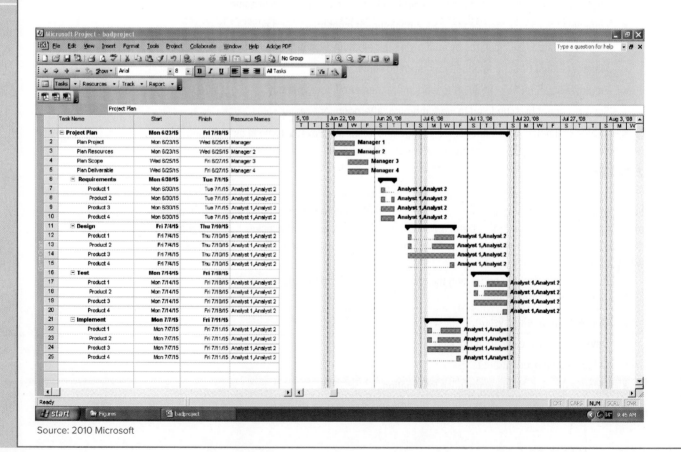

Source: 2010 Microsoft

at an airport in Washington State. Hering, a Marine, claimed he faked his death to avoid returning to Iraq, where he feared other soldiers would kill him because of something incriminating he had witnessed.

- One Florida woman, Alison Matera, informed her friends, family, and church choir that she was entering hospice because she was dying of cancer. Matera's plan unraveled when she appeared at her own funeral service, claiming to be her own long-lost identical twin sister. Police were called, and Matera admitted faking both her cancer and death.

Unexpected situations happen all the time, and the more you plan for them the better prepared you'll be when developing software. Hopefully, your employees are not faking their own deaths, but they will get into accidents, have babies, contract viruses and diseases, and face other life issues. All of these scenarios lead to unplanned absenteeism, which can throw your project plan into a tailspin. What can happen to a project when a key employee suddenly quits or is forced to go on short-term disability? When reviewing all of the different SDLC methodologies, which one offers the greatest flexibility for unplanned employee downtime? If you could choose when your employee was absent, during which phase in the SDLC would it be the safest if your project were to still continue and achieve success? What can you do to ensure you are preparing for unplanned absenteeism on your project plan?

5. Methods Behind Methodologies

Signatures Inc. specializes in producing personalized products such as coffee mugs and pens with company logos. The company generates more than $40 million in annual revenues and has more than 300 employees. The company is in the middle of a large multimillion-dollar SCM implementation, and it has just hired your project management outsourcing firm to take over the project management efforts.

On your first day, your team is told that the project is failing for the following reasons:

- The project is using the traditional waterfall methodology.
- The SDLC was not followed and the developers decided to skip the testing phase.
- A project plan was developed during the analysis phase, but the old project manager never updated or followed the plan.

Determine what your first steps would be to get this project back on track.

6. The Travel Store

The Travel Store is facing a dilemma because it tripled in size over the past three years and finds its online sales escalating beyond a billion dollars. The company is having a hard time continuing with operations because its business processes can't scale to meet the new demand. In the past six months, sales and profits have dropped and the stock price is plummeting.

The Travel Store is determined to take quick and decisive action to restore profitability and improve its credibility in the marketplace. One of its top priorities is to overhaul its inventory management system in an effort to create optimal levels of inventory to support sales demand. This would prevent higher-volume stores from running out of key sale items while also ensuring that lower-sales stores would not be burdened with excess inventory that could be moved only at closeout prices. The company would like to outsource this function but is worried about the challenges of transferring the responsibility of this important business function as well as the issues surrounding confidentiality and scope definition. List the competitive advantages outsourcing could give The Travel Store and recommendations for addressing the company's outsourcing concerns.

7. GEM Athletic Center

First Information Corporation is a large consulting company that specializes in systems analysis and design. The company has more than 2,000 employees, and first-quarter revenues reached $15 million. The company prides itself on maintaining an 85 percent success rate for all project implementations. The primary reason attributed to the unusually high project success rate is the company's ability to define accurate, complete, and high-quality business requirements.

The GEM Athletic Center located in Cleveland, Ohio, is interested in implementing a new payroll system. The current payroll process is manual and takes three employees two days each month to complete. The GEM Athletic Center does not have an IT department and is outsourcing the entire procurement, customization, and installation of the new payroll system to First Information Corporation.

You have been working for First Information for a little over one month. Your team has just been assigned the GEM Athletic Center project, and your first task is to define the initial business requirements for the development of the new payroll system.

a. Review the testimony of three current GEM Athletic Center accounting employees who detail the current payroll process along with their wish list for the new system. Figure AYK.2 displays the testimonies of Maggie Cleaver, Anne Logan, and Jim Poulos.

b. Review Chapter 17 Case, "Reducing Ambiguity in Business Requirements," and highlight several techniques you can use to develop solid business requirements.

c. After careful analysis, create a report detailing the business requirements for the new system. Be sure to list any assumptions, issues, or questions in your document.

Jim Poulos, Director of Sales

Each week I have to review all of the new memberships sold in our club. Each of my seven sales representatives receives $50 from a new sale for the initiation fee. They also receive 10 percent of the type of membership sold. Membership types include:

- Adult, $450/month
- Youth, $300/month
- Family, $750/month
- Senior, $300/month

Each sales representative is also paid $4.50/hour and receives a 25 percent bonus for working overtime and holidays. If the sales representative sells over 200 percent of expected sales they receive an additional 25 percent bonus on their commissions. If the membership is sold during a promotion, the commission rate decreases. The payroll department uses time sheets to track my sales representatives' hourly pay. I have to sign all time sheets once they are completed by the payroll department. I check my sales representatives' schedule to validate the times on the employee time sheets. I then have to submit a separate listing of each employee and their corresponding commissions for initiation fees and memberships sold. I track all of my sales representatives' vacation and sick time. If they are over their vacation or sick time, I have them sign a form stating that if they quit they will pay back all negative vacation or sick time.

I would like a system that can automatically calculate commissions and be able to handle sales forecasting and "what if" analysis on my sales representatives' commission rates. I would like to be able to walk up to my sales representatives and tell them that if they sell four more family memberships and one adult, they will receive their bonus. I would also like to be able to design promotions for our best customers. These types of things would really help boost sales at our club.

Maggie Cleaver, Payroll Manager

The first thing I do each week is collect the time sheets. I review each time sheet to ensure that the employee punched in and out correctly. If the employee forgot to clock out, I contact that person's director to find the time that the employee should have clocked out. I then calculate all regular hours, overtime hours, and holiday hours and total these on the time sheet. I also track sick time and vacation time and total these on the time sheet. Once completed, I send the time sheet to the directors of each department for approval.

When I receive the signed time sheets back, I begin to calculate payments. First, I calculate regular pay, then overtime pay, and finally holiday pay. I then add in the sales representatives' commissions, which I receive from the director of sales. I then calculate payment amounts for aerobics instructors because they are paid by class, not by hour. I receive the aerobics class schedule from the fitness coordinator. I then total the entire pay and send a sheet with payment amounts to my co-worker Anne, who calculates taxes. I then calculate all sick time and vacation time and track this in a separate document. I then print labels that state each employee's name, department, and the pay period. I place the labels on a new time sheet, which is returned to the employee punch clock.

I would like a system that automatically tracks employee sick time and vacation time. I would also like a system that can automatically calculate regular pay, overtime pay, and holiday pay. I don't know if there is a system that can validate employee time sheets, but if there is, that would be great.

Anne Logan, Tax Manager

I receive the payment amounts from Maggie. I then calculate all city, state, and federal taxes. I also deduct health benefits and retirement plan benefits. I then cut the check to the employee and the corresponding checks for the taxes to the government. I manually calculate W2s and all quarterly taxes. I'm also responsible for correcting personal information such as a change of address. I'm also responsible for cutting checks if an incorrect amount was issued. I also track amounts owed by employees that have gone over their sick time or vacation time. I also generate checks for all salaried employees.

The part of my job that takes the longest is correlating the total cash debit for all checks and the total amount calculated for all checks. It's amazing how many times these two figures do not match, which indithat a check was written for the wrong amount.

I would like a system that determines taxes automatically, along with quarterly tax filing statements. I would also like a system that can perform audits.

If you are looking for Excel projects to incorporate into your class, try any of the following to test your knowledge.

Project Number	Project Name	Project Type	Plug-In	Focus Area	Project Level	Skill Set	Page Number
9	Security Analysis	Excel	T3	Filtering Data	Intermediate	Conditional Formatting, Autofilter, Subtotal	AYK.7
10	Gathering Data	Excel	T3	Data Analysis	Intermediate	Conditional Formatting	AYK.8
11	Scanner System	Excel	T2	Strategic Analysis	Intermediate	Formulas	AYK.8
12	Competitive Pricing	Excel	T2	Profit Maximization	Intermediate	Formulas	AYK.9
13	Adequate Acquisitions	Excel	T2	Break Even Analysis	Intermediate	Formulas	AYK.9
15	Assessing the Value of Information	Excel	T3	Data Analysis	Intermediate	PivotTable	AYK.10
16	Growth, Trends, and Forecasts	Excel	T2, T3	Data Forecasting	Advanced	Average, Trend, Growth	AYK.11
18	Formatting Grades	Excel	T3	Data Analysis	Advanced	If, LookUp	AYK.12
22	Turnover Rates	Excel	T3	Data Mining	Advanced	PivotTable	AYK.15
23	Vital Information	Excel	T3	Data Mining	Advanced	PivotTable	AYK.15
24	Breaking Even	Excel	T4	Business Analysis	Advanced	Goal Seek	AYK.16
25	Profit Scenario	Excel	T4	Sales Analysis	Advanced	Scenario Manager	AYK.16

PLUG-IN

B1

Business Basics

LEARNING OUTCOMES

1. Define the three common business forms.
2. List and describe the seven departments commonly found in most organizations.

LO 1 **Define the three common business forms.**

Introduction

A sign posted beside a road in Colorado states, "Failing to plan is planning to fail." Playnix Toys posted the sign after successfully completing its 20th year in the toy business in Colorado. The company's mission is to provide a superior selection of high-end toys for children of all ages. When the company began, it generated interest by using unique marketing strategies and promotions. The toy business has a lot of tough competition. Large chain stores such as Walmart and Target offer toys at deep discount prices. Finding the right strategy to remain competitive is difficult in this industry, as FAO Schwarz discovered when it filed for bankruptcy after 143 years in the toy business.

This plug-in introduces basic business fundamentals beginning with the three most common business structures—sole proprietorship, partnership, and corporation. It then focuses on the internal operations of a corporation including accounting, finance, human resources, sales, marketing, operations/production, and management information systems.

Types of Business

Businesses come in all shapes and sizes and exist to sell products or perform services. Businesses make profits or incur losses. A *profit* occurs when businesses sell products or services for more than they cost to produce. A *loss* occurs when businesses sell products or services for less then they cost to produce. Businesses typically organize in one of the following types:

1. Sole proprietorship
2. Partnership
3. Corporation

SOLE PROPRIETORSHIP

The *sole proprietorship* is a business form in which a single person is the sole owner and is personally responsible for all the profits and losses of the business. The sole proprietorship is the quickest and easiest way to set up a business operation. No prerequisites or specific costs are associated with starting a sole proprietorship. A simple business license costing around $25 from the local county clerk is all that is required to start a sole proprietorship. The person who starts the sole proprietorship is the sole owner.

PARTNERSHIP

Partnerships are similar to sole proprietorships, except that this legal structure allows for more than one owner. Each partner is personally responsible for all the profits and losses of the business. Similar to the sole proprietorship, starting a partnership is a relatively easy process since there are no prerequisites or specific costs required. When starting a partnership, it is wise to have a lawyer draft a partnership agreement. A *partnership agreement* is a legal agreement between two or more business partners that outlines core business issues. Partnership agreements typically include:

- Amount of capital each partner expects to contribute. *Capital* represents money whose purpose is to make more money, for example, the money used to buy a rental property or a business.
- Duties and responsibilities expected from each partner.
- Expectations for sharing profits and losses.
- Partners' salary requirements.
- Methods for conflict resolution.
- Methods for dissolving the partnership.

Limited Partnership

A *limited partnership* is much like a general partnership except for one important fundamental difference; the law protects the limited partner from being responsible for all of the partnership's losses. The limited partner's legal liability in the business is limited to the amount of his or her investment. The limited partnership enables this special type of investor to share in the partnership profits without being exposed to its losses in the event the company goes out of business. However, this protection exists only as long as the limited partner does not play an active role in the operation of the business.

CORPORATION

The corporation is the most sophisticated form of business entity and the most common among large companies. The *corporation (also called organization, enterprise, or business)* is an artificially created legal entity that exists separate and apart from those individuals who created it and carry on its operations. In a corporation, the business entity is separate from the business owners. *Shareholder* is another term for business owners. An important advantage of using a corporation as a business form is that it offers the shareholders limited liability. *Limited liability* means that the shareholders are not personally liable for the losses incurred by the corporation. In most instances, financial losses incurred by a corporation are limited to the assets owned by the corporation. Shareholders' personal assets, such as their homes or investments, cannot be claimed to pay off debt or losses incurred by the corporation.

There are two general types of corporations—for profit and not for profit. *For profit corporations* primarily focus on making money and all profits and losses are shared by the business owners. *Not for profit (or nonprofit) corporations* usually exist to accomplish some charitable, humanitarian, or educational purpose, and the profits and losses are not shared by the business owners. Donations to nonprofit businesses may be tax deductible for the donor. Typical examples include hospitals, colleges, universities, and foundations.

Eleanor Josaitis is a tiny 72-year-old woman who cofounded the Detroit civil-rights group Focus: HOPE. Focus: HOPE, founded in 1968, began as a food program serving pregnant women, new mothers, and their children. Josaitis has built the nonprofit organization from a basement operation run by a handful of friends into a sprawling 40-acre campus in Detroit that now employs over 500 people, boasts more than 50,000 volunteers and donors, and has helped over 30,000 people become gainfully employed.

Josaitis and her team developed a technical school to help job seekers gain certifications in IT support. They operate a machinists' training program that funnels people into the employment pipeline at local automotive companies. The organization also teams up with local universities to help disadvantaged students receive college educations, and it runs a child care center to make sure all these opportunities are available to working and single parents. Josaitis states that the most courageous act she has performed in her life occurred 36 years ago when she turned off her television, got up off the couch, and decided to do something. "You have to have the guts to try something, because you won't change a thing by sitting in front of the TV with the clicker in your hand," Josaitis said.

Forming a corporation typically costs several hundred dollars in fees, and the owners must file a charter within the respective state. The charter typically includes:

- Purpose of the intended corporation.
- Names and addresses of the incorporators.
- Amount and types of stock the corporation will be authorized to issue.
- Rights and privileges of the shareholders.

The most common reason for incurring the cost of setting up a corporation is the recognition that the shareholder is not legally liable for the actions of the corporation. Figure B1.1 displays the primary reasons businesses choose to incorporate.

The Limited Liability Corporation (LLC)

The *limited liability corporation (LLC)* is a hybrid entity that has the legal protections of a corporation and the ability to be taxed (one time) as a partnership. A company can form an LLC for any lawful business as long as the nature of the business is not banking, insurance, and certain professional service operations. By simply filing articles of organization with the respective state agency, an LLC takes on a separate identity similar to a corporation, but without the tax problems of the corporation. Figure B1.2 summarizes the primary differences between the three most common business structures.

FIGURE B1.1

Reasons Businesses Choose to Incorporate.

	Reasons Businesses Choose to Incorporate
Limited liability	In most instances, financial losses or judgments against the corporation are limited to the assets owned by the corporation.
Unlimited life	Unlike sole proprietorships and partnerships, the life of the corporation is not dependent on the life of a particular individual or individuals. It can continue indefinitely until it accomplishes its objective, merges with another business, or goes bankrupt. Unless stated otherwise, it could go on indefinitely.
Transferability of shares	It is easy to sell, transfer, or give the ownership interest in a corporation to another person. The process of divesting sole proprietorships or partnerships can be cumbersome and costly. Property has to be re-titled, new deeds drawn, and other administrative steps taken any time the slightest change of ownership occurs. With a corporation, all of the individual owners' rights and privileges are represented by the shares of stock they own. Corporations can quickly transfer ownership by simply having the shareholders endorse the back of each stock certificate to another party.
Ability to raise investment capital	It is easy to attract new investors into a corporate entity because of limited liability and the easy transferability of ownership.

	Sole Proprietorship	Partnership	Corporation
Licensing	Local license, $25–$100	Partnership agreement, legal fees	Articles of incorporation through the Secretary of State
Income	Business flows directly into personal income	Distributions taken by partners, as agreed by partners	Business and personal earnings separate, depending on corporate structure
Liability	Owner is liable	Owners are liable	Only business is liable

FIGURE B1.2

Comparison of Business Structures.

Internal Operations of a Corporation

The majority of corporations use different specialized departments to perform the unique operations required to run the business. These departments commonly include accounting, finance, human resources, sales, marketing, operations/production, and management information systems (see Figure B1.3).

LO 2 List and describe the seven departments commonly found in most organizations.

Accounting

The *accounting department* provides quantitative information about the finances of the business including recording, measuring, and describing financial information. People tend to use the terms *accounting* and *bookkeeping* synonymously; however, the two are different. *Bookkeeping* is the actual recording of the business's transactions, without any analysis of the information. *Accounting* analyzes the transactional information of the business so the owners and investors can make sound economic decisions.

The two primary types of accounting are financial and managerial. *Financial accounting* involves preparing financial reports that provide information about the business's performance to external parties such as investors, creditors, and tax authorities. Financial accounting must follow strict guidelines known as Generally Accepted Accounting Principles (GAAP). *Managerial accounting* involves analyzing business operations for internal decision making and does not have to follow any rules issued by standard-setting bodies such as GAAP.

FINANCIAL STATEMENTS

All businesses operate using the same basic element, the transaction. A *transaction* is an exchange or transfer of goods, services, or funds involving two or more people. Each time a transaction occurs a source document captures all of the key data involved with the transaction. The source document describes the basic transaction data such as its date, purpose, and amount and includes cash receipts, canceled checks, invoices, customer refunds, employee

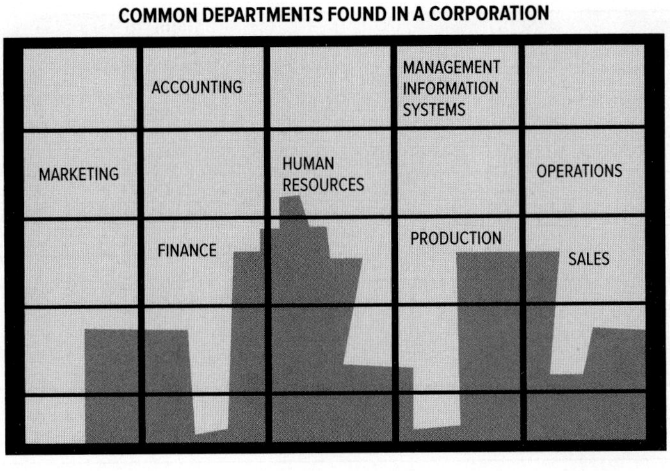

COMMON DEPARTMENTS FOUND IN A CORPORATION

FIGURE B1.3

Departmental Structure of a Typical Organization.

time sheet, etc. The source document is the beginning step in the accounting process and serves as evidence that the transaction occurred. *Financial statements* are the written records of the financial status of the business that allow interested parties to evaluate the profitability and solvency of the business. *Solvency* represents the ability of the business to pay its bills and service its debt. The financial statements are the final product of the accountant's analysis of the business transactions. Preparing the financial statements is a major undertaking and requires a significant amount of effort. Financial statements must be understandable, timely, relevant, fair, and objective in order to be useful. The four primary financial statements include:

- Balance sheet.
- Income statement.
- Statement of owner's equity.
- Statement of cash flows.

Balance Sheet

The *balance sheet* gives an accounting picture of property owned by a company and of claims against the property on a specific date. The balance sheet is based on the fundamental accounting principle that assets = liabilities + owner's equity. An *asset* is anything owned that has value or earning power. A *liability* is an obligation to make financial payments. *Owner's equity* is the portion of a company belonging to the owners. The left (debit) side of a balance sheet states assets. The right (credit) side shows liabilities and owners' equity. The two sides must be equal (balance). The balance sheet is like a snapshot of the position of an individual or business at one point in time (see Figure B1.4).

Income Statement

The *income statement* (also referred to as earnings report, operating statement, and profit-and-loss (P&L) statement) reports operating results (revenues minus expenses) for a given time period ending at a specified date. *Revenue* refers to the amount earned resulting from the delivery or manufacture of a product or from the rendering of a service. Revenue can include sales from a product or an amount received for performing a service. *Expenses* refer to the costs incurred in operating and maintaining a business. The income statement reports a company's *net income*, or the amount of money remaining after paying taxes (see Figure B1.5).

Statement of Owner's Equity

The *statement of owner's equity* (also called the statement of retained earnings or equity statement) tracks and communicates changes in the shareholder's earnings. Profitable organizations typically pay the shareholders dividends. *Dividends* are a distribution of earnings to shareholders.

FIGURE B1.4

Balance Sheet Example.

ASSETS		LIABILITIES	
Current Assets		**Current Liabilities**	
Cash	$ 250,000	Accounts Payable	$ 150,000
Securities	$ 30,000	Loans (due < 1 year)	$ 750,000
Accounts Receivable	$ 1,500,000	Taxes	$ 200,000
Inventory	$ 2,920,000		
		Long-term Liabilities	
Fixed Assets	$ 7,500,000	Loans (due > 1 year)	$ 2,500,000
		Total Liabilities	$ 3,600,000
		Owner's Equity	$ 8,600,000
Total Assets	$12,200,000	**Total Liabilities + Owner's Equity**	$12,200,000

ASSETS = LIABILITIES + OWNER'S EQUITY

Statement of Cash Flows

Cash flow represents the money an investment produces after subtracting cash expenses from income. The **statement of cash flows** summarizes sources and uses of cash, indicates whether enough cash is available to carry on routine operations, and offers an analysis of all business transactions, reporting where the firm obtained its cash and how it chose to allocate the cash. The cash flow statement shows where money comes from, how the company is going to spend it, and when the company will require additional cash. Companies typically project cash flow statements on a monthly basis for the current year and a quarterly basis for the next two to five years. A **financial quarter** indicates a three-month period (four quarters per year). Cash flow statements become less valid over time since numerous assumptions are required to project into the future.

When it comes to decreasing expenses and managing a company's cash flow, managers need to look at all costs. Ben Worthen, executive vice president and CIO of Manufacturers Bank in Los Angeles, states that everyone notices the million-dollar negotiation; however, a couple of thousand dollars here and there are just as important. When attempting to cut costs, Worthen listed every contract the bank had. He saved $5,000 by renegotiating a contract with the vendor who watered the plants, a vendor that most employees did not even know existed. He also saved $50,000 by renegotiating the contract with the bank's cleaning agency. "You need to think of everything when cutting costs," Worthen said. "$5,000 buys three or four laptops for salespersons."

Income Statement	
Revenue (Sales)	$60,000,000
Cost of Goods Sold	$30,000,000
Gross Profit (Sales – Cost of Goods Sold)	$30,000,000
Operating Expenses	$7,000,000
Profit Before Taxes (Gross Profit – Operating Expenses)	$23,000,000
Taxes	$18,000,000
Net Profit (or Loss)	**$5,000,000**

FIGURE B1.5

Income Statement Example.

Finance

Finance deals with the strategic financial issues associated with increasing the value of the business while observing applicable laws and social responsibilities. Financial decisions include such things as:

- How the company should raise and spend its capital.
- Where the company should invest its money.
- What portion of profits will be paid to shareholders in the form of dividends.
- Whether the company should merge with or acquire another business.

Financial decisions are short term (usually up to one year), medium term (one to seven years), or long term (more than seven years). The typical forms of financing include loans (debt or equity) or grants. Financing may be required for immediate use in business operations or for an investment.

FINANCIAL ANALYSIS

Different financial ratios are used to evaluate a company's performance. Companies can gain additional insight into their performance by comparing financial ratios against other companies in their industry. A few of the more common financial ratios include:

- **Internal rate of return (IRR)**—the rate at which the net present value of an investment equals zero.
- **Return on investment (ROI)**—indicates the earning power of a project and is measured by dividing the benefits of a project by the investment.
- **Cash flow analysis**—a means to conduct a periodic check on the company's financial health. A projected cash flow statement estimates what the stream of money will be in coming months or years, based on a history of sales and expenses. A monthly cash flow statement reveals the current state of affairs. The ability to perform a cash flow analysis is an essential skill for every business owner; it can be the difference between being able to open a business and being able to stay in business.

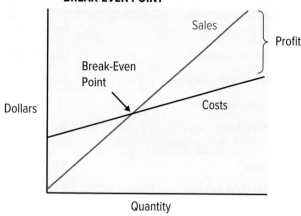

BREAK-EVEN POINT

Dollars

Sales

Profit

Break-Even
Point

Costs

Quantity

FIGURE B1.6

Break-Even Analysis.

- **Break-even analysis**—a way to determine the volume of business required to make a profit at the current prices charged for the products or services. For example, if a promotional mailing costs $1,000 and each item generates $50 in revenue, the company must generate 20 sales to break even and cover the cost of the mailing. The ***break-even point*** is the point at which revenues equal costs. The point is located by performing a break-even analysis. All sales over the break-even point produce profits; any drop in sales below that point will produce losses (see Figure B1.6).

Human Resources

Human resources (HR) includes the policies, plans, and procedures for the effective management of employees (human resources). HR typically focuses on the following:

- Employee recruitment.
- Employee selection.
- Employee training and development.
- Employee appraisals, evaluations, and rewards.
- Employee communications.

The primary goal of HR is to instill employee commitment by creating an environment of shared values, innovation, flexibility, and empowerment. Most organizations recognize that focusing on strong HR practices that foster employee growth and satisfaction can significantly contribute to achieving business success. The most obvious way HR practices create business success is through quality employee selection. Hiring the right employee who suits the company's culture is difficult. Organizations create employee value by implementing employment practices such as training, skill development, and rewards. An organization that focuses on HR creates valuable employees with strategic business competencies.

MANAGEMENT TECHNIQUES

There may be no such thing as a best practice for managing people. Numerous management techniques are used by all different types of managers in a variety of industries. For example, Sears and Nordstrom are legends in the retailing industry; however, their approaches to HR are completely different. Sears is one of the pioneering companies in the science of employee selection, relying on some of the most sophisticated selection tests in American industry. Sears employees receive extensive training in company practices; management tracks employee attitudes and morale through frequent and rigorous employee surveys. The company provides its sales representatives, who work on salary rather than commission, with intensive training in Sears products, the company's operating systems, and sales techniques.

Nordstrom operates with virtually no formal personnel practices. Its hiring is decentralized, using no formal selection tests. Managers look for applicants with experience in customer contact, but the main desirable quality appears to be pleasant personalities and motivation. The company has only one rule in its personnel handbook: "Use your best judgment at all times." Individual salesclerks virtually run their areas as private stores. Nordstrom maintains a continuous stream of programs to motivate employees to provide intensive service, but it offers very little training. Its commission-based payroll system makes it possible for salesclerks to earn sizable incomes. Nordstrom sales personnel are ranked within each department according to their monthly sales; the most successful are promoted (almost all managers are promoted from within the company) and the least successful are terminated.

Sears and Nordstrom are both highly successful retailers, yet they operate using widely different recruitment policies. One of the biggest success factors for any business is the company's management and personnel. Employees must possess certain critical skills for the company to succeed. The HR department takes on the important task of hiring, training, evaluating, rewarding, and terminating employees. Effective HR goes far beyond executing a standard set of policies and procedures; it requires questioning and understanding the relationships between choices in managing people, the strategies and goals of the organization, and the possibilities presented by the external environment. Today's competitive environment features rapid technological change, increasingly global markets, and a diverse workforce comprising not just men and women with different sorts of career objectives, but also potential workers from diverse cultural and ethnic backgrounds. HR must ensure that the choices made in managing people are made sensibly and with clear purposes in mind.

Sales

Sales is the function of selling a good or service and focuses on increasing customer sales, which increases company revenues. A salesperson has the main activity of selling a product or service. Many industries require a license before a salesperson can sell the products, such as real estate, insurance, and securities.

A common view of the sales department is to see the salespersons only concerned with making the sale now, without any regard to the cost of the sale to the business. This is called the hard sell, where the salesperson heavily pushes a product (even when the customer does not want the product) and where price cuts are given even if they cause financial losses for the company. A broader view of the sales department sees it as taking on the task of building strong customer relationships where the primary emphasis is on securing new customers and keeping current customers satisfied. Many sales departments are currently focusing on building strong customer relationships.

THE SALES PROCESS

Figure B1.7 depicts the typical sales process, which begins with an opportunity and ends with billing the customer for the sale. An opportunity is a name of a potential customer who might be interested in making a purchase (opportunities are also called *leads*). The company finds opportunities from a variety of sources such as mailing lists and customer inquiries. The name is sent to a salesperson who contacts the potential customer and sets up a meeting to discuss the products. During the meeting, all problems and issues are identified and resolved, and the salesperson generates a quote for the customer. If the customer decides to accept the quote, a sales order is placed. The company fulfills the order and delivers the product, and the process ends when the customer is billed.

MARKET SHARE

Sales figures offer a good indication of how well a company is performing. For example, high sales volumes typically indicate that a company is performing well. However, they do not always indicate how a firm is performing relative to its competitors. For example, changes in sales might simply reflect shifts in market size or in economic conditions. A sales increase might occur because the market increased in size, not because the company is performing better.

Measuring the proportion of the market that a firm captures is one way to measure a firm's performance relative to its competitors. This proportion is the firm's market share and is calculated by dividing the firm's sales by the total market sales for the entire industry. For example, if a firm's total sales (revenues) were $2 million and the sales for the entire industry were $10 million, the firm would have captured 20 percent of the total market, or have a 20 percent market share.

Many video game products launch with great enthusiasm and die a quick death such as Sega's GameGear and DreamCast, Atari's Lynx, and Nintendo's Virtual Boy. Video game consoles die quickly when only a limited number of game publishers sign up to supply games for the particular product. Producing video game products is a tough competitive business in a finicky market.

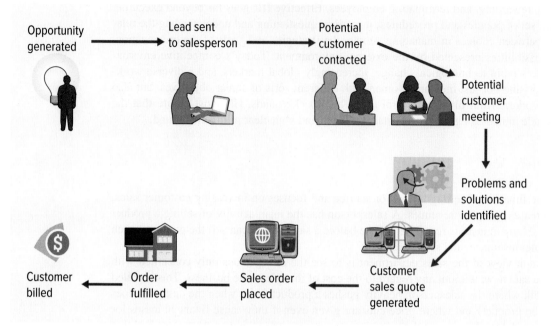

Sales Process

Opportunity generated → Lead sent to salesperson → Potential customer contacted → Potential customer meeting → Problems and solutions identified

Customer billed ← Order fulfilled ← Sales order placed ← Customer sales quote generated

FIGURE B1.7

The Sales Process.

Reasons to Increase Market Share

Many organizations seek to increase their market share because many individuals associate market share with profitability. Figure B1.8 indicates the primary reasons organizations seek to increase their market share.

Ways to Increase Market Share

A primary way to increase market share is by changing one of the following variables: product, price, place, or promotion (see Figure B1.9). It is common to refer to these four variables as the marketing mix, discussed in detail below.

FIGURE B1.8

Reasons to Increase Market Share.

Reasons to Increase Market Share
Economies of scale—An organization can develop a cost advantage by selling additional products or higher volumes.
Sales growth in a stagnant industry—If an industry stops growing, an organization can increase its sales by increasing its market share.
Reputation—A successful organization with a solid reputation can use its clout to its advantage.
Increased bargaining power—Larger organizations have an advantage in negotiating with suppliers and distributors.

FIGURE B1.9

Ways to Increase Market Share.

Ways to Increase Market Share
Product—An organization can change product attributes to provide more value to the customer. Improving product quality is one example.
Price—An organization can decrease a product's price to increase sales. This strategy will not work if competitors are willing to match discounts.
Place (Distribution)—An organization can add new distribution channels. This allows the organization to increase the size of its market, which should increase sales.
Promotion—An organization can increase spending on product advertising, which should increase sales. This strategy will not work if competitors also increase advertising.

Reasons Not to Increase Market Share
If an organization is near its production capacity and it experiences an increase in market share, it could cause the organization's supply to fall below its demand. Not being able to deliver products to meet demand could damage the organization's reputation.
Profits could decrease if an organization gains market share by offering deep discounts or by increasing the amount of money it spends on advertising.
If the organization is not prepared to handle the new growth, it could begin to offer shoddy products or less attentive customer service. This could result in the loss of its professional reputation and valuable customers.

Reasons Not to Increase Market Share

Surprisingly, it is not always a good idea to increase an organization's market share. Figure B1.10 offers a few reasons increasing an organization's market share can actually decrease an organization's revenues.

Marketing

Marketing is the process associated with promoting the sale of goods or services. The marketing department supports the sales department by creating promotions that help sell the company's products. *Marketing communications* seek to build product or service awareness and to educate potential consumers on the product or service.

Jenny Ming, president of Old Navy, a division of Gap Inc., believes that unique marketing ideas for Old Navy's original designs heavily contributed to the success of the $6.5 billion brand. Ideas come from anywhere, and Ming found one of the company's most successful products when she was dropping her daughter off at school. It was pajama day at school, and all of the girls were wearing pajama bottoms with a tank top. Ming began wondering why they even created and sold pajama tops; nobody seemed to wear them. The company, having problems selling pajama sets, quickly introduced "just bottoms," a line of pajama bottoms selling at $15. A full pajama set cost $25. Along with the bottoms, the company offered tank tops in different colors so the customer could mix and match the items. The company built a huge business from the "just bottoms" line. Ming encourages her staff to look for marketing and product opportunities everywhere, even in the most unlikely of places.

MARKETING MIX

The classic components of marketing include the four Ps in the marketing mix: product, price, place, and promotion. The *marketing mix* includes the variables that marketing managers can control in order to best satisfy customers in the target market (see Figure B1.11). The organization attempts to generate a positive response in the target market by blending these four marketing mix variables in an optimal manner.

Figure B1.12 summarizes the primary attributes involved with each decision made in the marketing mix.

CUSTOMER SEGMENTATION

Market segmentation is the division of a market into similar groups of customers. It is not always optimal for an organization to offer the same marketing mix to vastly different customers. Market segmentation makes it possible for organizations to tailor the marketing mix for specific target markets, hence better satisfying its customer needs. Not all attributes of the marketing mix need to be changed for each market segment. For example, one market segment might require a discounted price, while another market segment might require better customer service. An organization uses marketing research, market trends,

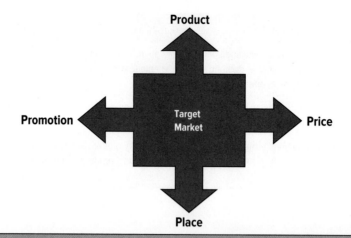

1. **Product**—the physical product or service offered to the consumer. Product decisions include function, appearance, packaging, service, warranty, etc.

2. **Price**—takes into account profit margins and competitor pricing. Pricing includes list price, discounts, financing, and other options such as leasing.

3. **Place** (distribution)—associated with channels of distribution that serve as the means for getting the product to the target customers. Attributes involved in place decisions include market coverage, channel member selection, logistics, and levels of service.

4. **Promotion**—related to communication to and selling to potential consumers. An organization can perform a break-even analysis when making promotion decisions. If an organization knows the value of each customer, it can determine whether additional customers are worth the cost of acquisition. Attributes involved in promotion decisions involve advertising, public relations, media types, etc.

FIGURE B1.12

Common Attributes Involved with Each P in the Marketing Mix.

Product	Price	Place (Distribution)	Promotion
Quality	Discount	Channel	Advertising
Brand	Financing	Market	Sales
Appearance	Lease	Location	Public relations
Package		Logistics	Marketing Message
Function		Service Level	Media Type
Warranty			Budget
Service/Support			

and managerial judgment when deciding the optimal way to segment a market. Market segmentation typically includes:

- **Geographic segmentation**—based on regional variables such as region, climate, population density, and population growth rate.
- **Demographic segmentation**—based on variables such as age, gender, ethnicity, education, occupation, income, and family status.
- **Psychographic segmentation**—based on variables such as values, attitudes, and lifestyles.
- **Behavioral segmentation**—based on variables such as usage rate, usage patterns, price sensitivity, and brand loyalty.

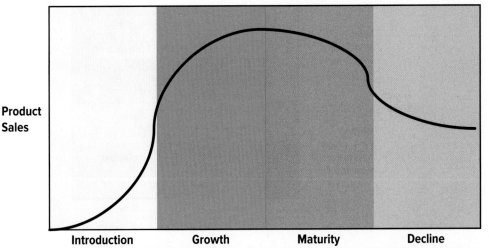

Product Sales

Introduction	Growth	Maturity	Decline

- **Introduction Stage**—The organization seeks to build product awareness and develop the product's market. The organization will use the marketing mix to help impact the target market. Product branding and quality level are established.

- **Growth Stage**—The organization seeks to build brand preference and increase market share. The organization maintains or increases the quality of the product and might add additional features or better customer service. The organization typically enjoys increases in demand with little competition allowing the price to remain constant.

- **Maturity Stage**—The strong growth in sales diminishes. Competition begins to appear with similar products. The primary objective at this point is to defend market share while maximizing profits. Some companies enhance product features to differentiate the product in the market.

- **Decline Stage**—Sales begin to decline. At this point, the organization has several options. It can maintain the product, possibly rejuvenating it by adding new features and finding new uses. It can reduce costs and continue to offer it, possibly to a loyal niche segment. It can discontinue the product, liquidating remaining inventory or selling it to another firm that is willing to continue the product.

THE PRODUCT LIFE CYCLE

The *product life cycle* includes the four phases a product progresses through during its life cycle including introduction, growth, maturity, and decline. An organization's marketing of a product will change depending on its stage in the product life cycle. An organization can plot a product's profits as a function of the product life cycle (see Figure B1.13).

Operations/Production

Operations management (also called production management) is the management of systems or processes that convert or transform resources (including human resources) into goods and services. The operations department oversees the transformation of input resources (i.e., labor, materials, and machines) into output resources (i.e., products and services). The operations department is critical because it manages the physical processes by which companies take in raw materials, convert them into products, and distribute them to customers. The operations department generally ranks high in the responsibilities of general management.

TRANSFORMING CORPORATIONS

Complete transformation of an organization, or an entire industry, is the ultimate goal of successful business process reengineering. Figure B1.14 displays a matrix that has project scope on one axis and project speed on the other. For a project with a relatively narrow scope where

Organizational
Transformation through BPR.

the speed is fast, reengineering occurs. Fast speed with broad scope may be a turnaround situation requiring downsizing and tough decision making. A project with a relatively slow speed and narrow scope results in continuous improvement. In the upper right-hand corner of Figure B1.14, where the project scope is broad and the time frame for achieving that change is longer, the term *transformation* is appropriate.

Progressive Insurance offers a great example of a corporation that transformed its entire industry by reengineering the insurance claims process. Progressive Insurance has seen phenomenal growth in an otherwise staid auto insurance market. Progressive's growth came not through acquisitions or mergers—the stuff that puts CEOs on the front page of *The Wall Street Journal*—but through substantial innovations in everyday operations. Progressive reengineered the insurance claim process. When a customer has an auto accident, Progressive representatives are on hand 24 hours a day to take the call and schedule a claims adjustor. The claims adjustor works out of a mobile van, enabling a nine-hour turnaround rather than the industry standard of 10 to 17 days. The Progressive adjustor prepares an estimate on the spot and will, in most cases, write the customer a check immediately and even offer a ride home.

What provoked this innovation? Progressive says it was the strong connection it has to its customers, its willingness to listen to customers' frustrations, and the common sense to act on those frustrations by changing the core of its business operations. As a result of customer feedback, the company did not merely tweak the details of the claims adjustment process. It dramatically rewrote the process, resulting in significant cost savings for the company. More important, however, the hassle-free claims process keeps customers happy and loyal, reducing the significant burden of constantly replacing lapsed customers with new ones.

Management Information Systems

Management information systems is a business function just as marketing, finance, operations, and human resources management are business functions. Formally defined, management information systems (MIS) is a general name for the business function and academic discipline covering the application of people, technologies, and procedures—collectively called information systems—to solve business problems. Other names for MIS include information services (IS), management information services (MIS), or managed service provider (MSP). In business, MIS supports business processes and operations, decision making, and competitive strategies. MIS involves collecting, recording, storing, and basic processing of information including:

- Accounting records such as sales, purchase, investment, and payroll information, processed into financial statements such as income statements, balance sheets, ledgers, management reports, and so on.

- Operations records such as inventory, work-in-process, equipment repair and maintenance, supply chain, and other production/operations information, processed into production schedules, production controllers, inventory systems, and production monitoring systems.

- Human resources records such as personnel, salary, and employment history information, processed into employee expense reports and performance-based reports.

- Marketing records such as customer profiles, customer purchase histories, marketing research, advertising, and other marketing information, processed into advertising reports, marketing plans, and sales activity reports.

- Strategic records such as business intelligence, competitor analysis, industry analysis, corporate objectives, and other strategic information, processed into industry trends reports, market share reports, mission statements, and portfolio models.

The bottom line is that management information systems must incorporate all aspects of the business to implement, control, and monitor plans, strategies, tactics, new products, new business models, or new business ventures.

The study of business begins with understanding the different types of businesses including a sole proprietorship, partnership, or a corporation. Figure B1.15 highlights seven departments found in a typical business.

All of these departments must be able to execute activities specific to their business function and also be able to work with the other departments to create synergies throughout the entire business.

- **Accounting** provides quantitative information about the finances of the business including recording, measuring, and describing financial information.

- **Finance** deals with the strategic financial issues associated with increasing the value of the business, while observing applicable laws and social responsibilities.

- **Human resources (HR)** includes the policies, plans, and procedures for the effective management of employees (human resources).

- **Sales** is the function of selling a good or service and focuses on increasing customer sales, which increases company revenues.

- **Marketing** is the process associated with promoting the sale of goods or services. The marketing department supports the sales department by creating promotions that help sell the company's products.

- **Operations management** (also called **production management**) is the management of systems or processes that convert or transform resources (including human resources) into goods and services.

- **Management information systems (MIS)** is a general name for the business function and academic discipline covering the application of people, technologies, and procedures—collectively called information systems—to solve business problems.

FIGURE B1.15

Common Departments in a Business.

✱ KEY TERMS

1. **Setting Up a Business**

   Your friend, Olivia Graves, is going to start her own chocolate shop, called Chocolate-By-Design. Olivia is an expert candy maker and one of the city's top pastry chefs. Olivia has come to you for advice on what type of business Chocolate-By-Design should be—a sole proprietorship, partnership, or corporation. Create a report comparing the three different types of businesses, along with your recommendation for Chocolate-By-Design's business structure.

2. **Guest Lecturing on Business**

   As a recent college graduate, your favorite professor, Dr. Henning, has asked you to come back and guest lecture at his introduction to business course. Create a presentation defining the different departments in a typical business, what roles each play, and why it is important that they all work together.

3. **Expanding Markets**

   J. R. Cash created a small business selling handmade cowboy boots, and within a year his business is booming. J. R. currently builds all of the boots in his store and takes orders over the phone and from walk-in customers. There is currently a three-month waiting list for boots. J. R. is not sure how to grow his business and has come to you for advice. Describe the reasons and ways some businesses increase market share and why J. R. might choose not to increase his market share.

4. **Segmenting Customers**

   Due to your vast marketing experience, you have been hired by a new company, Sugar, to perform a strategic analysis on chewing gum. The company wants to understand the many market segments for the different brands, flavors, sizes, and colors of gum. Create an analysis of the different market segments for chewing gum. What market segment would you recommend Sugar pursue?

5. **Product Life Cycle**

   An associate, Carl Deadmarsh, has developed a new brand of laundry detergent called Clean. Carl wants your opinion on his potential to enter and dominate the laundry detergent market. Using the product life cycle create a recommendation for Carl's new product.

6. **Redesigning a Business**

   Tom Walton is the new CEO for Lakeside, a large cereal manufacturing company. Tom's predecessor had run the company for 50 years and did little in terms of process improvement; in fact, his motto was "if it isn't broke, why fix it?" Tom wants to take advantage of technology to create new processes for the entire company. He believes that improving operations will increase efficiency and lower costs.

   Tom has a major hurdle to overcome before he can begin revamping the company—its employees. Many of the employees have worked at the company for decades and are comfortable with the motto "if it isn't broke, why fix it?" Develop a plan Tom can use to communicate to his employees the potential value gained from business process reengineering.

PLUG-IN

B2 Business Process

LEARNING OUTCOMES

1. Describe business processes and their importance to an organization.
2. Compare the continuous process improvement model and business process reengineering.
3. Describe the importance of business process modeling (or mapping) and business process models.
4. Explain business process management along with the reason for its importance to an organization.

LO 1 Describe business processes and their importance to an organization.

Introduction

The benefits of business process improvement vary, but a rough rule of thumb is that it will, at a minimum, double the gains of a project by streamlining outdated practices, enhancing efficiency, promoting compliance and standardization, and making an organization more agile. Business process improvement involves three key steps:

1. Measure what matters to most customers.
2. Monitor the performance of key business processes.
3. Assign accountability for process improvement.

Comprehensive business process management systems help organizations model and define complete business processes, implement those processes integrated with existing systems, and provide business leaders with the ability to analyze, manage, and improve the execution of processes in real time.

Examining Business Processes

Waiting in line at a grocery store is a great example of the need for process improvement. In this case, the "process" is called checkout, and the purpose is to pay for and bag groceries. The process begins when a customer steps into line and ends when the customer receives the receipt and leaves the store. The *process* steps are the activities the customer and store personnel do to complete the transaction. A ***business process*** is a standardized set of activities that accomplish a specific task, such as processing a customer's order. Business processes transform a set of inputs into a set of outputs (goods or services) for another person or process by using people and tools. This simple example describes a customer checkout process. Imagine other business processes: developing new products, building a new home, ordering clothes from mail-order companies, requesting new telephone service from a telephone company, administering Social Security payments, and so on.

Examining business processes helps an organization determine bottlenecks and identify outdated, duplicate, and smoothly running processes. To stay competitive, organizations must optimize and automate their business processes. To identify which business processes need to be optimized, the organization must clearly understand its business processes, which typically have the following important characteristics:

- The processes have internal and external users.

- A process is cross-departmental. Departments are functional towers of expertise, but processes cut across departments.

- The processes occur across organizations.

- The processes are based on how work is done in the organization.

- Every process should be documented and fully understood by everyone participating in the process.

- Processes should be modeled to promote complete understanding.

A business process can be viewed as a "value chain." By contributing to the creation or delivery of a product or service, each step in a process should add value to the preceding step. For example, one step in the product development process consists of conducting market acceptance tests. This step adds value by ensuring that the product meets the needs of the market before the product or service is finalized. A tremendous amount of learning and improvement can result from the documentation and examination of the input-output linkages. However, between every input and every output is a process. Knowledge and improvement can only be completed by peeling the layers of the onion and examining the processes through which inputs are converted into outputs. Figure B2.1 displays several sample business processes.

Organizations are only as effective as their business processes. Developing logical business processes can help an organization achieve its goals. For example, an automobile manufacturer might have a goal to reduce the time it takes to deliver a car to a customer. The automobile manufacturer cannot hope to meet this goal with an inefficient ordering process or a convoluted distribution process. Sales representatives might be making mistakes when completing order forms, data-entry clerks might not accurately code order information, and dock crews might be inefficiently loading cars onto trucks. All of these errors increase the time it will take to get the car to the customer. Improving any one of these business processes can have a significant effect on the total distribution process, made up of the order entry, production scheduling, and transportation processes.

FIGURE B2.1

Sample Business Processes.

Sample Business Processes	
ACCOUNTING BUSINESS PROCESSES	
- Accounts payable	- Check signing authority
- Accounts receivable	- Depreciation
- Bad/NSF checks	- Invoice billings
- Bank account reconciliation	- Petty cash
- Cash receipts	- Month-end closing procedures
- Check requests	
CUSTOMER SERVICE BUSINESS PROCESSES	
- Customer satisfaction survey	- Postsale customer follow-up
- Customer service contact/complaint handling	- Warranty and service policies
- Guarantee customer service satisfaction	

ENVIRONMENTAL BUSINESS PROCESSES

- Environmental protection
- Hazardous waste management
- Air/water/soil resource management

FINANCE BUSINESS PROCESSES

- Account collection
- Bank loan applications
- Banking policy and relations
- Business plans and forecasts
- Customer credit approval and credit terms
- Exercise of incentive stock options
- Property tax assessments
- Release of financial or confidential information
- Stock transactions
- Weekly financial and six-week cash flow reports

HUMAN RESOURCES BUSINESS PROCESSES

- Board of directors and shareholders meetings, minutes, and protocol
- Disabilities employment policies
- Drug-free workplace employment policies
- Employee hiring policies
- Employee orientation
- Family and Medical Leave Act
- Files and records management
- Health care benefits
- Paid and unpaid time off
- Pay and payroll matters
- Performance appraisals and salary adjustments
- Resignations and terminations
- Sexual harassment policies
- Training/tuition reimbursement
- Travel and entertainment
- Workplace rules and guidelines
- Workplace safety

MANAGEMENT INFORMATION SYSTEMS BUSINESS PROCESSES

- Disaster recovery procedures
- Backup/recovery procedures
- Service agreements, emergency services, and community resources
- Emergency notification procedures
- Office and department recovery
- User workstation standards
- Use of personal software
- Computer security incident reporting
- Control of computer virus programs
- Computer user/staff training plan
- Internet use policy
- Email policy
- Computer support center

MANUFACTURING BUSINESS PROCESSES

- Assembly manuals
- Bill of materials
- Calibration for testing and measuring equipment
- FDA inspections
- Manufacturing change orders
- Master parts list and files
- Serial number designation
- Quality control for finished goods
- Quality assurance audit procedure

SALES AND MARKETING BUSINESS PROCESSES

- Collection of sales tax
- Copyrights and trademarks
- Marketing plans model number
- Designation public relations
- Return of goods from customers
- Sales leads
- Sales order entry
- Sales training
- Trade shows

SHIPPING, PURCHASING, AND INVENTORY CONTROL BUSINESS PROCESSES

- Packing, storage, and distribution
- Physical inventory procedures
- Purchasing procedures
- Receiving, inspection, and stocking of parts and materials
- Shipping and freight claims
- Vendor selection, files, and inspections

Business Process Improvement

Improving business processes is paramount for businesses to stay competitive in today's marketplace. Over the past 10 to 15 years, companies have been forced to improve their business processes because customers are demanding better products and services; if they do not receive what they want from one supplier, they have many others to choose from (hence the competitive issue for businesses). Figure B2.2 displays several opportunities for business process improvement.

Many organizations began business process improvement with a continuous improvement model. A *continuous process improvement model* attempts to understand and measure the current process, and make performance improvements accordingly. Figure B2.3 illustrates the basic steps for continuous process improvement. Organizations begin by documenting what they do today, establish some way to measure the process based on what customers want, perform the process, measure the results, and then identify improvement opportunities based on the collected information. The next step is to implement process improvements, and then measure the performance of the new process. This loop repeats over and over again and is called continuous process improvement. It might also be called business process improvement or functional process improvement.

This method for improving business processes is effective to obtain gradual, incremental improvement. However, several factors have accelerated the need to improve business processes. The most obvious is technology. New technologies (like the Internet and wireless) rapidly bring new capabilities to businesses, thereby raising the competitive bar and the need to improve business processes dramatically.

Another apparent trend is the opening of world markets and increased free trade. Such changes bring more companies into the marketplace, adding to the competition. In today's marketplace, major changes are required just to stay in the game. As a result, companies have requested methods for faster business process improvement. Also, companies want breakthrough performance changes, not just incremental changes, and they want this now. Because the rate of change has increased for everyone, few businesses can afford a slow change process. One approach for rapid change and dramatic improvement is business process reengineering (BPR).

Business Process Improvement Examples
Eliminate duplicate activities
Combine related activities
Eliminate multiple reviews and approvals
Eliminate inspections
Simplify processes
Reduce batch sizes
Process in parallel
Implement demand pull
Outsource inefficient activities
Eliminate movement of work
Organize multifunctional teams
Design cellular workplaces
Centralize/decentralize

FIGURE B2.2

Opportunities for Business Process Improvement.

BUSINESS PROCESS REENGINEERING (BPR)

An organization must continuously revise and reexamine its decisions, goals, and targets to improve its performance. A bank may have many activities, such as investing, credit cards, loans, and so on, and it may be involved in cross-selling (e.g., insurance) with other preferred vendors in the market. If the credit card department is not functioning in an efficient manner, the bank might reengineer the credit card business process. This activity, **business process reengineering (BPR),** is the analysis and redesign of workflow within and between enterprises. BPR relies on a different school of thought than continuous process improvement. *In the extreme,* BPR assumes the current process is irrelevant, does not work, or is broken and must be overhauled from scratch. Such a clean slate enables business process designers to disassociate themselves from today's process and focus on a new process. It is like the designers projecting themselves into the future and asking: What should the process look like? What do customers want it to look like? What do other employees want it to look like? How do best-in-class companies do it? How can new technology facilitate the process?

Figure B2.4 displays the basic steps in a business process reengineering effort. It begins with defining the scope and objectives of the reengineering project, then goes through a learning process (with customers, employees, competitors, noncompetitors, and new technology).

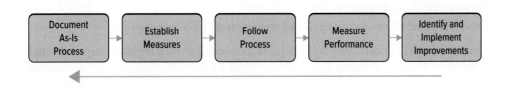

FIGURE B2.3

Continuous Process Improvement Model.

FIGURE B2.5

Managerial Approach to
Reengineering Projects.

Managerial Approach to Reengineering Projects
1. **Define the scope.** Define functional objectives; determine the management strategy to be followed in streamlining and standardizing processes; and establish the process, data, and information systems baselines from which to begin process improvement.
2. **Analyze.** Analyze business processes to eliminate non-value-added processes; simplify and streamline processes of little value; and identify more effective and efficient alternatives to the process, data, and system baselines.
3. **Evaluate.** Conduct a preliminary, functional, economic analysis to evaluate alternatives to baseline processes and select a preferred course of action.
4. **Plan.** Develop detailed statements of requirements, baseline impacts, costs, benefits, and schedules to implement the planned course of action.
5. **Approve.** Finalize the functional economic analysis using information from the planning data, and present to senior management for approval to proceed with the proposed process improvements and any associated data or system changes.
6. **Execute.** Execute the approved process and data changes, and provide functional management oversight of any associated information system changes.

Given this knowledge base, the designers can create a vision for the future and design new business processes by creating a plan of action based on the gap between current processes, technologies, and structures, and process vision. It is then a matter of implementing the chosen solution. The Department of Defense (DoD) is an expert at reengineering business processes. Figure B2.5 highlights the Department of Defense's best-in-class suggestions for a managerial approach to a reengineering effort.

LO 3 Describe the importance of business process modeling (or mapping) and business process models.

Business Process Design

After choosing the method of business process improvement that is appropriate for the organization, the process designers must determine the most efficient way to begin revamping the processes. To determine whether each process is appropriately structured, organizations should create a cross-functional team to build process models that display input-output relationships among process-dependent operations and departments. They should create business process models documenting a step-by-step process sequence for the activities that are required to convert inputs to outputs for the specific process.

Business process modeling (or mapping) is the activity of creating a detailed flowchart or process map of a work process, showing its inputs, tasks, and activities in a structured sequence. A *business process model* is a graphic description of a process, showing the sequence of process tasks, which is developed for a specific purpose and from a selected viewpoint. A set of one or more process models details the many functions of a system or subject area with graphics and text and its purpose is to:

- Expose process detail gradually and in a controlled manner.
- Encourage conciseness and accuracy in describing the process model.
- Focus attention on the process model interfaces.
- Provide a powerful process analysis and consistent design vocabulary.

A process model typically displays activities as boxes and uses arrows to represent data and interfaces. Process modeling usually begins with a functional process representation of

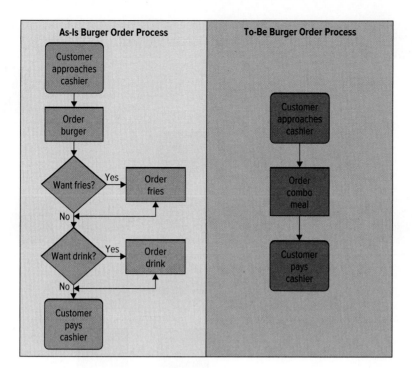

what the process problem is or an As-Is process model. ***As-Is process models*** represent the current state of the operation that has been mapped, without any specific improvements or changes to existing processes. The next step is to build a To-Be process model that displays *how* the process problem will be solved or implemented. ***To-Be process models*** show the results of applying change improvement opportunities to the current (As-Is) process model. This approach ensures that the process is fully and clearly understood before the details of a process solution are decided. The To-Be process model shows *how* the *what* is to be realized. Figure B2.6 displays the As-Is and To-Be process models for ordering a hamburger.

Analyzing As-Is business process models leads to success in business process reengineering since these diagrams are very powerful in visualizing the activities, processes, and data flow of an organization. As-Is and To-Be process models are integral in process reengineering projects. Figure B2.7 illustrates an As-Is process model of an order-filling process developed by a process modeling team representing all departments that contribute to the process. The process modeling team traces the process of converting the input (orders) through all the intervening steps until the final required output (payment) is produced. The map shows how all departments are involved as the order is processed.

It is easy to become bogged down in excessive detail when creating an As-Is process model. The objective is to aggressively eliminate, simplify, or improve the To-Be processes. Successful process improvement efforts result in positive answers to the key process design or improvement question: Is this the most efficient and effective process for accomplishing the process goals? This process modeling structure allows the team to identify all the critical interfaces, overlay the time to complete various processes, start to define the opportunities for process simulation, and identify disconnects (illogical, missing, or extraneous steps) in the processes. Figure B2.8 displays sample disconnects in the order-filling process in Figure B2.7.

The team then creates a To-Be process model, which reflects a disconnect-free order fulfillment process (see Figure B2.9). Disconnects fixed by the new process include

- Direct order entry by sales, eliminating sales administration.
- Parallel order processing and credit checking.
- Elimination of multiple order-entry and order-logging steps.

The consulting firm KPMG Peat Marwick uses process modeling as part of its business reengineering practice. Recently the firm helped a large financial services company slash

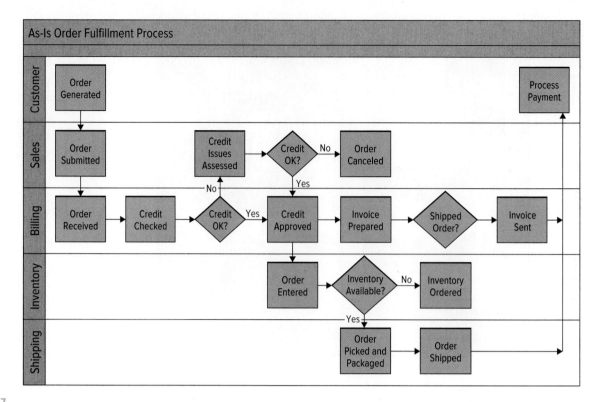

As-Is Order Fulfillment Process

FIGURE B2.7

As-Is Process Model for Order Entry.

costs and improve productivity in its Manufactured Housing Finance Division. Turnaround time for loan approval was reduced by half, using 40 percent fewer staff members.

Modeling helped the team analyze the complex aspects of the project. "In parts of the loan origination process, a lot of things happen in a short period of time," according to team leader Bob Karrick of KPMG. "During data capture, information is pulled from a number of different sources, and the person doing the risk assessment has to make judgment calls at different points throughout the process. There is often a need to stop, raise questions, make follow-up calls, and so on and then continue with the process modeling effort. Modeling allows us to do a thorough analysis that takes into account all these decision points and variables."

LO 4 Explain business process management along with the reason for its importance to an organization.

Business Process Management (BPM)

A key advantage of technology is its ability to improve business processes. Working faster and smarter has become a necessity for companies. Initial emphasis was given to areas such as production, accounting, procurement, and logistics. The next big areas to discover technology's value in business process were sales and marketing automation, customer relationship management, and supplier relationship management. Some of these processes involve several departments of the company and some are the result of real-time interaction of the company with its suppliers, customers, and other business partners. The latest area to discover the

FIGURE B2.8

Issues in the As-Is Process Model for Order Entry.

Issues in the As-Is Order Process Model
■ Sales representatives take too long to submit orders.
■ There are too many process steps.
■ Sales administration slows down the process by batch-processing orders.
■ Credit checking is performed for both old and new customers.
■ Credit checking holds up the process because it is done before (rather than concurrently with) order picking.

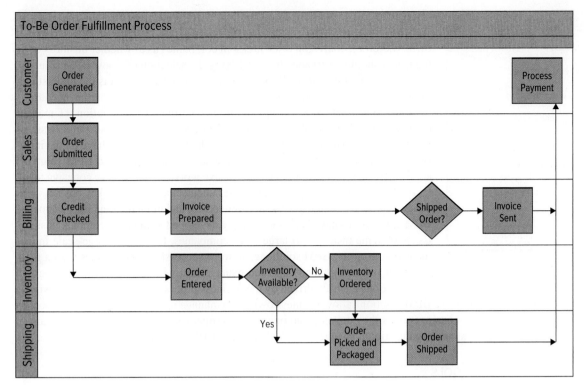

To-Be Order Fulfillment Process

Customer: Order Generated, Process Payment

Sales: Order Submitted

Billing: Credit Checked → Invoice Prepared → Shipped Order? → Invoice Sent

Inventory: Order Entered → Inventory Available? → No → Inventory Ordered

Yes

Shipping: Order Picked and Packaged → Order Shipped

FIGURE B2.9

To-Be Process Model for Order Entry.

power of technology in automating and reengineering business process is business process management. ***Business process management (BPM)*** integrates all of an organization's business process to make individual processes more efficient. BPM can be used to solve a single glitch or to create one unifying system to consolidate a myriad of processes.

Many organizations are unhappy with their current mix of software applications and dealing with business processes that are subject to constant change. These organizations are turning to BPM systems that can flexibly automate their processes and glue their enterprise applications together. Figure B2.10 displays the key reasons organizations are embracing BPM technologies.

BPM technologies effectively track and orchestrate the business process. BPM can automate tasks involving information from multiple systems, with rules to define the sequence in which the tasks are performed as well as responsibilities, conditions, and other aspects of the process (see Figure B2.11 for BPM benefits). BPM not only allows a business process to be executed more efficiently, but also provides the tools to measure performance and identify opportunities for improvement—as well as to easily make changes in processes to act upon those opportunities such as:

- Bringing processes, people, and information together.
- Identifying the business processes is relatively easy. Breaking down the barriers between business areas and finding owners for the processes are difficult.
- Managing business processes within the enterprise and outside the enterprise with suppliers, business partners, and customers.
- Looking at automation horizontally instead of vertically.

FIGURE B2.10

Key Reasons for BPM.

IS BPM FOR BUSINESS OR IT?

A good BPM solution requires two great parts to work together as one. Since BPM solutions cross application and system boundaries, they

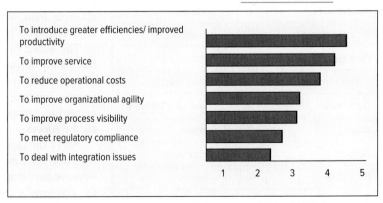

To introduce greater efficiencies/ improved productivity

To improve service

To reduce operational costs

To improve organizational agility

To improve process visibility

To meet regulatory compliance

To deal with integration issues

1 2 3 4 5

Scale 1 to 5 where 1 = not important and 5 = very important

BPM Benefits
■ Update processes in real time
■ Reduce overhead expenses
■ Automate key decisions
■ Reduce process maintenance cost
■ Reduce operating cost
■ Improve productivity
■ Improve process cycle time
■ Improve forecasting
■ Improve customer service

FIGURE B2.11

Benefits of BPM.

often need to be sanctioned and implemented by the IT organization, while at the same time BPM products are business tools that business managers need to own. Therefore, confusion often arises in companies as to whether business or IT managers should be responsible for driving the selection of a new BPM solution.

The key requirement for BPM's success in an organization is the understanding that it is a collaboration of business and IT, and thus both parties need to be involved in evaluating, selecting, and implementing a BPM solution. IT managers need to understand the business drivers behind the processes, and business managers need to understand the impact the BPM solution may have on the infrastructure. Generally, companies that have successfully deployed BPM solutions are those whose business and IT groups have worked together as a cohesive team.

All companies can benefit from a better understanding of their key business processes, analyzing them for areas of improvement and implementing improvements. BPM applications have been successfully developed to improve complex business issues of some medium- to large-sized companies. Like many large-scale implementation projects, BPM solutions are most successful in companies with a good understanding of their technology landscape and management willing to approach business in a new way. BPM solutions are truly driven by the business process and the company's owners.

Effective BPM solutions allow business owners to manage many aspects of the technology through business rules they develop and maintain. Companies that cannot support or manage cultural and organizational changes may lack positive BPM results.

BPM TOOLS

Business process management tools are used to create an application that is helpful in designing business process models and helpful in simulating, optimizing, monitoring, and maintaining various processes that occur within an organization. Many tasks are involved in achieving a goal, and these tasks are done either manually or with the help of software systems. For example, if an organization needs to buy a software application that costs $6 million, then a request has to be approved by several authorities and managers. The request approval may be done manually. However, when a person applies for a loan of $300,000, several internal and external business processes are triggered to find out details about that person before approving the loan. For these activities the BPM tool creates an application that coordinates the manual and automated tasks. Figure B2.12 displays several popular BPM tools.

BPM RISKS AND REWARDS

FIGURE B2.12

Popular BPM Tools.

Tool Name	Company Name
BPM Suite	Ultimus
Process Suite	Stalfware
Business Manager	Savvion
Pega Rules Process Commander	PegaSystem
E Work Vision	MetaStorm
Team Works	Lombardi Software
Intalio	Intalio
Bizflow	Handysoft
FugeoBPM	Fugeo
Business Process Manager	Filenet

If an organization is considering BPM, it must be aware of the risks involved in implementing these systems. One factor that commonly derails a BPM project has nothing to do with technology and everything to do with people. BPM projects involve cultural and organizational changes that companies must make to support the new management approach required for success. Where 10 area leaders once controlled 10 pieces of an end-to-end process, now a new group is involved in implementing a BPM solution across all these areas. Suddenly the span of control is consolidated and all are accountable to the whole process, not just one piece of the puzzle.

The added benefit of BPM is not only a technology solution, but also a business solution. BPM is a new business architecture and approach to managing the process and enabling proactive, continuous improvement. The new organizational structure and roles created to support BPM help maximize the continuous benefits to ensure success.

An IT director from a large financial services company gave this feedback when asked about his experience in using a BPM solution to improve the company's application help desk process. "Before BPM, the company's application help desk was a manual process, filled with inefficiencies, human error, and no personal accountability. In addition, the old process provided no visibility into the process. There was absolutely no way to track requests, since it was all manual. Business user satisfaction with the process was extremely low. A BPM solution provided a way for the company to automate, execute, manage, and monitor the process in real time. The biggest technical challenge in implementation was ensuring that the user group was self-sufficient. While the company recognized that the IT organization is needed, it wanted to be able to maintain and implement any necessary process changes with little reliance on IT. It views process management as empowering the business users to maintain, control, and monitor the process. BPM goes a long way to enable this process."

CRITICAL SUCCESS FACTORS

In a publication for the National Academy of Public Administration, Dr. Sharon L. Caudle identified six critical success factors that ensure government BPM initiatives achieve the desired results (see Figure B2.13).

FIGURE B2.13

Critical Success Factors for BPM Projects.

Critical Success Factors for BPM Projects

1. **Understand reengineering.**
   - Understand business process fundamentals.
   - Know what reengineering is.
   - Differentiate and integrate process improvement approaches.

2. **Build a business and political case.**
   - Have necessary and sufficient business (mission delivery) reasons for reengineering.
   - Have the organizational commitment and capacity to initiate and sustain reengineering.
   - Secure and sustain political support for reengineering projects.

3. **Adopt a process management approach.**
   - Understand the organizational mandate and set mission strategic directions and goals cascading to process-specific goals and decision making across and down the organization.
   - Define, model, and prioritize business processes important for mission performance.
   - Practice hands-on senior management ownership of process improvement through personal involvement, responsibility, and decision making.
   - Adjust organizational structure to better support process management initiatives.
   - Create an assessment program to evaluate process management.

4. **Measure and track performance continuously.**
   - Create organizational understanding of the value of measurement and how it will be used.
   - Tie performance management to customer and stakeholder current and future expectations.

5. **Practice change management and provide central support.**
   - Develop human resource management strategies to support reengineering.
   - Build information resources management strategies and a technology framework to support process change.
   - Create a central support group to assist and integrate reengineering efforts and other improvement efforts across the organization.
   - Create an overarching and project-specific internal and external communication and education program.

6. **Manage reengineering projects for results.**
   - Have a clear criterion to select what should be reengineered.
   - Place the project at the right level with a defined reengineering team purpose and goals.
   - Use a well-trained, diversified, expert team to ensure optimum project performance.
   - Follow a structured, disciplined approach for reengineering.

Business Process Modeling Examples

A picture is worth a thousand words. Just ask Wayne Kendrick, a system analyst for Mobil Oil Corporation in Dallas, Texas. Kendrick, whose work involves planning and designing complex processes, was scheduled to make a presentation to familiarize top management with a number of projects his group was working on. "I was given 10 minutes for my presentation, and I had 20 to 30 pages of detailed documentation to present. Obviously, I could not get through it all in the time allocated." Kendrick turned to business process models to help communicate his projects. "I think people can relate to pictures better than words," Kendrick said. He applied his thinking to his presentation by using Microsoft's Visio to create business process models and graphs to represent the original 30 pages of text. "It was an effective way to get people interested in my projects and to quickly see the importance of each project," he stated. The process models worked and Kendrick received immediate approval to proceed with all of his projects. Figures B2.14 through B2. 20 offer examples of business process models.

FIGURE B2.14

Ebusiness Process Model.

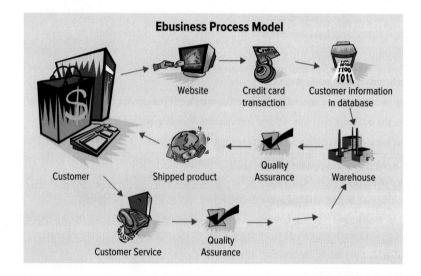

FIGURE B2.15

Online Banking Business Process Model.

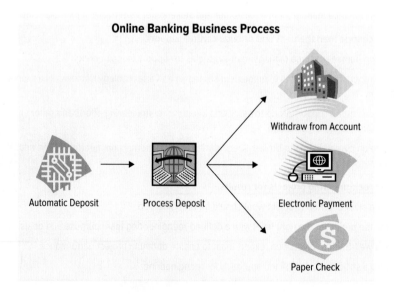

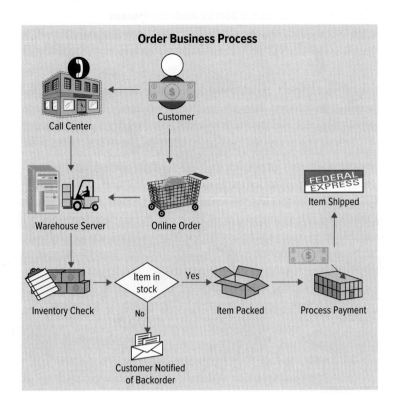

Order Business Process

Customer

Call Center

Warehouse Server

Online Order

Inventory Check

Item in stock

Yes

No

Customer Notified of Backorder

Item Packed

Process Payment

Item Shipped

FIGURE B2.16

Customer Order Business Process Model.

Purchase an Item on eBay Business Process

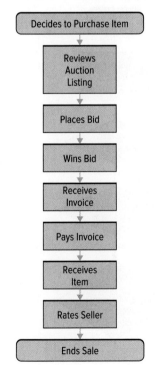

Decides to Purchase Item

Reviews Auction Listing

Places Bid

Wins Bid

Receives Invoice

Pays Invoice

Receives Item

Rates Seller

Ends Sale

FIGURE B2.17

eBay Buyer Business Process Model.

Sell an Item on eBay Business Process

Decides to Sell Item

Lists Item on eBay

Sets Initial Price

Sets Auction Length

Invoices Winning Bid

Receives Payment

Ships Item

Rates Buyer

Ends Sale

FIGURE B2.18

eBay Seller Business Process Model.

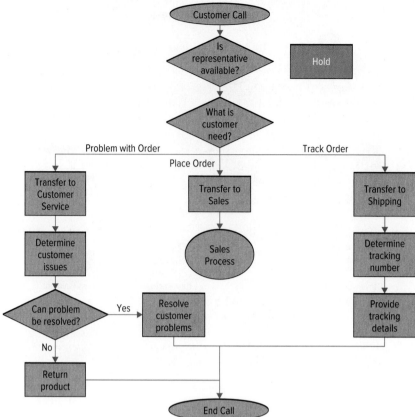

Customer Service Business Process

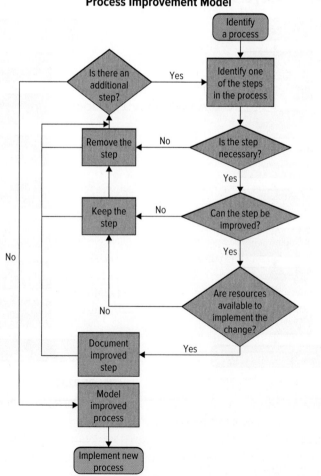

Process Improvement Model

Investment in continuous process improvement, business process reengineering, or business process management is the same as any other technology-related investment. Planning the project properly, setting clear goals, educating those people who have to change their mind-set once the system is implemented, and retaining strong management support will help with a successful implementation generating a solid return on investment.

Organizations must go beyond the basics when implementing business process improvement and realize that it is not a one-time project. Management and improvement of end-to-end business processes is difficult and requires more than a simple, one-time effort. Continuously monitoring and improving core business processes will guarantee performance improvements across an organization.

* KEY TERMS

As-Is process model   385
Business process   385
Business process
   management (BPM)   387
Business process
   management tool   389

Business process model   385
Business process modeling
   (or mapping)   385
Business process reengineering
   (BPR)   384

Continuous process improvement
   model   384
To-Be process model   385

* MAKING BUSINESS DECISIONS

1. **Discovering Reengineering Opportunities**

   In an effort to increase efficiency, your college has hired you to analyze its current business processes for registering for classes. Analyze the current business processes from paying tuition to registering for classes and determine which steps in the process are:

   - Broken
   - Redundant
   - Antiquated

   Be sure to define how you would reengineer the processes for efficiency.

2. **Modeling a Business Process**

   Do you hate waiting in line at the grocery store? Do you find it frustrating when you go to the movie store and cannot find the movie you wanted to rent? Do you get annoyed when the pizza delivery person brings you the wrong order? This is your chance to reengineer the annoying process that drives you crazy. Choose a problem you are currently experiencing and reengineer the process to make it more efficient. Be sure to provide an As-Is and To-Be process model.

3. **Revamping Business Processes**

   The following is the sales order business process for MusicMan. Draw the As-Is process model based on the following narrative:

   1. A customer submits an order for goods to MusicMan, a music retailer, through an online mechanism such as a browser-based order form. The customer supplies his or her name, the appropriate email address, the state to which the order will be shipped, the desired items (IDs and names), and the requested quantities.

2. The order is received by a processing system, which reads the data and appends an ID number to the order.

3. The order is forwarded to a customer service representative, who checks the customer's credit information.

4. If the credit check fails, the customer service representative is assigned the task of notifying the customer to obtain correct credit information, and the process becomes manual from this point on.

5. If the credit check passes, the system checks a database for the current inventory of the ordered item, according to the item ID, and it compares the quantity of items available with the quantity requested.

6. If the amount of stock is not sufficient to accommodate the order, the order is placed on hold until new inventory arrives. When the system receives notice of new incoming inventory, it repeats step 5 until it can verify that the inventory is sufficient to process the order.

7. If the inventory is sufficient, the order is forwarded simultaneously to a shipping agent who arranges shipment and an accounting agent who instructs the system to generate an invoice for the order.

8. If the system encounters an error in processing the input necessary to calculate the total price for the invoice, including state sales tax, the accounting agent who initiated the billing process is notified and prompted to provide the correct information.

9. The system calculates the total price of the order.

10. The system confirms that the order has been shipped and notifies the customer via email.

11. At any point in the transaction before shipping, the order can be canceled by notification from the customer.

4. Revamping Accounts

The accounting department at your company deals with the processing of critical documents. These documents must arrive at their intended destination in a secure and efficient manner. Such documents include invoices, purchase orders, statements, purchase requisitions, financial statements, sales orders, and quotes.

The current processing of documents is done manually, which causes a negative ripple effect. Documents tend to be misplaced or delayed through the mailing process. Unsecured documents are vulnerable to people making changes or seeing confidential documents. In addition, the accounting department incurs costs such as preprinted forms, inefficient distribution, and storage. Explain BPM and how it can be used to revamp the accounting department.

5. Revamp The Broadway Cafe

Your friends have asked you to review the customer ordering process for their restaurant, The Broadway Café. To make the café as efficient and effective as possible, you want to redesign processes to remove bottlenecks, reduce redundancies, and streamline workflow.

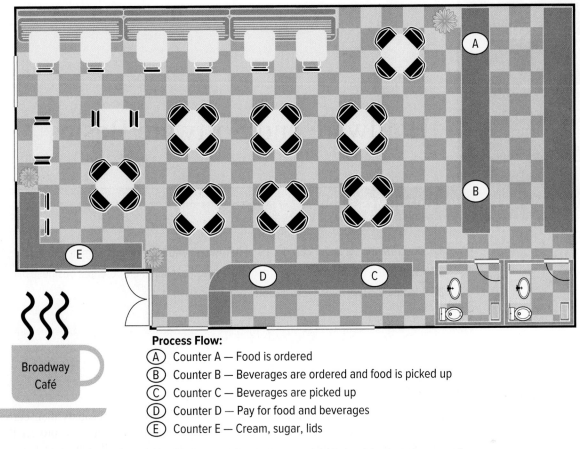

Process Flow:
- (A) Counter A — Food is ordered
- (B) Counter B — Beverages are ordered and food is picked up
- (C) Counter C — Beverages are picked up
- (D) Counter D — Pay for food and beverages
- (E) Counter E — Cream, sugar, lids

Review The Broadway Café's customer ordering process highlighted in the accompanying image and reengineer it for improvements in efficiency and effectiveness. If you are looking for a real challenge, create your As-Is and To-Be process diagrams by using PowerPoint or Visio.

Hardware and Software Basics

LEARNING OUTCOMES

1. Describe the six major categories of hardware, and provide an example of each.

2. Identify the different computer categories, and explain their potential business uses.

3. Identify the two main types of software.

LO 1 Describe the six major categories of hardware, and provide an example of each.

Introduction

Managers need to determine what types of hardware and software will satisfy their current and future business needs, the right time to buy the equipment, and how to protect their investments. This does not imply that managers need to be experts in all areas of technology; however, building a basic understanding of hardware and software can help them make the right investment choices.

Information technology can be an important enabler of business success and innovation. Information technology can be composed of the Internet, a personal computer, a cell phone that can access the web, a personal digital assistant, or presentation software. All of these technologies help to perform specific information processing tasks. There are two basic categories of information technology: hardware and software. ***Hardware*** consists of the physical devices associated with a computer system. ***Software*** is the set of instructions the hardware executes to carry out specific tasks. Software, such as Microsoft Excel, and various hardware devices, such as a keyboard and a monitor, interact to create a spreadsheet or a graph. This plug-in coversthe basics of computer hardware and software including terminology, characteristics, and the associated managerial responsibilities for building a solid enterprise architecture.

Hardware Basics

In many industries, exploiting computer hardware is key to gaining a competitive advantage. Frito-Lay gained a competitive advantage by using mobile devices to track the strategic placement and sale of items in convenience stores. Sales representatives track prices, competitor information, the number of items sold, and item location in the store all from their mobile device.[1]

A *computer* is an electronic device operating under the control of instructions stored in its own memory that can accept, manipulate, and store data. Figure B3.1 displays the two primary components of a computer—hardware and software. A computer system consists of six hardware components (see Figure B3.2). Figure B3.3 displays how these components work together to form a computer system.

CENTRAL PROCESSING UNIT

The *central processing unit (CPU)* (or *microprocessor*) is the actual hardware that interprets and executes the program (software) instructions and coordinates how all the other hardware devices work together. The CPU is built on a small flake of silicon and can contain the equivalent of several million transistors. CPUs are unquestionably one of the 20th century's greatest technological advances.

A CPU contains two primary parts: control unit and arithmetic/logic unit. The *control unit* interprets software instructions and literally tells the other hardware devices what to do, based on the software instructions. The *arithmetic-logic unit (ALU)* performs all arithmetic operations (for example, addition and subtraction) and all logic operations (such as sorting and comparing numbers). The control unit and ALU perform different functions. The control unit obtains instructions from the software. It then interprets the instructions, decides which tasks other devices perform, and finally tells each device to perform the task. The ALU responds to the control unit and does whatever it dictates, performing either arithmetic or logic operations.

The number of CPU cycles per second determines how fast a CPU carries out the software instructions; more cycles per second means faster processing, and faster CPUs cost more than their slower counterparts. CPU speed is usually quoted in megahertz and gigahertz. *Megahertz (MHz)* is the number of millions of CPU cycles per second. *Gigahertz (GHz)* is the number of billions of CPU cycles per second. Figure B3.4 displays the factors that determine CPU speed.

FIGURE B3.1

Hardware and Software Overview.

HARDWARE

The physical devices associated with a computer system

CENTRAL PROCESSING UNIT
CPU: The computer's "brains"
RAM: Integrated circuits; works with the CPU

INPUT DEVICE
• Keyboard; mouse; scanner

OUTPUT DEVICE
• Monitor; printer; headphones

STORAGE DEVICE
• DVD; memory stick; hard drive

COMMUNICATION DEVICE
• Modem; wireless card

CONNECTING DEVICE
• Cables; USB port

SOFTWARE

The set of instructions the hardware executes to carry out specific tasks

SYSTEM SOFTWARE
Controls how the various tools work together along with application software

OPERATING SYSTEM SOFTWARE
• Windows; Mac OS; Linux

UTILITY SOFTWARE
• Antivirus; screen savers; data recovery

APPLICATION SOFTWARE
Performs specific information processing needs

WORD PROCESSING SOFTWARE
• Microsoft Word

SPREADSHEET SOFTWARE
• Microsoft Excel

CPU	• The actual hardware that interprets and executes the program (software) instructions and coordinates how all the other hardware devices work together
Primary Storage	• The computer's main memory, which consists of the random access memory (RAM), the cache memory, and the read-only memory (ROM) that is directly accessible to the central processing unit (CPU)
Secondary Storage	• Equipment designed to store large volumes of data for long-term storage (diskette, CD, DVD, memory stick)
Input Devices	• Equipment used to capture information and commands (mouse, keyboard, scanner)
Output Devices	• Equipment used to see, hear, or otherwise accept the results of information processing requests (monitor, printer, microphone)
Communication Device	• Equipment used to send information and receive it from one location to another (modem, wireless card)

Advances in CPU Design

Chip makers are pressing more functionality into CPU technology. Most CPUs are *complex instruction set computer (CISC) chips*, which is a type of CPU that can recognize as many as 100 or more instructions, enough to carry out most computations directly. *Reduced instruction set computer (RISC) chips* limit the number of instructions the CPU can execute to increase processing speed. The idea of RISC is to reduce the instruction set to the bare minimum, emphasizing the instructions used most of the time and optimizing them for the fastest possible execution. An RISC processor runs faster than a CISC processor.

PRIMARY STORAGE

Primary storage is the computer's main memory, which consists of the random access memory (RAM), cache memory, and read-only memory (ROM) that is directly accessible to the CPU.

Random Access Memory

Random access memory (RAM) is the computer's primary working memory, in which program instructions and data are stored so that they can be accessed directly by the CPU via the processor's high-speed external data bus.

RAM is often called read/write memory. In RAM, the CPU can write and read data. Most programs set aside a portion of RAM as a temporary workspace for data so that one can modify (rewrite) as needed until the data are ready for printing or storage on secondary storage media, such as a hard drive or memory key. RAM does not retain its contents when the power to the computer is switched off; hence individuals should save their work frequently. When the computer is turned off, everything in RAM is wiped clean. *Volatility* refers to a device's ability to function with or without power. RAM is *volatile*, meaning it must have constant power to function; its contents are lost when the computer's electric supply fails.

© Royalty-Free/Corbis   © Stockbyte/Punchstock Images

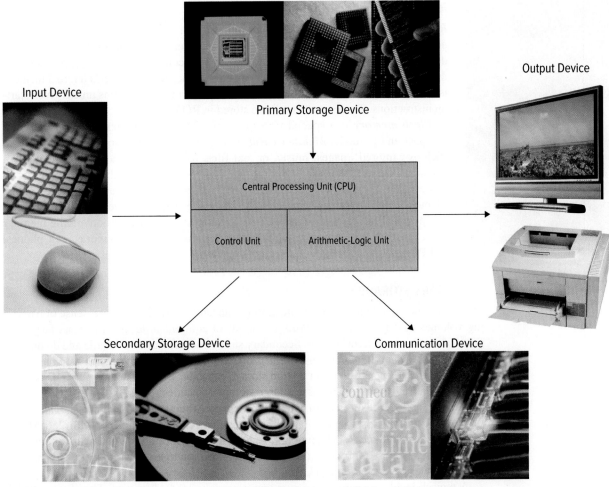

Input Device

Primary Storage Device

Output Device

Central Processing Unit (CPU)	
Control Unit	Arithmetic-Logic Unit

Secondary Storage Device

Communication Device

(clockwise, starting left to right):© Royalty-Free/Corbis,© Stockbyte/PunchStock Images,© Nick Rowe/Getty Images,© Digital Vision/Getty Images,© Image Club,© Royalty-Free/Corbis,© Getty Images/Photodisc,© Daisuke Morita/Getty Images,© Don Bishop/Photodisc/Getty Images/RF,© Stockbyte/PunchStock Images,© Stockbyte/PunchStock Images

FIGURE B3.3

How the Hardware Components Work Together.

Cache Memory

Cache memory is a small unit of ultra-fast memory that is used to store recently accessed or frequently accessed data so that the CPU does not have to retrieve this data from slower memory circuits such as RAM. Cache memory that is built directly into the CPU's circuits is called primary cache. Cache memory contained on an external circuit is called secondary cache.

FIGURE B3.4

Factors That Determine CPU Speed.

CPU Speed Factors
Clock speed—the speed of the internal clock of a CPU that sets the pace at which operations proceed within the computer's internal processing circuitry.
Word length—number of bits (0s and 1s) that can be processed by the CPU at any one time. Computers work in terms of bits and bytes using electrical pulses that have two states: on and off.
Bus width—the size of the internal electrical pathway along which signals are sent from one part of the computer to another. A wider bus can move more data, hence faster processing.
Chip line width—the distance between transistors on a chip. The shorter the chip line width the faster the chip since more transistors can be placed on a chip and the data and instructions travel short distances during processing.

Read-Only Memory (ROM)

Read-only memory (ROM) is the portion of a computer's primary storage that does not lose its contents when one switches off the power. ROM is *nonvolatile*, meaning it does not require constant power to function. ROM contains essential system programs that neither the user nor the computer can erase. Since the computer's internal memory is blank during start-up, the computer cannot perform any functions unless given start-up instructions. These instructions are stored in ROM.

Flash memory is a special type of rewritable read-only memory (ROM) that is compact and portable. *Memory cards* contain high-capacity storage that holds data such as captured images, music, or text files. Memory cards are removable; when one is full the user can insert an additional card. Subsequently, the data can be downloaded from the card to a computer. The card can then be erased and used again. Memory cards are typically used in digital devices such as cameras, cellular phones, and personal digital assistants (PDAs). *Memory sticks* provide nonvolatile memory for a range of portable devices including computers, digital cameras, cell phones, and PDAs.

© Nick Rowe/Getty Images

SECONDARY STORAGE

Storage is a hot area in the business arena as organizations struggle to make sense of exploding volumes of data. *Secondary storage* consists of equipment designed to store large volumes of data for long-term storage. Secondary storage devices are nonvolatile and do not lose their contents when the computer is turned off. Some storage devices, such as a hard disk, offer easy update capabilities and a large storage capacity. Others, such as CD-ROMs, offer limited update capabilities but possess large storage capacities.

Storage capacity is expressed in bytes, with megabytes being the most common. A *megabyte (MB or M or Meg)* is roughly 1 million bytes. Therefore, a computer with 256 MB of RAM translates into the RAM being able to hold roughly 256 million characters of data and software instructions. A *gigabyte (GB)* is roughly 1 billion bytes. A *terabyte (TB)* is roughly 1 trillion bytes (refer to Figure B3.5).[2]

A typical double-spaced page of pure text is roughly 2,000 characters. Therefore, a 40 GB (40 gigabyte or 40 billion characters) hard drive can hold approximately 20 million pages of text.

Common storage devices include:

- Magnetic medium
- Optical medium

Magnetic Medium

Magnetic medium is a secondary storage medium that uses magnetic techniques to store and retrieve data on disks or tapes coated with magnetically sensitive materials. Like iron filings on a sheet of waxed paper, these materials are reoriented when a magnetic field passes over them. During write operations, the read/write heads emit a magnetic field that orients the magnetic materials on the disk or tape to represent encoded data. During read operations, the read/write heads sense the encoded data on the medium.

One of the first forms of magnetic medium developed was magnetic tape. *Magnetic tape* is an older secondary storage medium that uses a strip of thin plastic coated with a magnetically sensitive recording medium. The most popular type of magnetic medium is a hard drive. A *hard drive* is a secondary storage medium that uses several rigid disks coated with a magnetically sensitive material and housed together with the recording heads in a hermetically sealed mechanism. Hard drive performance is measured in terms of access time, seek time, rotational speed, and data transfer rate.

A *solid state drive* is an all-electronic storage device that is an alternative to a hard disk and are faster than hard disks because there is zero latency (no read/write head to move). Instead of storing data magnetically like traditional hard drives, solid state drives store data using flash memory and have no moving parts so they do not need to "spin up" while in a

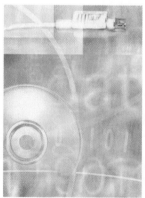
© Don Bishop/Photodisc/Getty Images/RF

Term	Size
Kilobyte (KB)	1,024 Bytes
Megabyte (MB)	1,024 KB
	1,048,576 Bytes
Gigabyte (GB)	1,024 MB (10^9 bytes)
Terabyte (TB)	1,024 GB (10^{12} bytes)
	1 TB = Printing of 1 TB would require 50,000 trees to be made into paper and printer
Petabyte (PB)	1,024 TB (10^{15} bytes)
	200 PB = All production of digital magnetic tape in 1995
Exabyte (EB)	1,024 PB (10^{18} bytes)
	2 EB = Total volume of information generated worldwide annually
	5 EB = All words ever spoken by human beings

sleep state and they don't need to move a drive head to different parts of the drive to access data. Therefore, solid state drives can access data faster than traditional hard drives and are far more rugged and reliable offering greater protection in hostile environments.

Optical Medium

Optical medium is a secondary storage medium for computers on which information is stored at extremely high density in the form of tiny pits. The presence or absence of pits is read by a tightly focused laser beam. Optical medium types include:

- **Compact disk-read-only memory (CD-ROM) drive**—an optical drive designed to read the data encoded on CD-ROMs and to transfer this data to a computer.
- **Compact disk-read-write (CD-RW) drive**—an optical drive that enables users to erase existing data and to write new data repeatedly to a CD-RW.
- **Digital video disk (DVD)**—a CD-ROM format capable of storing up to a maximum of 17 GB of data; enough for a full-length feature movie.
- **DVD-ROM drive**—a read-only drive designed to read the data encoded on a DVD and transfer the data to a computer.

© Daisuke Morita/Getty Images

- **Digital video disk-read/write (DVD-RW)**—a standard for DVD disks and player/recorder mechanisms that enables users to record in the DVD format.

CD-ROMs and DVDs offer an increasingly economical medium for storing data and programs. The overall trend in secondary storage is toward more direct-access methods, higher capacity with lower costs, and increased portability.

INPUT DEVICES

An *input device* is equipment used to capture information and commands. A keyboard is used to type in information, and a mouse is used to point and click on buttons and icons. *Adaptive computer devices* are input devices designed for special applications for use by people with different types of special needs. An example is a keyboard with tactile surfaces, which can be used by the visually impaired. A *stylus* is used as a pen-like device that taps the screen to enter commands. Numerous input devices are available in many different environments, some of

© Stockbyte/PunchStock Images

© Stockbyte/PunchStock Images

MANUAL INPUT DEVICES		AUTOMATED INPUT DEVICES	
KEYBOARD	• Provides a set of alphabetic, numeric, punctuation, symbol, and control keys	IMAGE SCANNER	• Captures images, photos, graphics, and text that already exist on paper
MOUSE	• One or more control buttons housed in a palm-sized case and designed so that one can move it about on the table next to the keyboard	BAR CODE SCANNER	• Captures information that exists in the form of vertical bars whose width and distance apart determine a number
TOUCH PAD	• Form of a stationary mouse on which the movement of a finger causes the pointer on the screen to move; typically found below the space bar on laptops	BIOMETRIC SCANNER	• Captures human physical attributes such as a fingerprint or iris for security purposes
TOUCH SCREEN	• Allows the use of a finger to point at and touch a monitor to execute commands	OPTICAL MARK READER	• Detects the presence or absence of a mark in a predetermined place (popular for multiple-choice exams)
POINTING DEVICE	• Devices used to navigate and select objects on a display screen	OPTICAL CHARACTER READER	• Converts text into digital format for computer input
GAME CONTROLLER	• Devices used for games to obtain better control screen action	DIGITAL STILL CAMERA	• Digitally captures still images in varying resolutions
		DIGITAL VIDEO CAMERA	• Digitally captures video
		WEBCAM	• Digitally captures video and uploads it directly to the Internet
		MICROPHONE	• Captures sounds such as a voice for voice-recognition software
		POINT-OF-SALE (POS)	• Captures information at the point of a transaction, typically in a retail environment

FIGURE B3.6

Input Devices.

which have applications that are more suitable in a personal setting than a business setting. A keyboard, mouse, and scanner are the most common forms of input devices (see Figure B3.6).

An *output device* is equipment used to see, hear, or otherwise accept the results of information processing requests. Among output devices, printers and monitors are the most common; however, speakers and plotters (special printers that draw output on a page) are widely used (see Figure B3.7). In addition, output devices are responsible for converting computer-stored information into a form that can be understood.

A new output device based on sensor technology aims to translate American Sign Language (ASL) into speech, enabling the millions of people who use ASL to better communicate with

MONITORS		PRINTERS	
CATHODE-RAY TUBE (CRT)	• A vacuum tube that uses an electron gun (cathode) to emit a beam of electrons that illuminates phosphors on a screen as the beam sweeps across the display repeatedly	**INK-JET PRINTER**	• Printer that makes images by forcing ink droplets through nozzles
LIQUID CRYSTAL DISPLAY (LCD)	• Low-powered displays used in laptop computers where rod-shaped crystal molecules change their orientation when an electrical current flows through them	**LASER PRINTER**	• Printer that forms images using an electrostatic process, the same way a photocopier works
LIGHT-EMITTING DIODE (LED)	• Tiny bulb used for backlight to improve the image on the screen	**MULTIFUNCTION PRINTER**	• Printer that can scan, copy, fax, and print all in one device
ORGANIC LIGHT-EMITTING DIODE (OLED)	• Displays use many layers of organic material emitting a visible light and therefore eliminating the need for backlighting	**PLOTTER**	• Printer that uses computer-directed pens for creating high-quality images, blueprints, schematics, etc.
		3-D PRINTER	• Printer that can produce solid, three-dimensional objects

FIGURE B3.7

Output Devices.

those who do not know the rapid gesturing system. The AcceleGlove is a glove lined on the inside with sensors embedded in rings. The sensors, called accelerometers, measure acceleration and can categorize and translate finger and hand movements. Additional, interconnected attachments for the elbow and shoulder capture ASL signs that are made with full arm motion. When users wear the glove while signing ASL, algorithms in the glove's software translate the hand gestures into words. The translations can be relayed through speech synthesizers or read on a PDA-size computer screen. Inventor Jose L. Hernandez-Rebollar started with a single glove that could translate only the ASL alphabet. Now, the device employs two gloves that contain a 1,000-word vocabulary.[3]

COMMUNICATION DEVICES

A *communication device* is equipment used to send information and receive it from one location to another. One of the first forms of communication devices was a telephone modem that connected a computer to a phone line in order to access another computer. The computer works in terms of digital signals, while a standard telephone line works with analog signals. Each digital signal represents a bit (either 0 or 1). The modem must convert the digital signals of a computer into analog signals so they can be sent across the telephone line. At the other end, another modem translates the analog signals into digital signals, which can then be used by the other computer. Figure B3.8 displays the different types of modems.

© Royalty-Free/Corbis

LO 2 Identify the different computer categories, and explain their potential business uses.

Computer Categories

Supercomputers today can hit processing capabilities of well over 200 teraflops—the equivalent of everyone on Earth performing 35,000 calculations per second (see Figure B3.9). For the past 20 years, federally funded supercomputing research has given birth to some of the computer industry's most significant technology breakthroughs including:

■ Clustering, which allows companies to chain together thousands of PCs to build mass-market systems.

■ Parallel processing, which provides the ability to run two or more tasks simultaneously and is viewed as the chip industry's future.

■ Mosaic browser, which morphed into Netscape and made the web a household name.

Federally funded supercomputers have also advanced some of the country's most dynamic industries, including advanced manufacturing, gene research in the life sciences, and real-time financial-market modeling.[4]

Carrier Technology	Description	Speed	Comments
Dial-up access	On demand access using a modem and regular telephone line (POT).	2,400 bps to 56 Kbps	■ Cheap but slow.
Cable	Special cable modem and cable line required.	512 Kbps to 20 Mbps	■ Must have existing cable access in area. ■ Bandwidth is shared.
DSL Digital Subscriber Line	This technology uses the unused digital portion of a regular copper telephone line to transmit and receive information. A special modem and adapter card are required.	128 Kbps to 8 Mbps	■ Doesn't interfere with normal telephone use. ■ Bandwidth is dedicated. ■ Must be within 5 km (3.1 miles) of telephone company switch.
Wireless (LMCS)	Access is gained by connection to a high-speed cellular like local multipoint communications system (LMCS) network via wireless transmitter/receiver.	30 Mbps or more	■ Can be used for high-speed data, broadcast TV, and wireless telephone service.
Satellite	Newer versions have two-way satellite access, removing need for phone line.	6 Mbps or more	■ Bandwidth is not shared. ■ Some connections require an existing Internet service account. ■ Setup fees can range from $500 to $1,000.

FIGURE B3.8

Comparing Modems.

Computers come in different shapes, sizes, and colors. And they meet a variety of needs. An *appliance* is a computer dedicated to a single function, such as a calculator or computer game. An *ebook* is an electronic book that can be read on a computer or special reading device. Some are small enough to carry around, while others are the size of a telephone booth. Size does not always correlate to power, speed, and price (see Figure B3.10).

MIT's Media Lab is developing a laptop that it will sell for $100 each to government agencies around the world for distribution to millions of underprivileged schoolchildren. Using a simplified sales model and reengineering the device helped MIT reach the $100 price point. Almost half the price of a current laptop comprises marketing, sales, distribution, and profit. Of the remaining costs, the display panel and backlight account for roughly half while the rest covers the operating system. The low-cost laptop will use a display system that costs less than $25, a 500 MHz processor from AMD, a wireless LAN connection, 1 GB of storage, and the Linux operating system. The machine will automatically connect with others. China and Brazil have already ordered 3 million and 1 million laptops, respectively. MIT's goal is to produce around 150 million laptops per year.[5]

FIGURE B3.9

Supercomputer.

© Digital Vision/Getty Images

Smartphone/Personal Digital Assistant (PDA)

Handheld/Ultra Portable/Pocket Computer

Laptop/Notebook/Portable Computer/Netbook

Tablet Computer

Personal/Desktop Computer

Workstation/Minicomputer

Mainframe Computer

Supercomputer

Computer Category	Description
Smartphone	A cellular telephone with a keypad that runs programs, music, photos, and email and includes many features of a PDA.
Personal digital assistant (PDA)	A small handheld computer that performs simple tasks such as taking notes, scheduling appointments, and maintaining an address book and a calendar. The PDA screen is touch-sensitive, allowing a user to write directly on the screen, capturing what is written.
Handheld (ultra portable, pocket) computer	Computer portable enough to fit in a purse or pocket and has its own power source or battery.
Laptop (portable, notebook) computer	Computer portable enough to fit on a lap or in a bag and has its own power source or battery. Laptops come equipped with all of the technology that a personal desktop computer has, yet weigh as little as two pounds.
Tablet computer	Computer with a flat screen that uses a mouse or fingertip for input instead of a keyboard. Similar to PDAs, tablet PCs use a writing pen or stylus to write notes on the screen and touch the screen to perform functions such as clicking on a link while visiting a website.
Personal computer (microcomputer)	Computer that is operated by a single user who can customize the functions to match personal preferences.
Desktop computer	Computer that sits on, next to, or under a user's desk and is too large to carry around. The computer box is where the CPU, RAM, and storage devices are held with a monitor on top, or a vertical system box (called a tower) usually placed on the floor within a work area.
Workstation computer	Similar to a desktop but has more powerful mathematical and graphics processing capabilities and can perform more complicated tasks in less time. Typically used for software development, web development, engineering, and ebusiness tools.
Minicomputer (server)	Designed to meet the computing needs of several people simultaneously in a small to medium-size business environment. A common type of minicomputer is a server and is used for managing internal company applications, networks, and websites.
Mainframe computer	Designed to meet the computing needs of hundreds of people in a large business environment. Mainframe computers are a step up in size, power, capability, and cost from minicomputers.
Supercomputer	The fastest, most powerful, and most expensive type of computer. Organizations such as NASA that are heavily involved in research and number crunching employ supercomputers because of the speed with which they can process information. Other large, customer-oriented businesses such as General Motors and AT&T employ supercomputers just to handle customer information and transaction processing.

Software Basics

Hardware is only as good as the software that runs it. Over the years, the cost of hardware has decreased while the complexity and cost of software have increased. Some large software applications, such as customer relationship management systems, contain millions of lines of code, take years to develop, and cost millions of dollars. The two main types of software are system software and application software.

SYSTEM SOFTWARE

System software controls how the various technology tools work together along with the application software. System software includes both operating system software and utility software.

Operating System Software

Linus Torvalds, a Finnish programmer, may seem an unlikely choice to be one of the world's top managers. However, Linux, the software project he created while a university student, is now one of the most powerful influences on the computer world. Linux is an operating system built by volunteers and distributed for free and has become one of the primary competitors to Microsoft. Torvalds coordinates Linux development with a few dozen volunteer assistants and more than 1,000 programmers scattered around the globe. They contribute code for the kernel—or core piece—of Linux. He also sets the rules for dozens of technology companies that have lined up behind Linux, including IBM, Dell, Hewlett-Packard, and Intel.

Operating system software controls the application software and manages how the hardware devices work together. When using Excel to create and print a graph, the operating system software controls the process, ensures that a printer is attached and has paper, and sends the graph to the printer along with instructions on how to print it. Some computers are configured with two operating systems so they can *dual boot*—provide the user with the option of choosing the operating system when the computer is turned on. An *embedded operating system* is used in computer appliances and special-purpose applications, such as an automobile or ATM and are used for a single purpose. A cell phone has a single-purpose embedded operating system.

Operating system software also supports a variety of useful features, one of which is multitasking. *Multitasking* allows more than one piece of software to be used at a time. Multitasking is used when creating a graph in Excel and simultaneously printing a word processing document. With multitasking, both pieces of application software are operating at the same time. There are different types of operating system software for personal environments and for organizational environments (see Figure B3.11).

FIGURE B3.11

Operating System Software.

Operating System Software	
Linux	An open source operating system that provides a rich environment for high-end workstations and network servers. Open source refers to any program whose source code is made available for use or modification as users or other developers see fit.
Mac OS X	The operating system of Macintosh computers.
Android Operating System	A Linux-based OS developed by the Open Handset Alliance (OHA) and Google used to run cell phones.
Microsoft Windows	Generic name for the various operating systems in the Microsoft Windows family.
MS-DOS	The standard, single-user operating system of IBM and IBM-compatible computers, introduced in 1981. MS-DOS is a command-line operating system that requires the user to enter commands, arguments, and syntax.
UNIX	A 32-bit multitasking and multiuser operating system that originated at AT&T's Bell Laboratories and is now used on a wide variety of computers, from mainframes to PDAs.

Types of Utility Software	
Crash-proof	Helps save information if a computer crashes.
Disk image for data recovery	Relieves the burden of reinstalling applications if a hard drive crashes or becomes irretrievably corrupted.
Disk optimization	Organizes information on a hard disk in the most efficient way.
Encrypt data	Protects confidential information from unauthorized eyes.
File and data recovery	Retrieves accidental deletion of photos or documents.
Uninstaller	Can remove software that is no longer needed.

FIGURE B3.12

Utility Software.

Utility Software

Utility software provides additional functionality to the operating system. Utility software includes antivirus software, screen savers, and anti-spam software. Operating systems are customized by using the *control panel,* which is a Windows feature that provides options that set default values for the Windows operating system. For example, the *system clock* works like a wristwatch and uses a battery mounted on the motherboard to provide power when the computer is turned off. If the user moves to a different time zone, the system clock can be adjusted in the control panel. *Safe mode* occurs if the system is failing and will load only the most essential parts of the operating system and will not run many of the background operating utilities. *System restore* enables a user to return to the previous operating system. Figure B3.12 displays a few types of available utility software.

APPLICATION SOFTWARE

Application software is used for specific information processing needs, including payroll, customer relationship management, project management, training, and many others. Application software is used to solve specific problems or perform specific tasks. From an organizational perspective, payroll software, collaborative software such as videoconferencing (within groupware), and inventory management software are all examples of application software (see Figure B3.13). *Personal information management (PIM) software* handles contact information, appointments, task lists, and email. *Course management software* contains course information such as a syllabus and assignments and offers drop boxes for quizzes and homework along with a grade book.

DISTRIBUTING APPLICATION SOFTWARE

After software has been deployed to its users, it is not uncommon to find bugs or additional errors that require fixing. *Software updates (software patch)* occur when the software vendor releases updates to software to fix problems or enhance features. *Software upgrade* occurs when the software vendor releases a new version of the software, making significant changes to the program. Application software can be distributed using one of the following methods:

- *Single user license*—restricts the use of the software to one user at a time.
- *Network user license*—enables anyone on the network to install and use the software.
- *Site license*—enables any qualified users within the organization to install the software, regardless of whether the computer is on a network. Some employees might install the software on a home computer for working remotely.
- *Application service provider license*—specialty software paid for on a license basis or per-use basis or usage-based licensing.

Types of Application Software	
Browser	Enables the user to navigate the World Wide Web. Common browsers include Internet Explorer, Microsoft Edge, Mozilla Firefox, Google Chrome, Safari.
Data management	Provides the tools for data retrieval, modification, deletion, and insertion; for example, Microsoft Access, MySQL, and Oracle.
Desktop publishing	Transforms a computer into a desktop publishing workstation. Leading packages include Microsoft Publisher, Serif, and QuarkXpress.
Email	Provides email services for computer users, including receiving mail, sending mail, and storing messages. Microsoft Outlook is a common email application.
Groupware	Increases the cooperation and joint productivity of small groups of co-workers.
Presentation graphics	Creates and enhances charts and graphs so that they are visually appealing and easily understood by an audience. A full-features presentation graphics package such as Microsoft PowerPoint or Visio includes facilities for making a wide variety of charts and graphs and for adding titles, legends, and explanatory text anywhere in the chart or graph.
Programming	Possesses an artificial language consisting of a fixed vocabulary and a set of rules (called syntax) that programmers use to write computer programs. Leading programming languages include SQL, Java, C#, Python, and PHP.
Spreadsheet	Simulates an accountant's worksheet onscreen and lets users embed hidden formulas that perform calculations on the visible data. Many spreadsheet programs also include powerful graphics and presentation capabilities to create attractive products. The leading spreadsheet application is Microsoft Excel.
Word processing	Transforms a computer into a tool for creating, editing, proofreading, formatting, and printing documents. Microsoft Word is the leading word processing application.

FIGURE B3.13

Application Software.

Information technology (IT) is a field concerned with the use of technology in managing and processing information. IT includes cell phones, PDAs, software such as spreadsheet software, and printers. There are two categories of IT: hardware and software. The six hardware components include CPU, primary storage, secondary storage, input devices, output devices, and communication devices. Computer categories include PDAs, laptops, tablets, desktops, workstations, minicomputers, mainframe computers, and supercomputers.

Software includes system software and application software. Operating system software and utility software are the two primary types of system software. There are many forms of application software from word processing to databases.

✳ KEY TERMS

Adaptive computer device   401
Appliance   404
Application service provider
   license   407
Application software   407
Arithmetic-logic unit (ALU)   397
Cache memory   399
Central processing unit (CPU)
   (or microprocessor)   397
Communication device   403
Complex instruction set computer
   (CISC) chip   398
Computer   396
Control panel   407
Control unit   397
Course management
   software   407
Dual boot   406
Ebook   404
Embedded operating system   406
Flash memory   400
Gigabyte (GB)   400

Gigahertz (GHz)   397
Hard drive   400
Hardware   396
Input device   401
Magnetic medium   400
Magnetic tape   400
Megabyte (MB, M, or
   Meg)   400
Megahertz (MHz)   397
Memory card   400
Memory stick   400
Multitasking   406
Network user license   407
Nonvolatile   400
Operating system
   software   406
Output device   402
Personal information management
   (PIM) software   407
Primary storage   398
Random access memory
   (RAM)   398

Read-only memory (ROM)   400
Reduced instruction set computer
   (RISC) chip   398
Safe mode   407
Secondary storage   400
Single user license   407
Site license   407
Software   407
Software updates (software
   patch)   407
Software upgrade   407
Solid state drive   400
Stylus   401
System clock   407
System restore   407
System software   396
Terabyte (TB)   400
Utility software   407
Volatile   398
Volatility   398

✳ MAKING BUSINESS DECISIONS

1. **Purchasing a Computer**

Dell specializes in computer customization. Connect to Dell's website at www.dell.com. Go to the portion of Dell's site that allows you to customize either a laptop or a desktop computer. First, choose an already prepared system and note its price and capability in terms of CPU speed, RAM size, monitor quality, and storage capacity. Now, customize that system to increase CPU speed, add more RAM, increase monitor size and quality, and add more storage capacity. What is the difference in price between the two? Which system is more in your price range? Which system has the speed and capacity you need?

2. Small Business Computers

Many different types of computers are available for small businesses. Use the Internet to find three different vendors of laptops or notebooks that are good for small businesses. Find the most expensive and the least expensive that the vendor offers and create a table comparing the different computers based on the following:

- CPU
- Memory
- Hard drive
- Optical drive
- Operating system
- Utility software
- Application software
- Support plan

Determine which computer you would recommend for a small business looking for an inexpensive laptop. Determine which computer you would recommend for a small business looking for an expensive laptop.

B4

MIS Infrastructures

1. Explain MIS infrastructure and its three primary types.
2. Identify the three primary areas associated with an information MIS infrastructure.
3. Describe the characteristics of an agile MIS infrastructure.

LO 1 Explain MIS infrastructure and its three primary types.

The Business Benefits of a Solid MIS Infrastructure

Management information systems have played a significant role in business strategies, affected business decisions and processes, and even changed the way companies operate. What is the foundation supporting all of these systems that enable business growth, operations, and profits? What supports the volume and complexity of today's user and application requirements? What protects systems from failures and crashes? It is the *MIS infrastructure*, which includes the plans for how a firm will build, deploy, use, and share its data, processes, and MIS assets. A solid MIS infrastructure can reduce costs, improve productivity, optimize business operations, generate growth, and increase profitability.

Briefly defined, *hardware* consists of the physical devices associated with a computer system, and *software* is the set of instructions the hardware executes to carry out specific tasks. In today's business environment, most hardware and software are run via a network. A *network* is a communications system created by linking two or more devices and establishing a standard methodology in which they can communicate. As more companies need to share more information, the network takes on greater importance in the infrastructure. Most companies use a specific form of network infrastructure called a client and server network. A *client* is a computer designed to request information from a server. A *server* is a computer dedicated to providing information in response to requests. A good way to understand this is when someone uses a web browser (this would be the client) to access a website (this would be a server that would respond with the web page being requested by the client).

In the physical world, a detailed blueprint would show how public utilities, such as water, electricity, and gas, support the foundation of a building. MIS infrastructure is similar, as it shows in detail how the hardware, software, and network connectivity support the firm's processes. Every company, regardless of size, relies on some form of MIS infrastructure, whether it is a few personal computers networked together sharing an Excel file or a large, multinational company with thousands of employees interconnected around the world.

MIS Infrastructure		
Information MIS Infrastructure Supports Operations	**Agile MIS Infrastructure** Supports Change	**Sustainable MIS Infrastructure** Supports Sustainability
Backup Recovery Disaster Recovery Business Continuity Planning	Accessibility Availability Maintainability Portability Reliability Scalability Usability	Grid Computing Cloud Computing Virtualization

An MIS infrastructure is dynamic; it continually changes as the business needs change. Each time a new form of Internet-enabled device, such as an iPhone or BlackBerry, is created and made available to the public, a firm's MIS infrastructure must be revised to support the device. This moves beyond just innovations in hardware to include new types of software and network connectivity. An ***enterprise architect (EA)*** is a person grounded in technology, fluent in business, and able to provide the important bridge between MIS and the business. Firms employ enterprise architects to help manage change and dynamically update MIS infrastructure. Figure B4.1 displays the three primary areas where enterprise architects focus when maintaining a firm's MIS infrastructure.

- **Supporting operations:** *Information MIS infrastructure* identifies where and how important information, such as customer records, is maintained and secured.
- **Supporting change:** *Agile MIS infrastructure* includes the hardware, software, and telecommunications equipment that, when combined, provides the underlying foundation to support the organization's goals.
- **Supporting the environment:** *Sustainable MIS infrastructure* identifies ways that a company can grow in terms of computing resources while simultaneously becoming less dependent on hardware and energy consumption.

Supporting Operations: Information MIS Infrastructure

LO 2 **Identify the three primary areas associated with an information MIS infrastructure.**

Imagine taking a quick trip to the printer on the other side of the room, and when you turn around you find that your laptop has been stolen. How painful would you find this experience? What types of information would you lose? How much time would it take you to recover all of that information? A few things you might lose include music, movies, emails, assignments, saved passwords, not to mention that all-important 40-page paper that took you more than a month to complete. If this sounds painful, then you want to pay particular attention to this section and learn how to eliminate this pain.

An information MIS infrastructure identifies where and how important information is maintained and secured. An information infrastructure supports day-to-day business operations and plans for emergencies such as power outages, floods, earthquakes, malicious attacks via the Internet, theft, and security breaches to name just a few. Managers must take every precaution to make sure their systems are operational and protected around the clock every day of the year. Losing a laptop or experiencing bad weather in one part of the country simply cannot take down systems required to operate core business processes. In the past, someone stealing company information would have to carry out boxes upon boxes of paper. Today, as data storage technologies grow in capabilities while shrinking in size, a person can simply walk out the front door of the building with the company's data files stored on a thumb drive or external hard drive. Today's managers must act responsibly to protect one of their most valued assets, information. To support continuous business operations, an information infrastructure provides three primary elements:

- Backup and recovery plan.
- Disaster recovery plan.
- Business continuity plan (see Figure B4.2).

BACKUP AND RECOVERY PLAN

Each year businesses lose time and money because of system crashes and failures. One way to minimize the damage of a system crash is to have a backup and recovery strategy in place. A **backup** is an exact copy of a system's information. **Recovery** is the ability to get a system up and running in the event of a system crash or failure that includes restoring the information backup. Many different types of backup and recovery media are available, including maintaining an identical replica or redundant of the storage server, external hard drives, thumb drives, and even DVDs. The primary differences between them are speed and cost.

Fault tolerance is the ability for a system to respond to unexpected failures or system crashes as the backup system immediately and automatically takes over with no loss of service. For example, fault tolerance enables a business to support continuous business operations if there is a power failure or flood. Fault tolerance is an expensive form of backup, and only

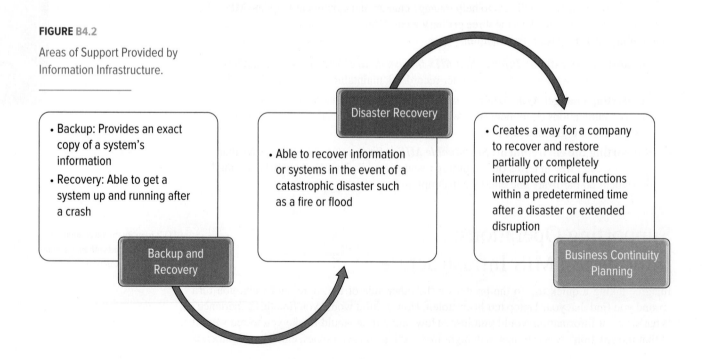

mission-critical applications and operations use it. ***Failover***, a specific type of fault tolerance, occurs when a redundant storage server offers an exact replica of the real-time data, and if the primary server crashes, the users are automatically directed to the secondary server or backup server. This is a high-speed and high-cost method of backup and recovery. ***Failback*** occurs when the primary machine recovers and resumes operations, taking over from the secondary server.

Using DVDs or thumb drives to store your data offers a low-speed and low-cost backup method. It is a good business practice to back up data at least once a week using a low-cost method. This will alleviate the pain of having your laptop stolen or your system crash as you will still have access to your data, and it will only be a few days old.

Deciding how often to back up information and what media to use is a critical decision. Companies should choose a backup and recovery strategy in line with their goals and operational needs. If the company deals with large volumes of critical information, it will require daily, perhaps hourly, backups to storage servers. If it relies on small amounts of noncritical information, then it might require only weekly backups to external hard drives or thumb drives. A company that backs up on a weekly basis is taking the risk that, if a system crash occurs, it could lose a week's worth of work. If this risk is acceptable, a weekly backup strategy will work. If it is unacceptable, the company needs more frequent backup.

DISASTER RECOVERY PLAN

Disasters such as power outages, fires, floods, hurricanes, and even malicious activities such as hackers and viruses strike companies every day. Disasters can have the following effects on companies and their business operations.

- **Disrupting communications:** Most companies depend on voice and data communications for daily operational needs. Widespread communications outages, from either direct damage to the infrastructure or sudden spikes in usage related to an outside disaster, can be as devastating to some firms as shutting down the whole business.

- **Damaging physical infrastructures:** Fire and flood can directly damage buildings, equipment, and systems, making structures unsafe and systems unusable. Law enforcement officers and firefighters may prohibit business professionals from entering a building, thereby restricting access to retrieve documents or equipment.

- **Halting transportation:** Disasters such as floods and hurricanes can have a deep effect on transportation. Disruption to major highways, roads, bridges, railroads, and airports can prevent business professionals from reporting to work or going home, slow the delivery of supplies, and stop the shipment of products.

- **Blocking utilities:** Public utilities, such as the supply of electric power, water, and natural gas, can be interrupted for hours or days even in incidents that cause no direct damage to the physical infrastructure. Buildings are often uninhabitable and systems unable to function without public utilities.

These effects can devastate companies by causing them to cease operations for hours, days, or longer and risk losing customers whom they cannot then supply. Therefore, to combat these disasters a company can create a ***disaster recovery plan***, which is a detailed process for recovering information or a system in the event of a catastrophic disaster. This plan includes such factors as which files and systems need to have backups and their corresponding frequency and methods along with the strategic location of the storage in a separate physical site that is geographically dispersed. A company might strategically maintain operations in New York and San Francisco, ensuring that a natural disaster would not impact both locations. A disaster recovery plan also foresees the possibility that not only the computer equipment but also the building where employees work may be destroyed. A ***hot site*** is a separate and fully equipped facility where the company can move immediately after a disaster and resume business. A ***cold site*** is a separate facility that does not have any computer equipment but is a place where employees can move after a disaster. A ***warm site*** is a separate facility with computer equipment that requires installation and configuration. Figure B4.3 outlines these resources that support disaster recovery.

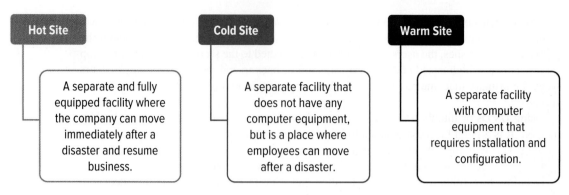

Hot Site	Cold Site	Warm Site
A separate and fully equipped facility where the company can move immediately after a disaster and resume business.	A separate facility that does not have any computer equipment, but is a place where employees can move after a disaster.	A separate facility with computer equipment that requires installation and configuration.

FIGURE B4.3

Sites to Support Disaster Recovery.

A disaster recovery plan usually has a disaster recovery cost curve to support it. A ***disaster recovery cost curve*** charts (1) the cost to the company of the unavailability of information and technology and (2) the cost to the company of recovering from a disaster over time. Figure B4.4 displays a disaster recovery cost curve and shows that the best recovery plan in terms of cost and time is where the two lines intersect. Creating such a curve is no small task. Managers must consider the cost of losing information and technology within each department or functional area, and across the whole company. During the first few hours of a disaster, those costs may be low, but they rise over time. With those costs in hand, a company must then determine the costs of recovery. Figure B4.5 displays TechTarget's disaster recovery strategies for business.

On April 18, 1906, San Francisco was rocked by an earthquake that destroyed large sections of the city and claimed the lives of more than 3,000 inhabitants. More than a century later, a rebuilt and more durable San Francisco serves as a central location for major MIS corporations as well as a major world financial center. Managers of these corporations are well aware of the potential disasters that exist along the San Andreas Fault and actively update their business continuity plans anticipating such issues as earthquakes and floods. The Union Bank of California is located in the heart of downtown San Francisco and maintains a highly detailed and well-developed business continuity plan. The company employs hundreds of business professionals scattered around the world that coordinate plans for addressing the potential loss of a facility, business professionals, or critical systems so that the company can continue to operate if a disaster happens. Its disaster recovery plan includes hot sites where staff can walk in and start working exactly as if they were in their normal location. It would be a matter of minutes, not hours, for the Union Bank of California to be up and running again in the event of a disaster.

FIGURE B4.4

Disaster Recovery Cost Curve.

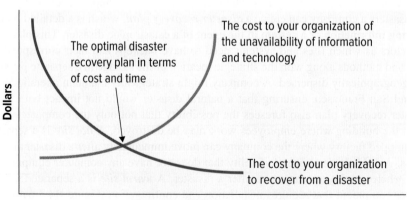

The cost to your organization of the unavailability of information and technology

The optimal disaster recovery plan in terms of cost and time

The cost to your organization to recover from a disaster

Dollars

Time from Disaster to Recovery

BUSINESS CONTINUITY PLAN

An *emergency* is a sudden, unexpected event requiring immediate action due to potential threat to health and safety, the environment, or property. *Emergency preparedness* ensures a company is ready to respond to an emergency in an organized, timely, and effective manner. Natural disasters and terrorist attacks are on the minds of business professionals who take safeguarding their information assets seriously. Disaster recovery plans typically focus on systems and data, ignoring cross-functional and intraorganizational business processes that can be destroyed during an emergency. For this reason many companies are turning to a more comprehensive and all-encompassing emergency preparedness plan known as *business continuity planning (BCP)*, which details how a company recovers and restores critical business operations and systems after a disaster or extended disruption. BCP includes such factors as identifying critical systems, business processes, departments, and the maximum amount of time the business can continue to operate without functioning systems. BCP contains disaster recovery plans along with many additional plans, including prioritizing business impact analysis, emergency notification plans, and technology recovery strategies (see Figures B4.6 and B4.7).

Business Impact Analysis

A *business impact analysis* identifies all critical business functions and the effect that a specific disaster may have upon them. A business impact analysis is primarily used to ensure a company has made the right decisions about the order of recovery priorities and strategies. For example, should the accounting department have its systems up and running before the sales and marketing departments? Will email be the first system for recovery to ensure employees can communicate with each other and outside stakeholders such as customers, suppliers, and partners? The business impact analysis is a key part of BCP as it details the order in which functional areas should be restored, ensuring the most critical are focused on first.

Emergency Notification Services

A business continuity plan typically includes an *emergency notification service*, that is, an infrastructure built for notifying people in the event of an emergency. Radio stations' occasional tests of the national Emergency Alert System are an example of a very large-scale emergency notification system. A firm will implement an emergency notification service

DISASTER RECOVERY STRATEGIES	
1. Activate backup and recovery facilities in secondary company data center; transfer production to that site	Assumes the secondary data center has sufficient resources, e.g., storage capacity, server hardware to accommodate additional processing requirements
2. Activate recovery resources in a cloud-based service; failover critical systems to that site and resume operations	Ensure that your contract for this service has the ability to flex as your needs dictate; ensure that security of your data can be maintained
3. Activate backup systems and data at a hot site; transfer operations to that site	Be sure you know what resources you have available at the hot site, what the declaration rules and fees are, and what your options are if multiple declarations are occurring at the same time
4. Replace damaged equipment with spare components	As much as possible, have available spare systems, circuit boards, and power supplies; backup disks with system software; and hard and soft copies of critical documentation
5. Recover virtual machines at an alternate site; assumes VMs have been updated to be current with production VMs	Create VM clones at an alternate site, keep them updated, and if needed they can quickly become production VMs
6. Activate alternate network routes and re-route data and voice traffic away from the failed network service	Ensure that network infrastructures have diverse routing of local access channels as well as diverse routing of high-capacity circuits[3]

FIGURE B4.5

TechTarget's Disaster Recovery Strategies.

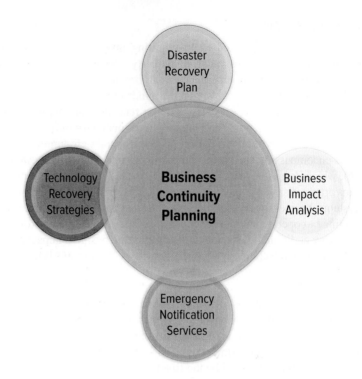

BUSINESS CONTINUITY STRATEGIES	
1. Evacuate existing building and relocate to a prear-ranged alternate work area	Assumes the alternate site is ready for occupancy, or can be made ready quickly, based on recovery time objectives; ensure that transportation is available
2. Work from home	Ensure that staff have broadband and Internet access at home; ensure that there are sufficient network access points to accommodate the increase in usage
3. Move selected staff to a hot site.	Assumes a hot site program is in place and that space is available at the site for staff
4. Move alternate staff into leadership roles in the absence of key leaders; ensure that they have been cross-trained	Succession planning is a key strategy in business continuity; it ensures that loss of a senior manager or someone with special expertise can be replaced with minimal disruption to the business
5. Move staff into local or nearby hotels and set up temporary work space	Make sure this kind of arrangement is set up with hotels in advance, especially in case of an incident that disrupts many other businesses in the same area
6. Relocate staff to another company office have access	Organizations with multiple offices that to the company network as well as work space can be leveraged to temporarily house employees[4]

to warn employees of unexpected events and provide them with instructions about how to handle the situation. Emergency notification services can be deployed through the firm's own infrastructure, supplied by an outside service provider on company premises, or hosted remotely by an outside service provider. All three methods provide notification using a variety of methods such as email, voice notification to a cell phone, and text messaging. The notifications can be sent to all the devices selected, providing multiple means in which to get critical information to those who need it.

Technology Recovery Strategies

Companies create massive amounts of data vital to their survival and continued operations. A *technology failure* occurs when the ability of a company to operate is impaired because of a hardware, software, or data outage. Technology failures can destroy large amounts of vital data, often causing *incidents*, unplanned interruption of a service. An *incident record* contains all of the details of an incident. *Incident management* is the process responsible for managing how incidents are identified and corrected. *Technology recovery strategies* focus specifically on prioritizing the order for restoring hardware, software, and data across the organization that best meets business recovery requirements. A technology recovery strategy details the order of importance for recovering hardware, software, data centers, and networking (or connectivity). If one of these four vital components is not functioning, the entire system will be unavailable, shutting down cross-functional business processes such as order management and payroll. Figure B4.8 displays the key areas a company should focus on when developing technology recovery strategies.

Supporting Change: Agile MIS Infrastructure

LO 3 Describe the characteristics of an agile MIS infrastructure.

Agile MIS infrastructure includes the hardware, software, and telecommunications equipment that, when combined, provides the underlying foundation to support the organization's goals. If a company grows by 50 percent in a single year, its infrastructure and systems must be able to handle a 50 percent growth rate. If they cannot, they can severely hinder the company's ability not only to grow but also to function.

The future of a company depends on its ability to meet its partners, suppliers, and customers anytime of the day in any geographic location. Imagine owning an ebusiness and everyone on the Internet is tweeting and collaborating about how great your business idea is and how successful your company is going to be. Suddenly, you have 5 million global customers interested in your website. Unfortunately, you did not anticipate this many customers so quickly, and the system crashes. Users typing in your URL find a blank message stating the website is unavailable and to try back soon. Or even worse, they can get to your website but it takes three minutes to reload each time they click on a button. The buzz soon dies about your business idea as some innovative web-savvy fast follower quickly copies your idea and creates a website that can handle the massive number of customers. The characteristics of agile MIS infrastructures can help ensure your systems can meet and perform under any unexpected or unplanned changes. Figure B4.9 lists the seven abilities of an agile infrastructure.

ACCESSIBILITY

Accessibility refers to the varying levels that define what a user can access, view, or perform when operating a system. Imagine the people at your college accessing the main student infor-

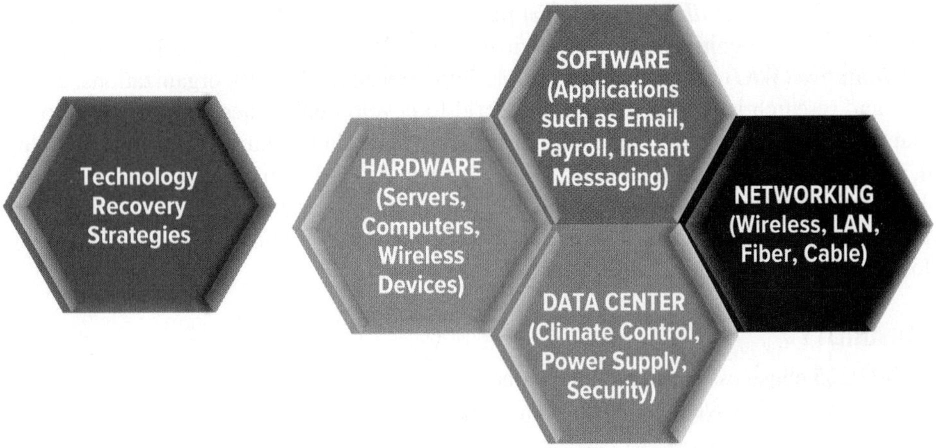

FIGURE B4.8

Key Areas of Technology Recovery Strategies.

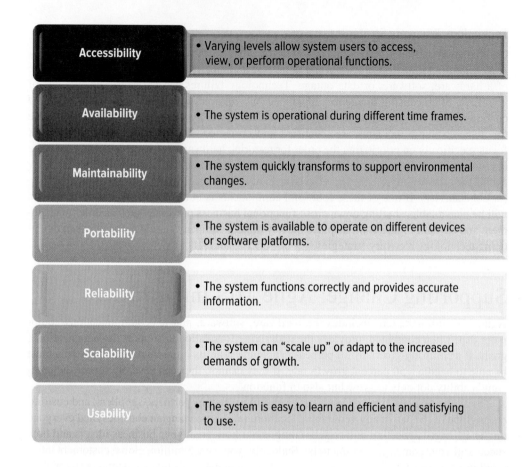

Accessibility	• Varying levels allow system users to access, view, or perform operational functions.
Availability	• The system is operational during different time frames.
Maintainability	• The system quickly transforms to support environmental changes.
Portability	• The system is available to operate on different devices or software platforms.
Reliability	• The system functions correctly and provides accurate information.
Scalability	• The system can "scale up" or adapt to the increased demands of growth.
Usability	• The system is easy to learn and efficient and satisfying to use.

mation system. Each person that accesses the system will have different needs and requirements; for example, a payroll employee will need to access vacation information and salary information, or a student will need to access course information and billing information. Each system user is provided with an access level that details which parts of the system the user can and cannot access and what the user can do when in the system. For example, you would not want your students to be able to view payroll information or professors' personal information; also, some users can only view information and are not allowed to create or delete information. Top-level MIS employees require *administrator access*, or unrestricted access to the entire system. Administrator access can perform functions such as resetting passwords, deleting accounts, and shutting down entire systems.

Tim Berners-Lee, W3C director and inventor of the World Wide Web, stated, "the power of the web is in its universality. Access by everyone regardless of disability is an essential aspect." *Web accessibility* means that people with disabilities, including visual, auditory, physical, speech, cognitive, and neurological disabilities, can use the web. The *web accessibility initiative (WAI)* brings together people from industry, disability organizations, government, and research labs from around the world to develop guidelines and resources to help make the web accessible to people with disabilities, including auditory, cognitive, neurological, physical, speech, and visual disabilities. The goal of WAI is to allow people to access the full potential of the web, enabling people with disabilities to participate equally. For example, Apple includes screen magnification and VoiceOver on its iPhone, iPad, and iPod, which allow the blind and visually impaired to use the devices.

AVAILABILITY

In a 24/7/365 ebusiness environment, business professionals need to use their systems whenever they want from wherever they want. *Availability* refers to the time frames when the system is operational. A system is called **unavailable** when it is not operating and cannot be used. **High availability** occurs when a system is continuously operational at all times. Availability is typically measured relative to "100 percent operational" or "never failing." A widely held but difficult-to-achieve standard of availability for a system is known as "five 9s" (99.999 percent) availability. Some companies have systems available around the clock to support ebusiness operations, global customers, and online suppliers.

Sometimes systems must be taken down for maintenance, upgrades, and fixes, which are completed during downtime. One challenge with availability is determining when to schedule system downtime if the system is expected to operate continuously. Performing maintenance during the evening might seem like a great idea, but evening in one city is morning somewhere else in the world, and business professionals scattered around the globe may not be able to perform specific job functions if the systems they need are unavailable. This is where companies deploy failover systems so they can take the primary system down for maintenance and activate the secondary system to ensure continuous operations.

MAINTAINABILITY

Companies must watch today's needs, as well as tomorrow's, when designing and building systems that support agile infrastructures. Systems must be flexible enough to meet all types of company changes, environmental changes, and business changes. **Maintainability (or flexibility)** refers to how quickly a system can transform to support environmental changes. Maintainability helps to measure how quickly and effectively a system can be changed or repaired after a failure. For example, when starting a small business you might not consider that you will have global customers, a common mistake. When building your systems, you might not design them to handle multiple currencies and different languages, which might make sense if the company is not currently performing international business. Unfortunately, when the first international order arrives, which happens easily with ebusiness, the system will be unable to handle the request because it does not have the flexibility to be easily reconfigured for a new language or currency. When the company does start growing and operating overseas, the system will need to be redeveloped, which is not an easy or cheap task, to handle multiple currencies and different languages.

Building and deploying flexible systems allow easy updates, changes, and reconfigurations for unexpected business or environmental changes. Just think what might have happened if Facebook had had to overhaul its entire system to handle multiple languages. Another social networking business could easily have stepped in and become the provider of choice. That certainly would not be efficient or effective for business operations.

PORTABILITY

Portability refers to the ability of an application to operate on different devices or software platforms, such as different operating systems. Apple's iTunes is readily available to users of Mac computers as well as users of PC computers, smartphones, iPods, iPhones, iPads, and so on. It is also a portable application. Because Apple insists on compatibility across its products, both software and hardware, Apple can easily add to its product, device, and service offerings without sacrificing portability. Many software developers are creating programs that are portable to all three devices—the iPhone, iPod, and iPad—which increases their target market and they hope their revenue.

RELIABILITY

Reliability (or accuracy) ensures a system is functioning correctly and providing accurate information. Inaccuracy can occur for many reasons, from the incorrect entry of information to the corruption of information during transmissions. Many argue that the information contained in Wikipedia is unreliable. Because the Wikipedia entries can be edited by any user, there are examples of rogue users inaccurately updating information. Many users skip over Google search findings that correlate to Wikipedia for this reason. Housing unreliable information on a website can put a company at risk of losing customers, placing inaccurate supplier orders, or even making unreliable business decisions. A *vulnerability* is a system weakness, such as a password that is never changed or a system left on while an employee goes to lunch, that can be exploited by a threat. Reliable systems ensure that vulnerabilities are kept at a minimum to reduce risk.

SCALABILITY

Estimating company growth is a challenging task, in part because growth can occur in a number of different forms—the firm can acquire new customers, new product lines, or new markets. *Scalability* describes how well a system can scale up, or adapt to the increased demands of growth. If a company grows faster than anticipated, it might experience a variety of problems, from running out of storage space to taking more time to complete transactions. Anticipating expected, and unexpected, growth is key to building scalable systems that can support that development.

Performance measures how quickly a system performs a process or transaction. Performance is a key component of scalability as systems that can't scale suffer from performance issues. Just imagine your college's content management system suddenly taking five minutes to return a page after a button is pushed. Now imagine if this occurs during your midterm exam and you miss the two-hour deadline because the system is so slow. Performance issues experienced by firms can have disastrous business impacts causing loss of customers, loss of suppliers, and even loss of help-desk employees. Most users will wait only a few seconds for a website to return a request before growing frustrated and either calling the support desk or giving up and moving on to another website.

Capacity represents the maximum throughput a system can deliver; for example, the capacity of a hard drive represents its size or volume. *Capacity planning* determines future environmental infrastructure requirements to ensure high-quality system performance. If a company purchases connectivity software that is outdated or too slow to meet demand, its employees will waste a great deal of time waiting for systems to respond to user requests. It is cheaper for a company to design and implement agile infrastructure that envisions growth requirements than to update all the equipment after the system is already operational. If a company with 100 workers merges with another company and suddenly there are 400 people using the system, performance time could suffer. Planning for increases in capacity can ensure systems perform as expected. Waiting for a system to respond to requests is not productive.

Web 2.0 is a big driver for capacity planning to ensure agile infrastructures can meet the business's operational needs. Delivering videos over the Internet requires enough bandwidth to satisfy millions of users during peak periods such as Friday and Saturday evenings. Video transmissions over the Internet cannot tolerate packet loss (blocks of data loss), and allowing one additional user to access the system could degrade the video quality for every user.

USABILITY

Usability is the degree to which a system is easy to learn and efficient and satisfying to use. Providing hints, tips, shortcuts, and instructions for any system, regardless of its ease of use, is recommended. Apple understood the importance of usability when it designed the first iPod. One of the iPod's initial attractions was the usability of the click wheel. One simple and efficient button operates the iPod, making it usable for all ages. And to ensure ease of use, Apple also made the corresponding iTunes software intuitive and easy to use. *Serviceability* is how quickly a third party can change a system to ensure it meets user needs and the terms of any contracts, including agreed levels of reliability, maintainability, or availability. When using a system from a third party, it is important to ensure the right level of serviceability for all users, including remote employees.

An MIS infrastructure is dynamic; it continually changes as the business needs change. Each time a new form of Internet-enabled device, such as an iPhone or BlackBerry, is created and made available to the public, a firm's MIS infrastructure must be revised to support the device. This moves beyond just innovations in hardware to include new types of software and network connectivity. The three primary areas where enterprise architects focus when maintaining a firm's MIS infrastructure are as follows:

- *Supporting operations:* Information MIS infrastructure identifies where and how important information, such as customer records, is maintained and secured.

- *Supporting change:* Agile MIS infrastructure includes the hardware, software, and telecommunications equipment that, when combined, provide the underlying foundation to support the organization's goals.

- *Supporting the environment:* Sustainable MIS infrastructure identifies ways that a company can grow in terms of computing resources while simultaneously becoming less dependent on hardware and energy consumption.

✱ KEY TERMS

Accessibility   419
Administrator access   420
Agile MIS infrastructure   413
Availability   420
Backup   414
Business continuity planning
   (BCP)   417
Business impact analysis   417
Capacity   422
Capacity planning   422
Client   412
Cold site   415
Disaster recovery cost curve   416
Disaster recovery plan   415
Emergency   417
Emergency notification
   service   417
Emergency preparedness   417

Enterprise architect (EA)   413
Failback   415
Failover   415
Fault tolerance   414
Hardware   412
High availability   421
Hot site   415
Incident   419
Incident management   419
Incident record   419
Information MIS
   infrastructure   413
Maintainability (or flexibility)   421
MIS infrastructure   412
Network   412
Performance   422
Portability   421
Recovery   414

Reliability (or accuracy)   421
Scalability   422
Server   412
Serviceability   422
Software   412
Sustainable MIS
   infrastructure   413
Technology failure   419
Technology recovery
   strategy   419
Unavailable   421
Usability   422
Vulnerability   422
Warm site   415
Web accessibility   420
Web accessibility initiative
   (WAI)   420

✱ MAKING BUSINESS DECISIONS

1. Creating Your BCP Plan

Business disruption costs money. In the event of a disaster or emergency, you will not only lose revenue, you will also incur additional expenses. If you are expecting your insurance to cover your losses, be careful—there are many losses your insurance will not cover such as lost sales, lost business intelligence, and lost customers. To mitigate the risks of a catastrophe, you will want to create a detailed business continuity plan. A business continuity plan (BCP) is not only a good idea but also one of the least expensive plans a company can develop. A BCP will detail how employees will contact each other and continue to keep operations functioning in the event of a disaster or emergency such as a fire or flood. Regrettably, many companies never take the time to develop such a plan until it is too late.

Research the web for sample BCP plans for a small business or a start-up. In a group, create a BCP for a start-up of your choice. Be sure to think of such things as data storage, data access, transaction processing, employee safety, and customer communications.

2. Disaster Recovery

Backup and recovery are essential for any computer system. How painful would it be if someone stole your laptop right now? How much critical information would you lose? How many hours would it take you to re-create your data? Perhaps that will motivate you to implement a backup procedure. How many of you have a disaster recovery plan? Disaster recovery is needed when your best friend dumps a grande latte on your computer or you accidently wash your thumb drive.

Disaster recovery plans are crucial for any business, and you should ensure that your company has everything it needs to continue operations if there is ever a disaster, such as 9/11. You need to decide which disasters are worth worrying about and which ones probably will never occur. For example, if you live in Colorado, chances are good you don't have to worry about hurricanes, but avalanches are another story.

How often does a company need to back up its data? Where should the backup be stored? What types of disasters should companies in your state prepare for in case of an emergency? Why is it important to test the backup? What could happen to a company if it failed to create a disaster recovery plan?

3. Ranking the Ab-"ilities"

Do you know how Google makes so much money? Unlike traditional businesses, Google does not make money from the users of its service. Google makes money by charging the companies that want to appear in the sponsored section of a search result. After performing a Google search, you will notice three sections on the resulting page. Along the top and side are the sponsored search results, and the middle lists the organic search results. Google's innovative marketing program, called AdWords, allows companies to bid on common search terms, and the highest bidder is posted first in the sponsored search results. Every time a user clicks a sponsored link, the company that owns the link has to pay Google. This is also called pay-per-click and can cost anywhere from a few cents to a few dollars for each click. A general search term such as "tropical vacation" costs less than a more specific search term such as "Hawaiian vacation." Whichever company bids the most for the search term appears at the top of the sponsored section. Clicking the links in the organic search results does not incur any charges for the company that owns the link.

Rank the agile infrastructure ab-"ilities" for Google from most important to least important in terms of supporting Google's MIS infrastructure and business operations. Be sure to provide the justification behind your ranking.

4. Laptop? Notebook? Netbook? Tablet?

Thanks to Moore's Law, computing devices are getting smaller, cheaper, and faster every year, allowing innovative companies to create new devices that are smaller and more powerful than current devices. Just look at desktop, laptop, notebook, and tablet computers. These are all different devices allowing users to connect and compute around the globe. Moore's Law has been accurate about computing power roughly doubling every 18 months. Do you agree or disagree that Moore's Law will continue to apply for the next 20 years? Why or why not?

5. Universities Are Switching to Gmail

Schools around the world are moving to cloud computing applications such as Google Docs & Spreadsheets and Google Calendar. Yale had planned to move from its own email system to Google Mail, but at the last minute decided to cancel the project because school administrators and faculty members did not believe the move could support their business requirements. Do you agree or disagree that Google Gmail would be unable to replace a university's private email system? What are the advantages and disadvantages of a private email system? What are the advantages and disadvantages of using a cloud application such as Google Gmail? What choice would you make if you were the primary decision maker for choosing your school's email system?

6. I Don't Have a Temperature, but I'm Positive I Have a Virus

Think how horrible it would be to finish your term paper at 4 a.m. and find out that your computer has a virus and you just lost your entire document. Or perhaps you submit your final paper, which is worth 50 percent of your grade, and then head off to Colorado for winter break. You return to find that you failed the course, and you frantically check email to find out what happened. A message from your professor informs you that your document was corrupt and couldn't be opened and that you had 24 hours to resend the file, which you missed because you were skiing down the slopes.

Have you ever experienced having a file corrupted? If so, what could you have done to recover from this situation? Do you think your instructor ever receives corrupted files? How did the file become corrupted? Do you think your instructor would be suspicious if you submitted a corrupted file?

7. Sustainable Departments

Energy prices and global warming are discussed daily in the news as the environmental impact of ewaste is just beginning to be recognized. Sustainability and corporate social responsibility need to be taken seriously by all managers because everyone should take an active role in helping to preserve the environment. List the different departments in a business and the types of environmental issues they typically encounter. Which department do you think creates the most ewaste? Which department uses the greatest amount of electricity or has the largest carbon footprint? What can each department do to help combat its environmental issues? Why do all managers, and for that matter all employees, need to be aware of environmental issues and ways they can create sustainable MIS infrastructures?

8. Facebook's Energy Use

Cheap electricity is great for keeping business costs down, but it often means relying on coal for power. Facebook recently commissioned a new computing facility in Oregon and is using power from PacifiCorp, a utility that gets the majority of its energy from coal-fired power stations, which are major contributors of greenhouse gas emissions. As more and more people subscribe to Facebook, its energy needs are increasing almost exponentially.

Do you agree that Facebook made a wise business decision in selecting a utility provider that uses coal-fired power stations? What alternative sources of energy could Facebook have used to power its computing facility? Do you think Facebook's core customers care about the environment? What types of business challenges might Facebook encounter if it continues using coal-fired power stations?

9. Planning for Disaster Recovery

You are the new senior analyst in the MIS department at Beltz, a large snack food manufacturing company. The company is located on the beautiful shoreline in Charleston, South Carolina. The company's location is one of its best and worst features. The weather and surroundings are beautiful, but the threat of hurricanes and other natural disasters is high. What types of information should be contained in Beltz's disaster recovery plan that will minimize any risks involved with a natural disaster?

10. Comparing Backup and Recovery Systems

Research the Internet to find three vendors of backup and recovery systems. Compare and contrast the three systems and determine which one you would recommend if you were installing a backup and recovery system for a medium-sized business, with 3,500 employees, that maintains information on the stock market. Compile your findings in a presentation that you can give to your class that details the three systems' strengths and weaknesses, along with your recommendation.

11. Cool Schools

Very large computers and data centers incur huge energy costs keeping electronic components cooled. Where is your school's data center located? How big is it? What security measures does the facility enforce? Can you get a tour of it? If it is on campus, how is the facility cooled? How is the power supplied? Heating and cooling computer systems are certainly a big issue. Think of ways you could reuse the heat from a data center, such as sending it to a college dorm. Could alternative resources, such as a nearby river or a lake, provide added cooling? What unanticipated environmental issues could this create?

Networks and Telecommunications

LO 1 Compare LANs, WANs, and MANs.

Introduction

Change is everywhere in the information technology domain, but nowhere is change more evident and more dramatic than the realm of networks and telecommunications. Most management information systems today rely on digital networks to communicate information in the form of data, graphics, video, and voice. Companies large and small from all over the world are using networks and the Internet to locate suppliers and buyers, to negotiate contracts with them, and to provide bigger, better, and faster services than ever before. *Telecommunication systems* enable the transmission of data over public or private networks. A *network* is a communications system created by linking two or more devices and establishing a standard methodology by which they can communicate. The world's largest and most widely used network is the Internet. The Internet is a global "network of networks" that uses universal standards to connect millions of different networks around the world. Telecommunication systems and networks are traditionally complicated and historically inefficient. However, businesses can benefit from today's network infrastructures that provide reliable global reach to employees and customers.

Network Basics

Networks range from small two-computer networks to the biggest network of all, the Internet. A network provides two principle benefits: the ability to communicate and the ability to share.

Today's corporate digital networks include a combination of local area networks, wide area networks, and metropolitan area networks. A *local area network (LAN)* is designed to connect a group of computers in proximity to each other such as in an office building, a school, or a home. A LAN is useful for sharing resources such as files, printers, games, or other applications. A LAN in turn often connects to other LANs, and to the Internet or wide area networks. A *wide area network (WAN)* spans a large geographic area, such as a state, province, or country. WANs often connect multiple smaller networks, such as local area networks or metropolitan area networks. The world's most popular WAN is the Internet. A *metropolitan area network (MAN)* is a large computer network usually spanning a city. Figure B5.1 highlights the three different types of networks, and Figure B5.2 illustrates each network type.

Direct data communication links between a company and its suppliers or customers, or both, have been successfully used to give the company a strategic advantage. The SABRE airline reservation system is a classic example of a strategic management information system that depends upon communication provided through a network. SABRE Airline Solutions pioneered technological advances for the industry in areas such as revenue management, pricing, flight scheduling, cargo, flight operations, and crew scheduling. In addition, not only did SABRE help invent ecommerce for the travel industry, the company holds claim to progressive solutions that defined—and continue to revolutionize—the travel and transportation marketplace.

A network typically includes four things (besides the computers themselves):

1. **Protocol**—a set of communication rules to make sure that everyone speaks the same language.
2. **Network interface card (NIC)**—a card that plugs into the back (or side) of your computers and lets them send and receive messages from other computers.
3. **Cable**—the medium to connect all of the computers.
4. **Hub (switch or router)**—hardware to perform traffic control.

We will continue to define many of these terms and concepts in the sections that follow. Networks are differentiated by the following:

- Architecture—peer-to-peer, client/server.
- Topology—bus, star, ring, hybrid, wireless.
- Protocols—Ethernet, transmission control protocol/Internet protocol (TCP/IP).
- Media—coaxial, twisted-pair, fiber-optic.

Architecture

LO 2 **Compare the two types of network architectures.**

The two primary types of network architectures are peer-to-peer networks and client/server networks.

Network Types	
Local area network (LAN)	Designed to connect a group of computers in proximity to each other such as in an office building, a school, or a home. A LAN is useful for sharing resources such as files, printers, games, or other applications. A LAN in turn often connects to other LANs, and to the Internet or wide area networks.
Wide area network (WAN)	Spans a large geographic area, such as a state, province, or country. WANs often connect multiple smaller networks, such as local area networks (LANs) or metropolitan area networks (MANs).
Metropolitan area network (MAN)	A large computer network usually spanning a city. Most colleges, universities, and large companies that span a campus use an infrastructure supported by a MAN.

FIGURE B5.1

Network Types.

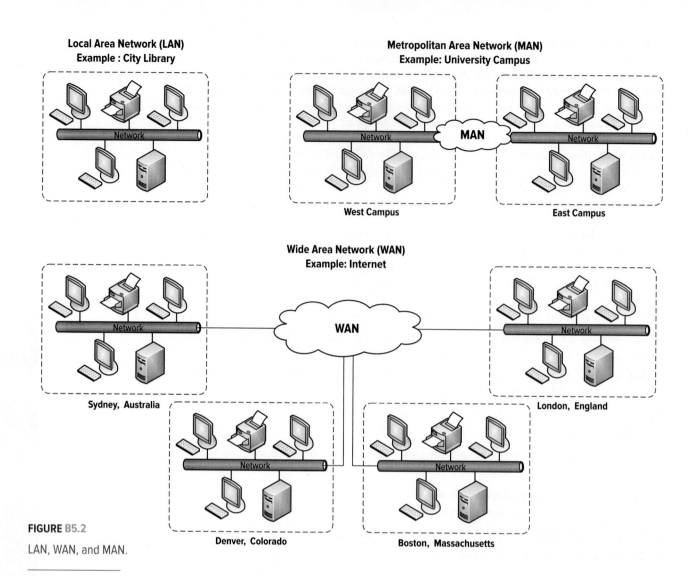

FIGURE B5.2

LAN, WAN, and MAN.

PEER-TO-PEER NETWORKS

A *peer-to-peer (P2P) network* is a computer network that relies on the computing power and bandwidth of the participants in the network rather than a centralized server, as illustrated in Figure B5.3. Each networked computer can allow other computers to access its files and use connected printers while it is in use as a workstation without the aid of a server.

FIGURE B5.3

Peer-to-Peer Networks.

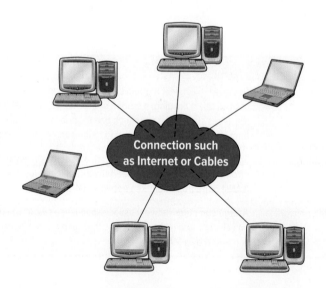

While Napster may be the most widely known example of a P2P implementation, it may also be one of the most narrowly focused since the Napster model takes advantage of only one of the many capabilities of P2P computing: file sharing. The technology has far broader capabilities, including the sharing of processing, memory, and storage, and the supporting of collaboration among vast numbers of distributed computers such as grid computing. Peer-to-peer computing enables immediate interaction among people and computer systems.[1]

CLIENT/SERVER NETWORKS

A *client* is a computer designed to request information from a server. A *server* is a computer dedicated to providing information in response to requests. A *client/server network* is a model for applications in which the bulk of the back-end processing, such as performing a physical search of a database, takes place on a server, while the front-end processing, which involves communicating with the users, is handled by the clients (see Figure B5.4). A *network operating system (NOS)* is the operating system that runs a network, steering information between computers and managing security and users. The client/server model has become one of the central ideas of network computing. Most business applications written today use the client/server model.

A fundamental part of client/server architecture is packet-switching. *Packet-switching* occurs when the sending computer divides a message into a number of efficiently sized units of data called packets, each of which contains the address of the destination computer. Each packet is sent on the network and intercepted by routers. A *router* is an intelligent connecting device that examines each packet of data it receives and then decides which way to send it onward toward its destination. The packets arrive at their intended destination, although some may have actually traveled by different physical paths, and the receiving computer assembles the packets and delivers the message to the appropriate application.

Topology

LO 3 Explain topology and the different types found in networks.

Networks are assembled according to certain rules. Cables, for example, have to be a certain length; each cable strand can support only a certain amount of network traffic. A *network topology* refers to the geometric arrangement of the actual physical organization of the computers (and other network devices) in a network. Topologies vary depending on cost and functionality. Figure B5.5 highlights the five common topologies used in networks, and Figure B5.6 displays each topology.

Protocols

LO 4 Describe protocols and the importance of TCP/IP.

A *protocol* is a standard that specifies the format of data as well as the rules to be followed during transmission. Simply put, for one computer (or computer program) to talk to another computer (or computer program) they must both be talking the same language, and this language is called a protocol.

FIGURE B5.4

Client/Server Network.

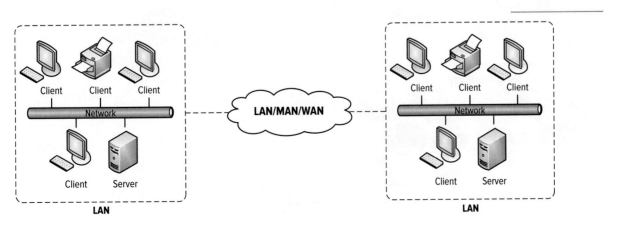

Network Topologies	
Bus	All devices are connected to a central cable, called the bus or backbone. Bus networks are relatively inexpensive and easy to install for small networks.
Star	All devices are connected to a central device, called a hub. Star networks are relatively easy to install and manage, but bottlenecks can occur because all data must pass through the hub.
Ring	All devices are connected to one another in the shape of a closed loop, so that each device is connected directly to two other devices, one on either side of it. Ring topologies are relatively expensive and difficult to install, but they offer high bandwidth and can span large distances.
Hybrid	Groups of star-configured workstations are connected to a linear bus backbone cable, combining the characteristics of the bus and star topologies.
Wireless	Devices are connected by signals between access points and wireless transmitters within a limited range.

A protocol is based on an agreed-upon and established standard, and this way all manufacturers of hardware and software that are using the protocol do so in a similar fashion to allow for interoperability. *Interoperability* is the capability of two or more computer systems to share data and resources, even though they are made by different manufacturers. The most popular network protocols used are Ethernet and transmission control protocol/Internet protocol (TCP/IP).

ETHERNET

Ethernet is a physical and data layer technology for LAN networking (see Figure B5.7). Ethernet is the most widely installed LAN access method, originally developed by Xerox

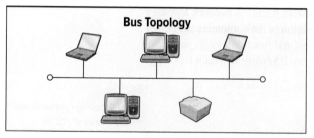

Bus Topology

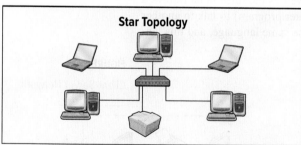

Star Topology

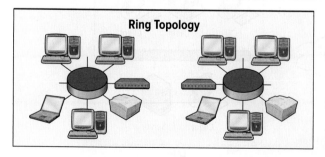

Ring Topology

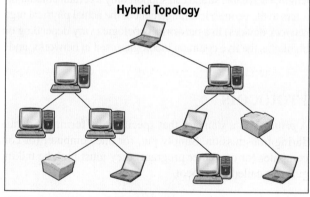

Hybrid Topology

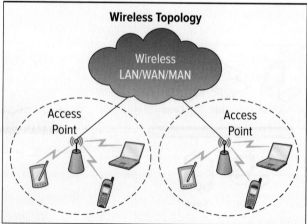

Wireless Topology

Wireless LAN/WAN/MAN

Access Point

Access Point

Ethernet LAN Diagram

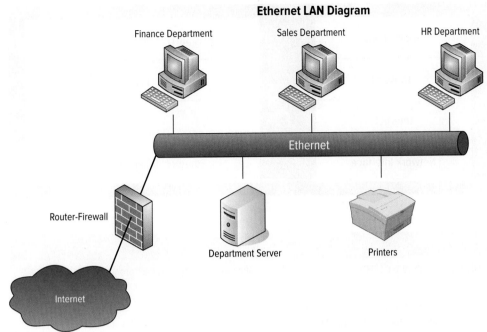

and then developed further by Xerox, Digital Equipment Corporation, and Intel. When it first began to be widely deployed in the 1980s, Ethernet supported a maximum theoretical data transfer rate of 10 megabits per second (Mbps). More recently, Fast Ethernet has extended traditional Ethernet technology to 100 Mbps peak, and Gigabit Ethernet technology extends performance up to 1,000 Mbps.

Ethernet is one of the most popular LAN technologies for the following reasons:

- Is easy to implement, manage, and maintain.
- Allows low-cost network implementations.
- Provides extensive flexibility for network installation.
- Guarantees interoperability of standards-compliant products, regardless of manufacturer.[2]

TRANSMISSION CONTROL PROTOCOL/INTERNET PROTOCOL

The most common telecommunication protocol is transmission control protocol/Internet protocol (TCP/IP), which was originally developed by the Department of Defense to connect a system of computer networks that became known as the Internet. *Transmission control protocol/Internet protocol (TCP/IP)* provides the technical foundation for the public Internet as well as for large numbers of private networks. The key achievement of TCP/IP is its flexibility with respect to lower-level protocols. TCP/IP uses a special transmission method that maximizes data transfer and automatically adjusts to slower devices and other delays encountered on a network. Although more than 100 protocols make up the entire TCP/IP protocol suite, the two most important of these are TCP and IP. **TCP** provides transport functions, ensuring, among other things, that the amount of data received is the same as the amount transmitted. **IP** provides the addressing and routing mechanism that acts as a postmaster. Figure B5.8 displays TCP/IP's four-layer reference model:

- Application layer—serves as the window for users and application processes to access network services.
- Transport layer—handles end-to-end packet transportation.

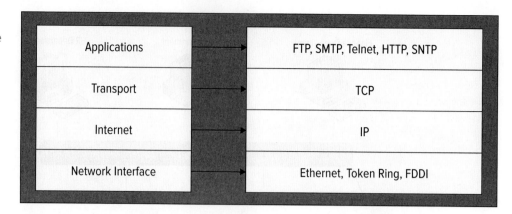

TCP/IP Applications	
File Transfer Protocol (FTP)	Allows files containing text, programs, graphics, numerical data, and so on to be downloaded off or uploaded onto a network.
Simple Mail Transfer Protocol (SMTP)	TCP/IP's own messaging system for email.
Telnet Protocol	Provides terminal emulation that allows a personal computer or workstation to act as a terminal, or access device, for a server.
Hypertext Transfer Protocol (HTTP)	Allows web browsers and servers to send and receive web pages.
Simple Network Management Protocol (SNMP)	Allows the management of networked nodes to be managed from a single point.

■ Internet layer—formats the data into packets, adds a header containing the packet sequence and the address of the receiving device, and specifies the services required from the network.

■ Network interface layer—places data packets on the network for transmission.[3]

OSI Model
7. Application
6. Presentation
5. Session
4. Transport
3. Network
2. Data Link
1. Physical

For a computer to communicate with other computers and web servers on the Internet, it must have a unique numeric IP address. IP provides the addressing and routing mechanism that acts as a postmaster. An IP address is a unique 32-bit number that identifies the location of a computer on a network. It works like a street address—as a way to find out exactly where to deliver information.

When IP addressing first came out, everyone thought that there were plenty of addresses to cover any need. Theoretically, you could have 4,294,967,296 unique addresses. The actual number of available addresses is smaller (somewhere between 3.2 and 3.3 billion) due to the way that the addresses are separated into classes, and some addresses are set aside for multicasting, testing, or other special uses.[4]

With the explosion of the Internet and the increase in home networks and business networks, the number of available IP addresses is simply not enough. The obvious solution is to redesign the address format to allow for more possible addresses. ***Internet protocol version 6 (IPv6)*** is the "next generation" protocol designed to replace the current version Internet protocol, IP version 4 (IPv4). However, IPv6 will take several years to implement because it requires modification of the entire infrastructure of the Internet. The main change brought by IPv6 is a much larger address space that allows greater flexibility in assigning addresses. IPv6 uses a 128-bit addressing scheme that produces 3.4×10^{38} addresses.[5]

The TCP/IP suite of applications includes five protocols—file transfer, simple mail transfer, telnet, hypertext transfer, and simple network management (see Figures B5.9 and B5.10).[6]

Media

Network transmission media refers to the various types of media used to carry the signal between computers. When information is sent across the network, it is converted into electrical signals. These signals are generated as electromagnetic waves (analog signaling) or as a sequence of voltage pulses (digital signaling). To be sent from one location to another, a signal must travel along a physical path. The physical path that is used to carry a signal between a signal transmitter and a signal receiver is called the transmission media. The two types of transmission media are wire (guided) and wireless (unguided).

WIRE MEDIA

Wire media are transmission material manufactured so that signals will be confined to a narrow path and will behave predictably. The three most commonly used types of guided media are (see Figure B5.11):

- Twisted-pair cable
- Coaxial cable
- Fiber-optic cable

Twisted-Pair Cable

Twisted-pair cable refers to a type of cable composed of four (or more) copper wires twisted around each other within a plastic sheath. The wires are twisted to reduce outside electrical interference. Twisted-pair cables come in shielded and unshielded varieties. Shielded cables have a metal shield encasing the wires that acts as a ground for electromagnetic interference. Unshielded twisted-pair (UTP) is the most popular and is generally the best option for LAN networks. The quality of UTP may vary from telephone-grade wire to high-speed cable. The cable has four pairs of wires inside the jacket. Each pair is twisted with a different number of twists per inch to help eliminate interference from adjacent pairs and other electrical devices. The connectors (called RF-45) on twisted-pair cables resemble large telephone connectors.

Coaxial Cable

Coaxial cable is cable that can carry a wide range of frequencies with low signal loss. It consists of a metallic shield with a single wire placed along the center of a shield and isolated from the shield by an insulator. Coaxial cable is similar to that used for cable television. This type of cable is referred to as coaxial because it contains one copper wire (or physical data channel) that carries the signal and is surrounded by another concentric physical channel consisting of a wire mesh. The outer channel serves as a ground for electrical interference.

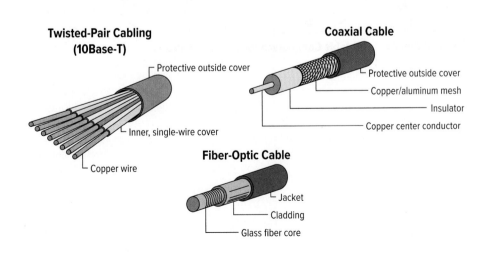

Twisted-Pair Cabling (10Base-T)
- Protective outside cover
- Inner, single-wire cover
- Copper wire

Coaxial Cable
- Protective outside cover
- Copper/aluminum mesh
- Insulator
- Copper center conductor

Fiber-Optic Cable
- Jacket
- Cladding
- Glass fiber core

FIGURE B5.11

Twisted-Pair, Coaxial Cable, and Fiber-Optic.

Because of this grounding feature, several coaxial cables can be placed within a single conduit or sheath without significant loss of data integrity.

Fiber-Optic Cable

Fiber-optic (**or** *optical fiber*) refers to the technology associated with the transmission of information as light impulses along a glass wire or fiber. Fiber-optic cable is the same type used by most telephone companies for long-distance service. Fiber-optic cable can transmit data over long distances with little loss in data integrity. In addition, because data are transferred as a pulse of light, fiber-optic is not subject to interference. The light pulses travel through a glass wire or fiber encased in an insulating sheath.

Fiber-optic's increased maximum effective distance comes at a price. Optical fiber is more fragile than wire, difficult to split, and labor intensive to install. For these reasons, fiber-optic is used primarily to transmit data over extended distances where the hardware required to relay the data signal on less expensive media would exceed the cost of fiber-optic installation. It is also used where large amounts of data need to be transmitted on a regular basis.

WIRELESS MEDIA

Wireless media are natural parts of the Earth's environment that can be used as physical paths to carry electrical signals. The atmosphere and outer space are examples of wireless media that are commonly used to carry these signals. Today, technologies for wireless data transmission include microwave transmission, communication satellites (see Figure B5.12), mobile phones, personal digital assistants (PDAs), personal computers (e.g., laptops), and mobile data networks.

Network signals are transmitted through all media as a type of waveform. When transmitted through wire and cable, the signal is an electrical waveform. When transmitted through fiber-optic cable, the signal is a light wave, either visible or infrared light. When transmitted through the Earth's atmosphere, the signal can take the form of waves in the radio spectrum, including microwaves, infrared, or visible light.

FIGURE B5.12

Communication Satellite Example.

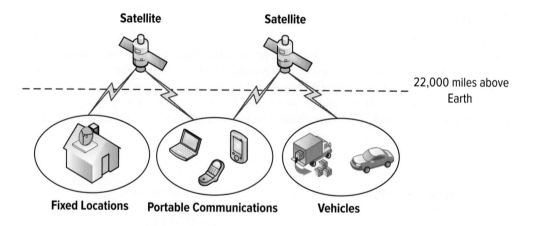

Satellite   Satellite

22,000 miles above Earth

Fixed Locations   **Portable Communications**   **Vehicles**

Networks come in all sizes, from two computers connected to share a printer to the Internet, which is the largest network of all, joining millions of computers of all types all over the world. In between are business networks, which vary in size from a dozen or fewer computers to many thousands. There are three primary types of networks: local area network (LAN), wide area network (WAN), and metropolitan area network (MAN). The following differentiate networks:

- Architecture—peer-to-peer, client/server.
- Topology—bus, star, ring, hybrid, wireless.
- Protocols—Ethernet, transmission control protocol/Internet protocol (TCP/IP).
- Media—coaxial, twisted-pair, fiber-optic.

★ KEY TERMS

Client   431
Client/server network   431
Coaxial cable   435
Ethernet   432
Fiber-optic (or optical fiber)   436
Internet protocol version 6
   (IPv6)   434
Interoperability   432
Local area network (LAN)   428
Metropolitan area network
   (MAN)   429

Network   435
Network operating system
   (NOS)   431
Network topology   431
Network transmission media   435
Packet-switching   431
Peer-to-peer (P2P) network   430
Protocol   431
Router   431
Server   431

Telecommunication system   428
Transmission control protocol/
   Internet protocol (TCP/IP)   433
Twisted-pair cable   435
Wide area network (WAN)   429
Wire media   435
Wireless media   436

★ MAKING BUSINESS DECISIONS

1. Secure Access

Organizations that have traditionally maintained private, closed systems have begun to look at the potential of the Internet as a ready-made network resource. The Internet is inexpensive and globally pervasive: Every phone jack is a potential connection. However, the Internet lacks security. What obstacles must organizations overcome to allow secure network connections?

2. Rolling Out with Networks

As organizations begin to realize the benefits of adding a wireless component to their network, they must understand how to leverage this emerging technology. Wireless solutions have come to the forefront for many organizations with the rollout of more standard, cost-effective, and secure wireless protocols. With wireless networks, increased business agility may be realized by continuous data access and synchronization. However, with the increased flexibility comes many challenges. Develop a report detailing the benefits an organization could obtain by implementing wireless technology. Also, include the challenges that a wireless network presents along with recommendations for any solutions.

3. Wireless Fitness

Sandifer's Fitness Club is located in beautiful South Carolina. Rosie Sandifer has owned and operated the club for 20 years. The club has three outdoor pools, two indoor pools, 10 racquetball courts, 10 tennis courts, an indoor and outdoor track, along with a four-story exercise equipment and massage therapy building. Rosie has hired you as a summer intern specializing in information technology. The extent of Rosie's current technology includes a few PCs in the accounting department and two PCs with Internet access for the rest of the staff. Your first assignment is to create a report detailing networks and wireless technologies. The report should explain how the club could gain a business advantage by implementing a wireless network. If Rosie likes your report, she will hire you as the full-time employee in charge of information technology. Be sure to include all of the different uses for wireless devices the club could implement to improve its operations.

4. Network Analysis

Global Manufacturing is considering a new technology application. The company wants to process orders in a central location and then assign production to different plants. Each plant will operate its own production scheduling and control system. Data on work in process and completed assemblies will be transmitted back to the central location that processes orders. At each plant, Global uses personal computers that perform routine tasks such as payroll and accounting. The production scheduling and control systems will be a package program running on a new computer dedicated to this application.

The MIS personnel at Global have retained you as a consultant to help with further analysis. What kind of network configuration seems most appropriate? How much bandwidth is needed? What data should be collected? Prepare a plan showing the information Global must develop to establish this network system. Should Global use a private network or can it accomplish its objectives through the Internet?

5. Frying Your Brains?

Radio waves, microwaves, and infrared all belong to the electromagnetic radiation spectrum used. These terms reference ranges of radiation frequencies we use every day in our wireless networking environments. However, the very word *radiation* strikes fear in many people. Cell towers have sprouted from fields all along highways. Tall rooftops harbor many more cell stations in cities. Millions of cell phone users place microwave transmitters/receivers next to their heads each time they make a call. With all this radiation zapping around, should we be concerned? Research the Internet to find out what the World Health Organization (WHO) has had to say about this.

6. Home Network Experience

If you maintain a home computer network (or have set one up in the past), create a document that describes the benefits that the network provides along with the difficulties that you have experienced. Include in your document a network topology, a detailed description of the type of network you have, and the equipment you use. If you have no experience with home networking, interview someone who does, and write up his or her comments. Compare this with several classmates, and discuss the benefits and challenges.

B6

Information Security

1. Describe the relationship between information security policies and an information security plan.
2. Provide an example of each of the three primary information security areas: (1) authentication and authorization, (2) prevention and resistance, and (3) detection and response.

LO 1 Describe the relationship between information security policies and an information security plan.

The First Line of Defense—People

Organizations today are able to mine valuable information such as the identity of the top 20 percent of their customers, who usually produce 80 percent of revenues. Most organizations view this type of information as intellectual capital and implement security measures to prevent it from walking out the door or falling into the wrong hands. At the same time, they must enable employees, customers, and partners to access needed information electronically. Organizations address security risks through two lines of defense; the first is people, the second technology.

Surprisingly, the biggest problem is people, as the majority of information security breaches result from people misusing organizational information. *Insiders* are legitimate users who purposely or accidentally misuse their access to the environment and cause some kind of business-affecting incident. For example, many individuals freely give up their passwords or write them on sticky notes next to their computers, leaving the door wide open for hackers. Through *social engineering*, hackers use their social skills to trick people into revealing access credentials or other valuable information. *Dumpster diving*, or looking through people's trash, is another way hackers obtain information. *Pretexting* is a form of social engineering in which one individual lies to obtain confidential data about another individual.

Information security policies identify the rules required to maintain information security, such as requiring users to log off before leaving for lunch or meetings, never sharing passwords with anyone, and changing passwords every 30 days. An *information security plan* details how an organization will implement the information security policies (see Figure B6.1). The best way a company can safeguard itself from people is by implementing and communicating its information security plan. This becomes even more important with Web 2.0 and as

Information Security Policies	Information Security Plan
Identifies the rules required to maintain information security	Details how an organization will implement the information security policies
Acceptable Encryption Policy	On-premise network servers must be encrypted and kept behind locked doors at a minimum. Limit employee access to servers.
Clean Desk Policy	Clear desk clear screen policy—all employees should be required to adhere to a clear desk, clear screen policy. When they leave their work computer, they should sign off to prevent an unauthorized user from accessing. You can set up a password-protected screensaver that will activate after 10 minutes in case the employee forgets to sign out. In addition ensure that employees do not leave sensitive printed information on their desks unattended.
Disaster Recovery Plan Policy	All networked computers must be accessed via a firewall.
Digital Signature Acceptance Policy	Keep filing cabinets locked at all times, and if feasible keep them behind locked doors. Keep keys locked in a single location with limited access.
Password Construction Guidelines	Require all employees to use password authentication to access their computers, the corporate network, and email.
Password Protection Policy	Set computer passwords to expire every 90 days.
Security Response Plan Policy	Client confidential information is defined as proprietary and confidential information received from customers. An example of this type of information is customer bank account info. This information type is restricted to management-approved internal access only.

FIGURE B6.1

Information Security Policies and Information Security Plan.

the use of mobile devices, remote workforce, and contractors are growing. A few details managers should consider surrounding people and information security policies include defining the best practices for:

- Applications allowed to be placed on the corporate network, especially various file sharing applications, IM software, and entertainment or freeware created by unknown sources (iPhone applications).
- Corporate computer equipment used for personal reason on personal networks.
- Password creation and maintenance including minimum password length, characters to be included while choosing passwords, and frequency for password changes.
- Personal computer equipment allowed to connect to the corporate network.
- Virus protection including how often the system should be scanned and how frequently the software should be updated. This could also include if downloading attachments is allowed and practices for safe downloading from trusted and untrustworthy sources.

The Second Line of Defense—Technology

Once an organization has protected its intellectual capital by arming its people with a detailed information security plan, it can begin to focus on deploying technology to help combat attackers. **Destructive agents** are malicious agents designed by spammers and other Internet attackers to farm email addresses off websites or deposit spyware on machines. Figure B6.2 displays the three areas where technology can aid in the defense against attacks.

LO 2 Provide an example of each of the three primary information security areas: (1) authentication and authorization, (2) prevention and resistance, and (3) detection and response.

PEOPLE: AUTHENTICATION AND AUTHORIZATION

Identity theft is the forging of someone's identity for the purpose of fraud. The fraud is often financial, because thieves apply for and use credit cards or loans in the victim's name. Two means of stealing an identity are phishing and pharming. **Information secrecy** is the category

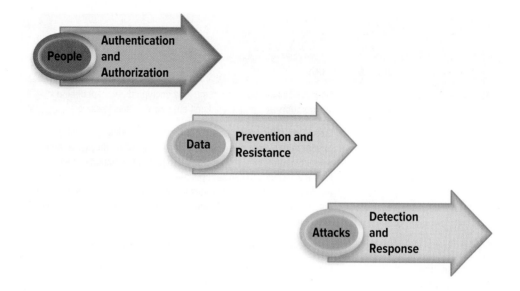

FIGURE B6.2

Three Areas of Information Security.

of computer security that addresses the protection of data from unauthorized disclosure and confirmation of data source authenticity. ***Phishing*** is a technique to gain personal information for the purpose of identity theft, usually by means of fraudulent emails that look as though they came from legitimate businesses. The messages appear to be genuine, with official-looking formats and logos, and typically ask for verification of important information such as passwords and account numbers, ostensibly for accounting or auditing purposes. Since the emails look authentic, up to one in five recipients responds with the information and subsequently becomes a victim of identity theft and other fraud. Figure B6.3 displays a phishing scam attempting to gain information for Skyline Bank; you should never click on emails asking you to verify your identity, as companies will never contact you directly asking for your username or password.[1]

Phishing expedition is a masquerading attack that combines spam with spoofing. The perpetrator sends millions of spam emails that appear to be from a respectable company. The emails contain a link to a website that is designed to look exactly like the company's website. The victim is encouraged to enter his or her username, password, and sometimes credit card information. ***Spear phishing*** is a phishing expedition in which the emails are carefully designed to target a particular person or organization. ***Vishing*** (**or** *voice phishing*) is a phone scam that attempts to defraud people by asking them to call a bogus telephone number to "confirm" their account information.

Pharming reroutes requests for legitimate websites to false websites. For example, if you were to type in the URL to your bank, pharming could redirect to a fake site that collects your information. A ***zombie*** is a program that secretly takes over another computer for the purpose of launching attacks on other computers. Zombie attacks are almost impossible to trace back to the attacker. A ***zombie farm*** is a group of computers on which a hacker has planted zombie programs. A ***pharming attack*** uses a zombie farm, often by an organized crime association, to launch a massive phishing attack.

Authentication and authorization technologies can prevent identity theft, phishing, and pharming scams. ***Authentication*** is a method for confirming users' identities. Once a system determines the authentication of a user, it can then determine the access privileges (or authorization) for that user. ***Authorization*** is the process of providing a user with permission including access levels and abilities such as file access, hours of access, and amount of allocated storage space. Authentication and authorization techniques fall into three categories; the most secure procedures combine all three:

1. Something the user knows, such as a user ID and password.
2. Something the user has, such as a smart card or token.
3. Something that is part of the user, such as a fingerprint or voice signature.

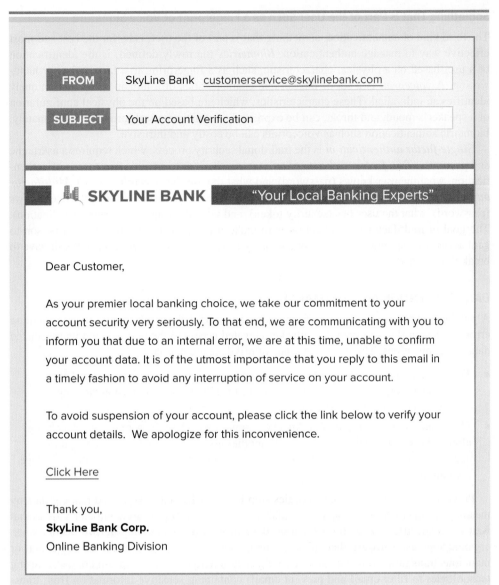

FROM	SkyLine Bank customerservice@skylinebank.com
SUBJECT	Your Account Verification

🏢 SKYLINE BANK   "Your Local Banking Experts"

Dear Customer,

As your premier local banking choice, we take our commitment to your account security very seriously. To that end, we are communicating with you to inform you that due to an internal error, we are at this time, unable to confirm your account data. It is of the utmost importance that you reply to this email in a timely fashion to avoid any interruption of service on your account.

To avoid suspension of your account, please click the link below to verify your account details. We apologize for this inconvenience.

Click Here

Thank you,
SkyLine Bank Corp.
Online Banking Division

Something the User Knows Such as a User ID and Password

A *password* is string of alphanumeric characters used to authenticate a user and provide access to a system. The first type of authentication, using something the user knows, is the most common way to identify individual users and typically consists of a unique user ID and password. However, this is actually one of the most *ineffective* ways for determining authentication because passwords are not secure. All it typically takes to crack one is enough time. More than 50 percent of help-desk calls are password related, which can cost an organization significant money, and a social engineer can coax a password from almost anybody.

Something the User Has Such as a Smart Card or Token

The second type of authentication, using something the user has, offers a much more effective way to identify individuals than a user ID and password. Tokens and smart cards are two of the primary forms of this type of authentication. *Tokens* are small electronic devices that change user passwords automatically. The user enters his or her user ID and token-displayed password to gain access to the network. A *smart card* is a device about the size of a credit card, containing embedded technologies that can store information and small amounts of software to perform some limited processing. Smart cards can act as identification instruments, a form of digital cash, or a data storage device with the ability to store an entire medical record.

Something That Is Part of the User Such as a Fingerprint or Voice Signature

The third kind of authentication, something that is part of the user, is by far the best and most effective way to manage authentication. *Biometrics* (narrowly defined) is the identification of a user based on a physical characteristic, such as a fingerprint, iris, face, voice, or handwriting. A *voiceprint* is a set of measurable characteristics of a human voice that uniquely identifies an individual. These characteristics, which are based on the physical configuration of a speaker's mouth and throat, can be expressed as a mathematical formula. Unfortunately, biometric authentication such as voiceprints can be costly and intrusive.

Single-factor authentication is the traditional security process, which requires a username and password. *Two-factor authentication* requires the user to provide two means of authentication, what the user knows (password) and what the user has (security token). *Multifactor authentication* requires more than two means of authentication such as what the user knows (password), what the user has (security token), and what the user is (biometric verification). The goal of multifactor authentication is to make it difficult for an unauthorized person to gain access to a system because, if one security level is broken, the attacker will still have to break through additional levels.

DATA: PREVENTION AND RESISTANCE

A *privilege escalation* is a network intrusion attack that takes advantage of programming errors or design flaws to grant the attacker elevated access to the network and its associated data and applications. There are two kinds of privilege escalation:

- *Vertical privilege escalation* Attackers grant themselves a higher access level such as administrator, allowing the attacker to perform illegal actions such as running unauthorized code or deleting data.

- *Horizontal privilege escalation* Attackers grant themselves the same access levels they already have but assume the identity of another user. For example, someone gaining access to another person's online banking account would constitute horizontal privilege escalation.

Prevention and resistance technologies stop intruders from accessing and reading data by means of content filtering, encryption, and firewalls. *Time bombs* are computer viruses that wait for a specific date before executing their instructions. *Content filtering* occurs when organizations use software that filters content, such as emails, to prevent the accidental or malicious transmission of unauthorized information. Organizations can use content filtering technologies to filter email and prevent emails containing sensitive information from transmitting, whether the transmission was malicious or accidental. It can also filter emails and prevent any suspicious files from transmitting such as potential virus-infected files. Email content filtering can also filter for spam, a form of unsolicited email.

Encryption scrambles information into an alternative form that requires a key or password to decrypt. If there were a security breach and the stolen information were encrypted, the thief would be unable to read it. Encryption can switch the order of characters, replace characters with other characters, insert or remove characters, or use a mathematical formula to convert the information into a code. Companies that transmit sensitive customer information over the Internet, such as credit card numbers, frequently use encryption. To *decrypt* information is to decode it and is the opposite of *encrypt*. *Cryptography* is the science that studies encryption, which is the hiding of messages so that only the sender and receiver can read them. The National Institute of Standards and Technology (NIST) introduced an *advanced encryption standard (AES)* designed to keep government information secure.

Some encryption technologies use multiple keys. *Public key encryption (PKE)* uses two keys: a public key that everyone can have and a private key for only the recipient (see Figure B6.4). The organization provides the public key to all customers, whether end consumers or other businesses, who use that key to encrypt their information and send it via the Internet. When it arrives at its destination, the organization uses the private key to unscramble it.

Public keys are becoming popular to use for authentication techniques consisting of digital objects in which a trusted third party confirms correlation between the user and the

Originating Business

• Sends the same public key to all customers

• Uses a private key to decrypt the information received

Public Key

Encrypted Information

Public Key

Encrypted Information

Public Key

Encrypted Information

public key. A *certificate authority* is a trusted third party, such as VeriSign, that validates user identities by means of digital certificates. A *digital certificate* is a data file that identifies individuals or organizations online and is comparable to a digital signature.

A *firewall* is hardware and/or software that guards a private network by analyzing incoming and outgoing information for the correct markings. If they are missing, the firewall prevents the information from entering the network. Firewalls can even detect computers communicating with the Internet without approval. As Figure B6.5 illustrates, organizations typically place a firewall between a server and the Internet. Think of a firewall as a gatekeeper that protects computer networks from intrusion by providing a filter and safe transfer points for access to and from the Internet and other networks. It screens all network traffic for proper passwords or other security codes and allows only authorized transmissions in and out of the network.

Firewalls do not guarantee complete protection, and users should enlist additional security technologies such as antivirus software and antispyware software. *Antivirus software* scans and searches hard drives to prevent, detect, and remove known viruses, adware, and spyware. Antivirus software must be frequently updated to protect against newly created viruses.

ATTACK: DETECTION AND RESPONSE

Cyberwar is an organized attempt by a country's military to disrupt or destroy information and communication systems for another country. *Cyberterrorism* is the use of computer and networking technologies against persons or property to intimidate or coerce governments, individuals, or any segment of society to attain political, religious, or ideological goals.

FIGURE B6.5

Sample Firewall Architecture Connecting Systems Located in Chicago, New York, and Boston.

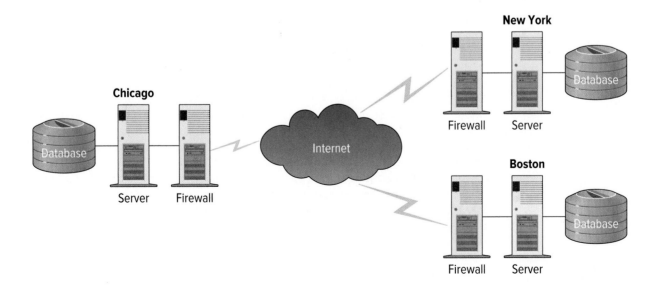

With so many intruders planning computer attacks, it is critical that all computer systems are protected. The presence of an intruder can be detected by watching for suspicious network events such as bad passwords, the removal of highly classified data files, or unauthorized user attempts. *Intrusion detection software (IDS)* features full-time monitoring tools that search for patterns in network traffic to identify intruders. IDS protects against suspicious network traffic and attempts to access files and data. If a suspicious event or unauthorized traffic is identified, the IDS will generate an alarm and can even be customized to shut down a particularly sensitive part of a network. After identifying an attack, an MIS department can implement response tactics to mitigate the damage. Response tactics outline procedures such as how long a system under attack will remain plugged in and connected to the corporate network, when to shut down a compromised system, and how quickly a backup system will be up and running.

Guaranteeing the safety of organization information is achieved by implementing the two lines of defense: people and technology. To protect information through people, firms should develop information security policies and plans that provide employees with specific precautions they should take in creating, working with, and transmitting the organization's information assets. Technology-based lines of defense fall into three categories: authentication and authorization, prevention and resistance, and detection and response.

Implementing information security lines of defense through people first and through technology second is the best way for an organization to protect its vital intellectual capital. The first line of defense is securing intellectual capital by creating an information security plan detailing the various information security policies. The second line of defense is investing in technology to help secure information through authentication and authorization, prevention and resistance, and detection and response.

※ KEY TERMS

Advanced encryption standard (AES) 444
Antivirus software 445
Authentication 442
Authorization 442
Biometrics 444
Certificate authority 445
Content filtering 444
Cryptography 444
Cyberterrorism 445
Cyberwar 445
Decrypt 444
Destructive agents 441
Digital certificate 445
Dumpster diving 440
Encryption 444
Firewall 445

Horizontal privilege escalation 444
Identity theft 441
Information secrecy 441
Information security plan 440
Information security policies 440
Insiders 440
Intrusion detection software (IDS) 446
Multifactor authentication 444
Password 443
Pharming 442
Pharming attack 442
Phishing 442
Phishing expedition 442
Pretexting 440

Privilege escalation 444
Public key encryption (PKE) 444
Single-factor authentication 444
Smart card 443
Social engineering 440
Spear phishing 442
Time bombs 444
Tokens 443
Two-factor authentication 444
Vertical Privilege Escalation 444
Vishing (or voice phishing) 442
Voiceprint 442
Zombie 442
Zombie farm 442

※ MAKING BUSINESS DECISIONS

1. Firewall Decisions

You are the CEO of Inverness Investments, a medium-size venture capital firm that specializes in investing in high-tech companies. The company receives more than 30,000 email messages per year. On average, there are two viruses and three successful hackings against the company each year, which result in losses to the company of about $250,000. Currently, the company has antivirus software installed but does not have any firewalls.

Your CIO is suggesting implementing 10 firewalls for a total cost of $80,000. The estimated life of each firewall is about three years. The chances of hackers breaking into the system with the firewalls installed are about 3 percent. Annual maintenance costs on the firewalls are estimated around $15,000. Create an argument for or against supporting your CIO's recommendation to purchase the firewalls. Are there any considerations in addition to finances?

2. Preventing Identity Theft

The FBI states that identity theft is one of the fastest-growing crimes. If you are a victim of identity theft, your financial reputation can be ruined, making it impossible for you to cash a check or receive a bank loan. Learning how to avoid identity theft can be a valuable activity. Using the Internet, research the most current ways the government recommends for you to prevent identity theft.

3. Discussing the Three Areas of Information Security

Great Granola Inc. is a small business operating out of northern California. The company specializes in selling homemade granola, and its primary sales vehicle is through its website. The company is growing exponentially and expects its revenues to triple this year to $12 million. The company also expects to hire 60 additional employees to support its growth. Joan Martin, the CEO, is aware that if her competitors discover the recipe for her granola, or who her primary customers are, it could easily ruin her business. Martin has hired you to draft a document discussing the different areas of information security, along with your recommendations for providing a secure ebusiness environment.

4. Beyond the Password

The password, a combination of a username and personal code, has been the primary way to secure systems since computers first hit the market in the 1980s. Of course, in the 1980s, users had only one password to maintain and remember, and chances are they still probably had to write it down. Today, users have dozens of usernames and passwords they have to remember to multiple systems and websites—it is simply no longer sustainable! A few companies are creating new forms of identification, hoping to eliminate the password problem.

- Bionym is developing the Nymi, a wristband with two electrodes that reads your heart's unique electrocardiogram signal and can unlock all your devices.
- Clef is developing the Clef Wave, a free app that generates a unique image on your smartphone that you can point at your webcam, which reads the image and unlocks your websites. The image cannot be stolen because it only stays on your screen for a few seconds. More than 300 websites have enabled the Clef Wave service.
- Illiri is developing an app that emits a unique sound on your smartphone that can be used to unlock other devices, process payments, and access websites. The sound lasts for 10 seconds and can be heard within 1 foot of your device.

In a group, evaluate the three preceding technologies and determine which one you would choose to implement at your school.

5. LifeLock: Keeping Your Identity Safe

Have you ever seen a LifeLock advertisement? If so, you know the Social Security number of LifeLock CEO Todd Davis because he posts it in all ads daring hackers to try to steal his identity. Davis has been a victim of identity theft at least 13 times. The first theft occurred when someone used his identity to secure a $500 loan from a check-cashing company. Davis discovered the crime only after the company called his wife's cell phone to recover the unpaid debt.

If you were starting an identity theft prevention company, do you think it would be a good idea to post your Social Security number in advertisements? Why or why not? What do you think happened that caused Davis's identity to be stolen? What types of information security measures should LifeLock implement to ensure that Davis's Social Security number is not stolen again? If you were LifeLock's CEO, what type of marketing campaign would you launch next?

PLUG-IN

B7 Ethics

1. **Identify the six epolicies organizations should implement to protect themselves.**

LO 1 Identify the six epolicies organizations should implement to protect themselves.

Developing Information Management Policies

Treating sensitive corporate information as a valuable resource is good management. Building a corporate culture based on ethical principles that employees can understand and implement is responsible management. Organizations should develop written policies establishing employee guidelines, employee procedures, and organizational rules for information. These policies set employee expectations about the organization's practices and standards and protect the organization from misuse of computer systems and IT resources. If an organization's employees use computers at work, the organization should, at a minimum, implement epolicies. *Epolicies* are policies and procedures that address information management along with the ethical use of computers and the Internet in the business environment. Figure B7.1 displays the epolicies a firm should implement to set employee expectations.

ETHICAL COMPUTER USE POLICY

In a case that illustrates the perils of online betting, a leading Internet poker site reported that a hacker exploited a security flaw to gain an insurmountable edge in high-stakes, no-limit Texas hold-'em tournaments—the ability to see his opponents' hole cards. The cheater, whose

FIGURE B7.1

Overview of Epolicies.

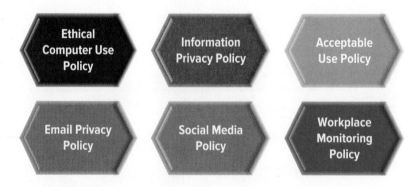

illegitimate winnings were estimated at between $400,000 and $700,000 by one victim, was an employee of AbsolutePoker.com and hacked the system to show that it could be done. Regardless of what business a company operates—even one that many view as unethical—the company must protect itself from unethical employee behavior. **Cyberbullying** includes threats, negative remarks, or defamatory comments transmitted via the Internet or posted on the website. A **threat** is an act or object that poses a danger to assets. **Click-fraud** is the abuse of pay-per-click, pay-per-call, and pay-per-conversion revenue models by repeatedly clicking on a link to increase charges or costs for the advertiser. **Competitive click-fraud** is a computer crime where a competitor or disgruntled employee increases a company's search advertising costs by repeatedly clicking on the advertiser's link. Cyberbullying and click-fraud are just a couple of examples of the many types of unethical computer use found today.

One essential step in creating an ethical corporate culture is establishing an ethical computer use policy. An **ethical computer use policy** contains general principles to guide computer user behavior. For example, it might explicitly state that users should refrain from playing computer games during working hours. This policy ensures the users know how to behave at work and the organization has a published standard to deal with infractions. For example, after appropriate warnings, the company may terminate an employee who spends significant amounts of time playing computer games at work.

Organizations can legitimately vary in how they expect employees to use computers, but in any approach to controlling such use, the overriding principle should be informed consent. The users should be *informed* of the rules and, by agreeing to use the system on that basis, *consent* to abide by them.

Managers should make a conscientious effort to ensure all users are aware of the policy through formal training and other means. If an organization were to have only one epolicy, it should be an ethical computer use policy because that is the starting point and the umbrella for any other policies the organization might establish.

Part of an ethical computer use policy can include a BYOD policy. A **bring your own device (BYOD)** policy allows employees to use their personal mobile devices and computers to access enterprise data and applications. BYOD policies offer four basic options, including:

- Unlimited access for personal devices.
- Access *only* to nonsensitive systems and data.
- Access, but with MIS control over personal devices, apps, and stored data.
- Access, but preventing local storage of data on personal devices.

INFORMATION PRIVACY POLICY

An organization that wants to protect its information should develop an **information privacy policy**, which contains general principles regarding information privacy. Visa created Inovant to handle all its information systems including its coveted customer information, which details how people are spending their money, in which stores, on which days, and even at what time of day. Just imagine what a sales and marketing department could do if it gained access to this information. For this reason, Inovant bans the use of Visa's customer information for anything outside its intended purpose—billing. Inovant's privacy specialists developed a strict credit card information privacy policy, which it follows.

Now Inovant is being asked if it can guarantee that unethical use of credit card information will never occur. In a large majority of cases, the unethical use of information happens not through the malicious scheming of a rogue marketer, but rather unintentionally. For instance, information is collected and stored for some purpose, such as record keeping or billing. Then, a sales or marketing professional figures out another way to use it internally, share it with partners, or sell it to a trusted third party. The information is "unintentionally" used for new purposes. The classic example of this type of unintentional information reuse is the Social Security number, which started simply as a way to identify government retirement benefits and then was used as a sort of universal personal ID, found on everything from drivers' licenses to savings accounts.

Fair information practices is a general term for a set of standards governing the collection and use of personal data and addressing issues of privacy and accuracy. Different organizations and countries have their own terms for these concerns. The United Kingdom terms it "Data Protection," and the European Union calls it "Personal Data Privacy"; the Organisation for Economic Co-operation and Development (OECD) has written *Guidelines on the Protection of Privacy and Transborder Flows of Personal Data,* which can be found at www.oecd.org/unitedstates.

ACCEPTABLE USE POLICY

An *acceptable use policy (AUP)* requires a user to agree to follow it to be provided access to corporate email, information systems, and the Internet. *Nonrepudiation* is a contractual stipulation to ensure that ebusiness participants do not deny (repudiate) their online actions. A nonrepudiation clause is typically contained in an acceptable use policy. Many businesses and educational facilities require employees or students to sign an acceptable use policy before gaining network access. When signing up with an email provider, each customer is typically presented with an AUP, which states the user agrees to adhere to certain stipulations. Users agree to the following in a typical acceptable use policy:

- Not using the service as part of violating any law.
- Not attempting to break the security of any computer network or user.
- Not posting commercial messages to groups without prior permission.
- Not performing any nonrepudiation.

Some organizations go so far as to create a unique information management policy focusing solely on Internet use. An *Internet use policy* contains general principles to guide the proper use of the Internet. Because of the large amounts of computing resources that Internet users can expend, it is essential that such use be legitimate. In addition, the Internet contains numerous materials that some believe are offensive, making regulation in the workplace a requirement. *Cybervandalism* is the electronic defacing of an existing website. *Typosquatting* is a problem that occurs when someone registers purposely misspelled variations of well-known domain names. These variants sometimes lure consumers who make typographical errors when entering a URL. *Website name stealing* is the theft of a website's name that occurs when someone, posing as a site's administrator, changes the ownership of the domain name assigned to the website to another website owner. These are all examples of unacceptable Internet use. *Internet censorship* is government attempts to control Internet traffic, thus preventing some material from being viewed by a country's citizens. Generally, an Internet use policy:

- Describes the Internet services available to users.
- Defines the organization's position on the purpose of Internet access and what restrictions, if any, are placed on that access.
- Describes user responsibility for citing sources, properly handling offensive material, and protecting the organization's good name.
- States the ramifications if the policy is violated.

EMAIL PRIVACY POLICY

An *email privacy policy* details the extent to which email messages may be read by others. Email is so pervasive in organizations that it requires its own specific policy. Most working professionals use email as their preferred means of corporate communications. While email and instant messaging are common business communication tools, there are risks associated with using them. For instance, a sent email is stored on at least three or four computers (see Figure B7.2). Simply deleting an email from one computer does not delete it from the others. Companies can mitigate many of the risks of using electronic messaging systems by implementing and adhering to an email privacy policy.

One major problem with email is the user's expectations of privacy. To a large extent, this expectation is based on the false assumption that email privacy protection exists somehow analogous to that of U.S. first-class mail. Generally, the organization that owns the email

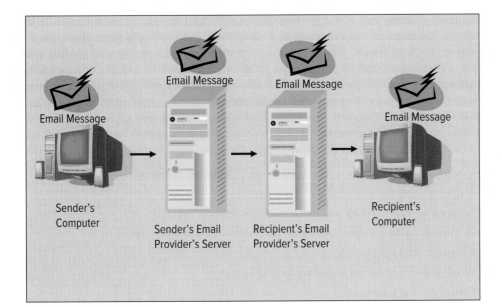

system can operate the system as openly or as privately as it wishes. Surveys indicate that the majority of large firms regularly read and analyze employees' email looking for confidential data leaks such as unannounced financial results or the sharing of trade secrets that result in the violation of an email privacy policy and eventual termination of the employee. That means that if the organization wants to read everyone's email, it can do so. Basically, using work email for anything other than work is not a good idea. A typical email privacy policy:

- Defines legitimate email users and explains what happens to accounts after a person leaves the organization.

- Explains backup procedure so users will know that at some point, even if a message is deleted from their computer, it is still stored by the company.

- Describes the legitimate grounds for reading email and the process required before such action is performed.

- Discourages sending junk email or spam to anyone who does not want to receive it.

- Prohibits attempting to mail bomb a site. A *mail bomb* sends a massive amount of email to a specific person or system that can cause that user's server to stop functioning.

- Informs users that the organization has no control over email once it has been transmitted outside the organization.

Spam is unsolicited email. It plagues employees at all levels within an organization, from receptionist to CEO, and clogs email systems and siphons MIS resources away from legitimate business projects. An *anti-spam policy* simply states that email users will not send unsolicited emails (or spam). It is difficult to write anti-spam policies, laws, or software because there is no such thing as a universal litmus test for spam. One person's spam is another person's newsletter. End users have to decide what spam is, because it can vary widely not just from one company to the next, but from one person to the next. A user can *opt out* of receiving emails by choosing to deny permission to incoming emails. A user can *opt in* to receive emails by choosing to allow permissions to incoming emails. *Teergrubing* is an anti-spamming approach where the receiving computer launches a return attack against the spammer, sending email messages back to the computer that originated the suspected spam.

SOCIAL MEDIA POLICY

Did you see the YouTube video showing two Domino's Pizza employees violating health codes while preparing food by passing gas on sandwiches? Millions of people did and the company took notice when disgusted customers began posting negative comments all over Twitter. Not having a Twitter account, corporate executives at Domino's did not know about the damaging tweets until it was too late. The use of social media can contribute many benefits to an organization, and implemented correctly it can become a huge opportunity for employees to build brands. But there are also tremendous risks as a few employees representing an entire company can cause tremendous brand damage. Defining a set of guidelines implemented in a social media policy can help mitigate that risk. Companies can protect themselves by implementing a *social media policy* outlining the corporate guidelines or principles governing employee online communications. Having a single social media policy might not be enough to ensure the company's online reputation is protected. Additional, more specific social media policies a company might choose to implement include:

- Employee online communication policy detailing brand communication.
- Employee blog and personal blog policies.
- Employee social network and personal social network policies.
- Employee Twitter, corporate Twitter, and personal Twitter policies.
- Employee LinkedIn policy.
- Employee Facebook usage and brand usage policy.
- Corporate YouTube policy.

Social media monitoring is the process of monitoring and responding to what is being said about a company, individual, product, or brand. Social media monitoring typically falls to the *social media manager,* a person within the organization who is trusted to monitor, contribute, filter, and guide the social media presence of a company, individual, product, or brand. Organizations must protect their online reputations and continuously monitor blogs, message boards, social networking sites, and media sharing sites. However, monitoring the hundreds of different social media sites can quickly become overwhelming. To combat these issues, a number of companies specialize in online social media monitoring; for example, Trackur.com creates digital dashboards allowing executives to view at a glance the date published, source, title, and summary of every item tracked. The dashboard highlights not only what's being said but also the influence of the particular person, blog, or social media site.

WORKPLACE MONITORING POLICY

Increasingly, employee monitoring is not a choice; it is a risk-management obligation. Michael Soden, CEO of the Bank of Ireland, issued a mandate stating that company employees could not surf illicit websites with company equipment. Next, he hired Hewlett-Packard to run the MIS department and illicit websites were discovered on Soden's own computer, forcing Soden to resign. Monitoring employees is one of the biggest challenges CIOs face when developing information management policies.

Physical security is tangible protection such as alarms, guards, fireproof doors, fences, and vaults. New technologies make it possible for employers to monitor many aspects of their employees' jobs, especially on telephones, computer terminals, through electronic and voice mail, and when employees are using the Internet. Such monitoring is virtually unregulated. Therefore, unless company policy specifically states otherwise (and even this is not assured), your employer may listen, watch, and read most of your workplace communications. *Workplace MIS monitoring* tracks people's activities by such measures as number of keystrokes, error rate, and number of transactions processed (see Figure B7.3 for an overview). The best path for an organization planning to engage in employee monitoring is open communication including an *employee monitoring policy* stating explicitly how, when, and where the company monitors its employees. Several common stipulations an organization can follow when creating an employee monitoring policy include:

- Be as specific as possible stating when and what (email, IM, Internet, network activity, etc.) will be monitored.
- Expressly communicate that the company reserves the right to monitor all employees.
- State the consequences of violating the policy.
- Always enforce the policy the same for everyone.

Common Internet Monitoring Technologies	
Key logger, or key trapper, software	A program that records every keystroke and mouse click.
Hardware key logger	A hardware device that captures keystrokes on their journey from the keyboard to the motherboard.
Cookie	A small file deposited on a hard drive by a website containing information about customers and their web activities. Cookies allow websites to record the comings and goings of customers, usually without their knowledge or consent.
Adware	Software that generates ads that install themselves on a computer when a person downloads some other program from the Internet.
Spyware (sneakware or stealthware)	Software that comes hidden in free downloadable software and tracks online movements, mines the information stored on a computer, or uses a computer's CPU and storage for some task the user knows nothing about.
Web log	Consists of one line of information for every visitor to a website and is usually stored on a web server.
Clickstream	Records information about a customer during a web surfing session such as what websites were visited, how long the visit was, what ads were viewed, and what was purchased.

FIGURE B7.3

Internet Monitoring Technologies.

Many employees use their company's high-speed Internet access to shop, browse, and surf the web. Most managers do not want their employees conducting personal business during working hours, and they implement a Big Brother approach to employee monitoring. Many management gurus advocate that organizations whose corporate cultures are based on trust are more successful than those whose corporate cultures are based on mistrust. Before an organization implements monitoring technology, it should ask itself, "What does this say about how we feel about our employees?" If the organization really does not trust its employees, then perhaps it should find new ones. If an organization does trust its employees, then it might want to treat them accordingly. An organization that follows its employees' every keystroke might be unwittingly undermining the relationships with its employees, and it might find the effects of employee monitoring are often worse than lost productivity from employee web surfing.

Advances in technology have made ethics a concern for many organizations. Consider how easy it is for an employee to email large amounts of confidential information, change electronic communications, or destroy massive amounts of important company information all within seconds. Electronic information about customers, partners, and employees has become one of corporate America's most valuable assets. However, the line between the proper and improper use of this asset is at best blurry. Should an employer be able to search employee files without employee consent? Should a company be able to sell customer information without informing the customer of its intent? What is a responsible approach to document deletion?

The law provides guidelines in many of these areas, but how a company chooses to act within the confines of the law is up to the judgment of its officers. Since CIOs are responsible for the technology that collects, maintains, and destroys corporate information, they sit smack in the middle of this potential ethical quagmire.

One way an organization can begin dealing with ethical issues is to create a corporate culture that encourages ethical considerations and discourages dubious information dealings. Not only is an ethical culture an excellent idea overall, but it also acts as a precaution, helping prevent customer problems from escalating into front-page news stories. The establishment of and adherence to well-defined rules and policies will help organizations create an ethical corporate culture. These policies include:

- Ethical computer use policy.
- Information privacy policy.
- Acceptable use policy.
- Email privacy policy.
- Social media policy.
- Workplace monitoring policy.

* KEY TERMS

Acceptable use policy (AUP)   452
Anti-spam policy   453
Bring your own device
    (BYOD)   451
Click-fraud   451
Competitive click-fraud   451
Cyberbullying   451
Cybervandalism   452
Email privacy policy   452
Employee monitoring policy   454
Epolicies   450

Ethical computer use
    policy   451
Fair information practices   451
Information privacy policy   451
Internet censorship   452
Internet use policy   452
Mail bomb   453
Nonrepudiation   452
Opt in   453
Opt out   453
Physical security   454

Social media manager   454
Social media monitoring   454
Social media policy   454
Spam   453
Teergrubing   453
Threat   451
Typosquatting   452
Website name stealing   452
Workplace MIS
    monitoring   454

* MAKING BUSINESS DECISIONS

1. Information—Does It Have Ethics?

A high school principal decided it was a good idea to hold a confidential conversation about teachers, salaries, and student test scores on his cellular phone in a local Starbucks. Not realizing that one of the students' parents was sitting next to him, the principal accidentally divulged sensitive information about his employees and students. The irate parent soon notified the school board about the principal's inappropriate behavior and a committee was formed to decide how to handle the situation.

With the new wave of collaboration tools, electronic business, and the Internet, employees are finding themselves working outside the office and beyond traditional office hours. Advantages associated with remote workers include increased productivity, decreased expenses, and boosts in morale as employees are given greater flexibility to choose their work location and hours. Unfortunately, disadvantages associated with workers working remotely include new forms of ethical challenges and information security risks.

In a group, discuss the following statement: Information does not have any ethics. If you were elected to the committee to investigate the principal's inappropriate Starbucks phone conversation, what types of questions would you want answered? What type of punishment, if any, would you enforce on the principal? What types of policies would you implement across the school district to ensure that this scenario is never repeated? Be sure to highlight how workers working remotely affect business along with any potential ethical challenges and information security issues.

2. Is IT Really Worth the Risk?

Ethics. It's just one tiny word, but it has monumental impact on every area of business. From the magazines, blogs, and newspapers you read to the courses you take, you will encounter ethics because it is a hot topic in today's electronic world. Technology has provided so many incredible opportunities, but it has also provided those same opportunities to unethical people. Discuss the ethical issues surrounding each of the following situations (yes, these are true stories):

- A student raises her hand in class and states, "I can legally copy any DVD I get from Netflix because Netflix purchased the DVD and the copyright only applies to the company who purchased the product."

- A student stands up the first day of class before the professor arrives and announces that his fraternity scans textbooks and he has the textbook for this course on his thumb drive, which he will gladly sell for $20. Several students pay on the spot and upload the scanned textbook to their PCs. One student takes down the student information and contacts the publisher about the incident.

- A senior marketing manager is asked to monitor his employee's email because there is a rumor that the employee is looking for another job.

- A vice president of sales asks her employee to burn all of the customer data onto an external hard drive because she made a deal to provide customer information to a strategic partner.

- A senior manager is asked to monitor his employee's email to discover whether she is sexually harassing another employee.

- An employee is looking at the shared network drive and discovers that his boss's entire hard drive, including his email backup, has been copied to the network and is visible to all.

- An employee is accidently copied on an email listing the targets for the next round of layoffs.

3. 15 Million Identity Theft Victims

Identity theft has quickly become the most common, expensive, and pervasive crime in the United States. The identities of more than 15 million U.S. citizens are stolen each year, with financial losses exceeding $50 billion. This means that the identities of almost 10 percent of U.S. adults will be stolen this year, with losses of around $4,000 each, not to mention the 100 million U.S. citizens whose personal data will be compromised due to data breaches on corporate and government databases.

The growth of organized crime can be attributed to the massive amounts of data collection along with the increased cleverness of professional identity thieves. Starting with individually tailored phishing and vishing scams, increasingly successful corporate and government databases hackings, and intricate networks of botnets that hijack millions of computers without a trace, we must wake up to this ever-increasing threat to all Americans.

You have the responsibility to protect yourself from data theft. In a group, visit the Federal Trade Commission's Consumer Information Identity Theft website at http://www.consumer.ftc.gov/

features/feature-0014-identity-theft and review what you can do today to protect your identity and how you can ensure that your personal information is safe.

4. Monitoring Employees

Every organization has the right to monitor its employees. Organizations usually inform their employees when workplace monitoring is occurring, especially regarding organizational assets such as networks, email, and Internet access. Employees traditionally offer their consent to be monitored and should not have any expectations of privacy when using organizational assets.

Do you agree or disagree that organizations have an obligation to notify employees about the extent of workplace monitoring, such as how long employees are using the Internet and which websites they are visiting? Do you agree or disagree that organizations have the right to read all employees' email sent or received on an organizational computer, including personal Gmail accounts?

5. The Right to Be Forgotten

The European Commissioner for Justice, Fundamental Rights, and Citizenship, Viviane Reding, announced the European Commission's proposal to create a sweeping new privacy right—the right to be forgotten, allowing individuals to request to have all content that violates their privacy removed. The right to be forgotten addresses an urgent problem in the digital age: the great difficulty of escaping your past on the Internet now that every photo, status update, and tweet lives forever in the cloud. To comply with the European Court of Justice's decision, Google created a new online form by which individuals can request search providers to remove links that violate their online privacy. In the first month, Google received more than 50,000 submissions from people asking the company to remove links. Many people in the United States believe that the right to be forgotten conflicts with the right to free speech. Do people who want to erase their past deserve a second chance? Do you agree or disagree?

6. Spying on Email

Technology advances now allow individuals to monitor computers that they do not even have physical access to. New types of software can capture an individual's incoming and outgoing email and then immediately forward that email to another person. For example, if you are at work and your child is home from school and she receives an email from John at 3:00 p.m., at 3:01 p.m. you can receive a copy of that email sent to your email address. If she replies to John's email, within seconds you will receive a copy of what she sent to John. Describe two scenarios (other than those described here) for the use of this type of software: one in which the use would be ethical and one in which it would be unethical.

7. Stealing Software

The software industry fights against pirated software on a daily basis. The major centers of software piracy are in places such as Russia and China where salaries and disposable income are comparatively low. People in developing and economically depressed countries will fall behind the industrialized world technologically if they cannot afford access to new generations of software. Considering this, is it reasonable to blame someone for using pirated software when it could cost him or her two months' salary to purchase a legal copy? Create an argument for or against the following statement: Individuals who are economically less fortunate should be allowed access to software free of charge to ensure that they are provided with an equal technological advantage.

8. Censoring Google

The Google debate over operations in China is an excellent example of types of global ethical and security issues U.S. companies face as they expand operations around the world. Google's systems were targeted by highly sophisticated hacker attacks aimed at obtaining proprietary information, including personal data belonging to Chinese human rights activists who use Google's Gmail service.

Google, which originally agreed to filter search results based on Chinese government censorship rules, decided to unfilter search results after what it called an infiltration of its technology and the email accounts of Chinese human-rights activists. China called Google's plan to defy government censorship rules unfriendly and irresponsible and demanded Google to shut down all operations in China.

Why would China want to filter search results? Do you agree or disagree with China's censorship rules? Do you think Google was acting ethically when it agreed to implement China's censorship rules? Why do companies operating abroad need to be aware of the different ethical perspective found in other cultures?

9. Sources Are Not Friends

The Canadian Broadcasting Company (CBC) has issued a social networking policy directing journalists to avoid adding sources or contacts as friends on social networking sites such as Facebook or LinkedIn. Basic rules state that reporters must never allow one source to view what another source says, and reporters must ensure that private conversations with sources remain private. Adding sources as friends can compromise a journalist's work by allowing friends to view other friends in the network. It may also not be in a journalist's best interest to become a friend in a source's network. The CBC also discourages posting any political preferences in personal profiles, comments on bulletin boards, or people's Facebook wall.

This might seem like common sense, but for employees who do not spend countless hours on the Internet, using social networking sites can be confusing and overwhelming. Why is it critical for any new hire to research and review all policies, especially social media policies? Research three companies you would like to work for after graduation and detail the types of social media policies that the company currently has or should implement.

10. Cheerleader Charged $27,750 for File Sharing 37 Songs

A federal appeals court is ordering a university student to pay the Recording Industry Association of America $27,750—$750 a track—for file sharing 37 songs when she was a high school cheerleader. Have you ever illegally copied or downloaded a song or movie? If you have and you were forced to pay $750 per track, how much would you owe? What is the difference between file sharing and Internet radio streaming? Do you agree or disagree with the federal appeals decision? Why or why not? Why is claiming a lack of copyright knowledge not a good defense against illegally sharing movies or music? If you do not have a good understanding of information laws, what can you do to ensure that you are never named in a federal lawsuit for violating information laws?

11. Police Records Found in Old Copy Machine

Copy machines made after 2002 all contain a hard drive that stores a copy of every document the machine has ever scanned, printed, copied, or faxed. If the hard drive is not erased or scrubbed when the copy machine is resold, all of that digital information is still maintained inside the machine. The Buffalo, New York, Police Sex Crimes Division recently sold several copy machines without scrubbing the hard drives. The hard drives yielded detailed domestic violence complaints and a list of wanted sex offenders. A machine from the Buffalo Police Narcotics Unit contained targets in a major drug raid, and a copier once used by a New York construction company stored 95 pages of pay stubs with names, addresses, and Social Security numbers.

Who do you think should be held responsible for the information issues caused at the Buffalo police department? What types of ethical issues and information security issues are being violated? What types of epolicies could a company implement to ensure that these situations do not occur? What forms of information security could a company implement to ensure that these situations do not occur? How does this case support the primary reason that ediscovery is so important to litigation?

B8 Operations Management

1. Explain operations management's role in business.
2. Describe the correlation between operations management and information technology.
3. Describe the five characteristics of competitive priorities.

LO 1 Explain operations management's role in business.

Introduction

Production is the creation of goods and services using the factors of production: land, labor, capital, entrepreneurship, and knowledge. Production has historically been associated with manufacturing, but the nature of business has changed significantly in the last 20 years. The service sector, especially Internet services, has grown dramatically. The United States now has what is called a service economy—that is, one dominated by the service sector.

Organizations that excel in operations management, specifically supply chain management, perform better in almost every financial measure of success, according to a report from Boston-based AMR Research Inc. When supply chain excellence improves operations, companies experience a 5 percent higher profit margin, 15 percent less inventory, 17 percent stronger "perfect order" ratings, and 35 percent shorter cycle times than their competitors. "The basis of competition for winning companies in today's economy is supply chain superiority," said Kevin O'Marah, vice president of research at AMR Research. "These companies understand that value chain performance translates to productivity and market-share leadership. They also understand that supply chain leadership means more than just low costs and efficiency: It requires a superior ability to shape and respond to shifts in demand with innovative products and services."

Operations Management Fundamentals

Books, DVDs, downloaded MP3s, and dental and medical procedures are all examples of goods and services. *Production management* describes all the activities managers do to help companies create goods. To reflect the change in importance from manufacturing to services, the term *production* often has been replaced by *operations* to reflect the manufacturing of both goods and services. ***Operations management (OM)*** is the management of systems or processes that convert or transform resources (including human resources) into goods and services. Operations management is responsible for managing the core processes used to manufacture goods and produce services.

Essentially, the creation of goods or services involves transforming or converting inputs into outputs. Various inputs such as capital, labor, and information are used to create goods or services using one or more transformation processes (e.g., storing, transporting, and cutting). A ***transformation process*** is often referred to as the technical core, especially in manufacturing organizations, and is the actual conversion of inputs to outputs. To ensure that the desired outputs are obtained, an organization takes measurements at various points in the transformation process (feedback) and then compares them with previously established standards to determine whether corrective action is needed (control). Figure B8.1 depicts the conversion system.

Figure B8.2 displays examples of inputs, transformation processes, and outputs. Although goods and services are listed separately in Figure B8.1 it is important to note that goods and services often occur jointly. For example, having the oil changed in a car is a service, but the oil that is delivered is a good. Similarly, house painting is a service, but the paint is a good. The goods–service combination is a continuum. It ranges from primarily goods with little service to primarily

FIGURE B8.1

Operations Involves the Conversion of Inputs into Outputs.

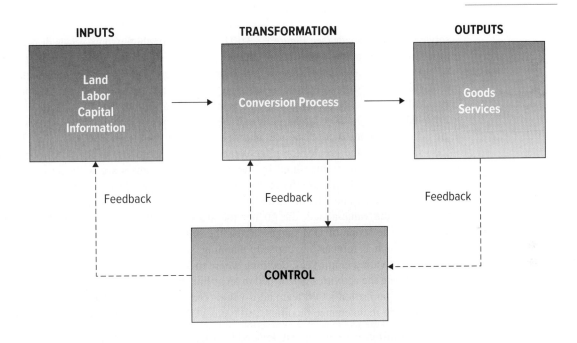

FIGURE B8.2

Examples of Inputs, Transformation, and Outputs.

Inputs	Transformation	Outputs
Restaurant inputs include hungry customers, food, wait staff.	Well-prepared food, well served: agreeable environment	Satisfied customers
Hospital inputs include patients, medical supplies, doctors, nurses.	Health care	Healthy individuals
Automobile inputs include sheet steel, engine parts, tires.	Fabrication and assembly of cars	High-quality cars
College inputs include high school graduates, books, professors, classrooms.	Imparting knowledge and skills	Educated individuals
Distribution center inputs include stock keeping units, storage bins, workers.	Storage and redistribution	Fast delivery of available products

FIGURE B8.3

The Goods–Service
Continuum: Most Products
Are a Bundle of Goods and
Services.

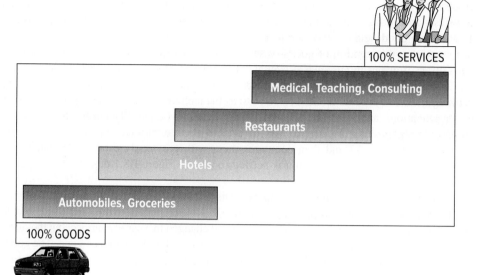

service with few goods (see Figure B8.3). There are relatively few pure goods or pure services; therefore, organizations typically sell product packages, which are a combination of goods and services. This makes managing operations more interesting, as well as more challenging.

Value-added is the term used to describe the difference between the cost of inputs and the value of price of outputs. OM is critical to an organization because of its ability to increase value-added during the transformation process. In nonprofit organizations, the value of outputs (highway construction, police, and fire protection) is their value to society; the greater the value-added, the greater the effectiveness of the operations. In for-profit organizations, the value of outputs is measured by the prices that customers are willing to pay for those goods or services. Firms use the money generated by value-added for research and development, investment in new facilities and equipment, worker salaries, and profits. Consequently, the greater the value-added, the greater the amount of funds available for these important activities. The scope of OM ranges across the organization and includes many interrelated activities, such as forecasting, capacity planning, scheduling, managing inventories, assuring quality, motivating employees, deciding where to locate facilities, and more.

Reviewing the activities performed in an airline company makes it easy to understand how a service organization's OM team adds value. The company consists of the airplanes, airport facilities, and maintenance facilities, and typical OM activities include:

- **Forecasting:** Estimating seat demand for flights, weather and landing conditions, and estimates for growth or reduction in air travel are all included in forecasting.
- **Capacity planning:** This is the key essential metric for the airline to maintain cash flow and increase revenues. Underestimating or overestimating flights will hurt profits.
- **Scheduling:** The airline operates on tight schedules that must be maintained including flights, pilots, flight attendants, ground crews, baggage handlers, and routine maintenance.
- **Managing inventory:** Inventory of such items as foods, beverages, first-aid equipment, in-flight magazines, pillows, blankets, and life jackets is essential for the airline.
- **Assuring quality:** Quality is indispensable in an airline where safety is the highest priority. Today's travelers expect high-quality customer service during ticketing, check-in, curb service, and unexpected issues where the emphasis is on efficiency and courtesy.
- **Motivating and training employees:** Airline employees must be highly trained and continually motivated, especially when dealing with frustrated airline travelers.
- **Locating facilities:** Key questions facing airlines include which cities to offer services, where to host maintenance facilities, and where to locate major and minor hubs.

Opposite from an airline is a bike factory, which is typically an assembly operation: buying components such as frames, tires, wheels, gears, and other items from suppliers, and then assembling bicycles. A bike factory also does some of the fabrication work itself, forming frames and making the gears and chains. Obviously, an airline company and a bike factory are completely different types of operations. One is primarily a service operation, the other a producer of goods. Nonetheless, these two operations have much in common. The same as the airline, the bike factory must schedule production, deal with components, order parts and materials, schedule and train employees, ensure quality standards are met, and above all satisfy customers. In both organizations, the success of the business depends on short- and long-term planning and the ability of its executives and managers to make informed decisions.

MIS's Role in OM

LO 2 Describe the correlation between operations management and information technology.

Managers can use MIS to heavily influence OM decisions including productivity, costs, flexibility, quality, and customer satisfaction. One of the greatest benefits of MIS on OM is in making operational decisions because operations management exerts considerable influence over the degree to which the goals and objectives of the organization are realized. Most OM decisions involve many possible alternatives that can have varying impacts on revenues and expenses. OM information systems are critical for managers to be able to make well-informed decisions.

Decision support systems and *executive information systems* can help an organization perform what-if analysis, sensitivity analysis, drill-down, and consolidation. Numerous managerial and strategic key decisions are based on OM information systems that affect the entire organization, including:

- **What:** What resources will be needed, and in what amounts?
- **When:** When will each resource be needed? When should the work be scheduled? When should materials and other supplies be ordered? When is corrective action needed?
- **Where:** Where will the work be performed?
- **How:** How will the product or service be designed? How will the work be done (organization, methods, equipment)? How will resources be allocated?
- **Who:** Who will perform the work?

OM STRATEGIC BUSINESS SYSTEMS

UPS uses package flow information systems at each of its locations. The custom-built systems combine operations strategy and mapping technology to optimize the way boxes are loaded and delivered. The goal is to use the package flow software to cut the distance that delivery trucks travel by more than 100 million miles each year. The project will also help UPS streamline the profitability of each of its facility locations.

Operations strategy is concerned with the development of a long-term plan for determining how to best utilize the major resources of the firm so that there is a high degree of compatibility between these resources and the firm's long-term corporate strategy. Operations strategy addresses very broad questions about how these major resources should be configured to achieve the desired corporate objectives. Some of the major long-term issues addressed in operations strategy include:

- How big to make the facilities.
- Where to locate the facilities.
- When to build additional facilities.
- What type of process(es) to install to make the products.

Each of these issues can be addressed by OM decision support systems. In developing an operations strategy, management needs to consider many factors. These include (*a*) the level of technology that is or will be available, (*b*) the required skill levels of the workers, and (*c*) the degree of vertical integration, in terms of the extent to which outside suppliers are used.

Type of Planning	Time Frame	Issues	Decisions	Systems
Strategic Planning	Long range	Plant size, location, type of processes	How will we make the products? Where do we locate the facility or facilities? How much capacity do we require? When should we add additional capacity?	Materials requirement planning (MRP) systems
Tactical Planning	Intermediate range	Workforce size, material requirements	How many workers do we need? When do we need them? Should we work overtime or put on a section shift? When should we have material delivered? Should we have a finished goods inventory?	Global inventory management systems
Operational Planning and Control (OP&C)	Short range	Daily scheduling of employees, jobs, and equipment, process management, inventory management	What jobs do we work on today or this week? To whom do we assign what tasks? What jobs have priority?	Inventory management and control systems, transportation planning systems, distribution management systems

FIGURE B8.4

Hierarchy of Operational Planning.

Today, many organizations, especially larger conglomerates, operate in terms of *strategic business units (SBUs)*, which consist of several stand-alone businesses. When companies become really large, they are best thought of as being composed of a number of businesses (or SBUs). As displayed in Figure B8.4, operations strategy supports the long-range strategy developed at the SBU level.

Decisions at the SBU level focus on being effective, that is, "on doing the right things." These decisions are sometimes referred to as *strategic planning,* which focuses on long-range planning such as plant size, location, and type of process to be used. The primary system used for strategic planning is a materials requirement planning system. *Materials requirement planning (MRP) systems* use sales forecasts to make sure that needed parts and materials are available at the right time and place in a specific company. The latest version of MRP is enterprise resource planning.

Strategic decisions impact intermediate-range decisions, often referred to as tactical planning, which focuses on being efficient, that is, "doing things right." *Tactical planning* focuses on producing goods and services as efficiently as possible within the strategic plan. Here the emphasis is on producing quality products, including when material should be delivered, when products should be made to best meet demand, and what size the workforce should be. One of the primary systems used in tactical planning includes global inventory management. *Global inventory management systems* provide the ability to locate, track, and predict the movement of every component or material anywhere upstream or downstream in the production process. This allows an organization to locate and analyze its inventory anywhere in its production process.

Finally, *operational planning and control (OP&C)* deals with the day-to-day procedures for performing work, including scheduling, inventory, and process management. *Inventory management and control systems* provide control and visibility to the status of individual items maintained in inventory. The software maintains inventory record accuracy, generates material requirements for all purchased items, and analyzes inventory performance. Inventory management and control software provides organizations with the information from a variety of sources including:

- Current inventory and order status.
- Cost accounting.
- Sales forecasts and customer orders.
- Manufacturing capacity.
- New-product introductions.

Two additional OP&C systems are transportation planning and distribution management. *Transportation planning systems* track and analyze the movement of materials and products to ensure the delivery of materials and finished goods at the right time, the right place, and the lowest cost. *Distribution management systems* coordinate the process of transporting materials from a manufacturer to distribution centers to the final customers. Transportation routes directly affect the speed and cost of delivery. An organization will use these systems to help it decide if it wants to use an effectiveness route and ship its products directly to its customers or use an efficiency route and ship its products to a distributor that ships the products to customers.

Competitive OM Strategy

LO 3 **Describe the five characteristics of competitive priorities.**

The key to developing a competitive OM strategy lies in understanding how to create value-added goods and services for customers. Specifically, value is added through the competitive priority or priorities that are selected to support a given strategy. Five key competitive priorities translate directly into characteristics that are used to describe various processes by which a company can add value to its OM decisions:

1. Cost
2. Quality
3. Delivery
4. Flexibility
5. Service

COST

Every industry has low-cost providers. However, being the low-cost producer does not always guarantee profitability and success. Products sold strictly on the basis of cost are typically commodity-like products including such goods as flour, petroleum, and sugar. In other words, customers cannot distinguish the products made by one firm from those of another. As a result, customers use cost as the primary determinant in making a purchasing decision.

Low-cost market segments are frequently very large, and many companies are lured by the potential for significant profits, which are associated with large unit volumes of product. As a consequence, the competition in this segment is exceedingly fierce—and so is the failure rate. After all, there can be only one lowest-cost producer, and that firm usually establishes the selling price in the market.

QUALITY

Quality can be divided into two categories—product quality and process quality. Product quality levels vary as to the particular market that it aims to serve. For example, a generic bike is of significantly different quality than the bike of a world-class cyclist. Higher-quality products command higher prices in the marketplace. Organizations must establish the "proper level" of product quality by focusing on the exact requirements of their customers. Overdesigned products with too much quality will be viewed as being prohibitively expensive. Underdesigned products, on the other hand, will lose customers to products that cost a little more but are perceived by the customers as offering greater value.

Process quality is critical in every market segment. Regardless of whether the product is a generic bike or a bike for an international cyclist, customers want products without defects. Thus, the primary goal of process quality is to produce error-free products. The investment in improving quality pays off in stronger customer relationships and higher revenues. Many organizations use modern quality control standards, including:

- **Six sigma quality:** The goal is to detect potential problems to prevent their occurrence and achieve no more than 3.4 defects per million opportunities. That is important to companies like Bank of America, which makes 4 million transactions a day.

- **Malcolm Baldrige National Quality Awards:** In 1987 in the United States, a standard was set for overall company quality with the introduction of the Malcolm Baldrige National Quality Awards, named in honor of the late U.S. secretary of commerce. Companies can apply for these awards in each of the following areas: manufacturing, services, small businesses, education, and health care. To qualify, an organization has to show quality in seven key areas: leadership, strategic planning, customer and market focus, information and analysis, human resources focus, process management, and business results.

- **ISO 900:** The common name given to quality management and assurance standards comes from the ***International Organization for Standardization (ISO),*** a nongovernmental organization established in 1947 to promote the development of world standards to facilitate the international exchange of goods and services. ISO is a worldwide federation of national standards bodies from more than 140 countries. ISO 900 standards require a company to determine customer needs, including regulatory and legal requirements. The company must also make communication arrangements to handle issues such as complaints. Other standards involve process control, product testing, storage, and delivery.

- **ISO 14000:** This collection of the best practices for managing an organization's impact on the environment does not prescribe specific performance levels, but establishes environmental management systems. The requirements for certification include having an environmental policy, setting specific improvement targets, conducting audits of environmental programs, and maintaining top management review of processes. Certification in ISO 14000 displays that a firm has a world-class management system in both quality and environmental standards.

- **CMMI:** Capability Maturity Model Integration is a framework of best practices. The current version, CMMI-DEV, describes best practices in managing, measuring, and monitoring software development processes. CMMI does not describe the processes themselves; it describes the characteristics of good processes, thus providing guidelines for companies developing or honing their own sets of processes.

DELIVERY

Another key factor in purchasing decisions is delivery speed. The ability of a firm to provide consistent and fast delivery allows it to charge a premium price for its products. George Stalk, Jr., of the Boston Consulting Group, has demonstrated that both profits and market share are directly linked to the speed with which a company can deliver its products relative to its competition. In addition to fast delivery, the reliability of the delivery is also important. In other words, products should be delivered to customers with minimum variance in delivery times.

FLEXIBILITY

Flexibility, from a strategic perspective, refers to the ability of a company to offer a wide variety of products to its customers. Flexibility is also a measure of how fast a company can convert its process(es) from making an old line of products to producing a new product line. Product variety is often perceived by the customers to be a dimension of quality.

The flexibility of the manufacturing process at John Deere's Harvester Works in Moline, Illinois, allows the firm to respond to the unpredictability of the agricultural industry's equipment needs. By manufacturing such small-volume products as seed planters in "modules," or factories within a factory, Deere can offer farmers a choice of 84 different planter models with such a wide variety of options that farmers can have planters virtually customized to meet their individual needs. Its manufacturing process thus allows Deere to compete on both speed and flexibility.

Currently, there appears to be a trend toward offering environmentally friendly products that are made through environmentally friendly processes. As consumers become more aware of the fragility of the environment, they are increasingly turning toward products that are safe for the environment. Several flexible manufacturers now advertise environmentally friendly products, energy-efficient products, and recycled products.

SERVICE

With shortened product life cycles, products tend to migrate toward one common standard. As a consequence, these products are often viewed as commodities in which price is the primary differentiator. For example, the differences in laptops offered among PC manufactures are relatively insignificant so price is the prime selection criterion. For this reason, many companies attempt to place an emphasis on high-quality customer service as a primary differentiator. Customer service can add tremendous value to an ordinary product.

Businesses are always looking toward the future to find the next competitive advantage that will distinguish their products in the marketplace. To obtain an advantage in such a competitive environment, firms must provide "value-added" goods and services, and the primary area where they can capitalize on all five competitive priorities is in the supply chain.

OM and the Supply Chain

A *supply chain* consists of all parties involved, directly or indirectly, in the procurement of a product or raw material. *Supply chain management (SCM)* involves the management of information flows between and among stages in a supply chain to maximize total supply chain effectiveness and profitability. SCM software can enable an organization to generate efficiencies within these steps by automating and improving the information flows throughout and among the different supply chain components. Figures B8.5 and B8.6 display the typical supply chains for goods and services.

FIGURE B8.5

A Typical Manufacturing Supply Chain.

FIGURE B8.6

A Typical Service Supply Chain.

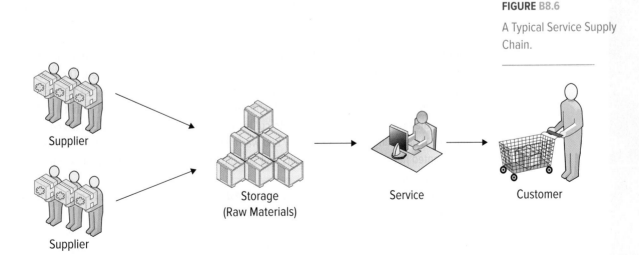

Supporting the Environment: Sustainable MIS Infrastructure

Combating ewaste, energy consumption, and carbon emissions requires a firm to focus on creating sustainable MIS infrastructures. A sustainable MIS infrastructure identifies ways that a company can grow in terms of computing resources while simultaneously becoming less dependent on hardware and energy consumption. The components of a sustainable MIS infrastructure are displayed in Figure B9.2.

FIGURE B9.2

Sustainable MIS Infrastructure Components.

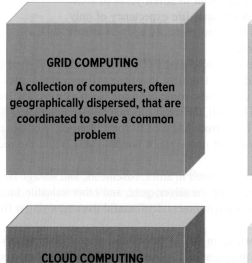

GRID COMPUTING

A collection of computers, often geographically dispersed, that are coordinated to solve a common problem

VIRTUALIZATION

Creates multiple "virtual" machines on a single computing device

CLOUD COMPUTING

Accesses shared resources that can be rapidly provisioned and released with minimal management

UTILITY COMPUTING

Offers a pay-per-use revenue model similar to a metered service such as gas or electricity

GRID COMPUTING

When a light is turned on, the power grid delivers exactly what is needed, instantly. Computers and networks can now work that way using grid computing. *Grid computing* is a collection of computers, often geographically dispersed, that are coordinated to solve a common problem. With grid computing a problem is broken into pieces and distributed to many machines, allowing faster processing than could occur with a single system (see Figure B9.3). Computers typically use less than 25 percent of their processing power, leaving more than 75 percent available for other tasks. Innovatively, grid computing takes advantage of this unused processing power by linking thousands of individual computers around the world to create a "virtual supercomputer" that can process intensive tasks. Grid computing makes better use of MIS resources, allowing greater scalability as systems can easily grow to handle peaks and valleys in demand, become more cost efficient, and solve problems that would be impossible to tackle with a single computer (see Figures B9.4 and B9.5).

The uses of grid computing are numerous, including the creative environment of animated movies. DreamWorks Animation used grid computing to complete many of its hit films including *Antz, Shrek, Madagascar,* and *How to Train Your Dragon.* The third *Shrek* film required more than 20 million computer hours to make (compared to 5 million for the first *Shrek* and 10 million for the second). At peak production times, DreamWorks dedicated more than 4,000 computers to its *Shrek* grid, allowing it to complete scenes in days and hours

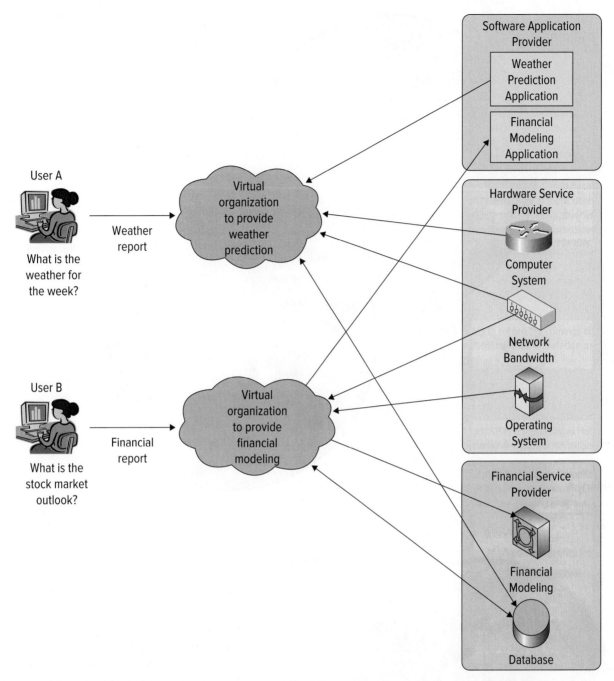

User A

What is the weather for the week?

Weather report

Virtual organization to provide weather prediction

User B

What is the stock market outlook?

Financial report

Virtual organization to provide financial modeling

Software Application Provider

Weather Prediction Application

Financial Modeling Application

Hardware Service Provider

Computer System

Network Bandwidth

Operating System

Financial Service Provider

Financial Modeling

Database

FIGURE B9.3

Virtual Organizations Using Grid Computing.

instead of months. With the increased grid computing power, the DreamWork's animators were able to add more realistic movement to water, fire, and magic scenes (see Figure B9.6). With grid computing a company can work faster or more efficiently, providing a potential competitive advantage and additional cost savings.

Solving the Energy Issue with Smart Grids

A *smart grid* delivers electricity using two-way digital technology. It is meant to solve the problem of the world's outdated electrical grid, making it more efficient and reliable by adding the ability to remotely monitor, analyze, and control the transmission of power. The current U.S. power grid is said to have outlived its life expectancy by as much as 30 years. Smart grids provide users with real-time usage monitoring, allowing them to choose off-peak times for noncritical or less urgent applications or processes. Residents of Boulder, Colorado, can monitor their use of electricity and control appliances remotely due to the city's large-scale

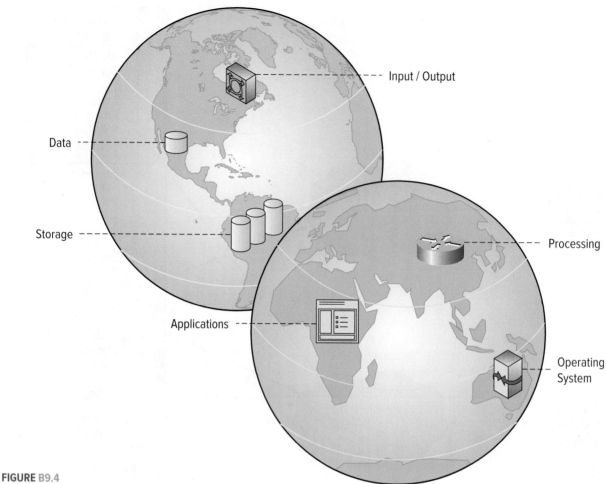

FIGURE B9.4

Grid Computer Network.

FIGURE B9.5

Grid Computing Example.

smart grid system. Xcel Energy has installed 21,000 smart grid meters since the $100 million program started several years ago. Energy use by early adopters is down as much as 45 percent.[2]

VIRTUALIZED COMPUTING

Most computers and even servers typically run only one operating system, such as Windows or Mac OS, and only one application. When a company invests in a large system such as inventory management, it dedicates a single server to house the system. This ensures the system has enough capacity to run during peak times and to scale to meet demand. Also, many systems have specific hardware requirements along with detailed software requirements, making it difficult to find two systems with the same requirements that could share the same machine. Through the use of virtualization, computers can run multiple operating systems along with multiple software applications—all at the same time. *Virtualization* the creation of a virtual (rather than actual) version of computing resources, such as an operating system, a server, a storage device, or network resources. A good analogy is a computer printer. In the past you had to purchase a fax machine, copy machine, answering machine, and computer printer separately. This was expensive, required enough energy to run four separate machines, not to mention created

How Grid Computing **Works**
Here's how DreamWorks Animation uses technologies to create films such as *Shrek 2* and *Shark Tale.*

1 Artists create digital 3-D characters and scenes on graphics work-stations. These can handle design, but not the heavy data-crunching needed to flesh out the figures.

2 Grid software deals out the animations in bite-size pieces to a cluster of server computers in DreamWorks data centers. These add color, texture, and lighting.

3 If more computing is needed, work is farmed out to more computers at a Hewlett-Packard data center. When all the pieces are complete, they are reassembled for editing.

FIGURE B9.6

Making *Shrek 2* with Grid Computing.

additional amounts of ewaste. Today, you can buy a virtualized computer printer that functions as a fax machine, answering machine, and copy machine all on one physical machine, thereby reducing costs, power requirements, and ewaste. Virtualization is essentially a form of consolidation that can benefit sustainable MIS infrastructures in a variety of ways, for example:

- By increasing availability of applications that can give a higher level of performance depending on the hardware used.
- By increasing energy efficiency by requiring less hardware to run multiple systems or applications.
- By increasing hardware usability by running multiple operating systems on a single computer.

Originally, computers were designed to run a single application on a single operating system. This left most computers vastly underutilized (as mentioned earlier, 75 percent of most computing power is available for other tasks). Virtualization allows multiple virtual computers to exist on a single machine, which allows it to share its resources, such as memory and hard disk space, to run different applications and even different operating systems. Mac computers have the ability to run both the Apple operating system and the Windows PC operating system, with the use of virtualization software (see Figure B9.7). Unfortunately, virtualization, at least at the moment, is not available for a PC to run Mac software. There are three basic categories of virtualization:

- *Storage virtualization* combines multiple network storage devices so they appear to be a single storage device.
- *Network virtualization* combines networks by splitting the available bandwidth into independent channels that can be assigned in real time to a specific device.
- *Server virtualization* combines the physical resources, such as servers, processors, and operating systems, from the applications. (This is the most common form and typically when you hear the term *virtualization,* you can assume server virtualization.)

Virtualization is also one of the easiest and quickest ways to achieve a sustainable MIS infrastructure because it reduces

FIGURE B9.7

Virtualization Allows an Apple Macintosh Computer to Run OS X and Windows 8.

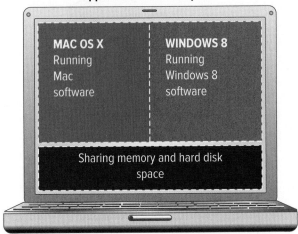

Apple Macintosh Computer

MAC OS X	WINDOWS 8
Running Mac software	Running Windows 8 software

Sharing memory and hard disk space

power consumption and requires less equipment that needs to be manufactured, maintained, and later disposed of safely. Managers no longer have to assign servers, storage, or network capacity permanently to single applications. Instead, they can assign the hardware resources when and where they are needed, achieving the availability, flexibility, and scalability a company needs to thrive and grow. Also, by virtually separating the operating system and applications from the hardware, if there is a disaster or hardware failure, it is easy to port the virtual machine to a new physical machine allowing a company to recover quickly from disasters. One of the primary uses of virtualization is for performing backup, recovery, and disaster recovery. Using virtual servers or a virtualization service provider, such as Google, Microsoft, or Amazon, to host disaster recovery is more sustainable than a single company incurring the expense of having redundant physical systems. Also, these providers' data centers are built to withstand natural disasters and are typically located far away from big cities (see Figure B9.8).

System virtualization is the ability to present the resources of a single computer as if it is a collection of separate computers ("virtual machines"), each with its own virtual CPUs, network interfaces, storage, and operating system.

Virtual machine technology was first implemented on mainframes in the 1960s to allow the expensive systems to be partitioned into separate domains and used more efficiently by more users and applications. As standard PC servers became more powerful in the past decade, virtualization has been brought to the desktop and notebook processors to provide the same benefits.

Virtual machines appear both to the user within the system and the world outside as separate computers, each with its own network identity, user authorization and authentication capabilities, operating system version and configuration, applications, and data. The hardware is consistent across all virtual machines: While the number or size of them may differ, devices are used that allow virtual machines to be portable, independent of the actual hardware type on the underlying systems. Figure B9.9 shows an overview of what a system virtualization framework looks like.

FIGURE B9.8

Virtualization Architecture.

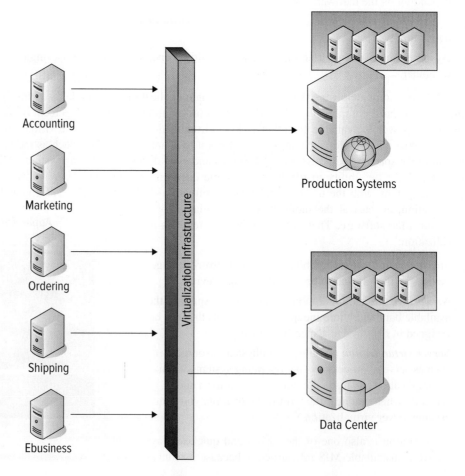

Accounting

Marketing

Ordering

Shipping

Ebusiness

Virtualization Infrastructure

Production Systems

Data Center

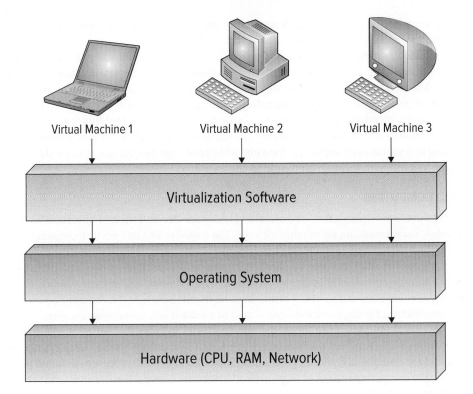

Virtual Machine 1   Virtual Machine 2   Virtual Machine 3

Virtualization Software

Operating System

Hardware (CPU, RAM, Network)

Virtual Data Centers

A *data center* is a facility used to house management information systems and associated components, such as telecommunications and storage systems. Data centers, sometimes referred to as server farms, consume power and require cooling and floor space while working to support business growth without disrupting normal business operations and the quality of service. The amount of data a data center stores has grown exponentially over the years as our reliance on information has increased. Backups, graphics, documents, presentations, photos, audio files, and video files all contribute to the ever-expanding information footprint that requires storage. One of the most effective ways to limit the power consumption and cooling requirements of a data center is to consolidate parts of the physical infrastructure, particularly by reducing the number of physical servers through virtualization. For this reason, virtualization is having a profound impact on data centers as the sheer number of servers a company requires to operate decreases, thereby boosting growth and performance while reducing environmental impact, as shown in Figure B9.10. Google, Microsoft, Amazon, and Yahoo! have all created data centers along the Columbia River in the northwestern United States. In this area, each company can benefit from affordable land, high-speed Internet access, plentiful water for cooling, and even more important, inexpensive electricity. These factors are critical to today's large-scale data centers, whose sheer size and power needs far surpass those of the previous generation. Microsoft's data center in Quincy, Washington, is larger than 10 football

FIGURE B9.10

Ways for Data Centers to Become Sustainable.

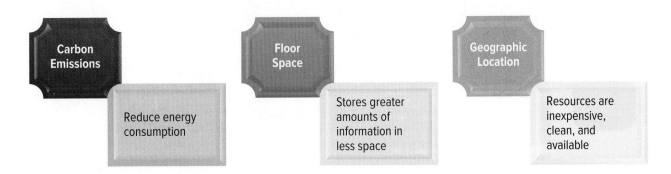

Carbon Emissions	Floor Space	Geographic Location
Reduce energy consumption	Stores greater amounts of information in less space	Resources are inexpensive, clean, and available

fields and is powered entirely by hydroelectricity, power generated from flowing water rather than from the burning of coal or other fossil fuel.

If we take a holistic and integrated approach to overall company growth, the benefits of integrating information MIS infrastructures, environmental MIS infrastructures, and sustainable MIS infrastructures become obvious. For example, a company could easily create a backup of its software and important information in one or more geographically dispersed locations using cloud computing. This would be far cheaper than building its own hot and cold sites in different areas of the country. In the case of a security breach, failover can be deployed as a virtual machine in one location of the cloud can be shut down as another virtual machine in a different location on the cloud comes online.

CLOUD COMPUTING

Imagine a cyclical business that specializes in Halloween decorations and how its sales trends and orders vary depending on the time of year. The majority of sales occur in September and October, and the remaining 10 months have relatively small sales and small system usage. The company does not want to invest in massive, expensive servers that sit idle 10 months of the year just to meet its capacity spikes in September and October. The perfect solution for this company is cloud computing, which makes it easier to gain access to the computing power that was once reserved for large corporations. Small to medium-size companies no longer have to make big capital investments to access the same powerful systems that large companies run.

According to the National Institute of Standards and Technology (NIST), *cloud computing* is a model for enabling ubiquitous, convenient, on-demand network access to a shared pool of configurable computing resources (e.g., networks, servers, storage, applications, and services) that can be rapidly provisioned and released with minimal management effort or service provider interaction. Cloud computing offers new ways to store, access, process, and analyze information and connect people and resources from any location in the world where an Internet connection is available. The easiest way to understand how cloud computing works is to imagine your home computer in a remote location. It has all of your applications and data on it and instead of turning it on, you contact it via the internet and sign in with a username and password. Your applications and data/media are them immediately available and changeable from any device you own that can log into it. Each time you log in, your changed data and media are then viewable from any other device.

As shown in Figure B9.11, users connect to the cloud from their personal computers or portable devices using a client, such as a web browser. To these individual users, the cloud

FIGURE B9.11

Cloud Computing Example.

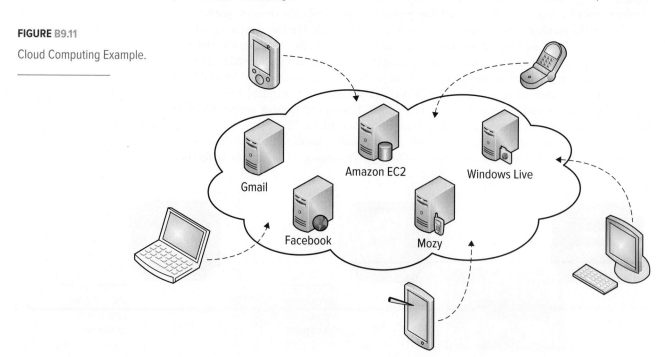

appears as their personal application, device, or document. It is like storing all of your software and documents "in the cloud," and all you need is a device to access the cloud. No more hard drives, software, or processing power—that is all located in the cloud, transparent to the users. Users are not physically bound to a single computer or network; they can access their programs and documents from wherever they are, whenever they need to. Just think of having your hard drive located in the sky and you can access your information and programs using any device from wherever you are. The best part is that even if your machine crashes, is lost, or is stolen, the information hosted in the cloud is safe and always available. (See Figure B9.12 for cloud providers and Figure B9.13 for cloud computing advantages.)

Multi-tenancy in the cloud means that a single instance of a system serves multiple customers. In the cloud, each customer is called a tenant and multiple tenants can access the same system. Multi-tenancy helps to reduce operational costs associated with implementing large systems as the costs are dispersed across many tenants as opposed to single-tenancy, in which each customer or tenant must purchase and maintain an individual system. With a multi-tenancy cloud approach, the service provider only has one place to update its system. With a single-tenancy cloud approach, the service provider would have to update its system in every company where the software was running. The *cloud fabric* is the software that makes possible the benefits of cloud computing, such as multi-tenancy. A *cloud fabric controller* is an individual who monitors and provisions cloud resources, similar to a server administrator at an individual company. Cloud fabric controllers provision resources, balance loads, manage servers, update systems, and ensure all environments are available and

Cloud Providers	
Amazon—Cloud Drive, Cloud Player, Amazon Prime	Amazon Kindle Fire is sold at a loss to push various types of media through Amazon Prime and Cloud Player where users can stream videos and music.
Apple—iCloud, iWork, iBooks, iTunes	iCloud brings together iPhones, iPads, and Mac to synchronize data across Apple devices. iWork helps users collaborate.
Google—Google Apps, Google Drive, Gmail, Google Calendar	Google offers a number of cloud services, including Google apps, Gmail, and Google Drive to store data.
Microsoft—Office 365, OneDrive, OneNote, Exchange	OneDrive and Office 365 offer ways to collaborate and share data, photos, email, and documents.

FIGURE B9.12

Overview of Cloud Providers.

FIGURE B9.13

Cloud Computing Advantages.

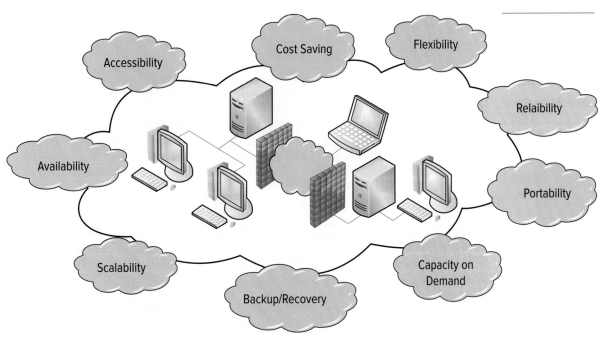

operating correctly. Cloud fabric is the primary reason cloud computing promotes all of the seven abilities, allowing a business to make its data and applications accessible, available, maintainable, portable, reliable, scalable, and usable. Figure B9.14 displays the top buisness cloud applications.

The cloud offers a company higher availability, greater reliability, and improved accessibility—all with affordable high-speed access. For flexibility, scalability, and cost efficiency, cloud computing is quickly becoming a viable option for companies of all sizes. With the cloud, you could simply purchase a single license for software such as Microsoft Office or Outlook at a far discounted rate and not worry about the hassle of installing and upgrading the software on your computer. No more worries that you don't have enough

FIGURE B9.14

Top Cloud-Based Business Applications.

CLOUD APPLICATIONS	
Box box.com	Box.com is like a file folder that all your gadgets and devices can access. You simply drag a file into Box, and you can instantly access it from anywhere.
Chatter.com! Chatter.com	Chatter is essentially an in-house social network. It allows your employees to share files, collaborate easily on projects, and pose questions to the whole company, which cuts down on meeting times, decreases the number of emails sent, and increases how quickly employees can gather information.
Evernote evernote.com	Evernote makes organizing notes simple. It organizes online all the sticky notes, scribbled-on notepads, and random pictures that you would have cluttering up your desk. It can even recognize writing in images, so if you take a picture of a whiteboard full of notes, you can find that image by searching for one of the phrases in it.
Google Apps Google.com	Google Apps pretty much eliminates the need for many computer programs. You can create and save text documents, spreadsheets, slide shows and more on Google Docs, and several people can work on one file simultaneously. Google Calendar makes creating and sharing calendars easy, and event reminders can be emailed to invitees. Gmail for Business gives companies personalized email accounts that are easy to set up and amend and that have the flexibility and storage space of Gmail.
MailChimp mailchimp.com	MailChimp is an email publishing platform that allows businesses of all sizes to design and send their email campaigns. Measuring the success of your email campaigns is really easy because the software integrates with Google Analytics for tracking purposes.
Moo uk.moo.com	Moo offers a design and printing service for business cards, postcards, and minicards. Users can customize existing Moo designs, upload their own designs, or import their own images from their Etsy, Facebook, Flickr, Picasa, or SmugMug account.
Mozy mozy.co.uk	Mozy is an online backup service that continuously backs up the files on your computer or server. It gives small businesses the space to back up all their computer and server files for a very reasonable price, so owners know their files are retrievable, even during a data loss crisis.
Outright outright.com	Outright is a cloud finance app that helps small businesses with their business accounting. It allows you to track income/expenses, tax obligations, and profits/losses in real time. Ideal for small companies or just entrepreneurs looking to get a hold on their finances.
Quickbooks quickbooks.intuit.co.uk	Quickbooks is an online accounting service and can help with all accounting needs, including monitoring cash flow, creating reports, and setting budgets, and is accessible from anywhere in the world.
Skype skype.com	Skype turns your computer into a phone; you can call or chat (with or without video) to other Skype users for free.
Toggl toggl.com	Toggl is a time-tracking application. It allows you to create tasks and projects and assign a certain amount of time to each project. It also logs how long tasks take to complete and how much time you have left to spend in a project.

ON-DEMAND SELF-SERVICE Users can increase storage and processing power as needed	BROAD NETWORK ACCESS All devices can access data and applications	MULTI-TENANCY Customers share pooled computing resources
RAPID ELASTICITY Storage, network bandwidth, and computing capacity can be increased or decreased immediately, allowing for optimal scalability	**MEASURED SERVICE** Clients can monitor and measure transactions and use of resources	

FIGURE B9.15

Benefits of Cloud Computing.

memory to run a new program because the hardware is provided in the cloud, along with the software. You simply pay to access the program. Think of this the same way you do your telephone service. You simply pay to access a vendor's service, and you do not have to pay for the equipment required to carry the call around the globe. You also don't have to worry about scalability because the system automatically handles peak loads, which can be spread out among the systems in the cloud. Figure B9.15 displays the benefits of cloud computing.

Because additional cloud resources are always available, companies no longer have to purchase systems for infrequent computing tasks that need intense processing power, such as preparing tax returns during tax season or increased sales transactions during certain holiday seasons. If a company needs more processing power, it is always there in the cloud—and available on a cost-efficient basis.

With cloud computing, individuals or businesses pay only for the services they need, when they need them, and where, much as we use and pay for electricity. In the past, a company would have to pay millions of dollars for the hardware, software, and networking equipment required to implement a large system such as payroll or sales management. A cloud computing user can simply access the cloud and request a single license to a payroll application. The user does not have to incur any hardware, software, or networking expenses. As the business grows and the user requires more employees to have access to the system, the business simply purchases additional licenses. Rather than running software on a local computer or server, companies can now reach to the cloud to combine software applications, data storage, and considerable computing power.

Regardless of which cloud model a business chooses, it can select from four different cloud computing environments—public, private, community, and hybrid (see Figure B9.16).

Public Cloud

Public cloud promotes massive, global, and industrywide applications offered to the general public. In a public cloud, customers are never required to provision, manage, upgrade, or replace hardware or software. Pricing is utility-style and customers pay only for the resources they use. Public clouds are the type used by service providers to offer free or paid-for services to the general public. They are open, but often with standard restrictions requiring passwords. A few great examples of public cloud computing include Amazon Web Services (AWS), Windows Azure, and Google Cloud Connect.

Private Cloud

Private cloud serves only one customer or organization and can be located on the customer's premises or off the customer's premises. A private cloud is the optimal solution for an organization such as the government that has high data security concerns and values information privacy. Private clouds are far more expensive than public clouds because costs are not shared

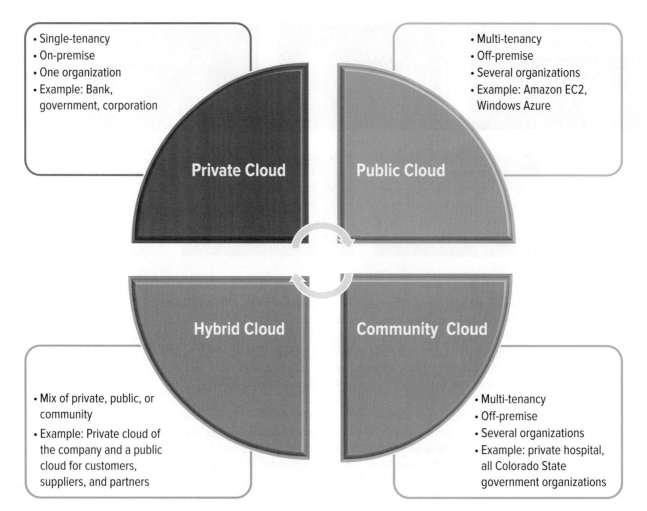

• Single-tenancy
• On-premise
• One organization
• Example: Bank, government, corporation

Private Cloud

Public Cloud

• Multi-tenancy
• Off-premise
• Several organizations
• Example: Amazon EC2, Windows Azure

Hybrid Cloud

Community Cloud

• Mix of private, public, or community
• Example: Private cloud of the company and a public cloud for customers, suppliers, and partners

• Multi-tenancy
• Off-premise
• Several organizations
• Example: private hospital, all Colorado State government organizations

FIGURE B9.16

Cloud Computing Environments.

across multiple customers. Private clouds are mostly used by firms and groups who need to keep data secure. The main downside is that they still require significant investment of time and money to set them up.

Community Cloud

Community cloud serves a specific community with common business models, security requirements, and compliance considerations. Community clouds are emerging in highly regulated industries such as financial services and pharmaceutical companies. Community clouds are private, but spread over a variety of groups within one organization. Different sections of the cloud can be set up specifically for each department or group.

Hybrid Cloud

Hybrid cloud includes two or more private, public, or community clouds, but each cloud remains separate and is only linked by technology that enables data and application portability. For example, a company might use a private cloud for critical applications that maintain sensitive data and a public cloud for nonsensitive data applications. The usage of both private and public clouds together is an example of a hybrid cloud. Hybrid clouds offer services even if connectivity faults occur and are often used to provide backup to critical online services. ***Cloud bursting*** is when a company uses its own computing infrastructure for normal usage and accesses the cloud when it needs to scale for peak load requirements, ensuring a sudden spike in usage does not result in poor performance or system crashes.

Deploying an MIS infrastructure in the cloud forever changes the way an organization's MIS systems are developed, deployed, maintained, and managed. Moving to the cloud is a fundamental shift from moving from a physical world to a logical world, making irrelevant the notion of which individual server applications or data reside on. As a result, organizations and MIS departments need to change the way they view systems and the new opportunities to find competitive advantages.

UTILITY COMPUTING

Utility computing offers a pay-per-use revenue model similar to a metered service such as gas or electricity. Many cloud computing service providers use utility computing cloud infrastructures, which are detailed in Figure B9.17.

Infrastructure as a Service (IaaS)

Infrastructure as a Service (IaaS) delivers hardware networking capabilities, including the use of servers, networking, and storage, over the cloud using a pay-per-use revenue model. With IaaS the customer rents the hardware and provides its own custom applications or programs. IaaS customers save money by not having to spend a large amount of capital purchasing expensive servers, which is a great business advantage considering some servers cost more than $100,000. The service is typically paid for on a usage basis, much like a basic utility service such as electricity or gas. IaaS offers a cost-effective solution for companies that need their computing resources to grow and shrink as business demand changes. This is known as *dynamic scaling*, which means the MIS infrastructure can be automatically scaled up or down based on needed requirements. *Disaster Recovery as a Service (DRaaS)* offers backup services that use cloud resources to protect applications and data from disruption caused by disaster. It gives an organization a total system backup that allows for business continuity in the event of system failure. DRaaS is typically part of a disaster recovery plan or business continuity plan.

Currently the most popular IaaS operation is Amazon's Elastic Compute Cloud, generally known as Amazon EC2, or simply EC2. EC2 provides a web interface through which customers can load and run their own applications on Amazon's computers. Customers control their own operating environment, so they can create, run, and stop services as needed, which is why Amazon describes EC2 as *elastic*. IaaS is a perfect fit for companies with research-intensive projects that need to process large amounts of information at irregular intervals, such as those in the scientific or medical fields. Cloud computing services offer these companies considerable cost savings because they can perform testing and analysis at levels that are not possible without access to additional and very costly computing infrastructure.

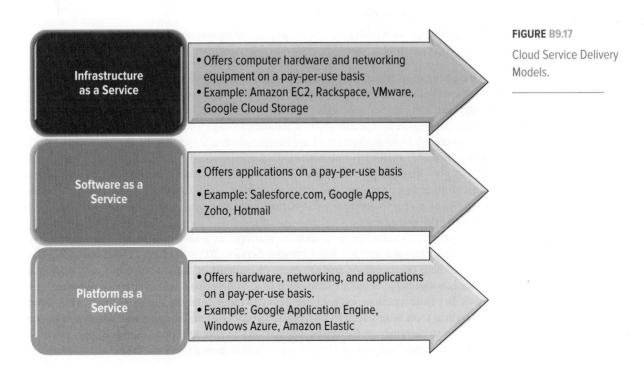

FIGURE B9.17

Cloud Service Delivery Models.

Software as a Service (SaaS)

Software as a Service (SaaS) delivers applications over the cloud using a pay-per-use revenue model. Before its introduction, companies often spent huge amounts of money implementing and customizing specialized applications to satisfy their business requirements. Many of these applications were difficult to implement, expensive to maintain, and challenging to use. Usability was one of the biggest drivers for creating interest in and success for cloud computing service providers.

SaaS offers a number of advantages; the most obvious is tremendous cost savings. The software is priced on a per-use basis with no up-front costs, so companies get the immediate benefit of reducing capital expenditures. They also get the added benefits of scalability and flexibility to test new software on a rental basis.

Salesforce.com is one of the most popular SaaS providers. Salesforce.com built and delivered a sales automation application, suitable for the typical salesperson, that automates functions such as tracking sales leads and prospects and forecasting. Tapping the power of SaaS can provide access to a large-scale, secure infrastructure, along with any needed support, which is especially valuable for a start-up or small company with few financial resources.

Data as a Service (DaaS) facilitates the accessibility of business-critical data in a timely, secure, and affordable manner. DaaS depends on the principle that specified, useful data can be supplied to users on demand, irrespective of any organizational or geographical separation between consumers and providers.

Platform as a Service (PaaS)

Platform as a Service (PaaS) supports the deployment of entire systems including hardware, networking, and applications using a pay-per-use revenue model. PaaS is a perfect solution for a business as it passes on to the service provider the headache and challenges of buying, managing, and maintaining web development software. With PaaS the development, deployment, management, and maintenance are based entirely in the cloud and performed by the PaaS provider, allowing the company to focus resources on its core initiatives. Every aspect of development, including the software needed to create it and the hardware to run it, lives in the cloud. PaaS helps companies minimize operational costs and increase productivity by providing all the following without up-front investment:

- Increased security.
- Access to information anywhere and anytime.
- Centralized information management.
- Easy collaboration with partners, suppliers, and customers.
- Increased speed to market with significantly less cost.

One of the most popular PaaS services is Google's Application Engine, which builds and deploys web applications for a company. Google's Application Engine is easy to build, easy to maintain, and easy to scale as a company's web-based application needs grow. Google's Application Engine is free and offers a standard storage limit and enough processing power and network usage to support a web application serving about 5 million page views a month. When a customer scales beyond these initial limits, it can pay a fee to increase capacity and performance. This can turn into some huge cost savings for a small business that does not have enough initial capital to buy expensive hardware and software for its web applications. Just think, a two-person company can access the same computing resources as Google. That makes good business sense.

Combining infrastructure as a service, platform as a service, and data as a service we arrive at Big Data as a Service. *Big Data as a Service (BDaaS)* offers a cloud-based Big Data service to help organizations analyze massive amounts of data to solve business dilemmas. BDaaS is a somewhat nebulous term often used to describe a wide variety of outsourcing of various Big Data functions to the cloud. This can range from the supply of data, to the supply of analytical tools with which to interrogate the data (often through a web dashboard or control panel) to carrying out the actual analysis and providing reports. Some BDaaS providers also include consulting and advisory services within their BDaaS packages.

Organizations pay special attention to computing basics since these form the underlying foundation that supports a firm's information systems. A solid underlying infrastructure is a necessity for ensuring the security, reliability, quality, and responsiveness of a firm's information systems. These systems are the tools that companies utilize and heavily rely upon to run their businesses and compete in today's competitive environment. As a business student, it is important that you understand the components and activities underpinning an organization's computing infrastructure so that you may be attuned to what is involved and be able to take steps to ensure this infrastructure is kept up-to-date and running as smoothly as possible.

✻ KEY TERMS

Big Data as a Service (BDaaS) 484
Carbon emissions 471
Clean computing 470
Cloud bursting 482
Cloud computing 478
Cloud fabric 479
Cloud fabric controller 479
Community cloud 482
Corporate social responsibility 470
Data as a Service (DaaS) 484
Data center 477
Disaster Recovery as a Service (DRaaS) 483

Dynamic scaling 483
Energy consumption 471
Ewaste 471
Green personal computer (green PC) 470
Grid computing 472
Hybrid cloud 482
Infrastructure as a Service (IaaS) 483
Moore's Law 470
Multi-tenancy 479
Network virtualization 475
Platform as a Service (PaaS) 484
Private cloud 481
Public cloud 481

Server virtualization 475
Smart grid 473
Software as a Service (SaaS) 484
Storage virtualization 475
Sustainable, or green, MIS 470
Sustainable MIS disposal 471
System virtualization 476
Upcycle 471
Utility computing 483
Virtualization 474

✻ MAKING BUSINESS DECISIONS

1. Solving the Ewaste Problem (StEP)

The United States disposes of more than 384 million units of ewaste yearly and currently recycles less than 20 percent, according to the Electronics TakeBack Coalition. The remaining 80 percent is burned or dumped in landfills, leaking toxic substances such as mercury, lead, cadmium, arsenic, and beryllium into the environment. Reports predict that ewaste will weigh as much as 200 Empire State Buildings by 2017. **S**olving the **E**waste **P**roblem (**StEP**) Initiative is a group represented by the United Nations organizations, governments, and science organizations, and their mission is to ensure safe and responsible ewaste disposal. StEP predicts ewaste will grow by a third in the next five years with the United States and China being the biggest contributors. Until recently, comprehensive data on global ewaste has been hard to collect because the definition of ewaste differs among countries. For example, the United States only includes consumer electronics such as TVs and computers, whereas Europe includes everything that has a battery or power cord in the ewaste category.

The growth of ewaste is an opportunity for entrepreneurs. Research the web and find examples of schools around the country that are responsibly tackling the ewaste problem. In a group, create a plan for implementing an ewaste recycling program at your school.

2 Upcycle Your Old PCs

Imagine walking into your friend's home and seeing her computer with live fish swimming around inside it. Upon taking a second look, you realize she has upcycled her old Mac into an innovative macquarium. Some young entrepreneurs are making a fortune by upcycling old Mac desktops as fish tanks. An upcycle reuses or refurbishes ewaste and creates a new product. With the growing problem of ewaste, one alternative is to upcycle your old technology by creating innovative household products or personal accessories. Take a look at one of the devices you are currently using to see whether you can create an upcycled product. Here are a few great ideas to get you started:

- Keyboard magnets
- Computer aquariums
- Mac mailboxes
- Keyboard calendars
- Floppy disk pencil holders
- Circuit board key rings
- RAM key chains
- Circuit earrings
- Cable bracelets
- Motherboard clocks
- Mouse belt buckles

3. Ewaste and the Environment

By some estimates, there may be as many as 1 billion surplus or obsolete computers and monitors in the world. Consider California, where 6,000 computers become surplus every day. If not disposed of properly, this enormous ewaste stream, which can contain more than 1,000 toxic substances, is harmful to human beings and the environment. Beryllium is found in computer motherboards, chromium in floppy disks, lead in batteries and computer monitors, and mercury in alkaline batteries. One of the most toxic chemicals known is cadmium, found in many old laptops and computer chips.

In poorer countries, where the United States and Europe export some of their ewaste, the full impact of the environmental damage is quickly being realized. These areas have little use for obsolete electronic equipment so local recyclers resell some parts and burn the rest in illegal dumps, often near residential areas, releasing toxic and carcinogenic substances into the air, land, and water.

Have you ever participated in ewaste? What can you do to ensure that you are safely disposing of electronic equipment including batteries? What can governments do to encourage companies to dispose of ewaste safely? What can be done to protect poorer countries from receiving ewaste? Create a list of the ways you can safely dispose of cell phones, computers, printers, ink cartridges, MP3 players, and batteries. What could you do to inform citizens of the issues associated with ewaste and educate them on safe disposal practices?

4. How Big Is Your Carbon Footprint?

Inevitably, in going about our daily lives—commuting, sheltering our families, eating—each of us contributes to the greenhouse gas emissions that are causing climate change. Yet there are many things each of us, as individuals, can do to reduce our carbon emissions. The choices we make in our homes, our travel, the food we eat, and what we buy and throw away all influence our carbon footprint and can help ensure a stable climate for future generations.

The Nature Conservancy's carbon footprint calculator measures your impact on our climate. Its carbon footprint calculator estimates how many tons of carbon dioxide and other greenhouse gases your choices create each year. Visit the Nature Conservancy's carbon footprint calculator to determine your carbon footprint and what you can do to reduce your emissions (http://www .nature.org/greenliving/carboncalculator/).

5. **Universities Are Switching to Gmail**

   Schools around the world are moving to cloud computing applications such as Google Docs & Spreadsheets and Google Calendar. Yale had planned to move from its own email system to Google Mail, but at the last minute decided to cancel the project. The reason was because school administrators and faculty members did not believe the move could support their business requirements. Do you agree or disagree that Google Gmail would be unable to replace a university's private email system? What are the advantages and disadvantages of a private email system? What are the advantages and disadvantages of using a cloud application such as Google Gmail? What choice would you make if you were the primary decision maker for choosing your school's email system?

6. **Desktop Virtualization**

   Every day users are becoming more comfortable with accessing and storing information in the cloud. This creates increased demand on MIS personnel to help manage, control, and provide access to that information—not just on company-issued computers, but on any number of devices, including personal ones. More and more employees want to be able to utilize their own computing devices—cell phones, netbooks, laptops—instead of company-issued ones. For instance, many students graduating from college have been exposed to Macs and may even own one, yet they are finding PCs as the standard computer of choice for most companies. Do you think it is a good business practice to allow your employees to use their personal devices for work-related business? What are the challenges of allowing users to port business applications to their personal devices? What are the challenges of allowing users to connect to corporate systems with personal devices?

7. **iTunes in the Cloud**

   Apple is considering a cloud version of its iTunes software that could possibly provide a host of new services for its users, as they would no longer be required to save iTunes to their computers, as it would reside in the cloud. With cloud computing, the software for iTunes would reside in centralized servers in data centers, rather than on a specific user computer. What would be the benefits to customers if they could host iTunes in the clouds and access it using a variety of devices? What would be your fears if you were to use iTunes in the cloud?

8. **Sustainable Departments**

   Energy prices and global warming are discussed daily in the news as the environmental impact of ewaste is just beginning to be recognized. Sustainability and corporate social responsibility need to be taken seriously by all managers, as everyone should take an active role in helping to preserve the environment. List the different departments in a business and the types of environmental issues they typically encounter. Which department do you think creates the most ewaste? Which department uses the greatest amount of electricity or has the largest carbon footprint? What can each department do to help combat its environmental issues? Why do all managers, and for that matter all employees, need to be aware of environmental issues and ways they can create sustainable MIS infrastructures?

9. **Making the Smart Grid Smart**

   ISO, a regional electricity company in New England, has launched an $18 million project in part because of an $8 million three-year federal grant. The project is designed to speed up the installation of 30 smart-grid devices covering every state in New England. The smart-grid devices will provide control room operators at ISO with enhanced tools to monitor and measure performance of the region's electrical grid, allowing the company to improve its ability to detect and address problems on the system. System status information coming into ISO will increase from once every four seconds to 30 times per second. Would you invest in ISO if you had the chance? Why or why not? If you were awarded an $8 million three-year federal grant, what type of sustainable infrastructure would you create?

10. **Box.net in the Cloud**

    Box.net was started by two college students, Aaron Levie and Dylan Smith, who needed a secure place to collaborate on group projects. The two immediately understood the value of cloud computing, and they created Box.net to allow them to share ideas and collaborate on documents in a virtual work space located in the cloud. They knew the cloud would allow them to access their documents from anywhere and on any device and that there was no chance of their papers being stolen or accidently destroyed. Levie and Smith recognized the business opportunity of their site and jumped at turning Box.net into a real business. Explain how Box.net could help you if you were working on a project with four other students. What would be the challenges of using Box.net?

PLUG-IN

B10

Business Intelligence

1. Compare tactical, operational, and strategic BI.
2. Describe the four categories of BI business benefits.

LO 1 **Compare tactical, operational, and strategic BI.**

Operational, Tactical, and Strategic BI

Claudia Imhoff, president of Intelligent Solutions, believes it is useful to divide the spectrum of data-mining analysis and business intelligence (BI) into three categories: operational, tactical, and strategic. Two trends are displayed when viewing the spectrum from operational through tactical to strategic. First, the analysis becomes increasingly complex and ad hoc. That is, it is less repetitive, it is less predictable, and it requires varying amounts and types of data. Second, both the risks and rewards of the analysis increase. That is, the often time-consuming, more strategic queries produce value less frequently but, when they do, the value can be extraordinary. Figure B10.1 illustrates the differences among operational, tactical, and strategic BI.

These three forms are not performed in isolation from each other. It is important to understand that they must work with each other, feeding results from strategic to tactical to promote better operational decision making. Figure B10.2 demonstrates this synergy. In this example, strategic BI is used in the planning stages of a marketing campaign. The results of these analytics form the basis for the beginnings of a new campaign, targeting specific customers or demographics, for example. The daily analyses of the campaign are used by the more tactical form of BI to change the course of the campaign if its results are not tracking where expected.

FIGURE B10.1

Operational, Tactical, Strategic BI.

	Operational BI	Tactical BI	Strategic BI
Business focus	Manage daily operations, integrate BI with operational systems	Conduct short-term analysis to achieve strategic goals	Achieve long-term organizational goals
Primary users	Managers, analysts, operational users	Executives, managers	Executives, managers
Time frame	Intraday	Day(s) to weeks to months	Months to years
Data	Real-time metrics	Historical metrics	Historical metrics

For example, perhaps a different marketing message is needed, or the inventory levels are not sufficient to maintain the current sales pace so the scope of marketing might be changed. These results are then fed into the operational BI for immediate actions—offering a different product, optimizing the sale price of the product, or changing the daily message sent to selected customer segments.

For this synergy to work, the three forms of BI must be tightly integrated with each other. Minimal time should be lost transporting the results from one technological environment to another. Seamlessness in terms of data and process flow is a must. TruServ, the parent company of True Value Hardware, has used BI software to improve efficiency of its distribution operations and reap a $50 million reduction in inventory costs. The marketing department uses BI to track sales promotion results such as which promotions were most popular by store or by region. Now that TruServ is building promotion histories in its databases, it can ensure all stores are fully stocked with adequate inventory. TruServ was able to achieve a positive return on investment in about five to six months.

BI'S OPERATIONAL VALUE

A leading risk insurance company allows customers to access account information over the Internet. Previously, the company sent paper reports and diskettes to all of its customers. Any errors in the reports would take one to two months to correct because customers would first have to receive the report, catch the mistake, and then notify the company of the error. Now customers spot the errors in real time and notify the insurance company directly through an extranet, usually within a couple of days.

Richard Hackathorn of Bolder Technologies developed an interesting graph to demonstrate the value of operational BI. Figure B10.3 shows the three latencies that impact the speed of decision making. These are data, analysis, and decision latencies.

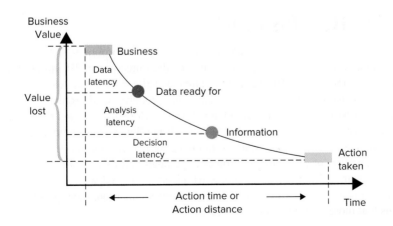

- **Data latency** is the time duration to make data ready for analysis (i.e., the time for extracting, transforming, and cleansing the data) and loading the data into the database. All this can take time depending on the state of the operational data to begin with.

- **Analysis latency** is the time from which data are made available to the time when analysis is complete. Its length depends on the time it takes a business to do analysis. Usually, we think of this as the time it takes a human to do the analysis, but this can be decreased by the use of automated analytics that have thresholds. When the thresholds are exceeded, alerts or alarms can be issued to appropriate personnel, or they can cause exception processes to be initiated with no human intervention needed.

- **Decision latency** is the time it takes a human to comprehend the analytic result and determine an appropriate action. This form of latency is very difficult to reduce. The ability to remove the decision-making process from the human and automate it will greatly reduce the overall decision latency. Many forward-thinking companies are doing just that. For example, rather than send a high-value customer a letter informing him of a bounced check (which takes days to get to the customer), an automated system can simply send an immediate email or voice message informing the customer of the problem.

The key is to shorten these latencies so that the time frame for opportunistic influences on customers, suppliers, and others is faster, more interactive, and better positioned. As mentioned above, the best time to influence customers is not after they have left the store or the website. It is while they are still in the store or still wandering around the website.

For example, a customer who is searching a website for travel deals is far more likely to be influenced by appropriate messaging actions then and there. Actions taken immediately, while customers are still in the site, might include:

- Offering customers an appropriate coupon for the trip they showed interest in while searching for cheap airfares.

- Giving customers information about their current purchase such as the suggestion that visas are needed.

- Congratulating them on reaching a certain frequent-buyer level and giving them 10 percent off an item.

A website represents another great opportunity to influence a customer, if the interactions are appropriate and timely. For example:

- A banner could announce the next best product to offer right after the customer puts an item in her basket.

- The customer could receive an offer for a product he just removed from his shopping basket.

- Appropriate instructions for the use of a product could come up on the customer's screen, perhaps warning a parent that the product should not be used by children under three.

LO 2 Describe the four categories of BI business benefits.

Business Benefits of BI

Agile BI is an approach to business intelligence (BI) that incorporates Agile software development methodologies to accelerate and improve the outcomes of BI initiatives. When an organization embraces Agile BI, it generally embeds Agile software developers in the organization's business intelligence team. As with all Agile initiatives, BI projects are broken down into a series of smaller projects that are planned for, developed, tested and rolled out on a continuous basis. This iterative development approach facilitates continuous improvement and helps an organization adapt more quickly to changing market conditions and organizational goals. Each iteration of an Agile BI project is planned and reviewed by both the software development team and the business owners who have requested work. This close collaboration between business and MIS results in better communication, clearly-defined goals and end results that more accurately meet expectations.

As with any Agile initiative, Agile BI tends to reduce total cost of change and promote a culture that values reflection, accepts change and understands how to respond flexibly to shifts in organizational value. Because BI project iterations are released on a regular basis, changes to a business intelligence dashboard or data warehouse can be made functional in a matter of weeks or months, providing business users with the information they need to make data-driven decisions much faster than could be realized with a more traditional waterfall project approach.

Rapid innovations in systems and data-mining tools are putting operational, tactical, and strategic BI at the fingertips of executives, managers, and even customers. With the successful implementation of BI systems an organization can expect to receive the following:

- **Single Point of Access to Information for All Users.** With a BI solution, organizations can unlock information held within their databases by giving authorized users a single point of access to data. Wherever the data reside, whether stored in operational systems, data warehouses, data marts, and/or enterprise applications, users can prepare reports and drill deep down into the information to understand what drives their business, without technical knowledge of the underlying data structures. The most successful BI applications allow users to do this with an easy-to-understand, nontechnical, graphical user interface.

- **BI across Organizational Departments.** There are many different uses for BI and one of its greatest benefits is that it can be used at every step in the value chain. All departments across an organization from sales to operations to customer service can benefit from the value of BI.

    Volkswagen AG uses BI to track, understand, and manage data in every department—from finance, production, and development, to research, sales and marketing, and purchasing. Users at all levels of the organization access supplier and customer reports relating to online requests and negotiations, vehicle launches, and vehicle capacity management and tracking.

- **Up-to-the-Minute Information for Everyone.** The key to unlocking information is to give users the tools to quickly and easily find immediate answers to their questions. Some users will be satisfied with standard reports that are updated on a regular basis, such as current inventory reports, sales per channel, or customer status reports. However, the answers these reports yield can lead to new questions. Some users will want dynamic access to information. The information that a user finds in a report will trigger more questions, and these questions will not be answered in a prepackaged report.

    While users may spend 80 percent of their time accessing standard or personalized reports, for 20 percent of their tasks, they need to obtain additional information not available in the original report. To address this need and to avoid frustration (and related report backlog for the IT team), a BI system should let users autonomously make ad hoc requests for information from corporate data sources.

    For merchants of MasterCard International, access to BI offers the opportunity to monitor their businesses more closely on a day-to-day basis. Advertising agencies are able to use information from an extranet when developing campaigns for merchants. On the authorization side, a call center can pull up cardholder authorization transactions to cut down on fraud. MasterCard expects that in the long term and as business partners increasingly demand access to system data, the system will support more than 20,000 external users.

CATEGORIES OF BI BENEFITS

Management is no longer prepared to sink large sums of money into IT projects simply because they are the latest and greatest technology. Information technology has come of age, and it is expected to make a significant contribution to the bottom line.

When looking at how BI affects the bottom line, an organization should analyze not only the organization-wide business benefits, but also the various benefits it can expect to receive

Most corporations today are inundated with data—from their own internal operational systems, their vendors, suppliers, and customers and from other external sources such as credit bureaus or industry sales data. The problem with understanding where your company is going is not in the amount of data coming into it. The problem is that this tidal wave of data is not in a form that can easily be digested, comprehended, or even accessed. Ask simple questions like who are your best customers or what are your most profitable products and you will most likely get as many answers as there are employees, not a comforting position to have in today's era of economic stress.

This is where business intelligence, or BI, comes in. The goal of BI is to provide the enterprise with a repository of "trusted" data—data that can be used in a multitude of applications to answer the questions about customers, products, supply and demand chains, production inefficiencies, financial trends, fraud, and even employees. It can be used to flag anomalies via alerts, provide visualization and statistical models, and understand the cause and effects of decisions upon the enterprise. Just about every aspect of an enterprise's business can benefit from the insights garnered from BI.

You, as a business student, must understand how technology can help you make intelligent decisions. But at the end of the day, how you interact with a customer face-to-face is the real test of your ability to foster and promote healthy customer relations.

 KEY TERMS

Analysis latency   492
Data latency   492
Decision latency   492

 MAKING BUSINESS DECISIONS

1. **Gaining Business Intelligence from Strategic Initiatives**

   You are a new employee in the customer service department at Premier One, a large pet food distributor. The company, founded by several veterinarians, has been in business for three years and focuses on providing nutritious pet food at a low cost. The company currently has 90 employees and operates in seven states. Sales over the past three years have tripled, and the manual systems currently in place are no longer sufficient to run the business. Your first task is to meet with your new team and create a presentation for the president and chief executive officer describing tactical, operational, and strategic business intelligence. The presentation should highlight the main benefits Premier One can receive from business intelligence along with any additional added business value that can be gained from the systems.

2. **Second Life BI**

   The virtual world of Second Life could become the first point of contact between companies and customers and could transform the whole customer experience. Since it began hosting the likes of Adidas, Dell, Reuters, and Toyota, Second Life has become technology's equivalent of India or China—everyone needs an office and a strategy involving it to keep their shareholders happy. But beyond opening a shiny new building in the virtual world, what can such companies do with their virtual real estate?

Like many other big brands, PA Consulting has its own offices in Second Life and has learned that simply having an office to answer customer queries is not enough. Real people, albeit behind avatars, must be staffing the offices—in the same way having a website is not enough if there is not a call center to back it up when a would-be customer wants to speak to a human being. The consultants believe call centers could one day ask customers to follow up a phone call with them by moving the query into a virtual world.

Unlike many corporate areas in the virtual world, the National Basketball Association incorporates capabilities designed to keep fans coming back, including real-time 3-D diagrams of games as they are being played.

You are the executive director of BI at StormPeak, an advanced AI company that develops robots. You are in charge of overseeing the first virtual site being built in Second Life. Create a BI strategy for gathering information in a virtual world. Here are a few questions to get you started:

- How will gathering BI for a business be different in a virtual world?
- How can BI help a business become more efficient in a virtual world?
- How will supporting BI in Second Life differ from supporting BI in a traditional company?
- What BI security issues might you encounter in Second Life?
- What BI ethical issues might you encounter in Second Life?

3. Searching for BI

Imagine being able to Google customer phone requests for information, sort through the recorded files of customer complaint calls, or decipher the exact moment when an interaction between a customer and store employee went awry. Being able to query voice records using the same methods as querying textual ones would open up boundless areas of business opportunity. Web surfers can already search audio files and audio/video feeds, but now enterprises can use this technology to help employees search voice mails or recorded calls for keywords and phrases and, in the end, to decode important customer concerns.

You have recently started your own marketing firm. You have built a BI tool that allows customers to query all of their unique data stores. Now all you need is to prepare your marketing materials to send to potential customers. Create a marketing pitch that you will deliver to customers detailing the business opportunities they could uncover if they purchased your product. Your marketing pitch can be a one-page document, a catchy tune, a video, or a PowerPoint presentation.

4. Mining Physician Data

NPR recently released a story discussing how large pharmaceutical companies are mining physician data. Thousands of pharmaceutical drug company sales representatives visit doctors and try to entice them to prescribe their company's newest drugs. The pharmaceutical companies buy prescription information from pharmacies all over the country describing which drugs are prescribed by which doctors. There is no patient information in the data. The sales representatives receive this BI from their companies and can tailor their sales pitch based on what that particular doctor has been prescribing to patients. Many doctors do not even realize that the sales representatives have this information and know exactly what drugs each individual doctor prescribes. The drug companies love mining data, but critics contend it is an invasion of privacy and drives up the cost of health care. Maine has just become the third state to pass a measure limiting access to the data.

You are working for your state government and your boss has asked you to create an argument for or against pharmaceutical data mining of physician data in your state. A few questions to get you started:

Do you agree that mining physician data should be illegal? Why or why not?

As a patient how do you feel about pharmaceutical companies mining your doctor's data?

As an employee of one of the pharmaceutical companies how do you feel about mining physician data?

5. **The Value of Plastic**

Accepting credit cards at Wendy's restaurants was a big decision facing corporate executives. There was no doubt that customers would appreciate the convenience of plastic, but could this option hurt overall sales? Wendy's executives decided that the best way to determine the value of plastic was to test it at several stores. The BI system was set to monitor how a credit card purchase affects sales, service speed, and cash sales. The intelligence gained from the system told executives that plastic sales were typically 35 percent higher than cash sales. Cash sales typically include a value meal—great for the customer but less profitable for the store. Plastic customers showed a trend of purchasing a la carte items generating a higher bill. Armed with BI, Wendy's introduced credit card readers nationally in June 2003.

You are the vice president of BI for McDonald's restaurants. The board of directors would like you to generate a report discussing the details of how you can use BI to analyze sales trends of menu items for all of its restaurants, including international locations. Identify several different variables you would monitor to determine menu item sales trends.

B11 Global Information Systems

1. Explain the cultural, political, and geoeconomic challenges facing global businesses.
2. Describe the four global MIS business drivers that should be included in all MIS strategies.
3. Describe governance and compliance and the associated frameworks an organization can implement.
4. Identify why an organization would need to understand global enterprise architectures when expanding operations abroad.
5. Explain the many different global information issues an organization might encounter as it conducts business abroad.
6. Identify global systems development issues organizations should understand before building a global system.

Introduction

Whether they are in Berlin or Bombay, Kuala Lumpur or Kansas City, San Francisco or Seoul, organizations around the globe are developing new business models to operate competitively in a digital economy. These models are structured yet agile, global yet local; and they concentrate on maximizing the risk-adjusted return from both knowledge and technology assets.

Globalization and working in an international global economy are integral parts of business today. Fortune 500 companies to mom-and-pop shops are now competing globally, and international developments affect all forms of business.

LO 1 Explain the cultural, political, and geoeconomic challenges facing global businesses.

Globalization

According to Thomas Friedman, the world is flat! Businesses are strategizing and operating on a global playing field. Traditional forms of business are simply not good enough in a global environment. Recall the way the Internet initially changed business by reviewing

Industry	How the Internet Changed Business
Travel	Travel site Expedia.com is now the biggest leisure-travel agency, with higher profit margins than even American Express. Thirteen percent of traditional travel agencies closed in 2002 because of their inability to compete with online travel.
Entertainment	The music industry has kept Napster and others from operating, but $35 billion annual online downloads are wrecking the traditional music business. U.S. music unit sales are down 20 percent since 2000. The next big entertainment industry to feel the effects of ebusiness will be the $67 billion movie business.
Electronics	Using the Internet to link suppliers and customers, Dell dictates industry profits. Its operating margins rose from 7.3 percent in 2002 to 8 percent in 2003, even as it took prices to levels where rivals couldn't make money.
Financial services	Nearly every public efinance company remaining makes money, with online mortgage service LendingTree growing 70 percent a year. Processing online mortgage applications is now 40 percent cheaper for customers.
Retail	Less than 5 percent of retail sales occur online, but eBay was on track in 2003 to become one of the nation's top 15 retailers, and Amazon.com will join the top 40. Walmart's ebusiness strategy is forcing rivals to make heavy investments in technology.
Automobiles	The cost of producing vehicles is down because of SCM and web-based purchasing. Also, eBay has become the leading U.S. used-car dealer, and most major car sites are profitable.
Education and training	Cisco saved $133 million by moving training sessions to the Internet, and the University of Phoenix online college classes please investors.

Figure B11.1. To succeed in a global business environment, cultural, political, and geoeconomic (geographic and economic) business challenges must be confronted.

CULTURAL BUSINESS CHALLENGES

Cultural business challenges include differences in languages, cultural interests, religions, customs, social attitudes, and political philosophies. Global businesses must be sensitive to such cultural differences. McDonald's, a truly global brand, has created several minority-specific websites in the United States: McEncanta for Hispanics, 365Black for African Americans, and i-am-asian for Asians. But these minority groups are not homogenous. Consider Asians: There are East Asian, Southeast Asian, Asian Indian, and, within each of these, divisions of national, regional, and linguistic nature. No company has the budget to create a separate website for every subsegment, but to assume that all Asian Americans fit into a single room— even a virtual room—risks a serious backlash. A company should ask a few key questions when creating a global website:

- Will the site require new navigational logic to accommodate cultural preferences?
- Will content be translated? If so, into how many languages?
- Will multilingual efforts be included in the main site or will it be a separate site, perhaps with a country-specific domain?
- Which country will the server be located in to support local user needs?
- What legal ramifications might occur by having the website targeted at a particular country, such as laws on competitive behaviors, treatment of children, or privacy?

POLITICAL BUSINESS CHALLENGES

Political business challenges include the numerous rules and regulations surrounding data transfers across national boundaries, especially personal information, tax implications, hardware and

Global IT Business
Management Areas.

software importing and exporting, and trade agreements. The protection of personal information is a real concern for all countries. For example, evidence from a national survey about citizen satisfaction with the Canadian government online services speaks to the importance of paying attention to privacy concerns. This highly publicized survey, known as Citizens First, was administered by the Institute for Citizen-Centered Service (ICCS) and the Institute for Public Administration in Canada (IPCA). Results from the survey indicate that although other factors help promote citizen satisfaction with the Internet, such as ease of finding information, sufficient information, site navigation, and visual appeal, the key driver that directly impacts whether citizens will conduct online transactions is their concerns over information security and privacy.

For security, there are high levels of concerns over information storage, transmission, and access and identity verification. For privacy and the protection of personal information, there are even stronger concerns about consolidation of information, unauthorized access, and sharing without permission.

GLOBAL GEOECONOMIC BUSINESS CHALLENGES

Geoeconomic refers to the effects of geography on the economic realities of international business activities. Even with the Internet, telecommunications, and air travel, the sheer physical distances across the globe make it difficult to operate multinational business. Flying MIS specialists into remote sites is costly, communicating in real-time across the globe's 24 time zones is challenging, and finding quality telecommunication services in every country is difficult. Skilled labor supplies, cost of living, and labor costs also differ among the various countries. When developing global business strategies, all of these geoeconomic challenges must be addressed.

Understanding the cultural, political, and geoeconomic business challenges is a good start to understanding global business, but the problems facing managers run far deeper. The remainder of this plug-in focuses on business management issues that are central to all global business. Business managers must understand four primary areas—global MIS business strategies, global enterprise architectures, global information issues, and global systems development—when running multinational companies (see Figure B11.2).

LO 2 Describe the four global MIS business drivers that should be included in all MIS strategies.

Global MIS Business Strategies

Global MIS business strategies must include detailed information on the application of information technology across the organization. MIS systems depend on global business drivers such as the nature of the industry, competitive factors, and environmental forces. For example, airlines and hotels have global customers who travel extensively and expect the same service regardless of location. Organizations require global MIS systems that can provide fast, convenient service to all international employees who are servicing these customers. When a high-end hotel customer checks into a hotel in Asia she expects to receive the same high-end service as when she is checking into a hotel in Chicago or London. Figure B11.3 displays the global MIS business drivers that should be included in all MIS strategies.

Many global MIS systems, such as finance, accounting, and operations management, have been in operation for years. Most multinational companies have global financial budgeting and cash management. As global operations expand and global competition heats up, pressure increases for companies to install global ebusiness applications for customers, suppliers, and employees. Examples include portals and websites geared toward customer service and supply chain management. In the past, such systems relied almost exclusively on privately

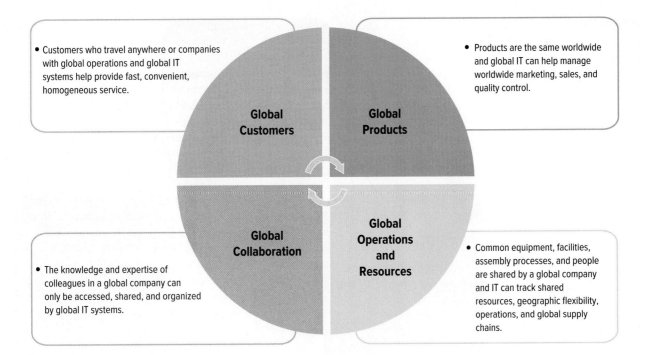

- Customers who travel anywhere or companies with global operations and global IT systems help provide fast, convenient, homogeneous service.

- Products are the same worldwide and global IT can help manage worldwide marketing, sales, and quality control.

Global Customers

Global Products

Global Collaboration

Global Operations and Resources

- The knowledge and expertise of colleagues in a global company can only be accessed, shared, and organized by global IT systems.

- Common equipment, facilities, assembly processes, and people are shared by a global company and IT can track shared resources, geographic flexibility, operations, and global supply chains.

FIGURE B11.3

Global MIS Business Drivers.

constructed or government-owned telecommunications networks. But the explosive business use of the Internet, intranets, and extranets for electronic commerce has made such applications more feasible for global companies.

GOVERNANCE AND COMPLIANCE

One fast-growing key area for all global business strategies is governance and compliance. *Governance* is a method or system of government for management or control. *Compliance* is the act of conforming, acquiescing, or yielding. A few years ago the ideas of governance and compliance were relatively obscure. Today, the concept of formal MIS governance and compliance is a must for virtually every company, both domestic and global. Key drivers for governance and compliance include financial and technological regulations as well as pressure from shareholders and customers.

Organizations today are subject to many regulations governing data retention, confidential information, financial accountability, and recovery from disasters. By implementing MIS governance, organizations have the internal controls they need to meet the core guidelines of many of these regulations, such as the Sarbanes-Oxley Act of 2002.

MIS governance essentially places structure around how organizations align MIS strategy with business strategy, ensuring that companies stay on track to achieve their strategies and goals, and implementing good ways to measure MIS's performance. Governance makes sure that all stakeholders' interests are considered and that processes provide measurable results. MIS governance should answer key questions including how the MIS department is functioning overall, what key metrics management requires, and what return the business is getting from its MIS investment. Figure B11.4 displays the five key areas of focus according to the MIS Governance Institute.

Organizations can follow a few different MIS governance frameworks, including:

- *CoBIT: Control Objectives for information and related technologies (CoBIT)* is a set of best practices that helps an organization to maximize the benefits of an information system, while at the same time establishing appropriate controls to ensure minimum errors.

- **ISACA:** *Information Systems Audit and Control Association (ISACA)* is a set of guidelines and supporting tools for IT governance that is accepted worldwide and generally used by auditors and companies as a way to integrate technology to implement controls and meet specific business objectives.

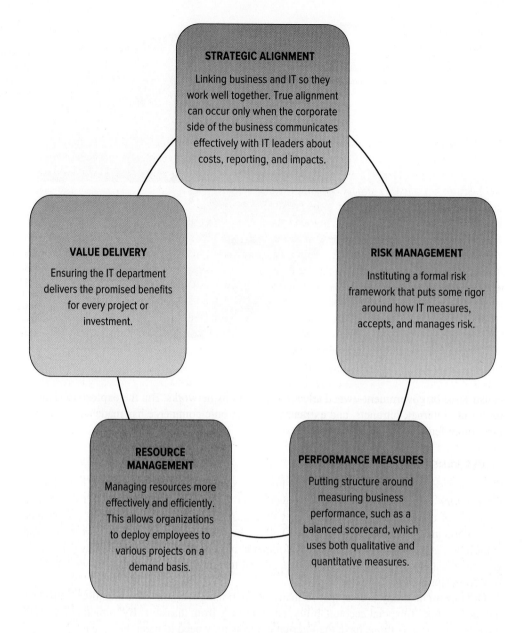

- **ITIL:** The *Information Technology Infrastructure Library (ITIL)* is a framework provided by the government of the United Kingdom and offers eight sets of management procedures: (1) service delivery, (2) service support, (3) service management, (4) Information and Communication Technology (ICT) infrastructure management, (5) software asset management, (6) business perspective, (7) security management, and (8) application management. ITIL is a good fit for organizations concerned about operations.

- **COSO:** The framework developed by the *Committee of Sponsoring Organizations (COSO)* is key for evaluating internal controls such as human resources, logistics, information technology, risk, legal, marketing and sales, operations, financial functions, procurement, and reporting. This is a more business-general framework that is less IT-specific.

- **CMMI:** Created by a group from government, industry, and Carnegie Mellon's Software Engineering Institute, the *Capability Maturity Model Integration (CMMI) method* is a process improvement approach that contains 22 process areas. It is divided into appraisal, evaluation, and structure. CMMI is particularly well suited to organizations that need help with application development, life cycle issues, and improving the delivery of products throughout the life cycle.

Global Enterprise Architectures

LO 4 Identify why an organization would need to understand global enterprise architectures when expanding operations abroad.

An *enterprise architecture* includes the plans for how an organization will build, deploy, use, and share its data, processes, and MIS assets. An organization must manage its global enterprise architecture to support its global business operations. Management of a global enterprise architecture not only is technically complex, but also has major political and cultural implications. For example, hardware choices are difficult in some countries because of high prices, high tariffs, import restrictions, long lead times for government approvals, lack of local service or replacement parts, and lack of documentation tailored to local conditions. Software choices also present issues; for example, European data standards differ from American or Asian standards, even when purchased from the same vendor. Some software vendors also refuse to offer service and support in countries that disregard software licensing and copyright agreements.

The Internet and the World Wide Web are critical to international business. This interconnected matrix of computers, information, and networks that reaches tens of millions of users in hundreds of countries is a business environment free of traditional boundaries and limits. Linking to online global businesses offers companies unprecedented potential for expanding markets, reducing costs, and improving profit margins at a price that is typically a small percentage of the corporate communications budget. The Internet provides an interactive channel for direct communication and data exchange with customers, suppliers, distributors, manufacturers, product developers, financial backers, information providers—in fact, with all parties involved in an international organization.

The Paris-based organization Reporters Without Borders notes that 45 countries restrict their citizens' access to the Internet. "At its most fundamental, the struggle between Internet censorship and openness at the national level revolves around three main means: controlling the conduits, filtering the flows, and punishing the purveyors. In countries such as Burma, Libya, North Korea, Syria, and the countries of Central Asia and the Caucasus, Internet access is either banned or subject to tight limitations through government-controlled ISPs. These countries face a lose-lose struggle against the information age. By denying or limiting Internet access, they stymie a major engine of economic growth. But by easing access, they expose their citizenry to ideas potentially destabilizing to the status quo. Either way, many people will get access to the electronic information they want. In Syria, for example, people go to Lebanon for the weekend to retrieve their email," said Virgini Locussol, Reporters Without Borders desk officer for the Middle East and North Africa.

Figure B11.5 displays the top 10 international telecommunication issues as reported by the MIS executives at 300 Fortune 500 multinational companies. Political issues dominate the listing over technology issues, clearly emphasizing their importance in the management of global enterprise architectures.

Estimating the operational expenses associated with international MIS operations is another global challenge. Companies with global business operations usually establish or contract with systems integrators for additional MIS facilities for their subsidiaries in other countries. These MIS facilities must meet local and regional computing needs, and even help balance global computing workloads through communications satellite links. However, offshore MIS facilities can pose major problems in headquarters' support, hardware and software acquisition, maintenance, and security. This is why many global companies prefer to outsource these facilities to application service providers or systems integrators such as IBM or Accenture to manage overseas operations. Managing global enterprise architectures, including Internet, intranet, extranet, and other telecommunication networks, is a key global MIS challenge for the 21st century.

Network Issues

- Improving the operational efficiency of networks
- Dealing with different networks
- Controlling data communication security

Regulatory Issues

- Dealing with transborder data flow restrictions
- Managing international telecommunication regulations
- Handling international politics

Technology and Country-Oriented Issues

- Managing network infrastructure across countries
- Managing international integration of technologies
- Reconciling national differences
- Dealing with international tariff structures

LO 5 Explain the many different global information issues an organization might encounter as it conducts business abroad.

Global Information Issues

While many consumer gadgets and software applications can benefit a company—for instance, by helping employees get their jobs done more efficiently—the security implications are legion, said Ken Silva, chief security officer at VeriSign, which specializes in network security software. "When we bolt those things onto corporate networks, we open up holes in the environment." Drugmaker Pfizer found this out the hard way. An employee's spouse loaded file-sharing software onto a Pfizer laptop at home, creating a security hole that appears to have compromised the names and Social Security numbers of 17,000 current and former Pfizer employees, according to a letter Pfizer sent to state attorneys general. Pfizer's investigation showed that 15,700 of those employees actually had their data accessed and copied.

Rather than fight the trend, some companies are experimenting with giving employees more choice regarding the technology they use—so long as they accept more responsibility for it. In 2005, BP began a pilot project that gives employees about $1,000 to spend on productivity-enhancing tools in addition to standard-issue equipment, according to a report from the Leading Edge Forum. But before they can participate, employees must pass a test of their computer literacy skills.

The company takes other steps to give employees free rein while mitigating risk. BP cordons off its network by letting employees link to the Internet via consumer connections, from outside the firewall, in the case of its 18,000 laptops. At the same time it beefs up security on those machines. This lets employees safely experiment with software such as Amazon's on-demand computing and storage services.

Deperimeterization occurs when an organization moves employees outside its firewall, a growing movement to change the way corporations address technology security. In a business world where many employees are off-site or on the road, or where businesses increasingly must collaborate with partners and customers, some say it's not practical to rely on a hardened perimeter of firewalls. Instead, proponents of deperimeterization say companies should focus on beefing up security in end-user devices and organizations' critical information assets.

INFORMATION PRIVACY

For many years, global data access issues have been the subject of political controversy and technology barriers in global business environments. These issues have become more prevalent with the growth of the Internet and the expansion of ebusinesses. ***Transborder data flows (TDF)*** occur when business data flows across international boundaries over the telecommunications networks of global information systems. Many countries view TDF as violating their national sovereignty because transborder data flows avoid customs duties and regulations for the import or export of goods and services. Others view transborder data flows as violating their laws to protect the local IT industry from competition or their labor regulations from protecting local jobs. In many cases, the data flow issues that seem particularly politically sensitive are those that affect the movement out of a country of personal data in ebusiness and human resource applications.

Many countries, especially those in the European Union (EU), may view transborder data flows as a violation of their privacy legislation since, in many cases, data about individuals are being moved out of the country without stringent privacy safeguards.

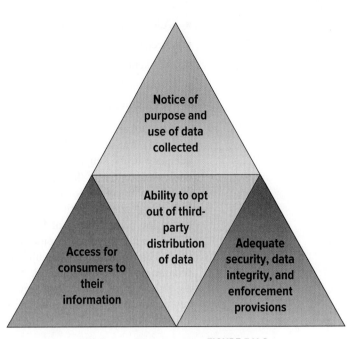

FIGURE B11.6

U.S.–EU Data Privacy Requirements.

Figure B11.6 highlights the key provisions of a data privacy agreement between the United States and the European Union. The agreement exempts U.S. companies engaging in international ebusiness from EU data privacy sanctions if they join a self-regulatory program that provides EU consumers with basic information about, and control over, how their personal data are used. Thus, the agreement is said to provide a "safe harbor" for such companies from the requirements of the EU's Data Privacy Directive, which bans the transfer of personal information on EU citizens to countries that do not have adequate data privacy protection.

Information privacy concerns the legal right or general expectation of individuals, groups, or institutions to determine for themselves when and to what extent information about them is communicated to others. In essence, information privacy is about how personal information is collected and shared. To facilitate information privacy, many countries have established legislation to protect the collection and sharing of personal information. However, this legislation varies greatly around the globe.

EUROPE

On one end of the spectrum lie European nations with their strong information privacy laws. Most notably, all member countries of the European Union adhere to a directive on the protection of personal data. A directive is a legislative act of the European Union that requires member states to achieve a particular result without dictating the means of how to achieve that result.

The directive on the protection of personal data grants European Union members the following rights:

- The right to know the source of personal data processing and the purposes of such processing.
- The right to access and/or rectify inaccuracies in one's own personal data.
- The right to disallow the use of personal data.

These rights are based on key principles pertaining to the collection or storage of personal data. The directive defines personal data to cover both facts and opinions about an individual. Any organization processing personal data of a person living in the European Union must comply with these key principles as outlined in the directive; these state that the data must be:

- Fairly and lawfully processed.
- Processed for limited purposes.

- Adequate, relevant, and not excessive.
- Accurate.
- Not kept longer than necessary.
- Processed in accordance with the data subject's rights.
- Not transferred to countries without adequate protection.

This last right restricts the flow of personal information outside the European Union by permitting its transfer to only countries that provide an "adequate" level of privacy protection—adequate in the sense that these other countries have to offer a level of privacy protection equivalent to that of the European Union. When first implemented, this part of the directive caused some concerns since countries outside the EU had much weaker privacy protection laws. Organizations in the United States were greatly concerned because they were at a legal risk if the personal data of EU citizens were transferred to computer servers in the United States—a likely scenario in today's global world of ebusiness. This led to extensive negotiations. The result was the establishment of a "safe harbor" program in the United States. This program provides a framework for U.S. organizations to show evidence of compliance with the EU directive. In this way, American companies can self-declare their compliance with the key principles of the directive and do business with EU nations without worrying about EU citizens suing them.

THE UNITED STATES

On the other end of the spectrum lies the United States. Information privacy is not highly legislated or regulated. There is no all-encompassing law that regulates the use of personal data or information. In many cases, access to public information is considered culturally acceptable, such as obtaining credit reports for employment or housing purposes. The reason for this may be historical. In the United States, the First Amendment protects free speech, and in many instances the protection of privacy might conflict with this amendment.

There are some exceptions. Though very few states recognize an individual's right to privacy, California's constitution protects an inalienable right to privacy. The California legislature has enacted several pieces of legislation aimed at protecting citizen information privacy. For example, California's Online Privacy Protection Act, established in 2003, requires commercial websites or online services that collect personal information of California residents to clearly post a privacy policy on the website or online service and to comply with this policy. Other nationwide exceptions include the Children's Online Privacy Protection Act (COPPA) and the Health Insurance Portability and Accountability Act (HIPAA).

COPPA is a federal law established in 1998 that applies to the collection of personal information from American children who are under 13 years of age. The act outlines what a website should include in its privacy policy, how to seek consent from a parent or guardian, and the responsibilities a website operator has to protect children's online safety and privacy. This law applies to any website that is perceived to be targeting American children. For example, if a toy company established in Canada wants to sell toys in the United States, the company's website should have to comply with the collection and use of information as outlined in COPPA. To show compliance requires a substantial amount of paperwork. As a result, many websites disallow underage users to join online communities and websites. Not complying with COPPA can be costly. In September 2006, the website Xanga, an online community, was fined $1 million for violating COPPA legislation.

HIPAA was enacted by the U.S. Congress in 1996. Provisions in HIPPA establish national standards for the electronic data interchange of health care–related transactions between health care providers, insurance plans, and employers. Embedded in these standards are rules for the handling and protection of personal health care information.

CANADA

Canada's privacy laws follow the European model very closely. Canada as a nation is quite concerned about protecting the personal information of its citizens. Its primary privacy law is the Personal Information Protection and Electronic Document Act (PIPEDA). The purpose of PIPEDA is to provide Canadians with a right of privacy with respect to how their personal information is collected, used, or disclosed by an organization. This is most important today, especially in the private sector, when information technology increasingly facilitates the collection and free flow of information.

Its precursor was the Privacy Act established in 1983, which restricted the handling of personal information within federal government departments and agencies only. This information concerned such things as pension and employment insurance files, medical records, tax records, and military records.

PIPEDA took effect in January 2001 and, like the Privacy Act, applied only to federally regulated organizations. By January 2004, PIPEDA's reach extended beyond government borders and applied to all other types of organizations, including commercial businesses. By doing so, Canada's PIPEDA law brought Canada into compliance with the European Union's directive on the protection of personal data. Hence, since January 2004, Canada no longer needed to implement safe harbor provisions for organizations wishing to collect and store personal information on European Union citizens.

Global Systems Development

LO 6 Identify global systems development issues organizations should understand before building a global system.

It is extremely difficult to develop a domestic information system, but the added complexity of developing a global information system quadruples the effort. Global information systems must support a diverse base of customers, users, products, languages, currencies, laws, and so on. Developing efficient, effective, and responsive information systems for multiple countries, differing cultures, and global ebusinesses is an enormous challenge for any organization. Managers should expect conflicts over local versus global system requirements and difficulties agreeing on common system features. For the project to succeed, the development environment should promote involvement and ownership by all local system users.

One of the most important global information systems development issues is the global standardization of data definitions. Common data definitions are necessary for sharing information among the parts of an international business. Differences in language, culture, and technology platforms can make global data standardization quite difficult. For example, what Americans call a "sale" may be called "an order booked" in the United Kingdom, an "order scheduled" in Germany, and an "order produced" in France. These are all referring to the exact same business event, but could cause problems if global employees have different versions of the data definition. Businesses are moving ahead to standardize data definitions and business processes. Many organizations are implementing corporate wikis where all global employees can post and maintain common business definitions.

Organizations can use several strategies to solve some of the problems that arise in global information systems development. First is transforming and customizing an information system used by the home office into a global application. This ensures the system uses the established business processes and supports the primary needs of the end users. Second is setting up a multinational development team with key people from several subsidiaries to ensure that the system design meets the needs of all local sites as well as corporate headquarters. Third, an organization could use centers of excellence where an entire system might be assigned for development to a particular subsidiary based on its expertise in the business or technical dimensions needed for successful development. A final approach that has rapidly become a major development option is to outsource the development work to global or offshore development countries that have the required skills and experience to build global information systems. All of these approaches require development team collaboration and managerial oversight to meet the global needs of the business.

Whether you aspire to be an entrepreneur, manager, or other type of business leader, it is increasingly important to think globally in planning your career. As this plug-in points out, global markets offer many opportunities yet are laced with significant challenges and complexities including cultural, political, and geoeconomic issues, such as:

- Global business strategies
- Global enterprise architectures
- Global information issues
- Global systems development

✳ **KEY TERMS**

Capability Maturity Model
    Integration (CMMI)
    method 504
Committee of Sponsoring
    Organizations
    (COSO) 504
Compliance 503

Control objectives for
    information and related
    technologies (CoBIT) 503
Deperimeterization 506
enterprise architecture 505
Geoeconomic 502
Governance 503

Information privacy 507
Information Systems Audit
    and Control Association
    (ISACA) 503
Information Technology
    Infrastructure Library (ITIL) 504
Transborder data flows (TDF) 507

✳ **MAKING BUSINESS DECISIONS**

1. Transforming an Organization

Your college has asked you to help develop the curriculum for a new course titled "Building a 21st-Century Organization." Use the materials in this text, the Internet, and any other resources to outline the curriculum that you would suggest the course cover. Be sure to include your reasons why the material should be covered and the order in which it should be covered.

2. Connecting Components

Components of a solid enterprise architecture include everything from documentation to business concepts to software and hardware. Deciding which components to implement and how to implement them can be a challenge. New IT components are released daily, and business needs continually change. An enterprise architecture that meets your organization's needs today may not meet those needs tomorrow. Building an enterprise architecture that is scalable, flexible, available, accessible, and reliable is key to your organization's success.

You are the enterprise architect for a large clothing company called Xedous. You are responsible for developing the initial enterprise architecture. Create a list of questions you will need answered to develop your architecture. Below is an example of a few questions you might ask.

- What are the company's growth expectations?
- Will systems be able to handle additional users?
- How long will information be stored in the systems?
- How much customer history must be stored?
- What are the organization's business hours?
- What are the organization's backup requirements?

3. IT Gets Its Say

CIOs need to speak the language of business to sell IT's strategic benefits. It is no secret that the most successful companies today are the ones that deliver the right products and services faster, more efficiently, more securely, and more cost-effectively than their competitors, and the key to that is a practical implementation of enterprise technology to improve business performance. IT executives and managers therefore must speak the language of business to articulate how technology can solve business problems.

CIOs of tomorrow will focus on a number of changing dynamics: enabling the business to grow versus just optimizing performance; saying yes instead of no; allowing open innovation rather than closed, traditional R&D practices; creating a culture of strategic growth and innovation; and empowering the customer to make decisions that drive a heightened value proposition for both the customer and supplier. You have been charged with creating a slogan for your company that explains the correlation of business and IT. A few examples include:

- IT should no longer be viewed as just an enabler of somebody else's business strategy.
- The distinction between technology and business is antediluvian—it's gone.

Create a slogan that you can use to explain to your employees the importance of business and IT.

4. Mom-and-Pop Multinationals

Global outsourcing is no longer just for big corporations as small businesses jump into the multisourcing game. Increasingly, Main Street businesses from car dealers to advertising agencies are finding it easier to farm out software development, accounting, support services, and design work to distant lands. For example, Randy and Nicola Wilburn run a micro-multinational organization right from their home. The Wilburns run real estate, consulting, design, and baby food companies from their home by taking outsourcing to the extreme. Professionals from around the globe are at their service. For $300, an Indian artist designed the cute logo of an infant peering over the words "Baby Fresh Organic Baby Foods" and Nicola's letterhead. A London freelancer wrote promotional materials. Randy has hired "virtual assistants" in Jerusalem to transcribe voice mail, update his website, and design PowerPoint graphics. Retired brokers in Virginia and Michigan handle real estate paperwork.

Elance, an online-services marketplace, boasts 48,500 small businesses as clients—up 70 percent in the past year—posting 18,000 new projects a month. Other online-services marketplaces such as Guru.com, Brickwork India, DoMyStuff.com, and RentACoder also report fast growth. You have decided to jump in the micro-multinational game and start your own online-services marketplace. Research the following as you compile your start-up business plan.

1. To compete in this market what types of services would you offer?

2. What types of cultural, political, and geoeconomic challenges would your business experience?

3. How would governance and compliance fit into your business strategy?

4. What types of global information issues might your company experience?

5. What types of customers would you want to attract and what vehicle would you use to find your customers?

6. What types of global systems development issues would your company experience?

7. What types of information security and ethical dilemmas should you anticipate?

PLUG-IN

B12 Global Trends

1. Explain why businesses use trends to assess the future.
2. Identify the global trends that will have the greatest impact on future business.
3. Identify the technologies that will have the greatest impact on future business.

Introduction

The core units brought out how important it is for organizations to anticipate and prepare for the future by studying emerging trends and new technologies. Having a broad view of emerging trends and new technologies as they relate to business can provide an organization with a valuable strategic advantage. Those organizations that can most effectively grasp the deep currents of technological evolution can use their knowledge to protect themselves against sudden and fatal technological obsolescence. This plug-in identifies several emerging trends that can help an organization prepare for future opportunities and challenges.

Reasons to Watch Trends

LO 1 Explain why businesses use trends to assess the future.

Organizations anticipate, forecast, and assess future events using a variety of rational, scientific methods including:

- **Trend analysis:** A trend is examined to identify its nature, causes, speed of development, and potential impacts.

- **Trend monitoring:** Trends viewed as particularly important in a specific community, industry, or sector are carefully monitored, watched, and reported to key decision makers.

- **Trend projection:** When numerical data are available, a trend can be plotted to display changes through time and into the future.

- **Computer simulation:** Complex systems, such as the U.S. economy, can be modeled by means of mathematical equations and different scenarios can be run against the model to conduct "what if" analysis.

Top Reasons to Study Trends	
1. Generate ideas and identify opportunities	Find new ideas and innovations by studying trends and analyzing publications.
2. Identify early warning signals	Scan the environment for potential threats and risks.
3. Gain confidence	A solid foundation of awareness about trends can provide an organization with the confidence to take risks.
4. Beat the competition	Seeing what is coming before others can give an organization the lead time it requires to establish a foothold in the new market.
5. Understand a trend	Analyzing the details within a trend can help separate truly significant developments from rapidly appearing and disappearing fads.
6. Balance strategic goals	Thinking about the future is an antidote to a "profit now, worry later" mentality that can lead to trouble in the long term.
7. Understand the future of specific industries	Organizations must understand everything inside and outside their industry.
8. Prepare for the future	Any organization that wants to compete in this hyperchanging world needs to make every effort to forecast the future.

- **Historical analysis:** Historical events are studied to anticipate the outcome of current developments.

Foresight is one of the secret ingredients of business success. Foresight, however, is increasingly in short supply because almost everything in our world is changing at a faster pace than ever before. Many organizations have little idea what type of future they should prepare for in this world of hyperchange. Figure B12.1 displays the top reasons organizations should look to the future and study trends.

Trends Shaping Our Future

According to the World Future Society, the following trends have the potential to change our world, our future, and our lives.

- The world's population will double in the next 40 years.
- People in developed countries are living longer.
- The growth in information industries is creating a knowledge-dependent global society.
- The global economy is becoming more integrated.
- The economy and society are dominated by technology.
- The pace of technological innovation is increasing.
- Time is becoming one of the world's most precious commodities.

THE WORLD'S POPULATION WILL DOUBLE IN THE NEXT 40 YEARS

The countries that are expected to have the largest increases in population between 2000 and 2050 are:

- Palestinian Territory—217 percent increase.
- Niger—205 percent increase.
- Yemen—168 percent increase.

LO 2 Identify the global trends that will have the greatest impact on future business.

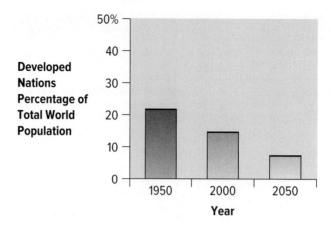

- Angola—162 percent increase.
- Democratic Republic of the Congo—161 percent increase.
- Uganda—133 percent increase.

In contrast, developed and industrialized countries are expected to see fertility rates decrease below population replacement levels, leading to significant declines in population (see Figure B12.2).

Potential Business Impact

- Global agriculture will be required to supply as much food as has been produced during all of human history to meet human nutritional needs over the next 40 years.
- Developed nations will find that retirees will have to remain on the job to remain competitive and continue economic growth.
- Developed nations will begin to increase immigration limits.

PEOPLE IN DEVELOPED COUNTRIES ARE LIVING LONGER

New pharmaceuticals and medical technologies are making it possible to prevent and cure diseases that would have been fatal to past generations. This is one reason that each generation lives longer and remains healthier than the previous generation. On average, each generation in the United States lives three years longer than the previous. An 80-year-old in 1950 could expect to live 6.5 years longer today. Many developed countries are now experiencing life expectancy over 75 years for males and over 80 years for females (see Figure B12.3).

FIGURE B12.3

Rising Life Expectancy in
Developed Countries.

Potential Business Impact

- Global demand for products and services for the elderly will grow quickly in the coming decades.
- The cost of health care is destined to skyrocket.
- Pharmaceutical companies will be pushed for advances in geriatric medicine.

THE GROWTH IN INFORMATION INDUSTRIES IS CREATING A KNOWLEDGE-DEPENDENT GLOBAL SOCIETY

Estimates indicate that 90 percent of American management personnel are knowledge workers. Estimates for knowledge workers in Europe and Japan are not far behind. Soon, large organizations will be composed of specialists who rely on information from co-workers, customers, and suppliers to

Rising Life Expectancy in Developed Countries		
Country	Life Expectancy (Born 1950–1955)	Life Expectancy (Born 1995–2020)
United States	68.9	76.5
United Kingdom	69.2	77.2
Germany	67.5	77.3
France	66.5	78.1
Italy	66.0	78.2
Canada	69.1	78.5
Japan	63.9	80.5

guide their actions. Employees will gain new power as they are provided with the authority to make decisions based on the information they acquire.

Potential Business Impact

- Top managers must be computer-literate to retain their jobs and achieve success.
- Knowledge workers are generally higher paid and their proliferation is increasing overall prosperity.
- Entry-level and unskilled positions are requiring a growing level of education.
- Information now flows from front-office workers to higher management for analysis. Thus, in the future, fewer mid-level managers will be required, flattening the corporate pyramid.
- Downsizing, restructuring, reorganization, outsourcing, and layoffs will continue as typical large organizations struggle to reinvent and restructure themselves for greater flexibility.

THE GLOBAL ECONOMY IS BECOMING MORE INTEGRATED

International outsourcing is on the rise as organizations refuse to pay high salaries for activities that do not contribute directly to the bottom line. The European Union has relaxed its borders and capital controls making it easier for companies to outsource support functions throughout the continent.

The Internet is one of the primary tools enabling our global economy. One of the primary reasons for the increase in Internet use is the increase in connectivity technology. The increase in Internet use is increasing revenues for ebusinesses.

Potential Business Impact

- Demand for personnel in distant countries will increase the need for foreign-language training, employee incentives suited to other cultures, and many other aspects of performing business globally.
- The growth of ebusiness and the use of the Internet to shop globally for raw materials and supplies will reduce the cost of doing business.
- The Internet will continue to enable small companies to compete with worldwide giants with relatively little investment.
- Internet-based operations require sophisticated knowledge workers and thus people with the right technical skills will be heavily recruited over the next 15 years.

THE ECONOMY AND SOCIETY ARE DOMINATED BY TECHNOLOGY

Computers are becoming a part of our environment. Mundane commercial and service jobs, environmentally dangerous jobs, standard assembly jobs, and even the repair of inaccessible equipment such as space stations will be increasingly performed by robots. Artificial intelligence and expert systems will help most companies and government agencies assimilate data and solve problems beyond the range of today's computers including energy prospecting, automotive diagnostics, insurance underwriting, and law enforcement.

Superconductors operating at economically viable temperatures are now in commercial use. Products eventually will include supercomputers the size of a three-pound coffee can, electronic motors 75 percent smaller and lighter than those in use today, and power plants.

Potential Business Impact

- New technologies provide dozens of new opportunities to create businesses and jobs.
- Automation will continue to decrease the cost of products and services, making it possible to reduce prices while improving profits.
- The Internet is expected to push prices of most products to the commodity level.
- The demand for scientists, engineers, and technicians will continue to grow.

Apply Your Knowledge Project Overview

Project Number	Project Name	Project Type	Plug-In	Focus Area	Project Level	Skill Set	Page Number
1	Financial Destiny	Excel	T2	Personal Budget	Introductory	Formulas	AYK.4
2	Cash Flow	Excel	T2	Cash Flow	Introductory	Formulas	AYK.4
3	Technology Budget	Excel	T1, T2	Hardware and Software	Introductory	Formulas	AYK.4
4	Tracking Donations	Excel	T2	Employee Relationships	Introductory	Formulas	AYK.4
5	Convert Currency	Excel	T2	Global Commerce	Introductory	Formulas	AYK.5
6	Cost Comparison	Excel	T2	Total Cost of Ownership	Introductory	Formulas	AYK.5
7	Time Management	Excel or Project	T12	Project Management	Introductory	Gantt Charts	AYK.6
8	Maximize Profit	Excel	T2, T4	Strategic Analysis	Intermediate	Formulas or Solver	AYK.6
9	Security Analysis	Excel	T3	Filtering Data	Intermediate	Conditional Formatting, Autofilter, Subtotal	AYK.7
10	Gathering Data	Excel	T3	Data Analysis	Intermediate	Conditional Formatting	AYK.8
11	Scanner System	Excel	T2	Strategic Analysis	Intermediate	Formulas	AYK.8
12	Competitive Pricing	Excel	T2	Profit Maximization	Intermediate	Formulas	AYK.9
13	Adequate Acquisitions	Excel	T2	Break-Even Analysis	Intermediate	Formulas	AYK.9
14	Customer Relations	Excel	T3	CRM	Intermediate	PivotTable	AYK.9
15	Assessing the Value of Information	Excel	T3	Data Analysis	Intermediate	PivotTable	AYK.10
16	Growth, Trends, and Forecasts	Excel	T2, T3	Data Forecasting	Advanced	Average, Trend, Growth	AYK.11
17	Shipping Costs	Excel	T4	SCM	Advanced	Solver	AYK.12
18	Formatting Grades	Excel	T3	Data Analysis	Advanced	If, LookUp	AYK.12

(Continued)

Project Number	Project Name	Project Type	Plug-In	Focus Area	Project Level	Skill Set	Page Number
19	Moving Dilemma	Excel	T2, T3	SCM	Advanced	Absolute vs. Relative Values	AYK.13
20	Operational Efficiencies	Excel	T3	SCM	Advanced	PivotTable	AYK.14
21	Too Much Information	Excel	T3	CRM	Advanced	PivotTable	AYK.14
22	Turnover Rates	Excel	T3	Data Mining	Advanced	PivotTable	AYK.15
23	Vital Information	Excel	T3	Data Mining	Advanced	PivotTable	AYK.15
24	Breaking Even	Excel	T4	Business Analysis	Advanced	Goal Seek	AYK.16
25	Profit Scenario	Excel	T4	Sales Analysis	Advanced	Scenario Manager	AYK.16
26	Electronic Résumés	HTML	T9, T10, T11	Electronic Personal Marketing	Introductory	Structural Tags	AYK.17
27	Gathering Feedback	Dreamweaver	T9, T10, T11	Data Collection	Intermediate	Organization of Information	AYK.17
28	Daily Invoice	Access	T5, T6, T7, T8	Business Analysis	Introductory	Entities, Relationships, and Databases	AYK.17
29	Billing Data	Access	T5, T6, T7, T8	Business Intelligence	Introductory	Entities, Relationships, and Databases	AYK.19
30	Inventory Data	Access	T5, T6, T7, T8	SCM	Intermediate	Entities, Relationships, and Databases	AYK.20
31	Call Center	Access	T5, T6, T7, T8	CRM	Intermediate	Entities, Relationships, and Databases	AYK.21
32	Sales Pipeline	Access	T5, T6, T7, T8	Business Intelligence	Advanced	Entities, Relationships, and Databases	AYK.23
33	Online Classified Ads	Access	T5, T6, T7, T8	Ecommerce	Advanced	Entities, Relationships, and Databases	AYK.23

NOTE: Many of the Excel projects support multiple data files. Therefore the naming convention that you see in the text may not be the same as what you see in a data folder. As an example, in the text we reference data files as AYK1_Data.xlsx; however, you may see a file named AYK1_Data_Version_1.xlsx, or AYK1_Data_Version_2.xlsx.

Project 1:

Financial Destiny

You have been introduced to Microsoft Excel and are ready to begin using it to help track your monthly expenses and take charge of your financial destiny. The first step is to create a personal budget so you can see where you are spending money and if you need to decrease your monthly expenses or increase your monthly income.

Project Focus

Create a template for a monthly budget of your income and expenditures, with some money set aside for savings (or you can use the data file, AYK1_Data.xlsx, we created). Create variations of this budget to show how much you could save if you cut back on certain expenses, found a room-mate, or got a part-time job. Compare the costs of a meal plan to costs of groceries. Consider how much interest would be earned if you saved $100 a month, or how much debt paid on student loans or credit card bills. To expand your data set, make a fantasy budget for 10 years from now, when you might own a home, have student loan payments, and have a good salary.

    Data File: AYK1_Data.xlsx

Project 2:

Cash Flow

Gears is a five-year-old company that specializes in bike components. The company is having trouble paying for its monthly supplies and would like to perform a cash flow analysis so it can understand its financial position. Cash flow represents the money an investment produces after subtracting cash expenses from income. The statement of cash flows summarizes sources and uses of cash, indicates whether enough cash is available to carry on routine operations, and offers an analysis of all business transactions, reporting where the firm obtained its cash and how it chose to allocate the cash. The cash flow statement shows where money comes from, how the company is going to spend it, and when the company will require additional cash. Gears would like to project a cash flow statement for the next month.

Project Focus

Using the data file AYK2_Data.xlsx complete the cash flow statement for Gears using Excel. Be sure to create formulas so the company can simply input numbers in the future to determine cash flow.

    Data File: AYK2_Data.xlsx

Project 3:

Technology Budget

Tally is a start-up website development company located in Seattle, Washington. The company currently has seven employees and is looking to hire six new employees in the next month.

Project Focus

You are in charge of purchasing for Tally. Your first task is to purchase computers for the new employees. Your budget is $250,000 to buy the best computer systems with a scanner, three color printers, and business software. Use the web to research various products and calculate the costs of different systems using Excel. Use a variety of Excel formulas as you analyze costs and compare prices. Use the data file AYK3_Data.xlsx as a template.

    Data File: AYK3_Data.xlsx

Project 4:

Tracking Donations

Lazarus Consulting is a large computer consulting company in New York. Pete Lazarus, the CEO and founder, is well known for his philanthropic efforts. Pete knows that most of his employees contribute to nonprofit organizations and wants to reward them for their efforts while encouraging others to contribute to charities. Pete began a program that matches 50 percent of each employee donation. The only stipulations are that the charity must be a nonprofit organization and the company will match only up to $2,000 per year per employee.

Project Focus

Open the data file AYK4_Data.xlsx and determine the following:

- What was the total donation amount per organization?
- What were the average donations per organization?

   Data File: AYK4_Data.xlsx

Project 5:

Convert Currency

You have decided to spend the summer traveling abroad with your friends. Your trip is going to take you to France, England, Italy, Switzerland, Germany, Norway, and Ireland. You want to use Excel to convert currencies as you travel around the world.

Project Focus

Locate one of the exchange rate calculators on the Internet (www.xe.com or www.x-rates.com). Find the exchange rates for each of the countries listed above and create formulas in Excel to convert $100, $500, and $1,000. Use the data file AYK5_Data.xlsx as a template.

   Data File: AYK5_Data.xls

Project 6:

Cost Comparison

You are thinking about purchasing a new computer because the machine you are using now is four years old, slow, and not always reliable, and it does not support the latest operating system. Your needs for the new computer are simple: anti-virus software, email, web browsing, word processing, spreadsheet, database, iTunes, and some lightweight graphical tools. Your concern is what the total cost of ownership will be for the next three years. You have to factor in a few added costs beyond just the initial purchase price for the computer itself, such as added hardware (this could include a new printer, docking station, or scanner), software (purchase of a new operating system), training (you're thinking about pursuing web training to get an internship next term), subsequent software upgrades, and maintenance.

Project Focus

- It is useful to think about costs over time—both direct as well as indirect costs. Part of the reason this distinction is important is that a decision should rest not on the nominal sum of the purchase, but rather on the present value of the purchase.

	A	B	C	D	E	F
1	COST OF NEW COMPUTER					
2	Discount Rate	1	0.9325	0.9109	0.7051	
3		Time 0	Year 1	Year 2	Year 3	Present Value Costs
4	Computer					
5	Software					
6	Additional Hardware					
7	Training					
8	Software upgrades					
9	Maintenance					
10						
11	Total Costs					
12						

FIGURE AYK.1

Sample Layout of New Computer Spreadsheet.

- A dollar today is worth more than a dollar one year from now.

- The relevant discount rate (interest rate) is your marginal cost of capital corresponding to a level of risk equal with the purchase.

- Use the data file AYK6_Data.xlsx as a template.

  Data File: AYK6_Data.xlsx

Project 7:

Time Management

You have just been hired as a business analyst by a new start-up company called Multi-Media. Multi-Media is an interactive agency that constructs phased and affordable website marketing, providing its clients with real and measurable solutions that are supported by easy-to-use tools. Because the company is very new to the business arena, it needs help in creating a project management plan for developing its own website. The major tasks for the development team have been identified but you need to create the timeline.

Project Focus

1. The task names, durations, and any prerequisites are:

   - Analyze and plan—two weeks. Cannot start anything else until done.

   - Create and organize content—four weeks. Can start to develop "look and feel" before this is done.

   - Develop the "look and feel"—four weeks. Start working on graphics and HTML at the same time.

   - Produce graphics and HTML documents—two weeks. Create working prototype after the first week.

   - Create a working prototype—two weeks. Give to test team when complete.

   - Test, test, test—four weeks.

   - Upload to a web server and test again—one week.

   - Maintain.

2. Using Microsoft Excel or Microsoft Project, create a Gantt chart using the information provided above.

Project 8:

Maximize Profit

Books, Books, Books is a wholesale distributor of popular books. The business buys overstocked books and sells them for a discount of more than 50 percent to local area bookstores. The owner of the company, BK Kane, would like to determine the best approach to boxing books so he can make the most profit possible. The local bookstores accept all shipments from Books, Books, Books because of BK's incredibly low prices. BK can order as many overstocked books as he requires, and this week's options include:

Title	Weight	Cost	Sale Price
Harry Potter and the Deathly Hallows, J. K. Rowling	5 lb	$9	$17
The Children of Húrin, J. R. R. Tolkien	4 lb	$8	$13
The Time Traveler's Wife, Audrey Niffenegger	3.5 lb	$7	$11
The Dark River, John Twelve Hawks	3 lb	$6	$9
The Road, Cormac McCarthy	2.5 lb	$5	$7
Slaughterhouse-Five, Kurt Vonnegut	1 lb	$4	$5

Project Focus

When packing a single box, BK must adhere to the following:

- 20 books or less.
- Books by three different authors.
- Between four and eight books from each author.
- Weight equal to or less than 50 pounds.

BK has come to you to help him determine which books he should order to maximize his profit based on the above information. Using the data file AYK8_Data.xlsx, determine the optimal book order for a single box of books.

Data File: AYK8_Data.xlsx

Project 9:

Security Analysis

SecureWorks Inc. is a small computer security contractor that provides computer security analysis, design, and software implementation for the U.S. government and commercial clients. SecureWorks competes for both private and U.S. government computer security contract work by submitting detailed bids outlining the work the company will perform if awarded the contracts. Because all of the work involves computer security, a highly sensitive area, almost all of SecureWorks tasks require access to classified material or company confidential documents. Consequently, all of the security engineers (simply known as "engineers" within the company) have U.S. government clearances of either Secret or Top Secret. Some have even higher clearances for the 2 percent of SecureWorks work that involves so-called black box security work. Most of the employees also hold clearances because they must handle classified documents.

Leslie Mamalis is SecureWorks's human resources (HR) manager. She maintains all employee records and is responsible for semiannual review reports, payroll processing, personnel records, recruiting data, employee training, and pension option information. At the heart of an HR system are personnel records. Personnel record maintenance includes activities such as maintaining employee records, tracking cost center data, recording and maintaining pension information, and absence and sick leave record keeping. While most of this information resides in sophisticated database systems, Leslie maintains a basic employee worksheet for quick calculations and ad hoc report generation. Because SecureWorks is a small company, Leslie can take advantage of Excel's excellent list management capabilities to satisfy many of her personnel information management needs.

Project Focus

Leslie has asked you to assist with a number of functions (she has provided you with a copy of her "trusted" personnel data file, AYK9_Data.xlsx):

1. Copy the worksheet Data to a new worksheet called Sort. Sort the employee list in ascending order by department, then by last name, then by first name.

2. Copy the worksheet Data to a new worksheet called Autofilter. Using the Autofilter feature, create a custom filter that will display employees whose birth date is greater than or equal to 1/1/1965 and less than or equal to 12/31/1975.

3. Copy the worksheet Data to a new worksheet called Subtotal. Using the subtotal feature create a sum of the salary for each department.

4. Copy the worksheet Data to a new worksheet called Formatting. Using the salary column, change the font color to red if the cell value is greater than or equal to 55000. You must use the conditional formatting feature to complete this step.

Data File: AYK9_Data.xlsx

Project 10:

Gathering Data

You have just accepted a new job offer from a firm that has offices in San Diego, Los Angeles, and San Francisco. You need to decide which location to move to. Because you have not visited any of these three cities and want to get in a lot of golf time, you determine that the main factor that will affect your decision is weather.

Go to www.weather.com and locate the box in which you can enter the city or zip code for which you want information. Enter San Diego, CA, and when the data appear, click the Averages and Records tab. Print this page and repeat this for Los Angeles and San Francisco. You will want to focus on the Monthly Average and Records section on the top of the page.

Project Focus

1. Create a spreadsheet to summarize the information you find.

2. Record the temperature and rainfall in columns, and group the cities into four groups of rows labeled Average High, Average Low, Mean, and Average Precipitation.

3. Fill in the appropriate data for each city and month.

4. Because rain is your greatest concern, use conditional formatting to display the months with an average precipitation below 2.5 inches in blue and apply boldface.

5. You also want to be in the warmest weather possible while in California. Use conditional formatting to display the months with average high temperatures above 65 degrees in green and apply an italic font face.

6. Looking at the average high temperatures above 65 degrees and average precipitation below two inches, to which city do you think you should relocate? Explain your answer.

Project 11:

Scanner System

FunTown is a popular amusement park filled with roller coasters, games, and water features. Boasting 24 roller coasters, 10 of which exceed 200 feet and 70 miles per hour, and five water parks, the park's attendance remains steady throughout the season. Due to the park's popularity, it is not uncommon for entrance lines to exceed one hour on busy days. FunTown would like your help to find a solution to decrease park entrance lines.

Project Focus

FunTown would like to implement a handheld scanner system that can allow employees to walk around the front gates and accept credit card purchases and print tickets on the spot. The park anticipates an overall increase in sales of 4 percent per year with online ticketing, with an expense of 6 percent of total sales for the scanning equipment. FunTown has created a data file for you to use, AYK11_Data.xlsx, that compares scanning sales and traditional sales. You will need to create the necessary formulas to calculate all the assumptions including:

- Tickets sold at the booth.
- Tickets sold by the scanner.
- Revenues generated by booth sales.
- Revenues generated by scanner sales.
- Scanner ticket expense.
- Revenue with and without scanner sales.
- Three year row totals.

Data File: AYK11_Data.xlsx

Project 12:

Competitive Pricing

Bill Schultz is thinking of starting a store that specializes in handmade cowboy boots. Bill is a longtime rancher in the town of Taos, New Mexico. Bill's reputation for honesty and integrity is well known around town, and he is positive that his new store will be highly successful.

Project Focus

Before opening his store, Bill is curious about how his profit, revenue, and variable costs will change depending on the amount he charges for his boots. Bill would like you to perform the work required for this analysis and has given you the data file AYK12_Data.xlsx. Here are a few things to consider while you perform your analysis:

- Current competitive prices for custom cowboy boots are between $225 and $275 a pair.
- Variable costs will be either $100 or $150 a pair depending on the types of material Bill chooses to use.
- Fixed costs are $10,000 a month.

   Data File: AYK12_Data.xlsx

Project 13:

Adequate Acquisitions

XMark.com is a major Internet company specializing in organic food. XMark.com is thinking of purchasing GoodGrow, another organic food Internet company. GoodGrow has current revenues of $100 million, with expenses of $150 million. Current projections indicate that GoodGrow's revenues are increasing at 35 percent per year and its expenses are increasing by 10 percent per year. XMark.com understands that projections can be erroneous, however; the company must determine the number of years before GoodGrow will return a profit.

Project Focus

You need to help XMark.com determine the number of years required to break even, using annual growth rates in revenue between 20 percent and 60 percent and annual expense growth rates between 10 percent and 30 percent. You have been provided with a template, AYK13_Data.xlsx, to assist with your analysis.

   Data File: AYK13_Data.xlsx

Project 14:

Customer Relations

Schweizer Distribution specializes in distributing fresh produce to local restaurants in the Chicago area. The company currently sells 12 different products through the efforts of three sales representatives to 10 restaurants. The company, like all small businesses, is always interested in finding ways to increase revenues and decrease expenses.

   The company's founder, Bob Schweizer, has recently hired you as a new business analyst. You have just graduated from college with a degree in marketing and a specialization in customer relationship management. Bob is eager to hear your thoughts and ideas on how to improve the business and help the company build strong, lasting relationships with its customers.

Project Focus

Bob has provided you with last year's sales information in the data file AYK14_Data.xlsx. Help Bob analyze his distribution company by using a PivotTable to determine the following:

1. Who is Bob's best customer by total sales?
2. Who is Bob's worst customer by total sales?

3. Who is Bob's best customer by total profit?

4. Who is Bob's worst customer by total profit?

5. What is Bob's best-selling product by total sales?

6. What is Bob's worst-selling product by total sales?

7. What is Bob's best-selling product by total profit?

8. What is Bob's worst-selling product by total profit?

9. Who is Bob's best sales representative by total profit?

10. Who is Bob's worst sales representative by total profit?

11. What is the best sales representative's best-selling product (by total profit)?

12. Who is the best sales representative's best customer (by total profit)?

13. What is the best sales representative's worst-selling product (by total profit)?

14. Who is the best sales representative's worst customer (by total profit)?

Data File: AYK14_Data.xlsx

Project 15:

Assessing the Value of Information

Recently Santa Fe, New Mexico, was named one of the safest places to live in the United States. Since then, housing development projects have been springing up all around Santa Fe. Six housing development projects are currently dominating the local market—Pinon Pine, Rancho Hondo, Creek Side, Vista Del Monte, Forest View, and Santa Fe South. These six projects each started with 100 homes, have sold all of them, and are currently developing phase two.

As one of the three partners and real estate agents of Affordable Homes Real Estate, it is your responsibility to analyze the information concerning the past 600 home sales and choose which development project to focus on for selling homes in phase two. Because your real estate firm is so small, you and your partners have decided that the firm should focus on selling homes in only one of the development projects.

From the New Mexico Real Estate Association you have obtained a spreadsheet file that contains information concerning each of the sales for the first 600 homes. It contains the following fields:

Column	Name	Description
A	LOT #	The number assigned to a specific home within each project.
B	PROJECT #	A unique number assigned to each of the six housing development projects (see table on the next page).
C	ASK PRICE	The initial posted asking price for the home.
D	SELL PRICE	The actual price for which the home was sold.
E	LIST DATE	The date the home was listed for sale.
F	SALE DATE	The date on which the final contract closed and the home was sold.
G	SQ. FT.	The total square footage for the home.
H	# BATH.	The number of bathrooms in the home.
I	# BDRMS	The number of bedrooms in the home.

The following numbers have been assigned to each of the housing development projects:

Project Number	Project Name
23	Pinon Pine
47	Rancho Hondo
61	Creek Side
78	Vista Del Monte
92	Forest View
97	Santa Fe South

It is your responsibility to analyze the sales list and prepare a report that details which housing development project your real estate firm should focus on. Your analysis should be from as many angles as possible.

Project Focus

1. You do not know how many other real estate firms will also be competing for sales in each of the housing development projects.

2. Phase two for each housing development project will develop homes similar in style, price, and square footage to their respective first phases.

3. As you consider the information provided to you, think in terms of what information is important and what information is not important. Be prepared to justify how you went about your analysis.

4. Upon completing your analysis, please provide concise, yet detailed and thorough, documentation (in narrative, numeric, and graphic forms) that justifies your decision.

Data file: AYK15_Data.xlsx

Project 16:

Growth, Trends, and Forecasts

Analytics Software provides innovative search software, website accessibility testing software, and usability testing software. All serve as part of its desktop and enterprise content management solutions for government, corporate, educational, and consumer markets. The company's solutions are used by website publishers, digital media publishers, content managers, document managers, business users, consumers, software companies, and consulting services companies. Analytics Software solutions help organizations develop long-term strategies to achieve web content accessibility, enhance usability, and comply with U.S. and international accessibility and search standards.

You manage the customer service group for the company and have just received an email from CIO Sue Downs that the number of phone calls from customers having problems with one of your newer applications is on the increase. This company has a 10-year history of approximately 1 percent in turnover a year, and its focus had always been on customer service. With the informal motto of "Grow big, but stay small," it takes pride in 100 percent callbacks in customer care, knowing that its personal service was one thing that made it outstanding.

The rapid growth to six times its original customer-base size has forced the company to deal with difficult questions for the first time, such as "How do we serve this many customers?"

One option might be for the company to outsource its customer service department. Before deciding to do that, Analytics Software needs to create a growth, trend, forecast analysis for future predictions.

Project Focus

1. Create a weekly analysis from the data provided in AYK16_Data.xlsx.

2. The price of the products, the actual product type, and any warrantee information is irrelevant.

3. Develop a growth, trend, and forecast analysis. You should use a three-day moving average; a shorter moving average might not display the trend well, and a much longer moving average would shorten the trend too much.

4. Upon completing your analysis, please provide concise yet detailed and thorough documentation (in narrative, numeric, and graphic forms) that justifies your recommendations.

Data File: AYK16_Data.xlsx

Project 17:

Shipping Costs

One of the main products of the Fairway Woods Company is custom-made golf clubs. The clubs are manufactured at three plants (Denver, Colorado; Phoenix, Arizona; and Dallas, Texas) and are then shipped by truck to five distribution warehouses in Sacramento, California; Salt Lake City, Utah; Chicago, Illinois; Albuquerque, New Mexico; and New York City, New York. Because shipping costs are a major expense, management has begun an analysis to determine ways to reduce them. For the upcoming golf season, the output from each manufacturing plant and how much each warehouse will require to satisfy its customers have been estimated.

The CIO from Fairway Woods Company has created a data file for you, AYK17_Data.xlsx, of the shipping costs from each manufacturing plant to each warehouse as a baseline analysis. Some business rules and requirements you should be aware of include:

- The problem presented involves the shipment of goods from three plants to five regional warehouses.

- Goods can be shipped from any plant to any warehouse, but it costs more to ship goods over long distances than over short distances.

Project Focus

1. Your goal is to minimize the costs of shipping goods from production plants to warehouses, thereby meeting the demand from each metropolitan area while not exceeding the supply available from each plant. To complete this project it is recommended that you use the Solver function in Excel to assist with the analysis.

2. Specifically you want to focus on:
   - Minimizing the total shipping costs.
   - Total shipped must be less than or equal to supply at a plant.
   - Total shipped to warehouses must be greater than or equal to the warehouse demand.
   - Number to ship must be greater than or equal to 0.

Data File: AYK17_Data.xlsx

Project 18:

Formatting Grades

Professor Streterstein is a bit absentminded. His instructor's grade book is a mess, and he would like your help cleaning it up and making it easier to use. In Professor Streterstein's course, the maximum possible points a student can earn is 750. The following table displays the grade equivalent to total points for the course.

Total Points	Calculated Grade
675	A
635	A–
600	B
560	B–
535	C
490	C–
450	D
0	F

Project Focus

Help Professor Streterstein rework his grade book. Open the data file AYK18_Data.xlsx and perform the following:

1. Reformat the workbook so it is readable, understandable, and consistent. Replace column labels, format and align the headings, and add borders and shading as appropriate.

2. Add a column in the grade book for final grade next to the total points earned column.

3. Use the VLookup Function to automatically assess final grades based on the total points column.

4. Using the If Function, format the workbook so each student's grade shows a pass or fail—P for pass, F for fail—based on the total points.

Data File: AYK18_Data.xlsx

Project 19:

Moving Dilemma

Pony Espresso is a small business that sells specialty coffee drinks at office buildings. Each morning and afternoon, trucks arrive at offices' front entrances, and the office employees purchase various beverages such as Java du Jour and Café de Colombia. The business is profitable. Pony Espresso offices, however, are located north of town, where lease rates are less expensive, and the principal sales area is south of town. This means the trucks must drive across town four times each day.

The cost of transportation to and from the sales area plus the power demands of the trucks' coffee brewing equipment are a significant portion of variable costs. Pony Espresso could reduce the amount of driving and, therefore, the variable costs, if it moved the offices closer to the sales area.

Pony Espresso presently has fixed costs of $10,000 per month. The lease of a new office, closer to the sales area, would cost an additional $2,200 per month. This would increase the fixed costs to $12,200 per month.

Although the lease of new offices would increase the fixed costs, a careful estimate of the potential savings in gasoline and vehicle maintenance indicates that Pony Espresso could reduce the variable costs from $0.60 per unit to $0.35 per unit. Total sales are unlikely to increase as a result of the move, but the savings in variable costs should increase the annual profit.

Project Focus

Consider the information provided to you from the owner in the data file AYK19_Data. xlsx. Especially look at the change in the variability of the profit from month to month. From

November through January, when it is much more difficult to lure office workers out into the cold to purchase coffee, Pony Espresso barely breaks even. In fact, in December, the business lost money.

1. Develop the cost analysis on the existing lease information using the monthly sales figures provided to you in the data file.

2. Develop the cost analysis from the new lease information provided above.

3. Calculate the variability that is reflected in the month-to-month standard deviation of earnings for the current cost structure and the projected cost structure.

4. Do not consider any association with downsizing such as overhead—simply focus on the information provided to you.

5. You will need to calculate the EBIT (earnings before interest and taxes).

Data File: AYK19_Data.xlsx

Project 20:

Operational Efficiencies

Hoover Transportation Inc. is a large distribution company located in Denver, Colorado. The company is currently seeking to gain operational efficiencies in its supply chain by reducing the number of transportation carriers that it is using to outsource. Operational efficiencies for Hoover Transportation, Inc., suggest that reducing the number of carriers from the Denver distribution center to warehouses in the selected states will lead to reduced costs. Brian Hoover, the CEO of Hoover Transportation, requests that the number of carriers transporting products from its Denver distribution center to wholesalers in Arizona, Arkansas, Iowa, Missouri, Montana, Oklahoma, Oregon, and Washington be reduced from the current five carriers to two carriers.

Project Focus

Carrier selection should be based on the assumptions that all environmental factors are equal and historical cost trends will continue. Review the historical data from the past several years to determine your recommendation for the top two carriers that Hoover Transportation should continue to use.

1. Analyze the last 24 months of Hoover's Transportation carrier transactions found in the data file AYK20_Data.xlsx.

2. Create a report detailing your recommendation for the top two carriers with which Hoover Transportation should continue to do business. Be sure to use PivotTables and PivotCharts in your report. A few questions to get you started include:

   - Calculate the average cost per carrier.
   - Calculate the total shipping costs per state.
   - Calculate the total shipping weights per state.
   - Calculate the average shipping costs per pound.
   - Calculate the average cost per carrier.

Data File: AYK20_Data.xlsx

Project 21:

Too Much Information

You have just landed the job of vice president of operations for The Pitt Stop Restaurants, a national chain of full-service, casual-themed restaurants. During your first week on the job, Suzanne Graham, your boss and CEO of the company, has asked you to provide an analysis of how well the company's restaurants are performing. Specifically, she would like to know which units and regions are performing extremely well, which are performing moderately well, and which are underperforming. Her goal is to identify where to spend time and focus efforts to improve the overall health of the company.

Project Focus

Review the data file AYK21_Data.xlsx and determine how best to analyze and interpret the data. Create a formal presentation of your findings. A few things to consider include:

- Should underperforming restaurants be closed or sold?
- Should high-performing restaurants be expanded to accommodate more seats?
- Should the company spend more or less on advertising?
- In which markets should the advertising budget be adjusted?
- How are The Pitt Stop Restaurants performing compared to the competition?
- How are units of like size performing relative to each other?

Data File: AYK21_Data.xlsx

Project 22:

Turnover Rates

Employee turnover rates are at an all-time high at Gizmo Manufacturing's plants. The company is experiencing severe worker retention issues, which are leading to productivity and quality control problems. The majority of the company's workers perform a variety of tasks and are paid by the hour. The company currently tests potential applicants to ensure they have the skills necessary for the intense mental concentration and dexterity required to fill the positions. Because significant costs are associated with employee turnover, Gizmo Manufacturing wants to find a way to predict which applicants have the characteristics of being a short-term versus a long-term employee.

Project Focus

1. Review the information that Gizmo Manufacturing has collected from two of its different data sources. The first data file, AYK22_Data_A.xlsx, contains information regarding employee wages. The second data file, AYK22_Data_B.xlsx, contains information regarding employee retention.

2. Using Excel analysis functions, determine the employee characteristics that you would recommend Gizmo Manufacturing look for when hiring new personnel. It is highly recommended that you use PivotTables as part of your analysis.

3. Prepare a report based on your findings (which should include several forms of graphical representation) for your recommendations.

Data Files: AYK22_Data_A.xlsx and AYK22_Data_B.xlsx

Project 23:

Vital Information

Martin Resorts Inc. owns and operates four Spa and Golf resorts in Colorado. The company has five traditional lines of business: (1) golf sales, (2) golf lessons, (3) restaurants, (4) retail and rentals, and (5) hotels. David Logan, director of marketing technology at Martin Resorts Inc., and Donald Mayer, the lead strategic analyst for Martin Resorts, are soliciting your input for their CRM strategic initiative.

Martin Resorts's IT infrastructure is pieced together with various systems and applications. Currently, the company has a difficult time with CRM because its systems are not integrated. The company cannot determine vital information such as which customers are golfing and staying at the hotel or which customers are staying at the hotel and not golfing.

For example, the three details that the customer Diego Titus (1) stayed four nights at a Martin Resorts managed hotel, (2) golfed three days, and (3) took an all-day spa treatment the first day are discrete facts housed in separate systems. Martin Resorts hopes that by using data warehousing technology to integrate its data, the next time Diego reserves lodging for another trip, sales associates may ask him if he would like to book a spa treatment as well, and even if he would like the same masseuse that he had on his prior trip.

Martin Resorts is excited about the possibility of taking advantage of customer segmentation and CRM strategies to help increase its business.

Project Focus

The company wants to use CRM and data warehouse technologies to improve service and personalization at each customer touch point. Using a data warehousing tool, important customer information can be accessed from all of its systems either daily, weekly, monthly, or once or twice per year. Analyze the sample data in AYK23_Data.xlsx for the following:

1. Currently, the quality of the data within the above disparate systems is low. Develop a report for David and Donald discussing the importance of high-quality information and how low-quality information can affect Martin Resorts's business.

2. Review the data that David and Donald are working with from the data warehouse in the data file AYK23_Data.xlsx.

   a. Give examples from the data showing the kind of information Martin Resorts might be able to use to gain a better understanding of its customers. Include the types of data quality issues the company can anticipate and the strategies it can use to help avoid such issues.

   b. Determine who are Martin Resorts's best customers, and provide examples of the types of marketing campaigns the company should offer these valuable customers.

   c. Prepare a report that summarizes the benefits Martin Resorts can receive from using business intelligence to mine the data warehouse. Include a financial analysis of the costs and benefits.

   Data File: AYK23_Data.xlsx

Project 24:

Breaking Even

Mountain Cycle specializes in making custom mountain bikes. The company founder, PJ Steffan, is having a hard time making the business profitable. Knowing that you have great business knowledge and solid financial sense, PJ has come to you for advice.

Project Focus

PJ would like you to determine how many bikes Mountain Cycle needs to sell per year to break even. Using Goal Seek in Excel solve using the following:

- Fixed cost equals $65,000
- Variable cost equals $1,575
- Bike price equals $2,500

Project 25:

Profit Scenario

Murry Lutz owns a small shop, Lutz Motors, that sells and services vintage motorcycles. Murry is curious how his profit will be affected by his sales over the next year.

Project Focus

Murry would like your help creating best, worst, and most-likely scenarios for his motorcycle sales over the next year. Using Scenario Manager, help Murry analyze the information in the data file AYK25_Data.xlsx.

   Data File: AYK25_Data.xlsx

Project 26:

Electronic Résumés

Résumés are the currency of the recruitment industry. They are the cornerstone of communication between candidates, recruiters, and employers. Technology is automating elements of the recruitment process, but a complete solution requires proper handling of the actual development of all the pieces and parts that comprise not just a résumé, but also an erésumé. Electronic résumés, or erésumés, have moved into the mainstream of today's job market at lightning speed. Erésumés have stepped up the efficiency of job placement to such a point that you could get a call from a recruiter just hours after submitting your erésumé. With this kind of opportunity, you cannot afford to be left in the dark ages of using only a paper résumé.

Project Focus

In the text or HTML editor of your choice, write your résumé as though you were really putting it online and inviting prospective employers to see it. We recommend typing in all the text and then later adding the HTML tags (rather than trying to type in the tags as you go).

Use the following checklist to make sure you're covering the basics. You do not need to match it exactly; it just shows what can be done.

- Add structural tags.
- Add paragraphs and headings.
- Find an opportunity to include a list.
- Add inline styles.
- Play with the alignment of elements.
- Add appropriate font selection, font size, and color.

Project 27:

Gathering Feedback

Gathering feedback from a website's visitors can be a valuable way of assessing a site's success, and it can help build a customer or subscriber database. For example, a business could collect the addresses of people who are interested in receiving product samples, email newsletters, or notifications of special offers.

Project Focus

Adding form elements to a web page is simple: They are created using a set of HTML form tags that define menus, text fields, buttons, and so on. Form elements are generally used to collect information from a web page.

In the text or HTML editor of your choice, create a web page form that would collect information for a customer ordering a customized bicycle. Use proper web page design and HTML tools to understand the process and function of form elements. Be sure to pay attention to:

- Form layout and design.
- Visual elements, including labels, alignment, font selection, font size, color.
- Required versus nonrequired fields.
- Drop-down boxes, text fields, and radio buttons.

Project 28:

Daily Invoice

Foothills Animal Hospital is a full-service small animal veterinary hospital located in Morrison, Colorado, specializing in routine medical care, vaccinations, laboratory testing, and surgery. The hospital has experienced tremendous growth over the past six months due to customer referrals. While Foothills Animal Hospital has typically kept its daily service records in a workbook format, it feels the need to expand its reporting capabilities to develop a relational database as a more functional structure.

Foothills Animal Hospital needs help developing a database, specifically:

- Create a customer table—name, address, phone, and date of entrance.
- Create a pet table—pet name, type of animal, breed, gender, color, neutered/spayed, weight, and comments.
- Create a medications table—medication code, name of medication, and cost of medication.
- Create a visit table—details of treatments performed, medications dispensed, and date of the visit.
- Produce a daily invoice report.

Figure AYK.2 displays a sample daily invoice report that the Foothills Animal Hospital accountants have requested. Foothills Animal Hospital organizes its treatments using the codes displayed in Figure AYK.3. The entities and primary keys for the database have been identified in Figure AYK.4. The following business rules have been identified:

1. A customer can have many pets but must have at least one.
2. A pet must be assigned to one and only one customer.
3. A pet can have one or more treatments per visit but must have at least one.
4. A pet can have one or more medications but need not have any.

Project Focus

Your job is to complete the following tasks:

1. Develop and describe the entity-relationship diagram.
2. Use normalization to assure the correctness of the tables (relations).

FIGURE AYK.2

Foothills Animal Hospital Daily Invoice Report.

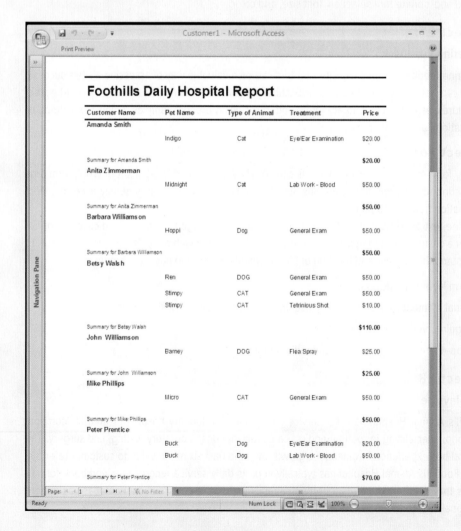

FIGURE AYK.3

Treatment Codes, Treatments, and Price Descriptions.

Treatment Code	Treatment	Price
0100	Tetrinious Shot	$10.00
0201	Rabonius Shot	$20.00
0300	General Exam	$50.00
0303	Eye/Ear Examination	$20.00
0400	Spay/Neuter	$225.00
0405	Reset Dislocation	$165.00
0406	Amputation of Limb	$450.00
0407	Wrap Affected Area	$15.00
0408	Cast Affected Area	$120.00
1000	Lab Work—Blood	$50.00
1003	Lab Work—Misc	$35.00
2003	Flea Spray	$25.00
9999	Other Not Listed	$10.00

FIGURE AYK.4

Entity Names and Primary Keys Foothills Animal Hospital.

Entity	Primary Key
CUSTOMER	Customer Number
PET	Pet Number
VISIT	Visit Number
VISIT DETAIL	Visit Number and Line Number (a composite key)
TREATMENT	Treatment Code
MEDICATION	Medication Code

3. Create the database using a personal DBMS package (preferably Microsoft Access).

4. Use the data in Figure AYK.3 to populate your tables. Feel free to enter your own personal information.

5. Use the DBMS package to create the basic report in Figure AYK.2.

Project 29:

Billing Data

On-The-Level Construction Company is a Denver-based construction company that specializes in subcontracting the development of single-family homes. In business since 1998, On-The-Level Construction has maintained a talented pool of certified staff and independent consultants providing the flexibility and combined experience required to meet the needs of its nearly 300 completed projects in the Denver metropolitan area. The field of operation methods that On-The-Level Construction is responsible for includes structural development, heating and cooling, plumbing, and electricity.

The company charges its clients by billing the hours spent on each contract. The hourly billing rate is dependent on the employee's position according to the field of operations (as noted above). Figure AYK.5 shows a basic report that On-The-Level Construction foremen would like to see every week concerning what projects are being assigned, the overall assignment hours, and the charges for the assignment. On-The-Level Construction organizes its internal structure in four different operations—Structure (500), Plumbing (501), Electrical (502), and Heating and Ventilation (503). Each of these operational departments can and should have many subcontractors who specialize in that area. On-The-Level Construction has decided to implement a relational database model to track project details according to project name, hours assigned, and charges per hour for each job description. Originally, On-The-Level Construction decided to let one of its employees handle the construction of the database. However, that employee has not had the time to completely implement the project. On-The-Level Construction has asked you to take over and complete the development of the database.

The entities and primary keys for the database have been identified in Figure AYK.6.

The following business rules have been identified:

1. A job can have many employees assigned but must have at least one.

2. An employee must be assigned to one and only one job number.

ON-THE-LEVEL CONSTRUCTION PROJECT DETAIL

PROJECT NAME	ASSIGN DATE	EMPLOYEE LAST NAME	FIRST NAME	JOB DESCRIPTION	ASSIGN HOUR	CHARGE/HOUR
Chatfield						
	6/10/2011	Olenkoski	Glenn	Structure	2.1	$35.75
	6/10/2011	Sullivan	David	Electrical	1.2	$105.00
	6/10/2011	Ramora	Anne	Plumbing	2.6	$96.75
	6/11/2011	Frommer	Matt	Plumbing	1.4	$96.75
Summary of Assignment Hours and Charges					7.30	$588.08
Evergreen						
	6/10/2011	Sullivan	David	Electrical	1.8	$105.00
	6/10/2011	Jones	Anne	Heating and Ventalation	3.4	$84.50
	6/11/2011	Frommer	Matt	Plumbing	4.1	$96.75
	6/16/2011	Bawangi	Terry	Plumbing	4.1	$96.75
	6/16/2011	Newman	John	Electrical	1.7	$105.00
Summary of Assignment Hours and Charges					15.10	$1,448.15
Roxborough						
	6/10/2011	Washberg	Jeff	Plumbing	3.9	$96.75
	6/10/2011	Ramora	Anne	Plumbing	2.6	$96.75
	6/11/2011	Smithfield	William	Structure	2.4	$35.75
	6/11/2011	Bawangi	Terry	Plumbing	2.7	$96.75
	6/16/2011	Johnson	Peter	Electrical	5.2	$105.00
	6/16/2011	Joen	Denise	Plumbing	2.5	$96.75
Summary of Assignment Hours and Charges					19.30	$1,763.78

FIGURE AYK.6

Entity Classes and Primary
Keys for On-The-Level
Construction.

Entity	Primary Key
PROJECT	Project Number
EMPLOYEE	Employee Number
JOB	Job Number
ASSIGNMENT	Assignment Number

3. An employee can be assigned to work on one or more projects.

4. A project can be assigned to only one employee but need not be assigned to any employee.

Project Focus

Your job is to complete the following tasks:

1. Develop and describe the entity relationship diagram.

2. Use normalization to assure the correctness of the tables (relations).

3. Create the database using a personal DBMS package (preferably Microsoft Access).

4. Use the DBMS package to create the basic report in Figure AYK.5.

5. You may not be able to develop a report that looks exactly like the one in Figure AYK.5. However, your report should include the same information.

6. Complete personnel information is tracked by another database. For this application, include only the minimum: employee number, last name, and first name.

7. Information concerning all projects, employees, and jobs is not readily available. You should create information for several fictitious projects, employees, and jobs to include in your database.

Project 30:
Inventory Data

An independent retailer of mobile entertainment and wireless phones, iToys.com has built its business on offering the widest selection, expert advice, and outstanding customer service. However, iToys.com does not use a formal, consistent inventory tracking system. Periodically, an iToys.com employee visually checks to see what items are in stock. Although iToys.com does try to keep a certain level of each "top seller" in stock, the lack of a formal inventory tracking system has led to the overstocking of some items and understocking of other items. On occasion, a customer will request a hot item, and it is only then that iToys.com realizes that the item is out of stock. If an item is not available, iToys.com risks losing a customer to a competitor.

Lately, iToys.com has become concerned with its inventory management methods. The owner of iToys.com, Dan Connolly, wants to better manage his inventory. The company receives orders by mail, by telephone, or through its website. Regardless of how the orders are received, Dan needs a database to automate the inventory checking and ordering process.

Project Focus

Dan has provided you with a simplified version of the company's current system (an Excel workbook) for recording inventory and orders in an Excel spreadsheet data file AYK30_Data.xlsx.

1. Develop an ERD diagram before you begin to create the database. You will need to use the information provided here as well as the data given in the Excel workbook.

2. Create the database using a personal DBMS package (preferably Microsoft Access) that will track items (i.e., products), orders, order details, categories, suppliers, and shipping methods.

3. In addition to what is mentioned above, the database needs to track the inventory levels for each product, according to a reorder level and lead time.

4. At this time, Dan does not need information stored about the customer; he simply needs you to focus on the inventory structure.

5. Develop a query that will display the products that need to be ordered from their supplier. To complete this, you will want to compare a reorder level with how many units are in stock.

6. Develop several reports that display:

   a. Each product ordered by its supplier. The report should include the product name, quantity on hand, and reorder level.

   b. Each supplier ordered by shipping method.

   c. Each product that requires more than five days lead time. (Hint: You will want to create a query for this first.)

   d. Each product ordered by category.

7. Here are some additional business rules to assist you in completing this task:

   a. An order must have at least one product, but can contain more than one product.

   b. A product can have one or more orders, but need not have any orders.

   c. A product must belong to one and only one category, but a category may contain many different products.

   d. A product can only be stocked by one supplier, but a supplier can provide more than one product.

   e. A supplier will use one type of shipping method, but shipping methods can be used by more than one supplier.

   Data File: AYK30_Data.xlsx

Project 31:

Call Center

A manufacturing company, Teleworks, has been a market leader in the wireless telephone business for the past 10 years. Other firms have imitated its product with some degree of success, but Teleworks occupies a dominant position in the marketplace because it has a first-mover advantage with a quality product.

Recently Teleworks began selling a new, enhanced wireless phone. This new phone does not replace its current product, but offers additional features, greater durability, and better performance for a somewhat higher price. Offering this enhanced phone has established a new revenue stream for the company.

Many sales executives at Teleworks seem to subscribe to the-more-you-have, the-more-you-want theory of managing customer data. That is, they believe they can never accumulate too much information about their customers, and that they can do their jobs more effectively by collecting infinite amounts of customer details. Having a firm grasp on a wide range of customer-focused details—specifically reports summarizing call center information—can be critical in enabling your company to successfully manage a customer relationship management (CRM) solution that creates a positive impact.

To continue to provide excellent customer support, and in anticipation of increased calls due to the release of its new product, Teleworks needs a database that it can use to record, track, and query call center information. Teleworks CIO KED Davisson has hired you to develop this database.

Project Focus

1. Teleworks has provided you with a data file AYK31_Data.xlsx; its current approach for recording cell center information is a spreadsheet file.

2. Develop an ERD diagram before you begin to create the database.

3. Create the database using a personal DBMS package (preferably Microsoft Access) that will allow data analysts to enter call center data according to the type of issue and the customer, assign each call to a consultant, and prioritize the call.

4. Develop a query that will display all issues that are "open."

5. Develop a screen form to browse all issues.

6. Develop several reports that display:

   a. All closed issues.

   b. Each issue in detail ordered by issue ID.

   c. Each issue in detail ordered by consultant.

   d. Each issue in detail ordered by category.

   e. Each issue in detail ordered by status.

7. Here are some additional business rules to assist you in completing this task:

   a. An issue must have at least one customer.

   b. A customer can have more than one issue.

   c. Each issue must be assigned to one consultant.

   d. Each consultant can be assigned to more than one issue.

   e. An issue can only belong to one category.

   f. An issue must be assigned only one status code.

   g. An issue must be assigned a priority code.

8. Priorities are assigned accordingly:

Priority Level
Critical
High
Moderate
Standard
Low

9. Status is recorded as either open or closed.

10. The categories of each issue need to be recorded as:

Category
Hardware/Phone
Software/Voice mail
Internet/Web

Data File: AYK31_Data.xlsx

Project 32:

Sales Pipeline

Sales drive any organization. This is true for every for-profit business irrespective of size or industry type. If customers are not buying your goods or services, you run the risk of not having a business. This is when tough decisions have to be made, like whether to slash budgets, lay off staff, or seek additional financing.

Unfortunately, you do not wield ultimate power over your customers' buying habits. While you can attempt to influence buying behavior through strategic marketing, smart businesses remain one step ahead by collecting and analyzing historical and current customer information from a range of internal and external sources to forecast future sales. In other words, managing the sales pipeline is an essential ingredient to business success.

You have recently been hired by RealTime Solutions, a new company that collects information to understand, manage, and predict specific sales cycle (including the supply chain and lead times) in the automobile business. Having an accurate forecast of future sales will allow the company to increase or decrease the production cycle as required and manage personnel levels, inventory, and cash flow.

Project Focus

Using a personal DBMS package (preferably Microsoft Access) create a sales pipeline database that will:

1. Track opportunities from employees to customers.

   - Opportunities should have a ranking, category, source of opportunity, open date, closed date, description.

2. Create a form for inputting customer, employee, and opportunity data.

3. Create a few reports that display:

   - All open opportunities, including relevant customer and employee information.

   - Closed opportunities, including relevant customer and employee information.

   - All customers.

4. Create your own data to test the integrity of the relationships. Use approximately 10 records per table.

Project 33:

Online Classified Ads

With the emergence of the Internet as a worldwide standard for communicating information, *The Morrison Post*, a medium-size community newspaper in central Colorado, is creating an electronic version of its paper-based classified ads.

Advertisers can place a small ad that lists items that they wish to sell and provide a means (e.g., telephone number and email) by which prospective buyers can contact them.

The nature of a sale via the newspaper's classified system goes as follows:

- During the course of the sale, the information flows in different directions at different stages.

- First, there is a downstream flow of information (from seller to buyer): the listing in print in the newspaper. (Thus, the classified ad listing is just a way of bringing a buyer and seller together.)

- When a potential purchaser's interest has been raised, then that interest must be relayed upstream, usually by telephone or by email.

- Finally, a meeting should result that uses face-to-face negotiation to finalize the sale, if the sale can be agreed.

By placing the entire system on the Internet, the upstream and downstream communications are accomplished using a web browser. The sale becomes more of an auction, because many potential buyers, all with equal status, can bid for the same item. So it is fairer for all purchasers and gets a better deal for the seller.

Any user who is trying to buy an item can:

- View items for sale.

- Bid on an item he or she wishes to purchase.

Any user who is trying to sell an item can:

- Place a new item for sale.

- Browse a list of the items that he or she is trying to sell, and examine the bids that have been made on each of those items.

- Accept a bid on an item that he or she is selling.

Your job is to complete the following:

1. Develop and describe the entity-relationship diagram for the database that will support the listed activities.

2. Use normalization to ensure the correctness of the tables.

3. Create the database using a personal DBMS package.

4. Use Figure AYK.7 as a baseline for your database design.

   Data File: AYK33_Data.xlsx

The Morrison Post Classified Section
New User Registration

In order to bid on existing "for-sale" items, or sell your own items, you need to register first. Once you have done that, you will have full access to the system.

E-Mail Address:	
First Name:	
Last Name:	
Address:	
City:	
State:	
Postal Code:	
Country:	
Password:	
Verify Password:	

Submit   Reset

3D printing   Builds—layer by layer in an additive process—a three-dimensional solid object from a digital model.

A

acceptable use policy (AUP)   A policy that a user must agree to follow in order to be provided access to a network or to the Internet.

access point (AP)   The computer or network device that serves as an interface between devices and the network.

accessibility   Refers to the varying levels that define what a user can access, view, or perform when operating a system.

accounting and finance ERP component   Manages accounting data and financial processes within the enterprise with functions such as general ledger, accounts payable, accounts receivable, budgeting, and asset management.

accounting department   Provides quantitative information about the finances of the business including recording, measuring, and describing financial information.

accounting   Analyzes the transactional information of the business so the owners and investors can make sound economic decisions.

active RFID tags   Have their own transmitter and a power source (typically a battery).

adaptive computer device   Input devices designed for special applications for use by people with different types of special needs.

administrator access   Unrestricted access to the entire system.

advanced encryption standard (AES)   Introduced by the National Institute of Standards and Technology (NIST), AES is an encryption standard designed to keep government information secure.

adware   Software that, although purporting to serve some useful function and often fulfilling that function, also allows Internet advertisers to display advertisements without the consent of the computer user.

adwords   Keywords that advertisers choose to pay for and appear as sponsored links on the Google results pages.

affinity grouping analysis   Reveals the relationship between variables along with the nature and frequency of the relationships.

Agile BI   An approach to business intelligence (BI) that incorporates Agile software development methodologies to accelerate and improve the outcomes of BI initiatives.

agile methodology   Aims for customer satisfaction through early and continuous delivery of useful software components developed by an iterative process with a design point that uses the bare minimum requirements.

agile MIS infrastructure   Includes the hardware, software, and telecommunications equipment that, when combined, provides the underlying foundation to support the organization's goals.

algorithm   A mathematical formula placed in software that performs an analysis on a data set.

alpha testing   Assess if the entire system meets the design requirements of the users.

ambient digital experience   A blend of the physical, virtual, and electronic environments creating a real-time ambient environment that changes as the user moves from one place to another.

analysis latency   The time from which data are made available to the time when analysis is complete.

analysis paralysis   Occurs when the user goes into an emotional state of over-analysis (or over-thinking) a situation so that a decision or action is never taken, in effect paralyzing the outcome.

analysis phase   Analyzing end-user business requirements and refining project goals into defined functions and operations of the intended system.

analytical CRM   Supports back-office operations and strategic analysis and includes all systems that do not deal directly with the customers.

analytical information   Encompasses all organizational information, and its primary purpose is to support the performing of managerial analysis tasks.

analytics   The science of fact-based decision making.

anomaly detection   The process of identifying rare or unexpected items or events in a data set that do not conform to other items in the data set.

anti-spam policy   States that email users will not send unsolicited emails (or spam).

antivirus software   Scans and searches hard drives to prevent, detect, and remove known viruses, adware, and spyware.

applet   A program that runs within another application such as a website.

appliance   A computer dedicated to a single function, such as a calculator or computer game.

application programming interface (API)   A set of routines, protocols, and tools for building software applications.

application service provider license   Specialty software paid for on a license basis or per-use basis or usage-based licensing.

application software   Used for specific information processing needs, including payroll, customer relationship management, project management, training, and many others.

arithmetic/logic unit (ALU)   Performs all arithmetic operations (for example, addition and subtraction) and all logic operations (such as sorting and comparing numbers).

artificial intelligence (AI)   Simulates human intelligence such as the ability to reason and learn.

As-Is process model   Represents the current state of the operation that has been mapped, without any specific improvements or changes to existing processes.

asset tracking   Occurs when a company places active or semipassive RFID tags on expensive products or assets to gather data on the items' location with little or no manual intervention.

asset   Anything owned that has value or earning power.

asynchronous communication   Communication such as email in which the message and the response do not occur at the same time.

attribute The data elements associated with an entity.

augmented reality The viewing of the physical world with computer-generated layers of information added to it.

authentication A method for confirming users' identities.

authorization The process of providing a user with permission including access levels and abilities such as file access, hours of access, and amount of allocated storage space.

automatic vehicle location (AVL) Uses GPS tracking to track vehicles.

autonomic computing A self-managing computing model named after, and patterned on, the human body's autonomic nervous system.

autonomous agent Software that carries out some set of operations on behalf of a user or another program with some degree of independence or autonomy, and employ some knowledge or representation of the user's goals or desires.

availability Refers to the time frames when the system is operational.

B

backup An exact copy of a system's information.

backward integration Takes information entered into a given system and sends it automatically to all upstream systems and processes.

balance sheet Gives an accounting picture of property owned by a company and of claims against the property on a specific date.

balanced scorecard A management system, in addition to a measurement system, that enables organizations to clarify their vision and strategy and translate them into action.

behavioral analytics Uses data about people's behaviors to understand intent and predict future actions.

benchmark Baseline values the system seeks to attain.

benchmarking The process of continuously measuring system results, comparing those results to optimal system performance (benchmark values), and identifying steps and procedures to improve system performance.

best practices The most successful solutions or problem-solving methods that have been developed by a specific organization or industry.

Big Data as a Service (BDaaS) Offers a cloud-based Big Data service to help organizations analyze massive amounts of data to solve business dilemmas.

big data A collection of large, complex data sets, including structured and unstructured data, which cannot be analyzed using traditional database methods and tools.

biological 3D printing Includes the printing of skin and organs and is progressing from theory to reality, however, politicians and the public do not have a full understanding of the implications.

biometrics The identification of a user based on a physical characteristic, such as a fingerprint, iris, face, voice, or handwriting.

blog An online journal that allows users to post their own comments, graphics, and video.

Bluetooth A wireless PAN technology that transmits signals over short distances among cell phones, computers, and other devices.

bookkeeping The actual recording of the business's transactions, without any analysis of the information.

brainstorming A technique for generating ideas by encouraging participants to offer as many ideas as possible in a short period of time without any analysis until all the ideas have been exhausted.

break-even point The point at which revenues equal costs.

bring your own device (BYOD) A policy allows employees to use their personal mobile devices and computers to access enterprise data and applications.

bug Defects in the code of an information system.

bullwhip effect Occurs when distorted product-demand information passes from one entity to the next throughout the supply chain.

business continuity planning (BCP) Details how a company recovers and restores critical business operations and systems after a disaster or extended disruption.

business impact analysis A process that identifies all critical business functions and the effect that a specific disaster may have upon them.

business intelligence (BI) Information collected from multiple sources such as suppliers, customers, competitors, partners, and industries that analyzes patterns, trends, and relationships for strategic decision making.

business intelligence dashboard Tracks corporate metrics such as critical success factors and key performance indicators and includes advanced capabilities such as interactive controls, allowing users to manipulate data for analysis.

business model A plan that details how a company creates, delivers, and generates revenues.

business process management (BPM) Integrates all of an organization's business processes to make individual processes more efficient.

business process management tool Used to create an application that is helpful in designing business process models and also helpful in simulating, optimizing, monitoring, and maintaining various processes that occur within an organization.

Business Process Model and Notation (BPMN) A graphical notation that depicts the steps in a business process.

business process model A graphic description of a process, showing the sequence of process tasks, which is developed for a specific purpose and from a selected viewpoint.

business process modeling (or mapping) The activity of creating a detailed flowchart or process map of a work process, showing its inputs, tasks, and activities in a structured sequence.

business process patent A patent that protects a specific set of procedures for conducting a particular business activity.

business process reengineering (BPR) The analysis and redesign of workflow within and between enterprises.

business process A standardized set of activities that accomplish a specific task, such as processing a customer's order.

business requirement The specific business requests the system must meet to be successful, so the analysis phase is critical because business requirements drive the entire systems development effort.

business rule Defines how a company performs a certain aspect of its business and typically results in either a yes/no or true/false answer.

business strategy A leadership plan that achieves a specific set of goals or objectives such as increasing sales, decreasing costs, entering new markets, or developing new products or services.

business unit A segment of a company (such as accounting, production, marketing) representing a specific business function.

business-critical integrity constraint Enforces business rules vital to an organization's success and often requires more insight and knowledge than relational integrity constraints.

business-facing process Invisible to the external customer but essential to the effective management of the business; they include goal setting, day-to-day planning, giving performance feedback and rewards, and resource allocation.

business-to-business (B2B)   Applies to businesses buying from and selling to each other over the Internet.

business-to-consumer (B2C)   Applies to any business that sells its products or services to consumers over the Internet.

buyer power   The ability of buyers to affect the price they must pay for an item.

C

cache memory   A small unit of ultra-fast memory that is used to store recently accessed or frequently accessed data so that the CPU does not have to retrieve this data from slower memory circuits such as RAM.

Call scripting system   Gathers product details and issue resolution information that can be automatically generated into a script for the representative to read to the customer.

campaign management system   Guides users through marketing campaigns by performing such tasks as campaign definition, planning, scheduling, segmentation, and success analysis.

Capability Maturity Model Integration (CMMI) method   A process improvement approach that contains 22 process areas.

capacity planning   Determines future environmental infrastructure requirements to ensure high-quality system performance.

capacity   Represents the maximum throughput a system can deliver; for example, the capacity of a hard drive represents the size or volume.

capital   Represents money whose purpose is to make more money, for example, the money used to buy a rental property or a business.

carbon emission   Includes the carbon dioxide and carbon monoxide in the atmosphere, produced by business processes and systems.

cartography   The science and art of making an illustrated map or chart.

central processing unit (CPU) (or microprocessor)   The actual hardware that interprets and executes the program (software) instructions and coordinates how all the other hardware devices work together.

certificate authority   A trusted third party, such as VeriSign, that validates user identities by means of digital certificates.

change agent   A person or event that is the catalyst for implementing major changes for a system to meet business changes.

chief automation officer   Determines if a person or business process can be replaced by a robot or software.

chief data officer   Responsible for determining the types of information the enterprise will capture, retain, analyze, and share.

chief information officer (CIO)   Responsible for (1) overseeing all uses of information technology and (2) ensuring the strategic alignment of MIS with business goals and objectives.

chief intellectual property officer   Manage and defend intellectual property, copyrights, and patents.

chief knowledge officer (CKO)   Responsible for collecting, maintaining, and distributing the organization's knowledge.

chief privacy officer (CPO)   Responsible for ensuring the ethical and legal use of information within an organization.

chief security officer (CSO)   Responsible for ensuring the security of MIS systems and developing strategies and MIS safeguards against attacks from hackers and viruses.

chief technology officer (CTO)   Responsible for ensuring the throughput, speed, accuracy, availability, and reliability of an organization's information technology.

chief user experience officer   Create the optimal relationship between user and technology.

Child Online Protection Act (COPA)   A law that protects minors from accessing inappropriate material on the Internet.

chipless RFID tags   Use plastic or conductive polymers instead of silicon-based microchips, allowing them to be washed or exposed to water without damaging the chip.

classification analysis   The process of organizing data into categories or groups for its most effective and efficient use.

clean computing   Refers to the environmentally responsible use, manufacture, and disposal of technology products and computer equipment.

click-fraud   The abuse of pay-per-click, pay-per-call, and pay-per-conversion revenue models by repeatedly clicking on a link to increase charges or costs for the advertiser.

click-to-talk   Allows customers to click a button and talk with a representative via the Internet.

clickstream data   Exact pattern of a consumer's navigation through a site.

client/server network   A model for applications in which the bulk of the back-end processing, such as performing a physical search of a database, takes place on a server, while the front-end processing, which involves communicating with the users, is handled by the clients.

client   Computer that is designed to request information from a server.

closed source   Any proprietary software licensed under exclusive legal right of the copyright holder.

cloud bursting   When a company uses its own computing infrastructure for normal usage and accesses the cloud when it needs to scale for high/peak load requirements, ensuring a sudden spike in usage does not result in poor performance or system crashes.

cloud computing   Stores, manages, and processes data and applications over the Internet rather than on a personal computer or server.

cloud fabric controller   An individual who monitors and provisions cloud resources similar to a server administrator at an individual company.

cloud fabric   The software that makes the benefits of cloud computing possible, such as multi-tenancy.

cluster analysis   A technique used to divide an information set into mutually exclusive groups such that the members of each group are as close together as possible to one another and the different groups are as far apart as possible.

coaxial cable   Cable that can carry a wide range of frequencies with low signal loss.

cold site   A separate facility that does not have any computer equipment, but is a place where employees can move after a disaster.

collaboration system   A set of tools that supports the work of teams or groups by facilitating the sharing and flow of information.

collective intelligence   Collaborating and tapping into the core knowledge of all employees, partners, and customers.

Committee of Sponsoring Organizations (COSO)   Key for evaluating internal controls such as human resources, logistics, information technology, risk, legal, marketing and sales, operations, financial functions, procurement, and reporting.

common data repository   Allows every department of a company to store and retrieve information in real-time allowing information to be more reliable and accessible.

communication device   Equipment used to send information and receive it from one location to another.

communication plan   Defines the how, what, when, and who regarding the flow of project information to stakeholders and is key for managing expectations.

community cloud   Serves a specific community with common business models, security requirements, and compliance considerations.

comparative analysis   Compares two or more data sets to identify patterns and trends.

competitive advantage   A feature of a product or service that an organization's customers place a greater value on than similar offerings from a competitor.

competitive click-fraud   A computer crime where a competitor or disgruntled employee increases a company's search advertising costs by repeatedly clicking on the advertiser's link.

competitive intelligence   The process of gathering information about the competitive environment, including competitors' plans, activities, and products, to improve a company's ability to succeed.

competitive monitoring   A company keeps tabs of its competitor's activities on the web using software that automatically tracks all competitor website activities such as discounts and new products.

complex instruction set computer (CISC) chip   Type of CPU that can recognize as many as 100 or more instructions, enough to carry out most computations directly.

compliance   The act of conforming, acquiescing, or yielding.

computer simulation   Complex systems, such as the U.S. economy, can be modeled by means of mathematical equations and different scenarios can be run against the model to determine "what if" analysis.

computer-aided design/computer-aided manufacturing (CAD/CAM)   Systems used to create the digital designs and then manufacture the products.

computer-aided software engineering (CASE)   Tools are software suites that automate systems analysis, design, and development.

computer   Electronic device operating under the control of instructions stored in its own memory that can accept, manipulate, and store data.

confidentiality   The assurance that messages and information are available only to those who are authorized to view them.

consolidation   Involves the aggregation of information and features simple roll-ups to complex groupings of interrelated information.

consumer-to-business (C2B)   Applies to any consumer that sells a product or service to a business over the Internet.

consumer-to-consumer (C2C)   Applies to customers offering goods and services to each other on the Internet.

contact center (or call center)   A place where customer service representatives answer customer inquiries and solve problems, usually by email, chat, or phone.

contact management CRM system   Maintains customer contact information and identifies prospective customers for future sales, using tools such as organizational charts, detailed customer notes, and supplemental sales information.

content creator   The person responsible for creating the original website content.

content editor   The person responsible for updating and maintaining website content.

content filtering   Occurs when organizations use software that filters content to prevent the transmission of unauthorized information.

content management system   Helps companies manage the creation, storage, editing, and publication of their website content.

continuous process improvement model   Attempts to understand and measure the current process, and make performance improvements accordingly.

control objectives for information and related technologies (COBIT)   A set of best practices that helps an organization to maximize the benefits of an information system, while at the same time establishing appropriate controls to ensure minimum errors.

control panel   A Windows feature that provides a group of options that sets default values for the Windows operating system.

control unit   Interprets software instructions and literally tells the other hardware devices what to do, based on the software instructions.

conversion   The process of transferring information from a legacy system to a new system.

copyright   The legal protection afforded an expression of an idea, such as a song, book, or video game.

core ERP component   Traditional components included in most ERP systems and they primarily focus on internal operations.

core processes   Business processes, such as manufacturing goods, selling products, and providing service, that make up the primary activities in a value chain.

corporate social responsibility   Companies' acknowledged responsibility to society.

corporation (also called organization, enterprise, or business)   An artificially created legal entity that exists separate and apart from those individuals who created it and carry on its operations.

corrective maintenance   Makes system changes to repair design flaws, coding errors, or implementation issues.

counterfeit software   Software that is manufactured to look like the real thing and sold as such.

course management software   Contains course information such as a syllabus and assignments and offers drop boxes for quizzes and homework along with a grade book.

Cradle-to-grave   Provides logistics support throughout the entire system or life of the product.

critical path   Estimates the shortest path through the project ensuring all critical tasks are completed from start to finish.

critical success factor (CSF)   Crucial steps companies perform to achieve their goals and objectives and implement their strategies.

CRM analysis technologies   Help organizations segment their customers into categories such as best and worst customers.

CRM predicting technologies   Help organizations make predictions regarding customer behavior such as which customers are at risk of leaving.

CRM reporting technologies   Help organizations identify their customers across other applications.

cross-selling   Selling additional products or services to an existing customer.

crowdfunding   Sources capital for a project by raising many small amounts from a large number of individuals, typically via the Internet.

crowdsourcing   Refers to the wisdom of the crowd.

cryptography   The science that studies encryption, which is the hiding of messages so that only the sender and receiver can read them.

cube   The common term for the representation of multidimensional information.

customer analytics   Involves gathering, classifying, comparing, and studying customer data to identify buying trends, at-risk customers, and potential future opportunities.

customer relationship management (CRM) Involves managing all aspects of a customer's relationship with an organization to increase customer loyalty and retention and an organization's profitability.

customer segmentation Divides a market into categories that share similar attributes such as age, location, gender, habits, and so on.

customer service and support (CSS) A part of operational CRM that automates service requests, complaints, product returns, and information requests.

customer-facing process Results in a product or service that is received by an organization's external customer.

cyberbullying Threats, negative remarks, or defamatory comments transmitted via the Internet or posted on a website.

cybermediation Refers to the creation of new kinds of intermediaries that simply could not have existed before the advent of ebusiness.

cyberterrorism The use of computer and networking technologies against persons or property to intimidate or coerce governments, individuals, or any segment of society to attain political, religious, or ideological goals.

cybervandalism The electronic defacing of an existing website.

cyberwar An organized attempt by a country's military to disrupt or destroy information and communication systems for another country.

D

data aggregation The collection of data from various sources for the purpose of data processing.

data artist A business analytics specialist who uses visual tools to help people understand complex data.

data as a service (DaaS) Facilitates the accessibility of business-critical data in a timely, secure, and affordable manner.

data broker A business that collects personal information about consumers and sells that information to other organizations.

data center A facility used to house management information systems and associated components, such as telecommunications and storage systems.

data dictionary Compiles all of the metadata about the data elements in the data model.

data element (or data field) The smallest or basic unit of information.

data flow diagram (DFD) Illustrates the movement of information between external entities and the processes and data stores within the system.

data gap analysis Occurs when a company examines its data to determine if it can meet business expectations, while identifying possible data gaps or where missing data might exist.

data governance Refers to the overall management of the availability, usability, integrity, and security of company data.

data lake A storage repository that holds a vast amount of raw data in its native format until it is needed.

data latency The time it takes for data to be stored or retrieved.

data map A technique for establishing a match, or balance, between the source data and the target data warehouse.

data mart Contains a subset of data warehouse information.

data mining The process of analyzing data to extract information not offered by the raw data alone.

data mining tools A variety of techniques to find patterns and relationships in large volumes of information that predict future behavior and guide decision making.

data model Logical data structures that detail the relationships among data elements using graphics or pictures.

data point An individual item on a graph or a chart.

data profiling The process of collecting statistics and information about data in an existing source.

data replication The process of sharing information to ensure consistency between multiple data sources.

data scientist Extracts knowledge from data by performing statistical analysis, data mining, and advanced analytics on big data to identify trends, market changes, and other relevant information.

data set An organized collection of data.

data steward Responsible for ensuring the policies and procedures are implemented across the organization and acts as a liaison between the MIS department and the business.

data stewardship The management and oversight of an organization's data assets to help provide business users with high-quality data that is easily accessible in a consistent manner.

data validation Includes the tests and evaluations used to determine compliance with data governance polices to ensure correctness of data.

data visualization tools Moves beyond Excel graphs and charts into sophisticated analysis techniques such as controls, instruments, maps, time-series graphs, and more.

data visualization Describes technologies that allow users to "see" or visualize data to transform information into a business perspective.

data warehouse A logical collection of information—gathered from many different operational databases—that supports business analysis activities and decision-making tasks.

data-driven decision management An approach to business governance that values decisions that can be backed up with verifiable data.

data-driven website An interactive website kept constantly updated and relevant to the needs of its customers through the use of a database.

data-mining tool Uses a variety of techniques to find patterns and relationships in large volumes of information and infer rules from them that predict future behavior and guide decision making.

data Raw facts that describe the characteristics of an event.

database management system (DBMS) Creates, reads, updates, and deletes data in a database while controlling access and security

database Maintains information about various types of objects (inventory), events (transactions), people (employees), and places (warehouses).

decision latency The time it takes a human to comprehend the analytic result and determine an appropriate action.

decision support system (DSS) Model information using OLAP, which provides assistance in evaluating and choosing among different courses of action.

decrypt Decodes information and is the opposite of encrypted.

dependency A logical relationship that exists between the project tasks, or between a project task and a milestone.

deperimeterization Occurs when an organization moves employees outside its firewall, a growing movement to change the way corporations address technology security.

design phase Involves describing the desired features and operations of the system including screen layouts, business rules, process diagrams, pseudo code, and other documentation.

destructive agents Malicious agents designed by spammers and other Internet attackers to farm email addresses off websites or deposit spyware on machines.

development phase   Involves taking all of the detailed design documents from the design phase and transforming them into the actual system.

development testing   Programmers test the system to ensure it is bug-free.

digital certificate   A data file that identifies individuals or organizations online and is comparable to a digital signature.

digital Darwinism   Organizations that cannot adapt to the new demands placed on them for surviving in the information age are doomed to extinction.

digital dashboard   Tracks key performance indicators (KPIs) and critical success factors (CSFs) by compiling information from multiple sources and tailoring it to meet user needs.

digital rights management   A technological solution that allows publishers to control their digital media to discourage, limit, or prevent illegal copying and distribution.

dirty data   Erroneous or flawed data.

Disaster Recovery as a Service (DRaaS)   Offers backup services that use cloud resources to protect applications and data from disruption caused by disaster.

disaster recovery cost curve   Charts (1) the cost to the organization of the unavailability of information and technology and (2) the cost to the organization of recovering from a disaster over time.

disaster recovery plan   A detailed process for recovering information or a system in the event of a catastrophic disaster.

discovery prototyping   Builds a small-scale representation or working model of the system to ensure it meets the user and business requirements.

disintermediation   Occurs when a business sells direct to the customer online and cuts out the intermediary.

disruptive technology   A new way of doing things that initially does not meet the needs of existing customers.

distributed computing   Processes and manages algorithms across many machines in a computing environment.

distribution management system   Coordinates the process of transporting materials from a manufacturer to distribution centers to the final customer.

dividend   A distribution of earnings to shareholders.

domain name hosting   A service that allows the owner of a domain name to maintain a simple website and provide email capacity.

downtime   Refers to a period of time when a system is unavailable

drill-down   Enables users to get details, and details of details, of information.

drive-by hacking   A computer attack where an attacker accesses a wireless computer network, intercepts data, uses network services, and/or sends attack instructions without entering the office or organization that owns the network.

drone   An unmanned aircraft that can fly autonomously, or without a human.

dual boot   Provides the user with the option of choosing the operating system when the computer is turned on.

dumpster diving   Looking through people's trash, another way hackers obtain information.

dynamic catalog   An area of a website that stores information about products in a database.

dynamic information   Includes data that change based on user actions.

dynamic process   Continuously changing and provides business solutions to ever-changing business operations.

dynamic report   A report that changes automatically during creation.

dynamic scaling   Means that the MIS infrastructure can be automatically scaled up or down based on needed requirements.

E

ebook   An electronic book that can be read on a computer or special reading device.

ebusiness model   A plan that details how a company creates, delivers, and generates revenues on the Internet.

ebusiness   Includes ecommerce along with all activities related to internal and external business operations such as servicing customer accounts, collaborating with partners, and exchanging real-time information.

ecommerce   The buying and selling of goods and services over the Internet.

edge matching (warping, rubber sheeting)   Occurs when paper maps are laid edge to edge, and items that run across maps but do not match are reconfigured to match.

ediscovery   Refers to the ability of a company to identify, search, gather, seize, or export digital information in responding to a litigation, audit, investigation, or information inquiry.

effectiveness MIS metric   Measures the impact MIS has on business processes and activities including customer satisfaction, conversion rates, and sell-through increases.

efficiency MIS metric   Measures the performance of the MIS system itself including throughput, speed, and availability.

egovernment   Involves the use of strategies and technologies to transform government(s) by improving the delivery of services and enhancing the quality of interaction between the citizen-consumer within all branches of government.

electronic data interchange (EDI)   A standard format for the electronic exchange of information between supply chain participants.

elogistics   Manages the transportation and storage of goods.

email privacy policy   Details the extent to which email messages may be read by others.

embedded operating system   Used for a single purpose in computer appliances and special-purpose applications, such as an automobile, ATM, or media player.

emergency notification service   An infrastructure built for notifying people in the event of an emergency.

emergency preparedness   Ensures a company is ready to respond to an emergency in an organized, timely, and effective manner.

emergency   A sudden, unexpected event requiring immediate action due to potential threat to health and safety, the environment, or property.

employee monitoring policy   Stating explicitly how, when, and where the company monitors its employees.

employee relationship management (ERM)   Provides employees with a subset of CRM applications available through a web browser.

encryption   Scrambles information into an alternative form that requires a key or password to decrypt the information.

energy consumption   The amount of energy consumed by business processes and systems.

enterprise application integration (EAI) middleware   Represents a new approach to middleware by packaging together commonly used functionality, such as providing prebuilt links to popular enterprise applications, which reduces the time necessary to develop solutions that integrate applications from multiple vendors.

enterprise architect (EA)   Person grounded in technology, fluent in business, a patient diplomat, and provides the important bridge between IT and the business.

enterprise architecture   Includes the plans for how an organization will build, deploy, use, and share its data, processes, and MIS assets.

enterprise resource planning (ERP)   Integrates all departments and functions throughout an organization into a single system (or integrated set of MIS systems) so that employees can make decisions by viewing enterprisewide information on all business operations.

entity   Stores information about a person, place, thing, transaction, or event.

entry barrier   A feature of a product or service that customers have come to expect and entering competitors must offer the same for survival.

epolicies   Policies and procedures that address the ethical use of computers and Internet usage in the business environment.

eprocurement   The business-to-business (B2B) purchase and sale of supplies and services over the Internet.

eshop (estore or etailer)   An online version of a retail store where customers can shop at any hour.

estimated time enroute (ETE)   The time remaining before reaching a destination using the present speed; typically used for navigation applications.

estimated time of arrival (ETA)   The time of day of an expected arrival at a certain destination; typically used for navigation applications.

estimation analysis   Determine values for an unknown continuous variable behavior or estimated future value.

ethernet   A physical and data layer technology for LAN networking.

ethical computer use policy   Contains general principles to guide computer user behavior.

ewaste   Refers to discarded, obsolete, or broken electronic devices.

executive information system (EIS)   A specialized DSS that supports senior-level executives within the organization.

executive sponsor   The person or group who provides the financial resources for the project.

expense   Refers to the costs incurred in operating and maintaining a business.

expert system   Computerized advisory programs that imitate the reasoning processes of experts in solving difficult problems.

explicit knowledge   Consists of anything that can be documented, archived, and codified, often with the help of IT.

extended ERP component   The extra components that meet the organizational needs not covered by the core components and primarily focus on external operations.

extensible markup language (XML)   A markup language for documents, containing structured information.

extraction, transformation, and loading (ETL)   A process that extracts information from internal and external databases, transforms the information using a common set of enterprise definitions, and loads the information into a data warehouse.

extreme programming (XP) methodology   Breaks a project into tiny phases, and developers cannot continue on to the next phase until the first phase is complete.

ezine   A magazine published only in electronic form on a computer network.

F

fact   The confirmation or validation of an event or object.

failback   Occurs when the primary machine recovers and resumes operations, taking over from the secondary server.

failover   Occurs when a redundant storage server offers an exact replica of the real-time data, and if the primary server crashes, the users are automatically directed to the secondary server or backup server.

Fair information practices   A general term for a set of standards governing the collection and use of personal data and addressing issues of privacy and accuracy.

fast data   The application of big data analytics to smaller data sets in near-real or real-time in order to solve a problem or create business value.

fault tolerance   The ability for a system to respond to unexpected failures or system crashes as the backup system immediately and automatically takes over with no loss of service.

feasibility   The measure of the tangible and intangible benefits of an information system.

feedback   Information that returns to its original transmitter (input, transform, or output) and modifies the transmitter's actions.

fiber-optic (optical fiber)   The technology associated with the transmission of information as light impulses along a glass wire or fiber.

finance   Deals with the strategic financial issues associated with increasing the value of the business while observing applicable laws and social responsibilities.

financial accounting   Involves preparing financial reports that provide information about the business's performance to external parties such as investors, creditors, and tax authorities.

financial quarter   A three-month period (four quarters per year).

financial statements   Written records of the financial status of the business that allow interested parties to evaluate the profitability and solvency of the business.

firewall   Hardware and/or software that guards a private network by analyzing the information leaving and entering the network.

first-mover advantage   Occurs when an organization can significantly impact its market share by being first to market with a competitive advantage.

flash memory   A special type of rewritable read-only memory (ROM) that is compact and portable.

folksonomy   Similar to taxonomy except that crowdsourcing determines the tags or keyword-based classification system.

for profit corporations   Primarily focus on making money and all profits and losses are shared by the business owners.

forecasting model   Predictions based on time-series information allowing users to manipulate the time series for forecasting activities.

foreign key   A primary key of one table that appears as an attribute in another table and acts to provide a logical relationship between the two tables.

forward integration   Takes information entered into a given system and sends it automatically to all downstream systems and processes.

fourth-generation language (4GL)   Programming languages that look similar to human languages.

fuzzy logic   A mathematical method of handling imprecise or subjective information.

G

Gantt chart   A simple bar chart that lists project tasks vertically against the project's time frame, listed horizontally.

genetic algorithm   An artificial intelligence system that mimics the evolutionary, survival-of-the-fittest process to generate increasingly better solutions to a problem.

geocache   A GPS technology adventure game that posts on the Internet the longitude and latitude location of an item for users to find.

geocoding   Spatial databases in a coding process that takes a digital map feature and assigns it an attribute that serves as a unique ID (tract number, node number) or classification (soil type, zoning category).

geocoin   A round, coin-sized object that is uniquely numbered and hidden in geocache.

geoeconomic   Refers to the effects of geography on the economic realities of international business activities.

geographic information system (GIS)   Stores, views, and analyzes geographic data creating multidimensional charts or maps.

gigabyte (GB)   Roughly 1 billion bytes.

gigahertz (GHz)   The number of billions of CPU cycles per second.

GIS map automation   Links business assets to a centralized system where they can be tracked and monitored over time.

global inventory management system   Provides the ability to locate, track, and predict the movement of every component or material anywhere upstream or downstream in the supply chain.

global positioning system (GPS)   A satellite-based navigation system providing extremely accurate position, time, and speed information.

goal-seeking analysis   Finds the inputs necessary to achieve a goal such as a desired level of output.

goods   Material items or products that customers will buy to satisfy a want or need.

governance   Method or system of government for management or control.

granularity   Refers to the level of detail in the model or the decision-making process.

graphical user interface (GUI)   The interface to an information system.

green personal computer (green PC)   Built using environment-friendly materials and designed to save energy.

grid computing   A collection of computers, often geographically dispersed, that are coordinated to solve a common problem.

H

hacker   Experts in technology who use their knowledge to break into computers and computer networks, either for profit or simply for the challenge.

hard drive   Secondary storage medium that uses several rigid disks coated with a magnetically sensitive material and housed together with the recording heads in a hermetically sealed mechanism.

hardware   Consists of the physical devices associated with a computer system.

hashtag   A keyword or phrase used to identify a topic and is preceded by a hash or pound sign (#).

help desk   A group of people who respond to internal system user questions.

high availability   Occurs when a system is continuously operational at all times.

historical analysis   Historical events are studied to anticipate the outcome of current developments.

horizontal privilege escalation   Attacker grants themselves the same access levels they already have but assumes the identity of another user.

hot site   A separate and fully equipped facility where the company can move immediately after a disaster and resume business.

hotspots   Designated locations where Wi-Fi access points are publicly available.

HTML 5   The current version of HTML delivers everything from animation to graphics and music to movies.

human resources (HR)   Includes the policies, plans, and procedures for the effective management of employees (human resources).

human resources ERP component   Tracks employee information including payroll, benefits, compensation, and performance assessment, and assures compliance with the legal requirements of multiple jurisdictions and tax authorities.

human-generated data   Data that humans, in interaction with computers, generate.

hybrid cloud   Includes two or more private, public, or community clouds, but each cloud remains separate and is only linked by technology that enables data and application portability.

hybrid ERP   Splits the ERP functions between an on-premises ERP system and one or more functions handled as Software as a Service (SaaS) in the cloud.

hypertext markup language (HTML)   Links documents allowing users to move from one to another simply by clicking on a hotspot or link.

I

identity management   A broad administrative area that deals with identifying individuals in a system (such as a country, a network, or an enterprise) and controlling their access to resources within that system by associating user rights and restrictions with the established identity.

identity theft   The forging of someone's identity for the purpose of fraud.

IEEE 802.11n (or Wireless-N)   The standard for wireless networking.

implementation phase   Involves placing the system into production so users can begin to perform actual business operations with the system.

in-sourcing (in-house development)   A common approach using the professional expertise within an organization to develop and maintain the organization's information technology systems.

incident management   The process responsible for managing how incidents are identified and corrected.

incident record   Contains all of the details of an incident.

incident   Unplanned interruption of a service.

income statement   Reports operating results (revenues minus expenses) for a given time period ending at a specified date.

infographics (information graphics)   Present the results of data analysis, displaying the patterns, relationships, and trends in a graphical format.

information age   A time when infinite quantities of facts are widely available to anyone who can use a computer.

information architecture   The set of ideas about how all information in a given context should be organized

information cleansing or scrubbing   A process that weeds out and fixes or discards inconsistent, incorrect, or incomplete information.

information ethics Governs the ethical and moral issues arising from the development and use of information technologies, as well as the creation, collection, duplication, distribution, and processing of information itself (with or without the aid of computer technologies) .

information granularity Refers to the extent of detail within the information (fine and detailed or "coarse" and abstract information).

information inconsistency Occurs when the same data element has different values.

information integrity A measure of the quality of information.

information MIS infrastructure Identifies where and how important information, such as customer records, is maintained and secured.

Information of Everything (IoE) A concept that extends the Internet of Things (IoT) emphasis on machine-to-machine communications to describe a more complex system that also encompasses people and processes.

information privacy policy Contains general principles regarding information privacy.

information privacy Concerns the legal right or general expectation of individuals, groups, or institutions to determine for themselves when and to what extent information about them is communicated to others.

information reach Measures the number of people a firm can communicate with all over the world.

information redundancy The duplication of data, or the storage of the same data in multiple places.

information richness Refers to the depth and breadth of information transferred between customers and businesses.

information secrecy The category of computer security that addresses the protection of data from unauthorized disclosure and confirmation of data source authenticity.

information security plan Details how an organization will implement the information security policies.

information security policy Identifies the rules required to maintain information security.

information security A broad term encompassing the protection of information from accidental or intentional misuse by persons inside or outside an organization.

information silo Occurs when one business unit is unable to freely communicate with other business units making it difficult or impossible for organizations to work cross-functionally.

Information Systems Audit and Control Association (ISACA) A set of guidelines and supporting tools for IT governance that is accepted worldwide and generally used by auditors and companies as a way to integrate technology to implement controls and meet specific business objectives.

Information Technology Infrastructure Library (ITIL) A framework provided by the government of the United Kingdom that offers eight sets of management procedures.

information Data converted into a meaningful and useful context.

Infrastructure as a Service (IaaS) Delivers hardware networking capabilities, including the use of servers, networking, and storage, over the cloud using a pay-per-use revenue model.

input device Equipment used to capture information and commands.

insider Legitimate users who purposely or accidentally misuse their access to the environment and cause some kind of business-affecting incident.

instant messaging (IM or IMing) A service that enables instant or real-time communication between people.

Institute of Electrical and Electronics Engineers (IEEE) An organization that researches and institutes electrical standards for communication and other technologies.

intangible benefits Difficult to quantify or measure.

integration testing Verifies that separate systems can work together passing data back and forth correctly.

integration Allows separate systems to communicate directly with each other, eliminating the need for manual entry into multiple systems.

integrity constraint The rules that help ensure the quality of information.

intellectual property Intangible creative work that is embodied in physical form and includes copyrights, trademarks, and patents.

intelligent agent A special-purpose knowledge-based information system that accomplishes specific tasks on behalf of its users.

intelligent system Various commercial applications of artificial intelligence.

interactivity Measures advertising effectiveness by counting visitor interactions with the target ad, including time spent viewing the ad, number of pages viewed, and number of repeat visits to the advertisement.

intermediary Agent, software, or business that brings buyers and sellers together to provide a trading infrastructure to enhance ebusiness.

International Organization for Standardization (ISO) A nongovernmental organization established in 1947 to promote the development of world standards to facilitate the international exchange of goods and services.

Internet censorship Government attempts to control Internet traffic, thus preventing some material from being viewed by a country's citizens.

Internet Corporation for Assigned Names and Numbers (ICANN) A nonprofit organization that has assumed the responsibility for Internet Protocol (IP) address space allocation, protocol parameter assignment, domain name system management, and root service system management functions previously performed under U.S. government.

Internet of things (IoT) A world where interconnected Internet-enabled devices or "things" have the ability to collect and share data without human intervention.

Internet protocol version 6 (IPv6) The "next generation" protocol designed to replace the current version Internet protocol.

Internet service provider (ISP) A company that provides access to the Internet for a monthly fee.

Internet use policy Contains general principles to guide the proper use of the Internet.

Internet A massive network that connects computers all over the world and allows them to communicate with one another.

interoperability Capability of two or more computer systems to share data and resources, even though they are made by different manufacturers.

intrusion detection software (IDS) Features full-time monitoring tools that search for patterns in network traffic to identify intruders.

inventory management and control system Provides control and visibility to the status of individual items maintained in inventory.

IT consumerization The blending of personal and business use of technology devices and applications.

iterative development Consists of a series of tiny projects.

J

joint application development (JAD) A session where employees meet, sometimes for several days, to define or review the business requirements for the system.

K

key performance indicator (KPI) Quantifiable metrics a company uses to evaluate progress toward critical success factors.

kill switch A trigger that enables a project manager to close the project prior to completion.

knowledge management (KM) Involves capturing, classifying, evaluating, retrieving, and sharing information assets in a way that provides context for effective decisions and actions.

knowledge management system (KMS) Supports the capturing, organization, and dissemination of knowledge (i.e., know-how) throughout an organization.

knowledge workers Individuals valued for their ability to interpret and analyze information.

knowledge Skills, experience, and expertise coupled with information and intelligence that creates a person's intellectual resources.

L

latitude Represents a north/south measurement of position.

legacy system An old system that is fast approaching or beyond the end of its useful life within an organization.

liability An obligation to make financial payments.

limited liability corporation (LLC) A hybrid entity that has the legal protections of a corporation and the ability to be taxed (one time) as a partnership.

limited liability Means that the shareholders are not personally liable for the losses incurred by the corporation.

limited partnership Much like a general partnership except for one important fundamental difference; the law protects the limited partner from being responsible for all of the partnership's losses.

list generator Compile customer information from a variety of sources and segment it for different marketing campaigns.

local area network (LAN) Designed to connect a group of computers in proximity to each other such as in an office building, a school, or a home.

location-based services (LBS) Applications that use location information to provide a service.

logical view of information Focuses on how users logically access information to meet their particular business needs.

logistics Includes the processes that control the distribution, maintenance, and replacement of materials and personnel to support the supply chain.

long tail Referring to the tail of a typical sales curve.

longitude Represents an east/west measurement of position.

loose coupling The capability of services to be joined on demand to create composite services or disassembled just as easily into their functional components.

loss Occurs when businesses sell products or services for less than they cost to produce.

loyalty program Rewards customers based on their spending.

M

machine learning A type of artificial intelligence that enables computers to both understand concepts in the environment, and also to learn.

machine-generated data Data created by a machine without human intervention.

machine-to-machine (M2M) Refers to devices that connect directly to other devices

magnetic medium Secondary storage medium that uses magnetic techniques to store and retrieve data on disks or tapes coated with magnetically sensitive materials.

magnetic tape Older secondary storage medium that uses a strip of thin plastic coated with a magnetically sensitive recording medium.

mail bomb A massive amount of email to a specific person or system that can cause that user's server to stop functioning.

maintainability (or flexibility) Refers to how quickly a system can transform to support environmental changes.

maintenance phase The organization performs changes, corrections, additions, and upgrades to ensure the system continues to meet business goals.

maker movement A cultural trend that places value on an individual's ability to be a creator of things as well as a consumer of things.

makerspace A community center that provides technology, manufacturing equipment, and educational opportunities to the public that would otherwise be inaccessible or unaffordable.

management information systems (MIS) A business function, like accounting and human resources, which moves information about people, products, and processes across the company to facilitate decision making and problem solving.

managerial accounting Involves analyzing business operations for internal decision making and does not have to follow any rules issued by standard-setting bodies such as GAAP.

managerial level Employees are continuously evaluating company operations to hone the firm's abilities to identify, adapt to, and leverage change.

market basket analysis Evaluates such items as websites and checkout scanner information to detect customers' buying behavior and predict future behavior by identifying affinities among customers' choices of products and services.

market segmentation The division of a market into similar groups of customers.

market share The proportion of the market that a firm captures.

marketing communication Seeks to build product or service awareness and to educate potential consumers on the product or service.

marketing mix Includes the variables that marketing managers can control in order to best satisfy customers in the target market.

marketing The process associated with promoting the sale of goods or services.

mashup editor WYSIWYGs (What You See Is What You Get) for mashups that provide a visual interface to build a mashup, often allowing the user to drag and drop data points into a web application.

mashup A website or web application that uses content from more than one source to create a completely new product or service.

mass customization Ability of an organization to give its customers the opportunity to tailor its products or services to the customers' specifications.

master data management   The practice of gathering data and ensuring that it is uniform, accurate, consistent, and complete, including such entities as customers, suppliers, products, sales, employees, and other critical entities that are commonly integrated across organizational systems.

materials management   Includes activities that govern the flow of tangible, physical materials through the supply chain such as shipping, transport, distribution, and warehousing.

materials requirement planning (MRP) system   Sales forecasts to make sure that needed parts and materials are available at the right time and place in a specific company.

megabyte (MB or M or Meg)   Roughly 1 million bytes.

megahertz (MHz)   The number of millions of CPU cycles per second.

memory card   Contains high-capacity storage that holds data such as captured images, music, or text files.

memory stick   Provides nonvolatile memory for a range of portable devices including computers, digital cameras, MP3 players, and PDAs.

metadata   Details about data.

methodology   A set of policies, procedures, standards, processes, practices, tools, techniques, and tasks that people apply to technical and management challenges.

metrics   Measurements that evaluate results to determine whether a project is meeting its goals.

metropolitan area network (MAN)   A large computer network usually spanning a city.

microblogging   The practice of sending brief posts (140 to 200 characters) to a personal blog, either publicly or to a private group of subscribers who can read the posts as IMs or as text messages.

middleware   Several different types of software that sit in the middle of and provide connectivity between two or more software applications.

MIS infrastructure   Includes the plans for how a firm will build, deploy, use, and share its data, processes, and MIS assets.

MIS skills gap   The difference between existing MIS workplace knowledge and the knowledge required to fulfill the business goals and strategies.

mobile application management   Administers and delivers applications to corporate and personal smartphones and tablets.

mobile business (mcommerce or mbusiness)   The ability to purchase goods and services through a wireless Internet-enabled device.

mobile device management (MDM)   Remotely controls smartphones and tablets, ensuring data security.

model   A simplified representation or abstraction of reality.

module software design   Divides the system into a set of functional units (named modules) that can be used independently or combined with other modules for increased business flexibility.

Moore's Law   Refers to the computer chip performance per dollar doubling every 18 months.

multi-tenancy   A single instance of a system serves multiple customers.

multifactor authentication   Requires more than two means of authentication such as what the user knows (password), what the user has (security token), and what the user is (biometric verification).

multiple-in/multiple-out (MIMO) technology   Multiple transmitters and receivers allow sending and receiving greater amounts of data than traditional networking devices.

multitasking   Allows more than one piece of software to be used at a time.

mutation   The process within a genetic algorithm of randomly trying combinations and evaluating the success (or failure) of the outcome.

N

native advertising   An online marketing concept in which the advertiser attempts to gain attention by providing content in the context of the user's experience in terms of its content, format, style, or placement.

nearshore outsourcing   Contracting an outsourcing agreement with a company in a nearby country.

net income   The amount of money remaining after paying taxes.

network effect   Describes how products in a network increase in value to users as the number of users increases.

network operating system (NOS)   The operating system that runs a network, steering information between computers and managing security and users.

network topology   Refers to the geometric arrangement of the actual physical organization of the computers (and other network devices) in a network.

network transmission media   Various types of media used to carry the signal between computers.

network user license   Enables anyone on the network to install and use the software.

network virtualization   Combines networks by splitting the available bandwidth into independent channels that can be assigned in real time to a specific device.

network   A communications system created by linking two or more devices and establishing a standard methodology in which they can communicate.

neural network (artificial neural network)   A category of AI that attempts to emulate the way the human brain works.

nonrepudiation   A contractual stipulation to ensure that ebusiness participants do not deny (repudiate) their online actions.

nonvolatile   Does not require constant power to function.

not for profit (or nonprofit) corporation   Usually exists to accomplish some charitable, humanitarian, or educational purpose, and the profits and losses are not shared by the business owners.

O

object-oriented languages   Languages that group data and corresponding processes into objects.

off-the-shelf application   Supports general business processes and does not require any specific software customization to meet the organization's needs.

offshore outsourcing   Using organizations from developing countries to write code and develop systems.

on-premise system   Includes a server at a physical location using an internal networkfor internal access and firewalls for remote user's access.

online analytical processing (OLAP) The manipulation of information to create business intelligence in support of strategic decision making.

online training Runs over the Internet or on a CD or DVD, and employees complete the training on their own time at their own pace.

online transaction processing (OLTP) The capturing of transaction and event information using technology to (1) process the information according to defined business rules, (2) store the information, and (3) update existing information to reflect the new information.

onshore outsourcing The process of engaging another company within the same country for services.

open source Refers to any software whose source code is made available free for any third party to review and modify.

open system Consists of nonproprietary hardware and software based on publicly known standards that allow third parties to create add-on products to plug into or interoperate with the system.

operating system software Controls the application software and manages how the hardware devices work together.

operational CRM Supports traditional transactional processing for day-to-day front-office operations or systems that deal directly with the customers.

operational level Employees develop, control, and maintain core business activities required to run the day-to-day operations.

operational planning and control (OP&C) Deals with the day-to-day procedures for performing work, including scheduling, inventory, and process management.

operations management The management of systems or processes that convert or transform resources (including human resources) into goods and services.

opportunity management CRM systems Targets sales opportunities by finding new customers or companies for future sales.

Opt in A user receives emails by choosing to allow permissions to incoming emails.

opt out Receiving emails by choosing to deny permission to incoming emails.

optimization analysis An extension of goal-seeking analysis, finds the optimum value for a target variable by repeatedly changing other variables, subject to specified constraints.

optimization model A statistical process that finds the way to make a design, system, or decision as effective as possible, for example, finding the values of controllable variables that determine maximal productivity or minimal waste.

outlier A data value that is numerically distant from most of the other data points in a set of data.

output device Equipment used to see, hear, or otherwise accept the results of information processing requests.

outsourcing An arrangement by which one organization provides a service or services for another organization that chooses not to perform them in-house.

owner's equity The portion of a company belonging to the owners.

P

packet-switching Occurs when the sending computer divides a message into a number of efficiently sized units called packets, each of which contains the address of the destination computer.

paradigm shift Occurs when a new radical form of business enters the market that reshapes the way companies and organizations behave.

parallel implementation Uses both the legacy system and new system until all users verify that the new system functions correctly.

partner relationship management (PRM) Focuses on keeping vendors satisfied by managing alliance partner and reseller relationships that provide customers with the optimal sales channel.

partnership agreement A legal agreement between two or more business partners that outlines core business issues.

partnership Similar to sole proprietorships, except that this legal structure allows for more than one owner.

passive RFID tags Do not have a power source.

password A string of alphanumeric characters used to authenticate a user and provide access to a system.

patent An exclusive right to make, use, and sell an invention granted by a government to the inventor.

pay-per-call Generates revenue each time users click on a link that takes them directly to an online agent waiting for a call.

pay-per-click Generates revenue each time a user clicks on a link to a retailer's website.

pay-per-conversion Generates revenue each time a website visitor is converted to a customer.

peer-to-peer (P2P) network A computer network that relies on the computing power and bandwidth of the participants in the network rather than a centralized server.

performance Measures how quickly a system performs a certain process or transaction.

personal area network (PAN) Provides communication for devices owned by a single user that work over a short distance.

personal information management (PIM) software Software handles contact information, appointments, task lists, and email.

personalization Occurs when a company can know enough about a person's likes and dislikes that it can fashion offers that are more likely to appeal to that person.

PERT (Program Evaluation and Review Technique) chart A graphical network model that depicts a project's tasks and the relationships between those tasks.

pharming attack Uses a zombie farm, often by an organized crime association, to launch a massive phishing attack.

pharming Reroutes requests for legitimate websites to false websites.

phased implementation Installs the new system in phases (for example, by department) until it is verified that it works correctly.

phishing expedition A masquerading attack that combines spam with spoofing.

phishing Technique to gain personal information for the purpose of identity theft, usually by means of fraudulent email.

physical security Tangible protection such as alarms, guards, fireproof doors, fences, and vaults.

physical view of information The physical storage of information on a storage device such as a hard disk.

pilot implementation A small group uses the new system until it is verified that it works correctly, then the remaining users migrate to the new system.

pirated software The unauthorized use, duplication, distribution, or sale of copyrighted software.

planning phase Involves establishing a high-level plan of the intended project and determining project goals.

Platform as a Service (PaaS) Supports the deployment of entire systems including hardware, networking, and applications using a pay-per-use revenue model.

plunge implementation Discards the legacy system and immediately migrates all users to the new system.

podcasting Converts an audio broadcast to a digital music player.

portability Refers to the ability of an application to operate on different devices or software platforms, such as different operating systems.

Porter's Five Forces Model Analyzes the competitive forces within the environment in which a company operates to assess the potential for profitability in an industry.

Porter's three generic strategies Generic business strategies that are neither organization nor industry specific and can be applied to any business, product, or service.

prediction A statement about what will happen or might happen in the future, for example, predicting future sales or employee turnover.

predictive analytics Extracts information from data and uses it to predict future trends and identify behavioral patterns.

pretexting A form of social engineering in which one individual lies to obtain confidential data about another individual.

preventive maintenance Makes system changes to reduce the chance of future system failure.

primary key A field (or group of fields) that uniquely identifies a given entity in a table.

primary storage Computer's main memory, which consists of the random access memory (RAM), cache memory, and read-only memory (ROM) that is directly accessible to the CPU.

primary value activities Found at the bottom of the value chain, these include business processes that acquire raw materials and manufacture, deliver, market, sell, and provide after-sales services.

privacy The right to be left alone when you want to be, to have control over your own personal possessions, and not to be observed without your consent.

private cloud Serves only one customer or organization and can be located on the customer's premises or off the customer's premises.

privilege escalation A network intrusion attack that takes advantage of programming errors or design flaws to grant the attacker elevated access to the network and its associated data and applications.

process owner The person responsible for the end-to-end functioning of a business process.

procurement The purchasing of goods and services to meet the needs of the supply chain.

product differentiation An advantage that occurs when a company develops unique differences in its products with the intent to influence demand.

product life cycle Includes the four phases a product progresses through during its life cycle including introduction, growth, maturity, and decline.

production and materials management ERP component Handles the various aspects of production planning and execution such as demand forecasting, production scheduling, job cost accounting, and quality control.

production management Describes all the activities managers do to help companies create goods.

production The process where a business takes raw materials and processes them or converts them into a finished product for its goods or services.

productivity The rate at which goods and services are produced based upon total output given total inputs.

profit Occurs when businesses sell products or services for more than they cost to produce.

project assumption Factor that is considered to be true, real, or certain without proof or demonstration.

project constraint Specific factor that can limit options.

project deliverable Any measurable, tangible, verifiable outcome, result, or item that is produced to complete a project or part of a project.

project management office (PMO) An internal department that oversees all organizational projects.

project management The application of knowledge, skills, tools, and techniques to project activities in order to meet or exceed stakeholder needs and expectations from a project.

project manager An individual who is an expert in project planning and management, defines and develops the project plan, and tracks the plan to ensure all key project milestones are completed on time.

project milestone Represents key dates when a certain group of activities must be performed.

project objective Quantifiable criteria that must be met for the project to be considered a success.

project plan A formal, approved document that manages and controls project execution.

project requirements document Defines the specifications for product/output of the project and is key for managing expectations, controlling scope, and completing other planning efforts.

project scope statement Links the project to the organization's overall business goals.

project scope Describes the business need (the problem the project will solve) and the justification, requirements, and current boundaries for the project.

project stakeholder Individuals and organizations actively involved in the project or whose interests might be affected as a result of project execution or project completion.

project A temporary endeavor undertaken to create a unique product or service.

protocol A standard that specifies the format of data as well as the rules to be followed during transmission.

prototype A modern design approach where the designers and system users use an iterative approach to building the system.

public cloud Promotes massive, global, industrywide applications offered to the general public.

public key encryption (PKE) Encryption system that uses two keys: a public key that everyone can have and a private key for only the recipient.

Q

query-by-example (QBE) tool Helps users graphically design the answer to a question against a database.

R

radio frequency identification (RFID) Uses electronic tags and labels to identify objects wirelessly over short distances.

random access memory (RAM) The computer's primary working memory, in which program instructions and data are stored so that they can be accessed directly by the CPU via the processor's high-speed external data bus.

ransomware A form of malicious software that infects your computer and asks for money.

rapid application development (RAD) (also called rapid prototyping) methodology Emphasizes extensive user involvement in the rapid and evolutionary construction of working prototypes of a system to accelerate the systems development process.

rational unified process (RUP) methodology Provides a framework for breaking down the development of software into four gates.

read-only memory (ROM) The portion of a computer's primary storage that does not lose its contents when one switches off the power.

Real Simple Syndication (RSS) A web format used to publish frequently updated works, such as blogs, news headlines, audio, and video, in a standardized format.

real-time adaptive security The network security model necessary to accommodate the emergence of multiple perimeters and moving parts on the network, and increasingly advanced threats targeting enterprises.

real-time communication Occurs when a system updates information at the same rate it receives it.

real-time information Immediate, up-to-date information.

real-time system Provides real-time information in response to query requests.

recommendation engine A data-mining algorithm that analyzes a customer's purchases and actions on a website and then uses the data to recommend complementary products.

record A collection of related data elements.

recovery The ability to get a system up and running in the event of a system crash or failure and includes restoring the information backup.

reduced instruction set computer (RISC) chip Limits the number of instructions the CPU can execute to increase processing speed.

regression model Includes many techniques for modeling and analyzing several variables when the focus is on the relationship between a dependent variable and one or more independent variables.

reintermediation Steps are added to the value chain as new players find ways to add value to the business process.

relational database management system Allows users to create, read, update, and delete data in a relational database.

relational database model A type of database that stores information in the form of logically related two-dimensional tables.

relational integrity constraint The rules that enforce basic and fundamental information-based constraints.

reliability (or accuracy) Ensures all systems are functioning correctly and providing accurate information.

report A document containing data organized in a table, matrix, or graphical format allowing users to easily comprehend and understand information.

repository A central location in which data is stored and managed.

reputation system Where buyers post feedback on sellers.

requirements definition document Prioritizes all of the business requirements by order of importance to the company.

requirements management The process of managing changes to the business requirements throughout the project.

responsibility matrix Defines all project roles and indicates what responsibilities are associated with each role.

return on investment (ROI) Indicates the earning power of a project.

revenue Refers to the amount earned resulting from the delivery or manufacture of a product or from the rendering of a service.

RFID accelerometer A device that measures the acceleration (the rate of change of velocity) of an item and is used to track truck speeds or taxi cab speeds.

RFID reader (RFID interrogator) A transmitter/receiver that reads the contents of RFID tags in the area.

RFID tag An electronic identification device that is made up of a chip and antenna.

RFID's electronic product code (RFID EPC) Promotes serialization or the ability to track individual items by using the unique serial number associated with each RFID tag.

rivalry among existing competitors High when competition is fierce in a market and low when competition is more complacent.

Robotics Focuses on creating artificial intelligence devices that can move and react to sensory input.

router An intelligent connecting device that examines each packet of data it receives and then decides which way to send it onward toward its destination.

S

safe mode Occurs if the system is failing and will load only the most essential parts of the operating system and will not run many of the background operating utilities.

sales analytics Involves gathering, classifying, comparing, and studying company sales data to analyze product cycles, sales pipelines, and competitive intelligence.

sales force automation (SFA) Automatically tracks all the steps in the sales process.

sales management CRM systems Automates each phase of the sales process, helping individual sales representatives coordinate and organize all their accounts.

sales The function of selling a good or service that focuses on increasing customer sales, which increases company revenues.

satellite A space station that orbits the Earth receiving and transmitting signals from Earth-based stations over a wide area.

scalability Describes how well a system can scale up, or adapt to the increased demands of growth.

scripting language A programming method that provides for interactive modules to a website.

scrum methodology Uses small teams to produce small pieces of deliverable software using sprints, or 30-day intervals, to achieve an appointed goal.

search engine optimization (SEO) Combines art along with science to determine how to make URLs more attractive to search engines resulting in higher search engine ranking.

search engine ranking Evaluates variables that search engines use to determine where a URL appears on the list of search results.

search engine Website software that finds other pages based on keyword matching.

secondary storage Consists of equipment designed to store large volumes of data for long-term storage.

selfie A self-photograph placed on a social media website.

selling chain management Applies technology to the activities in the order life cycle from inquiry to sale.

semantic web A component of Web 3.0 that describes things in a way that computers can understand.

semi-passive RFID tags Include a battery to run the microchip's circuitry, but communicate by drawing power from the RFID reader.

semistructured decisions   Occurs in situations in which a few established processes help to evaluate potential solutions, but not enough to lead to a definite recommended decision.

sensitivity analysis   The study of the impact on other variables when one variable is changed repeatedly.

server virtualization   Combines the physical resources, such as servers, processors, and operating systems, from the applications.

server   Computer that is dedicated to providing information in response to external requests.

service-oriented architecture (SOA)   A business-driven enterprise architecture that supports integrating a business as linked, repeatable activities, tasks, or services.

serviceability   How quickly a third party or vendor can change a system to ensure it meets user needs and the terms of any contracts, including agreed levels of reliability, maintainability, or availability.

services   Tasks performed by people that customers will buy to satisfy a want or need.

shareholder   Another term for business owners.

shopping bot   Software that will search several retailer websites and provide a comparison of each retailer's offerings including price and availability.

sign-off   The system users' actual signatures indicating they approve all of the business requirements.

single user license   Restricts the use of the software to one user at a time.

single-factor authentication   The traditional security process, which requires a username and password.

site license   Enables any qualified users within the organization to install the software, regardless of whether the computer is on a network.

slice-and-dice   The ability to look at information from different perspectives.

smart card   A device that is around the same size as a credit card, containing embedded technologies that can store information and small amounts of software to perform some limited processing.

smart grid   Delivers electricity using two-way digital technology.

smartphone   Offers more advanced computing ability and connectivity than basic cell phones.

snapshot   A view of data at a particular moment in time.

SOA service   A business task, such as checking a potential customer's credit rating when opening a new account.

social bookmarking   Allows users to share, organize, search, and manage bookmarks.

social engineering   Hackers use their social skills to trick people into revealing access credentials or other valuable information.

social graph   Represents the interconnection of relationships in a social network.

social media monitoring   The process of monitoring and responding to what is being said about a company, individual, product, or brand.

social media policy   Outlines the corporate guidelines or principles governing employee online communications.

social media   Refers to websites that rely on user participation and user-contributed content.

social network   An application that connects people by matching profile information.

social networking analysis (SNA)   Maps group contacts, identifying who knows each other and who works together.

social networking   The practice of expanding your business and/or social contacts by constructing a personal network.

social tagging   Describes the collaborative activity of marking shared online content with keywords or tags as a way to organize it for future navigation, filtering, or search.

Software as a Service (SaaS)   Delivers applications over the cloud using a pay-per-use revenue model.

software customization   Modifies existing software according to the business's or user's requirements.

software engineering   A disciplined approach for constructing information systems through the use of common methods, techniques, or tools.

software updates (software patch)   Occurs when the software vendor releases updates to software to fix problems or enhance features.

software upgrade   Occurs when the software vendor releases a new version of the software, making significant changes to the program.

software   The set of instructions that the hardware executes to carry out specific tasks.

sole proprietorship   A business form in which a single person is the sole owner and is personally responsible for all the profits and losses of the business.

solid state drive   An all-electronic storage device that is an alternative to a hard disk and is faster than hard disks because there is zero latency (no read/write head to move).

solvency   Represents the ability of the business to pay its bills and service its debt.

source code   Contains instructions written by a programmer specifying the actions to be performed by computer software.

source data   Identifies the primary location where data is collected.

source document   Describes the original transaction record along with details such as its date, purpose, and amount spent and includes cash receipts, canceled checks, invoices, customer refunds, employee time sheet, etc.

spam   Unsolicited email.

spatial data (geospatial data or geographic information)   Identifies the geographic location of features and boundaries on Earth, such as natural or constructed features, oceans, and more.

spear phishing   A phishing expedition in which the emails are carefully designed to target a particular person or organization.

spyware   A special class of adware that collects data about the user and transmits it over the Internet without the user's knowledge or permission.

stakeholder   A person or group that has an interest or concern in an organization.

statement of cash flows   Summarizes sources and uses of cash, indicates whether enough cash is available to carry on routine operations, and offers an analysis of all business transactions, reporting where the firm obtained its cash and how it chose to allocate the cash.

statement of owner's equity   Tracks and communicates changes in the shareholder's earnings.

static information   Includes fixed data that are not capable of change in the event of a user action.

static process   Uses a systematic approach in an attempt to improve business effectiveness and efficiency continuously.

static report   A report created once based on data that does not change.

status report   Periodic reviews of actual performance versus expected performance.

storage virtualization Combines multiple network storage devices so they appear to be a single storage device.

strategic business units (SBUs) Consists of several stand-alone businesses.

strategic level Managers develop overall business strategies, goals, and objectives as part of the company's strategic plan.

strategic planning Focuses on long-range planning such as plant size, location, and type of process to be used.

streaming A method of sending audio and video files over the Internet in such a way that the user can view the file while it is being transferred.

structured data Data that has a defined length, type, and format and includes numbers, dates, or strings such as Customer Address.

structured decisions Involves situations where established processes offer potential solutions.

structured query language Users write lines of code to answer questions against a database.

stylus A pen-like device used to tap the screen to enter commands.

supplier power The suppliers' ability to influence the prices they charge for supplies (including materials, labor, and services).

supplier relationship management (SRM) Focuses on keeping suppliers satisfied by evaluating and categorizing suppliers for different projects, which optimizes supplier selection.

supply chain design Determines how to structure a supply chain including the product, selection of partners, the location and capacity of warehouses, transportation methods, and supporting management information systems.

supply chain execution system Ensures supply chain cohesion by automating the different activities of the supply chain.

supply chain management (SCM) Involves the management of information flows between and among activities in a supply chain to maximize total supply chain effectiveness and corporate profitability.

supply chain planning system Uses advanced mathematical algorithms to improve the flow and efficiency of the supply chain while reducing inventory.

supply chain visibility The ability to view all areas up and down the supply chain in real time.

supply chain Consists of all parties involved, directly or indirectly, in the procurement of a product or raw material.

support value activities Found along the top of the value chain and includes business processes, such as firm infrastructure, human resource management, technology development, and procurement that support the primary value activities.

sustainable MIS disposal Refers to the safe disposal of MIS assets at the end of their life cycle.

sustainable MIS infrastructure Identifies ways that a company can grow in terms of computing resources while simultaneously becoming less dependent on hardware and energy consumption.

sustainable, or green, MIS Describes the production, management, use, and disposal of technology in a way that minimizes damage to the environment.

sustaining technology Produces an improved product customers are eager to buy, such as a faster car or larger hard drive.

swimlane diagram Documents the steps or activities of a workflow by grouping activities into swimlanes, which are horizontal or vertical columns containing all associated activities for that category or department.

switching cost The costs that can make customers reluctant to switch to another product or service.

SWOT analysis Evaluates an organization's **s**trengths, **w**eaknesses, **o**pportunities, and **t**hreats to identify significant influences that work for or against business strategies.

synchronous communication Communications that occur at the same time such as IM or chat.

system clock Works like a wristwatch and uses a battery mounted on the motherboard to provide power when the computer is turned off.

system restore Enables a user to return to the previous operating system.

system software Controls how the various technology tools work together along with the application software.

system testing Verifies that the units or pieces of code function correctly when integrated.

system virtualization The ability to present the resources of a single computer as if it is a collection of separate computers ("virtual machines"), each with its own virtual CPUs, network interfaces, storage, and operating system.

system A collection of parts that link to achieve a common purpose.

systems development life cycle (SDLC) The overall process for developing information systems from planning and analysis through implementation and maintenance.

systems thinking A way of monitoring the entire system by viewing multiple inputs being processed or transformed to produce outputs while continuously gathering feedback on each part.

T

tacit knowledge The knowledge contained in people's heads.

tactical planning Focuses on producing goods and services as efficiently as possible within the strategic plan.

tags Specific keywords or phrases incorporated into website content for means of classification or taxonomy.

tangible benefits Easy to quantify and typically measured to determine the success or failure of a project.

taxonomy The scientific classification of organisms into groups based on similarities of structure or origin.

technology failure Occurs when the ability of a company to operate is impaired because of a hardware, software, or data outage.

technology recovery strategy Focus specifically on prioritizing the order for restoring hardware, software, and data across the organization that best meets business recovery requirements.

teergrubbing Anti-spamming approach where the receiving computer launches a return attack against the spammer, sending email messages back to the computer that originated the suspected spam.

telecommunication system Enables the transmission of data over public or private networks.

terabyte (TB) Roughly 1 trillion bytes.

test condition The detailed steps the system must perform along with the expected results of each step.

testing phase Involves bringing all the project pieces together into a special testing environment to test for errors, bugs, and interoperability and verify that the system meets all of the business requirements defined in the analysis phase.

threat of new entrants High when it is easy for new competitors to enter a market and low when there are significant entry barriers to entering a market.

threat of substitute products or services High when there are many alternatives to a product or service and low when there are few alternatives from which to choose.

threat   An act or object that poses a danger to assets.

time bombs   Computer viruses that wait for a specific date before executing instructions.

time-series information   Time-stamped information collected at a particular frequency.

To-Be process model   Shows the results of applying change improvement opportunities to the current (As-Is) process model.

token   Small electronic devices that change user passwords automatically.

transaction processing system (TPS)   The basic business system that serves the operational level (analysts) in an organization.

transaction   Exchange or transfer of goods, services, or funds involving two or more people.

transactional information   Encompasses all of the information contained within a single business process or unit of work, and its primary purpose is to support the performing of daily operational tasks.

transborder data flows (TDF)   When business data flows across international boundaries over the telecommunications networks of global information systems.

transformation process   The technical core, especially in manufacturing organizations; the actual conversion of inputs to outputs.

transmission control protocol/Internet protocol (TCP/IP)   Provides the technical foundation for the public Internet as well as for large numbers of private networks.

transportation planning system   Tracks and analyzes the movement of materials and products to ensure the delivery of materials and finished goods at the right time, the right place, and the lowest cost.

trend analysis   A trend is examined to identify its nature, causes, speed of development, and potential impacts.

trend monitoring   Trends viewed as particularly important in a specific community, industry, or sector are carefully monitored, watched, and reported to key decision makers.

trend projection   When numerical data are available, a trend can be plotted to display changes through time and into the future.

twisted-pair cable   A type of cable composed of four (or more) copper wires twisted around each other within a plastic sheath.

two-factor authentication   Requires the user to provide two means of authentication, what the user knows (password) and what the user has (security token).

typosquatting   A problem that occurs when someone registers purposely misspelled variations of well-known domain names.

U

unavailable   When a system is not operating or cannot be used.

unit testing   Testing individual units or pieces of code for a system.

universal resource locator (URL)   The address of a file or resource on the web such as www.apple.com.

unstructured data   Data that is not defined and does not follow a specified format and is typically free-form text such as emails, Twitter tweets, and text messages.

unstructured decisions   Occurs in situations in which no procedures or rules exist to guide decision makers toward the correct choice.

up-selling   Increasing the value of the sale.

upcycle   Reuses or refurbishes ewaste and creates a new product.

uplift modeling   A form of predictive analytics for marketing campaigns that attempts to identify target markets or people who could be convinced to buy products.

usability   The degree to which a system is easy to learn, efficient, and satisfying to use.

user acceptance testing (UAT)   Determines if the system satisfies the user and business requirements.

user documentation   Highlights how to use the system and how to troubleshoot issues or problems.

user-contributed content (user-generated content)   Content created and updated by many users for many users.

utility computing   Offers a pay-per-use revenue model similar to a metered service such as gas or electricity.

utility software   Provides additional functionality to the operating system.

V

value chain analysis   Views a firm as a series of business processes that each add value to the product or service.

value-added   The term used to describe the difference between the cost of inputs and the value of price of outputs.

variable   A data characteristic that stands for a value that changes or varies over time.

vertical privilege escalation   Attackers grant themselves a higher access level such as administrator allowing the attacker to perform illegal actions such as running unauthorized code or deleting data.

videoconference   Allows people at two or more locations to interact via two-way video and audio transmissions simultaneously as well as share documents, data, computer displays, and whiteboards.

virtual assistant (VA)   A small program stored on a PC or portable device that monitors emails, faxes, messages, and phone calls.

virtual reality   A computer-simulated environment that can be a simulation of the real world or an imaginary world.

virtualization   The creation of a virtual (rather than actual) version of computing resources, such as an operating system, a server, a storage device, or network resources.

virus   Software written with malicious intent to cause annoyance or damage.

vishing (or voice phishing)   A phone scam that attempts to defraud people by asking them to call a bogus telephone number to "confirm" their account information.

Voice over LTE (VoLTE)   Allows mobile voice calls to be made over broadband networks, creating—under the right network conditions—clearer audio and fewer dropped calls.

voiceprint   A set of measurable characteristics of a human voice that uniquely identifies an individual.

volatile   Must have constant power to function; contents are lost when the computer's electric supply fails.

volatility   Refers to RAM's complete loss of stored information if power is interrupted.

vulnerability   A system weakness that can be exploited by a threat; for example, a password that is never changed or a system left on while an employee goes to lunch.

W

war chalking   The practice of tagging pavement with codes displaying where Wi-Fi access is available.

war driving   Deliberately searching for Wi-Fi signals from a vehicle.

warm site   A separate facility with computer equipment that requires installation and configuration.

waterfall methodology A sequence of phases in which the output of each phase becomes the input for the next.

Web 1.0 (or Business 1.0) Refers to the World Wide Web during its first few years of operation between 1991 and 2003.

Web 2.0 (or Business 2.0) The next generation of Internet use—a more mature, distinctive communications platform characterized by new qualities such as collaboration, sharing, and free.

web accessibility initiative (WAI) Brings together people from industry, disability organizations, government, and research labs from around the world to develop guidelines and resources to help make the web accessible to people with disabilities, including auditory, cognitive, neurological, physical, speech, and visual disabilities.

web accessibility Means that people with disabilities—including visual, auditory, physical, speech, cognitive, and neurological disabilities—can use the web.

web browser Allows users to access the WWW.

web conferencing (webinar) Blends videoconferencing with document sharing and allows the user to deliver a presentation over the web to a group of geographically dispersed participants.

web service An open-standards way of supporting interoperability.

Web-based self-service systems Allows customers to use the web to find answers to their questions or solutions to their problems.

website bookmark A locally stored URL or the address of a file or Internet page saved as a shortcut.

website name stealing The theft of a website's name that occurs when someone, posing as a site's administrator, changes the ownership of the domain name assigned to the website to another website owner.

website personalization Occurs when a website has stored enough data about a person's likes and dislikes to fashion offers more likely to appeal to that person.

what-if analysis Checks the impact of a change in an assumption on the proposed solution.

Wi-Fi infrastructure Includes the inner workings of a Wi-Fi service or utility, including the signal transmitters, towers, or poles, along with additional equipment required to send out a Wi-Fi signal.

Wi-Fi protected access (WPA) A wireless security protocol to protect Wi-Fi networks.

wide area network (WAN) Spans large geographic area, such as a state, province, or country.

wiki A type of collaborative web page that allows users to add, remove, and change content, which can be easily organized and reorganized as required.

wire media Transmission material manufactured so that signals will be confined to a narrow path and will behave predictably.

wired equivalent privacy (WEP) An encryption algorithm designed to protect wireless transmission data.

wireless access point (WAP) Enables devices to connect to a wireless network to communicate with each other.

wireless fidelity (Wi-Fi) A means by which portable devices can connect wirelessly to a local area network, using access points that send and receive data via radio waves.

wireless LAN (WLAN) A local area network that uses radio signals to transmit and receive data over distances of a few hundred feet.

wireless MAN (WMAN) A metropolitan area network that uses radio signals to transmit and receive data.

wireless media Natural parts of the Earth's environment that can be used as physical paths to carry electrical signals.

wireless WAN (WWAN) A wide area network that uses radio signals to transmit and receive data.

workflow control systems Monitor processes to ensure tasks, activities, and responsibilities are executed as specified.

workflow Includes the tasks, activities, and responsibilities required to execute each step in a business process.

workplace MIS monitoring Tracks people's activities by such measures as number of keystrokes, error rate, and number of transactions processed.

workshop training Held in a classroom environment and led by an instructor.

World Wide Web (WWW) A global hypertext system that uses the Internet as its transport mechanism.

World Wide Web consortium (W3C) An international community that develops open standards to ensure the long-term growth of the Web (www.w3.org).

Worldwide Interoperability for Microwave Access (WiMAX) A communications technology aimed at providing high-speed wireless data over metropolitan area networks.

worm Spreads itself not only from file to file but also from computer to computer.

Z

zombie farm A group of computers on which a hacker has planted zombie programs.

zombie A program that secretly takes over another computer for the purpose of launching attacks on other computers.

NOTES

CHAPTER 1

1. Hiroko Tabuchi, "Stores Suffer From a Shift of Behavior in Buyers", *NY Times,* August 13, 2015, accessed 4/15/2016 Travis Bradberry, "You Should Spend Your Money on Experiences, Not Things", *Entrepreneur,* March 1, 2016, accessed 4/14/2016.

2. Interesting Facts, www.interestingfacts.org, accessed June 2012.

3. http://www.intel.com/content/www/us/en/internet-of-things/ industrysolutions.html , accessed May 2014; Michael Chui, Markus Löffler, and Roger Roberts, "The Internet of Things," Mckinsey Quarterly, March 2010, http://www.mckinsey.com/ insights/high_tech_ telecoms_internet/the_internet_of_things; Stefan Ferber, "How the Internet of Things Changes Everything," Harvard Business Review, May 2013.

4. Thomas L. Friedman, The World Is Flat (New York: Farrar, Straus & Giroux, 2005); Thomas Friedman, "The World Is Flat," www.thomaslfriedman.com, accessed June 2010; Thomas L. Friedman, "The Opinion Pages," The New York Times, topics.nytimes.com/top/opinion/editorialsandoped/ oped/columnists/thomaslfriedman, accessed June 2012.

CHAPTER 2

1. Ina Fried, "Apple Earnings Top Estimates," CNET News, October 11, 2005, http://news.cnet.com/Appleearningstopesti-mates/2100-1041_3-5893289.html?tag=lia;rcol , accessed July 2012.

2. Frederic Paul, "Smart Social Networking for Your Small Business," Forbes.com, www.forbes.com/2009/06/05/social-networkinginterop-entrepreneurs-technology-bmighty.html, accessed July 2012.

3. Michael E. Porter, "The Five Competitive Forces That Shape Strategy," The Harvard Business Review Book Series, *Harvard Business Review,* January 2008; Michael E. Porter, "Competitive Strategy: Techniques for Analyzing Industries and Competitors," *Harvard Business Review,* January 2002; Michael E. Porter, "On Competition," *The Harvard Business Review Book Series* (Boston: Harvard Business School Publishing, 1985); Harvard Institute for Strategy and Competitiveness, www.isc.hbs.edu/, accessed June 2012.

4. Michael E. Porter, "The Five Competitive Forces That Shape Strategy," The Harvard Business Review Book Series, *Harvard Business Review,* January 2008; Michael E. Porter, "Competitive Strategy: Techniques for Analyzing Industries and Competitors," *Harvard Business Review,* January 2002; Michael E. Porter, "On Competition," *The Harvard Business Review Book Series* (Boston: Harvard Business School Publishing, 1985); Harvard Institute for Strategy and Competitiveness, www.isc.hbs.edu/, accessed June 2012.

5. Michael E. Porter, "The Five Competitive Forces That Shape Strategy," The Harvard Business Review Book Series, *Harvard Business Review,* January 2008; Michael E. Porter, "Competitive Strategy: Techniques for Analyzing Industries and Competitors," *Harvard Business Review,* January 2002; Michael E. Porter, "On Competition," *The Harvard Business Review Book Series* (Boston: Harvard Business School Publishing, 1985); Harvard Institute for Strategy and Competitiveness, www.isc.hbs.edu/, accessed June 2012.

6. Michael E. Porter, "The Five Competitive Forces That Shape Strategy," The Harvard Business Review Book Series, *Harvard Business Review,* January 2008; Michael E. Porter, "Competitive Strategy: Techniques for Analyzing Industries and Competitors," *Harvard Business Review,* January 2002; Michael E. Porter, "On Competition," *The Harvard Business Review Book Series* (Boston: Harvard Business School Publishing, 1985); Harvard Institute for Strategy and Competitiveness, www.isc.hbs.edu/, accessed June 2012.

7. Michael E. Porter, "The Five Competitive Forces That Shape Strategy," The Harvard Business Review Book Series, *Harvard Business Review,* January 2008; Michael E. Porter, "Competitive Strategy: Techniques for Analyzing Industries and Competitors," Harvard Business Review, January 2002; Michael E. Porter, "On Competition," *The Harvard Business Review Book Series* (Boston: Harvard Business School Publishing, 1985); Harvard Institute for Strategy and Competitiveness, www.isc.hbs.edu/, accessed June 2012.

8. Michael E. Porter, "The Five Competitive Forces That Shape Strategy," The Harvard Business Review Book Series, *Harvard Business Review,* January 2008; Michael E. Porter, "Competitive Strategy: Techniques for Analyzing Industries and Competitors," *Harvard Business Review,* January 2002; Michael E. Porter, "On Competition," *The Harvard Business Review Book Series* (Boston: Harvard Business School Publishing, 1985); Harvard Institute for Strategy and Competitiveness, www.isc.hbs.edu/, accessed June 2012.

9. Michael E. Porter, "The Five Competitive Forces That Shape Strategy," The Harvard Business Review Book Series, *Harvard Business Review,* January 2008; Michael E. Porter, "Competitive Strategy: Techniques for Analyzing Industries and Competitors," *Harvard Business Review,* January 2002; Michael E. Porter, "On Competition," *The Harvard Business Review Book Series* (Boston: Harvard Business School Publishing, 1985); Harvard Institute for Strategy and Competitiveness, www.isc.hbs.edu/, accessed June 2012.

10. Michael E. Porter, "The Five Competitive Forces That Shape Strategy," The Harvard Business Review Book Series, *Harvard Business Review,* January 2008; Michael E. Porter, "Competitive Strategy: Techniques for Analyzing Industries and Competitors," *Harvard Business Review,* January 2002; Michael

E. Porter, "On Competition," *The Harvard Business Review Book Series* (Boston: Harvard Business School Publishing, 1985); Harvard Institute for Strategy and Competitiveness, www.isc.hbs.edu/, accessed June 2012.

11. Michael E. Porter, "The Five Competitive Forces That Shape Strategy," The Harvard Business Review Book Series, *Harvard Business Review*, January 2008; Michael E. Porter, "Competitive Strategy: Techniques for Analyzing Industries and Competitors," *Harvard Business Review*, January 2002; Michael E. Porter, "On Competition," *The Harvard Business Review Book Series* (Boston: Harvard Business School Publishing, 1985); Harvard Institute for Strategy and Competitiveness, www.isc.hbs.edu/, accessed June 2012.

12. Michael E. Porter, "The Five Competitive Forces That Shape Strategy," The Harvard Business Review Book Series, Harvard Business Review, January 2008; Michael E. Porter, "Competitive Strategy: Techniques for Analyzing Industries and Competitors," Harvard Business Review, January 2002; Michael E. Porter, "On Competition," The Harvard Business Review Book Series (Boston: Harvard Business School Publishing, 1985); Harvard Institute for Strategy and Competitiveness, www.isc.hbs.edu/, accessed June 2012.

13. "Harvard Business Review on Managing the Value Chain," Harvard Business School Press, January 2000.

14. "Harvard Business Review on Managing the Value Chain," Harvard Business School Press, January 2000.

15. Michael Porter, TED talk live, https://www.ted.com/talks/michael_porter_why_business_can_be_good_at_solving_social_problems, accessed 2015.

CHAPTER 3

1. Christopher Koch, "The ABC's of Supply Chain Management," www.cio.com, accessed October 2012.

2. Amazon Reveals Impressive Prime Air Drone, www.247supplychain.com, accessed November 2015.

CHAPTER 4

1. Michael Schrage, "Rebuilding the Business Case," *CIO Magazine Online*, www.cio.com, accessed November 2012.

2. "Integrating Information at Children's Hospital," *KMWorld*, www.kmworld.com/Articles/ReadArticle.aspx, accessed April 2012.

3. The Future of Work, Fast Company, Accessed December 2015, http://www.fastcompany.com/3048398/the-future-of-work/10-c-suite-jobs-of-the-future

4. Peter Drucker, "The Man Who Invented Management: Why Peter Drucker's Ideas Still Matter," www.businessweek.com/magazine/content/05_48/b3961001.htm, accessed October 2010.

5. Neustar Webmetrics, www.webmetrics.com/, accessed April 2015.

6. Neustar Webmetrics, www.webmetrics.com/, accessed April 2015.

7. Neustar Webmetrics, www.webmetrics.com/, accessed April 2015.

8. The Balanced Scorecard, www.balancedscorecard.org, accessed February 2015.

9. Clive Thompson, "Do You Speak Statistics?" *Wired*, May 2010, p. 36.

CHAPTER 5

1. Scott Berinato, "The CIO Code of Ethical Data Management," *CIO Magazine*, www.cio.com, accessed April 2015.

2. http://www.intel.com/content/www/us/en/internet-of-things/industrysolutions.html, accessed May 2014; Michael Chui, Markus Löffler, and Roger Roberts, "The Internet of Things," *Mckinsey Quarterly*, March 2010, http://www.mckinsey.com/insights/high_tech_telecoms_internet/the_internet_of_things; Stefan Ferber, "How the Internet of Things Changes Everything," *Harvard Business Review*, May 2013.

CHAPTER 6

1. http://www.intel.com/content/www/us/en/internet-of-things/industrysolutions.html , accessed May 2014; Michael Chui, Markus Löffler, and Roger Roberts, "The Internet of Things," *Mckinsey Quarterly*, March 2010, http://www.mckinsey.com/insights/high_tech_telecoms_internet/the_internet_of_things; Stefan Ferber, "How the Internet of Things Changes Everything," *Harvard Business Review*, September 2015.

2. Julia Kiling, "OLAP Gains Fans among Data-Hungry Firms," *ComputerWorld*, January 8, 2014, p. 54.

3. www.ellisisland.org, accessed October 2015

4. www.zappos.com, accessed April, 2015.

5. Stephen Baker, "What Data Crunchers Did for Obama," *Bloomberg Businessweek*, January 2009.

CHAPTER 7

1. Prashant Gopal, "Zillow Opens Online Mortgage Marketplace," *BusinessWeek*, April 3, 2012, http://www.businessweek.com/lifestyle/content/apr2008/bw2008043_948040.htm.

CHAPTER 8

1. Julie Schlosser, "Looking for Intelligence in Ice Cream," *Fortune*, March 2009; Leslie Goff, "Summertime Heats Up IT at Ben & Jerry's," *ComputerWorld*, July 2010; Customer Success Stories, www.cognos.com, accessed January 2012

2. Maria Popova, "Data Visualization: Stories for the Information Age," Bloomberg Businessweek, April 2011.

3. www.webdesignerdepot.com, accessed April 2012; flowingdata.com/2011/12/21/the-best-data-visualization-projects-of-2011/, accessed April 2012.

CHAPTER 9

1. Tim Kelly, *Wired*, Consumers are in the Connected Car's Driver Seat in 2015, http://www.wired.com/insights/2015/01/consumers-are-in-the-connected-cars-driver-seat-in-2015/, accessed April 2016

2. Tom Davenport, "Tom Davenport: Back to Decision-Making Basics," Bloomberg Businessweek, March 2008.

3. "What Is Systems Thinking," SearchCIO.com, http://searchcio.tech.

4. Rachel King, "Soon That Nearby Worker Might Be a Robot," Bloomberg Businessweek, June 1, 2014.

5. Sharon Begley, "Software au Natural"; Neil McManus, "Robots at Your Service"; Santa Fe Institute, www.dis.anl.gov/abms/, accessed June 24, 2007; Michael A. Arbib (Ed.), *The Handbook of Brain Theory and Neural Networks* (MIT Press, mitpress.mit.edu, 1995); L. Biacino and G. Gerla, "Fuzzy Logic, Continuity and Effectiveness," Archive for Mathematical Logic.

6. "Darpa Grand Challenge," www.darpa.mil/grandchallenge/, accessed September 1, 2015.

CHAPTER 10

1. http://www.fastcodesign.com/3042352/how-one-knitter-makes-almost-1-million-a-year-on-etsy, accessed January 2016.

CHAPTER 11

1. www.zappos.com, accessed April 9, 2010.

CHAPTER 12

1. http://www.cio.com/article/2429865/enterprise-resource-planning/10-famous-erp-disasters--dustups-and-disappointments.html, accessed February 2016.

2. Tim Kelly, *Wired*, Consumers are in the Connected Car's Driver Seat in 2015, http://www.wired.com/insights/2015/01/consumers-are-in-the-connected-cars-driver-seat-in-2015/, accessed April 2016.

3. www.actionaly.com, accessed April 2012; www.socialmedia.biz/2011/01/12/top-20-social-media-monitoring-vendors-forbusiness, accessed April 2012; www.radian6.com, accessed April 2012; www.collectiveintellect.com, accessed April 2012.

CHAPTER 13

1. Eugene Kim, Business Insider, The Man Behind One Of The Hottest Apps In The World Tells Us How Even Boring Enterprise Apps Can Go Viral, accessed August 2014.

2. "Polaroid Files for Bankruptcy Protection," www.dpreview.com/news/0110/01101201polaroidch11.asp, accessed July 2012.

3. Clayton Christensen, *The Innovator's Dilemma* (Boston: Harvard Business School, 1997); Adam Lashinsky, "The Disrupters," *Fortune,* August 11, 2003, pp. 62–65.

4. Timothy Mullaney, "Netflix," *Bloomberg Businessweek,* www.businessweek.com/smallbiz/, accessed June 2010.

5. "Disintermediation," *TechTarget,* http://whatis.techtarget.com/defition.html, accessed April 2010.

6. http://www.economist.com/blogs/economist-explains/2015/01/economist-e, accessed January 2016.

CHAPTER 14

1. "The Complete Web 2.0 Directory," www.go2web20.net/, accessed June 2012 "Web 2.0 for CIOs," www.cio.com/article/16807; www.emarketer.com, accessed January 2012.About.com.

CHAPTER 15

1. "The Complete Web 2.0 Directory," www.go2web20.net/, accessed June 24, 2007; "Web 2.0 for CIOs," www.cio.com/article/16807;www.emarketer.com, accessed January 2010; Daniel Nations, "What Is Social Bookmarking," About.com, "Web Trends," http://webtrends.about.com/od/socialbookmarking101/p/aboutsocialtags.htm, accessed April 5, 2010.

2. Ibid.

3. Ibid.

4. Ibid.

5. Ibid.

6. Ibid.

7. Ibid.

8. Ibid.

9. Ibid.

10. Ibid.

11. Ibid.

12. Tim Berners-Lee, "Semantic Web Road Map," October 14, 1998, www.w3.org/DesignIssues/Semantic.html, accessed April 12, 2012.

13. Ingrid Lunden, "Pinterest Updates Terms of Service as It Preps an API and Private Pinboards: More Copyright Friendly," Tech Crunch, April 2012; Chad McCloud, "What Pinterest Teaches Us About Innovation in Business," Bloomberg Businessweek, May 2012; Courteney Palis, "Pinterest Traffic Growth Soars to New Heights: Experian Report," The Huffington Post, April 6, 2012.

14. www.kiva.org, accessed 10/31/2015.

CHAPTER 16

1. "How Do Cellular Devices Work," www.cell-phone101.info/devices.php, accessed February 9, 2008.

2. Ibid.

3. Deepak Pareek, *WiMAX: Taking Wireless to the MAX* (Boca Raton, FL: CRC Press, 2006), pp. 150–51; V. C. Gungor and F. C. Lambert, "A Survey on Communication Networks for Electric System Automation, Computer Networks," *International Journal of Computer and Telecommunications Networking*, May 15, 2006, pp. 877–97.

4. Ibid.

5. Ibid.

6. Ibid.

7. Ibid.

8. Ibid.

9. "RFID Privacy and You," www.theyaretrackingyou.com/rfid-privacy-and-you.html, accessed February 12, 2012. "RFID Roundup," www.rfidgazette.org, accessed February 10, 2012. "Security-Free Wireless Networks," www.wired.com, accessed February 11, 2012.

10. "RFID Privacy and You," www.theyaretrackingyou.com/rfid-privacy-and-you.html, accessed February 12, 2012. "RFID Roundup," www.rfidgazette.org, accessed February 10, 2012. "Security-Free Wireless Networks," www.wired.com, accessed February 11, 2012.

11. Natasha Lomas, "Location Based Services to Boom in 2008," *Bloomberg Businessweek*, February 11, 2008, www.businessweek.com/globalbiz/content/feb2008/gb20080211_420894.htm.

12. http://www.theverge.com/2014/8/12/5991005/slack-is-killing-email-yes-really, www.slack.com, accessed April 2016.

13. www.bitcoin.com, accessed January 2016.

14. Brad Stone, "Invasion of the Taxi Snatchers: Uber Leads an Industry's Disruption," *Bloomberg Businessweek*, February 2014, http://www.businessweek.com/articles/2014-02-20/uber-leads-taxi-industry-disruption-amid-fight-for-riders-drivers.

CHAPTER 17

1. http://www.gameindustrycareerguide.com/video-game-programmer-salary/, accessed 4/15/2016.

CHAPTER 18

1. "Four Steps to Getting Things on Track," *Bloomberg Businessweek*, July 7, 2010, www.businessweek.com/idg/2010-07-07/project-management-4-steps-to-getting-things-on-track.html.

CHAPTER 19

1. "Baggage Handling System Errors," www.flavors.com, accessed November 16, 2003.

2. Edward Yourdon, Death March: *The Complete Software Developer's Guide to Surviving "Mission Impossible" Projects* (Upper Saddle River, NJ: Prentice Hall PTR, 1999).

3. Charles Bryant, "Top 10 Things You Should Not Share on Social Networks," *Howstuffworks*, howstuffworks.com, accessed May 2012.

4. Rachel King; "How Aaron Levie and his childhood friends built Box into a $2 billion business, without stabbing each other in the back," March 8, 2014, http://www.techrepublic.com/article/how-aaronlevie-and-his-childhood-friends-built-box-into-a-2-billion-businesswithout-stabbing-each-other-in-the-back/.

PLUG-IN B3

1. Aaron Ricadela, "Seismic Shift," *Information Week,* March 14, 2005.

2. "Electronic Breaking Points," *PC World,* August 2005.

3. "The Linux Counter," counter.li.org, accessed October 2005.

4. www.mit.com, accessed October 2005.

5. www.needapresent.com, accessed October 2005.

PLUG-IN B5

1. Andy Patrizio, "Peer-to-Peer Goes Beyond Napster," *Wired,* February, 14, 2001, www.wired.com/science/discoveries/news/2001/02/41768, accessed January 2009.

2. Cisco, "Network Media Types," www.ciscopress.com/articles/article.asp?p=31276, accessed January 2009.

3. Cisco, "TCP/IP Overview," www.cisco.com/en/US/tech/tk365/technologies_white_paper09186a008014f8a9.shtml, accessed January 2009.

4. Cisco, "TCP/IP Overview."

5. Intel in Communications, "10 Gigabit Ethernet Technology Overview," www.intel.com/network/connectivity/resources/doc_library/white_papers/pro10gbe_lr_sa_wp.pdf, accessed January 2009.

6. "IPv6," www.ipv6.org, accessed January 2009.

PLUG-IN B6

1. www.ftc.gov/ogc/coppa1.htm, accessed April 2013.

PLUG-IN B9

1. "Center Energy Efficiency," www.energystar.gov/ia/partners/prod_development/downloads/EPA_Report_Exec_Summary_Final.pdf, accessed January 23, 2008.

2. *Google Docs,* docs.google.com, accessed June 4, 2010.

PLUG-IN B12

1. Heather Pemberton Levy, Top 10 Technology Trends Signal the Digital Mesh www.gartner.com, accessed January 2016.

Pattern recognition analysis, 141
Pay-per-call, 257
Pay-per-click, 257
Pay-per-conversion, 257
Payback method, 62
Payless Shoes, 28
PDA (personal digital assistant), 405
Peer-to-peer (P2P) network, 430–431
Peninsular and Oriental Steam Navigation Co. (P&O), 234
Perform, 207
Performance, 422
Performance measures, 504
Personal area network (PAN), 282–283
Personal career SWOT analysis, 33–34
Personal computer, 405
Personal digital assistant (PDA), 405
Personal information management (PIM) software, 407
Personal Information Protection and Electronic Document
    Act (PIPEDA), 509
Personalization, 246
PERT (Program Evaluation and Review Technique) chart,
    343, 344
Petabyte (PB), 131, 401
Petraeus, David, 90
Pfizer, 506
Pharming, 442
Pharming attack, 442
Phased implementation, 319
Phillips Petroleum, 243
Phishing, 85, 86, 442, 443
Phishing expedition, 442
Physical security, 454
Physical view of information, 108
Pilot implementation, 319
PIM (personal information management) software, 407
Pinterest, 275–277
PIPEDA (Personal Information Protection and Electronic
    Document Act), 509
Pirated software, 71
Pivot, 172
PivotTable, 111
Pixie Scientific, 84
PKE (public key encryption), 444, 445
P&L (profit-and-loss) statement, 368
Place, 374
Plagiarism, 273
Planning phase, 314
Platform as a Service (PaaS), 484
Playnix Toys, 364
Plotter, 403
Plug-ins, 5. See also individual plug-in names
Plunge implementation, 319
Pocket computer, 405
Podcasting, 259
Point-of-sale (POS), 402
Pointing device, 402
Polaroid, 25, 242
Political feasibility, 340
Political microtargeting (2008 presidential election),
    114–115
Polymorphic viruses and worms, 76
Pop-up ad, 249
Population increase, 513–514
Portability, 421
Portal, 257
Porter, Michael, 164
    business and social problems, 31
    five forces model. See Five forces model
    three generic strategies, 27–28
    value chain analysis, 28–30
Post-implementation report, 320
Postal Service, 90–91, 193
Pragmatic Chaos, 157
Prediction, 139–140
Predictive analytics, 11
Presentation graphics, 408
Presidential election (2008), 114–115
Pretexting, 440

Preventive maintenance, 319
Price, 374
Priceline.com, 256, 275
Primary key, 105, 106
Primary storage, 398–400
Primary value activities, 29, 30
Prime Air, 52
Printer, 403
Privacy, 71
    Canada, 509
    chief privacy officer (CPO), 57
    email privacy policy, 452–453
    EU, 507–508
    information, 507
    information privacy policy, 451–452
    United States, 508
Privacy Act (Canada), 509
Private cloud, 481–482
Privilege escalation, 444
PRM (partner relationship management), 202–203
Process improvement model, 393
Process owner, 42
Process quality, 465
Procter & Gamble (P&G), 44, 243
Procurement, 29, 182–183
Product, 374
Product differentiation, 26
Product life cycle, 375
Product quality, 465
Product realization, 37
Production, 15, 460
Production and materials management ERP
    components, 215
Production management, 375, 460
Production planning process, 215
Productivity, 15
Profit, 364
Profit-and-loss (P&L) statement, 368
Programming, 408
Programming languages, 318
Progressive Insurance, 39, 376
Project, 59, 314
Project assumption, 342
Project constraint, 342
Project deliverable, 342
Project failure, 338–341
Project management, 314. See also Organizational project
    management
Project Management Body of Knowledge
    (PMBOK), 342
Project Management Institute (PMI), 314, 341, 342
Project management office (PMO), 342
Project manager, 314
Project milestone, 342
Project objectives, 342, 343
Project plan, 314
Project requirements document, 342
Project scope, 314
Project scope statement, 342
Project stakeholder, 342
Promotion, 374
Protocol, 431–434
Prototyping, 326
Psychographic segmentation, 374
Public cloud, 481
Public key encryption (PKE), 444, 445
Publishing industry, 245
Pure-play business, 256

Q

QBE (query-by-example) tool, 104
Quality, 465–466
Quantum, 243
Queisser, Jeff, 356
Query-by-example (QBE) tool, 104
Quickbooks, 480

R

Rackspace, 203, 206–207
RAD (rapid application development)
    methodology, 327
Radio-frequency identification (RFID), 185–186,
    289–290
RAM (random access memory), 398
Random access memory (RAM), 398
Ransomware, 76, 86
Rapid application development (RAD) methodology, 327
Rapid prototyping, 327
Rational unified process (RUP) methodology, 328
Read-only memory (ROM), 400
Real simple syndication (RSS), 271
Real-time adaptive security, 518
Real-time communication, 259
Real-time information, 101
Real-time systems, 101
Recommendation engine, 136
Record, 105, 106
Recovery, 414
Reding, Viviane, 458
Reduced instruction set computer (RISC) chips, 398
Redundant data, 109
Regression model of prediction, 140
Reidenberg, Joe, 72
Reintermediation, 247–248
Relational database, 140
Relational database management system, 104–110
    advantages, 108–110
    Coca-Cola, 106–107
    entities/attributes, 105, 106
    increased flexibility, 108
    increased scalability and performance, 108–109
    information integrity, 109
    information redundancy, 109
    information security, 109–110
    primary/foreign key, 105, 106
    records, 105, 106
Relational database model, 105
Relational integrity constraints, 109
Reliability, 421–422
RentACoder, 511
Report, 9
Reporters Without Borders, 505
Repository, 119
Reputation system, 267
Requirements definition document, 314
Requirements management, 314
Resource management, 504
Response time, 61
Responsibility matrix, 342
Résumé, lying on your, 81
Retail industry, 245
Return of investment (ROI), 60, 62, 369
Revenue, 368
RFID (radio-frequency identification), 185–186
RFID accelerometer, 290
RFID electronic product code (EPC), 185
RFID interrogator, 289
RFID reader, 186, 289
RFID tags, 185, 186, 289
RFM formula, 48
Richter, Dominik, 262
Right to be forgotten, 458
Ring topology, 432
RISC (reduced instruction set computer) chips, 398
Risk management, 504
Rivalry among existing competitors, 26
Robotic prosthetic, 231
Robotics, 187–188
RobotLAB, 519–520
ROI (return of investment), 60, 62, 369
ROM (read-only memory), 400
Romm, Joseph, 66
Rotation, 172
Router, 431